THE ENGLISH FAMILIAR ESSAY

REPRESENTATIVE TEXTS

EDITED, WITH INTRODUCTION AND NOTES

BY

WILLIAM FRANK BRYAN, Ph.D.

AND

RONALD S. CRANE, Ph.D.

OF THE DEPARTMENT OF ENGLISH OF NORTHWESTERN UNIVERSITY

GINN AND COMPANY

BOSTON · NEW YORK · CHICAGO · LONDON
ATLANTA · DALLAS · COLUMBUS · SAN FRANCISCO

𝕿𝖍𝖊 𝕬𝖙𝖍𝖊𝖓𝖆𝖚𝖒 𝕻𝖗𝖊𝖘𝖘
GINN AND COMPANY · PRO-
PRIETORS · BOSTON · U.S.A.

PREFACE

Probably no one will undertake to controvert the statement that a definition of the essay has not yet been made both inclusive enough to cover all the different kinds of prose to which the name has been given and still sufficiently restrictive to mark out any particular qualities which distinguish the essay from any other comparatively brief composition. An attempt to discover the characteristics common to Locke's " Essay on the Human Understanding," Lamb's " Dissertation on Roast Pig," Macaulay's " Warren Hastings," Carlyle's " Essay on Burns," and Arnold's " Sweetness and Light" would pretty surely demonstrate that these various pieces of literature do not belong to any single, unified genre. There are, however, a large number of writings commonly called " essays " which have traditionally been felt to constitute a distinct type. These are characterized by a personal, confidential attitude of the writers toward their subjects and their readers, by an informal, familiar style, and by a concern with everyday manners and morals or with individual emotions and experiences rather than with public affairs or the material of systematic thinking. It is with the essay of this more narrowly limited type — perhaps best called the Familiar Essay — that the present volume is exclusively concerned.

In treating the Familiar Essay the editors have designed not to furnish models for a course in English composition or to compile an anthology, but to present such a selection of texts as will exhibit clearly the development of the genre in England. The complete accomplishment of this purpose has made it necessary, of course, to begin outside of England with Montaigne, the originator of the type, and to include specimens of his essays. A similar consideration has led to the inclusion of a brief extract from La Bruyère. But with these exceptions only British writers are represented. However delightful or stimulating are the essays of Irving and Emerson and Lowell, they have not affected the development of the type ; and regard for unity of purpose, combined with lack of space, compels their exclusion. Further, instead of presenting one or two essays each by a great

iii

number of writers, the collection is confined to the works of the most significant and influential essayists, in the belief that an adequate representation of their work is the truest way of making clear the evolution of the type. The selection of the individual essays, however, has been made with as much regard to their intrinsic interest and charm as to their historical significance.

As this collection is prepared not for the scholar-specialist but for the general reader and the college undergraduate, the spelling and the punctuation have been revised wherever adherence to earlier usage would baffle or seriously annoy the reader. The essays of the seventeenth and the eighteenth centuries have been modernized to this extent; those of the nineteenth century, in this respect, have been left almost wholly untouched. In every case the texts of the essays are those of standard editions, and they have been carefully collated wherever collation has seemed advisable.

The introduction tries to present in the briefest possible compass an ordered account of the historical development of the Familiar Essay in England; and for this sketch especial effort has been made to secure accuracy in matters of both fact and inference. For the section on Montaigne, and Bacon's relationship to Montaigne, the editors are deeply indebted to the careful and illuminating monographs of M. Pierre Villey; their obligations to other studies of the various essayists, though very considerable, do not demand here such particularization. A large part of the material for the introduction they have gathered from the original sources.

The notes, it is hoped, will contribute directly to an intelligent appreciation of the text. Quotations and allusions have been definitely placed, in order to throw light upon the extent and the character of the reading of the various essayists; and wherever it has appeared that an explanation or a statement of fact would really be of service to the reader, a note has been supplied. The notes, though full, are not compendiums of general information, but each concerns immediately the passage in the text to which it is related. All foreign words and phrases have been translated; the meaning of an English word, however, has been given only when the word is used in a sense not made clear in the sort of dictionary presumably owned by any person who wishes to read intelligently. The bibliographical essay, like the notes, is intended to be of practical utility to the general student and

reader. It includes the titles of only the most notable complete editions, of the most satisfactory inexpensive editions of the essays or of
selections from them, and of a small number of studies which contain
pertinent and valuable information on the development of the type
or on the individual essayists, or which will be of definite assistance
to the reader who desires fuller information than he can obtain from
the necessarily compacted introduction and notes of this volume.

Throughout this work both editors have collaborated closely, and
both are equally responsible for selection and arrangement; but each
acknowledges a more definite accountability for certain sections. The
preparation of the text for the seventeenth and the eighteenth centuries, with the accompanying notes and the corresponding section of
the introduction, is the work of Dr. Crane; for the material of the
nineteenth century Dr. Bryan is similarly responsible.

The editors desire to acknowledge gratefully their obligations to
Charles Scribner's Sons for permission to reprint Stevenson's "The
Lantern Bearers," and to the Newberry Library and the libraries of
Harvard University and of Northwestern University for services that
have made the work possible. To their former colleague, Mr. Herbert
K. Stone, now of the University of Illinois, and to their present colleagues and friends, Professor Keith Preston, Messrs. George B.
Denton, J. B. McKinney, and Arthur H. Nethercot, they desire also
to express their appreciation of assistance generously given. Almost
every page of the introduction owes something to Mr. Denton's
keen and thoughtful criticism.

W. F. B.
R. S. C.

Evanston, Illinois

CONTENTS[1]

    [1] Titles of essays in brackets have been supplied by the editors.

A HISTORY OF THE ENGLISH FAMILIAR ESSAY

I. MONTAIGNE AND THE BEGINNINGS OF THE ESSAY IN ENGLAND

The Familiar Essay made its first appearance in England during one of the most crowded and prolific periods of her literary history — the last decade of the sixteenth century. As a distinct type of prose writing it was not native to England, although many of the literary practices out of which it developed were to be found there, as in most of the countries of Europe. The direct stimulus to its cultivation by English writers came from France.

In the year 1570 a French gentleman, Michel de Montaigne, gave up his post as a lawyer in Bordeaux and retired to his country

Montaigne (1533-1592): his education and tastes estates, for the purpose, as he himself expressed it, of " living in quiet and reading." In his education and tastes Montaigne was a typical cultured Frenchman of the Renaissance. At the instance of his father, an enthusiastic admirer of Italian humanism, he was taught Latin before he learned French, and at college he had among his tutors some of the most accomplished classical scholars of the time. His culture consequently took on a very pronounced Latin and Italian tinge ; Greek writers he read with difficulty, and by preference in translations ; and his interest in earlier and contemporary French literature was limited to a few authors and books, principally in the field of history. Above all, as he grew older he became absorbed in the moral problems which the revival of the literatures and philosophies of antiquity, together with the discovery of America, had brought to the fore all over Europe. It was doubtless to gain more time for reflection on these questions that at the age of thirty-seven he abandoned active life for a quiet existence in his library at Montaigne. He had not been there long before a natural desire to " preserve his memories " and to " clarify his reflections " led him to write.

The form which his first compositions took was in no sense original with him. By the middle of the sixteenth century there had come
into existence, in nearly all the countries touched by the
Renaissance, various types of works designed to make accessible the knowledge and ideas of antiquity. Some of
these had themselves an antique origin. Thus, from the
so-called *Distichs of Cato*, a work dating from the late Roman Empire,
proceeded a long line of collections of " sentences," or moral maxims,
of which Erasmus's *Adagia* (1500) was perhaps the most celebrated
— books in which were brought together, sometimes under general
heads such as " education," " the brevity of life," " death," " youth
and age," " riches," etc., wise sayings of ancient and often, too, of modern authors. Similarly, the influence of Plutarch (born cir. 46 A.D.)
and of Valerius Maximus (first century A.D.) led to the compilation
of numerous books of apothegms, or " sentences " put into the mouths
of historical personages, and of " examples," or significant anecdotes
culled from the writings of historians and moralists. Works of this
kind enjoyed an extraordinary vogue during the Renaissance ; they
existed in nearly all the modern languages as well as in Latin, and
some of them ran through literally hundreds of editions. Strictly
speaking, however, they were not so much books as extremely arid
compilations of raw material. To supplement them, and to present
the wisdom of antiquity in a more readable form, certain humanists
developed, chiefly from hints furnished by such ancient authors as
Aulus Gellius (2d century A.D.) and Macrobius (5th century A.D.), a
special type of writing, commonly called in France the *leçon morale*, in
which " sentences," apothegms, and " examples " were fused together
in short dissertations on ethical subjects. The writers who cultivated
this genre, whether in Latin or in the various vernaculars, had for
the most part a purely practical object — to collect and make readily
accessible the views and discoveries of the ancients on all questions
relating to the conduct of life. They attached themselves by preference to subjects of a general and commonplace sort, such as strange
customs and singular happenings, the grandeur and misery of man,
the intelligence of animals, the moral virtues, the force of the imagination, death ; and in treatment they seldom went beyond an impersonal, unoriginal grouping of maxims and " examples."

*Sources and
character of
his early
essays*

When Montaigne began to write, probably in 1571, it was to the compilers of *leçons* that he looked for literary inspiration. It was, indeed, only natural that he should do so; for his own aims in writing were at first almost precisely the same as theirs. He had no ambition to write an original book; he wished only to bring together, with a minimum of effort, the interesting and helpful passages which he encountered in his reading. Accordingly, his first compositions belonged essentially in both manner and matter to the genre which these compilers had popularized. Some of them, as, for example, a little piece entitled " That the Hour of Parley is Dangerous," were merely brief collections of anecdotes and " sentences," unified by a common subject; others, such as " Of the Inequality Amongst Us " and " Of Sorrow,"[1] had a somewhat more elaborate organization, but were constructed out of the same elements. The subjects, all of them questions of morals or practical affairs, had nearly all been treated already by one or another of the numerous writers of *leçons*. In dealing with them afresh Montaigne displayed an impersonality of method quite as marked as that of any of his predecessors. Now and then he developed in his own way a maxim from an ancient writer, added a word of comment to one of his numerous moral stories, or contributed a sentence or two of transition; but beyond that his ambition did not go; there were no personal confidences, no revelations of his own experience and ideas.

Such was the character of the writings with which Montaigne occupied himself during the year or two following his retirement. His **His creation** subservience to the ideals and methods of the *leçon* was **of the per-** complete. About 1574, however, before he had published **sonal essay** anything, a change began in his conception and practice of composition which was to result, before 1580, in the creation of an entirely new literary form — the personal essay. Among the influences which contributed to this change one of the most potent certainly was that of his own temperament. Montaigne had brought into his retirement a strong native tendency to moral reflection and self-analysis — a tendency which his isolation from affairs, and especially a severe illness which he underwent about 1578, no doubt helped to intensify. But there were literary factors also at work. Shortly after

---

[1] See pp. 2–5, below.

1572 he fell under the spell of the writings of Plutarch, then lately translated into French by Jacques Amyot. In these, particularly in the collection of short moral discourses known as *Moralia*, he found models of a very different sort from the dry and impersonal compilations he had imitated hitherto. Plutarch's chapters were, it is true, full of maxims and "examples"; but the maxims and "examples" did not form the substance of the composition — they were wholly subordinate to the personal reflections of the author. The naturalness and freedom from pedantry of the old Greek moralist made a profound impression on Montaigne; he seems to have had the *Moralia* almost constantly before him during a period of several years, and their influence had much to do with the transformation of his own methods of composition.

This transformation first appeared clearly in a number of pieces written between 1578 and 1580.[2] Content no longer with a mere compilation of striking passages from his reading, Montaigne now aimed to give primarily his own reflections on moral and psychological subjects. The quotations and "examples," it is true, still abounded; but their function was changed; they were not, as before, the basis of the composition, but rather simply a means of illustrating the writer's thought. Moreover, to the "examples" drawn from books Montaigne began now to add anecdotes taken from his own memory and observation. Thus, in a chapter entitled "Of the Education of Children," after setting forth the general principles which should govern in the training of children, he proceeded to give a sketch, full of intimate details, of his own education. Again, in the chapter "Of Books" he discoursed not so much of books in general as of his own individual tastes and prejudices in literature. In short, the chapters written during this second period of Montaigne's career tended to become each a tissue of personal reflections, colored, to be sure, but no longer dominated, by their writer's reading. For the most part, too, they were considerably longer than those of the first period, and far less regular and orderly in composition.

[2] Especially, "Of the Education of Children," "Of the Affection of Fathers to their Children," "Of Books," "Of Cruelty," "Of Presumption," and "Of the Resemblance of Children to their Fathers." With the exception of the first, all of these pieces are to be found in the second book of the *Essais*. The first book is almost entirely made up of impersonal essays of Montaigne's earliest period.

In 1580 Montaigne assembled the chapters he had written up to that time — ninety-four in all — and published them at Bordeaux in two books, entitling them modestly *Essais*. The name, a new one in European literature, itself gave warning that the collection was no mere book of conventional *leçons*, but, in however tentative a way, an original work. But Montaigne was not content with this indirect advertisement of his new-found purpose. Forgetful of nearly the whole of the first book, and thinking only of a few chapters in the second, he insisted, in his prefatory epistle to the reader, on the personal character of his undertaking. " It is," he wrote, " myself I portray."

First edition of Montaigne's Essais

Between 1580 and 1588 Montaigne continued to busy himself with his book, and in the latter year brought out a new edition, in which, along with revised versions of the essays written before 1580, he included thirteen entirely new chapters.[8] In these last pieces the traits which had been slowly coming to characterize his writing since about 1574 became still more marked. The individual essays were longer; the composition was if anything more rambling and discursive; and, though the quotations and the "examples" remained, the personal experiences and reflections of the writer formed even more notably the center of the work. Everywhere, no matter what the subject announced at the beginning of the chapter, Montaigne talked of himself — of his memories of youth, of the curious and interesting things which had happened to him in manhood, of his habits of body and mind, of his whims and prejudices, of his ideas. Like the good moralist he was, he took on the whole more interest in what happened within him than in the external events of his life. " I can give no account of my life by my actions," he wrote in the essay " Of Vanity "; " fortune has placed them too low; I must do it by my fancies." But it was not his intention to write anything like a formal autobiography even of his inner life. He wished rather to find in his own experiences, commonplace as many of them were, light on the general moral problems which were always the primary subject of his reflections. " I propose," he said, speaking of his design

Montaigne's later essays

---

[8] These formed a third book. Among them were the essays on which Montaigne's fame has perhaps most largely rested: "Of Repentance," "Upon Some Verses of Virgil," " Of Coaches," " Of the Inconvenience of Greatness," " Of Vanity," " Of Experience."

to picture himself, "a life ordinary and without luster; 't is all one; all moral philosophy may as well be applied to a common and private life, as to one of richer composition; every man carries the entire form of human condition." Such was the philosophical conception which underlay the personal essay as it was finally developed by Montaigne.

The *Essais*, popular from the first in France, were not long in making their way across the Channel into England. In 1595, three **The *Essais*** years after Montaigne's death, a copyright was issued for **in England** an English translation, possibly the one which appeared in 1603. This version was the work of a literary schoolmaster named John Florio. As a representation of the original it was far from faithful. It was written, however, in picturesque if somewhat obscure English, and it acquired enough popularity in the early seventeenth century to make necessary at least two reprintings. In this translation, or in the original French, the *Essais* were read by an extensive public, which numbered some of the most eminent names in Elizabethan letters. Under these circumstances it is not strange that the literary genre which Montaigne created — the informal, personal essay — should have become naturalized in England.

The first work by an English writer to bear the name of the new form appeared in 1597. Early in that year Francis Bacon, then a **Bacon's** rising lawyer in the service of the queen, published a **first essays:** small volume entitled *Essayes. Religious Meditations.* **their source** *Places of perswasion and disswasion.* The "essayes" **in sixteenth-** **century col-** were ten in number: "Of Study," "Of Discourse," "Of **lections of** Ceremonies and Respects," "Of Followers and Friends," **"sentences"** "Of Suitors," "Of Expense," "Of Regiment of Health," "Of Honour and Reputation," "Of Faction," and "Of Negotiating." In reality they were not essays in the Montaigne sense at all, but rather short collections of "sentences" or aphorisms, of a type which had been familiar throughout Europe during the whole of the sixteenth century. Each piece consisted of a series of brief, pointed maxims relating to the general subject proposed at the beginning; there was little attempt at order; and the individual maxims were quite devoid of concrete illustration or development of any kind. Fundamentally Bacon's purpose in writing the book was not to discuss questions of morals or psychology in the light of his own experience in life, but to furnish in a condensed, memorable form practical counsel to those ambitious of success in public affairs. Only the title, it would seem, came from Montaigne, and that was doubtless added some time after the book itself was completed.

It was not long, however, before essays really of the Montaigne type made their appearance. In two volumes, published in 1600 and **Cornwallis's** 1601, Sir William Cornwallis, a friend of Ben Jonson, **Essays** brought out a collection of fifty-two pieces, for the most part short, dealing with such general themes as resolution, patience, love, glory, ambition, discourse, fame, judgment, sorrow, vanity, fortune, and the like. Like Montaigne, to whom in several passages of warm praise he acknowledged his debt, Cornwallis wrote his *Essays* largely in the first person, made abundant illustrative use of " examples," some from ancient historians and poets, some from his own experience, and in general afforded a rather full revelation of his ideas, tastes, and sentiments. As a result, in part no doubt, of this strong personal note, his book shared during the first third of the seventeenth century not a little of the popularity of its model.

The next important occurrence in the history of the new genre in England was the appearance in 1612 of an enlarged edition of **Bacon's** the *Essays* of Bacon. From ten in the edition of 1597 the **Essays** number of chapters had now become thirty-eight. The **of 1612** first essays were reprinted without fundamental change; here and there new maxims were added, and some of the old ones given a slight degree of development; but on the whole their original character remained unaltered. Of the newer essays a few, such as "Of Praise," "Of Delay," and "Of Fortune," belonged essentially to the old type of " sentences "; the majority, however, exhibited traits which showed that Bacon's conception of the essay as a form and his own methods of writing were beginning to change. Thus, in many of the pieces there appeared a more marked element of order and composition; quotations and " examples," usually very briefly indicated, became an established feature of the exposition; in a word, the old ideal of a collection of detached maxims began to give place, in Bacon's mind, to that of a more continuous and living discourse.

This evolution, clearly apparent in the essays first published in 1612, became still more pronounced in the final collection which Bacon put forth in 1625. The total number of essays was now increased to fifty-eight. Of the old ones nearly all had been subjected to some revision, those of 1612 undergoing the greatest change.

Bacon's Essays of 1625   The result was a body of writing which differed in several important features from the *Essays* of 1597. For one thing, many of the pieces now exhibited something like orderly and planned composition; instead of merely juxtaposed maxims, there was now, in many cases (as in the essay "Of Friendship"), a clear and explicit development by points. The average length also had increased; many of the new essays covered from six to ten pages. Furthermore, the style was different — without losing its epigrammatic flavor, it was fuller, richer in imagery, more circumstantial. But the most significant changes were the increase in the number of historical "examples" and the introduction of a certain amount of personal opinion and reminiscence. Scarcely an essay now but had its illustrations from ancient or modern history; in some pieces (as, for example, "Of Empire") they occupied nearly as much space as the general reflections which they served to clarify and illuminate. Along with them appeared for the first time anecdotes derived from Bacon's own experience in life; as when, in the essay "Of Prophecies," he reported the "trivial prophecy, which I heard when I was a child," that "When hempe is sponne, England's done." More and more, too, he formed the habit of stating his opinions in the first person.

Such were some of the differences in form and spirit which separated Bacon's essays of 1625 from their predecessors of 1597. Sev-

Causes of the transformation in Bacon's Essays   eral influences probably combined to produce the change. In the first place, one of Bacon's dreams for a number of years past had been the construction of a science of morals. In his *De Augmentis Scientiarum* (1623) he had proposed as a means to this end the writing of short monographs on each of the passions, virtues, and types of character. He never carried out his design in full; but it is not unlikely that such essays as those "Of Envy" and "Of Simulation and Dissimulation," which were among the most finished and orderly of the 1625 group, were composed as examples of the monographs he had in view. Another probable influence was that of the *Epistles* of Seneca (first century A.D.), one of the most widely read of ancient works on morals, a book constantly quoted by Bacon. In a canceled preface to the edition of

1612 he had remarked of the title of his own book: "The word is late, but the thing is ancient. For Seneca's Epistles to Lucilius, if one mark them well, are but essays, — that is, dispersed meditations, — though conveyed in the form of epistles." Finally, much of the impetus to the change in his methods of writing, particularly after 1612, would appear to have come from Montaigne. Montaigne's influence it was, in all likelihood, that led Bacon to cultivate a more picturesque style, to develop his meager aphorisms into connected discourses, to multiply illustrations of all kinds, and — though to a very limited degree — to speak of himself.

Yet, in spite of this influence, the type of essay which Bacon developed resembled only superficially that of Montaigne. In form it was Differences shorter, more compact and orderly, and far less personal; between the in content it had a practical bias which for the most part essays of Montaigne's wanted. From first to last Bacon's purpose Bacon and was to give, from his own extensive knowledge of life Montaigne and history, sound advice which would profit those whose ambition it was to rise in the world of courts and council chambers. The title which he prefixed to the edition of 1625 — Essays, or Counsels Civil and Moral — exactly expressed his aim. His book was to be a manual of morality and policy for aspiring courtiers and statesmen. It is true that in the second and third editions he included essays of a more general sort — meditations on truth, death, beauty, friendship. But, aside from the fact that even here a certain amount of worldly wisdom crept in, these essays were far less typical of the work as a whole than those which dealt with such themes as the practice of dissimulation, the relative advantage of marriage and single life to public men, the means of rising to great place, the best method of dealing with rebellious subjects, the value of travel in the education of a gentleman, the management of an estate, the causes which make nations great, the best way to govern colonies, the economy of princely buildings and gardens. In short, though almost certainly indebted to Montaigne for a number of characteristic features,— for the most part, to be sure, features which Montaigne derived from the writers of leçons,— Bacon's Essays really introduced a new and distinct variety of the genre.

During the thirty-five years which elapsed between the completion of Bacon's work and the Restoration, several other writers tried their hands at the familiar essay. With some of these the dominant inspiration was Bacon, with others Montaigne. Thus Owen Felltham **Decline of** in his *Resolves: Divine, Moral, Political* (cir. 1620; a **the essay be-** second part in 1628) adapted Bacon's later method and **tween Bacon** style to the exposition of ideas quite unlike Bacon's in **and the** **Restoration** their emphasis on the religious and devotional side of life; while Sir Thomas Browne in his *Religio Medici* (written about 1635, published in 1642) united with a quaint picturesqueness of thought and expression peculiar to himself, not a little of Montaigne's characteristic manner of personal revelation. Neither of these writers, however, nor any of their fellows, had any appreciable influence on the development of the essay. They wrote, moreover, at a time when the essay as a type was undergoing a marked eclipse of its earlier popularity. No doubt in part this eclipse was due to the superior attractiveness for the men of this generation of the " character " [4]; no doubt in part also it reflected the absorption of the ablest minds of the period in the political and religious controversies which preceded and accompanied the Civil War. Whatever the causes, an eclipse took place, and it was not until the more peaceful days of the Restoration that essay-writing again assumed a place of prominence among the activities of literary Englishmen.

In this revival, as in the original introduction of the form, the all-important factor was the influence of Montaigne. After suffering **Revival of** a temporary obscuration during the period of the Civil **the essay** War, Montaigne's popularity became greater than ever **after the** during the last forty years of the seventeenth century. **Restoration** **—the influ-** The causes that contributed to this result were principally **ence of Mon-** two: the greatly increased interest in French literature **taigne** which characterized the public of the generation after the Restoration, and the appeal which Montaigne made to the growing current of scepticism and free-thought. In 1685 Charles Cotton, a poet and translator, the joint author with Izaak Walton of *The Compleat Angler*, published a new version of the *Essais*, which went through three editions by 1700 and completely superseded Florio's now largely obsolete translation. The admirers of Montaigne included some of the most distinguished and influential persons of the age. He was a favorite author of the poet Cowley; Dryden referred to

[4] See below, p. xxxi.

him, in the preface to *All for Love*, as "honest Montaigne"; he was one of the writers with whom Wycherley, according to his friend Pope, used to "read himself to sleep"; the Marquis of Halifax confessed that the *Essais* was "the book in the world I am best entertained with." In this atmosphere of enthusiasm for Montaigne the form which he had created began once more to attract English writers.

The man who most successfully cultivated the familiar essay in the period after the Restoration was Abraham Cowley. Cowley brought
Abraham to the writing of essays not only a mind stored with the
Cowley best classical learning of the day and a sensibility made
(1618-1667) delicate by long practice as a poet, but also a somewhat extensive experience in active affairs. A graduate of Trinity College, Cambridge, he was expelled from his fellowship in 1643 by the Puritans, and in 1646 followed the exiled queen of Charles I to France, where he was employed on various Royalist missions until the Restoration. On his return to England he looked confidently for some reward of his services from Charles II. Like many another good Royalist, however, he was disappointed in this expectation, and in 1663 he withdrew completely from public life and finally settled on a small estate in the country secured to him by his patrons the Earl of St. Albans and the Duke of Buckingham. Here he lived until his death in 1667. During the last four or five years of his life he amused himself by composing at intervals a number of short prose essays, each concluding with one or more verse translations from his favorite Roman poets. In them he dwelt on the superior advantages of liberty over dependence, of obscurity over greatness, of agriculture over business, and of a quiet life of reflection in the country over a crowded existence in city or court — all in a familiar style, enlivened by illustrations from his own experience and from the accumulated wisdom of ancient moralists and poets. The eleven essays thus written were published in the 1668 folio of his works under the title of *Several Discourses, by Way of Essays, in Verse and Prose.*

Of all the English essayists of the seventeenth century, Cowley was most fully indebted to Montaigne. His interests in life, it is true, were narrower; he had little of Montaigne's spirit of free inquiry and criticism; he was more restrained in his revelation of himself:

his language was less vigorous and picturesque. Nevertheless Montaigne — the Montaigne of the later, more personal *Essais* — was his master. He it was who taught him, in large part at least, the habit of self-analysis, the trick of weaving into his discourse quotations and anecdotes from ancient writers, the secret of a free, informal composition and of a familiar, colloquial style.

Cowley's indebtedness to Montaigne

Toward the end of the century another lover of Montaigne and of country life made a contribution to the essay almost if not quite as notable as that of Cowley. This was Sir William Temple, perhaps best known to the public of his time as an astute diplomat, the chief promoter of that Triple Alliance which united Holland, Denmark, and England against the growing power of Louis XIV. In intervals of official business, and especially during several periods of enforced retirement from public life, Temple was accustomed to spend his time on his country estate in Surrey. Here he cultivated his garden, cared for his fruit trees, which were famous throughout Europe, and diverted himself by setting down his thoughts on various subjects in the form of loosely organized essays modeled more or less closely on those of Montaigne. Sometimes his themes were literary, as in the discourses " Upon the Ancient and Modern Learning " and " Of Poetry." More frequently, however, they were suggested by his experiences and reflections as a country gentleman upon his estate, as when he wrote of the cure of the gout, of gardening, of health and long life, of conversation. These essays, composed at different times between the late seventies and Temple's death in 1699, were published in three volumes, entitled *Miscellanea*, in 1680, 1690, and 1701.

Sir William Temple (1628–1699)

If Cowley and Temple were the most important essayists of the last forty years of the seventeenth century, they were by no means the only ones. George Savile (Marquis of Halifax), John Sheffield (Duke of Buckingham), Charles Blount, Joseph Glanvill, Jeremy Collier — all these men in various ways carried on the traditions of Montaigne or of Bacon. As they initiated, however, no new departures in essay-writing, and had little influence on succeeding essayists, their activity was of small significance in the evolution of the type.

Other essayists contemporary with Cowley and Temple

With their passing, the first stage in the history of the essay in

England came to a close. It was a stage characterized not so much by abundant and varied production or widespread popularity as by experimentation on rather narrow lines. The great models of the genre, the writers whose methods and spirit animated the work of the lesser men, were Montaigne and Bacon — the one presenting an ideal of frank and lively self-portraiture, the other inspiring to a concise and sententious, if somewhat impersonal, handling of general ideas. The influence of both men coincided on at least two points: with both of them, and consequently with all of their followers during the seventeenth century, the essay was primarily concerned with problems of morality, in the large sense of the word; and it treated these problems for the most part in the light of classical example and precept, or at least in the spirit of classical ethical reflection. "An Essay," wrote a certain Ralph Johnson in 1665, "is a short discourse about any virtue, vice, or other commonplace." He might have added that the virtues and vices with which the essayists dealt were essentially individual virtues and vices — it was morality from the individual's point of view and in the individual's interest, and not from the point of view of society, that formed the burden of their reflections. The multifarious aspects of social life — manners, customs, institutions — interested them but slightly if at all. Of course in this they wrote but as children of their age. The period of the sixteenth and seventeenth centuries, dominated still by the intellectual tendencies of the Renaissance, was in its thinking on ethical questions an age of pronounced individualism. Little wonder then that Montaigne and Bacon and their disciples fixed their attention chiefly, if not altogether, on the cultivation and expression of personality. Equally representative of the culture of the time were the drafts which all of the essayists made upon ancient literature for aphorism and illustration. The abundance of "sentences" and "examples" derived from Greek and especially Latin sources, the frequency of allusions to classical poets, moralists, and historians, the general disposition to find in ancient civilization and literature guidance for modern times — all these things clearly reflected the humanism out of which the essay originally developed and which still survived in cultured circles to the end of the seventeenth century.

General character of the essay in the seventeenth century

II. THE PERIODICAL ESSAY OF THE EIGHTEENTH CENTURY

Shortly after 1700 a new period opened in the history of the English familiar essay. During the preceding hundred years the essay had been essentially a minor form; it had been neglected by most of the prominent writers, and cultivated by those who did attempt it only in their moments of leisure from more serious writing; its public had been small and select. Now, however, it took its place among the three or four most important and widely popular literary types. Scarcely one of the great writers of the period, from Addison and Pope to Dr. Johnson and Goldsmith, but concerned himself with it at one time or another; and its readers included Englishmen of all classes and tastes. Moreover, along with this rise in prominence, there took place a notable change in its aim and spirit. Whereas in the seventeenth century the essay had been almost universally conceived as an informal, more or less personal, discourse on some phase of individual morality, it now became oriented definitely toward the analysis and criticism of contemporary social life. Stylistic changes, too, accompanied these modifications in substance; new methods of composition, new devices of exposition appeared alongside the old; with the result that the essay of the eighteenth century constituted in many respects an entirely new literary type.

Increased prominence and changed character of the essay in the eighteenth century

This type was the joint creation of two men, Richard Steele (1672–1729) and Joseph Addison (1672–1719), and as such it bore in unmistakable manner the impress of their personalities. However, as neither Steele nor Addison could escape the influence of their environment, the particular form and direction which they gave to the essay were in large measure determined by external conditions.

Among these conditions none was of greater moment in shaping the essay in the eighteenth century than the development of literary periodicals. During the years immediately following the Revolution of 1688, when, under the stimulus of an aroused interest in politics and a relaxed censorship, newspapers in the strict sense of the word began to appear in considerable numbers, certain persons conceived the idea of publishing journals that should deal, not primarily with news, but with some of the numerous miscellaneous matters of

Influences on the new essay: the rise of literary periodicals

fashions, literature, and morals that engaged the attention of the public. One of these persons, a bookseller named John Dunton, *The Athe-* began in 1691 to print a sheet which he called at first *nian Mercury The Athenian Gazette* and later *The Athenian Mercury.* (1691-1697) He and the men that he associated with him in writing it aimed to furnish instruction mingled with entertainment. Their characteristic device was questions and answers; they invited queries on all manner of subjects from their readers and undertook to reply to them in their paper. Thus, in one number they discussed the question "whether the torments of the damned are visible to the saints in heaven," and vice versa. But not all their space was devoted to merely curious matters like this. Even more frequently they were called upon to supply useful information regarding history or natural science, to pronounce upon questions of taste, or to resolve nice problems of conduct and manners. Dunton continued to publish the *Athenian Mercury* for six years. It was the first journal of a miscellaneous character, not primarily concerned with politics, that England had seen.

It was followed, after an interval, by others. Of these by far the most important and successful was *A Weekly Review of the Affairs* *Defoe's* *of France*, published between 1704 and 1713 by Daniel *Review* Defoe. Defoe's primary object in issuing the *Review* was (1704-1713) to provide himself with a medium through which he could express his opinions on public affairs, particularly on the struggle then going on with France, and on the progress of English trade. Each number, therefore, contained an essay from his pen on one or the other of these subjects. But he was too shrewd a man of business, and too well acquainted with the tastes of his readers, to confine himself to the serious matters of politics. "When I first found the design of this paper," he wrote in one of his prefaces, ". . . I considered it would be a thing very historical, very long, and though it could be much better performed than ever I was like to do it, this age had such a natural aversion to a solemn and tedious affair that, however profitable, it would never be diverting, and the world would never read it. To get over this difficulty that secret hand, I make no doubt, that directed this birth into the world dictated to make some sort of entertainment or amusement at the end of each paper, upon the immediate subject then on the tongues of the Town, which innocent diversion would hand on the more weighty and serious part of the design into the heads and thoughts of those to whom it might be useful." This "entertaining part," which Defoe hoped would make readers for his more serious reflections, he called "Mercure Scandale: or, Advice from the Scandalous Club." It consisted of short discourses on questions of fashions, manners, morals, taste, and the like, purporting to be written by the members of the "Scandalous Club," usually in answer to inquiries sent to them from readers. For about a year it was published regularly in the *Review*; then, on account of a press of other matter, it was taken out and issued separately, under the title of *The Little Review*; presently it was discontinued altogether.

These journals were important in that they established in England the tradition of the literary or miscellaneous periodical. Of direct influence upon the essay, however, they exerted but little. Neither the *Athenian Mercury* nor Defoe's *Review* had much to do with determining the character of this genre as it was written in the eighteenth century. That rôle was reserved for two papers which followed shortly upon them, appealed to the same general interests, and profited by the taste which they had helped to create.

On April 12, 1709, while the *Review* was still coming out, there appeared the first number of a new journal, *The Tatler*. In external **The Tatler** form it consisted of a single folio leaf printed on both **(1709-1711)** sides; and a prospectus at the beginning announced that it would be published on Tuesdays, Thursdays, and Saturdays, "for the convenience of the post." At first the name of the editor was not known. But it was presently whispered about that he was Richard Steele, a writer and politician of strong Whig sympathies, who at the time was editor of the official government newspaper, *The London Gazette*. As Gazetteer, Steele had access to the latest news, especially of foreign affairs — to a great deal, moreover, that he could not use in the *Gazette* itself. This circumstance, combined with the recent success of Defoe's "Scandalous Club," had given him the idea of publishing a journal of his own that should be at once a newspaper and a collection of essays on miscellaneous subjects. For various reasons he did not wish his own name to appear as editor. He therefore announced the *Tatler* as the work of Isaac Bickerstaff, Esq., a benevolent astrologer in whose name Swift had diverted the town in a humorous pamphlet controversy of the previous year.

The prospectus in the first number announced that the *Tatler* was to consist of two parts — accounts of news and essays. For a time this program was carried out. Until October, 1709, the numbers of the paper regularly contained, under the heading of St. James Coffee-house, a paragraph of foreign news condensed from the latest dispatches from the Continent. After No. 80 (October 13, 1709), however, this disappeared as a regular feature and reappeared only occasionally thereafter. The essays also appeared from the first. In the beginning they were as a rule short, and each number contained several. Thus in No. 5 there was a discourse on love, a notice of a new book, a story of two brave English soldiers, besides several paragraphs of news. As time went on, the length of the essays was increased, and the number ultimately reduced to one to each issue; when the *Tatler* was discontinued, this had become the usual practice.

Steele began his periodical entirely by himself; the plan was his, and he wrote the first few numbers without any assistance. With No. 18, however, he began to receive help from an old school friend and fellow Whig, Joseph Addison, then under-secretary to the Lord Lieutenant of Ireland. Addison wrote for the *Tatler* off and on until its withdrawal, contributing in all some forty-one papers and parts of thirty-four others, a little over a third of the total number. At no time did he become a dominant influence in the journal.

The Tatler continued to appear for twenty-one months. Finally, on the 2d of January, 1711, it was suddenly withdrawn, greatly to the regret of the large public which had come to welcome its half-humorous, half-satirical comment on the life of the day. "Everyone," wrote the poet Gay, "wanted so agreeable an amusement, and the coffee-houses began to be sensible that the Esquire's Lucubrations alone had brought them more customers than all other newspapers put together." It was not long, however, before a new periodical took its place.

On March 1, 1711, two months after the cessation of the *Tatler*, appeared the first number of the *Spectator*. The new paper resembled **The Spectator (1711-1712)** the *Tatler* in external form, but, unlike the *Tatler*, it was published daily, and at no time contained news. A single essay, headed by a Latin or Greek motto, and followed by a group of advertisements, made up the contents of each number. The editor was announced to be a silent but very observing man named Mr. Spectator, who was assisted in his conduct of the paper by a club composed of an old country knight, a lawyer, a merchant, a soldier, a man of the world, and a clergyman. The general editorial charge of the new periodical was in the hands of Steele. Addison was a very frequent contributor, and indeed wrote more essays than his friend; his assistance extended also to the general design of the work. A few other persons, such as Addison's cousin Eustace Budgell, John Hughes, Henry Grove, and Henry Martin, contributed papers occasionally.

The audience which the *Spectator* was designed to reach was a diversified one. It included persons of quality, students and professional men, merchants of the City, and, above all, women. "I take it for a particular happiness," wrote Steele in No. 4, "that I have always had an easy and familiar admittance to the fair sex . . . As these compose half the world, and are, by the just complaisance and gallantry of our nation, the more powerful part of our people, I shall dedicate a considerable share of these my speculations to their service, and shall lead the young through all the becoming duties of virginity, marriage, and widowhood . . . In a word, I shall take it for the greatest glory of my work if among reasonable women this paper may furnish tea-table talk."

With this variety of appeal, it is not strange that the new journal became popular. Gay wrote in May, 1711, two months after it began to appear: "the Spectator . . . is in every one's hand, and a constant topic of our morning conversation at tea-tables and coffee-houses."[1] In August, 1712, when this popularity was at its height, the government imposed on all periodicals a stamp tax of a halfpenny for each half-sheet and a shilling a week for each advertisement. As a consequence, a great many papers went under. For a time the *Spectator* continued to appear, though, as its price was doubled, many of its subscribers fell off. But the loss of the subscribers was a less serious blow to the paper than the loss of a great number of its advertisers as a result of the shilling tax. From this blow it never recovered, and was discontinued, with the 555th number, on December 6, 1712.

It was in the *Tatler* and the *Spectator*, and under the conditions imposed by the nature of these papers, that the new essay of the eighteenth century had its birth. As was only natural, many of its

[1] For details concerning the circulation of the *Spectator*, see below, pp. 419–420.

distinguishing features betrayed clearly the character of its origin. Thus, the limits of the single sheet on which the journals were printed

Effect of periodical publication on the new essay

restricted the essays to a relatively brief compass; the efforts of the writers to conceal their authorship under the names of imaginary editors gave to their self-revelations an indirect and somewhat dramatic tone; and the fact of periodical publication resulted in the adoption of many devices of a purely occasional and journalistic nature, such as letters from correspondents, answers to criticisms, references to events of the day, and the like. Nor was the influence of the conditions under which the new essay was produced confined to these more or less external features. Written not as the seventeenth-century essay had been for a limited circle of cultured individuals, but for a large and growing periodical-reading public with diversified interests and tastes, it inevitably took on a popular tone entirely absent from the older essay. Finally, as an indirect result of its connection with the periodicals, the new essay came strongly under the influence of the social movement of the time.

Both Steele and Addison, in numerous passages in the *Tatler* and the *Spectator*, laid great stress on the didactic character of their

The influence of the social movement on the new essay

undertaking. Steele, in particular, made no secret of his reformatory zeal. "I own myself of the Society for Reformation of Manners," he wrote in *Tatler* No. 3. "We have lower instruments than those of the family of Bickerstaff for punishing great crimes and exposing the abandoned. Therefore, as I design to have notices from all public assemblies, I shall take upon me only indecorums, improprieties, and negligencies, in such as should give us better examples. After this declaration, if a fine lady thinks fit to giggle at church, or a great beau to come in drunk to a play, either shall be sure to hear of it in my ensuing paper; for merely as a well-bred man I cannot bear these enormities." And again, with perhaps a growing seriousness, he declared in No. 39: "I am called forth by the immense love I bear to my fellow creatures, and the warm inclination I feel within me, to stem, as far as I can, the prevailing torrent of vice and ignorance." Addison was scarcely less explicit, though he perhaps emphasized more than Steele had done his intention to make his teaching agreeable. "I shall endeavor," he wrote in a famous passage in *Spectator* No. 10, "to enliven morality with wit, and to temper wit with morality, that my readers may, if possible, both ways find their account in the speculation of the day. And to the end that their virtue and discretion may not be short, transient, intermitting starts of thoughts, I have resolved to refresh their memories from day to day, till I have recovered them out of that desperate state of vice and folly into which the age is fallen. . . . I shall be ambitious to have it said of me that I have brought philosophy out of closets and libraries, schools and colleges, to dwell in clubs and assemblies, at tea-tables and in coffee-houses."

In thus adopting as the aim of their journals moral and social reformation, Steele and Addison were simply placing themselves in line with one of the most powerful tendencies of early eighteenth-century England — the reaction against the moral license of Restoration society which came with the rise into prominence and affluence of the middle classes. This was not, however, the only way in which the social movement affected the periodicals, and through them the new essay. By the beginning of the eighteenth century the coffee-house had come to be one of the most influential of London institutions, the center of innumerable discussions on morals, literature, politics, society, in which members of the reading public sharpened their wits, learned to have opinions of their own on all manner of subjects, and acquired a taste for a simple, colloquial, unbookish style of speech. The periodicals became in a very real sense the organs of this coffee-house world. Their writers were members of it; they reported its conversation, described and sometimes satirized its characters, attempted to reform its evil tendencies, and in general reflected its spirit and tone. In short, more than any other literary form of the eighteenth century, the periodical essay was an outgrowth of the London coffee-houses.

A third group of influences affecting the new essay came from the field of literature. Confronted by the problem of promoting moral and social reform and at the same time holding the interest of a large and heterogeneous public, the periodical writers found the somewhat narrow formula of the seventeenth-century essay inadequate to their needs. Without abandoning it entirely (Steele, indeed, owed not a little to Cowley, and both Bacon and Montaigne continued to have an influence), they looked

Literary influences on the periodical essay

about for new methods and forms that would give to their writing the variety and flexibility which both their public and their material required.

Of the literary forms with which they thus attempted to vivify the essay one of the most influential was the " character." The fashion of writing " characters," or descriptive sketches of typical personages, had become established in England during the early years of the seventeenth century. The event which initiated the vogue was the publication in 1592 by Isaac Casaubon, a celebrated French classical scholar, of a Latin translation of the *Characters* of Theophrastus. Tyrtamus of Lesbos, commonly called Theophrastus, was a Greek of the fourth and third centuries B.C. (cir. 372–cir. 288), one of the most eminent of the disciples of Aristotle. The work by which he most affected modern literature consisted of a series of twenty-eight descriptions of the various qualities characteristic of human beings, such as garrulity, rusticity, newsmongering, impudence, superstition, tediousness, pride, timidity. In all these descriptions he followed a stereotyped method, first defining the quality in general terms, then illustrating this definition by an enumeration of typical actions. Under the influence of Casaubon's translation the genre thus conceived became widely popular in seventeenth-century England. The first writer to cultivate it was Bishop Joseph Hall, who published in 1608 *Characters of Vices and Virtues*, a collection of descriptions of typical personages, each embodying some moral quality, good or bad, such as the wise man, the humble man, the truly noble, the busybody, the malcontent, the vainglorious. Other collections followed. In 1614 appeared the " characters " ascribed to Sir Thomas Overbury, the subjects of which were somewhat more concrete than those of Hall, and included, in addition to moral qualities, social and national types. Another character-book of the same period was John Earle's *Microcosmographie, or a Piece of the World Discovered in Essays and Characters*, first issued in 1628 and frequently republished during the next fifty years. Earle's subjects were similar for the most part to those of the Overbury collection : he wrote of the " young raw preacher," of the " grave divine," of the " mere young gentleman of the university," of the " mere gull citizen," of the " plain country fellow." Numerous other collections of the same type made their appearance during the second half of the seventeenth century.

The "character"

Two features distinguished all of these attempts at character-writing: first, the human types they represented, whether ethical, social, or national, were but slightly individualized; and second, as compositions they formed an independent literary species, allied to the essay but seldom combined with it. It remained for a French writer of the latter part of the century at once to individualize the " character " and to combine it organically with the essay. In 1688, at the end of a new translation of Theophrastus, Jean La Bruyère (1645–1696) published a series of short chapters called collectively *Les Caractères, ou les Mœurs de ce Siècle*.[2] Each of these chapters treated some moral question or some phase of the social life of the time — personal merit, women, society and conversation, the city, the court, the nobility, judgments, fashion, man in general. In the first edition the essay element predominated: the chapters were very largely made up of general reflections, stated succinctly and without transitional phrases, in the form of maxims. Here and there, however, between two groups of maxims, appeared brief " characters " or portraits of representative individuals, each designated by a name of Latin or Greek origin, as, for example, Cléante, Sosie, Cresus, Narcisse. In later editions, while the reflections remained, the portraits greatly increased in number. They took various forms — descriptions, anecdotes, dialogues, typical narratives. Whatever the form, they had one feature in common — they were all thoroughly individualized. Not merely by the use of names, but by the inclusion of concrete detail of all kinds, La Bruyère succeeded in giving the impression that his portraits, while representative of a class, were none the less portraits of real persons.

To the writers of the *Tatler* and the *Spectator*, intent on a concrete presentation of the life around them, the generalized " characters " of the type of Overbury's and Earle's made less of an appeal than the individualized character-essays of La Bruyère. Steele, in particular, found *Les Caractères* a congenial work, and made no secret of his intention to imitate it.[3]

The " character," though perhaps the most influential, was not the only literary form from which the periodical writers took suggestions for the new essay. They learned much from the writings of earlier

---

[2] An English translation appeared in 1699.
[3] See *Tatler* No. 9.

and contemporary literary critics, notably the Englishman Dryden and the Frenchman Saint-Évremond. They adapted to their uses the popular genre of the epistle as it had been developed in England in the middle of the seventeenth century by such writers as James Howell and Robert Loveday and later applied to purposes of journalism by the editors of the *Athenian Mercury*. They showed themselves close students of the literature of visions and allegories, ancient and modern, from Plato to Edmund Spenser. They took hints of subject and style from the collections of oriental stories that were beginning, in the early eighteenth century, to penetrate into western Europe. They borrowed not a little in the way of method from the contemporary French novelists.

Other literary forms contributory to the new essay

Such were the varied influences under which Steele and Addison created and brought to perfection the periodical essay. Steele led the way: his was the design of the *Tatler* and, in part at least, of the *Spectator*; his were the first rough sketches of nearly all the types of papers which appeared in the two journals. But though more original than his associate and possessed of greater moral fervor and power of touching the feelings of his readers, he was less systematic, less scholarly, less subtly humorous; and it remained for Addison to exhibit the full possibilities of many lines of thought and many artistic devices which he had merely suggested. However, the collaboration between the two men was ever close, and the essays which they wrote possessed numerous characteristics in common.

The rôles of Steele and Addison in the development of the eighteenth-century essay

To a reader familiar with Montaigne, Bacon, or Cowley, the essays of Addison and Steele, while presenting some traditional features, must have seemed on the whole a new species. They were as a rule shorter than the essays of the seventeenth century and, what was perhaps even more striking, all of uniform or nearly uniform length. In character they were more occasional, more satirical, more social and citified, and a great deal less bookish; all in all, too, as compared with the work of Montaigne and Cowley, they were less intimately and directly personal. But, most of all, they exhibited a variety of subject and method quite unapproached by the essayists of the preceding century.

Distinguishing features of the new essay

The themes treated in the *Tatler* and *Spectator* essays belonged in general to two main classes, both of which were in a measure dictated by the program of social reform for which the periodicals stood. Addison in *Spectator* 435 clearly indicated this division. "Most of the papers I give the public," he said, "are written on subjects that never vary, but are forever fixed and immutable. Of this kind are all my more serious essays and discourses; but there is another sort of speculations, which I consider as occasional papers, that take their rise from the folly, extravagance, and caprice of the present age." Among the "fixed and immutable" subjects naturally appeared many of the themes of the older essayists: modesty, the government of the passions, fame, love, immortality, the vanity of ambition, conversation, friendship, honor, education, marriage, cheerfulness, hypocrisy, the enjoyments of a country life, faith. To this group belonged also such general literary subjects as humor, wit, taste, and the pleasures of the imagination. More distinctive of the spirit and aims of the new essay were the themes of the second class — those which inspired the "occasional papers." They included the whole range of contemporary social life, though, as was only natural, the emphasis fell on interests and customs especially characteristic of London. The absurdities of the Italian opera, the practice of the duel, the habit of taking snuff, the puppet-show, the lottery, the reading of newspapers, fashionable slang, the Midnight Masquerade, coffeehouses, "party-patches," the belief in witchcraft, the hoop-petticoat, the effect of the war on the English language, the street-cries of London, pin-money, the occupations of a young lady of fashion, the Mohocks — all these furnished material for kindly satirical essays which, though somewhat less numerous than the speculations on abstract subjects, were perhaps more popular with contemporary readers. Both groups of papers were pervaded by a common spirit — a spirit earnest and didactic, to be sure, and not particularly personal, but always urbane, and lightened when the subject demanded by touches of quiet humor.

The same variety which characterized the subject matter of the new essay appeared also in its form. The essay of the seventeenth century had been a relatively simple compound of three elements — general reflections, "examples" and "sentences" from books, and personal observations or reminiscences. To these familiar elements

the essayists who wrote for the *Tatler* and the *Spectator* added
several others — tales of real life, elaborate classical and oriental
Types of allegories, letters and diaries of correspondents, typical
essays moral and social "characters," reports of the conversation of London coffee-houses and tea-tables. The result was that,
instead of papers constructed more or less on the same pattern, they
were able to give their readers a considerable number of distinct
types of essays.

They were particularly fond of what Addison called "papers of
morality," that is to say, discourses devoted primarily to the exposition
Moralizing of some general ethical principle or quality, such as mod-
essays esty, cheerfulness, hypocrisy, affectation. In writing them
they followed no single method; sometimes they developed their
central theme in a formal, orderly way, with illustrations from the
classics, the Scriptures, or the more serious modern authors; sometimes they contented themselves with simply suggesting, in paragraphs devoid of concrete detail, a few of its significant phases. Their
models, so far as they were dependent upon any, were to be found
in part among the writings of the earlier essayists — Bacon in particular furnished them many hints of method — and in part among the
sermons of the great English divines of the preceding generation.

Many of the features of the "papers of morality" characterized
also another type of essays much cultivated in the periodicals —
Critical essays in literary criticism. These were of two classes,
essays according as the starting point was a general literary
idea or a particular work. Both classes were marked by like qualities of composition — great explicitness of plan, ample illustration,
and abundant generalization.

A third type of paper, somewhat less abstract than these two, included essays made up of general reflections interspersed with "char-
Character acters." This type was peculiarly Steele's; whenever,
essays from early in the *Tatler* to the end of the *Spectator*,
he had occasion to treat of the broader aspects of social life — types
of character, good breeding, conversation — it was in this mold
that he tended to cast his thought. As in the model of the genre,
Les Caractères of La Bruyère, the function of the "characters"
was primarily illustrative. They were embedded in the reflections,
sometimes one in an essay, sometimes several. In manner, too, they

owed much to La Bruyère. All his favorite devices of exposition — dialogue, apostrophe, description, narrative — reappeared in the work of Steele and his imitators. Even the names were largely of the same type. For a few characters who bore English names, such as Will Nice, Tom Folio, Ned Softly, there were numerous others — Clarissa, Nobilis, Senecio, Urbanus, Flavia, Eusebius — who clearly belonged with La Bruyère's Romans and Greeks. Such, in general, were the typical character-essays of the *Tatler* and the *Spectator*. In addition there were a few others, such as the account of the club at the Trumpet and the description of Mr. Spectator's friends, in which the portraits were presented for their own sake, independently of any general ideas they might serve to illustrate. But papers of this sort appeared too infrequently to constitute a separate type.

Sometimes, again, the essayist, instead of pointing his moral with a " character," employed for the same purpose an incident or scene **Anecdotal** from his observation of the life around him. Thus, **essays** Addison, who perhaps made most use of the device, introduced his remarks on popular superstitions in *Spectator* 7 with an account of a conversation at a friend's dinner table. In this case the anecdote preceded the reflections, which were represented as rising naturally out of it; in other cases the order was reversed. Whatever the order, the moral of the essay commonly appeared as subsidiary to the concrete happening which started the essayist's train of thought.

Still another group of essays was made up of those containing letters from correspondents, real or imaginary. This type, a favor- **Letter** ite with all contributors, flourished in several varieties. **essays** Sometimes the essayist presented his correspondent's words without comment; sometimes he added remarks of his own, intended to supplement or enforce the point of the letter. In many cases one letter only was given; in others the paper contained several, all perhaps dealing with different subjects. Nor were the letters themselves all of the same pattern. Some were sketches of character, others were requests for advice, still others were narratives of real life or satirical accounts of contemporary fashions and conditions.

Finally, the *Tatler* and the *Spectator* contained a great many essays of a type predominantly narrative. Some, perhaps most, of these dealt with simple incidents of everyday life set in a background of contemporary manners. Such, for example, were the accounts of Jenny Distaff's love affair and marriage, and the story of Orlando, **Narrative essays** in the *Tatler*; and the narratives of Mr. Spectator's visit to Sir Roger de Coverley's country place and of the old knight's return journey to London, in the *Spectator*. For the most part in these narrative papers the element of moralizing was slight, though it was nearly always present; and the interest of the essays for both writers and readers lay in their faithful pictures of the habits and acts of ordinary English people. Not all of the narratives in the periodicals, however, were of this realistic sort. With the serious-minded readers of the early eighteenth century few essays enjoyed a greater vogue than those cast in the form of visions or oriental allegories. Steele experimented with this type in one or two papers early in the *Tatler*; but it remained for Addison to develop it into a finished medium for the expression of moral and religious ideas.

These, then, were some of the typical forms into which the writers for the *Tatler* and the *Spectator* cast their ethical teaching and their critical comment on the life of the day. They were not, however, always content to limit themselves to these main types. On the contrary, they never ceased to invent new devices, which they employed perhaps no more than once or twice and then completely neglected. To this class of special essays belonged, in the *Tatler*, the papers on the Court of Honor, on the adventures of a shilling, and on frozen words; in the *Spectator*, the journal of the Indian kings, the anatomy of the coquette's heart, the diary of Clarinda, the minutes of the Everlasting Club, and the account of Pug the Monkey. Taken all together they furnished a striking manifestation of the diversity of method and device which the new conditions of publication made characteristic of the essay.

When the daily issue of the *Spectator* came to an end in December, 1712, the eighteenth-century essay in all its varieties was fully formed. Thenceforward for over a hundred years the history of **The later history of the periodical essay** the familiar essay in England was the history of the imitations made of this fixed and established type. Many, perhaps most, of these imitations appeared in single-sheet journals modeled closely on the *Tatler*; by 1809 no less than 220 such periodicals had seen the light in London and other cities of the

British Isles. Of the early ventures of this type the most notable were the *Guardian* (1713), edited by Steele and written by him in conjunction with Addison, Pope, and others, and the revived *Spectator* (1714), the work almost entirely of Addison. Then for a number of years the single-sheet papers took on a prevailingly political character, the reflection in large measure of the bitter party strife which raged under the first two Georges; and familiar essays, though they continued to appear, became almost swamped under the stream of purely controversial writing. Toward the middle of the century, however, journals of a more general nature again came into vogue. *The Champion* (1739–1741), a semi-political paper to which the chief contributor was Henry Fielding, was followed by the *Rambler* (1750–1752), a strictly literary production, written almost entirely by Dr. Johnson; the *Covent-Garden Journal* (1752), another enterprise of Fielding's; the *Adventurer* (1752–1754), a journal edited by John Hawkesworth with the aid of Johnson; the *World* (1753–1756); the *Connoisseur* (1754–1756); the *Bee* (1759); the *Mirror* (1779–1780); the *Lounger* (1785–1787); the *Observer* (1785–1790); and numerous others to the end of the century. But journals of this sort were not the only repositories in which the imitators of Addison and Steele published their works. Many essays of the *Tatler* and *Spectator* type appeared in the somewhat restricted columns of the daily and weekly newspapers; it was in a newspaper, for example, that Johnson printed his *Idler* papers, and Goldsmith his *Letters from a Citizen of the World*. Many also appeared in the monthly magazines which in constantly increasing numbers followed in the wake of the successful *Gentleman's Magazine* (founded 1731). And a few writers resorted to the practice, universal in the seventeenth century, of publishing essays for the first time in volumes. To this last class belonged Vicesimus Knox, whose *Essays Moral and Literary* (1778–1779) revealed a marked admiration for the great masters of the periodical form.

Of the many essayists who in the middle and later years of the eighteenth century carried on the traditions of Addison and Steele, two won in a peculiar measure the admiration of their contemporaries — Samuel Johnson and Oliver Goldsmith.

Johnson's career as a familiar essayist fell entirely within the decade of the fifties. In 1750 he began to publish the *Rambler*, a paper of the type of the *Tatler* and the *Spectator*; it ran until 1752, and though only moderately successful when first issued, took its place as one of the standard essay-collections of the century when reprinted in volumes. Between 1752 and 1754 he contributed a number of papers to Hawkesworth's *Adventurer*, and in 1758 he started in a weekly newspaper a series of essays entitled *The Idler*, which continued to appear during two years. In all of these ventures Johnson's aims closely resembled those of the great essayists of the beginning of the century. The name "periodical mentor," which he frequently applied to himself, exactly expressed the spirit and purpose of his work; he wrote primarily to satirize and correct. In his methods of composition, too, he approved himself a faithful follower of Addison and Steele, writing "papers of morality," oriental apologues, sketches of domestic life, character-essays, criticisms, letters, with little if any deviation from the model which they had set. Only in two respects, indeed, did his practice differ markedly from theirs. For one thing, though he did not entirely withhold his satire from the lighter aspects of social life, — witness the letter in the *Rambler* from the young lady who found country life a bore, and the Dick Minim papers in the *Idler*,— still his preference was for subjects of a serious moral and religious import — abstraction and self-examination, patience, the folly of anticipating misfortunes. Again, the style in which he clothed his thoughts, especially in the *Rambler*, drew little of its inspiration from the polished but colloquial English of the *Tatler* and the *Spectator*. Though he was to write, in *The Lives of the Poets*, perhaps the most sympathetic appreciation of the qualities of Addison's style which the eighteenth century produced, in his own work he strove for a stateliness and balance of rhythm and a Latinized dignity of vocabulary quite remote from the simplicity and ease of his predecessor.

(margin) **Samuel Johnson (1709–1784)**

Goldsmith appeared before the public as an essayist almost a decade later than Johnson. He began to contribute to the *Monthly Review* and other periodicals in 1757, but his characteristic manner first became manifest in a number of miscellaneous papers which he wrote in 1759 for a short-lived journal called *The Bee*. In 1760 and 1761 he contributed to the *Public Ledger* a series of 123 letters purporting to be written by a philosophical Chinaman sojourning in England, which were later

(margin) **Oliver Goldsmith (1728–1774)**

reprinted under the title of *The Citizen of the World*.[4] These letters constituted his most extensive and elaborate excursion into the field of the essay. With the exception of a collected edition of his various papers which appeared in 1765, they were also his last publication in that genre.

Goldsmith developed quite another side of his inheritance from the earlier essayists than did Johnson — the side of humor and social satire. He did not, to be sure, altogether neglect serious themes. Among his essays were numerous papers of literary criticism, a few general ethical discussions, and at least one oriental allegory — the story of Asem — the moral of which was quite as weighty as that of any similar production of Addison or Johnson. But these were not his favorite or most characteristic subjects. It was when he was recording his own or his Chinese traveler's opinions on the English passion for politics and newspapers, on the quack doctors of London, on the length of ladies' trains, on gambling among women, on the races at Newmarket, on the manners of fashionable shopkeepers, on the pride and luxury of the middle class, or picturing domestic life in the manner of Steele, or creating fantasies that Addison might have envied, that his true genius as an essayist appeared most clearly. And his manner was perfectly suited to his substance — in its simple diction and constructions and its conversational tone the direct antithesis of the manner of Johnson.

The type of essay established in the *Tatler* and the *Spectator*, and cultivated in a host of imitations throughout the eighteenth century, persisted in full vigor in the early years of the nineteenth. **The survival of the periodical essay in the early nineteenth century** Its survival was especially marked in such magazines of the period as the *Gentleman's* and the *European*. In the former, for example, from January, 1802, to November, 1809, there appeared regularly a series of essays in the manner of the *Spectator* under the general title of *The Projector*. After the latter date this series was apparently crowded out by the

---

[4] The method employed in these essays was by no means a new one. Used by Addison in *Spectator* 50, it had become especially popular after the publication in 1721 of Montesquieu's *Lettres persanes*, translated into English in 1735 as *Persian Letters*. In 1757, three years before Goldsmith began his series of essays in the *Public Ledger*, Horace Walpole published a *Letter from Xo Ho, a Chinese Philosopher at London, to his Friend Lien Chi at Peking*.

growing pressure of miscellaneous contributions from correspondents; no reason, however, was given for its somewhat sudden discontinuance, and it seems to have been popular to the last. In the *European Magazine* essays of the eighteenth-century type were published regularly and in considerable numbers for at least twenty years after the opening of the century. Thus the issue for August, 1800, had an " Essay on Fashion," manifestly modeled on the moralizing papers of the *Rambler*; and the numbers for November and December contained each an " Essay after the Manner of Goldsmith." Between January and June, 1805, imitations of Johnson were particularly numerous, two in the January number being described as " by the author of the ' Essays after the Manner of Goldsmith ' "; while from April to November of the same year a series called *The Jester* carried on the lighter traditions of the *Spectator*, with all the paraphernalia of correspondents and characters invented for illustration. In the numbers for July to December, 1811, the essays were about evenly divided between imitations of the *Spectator* and heavier imitations of the *Rambler*. Nor was this the end. For at least another ten years essays on the model of one or another of the great eighteenth-century writers continued to appear in the *European* — contributors who affected lightness and cleverness following Addison or Goldsmith, those who were oppressed with the seriousness of life finding their inspiration in Dr. Johnson.

III. THE NEW MAGAZINE ESSAY OF THE NINETEENTH CENTURY

Within the early years of the nineteenth century the type of familiar essay was developed which has continued to the present. By 1825 it had largely supplanted the imitations of the *Tatler* and *Spectator*, and Lamb, Hunt, Hazlitt, De Quincey, and other writers had won for it a popularity that the essay had not enjoyed for a long time. The new type differed from the old in many essential respects.

In the first place, the new essay had a much wider range of subject than the old. It was no longer confined largely to " the Town," to the fashions and foibles of society, to problems of conduct and manners, or to the general principles of morality. There was, indeed, no general uniformity of topic. Each essayist wrote upon whatever

presented itself to him as an attractive or congenial theme; his range
of subject was determined only by the breadth or narrowness of his
individual interests and sympathies. Lamb wrote of his
schoolboy life, of his daily occupations, his vacation
excursions, his friends and his family, his personal sympathies and antipathies; Leigh Hunt chatted about his
reading, his fireside comforts, the interesting individuals or types he
had observed or experiences he had encountered, or tried to discover
compensation for the deaths of little children; Hazlitt lingered over
his books or recalled his first meeting with poets later famous,
recounted the delights of a solitary tramp in the open country and
the evening comforts of an inn, presented the pleasures of painting
or of hating, or considered the basis of his deepest feelings; De
Quincey gossiped of his acquaintances or recalled gorgeous or
terrible dream fancies. As many writers of the new essay, including
Lamb and Hunt and Hazlitt, spent their most active years in London,
they frequently, of course, wrote on some aspect of London life,
but their subjects included such as had been in large measure
beneath the sympathetic regard of the eighteenth-century essayists —
chimney sweeps, the postman, clerks, artisans, and sailors.

Wide range of subject of the new essay

In manner of presentation and purpose, too, the new essay was
markedly different from the old. One of the most characteristic differences is that the essayist no longer hid his individuality
behind the elaborately sustained figure of an invented
Mr. Bickerstaff, or Mr. Spectator, or Chinese Traveler,
but wrote in his own person. Even when through diffidence he employed the editorial plural or adopted a pen-name, he
really expressed his own personality, and his thin disguise was easily
penetrable. Many other long-used conventions were almost wholly
discarded; for example, the machinery of clubs and correspondents,
the visions and apologues, and the invented characters with classical
or pseudo-classical names. The classics, too, and classical history
were less drawn upon for mottoes and quotations and illustrations.
In general, there was much less artificiality and much greater directness, and a strong tendency to rely for illustration upon the personal
experience of the writer or of his acquaintances, upon contemporary
events or those of comparatively recent history, and upon modern or
native literature. Nor, as a rule, was the new essay marked by the

Directness and individualism of the new essay

satiric or didactic tone that generally pervaded the old. The eighteenth-century essay was largely social in character, and professed as its principal aim a reformation of the delinquencies and peccadillos of society. The new essay was just as distinctly individualistic; as a literary form it was not the vehicle of any propaganda. The character of each essayist's work as a whole was determined purely by his peculiar temperament, and any single essay might reflect his mood of a moment or the deeply grounded philosophy of his lifetime. The one property common to the essayists of the early nineteenth century is their egotism; they were chiefly interested in themselves, and were frank, though by no means offensively so, in the expression of this interest. This frankness of egotism, however, is characteristic of the period rather than of the literary type, although, of course, a strongly personal coloring is never absent from the familiar essay of the nineteenth century.

Of all the differences between the essay of the eighteenth century and that of the nineteenth, the most obvious is the much greater length of the latter. As the content of a piece of writing is largely dependent upon the space it is to occupy, the greater length of the new essay is one of its essential characteristics. The eighteenth-century essay had space for only sketches and outlines or for the treatment of a very limited phase of a subject; the new essay could present full-length portraits or the development of ample themes, and it invited digression. The *Tatler* and *Spectator* papers, from their mode of publication and the temper of the particular reading public to whom they were directed, were very brief, ranging from about twelve hundred to fifteen hundred words each, and in this respect, as in others, they were followed by their imitators. Of the founders of the new essay, Leigh Hunt most closely resembled the writers of the preceding century in brevity; probably in part because of his temperament, and in part because, like the earlier essayists, he wrote principally for newspapers or for periodicals modeled upon the *Tatler*. Lamb was between the old and the new, the *Essays of Elia* averaging from one and a half to two times the length of the eighteenth-century periodical essay. The greater number of Hazlitt's essays were three or four times as long as those of the *Spectator* type; in this, as in so many other respects, they were wholly of the new order. Even within such expanded limits De Quincey was unable to confine himself, and some of his papers were inordinately long. Naturally, there cannot be any definitely fixed length for the essay, but so far as there is any standard, that set by Hazlitt became generally observed and is now usually followed. It permits the writer to treat his theme with reasonable fullness, but checks a presentation that would tax the capacity of the reader at a single sitting.

The changed character of the essay was the effect of a number of causes. The first was the progress of Romanticism, which, by 1820, **Causes of the change in the character of the essay** throughout the world of literature had resulted in the expression of new interests or of those long dormant, — particularly the interest the individual felt in himself, — in the abandonment of old standards and conventions, and in experimentation with new or long-disused forms. Individualism had been strongly stimulated. The essayists were moved by the same forces as the poets. Indeed, in practically all essentials there is a manifest similarity between the new poetry and the new essay. The second cause is closely related to the first: the new forces in life and literature affected men of original and responsive genius, capable of developing a new type of essay, and by the success of their own efforts influential in establishing it in popular favor. The services of Lamb and Hunt and Hazlitt are exactly comparable to those of Wordsworth and Byron and Keats. A less general and somewhat more tangible influence was the greatly heightened interest in Montaigne. His *Essais*, in Cotton's translation, was one of the small stock of books identified as certainly belonging to Lamb; he was quoted or appreciatively referred to several times by Leigh Hunt; and Hazlitt was thoroughly familiar with the *Essais* and a consistent admirer of both their matter and their manner.

But the single factor of greatest moment in the development of the new type was the establishment of the modern literary magazine. At **Establishment of modern literary magazines** the beginning of the nineteenth century, publication of essays as independent periodicals after the fashion of the *Tatler* and the *Spectator* had largely given way to publication in newspapers and magazines. Obviously, the small news sheets could not provide space for any considerable expansion of the essay, which, moreover, was merely an excrescent growth upon them. Nor did the existing magazines, such as the *Gentleman's* and the *European*, offer much greater possibilities. They were literally magazines, overcrowded depositories of miscellaneous matter — meteorological data, tables of the values of stocks, parliamentary reports, records of births and deaths, cursory reviews, notes of the stage and the arts, letters from correspondents and answers to them, and curious information on a variety of topics. Literature was usually represented in a small section devoted to whatever of essays, sketches, verse, etc. the editor needed to fill out his ninety-odd pages, or had not the heart to reject. Rarely did a number of one of the old magazines have a single article of genuine literary merit or interest. And the critical reviews were even more hopelessly dull and wanting in originality. Both classes of periodicals were almost wholly the product of amateurs or of poorly paid drudges.

Vivification of the literary periodical first manifested itself in the critical reviews with the establishment of the *Edinburgh Review* in 1802 and the *Quarterly Review* in 1809, the former a Whig, the latter a Tory organ. From the first the rivalry between them was intense; and the liberal payments to contributors soon attracted to each a group of vigorous young writers, whose pronouncements upon the social, political, and literary questions of the day, whatever they lacked in depth and poise, certainly wanted nothing in assurance and energy. Both the *Edinburgh* and the *Quarterly* became immediately and dominantly popular.

The first notable effort to establish a distinctly literary magazine was made by Leigh Hunt in the *Reflector* (1811–1812). Lack of financial support, however, and other causes not now known made the venture abortive. But only a few years later the first modern magazine was actually founded. The success of the new reviews prompted William Blackwood, an active and astute Edinburgh publisher, to set up a magazine which should be equally different from the dull and characterless miscellanies then in existence. He was unfortunate, however, in the first selection of his staff, and the initial number of *Blackwood's Magazine*, which appeared in April, 1817, gave no real promise of originality or increased attractiveness. But with the October number John Wilson ("Christopher North"), together with Lockhart, joined Blackwood's forces; and the former, particularly, imparted to the magazine a character derived from his own freshness and high spirits. Almost instantly *Blackwood's* leaped into a more than local popularity.

The success of *Blackwood's* encouraged the establishment of the first magazine of similar character in London. This was the *London Magazine*, the initial number of which appeared in January, 1820. Its first editor, John Scott, was apparently given a free hand by the owners; he, in turn, threw open the pages of the *London* to good writing on almost any subject and paid for it liberally. As a result of this policy the *London* commanded the pens of original and attractive writers and from the beginning was of interest and high standing. After the death of Scott in a duel, rapid changes in the control of the magazine ensued, the result of which was a swift descent in its fortunes. But it had shown the way to success and had set up a new standard for magazines. The conduct of the *New Monthly Magazine* illustrates the force of the example set by the *London*. The *New Monthly*, which was founded in 1814, during the first seven years of its existence was distinguished in no vital respect from the older miscellanies. In 1820, however, the popularity of the *London* forced a change of policy: it was placed under the editorship of Campbell, the poet, and inaugurating a new series with the first number for 1821, it became of the new order. Within a few more years many magazines of the older type had disappeared and very much the kind of magazine we know to-day had become definitely established.

Probably the most obvious contribution of the modern magazine to the development of the essay was the encouragement to expansion

Obligations of the new essay to the modern magazine beyond the former narrow limits, an expansion impossible in the newspapers or in the older magazines, divided as they were into numerous crowded departments. The new magazines, unburdened with the traditions that hampered the old, and thus excluding much of the journalistic matter appearing in their predecessors, were able to provide not merely a page or two for an essay, but six or eight, and on occasion, ten or twelve or twenty pages. They thus made possible the changed content and manner of the essay, which could result only from an enlargement of its physical limits.

But increased length and all that goes with it was not the only indebtedness of the new essay to the new magazine. *Blackwood's* and the *London* could make a place for themselves only by being different from the long-established magazines, by surpassing them in literary interest and attractiveness; their editors and owners accordingly vied with one another in offering inducements to writers of original power, paying them with hitherto unexampled liberality and leaving them free to write as their own genius might direct. Finally, the very fact that these magazines were new, that they were unfettered by hampering precedents, was in itself a strong incentive to break away from existing conventions and to test new forms and modes. Lamb, Hunt, Hazlitt, Wilson, and De Quincey are chief among the founders of the new essay; though Hunt, the least modern of the group, owed comparatively little to the new magazines, even he departed from his eighteenth-century models for the first time in the *Reflector*; and *Blackwood's* produced Wilson's sketches, and the *London* stimulated Lamb, Hazlitt, and De Quincey to discover their peculiar genius and to give it expression. Extremely significant is the fact that the great body of familiar essays produced within the last century has been written for the modern magazine, the direct successor of *Blackwood's* and the *London*.

During the period within which the new essay was established Lamb, Hunt, and Hazlitt were the most notable writers — notable for their relations to the older type or for their influence upon the development of the new, as well as for the permanent interest and attractiveness of their writings.

Lamb's first essay, " The Londoner," was printed in the *Morning Post* for February 1, 1802. " The Londoner " promised to be the first **Charles** of a series, but the promise was not carried out, and Lamb **Lamb** wrote no other essays until the establishment of Leigh **(1775–1834)** Hunt's *Reflector*. To the four issues of this magazine, which appeared probably in 1811–1812, he contributed a number of short essays as well as two important critical papers. Consequent upon the death of the *Reflector* was a period of scant productivity, which lasted until the appearance of the *London Magazine* in 1820. Lamb's first contribution to this magazine, " The South Sea House," appeared in the number for August, 1820; his last, " Stage Illusion," in that for August, 1825. Between these two dates, writing over the pen-name " Elia," which he had appropriated from an Italian fellow clerk of the South Sea House, Lamb published in the *London* practically all his most characteristic essays. After 1820 he wrote but little except for the *London*, and after 1826 he practically ceased writing at all, his only considerable papers being three or four for the ephemeral

Englishman's Magazine in 1831. Collections of Lamb's essays were made three times before his death in 1834: his *Works* (1818) contained most of his earlier pieces, and the *Essays of Elia* (1823) and the *Last Essays of Elia* (1833) included most of his contributions to the *London* as well as a few of both his earlier and his later papers.

Lamb's earlier essays were written under the influence of the long-established models. His first venture, "The Londoner," was obviously imitative, owing much in particular to the first number of the *Spectator*; and most of his brief papers in the *Reflector* were considerably indebted to the seventeenth-century "character" or to the *Tatler* and its successors.[1] Moreover, even in the period of Lamb's most thoroughly original work, when Elia was doing much to establish the new type of familiar essay, he at times reverted to the manner of the old: the first part of "Poor Relations" is patterned after the seventeenth-century "character"; the first part of "The Wedding" is wholly in the manner of Steele's sketches of domestic life; and "A Vision of Horns," one of the *Essays of Elia* not reprinted by Lamb, he himself characterized as "resembling the most laboured papers in the *Spectator*."

But by far the greater number of the Elia essays were no more imitative than they are imitable; they were wholly original and the expression of Lamb's own personality. They were the very perfection of that kind of intimate writing which wins not merely interest for itself but affection for the writer. The content of these essays was varied. A few were playful fantasies, a few were serious musings; a small number presented Lamb's satirical observation and comment upon incongruities of conduct, a larger number, his humorous observation of incident and character; and seven or eight were critical papers on books and the stage. In almost every one of these papers, even those professedly critical, Lamb's personality was warmly reflected, and by far the greater number of his essays were undisguised autobiography and reminiscence, written in the first person. They recorded ingenuously his sympathies and his prejudices,

---

[1] Something of the nature of the relationship between Lamb's early papers and the eighteenth-century periodical essay will appear from an examination of "A Bachelor's Complaint of the Behaviour of Married People," which appeared first in the *Reflector* and was later reprinted with some changes as an Elia essay.

presented him and his family and his friends, disclosed his habits, and unveiled his memories. They formed almost a complete record of his life, together with an intimate and candid commentary upon it. In them appeared his tenderness and manliness, his tolerance of everything but pretence and priggishness and complacent stupidity, his intensely social nature, his liking for people with some harmless idiosyncrasy, his keen observation of the unexpected hidden amid the commonplace, his devotion to his old folios, and his half-humorous, half-pathetic attitude toward life.

Lamb's most fundamental characteristic was his humor — tender, playful, fantastic, never bitter, usually warming the reader's feeling or flashing a glimpse of a truth hitherto unconsidered. Very frequently the vehicle of this humor was a comparison startlingly unexpected, but perfectly appropriate and owing much of its happiness of effect to a suggestion of incongruity. The illustrative or figurative half of such a comparison was usually drawn from Lamb's familiar acquaintance with English literature of the late sixteenth and the seventeenth century — Shakespeare and the Elizabethan dramatists, Milton and Marvell, Burton and Browne and Fuller, and the Bible. From the same sources came the abundance of allusion that enriched every page, and the choice of word and turn of phrase that gave to his diction its archaic flavor. The result was not the affectation and artificiality that might have been expected, but what Lamb called a " self-pleasing quaintness," a style and manner peculiarly his own and perfectly expressive of his individuality.

About two years after the appearance of Lamb's " The Londoner," Leigh Hunt began to contribute his juvenile essays to the *Traveller*

James Henry newspaper (1804–1805), and during the next fifty years,
Leigh Hunt amid much ephemeral matter, largely critical or journal-
(1784–1859) istic, a very considerable body of familiar essays appeared from his pen. Though in the *Reflector* (1811–1812) he made a notable attempt to found a literary magazine, yet the new type of magazine, when it was actually established, had much slighter effect upon his development than upon that of any of his contemporaries; by far the larger number of his essays were written for newspapers, family miscellanies, and independent sheets patterned somewhat closely after the *Tatler*. In fact, his most attractive and most characteristic work appeared in periodicals of the kind last mentioned. The most

important of these was the earliest, the *Indicator*, which was issued weekly from October 13, 1819, to March 21, 1821. Similar in character were the *Companion* (1828) and *Leigh Hunt's London Journal* (1834–1835). No approximately full collection of Hunt's essays was made before his death, in 1859, nor, indeed, has any been made since. Selections from the *Indicator* and the *Companion* were reprinted in 1834; and the *Seer* (1840–1841), *Men, Women, and Books* (1847), and *Table Talk* (1851) contained a good deal of matter that had previously appeared.[2]

The influence of the earlier types was even more pervasive and persistent in Hunt's work than in Lamb's. Hunt's papers in the *Traveller* were in avowed imitation of the *Connoisseur* (1754–1756), itself an imitation of the *Tatler* and the *Spectator*. In the *Reflector*, which he edited, most of his own essays, as well as many from other contributors, were similar in subject and manner to those of Addison and Goldsmith. A third literary venture of his, the *Round Table* papers in the *Examiner* (1815–1817), was confessedly designed after the *Tatler* and the *Spectator*, and most of Hunt's own writing was strongly suggestive of his reading in the essays of the eighteenth century. The influence of the early models persisted in a large proportion of even his most individual and most nearly original essays, such as those written for the *Indicator*. His " characters," particularly, a form which he cultivated as long as he wrote, owed much both to the seventeenth-century "characters" and to the more lifelike and dramatic studies of the *Tatler* and its successors.

Hunt's own everyday experiences and his observation of the everyday life about him formed the staple of his essays: he wrote upon books, the stage, clothes, manners and habits, the weather, animal pets, interesting types of character, the life of the London streets, the pleasures and the discomforts of a dweller in the suburbs, the joys and the sorrows of domestic life. Books were his chief interest, and his reading largely colored his observation. His distinctive manner first showed itself in " A Day by the Fire," in the last number of the *Reflector* — a cheery, familiarly gossiping presentation of a

---

[2] In the list of Hunt's collected essays, one feels tempted to include the *Autobiography* (1851, 1852, revised 1860); it is much more a series of sketches and reminiscences than a connected account of his life, and it has the chatty, intimate manner of his essays.

book lover's enjoyment of his snug fireside. Hunt's personality as revealed in his essays, unlike Lamb's, was not such as unfailingly to win the reader's appreciative sympathy, nor was he, like Hazlitt, keenly analytical or deeply reflective; he was merely a companionable sort of person who chatted entertainingly about everything that caught his own interest. His talk was sprightly, frequently interrupted to touch some topic that had suggested itself, now colored with sentiment, now shot through with gentle or tricksy humor. Few essayists have conveyed more perfectly than Hunt the sense of their own personality.

Hazlitt first appeared in the rôle of essayist as the principal associate of Leigh Hunt in the *Round Table* papers published in the

William Hazlitt (1778–1830) *Examiner* between January 1, 1815, and January 5, 1817. After the somewhat abrupt termination of this series Hazlitt turned his energies for a few years very largely to the preparation of lectures on English literature, in the meantime writing a few brief essays for the *Edinburgh Magazine*, New Series (1818). With the establishment of the *London Magazine*, in 1820, the period of his most abundant and characteristic work as essayist began. In the periodicals to which he had been contributing he had been cramped for room; now he had space in which to write himself out upon his chosen topics, and his papers accordingly expanded to two or three times their former length. His first essay in the *London* appeared in June, 1820, and he wrote regularly for this magazine until December, 1821. In February of the following year he allied himself with the revivified *New Monthly Magazine*, to which he was a more or less regular contributor until his death, in 1830. He occasionally wrote also for other magazines, for newspapers, and for the miscellanies then coming into popularity.

These contributions to periodicals did not exhaust Hazlitt's fertility. In 1821–1822 he published under the title *Table Talk* thirty-three essays, twenty-six of which had not been printed previously; and in 1826, *The Plain Speaker*, in which thirteen of the thirty-two essays were new. These two collections contained a great deal of his most attractive and most characteristic writing. Except in the *Round Table* (1817), *Table Talk*, and *The Plain Speaker*, Hazlitt did not collect and republish his essays. In 1839 this was in part done by his son in *Winterslow* and *Essays and Sketches*.

In the *Round Table* paper on the *Tatler*, Hazlitt declared Montaigne to be " a most magnanimous and undisguised egotist." In a sense — not the commonly accepted one, to be sure — the first half of this characterization might be applied to Hazlitt as well as to Montaigne; the second half, without any qualification, would be applied to him by anyone who knew him. In the earlier papers of *Round Table* series his individuality showed strongly, although he wrote under the restraint of the editorial and collective *we*; in his later papers he broke through even this thin disguise and wrote freely and openly in his own person. Very few of his essays were purely autobiographic or reminiscent; and yet he wrote the whole body of them out of himself, and into them he wrote himself completely. It would be difficult to discover a single important circumstance of his life to which he did not refer in his writing, and equally difficult to find a paper of his in which he did not exhibit clearly some phase of his many-angled personality. As a young man Hazlitt studied painting, and although he was unsuccessful as an artist, painting and the great painters remained one of his passions. He was deeply rather than widely read — in Cervantes and Boccaccio, in certain French writers from Montaigne and Rabelais to Rousseau, and in English literature from the time of Shakespeare. His personal acquaintance included most of the writers of the time, for whom and for whose works he had strong — and usually mixed — feelings of attachment or aversion. He was a dramatic critic whose enthusiasm had not become sated or dulled. He fancied himself a metaphysician, and was much given to reflection upon philosophical and psychological problems and processes, particularly upon his own ideas and emotions. This speculative and reflective habit of mind produced his somewhat cynical observation of society, in which he concerned himself much more with the springs of conduct than with speech and dress and manners, though these details did not wholly escape his animadversion. Finally, he remained throughout his life a political Radical, preserving unchanged his hatred of repression and his faith in the doctrines and ideas of the French Revolution. Curiously enough, however, he saw in Napoleon the embodiment of these principles and made him the " god of his idolatry."

Although Hazlitt was almost never wholly promiscuous and desultory, yet, except in the briefer and earlier *Round Table* papers, he rarely presented a carefully ordered treatment of a subject. His essays had much of the discursive character of talk — but the talk of a thinker who is always master of his subject and is never mastered by it. His manner combined a good deal of Montaigne's reflective self-curiosity with Rousseau's naked self-revelation of feeling; he lacked, however, something of the latter's hectic sentimentalism as well as the former's open-mindedness. Hazlitt's style, though thoroughly individual, was unusually free from mannerisms; two particulars of it, however, were very striking. The first was his fondness for quotation, frequently remembered inexactly and almost as frequently somewhat changed to secure greater appositeness. The quotations were never paraded, and appeared as congruous and native as Hazlitt's own diction. The second was his favorite practice of beginning a paper, particularly one on a speculative or reflective theme, by some striking statement, epigrammatic or paradoxical. This was, of course, the device employed by Bacon and somewhat frequently by essayists of the seventeenth and eighteenth centuries. Hazlitt's work showed other occasional resemblances to the " character " and to the papers in the *Tatler*, but the indebtedness, even in his earliest essays, was actually very slight — Hazlitt was a thoroughgoing individualist, who never willingly conformed to any convention, literary or social.

Next to Lamb, Hunt, and Hazlitt, probably John Wilson ("Christopher North") and Thomas De Quincey were most influential in the **John Wilson** establishment of the new type of familiar essay. Wilson **(1785–1854)** joined the staff of *Blackwood's* with the number for October, 1817, and soon became the most important contributor to that magazine. The *Noctes Ambrosianæ*, which for the most part were written by him and by which his reputation was chiefly established, were a series of dialogues constituting a symposium upon the topics of the day, and cannot strictly be classed as familiar essays; but they possessed many of the features of the essay, and their popularity encouraged indirectly the cultivation of the type. In addition Wilson wrote for *Blackwood's* a number of papers after the general pattern that was being set by Lamb and Hazlitt.

De Quincey's first essay was the " Confessions of an English Opium-Eater," published in the *London Magazine* for September and October, 1821. It commanded immediate and lasting popularity. In the succeeding thirty years De Quincey wrote for a number of magazines,

particularly *Blackwood's* and *Tait's*; for the former, the "Suspiria de
Profundis" (1845) and "The English Mail Coach" (1849); for the
latter, many articles presenting sections of his autobiography and reminiscences of his literary friends and acquaintances.[3] Most of the essays proper, such as the
"Suspiria" and the "Confessions," were largely dream phantasmagoria, the real or feigned result of De Quincey's consumption of
opium. They were characterized by their extreme length and discursiveness, and in many passages by a dignity of cadence and subtlety
of rhythm hardly before attempted in English prose.

Thomas De Quincey (1785–1859)

Though it is as a novelist that Dickens holds his place in literary
history, yet it was as an essayist that he first attracted notice. His
earliest departure from mere journalism was in the
Sketches by Boz, the first of which was published in the
Monthly Magazine for December, 1833, and others in
the *Monthly* and in the *Evening Chronicle* during the next two years.
Some of these sketches, particularly portrayals of characters, were
apparently written under the influence of Leigh Hunt. A quarter of
a century later Dickens began a new series of essays and sketches,
first collected in the *Uncommercial Traveller* and issued in December,
1860.[4] To this collection additions were made in 1868 and 1869.

Charles Dickens (1812–1870)

But the chief figure among the essayists of the mid-century was
Thackeray. A number of his contributions to *Punch* between 1846
and 1850 — the *Snobs of England* (1846–1847), *Travels
in London* (1847–1848), and *Mr. Brown's Letters to a
Young Man about Town* (1849) — presented most of the
features of the familiar essay, frequently differing from
the type only in the excessive heightening of burlesque or satirical
tone; and *The Proser* (1850) was really a series of familiar essays.

William Makepeace Thackeray (1811–1863)

[3] Although the contributions to *Tait's Magazine*, in their content and in their
intimate, almost gossiping style, are nearly related to the familiar essay, yet, as
De Quincey published them they are more accurately to be classified as
magazine articles than as essays.

[4] The inference seems warranted that the *Uncommercial Traveller* was
written in some measure to compete with Thackeray's *Roundabout Papers* in
the *Cornhill*, the initial number of which had appeared but a few weeks before
the first of the sketches by the *Uncommercial Traveller*. The competition did
not last long, however, as the series began January 28, 1860, and was concluded
October 13 of the same year.

They were written in the character of Dr. Solomon Pacifico, an " old Fogey " of kindly heart and much experience of the world and a very close relative of the later moralist of the *Roundabout Papers*. It is, however, to the *Roundabout Papers* in the *Cornhill Magazine* that Thackeray owes his place in the small group of writers who have given to the familiar essay in England its charm and distinction. When the *Cornhill* began publication in January, 1860, Thackeray was its editor, and he continued in this position until after the number for March, 1862. Then ill health and the irritating urgency of his editorial duties caused his resignation, though he remained a contributor to the magazine until his death, December 24, 1863. The first of the *Roundabout Papers* appeared in the initial number of the *Cornhill*, the last in the issue for November, 1863. The total number of essays included in the series is thirty-four, though six of them did not appear under this heading when they were first published in the *Cornhill*.

The various single *Roundabout Papers* rambled in such a pleasantly discursive fashion that they do not readily submit to any definite classification based on the subjects treated. A few were dream phantasmagoria ; several were inspired by events or situations of contemporaneous interest ; a goodly number were largely autobiographical or reminiscential, concerned particularly with Thackeray's boyhood, with his reading, and with his editorial trials and triumphs ; but by far the largest part of the whole body consisted of reflections — humorous, satirical, sympathetic — based upon the writer's observation of human life and conduct and character. Indeed, in nearly every essay, whatever the professed subject, there were almost sure to be shrewd thrusts at sham and disingenuousness, or whole-hearted attacks upon baseness and meanness hidden behind respectability, or the sympathetic consideration of human weakness, or grateful appreciation of such simple virtues as manly strength and honor and womanly purity and charity. In Thackeray's consideration of the human comedy, his point of view was the same as in his novels, particularly the later ones — that of a member of the upper ranks of society, a man of breeding and position and knowledge of the world, whose experience had made him thoroughly cognizant of human frailty but had also mellowed him to a kindly tolerance. The audience to whom he especially directed himself were men of his own station and the members of their families; his sympathy embraced servants and workhouse inmates, but his attitude toward them was that of the considerate master and the genuinely charitable gentleman.

In the essayist's point of view, in the audience particularly addressed, and in the generally prevalent tone of social satire the *Roundabout Papers* were strongly suggestive of the eighteenth century. A further resemblance in detail appeared in the frequent use of illustrative characters with descriptive or suggestive names. But the differences were even more noteworthy than the resemblances. Unlike the eighteenth-century essayists Thackeray as a social satirist was concerned not with externals of taste and dress and manners, but with character and its expression in conduct. Further, in their greater length, in their discursiveness, and in their intimate revelations of personality, his essays were closely related to those of Montaigne and Lamb and Hazlitt. Montaigne was Thackeray's "bedtime book."

The *Roundabout Papers* owed almost as much of their attractiveness to their style as to the personality of the writer. They possessed the greatest charm of familiar writing — conversational ease that does not lack vigor or suppleness and still does not degenerate into vulgarity.

Dr. John Brown, an active physician of Edinburgh and a valued friend of Thackeray's, occupies a small but significant position as

Dr. John Brown (1810–1882) essayist, chiefly by reason of his sketches of dog life and character. "Rab and his Friends," the best known of his works, was as much story as essay and claimed interest as much for its human figures as for its canine hero; but certain other very attractive papers were simply studies of the personality of dog companions by one who loved and understood them. Dr. Brown's essays also included some delightfully fresh out-of-door pieces, such as "Minchmoor" and "The Enterkin" which in many respects anticipated the travel essays of Stevenson. His writings, of which only a part are properly familiar essays, were first collected in the three volumes of *Horæ Subsecivæ*, published in 1858, 1861, and 1882, respectively.

Of the later nineteenth-century essayists Robert Louis Stevenson, a fellow townsman of Dr. Brown's, was the most conspicuous — notable for the character of his own work and for the stimulus he gave both to the writing and to the reading of essays. Stevenson first appeared in print in a half-dozen papers written for the *Edinburgh University Magazine* (January–April, 1871). After the demise of this

publication he practiced his art assiduously, but for some two and a half years he published nothing. Then, in December, 1873, an article of his entitled " Roads," which had been rejected by the *Saturday Review*, appeared in the *Portfolio*. In May, 1874, he contributed " Ordered South " to *Macmillan's Magazine*, and in the same year, through the discernment of Mr. Leslie Stephen, the editor of the *Cornhill*, his work was admitted to the pages of that magazine. From 1876 through 1882 the *Cornhill* was by far his most important medium of publication; after the latter year his writings appeared more at large. The most important body of essays of his later life was written for *Scribner's Magazine*, one paper appearing each month throughout 1888. In the summer of that year Stevenson sailed on his first voyage to the South Seas. Thereafter his voyages, the setting up of his establishment in Samoa and his interest in Samoan public affairs, letter writing, and absorption in fiction consumed his energies, and he published no essays.

Several small volumes of Stevenson's essays were collected and published before his death in 1894. The earliest of these, *Virginibus Puerisque* (1881), contained fourteen papers; *Memories and Portraits* (1887), sixteen; and *Across the Plains* (1892), twelve. All but three or four of the essays contained in these volumes had been printed previously in various periodicals. Even before *Virginibus Puerisque* two other slender volumes had appeared: *An Inland Voyage* (1878) — Stevenson's first book — and *Travels with a Donkey* (1879). The titles suggest narratives, but these little books were really series of travel essays, almost any one of which could be enjoyed separately, though the papers composing each volume were bound together by a slender thread of narrative. *Familiar Studies of Men and Books* (1882), despite its title, can hardly be considered a collection of familiar essays; it is rather a group of critical articles. For some years preceding Stevenson's death his essays were more widely read than were those of any one of his contemporaries; nevertheless, no full collection of them was issued before the publication of the first complete edition of his works in 1895.

Stevenson's essays presented chiefly four kinds of material: travel impressions, autobiography and reminiscence, moral and philosophical ideas, and a writer's interest in his craft. Probably Stevenson's most characteristic work was his development of the travel essay, the cultivation of this particular variety being the natural consequence of the nomadic habits which his search for health and his innate fondness for wandering confirmed in him. In his hands the travel sketch became not merely a narrative of travel or a description of places visited and objects and persons observed; it was both narrative and description, combined with recollections, comments, reflections, and all interpenetrated by his personality.

The title *Memories and Portraits* indicates the character of a considerable number of Stevenson's essays other than those included in the volume to which it was affixed. The portraits ranged from those of beggars, the family gardener, and an old shepherd, to the friends of Stevenson's youth and the members of his own family. The memories were largely of his childhood and young manhood — and naturally so, as he had scarcely reached middle age when his last essay was written. The most highly individual papers of this kind were those in which Stevenson recalled his very early sensations and impressions, and interpreted the actions and emotions of childhood in very much the same sympathetic spirit as in his *Child's Garden of Verse*.

The essays in which were embodied Stevenson's ethical and philosophical ideas varied in content from an appreciation of wisely spent idleness or a study of the comic incongruities incident upon falling in love, to a resolute, almost stoical facing of man's ultimate fate. They manifested his conviction that life is well worth the living and that this world is a very good place in which to live it, his admiration for the active and unafraid, and his remoteness from that spirit which is actuated to well-doing merely by the hope of bread-and-butter success in this world or by a promised reward of immortality in another. Almost everywhere in Stevenson's essays the moralist appeared;[5] not as the righteous Pharisee or the self-constituted reformer of society, but as an observer and thinker thoroughly human and richly endowed with a sense of humor.

Besides the distinctly critical articles a number of Stevenson's essays showed his interest in the craft of letters. These exhibited his

[5] In "Talk and Talkers" Stevenson declared that "you can keep no man long, nor Scotchman at all, off moral or theological discussion."

contempt for slovenly and dishonest writing, and insisted upon the blindness of the note-taking realists who transcribe the bare apparent facts and ignore the poetry and romance of life. They also recounted his own efforts to learn to write and his unwearied pursuit of style. For no writer of English has been more consciously a stylist, or has considered more nicely the effects he aimed to produce. In the choice of word and phrase, as in the attitude toward his subject, he carried almost to the extreme what Mr. Leslie Stephen has characterized as a " hatred for the commonplace formula." His style was fluid, always in process of change, but there was a fairly consistent difference between that of his earlier and of his later essays. The earlier papers, those in the *Virginibus Puerisque* collection, for example, were the more mannered — Stevenson himself declared that they were written in a " neat, brisk little style " ; the later, including most of the essays collected in *Across the Plains*, were less affected, less jaunty. While they were being written and afterwards, Stevenson was practicing what he called a " bald " style. He has named the models whom he chose to follow.[6] Significantly enough, the eighteenth-century essayists are not included in the list; and equally significant is a statement of his that he " could never read a word " of Addison. But of Montaigne and of Hazlitt — who of all the English essayists most resembles Montaigne — he was an eager and admiring student. And his relationship to these two was much closer than that of style in any narrowly restricted sense of the term.

With Stevenson the tale of the greater essayists of the nineteenth century is ended, and thus far in the twentieth century no one has **The essay** appeared to match him in charm and distinction. As, **to-day** moreover, no really important modification of the character of the familiar essay has occurred since his death, this sketch of the development of the type may well be concluded with the account of his work. But Stevenson is by no means the last of the

---

[6] In "A College Magazine" Stevenson wrote of having "played the sedulous ape to Hazlitt, to Lamb, to Wordsworth, to Sir Thomas Browne, to Defoe, to Hawthorne, to Montaigne, to Baudelaire, and to Obermann." And in a note book of 1871–1872 is a *Catalogus Librorum Carissimorum*, at the head of which is Montaigne's *Essays*, followed at a little distance by Hazlitt's *Table Talk*. The reader of this present collection may observe in " Walking Tours " Stevenson's enthusiasm for Hazlitt.

English essayists; to-day Chesterton and Benson and Galsworthy are notable names. And despite the popularity of the short story, which during the last twenty-five years has come more and more to occupy the magazines, the essay holds its place secure, and promises to continue to give pleasant half hours to the thoughtful and unhurried reader.

THE ENGLISH FAMILIAR ESSAY

MICHEL DE MONTAIGNE (1533–1592)

THE AUTHOR TO THE READER

(1580)

Reader, lo here a well-meaning book. It doth at the first entrance forewarn thee that in contriving the same I have proposed unto myself no other than a familiar and private end: I have no respect or consideration at all either to thy service or to my glory; my forces are not capable of any such design. I have vowed the same to the particular commodity of my kinsfolks and friends; to the end that losing me (which they are likely to do ere long) they may therein find some lineaments of my conditions and humours, and by that means reserve more whole and more lively foster the knowledge and acquaintance they have had of me. Had my intention been to forestall and purchase the world's opinion and favour, I would surely have adorned myself more quaintly, or kept a more grave and solemn march. I desire therein to be delineated in mine own genuine, simple, and ordinary fashion, without contention, art, or study; for it is myself I portray. My imperfections shall therein be read to the life, and my natural form discerned, so far forth as public reverence hath permitted me. For if my fortune had been to have lived among those nations which yet are said to live under the sweet liberty of Nature's first and uncorrupted laws, I assure thee I would most willingly have portrayed myself fully and naked. Thus, gentle Reader, myself am the groundwork of my book. It is then no reason thou shouldest employ thy time about so frivolous and vain a subject. Therefore farewell. From *Montaigne*, the first of March 1580.

OF SORROW

(1580)

No man living is more free from this passion than I, who yet neither like it in myself nor admire it in others, and yet generally the world, as a settled thing, is pleased to grace it with a particular esteem, clothing therewith wisdom, virtue, and conscience. Foolish and sordid guise! The Italians have more fitly baptized by this name malignity; for 'tis a quality always hurtful, always idle and vain; and as being cowardly, mean, and base, it is by the Stoics expressly and particularly forbidden to their sages.

But the story says that Psammitichus, King of Egypt, being defeated and taken prisoner by Cambyses, King of Persia, seeing his own daughter pass by him as prisoner, and in a wretched habit, with a bucket to draw water, though his friends about him were so concerned as to break out into tears and lamentations, yet he himself remained unmoved, without uttering a word, his eyes fixed upon the ground; and seeing, moreover, his son immediately after led to execution, still maintained the same countenance; till spying at last one of his domestic and familiar friends dragged away amongst the captives, he fell to tearing his hair and beating his breast, with all the other extravagances of extreme sorrow.

A story that may very fitly be coupled with another of the same kind, of recent date, of a prince of our own nation, who being at Trent, and having news there brought him of the death of his elder brother, a brother on whom depended the whole support and honour of his house, and soon after of that of a younger brother, the second hope of his family, and having withstood these two assaults with an exemplary resolution; one of his servants happening a few days after to die, he suffered his constancy to be overcome by this last accident; and, parting with his courage, so abandoned himself to sorrow and mourning, that some thence were forward to conclude that he was only touched to the quick by this last stroke of fortune:

but, in truth, it was, that being before brimful of grief, the least addition overflowed the bounds of all patience. Which, I think, might also be said of the former example, did not the story proceed to tell us that Cambyses asking Psammiti-chus, "Why, not being moved at the calamity of his son and daughter, he should with so great impatience bear the mis-fortune of his friend?" "It is," answered he, "because only this last affliction was to be manifested by tears, the two first far exceeding all manner of expression."

And, peradventure, something like this might be working in the fancy of the ancient painter, who having, in the sacri-fice of Iphigenia, to represent the sorrow of the assistants proportionably to the several degrees of interest every one had in the death of this fair innocent virgin, and having, in the other figures, laid out the utmost power of his art, when he came to that of her father, he drew him with a veil over his face, meaning thereby that no kind of countenance was capable of expressing such a degree of sorrow. Which is also the reason why the poets feign the miserable mother, Niobe, having first lost seven sons, and then afterwards as many daughters (overwhelmed with her losses), to be at last trans-formed into a rock—

Diriguisse malis,

thereby to express that melancholic, dumb, and deaf stupefac-tion, which benumbs all our faculties, when oppressed with accidents greater than we are able to bear. And, indeed, the violence and impression of an excessive grief must of necessity astonish the soul, and wholly deprive her of her ordinary func-tions: as it happens to every one of us, who, upon any sudden alarm of very ill news, find ourselves surprised, stupefied, and in a manner deprived of all power of motion, so that the soul, beginning to vent itself in tears and lamentations, seems to free and disengage itself from the sudden oppression, and to have obtained some room to work itself out at greater liberty.

Et via vix tandem voci laxata dolore est.

In the war that Ferdinand made upon the widow of King John of Hungary, about Buda, a man-at-arms was particularly taken notice of by every one for his singular gallant behaviour in a certain encounter; and, unknown, highly commended, and lamented, being left dead upon the place: but by none so much as by Raïsciac, a German lord, who was infinitely enamoured of so rare a valour. The body being brought off, and the count, with the common curiosity coming to view it, the armour was no sooner taken off but he immediately knew him to be his own son, a thing that added a second blow to the compassion of all the beholders; only he, without uttering a word, or turning away his eyes from the woeful object, stood fixedly contemplating the body of his son, till the vehemency of sorrow having overcome his vital spirits, made him sink down stone-dead to the ground.—

> Chi puo dir com' egli arde, è in picciol fuoco,

say the Innamoratos, when they would represent an insupportable passion:—

> Misero quod omneis
> Eripit sensus mihi: nam simul te,
> Lesbia, aspexi, nihil est super mi,
> Quod loquar amens.
> Lingua sed torpet: tenuis sub artus
> Flamma dimanat; sonitu suopte
> Tintinant aures; gemina teguntur
> Lumina nocte.

Neither is it in the height and greatest fury of the fit that we are in a condition to pour out our complaints or our amorous persuasions, the soul being at that time over-burdened, and labouring with profound thoughts; and the body dejected and languishing with desire; and thence it is that sometimes proceed those accidental impotencies that so unseasonably surprise the lover, and that frigidity which by the force of an immoderate ardour seizes him even in the very lap of fruition. For all passions that suffer themselves to be relished and digested are but moderate:—

> Curæ leves loquuntur, ingentes stupent.

A surprise of unexpected joy does likewise often produce the same effect : —

> Ut me conspexit venientem, et Troja circum
> Arma amens vidit, magnis exterrita monstris,
> Diriguit visu in medio, calor ossa reliquit,
> Labitur, et longo vix tandem tempore fatur.

Besides the examples of the Roman lady, who died for joy to see her son safe returned from the defeat of Cannæ ; and of Sophocles and of Dionysius the Tyrant, who died of joy ; and of Thalna, who died in Corsica, reading news of the honours the Roman Senate had decreed in his favour, we have, moreover, one in our time, of Pope Leo X, who, upon news of the taking of Milan, a thing he had so ardently desired, was rapt with so sudden an excess of joy that he immediately fell into a fever and died. And for a more notable testimony of the imbecility of human nature, it is recorded by the ancients that Diodorus the dialectician died upon the spot, out of an extreme passion of shame, for not having been able in his own school, and in the presence of a great auditory, to disengage himself from a nice argument that was propounded to him. I, for my part, am very little subject to these violent passions ; I am naturally of a stubborn apprehension, which also, by reasoning, I every day harden and fortify.

OF REPENTANCE

(1588)

Others form man ; I only report him : and represent a particular one, ill fashioned enough, and whom, if I had to model him anew, I should certainly make something else than what he is : but that 's past recalling. Now, though the features of my picture alter and change, 't is not, however, unlike : the world eternally turns round ; all things therein are incessantly moving, the earth, the rocks of Caucasus, and the pyramids of Egypt, both by the public motion and their own. Even constancy itself is no other but a slower and more languishing motion. I cannot fix my object; 't is always tottering and reeling by a natural giddiness; I take it as it is at the instant I consider it; I do not paint its being, I paint its passage; not a passing from one age to another, or, as the people say, from seven to seven years, but from day to day, from minute to minute. I must accommodate my history to the hour: I may presently change, not only by fortune, but also by intention. 'T is a counterpart of various and changeable accidents, and of irresolute imaginations, and, as it falls out, sometimes contrary: whether it be that I am then another self, or that I take subjects by other circumstances and considerations: so it is, that I may peradventure contradict myself, but, as Demades said, I never contradict the truth. Could my soul once take footing, I would not essay but resolve: but it is always learning and making trial.

I propose a life ordinary and without lustre: 't is all one; all moral philosophy may as well be applied to a common and private life, as to one of richer composition: every man carries the entire form of human condition. Authors communicate themselves to the people by some especial and extrinsic mark; I, the first of any, by my universal being; as Michel de Montaigne, not as a grammarian, a poet, or a lawyer. If the world find fault that I speak too much of myself, I find fault that they do not so much as think of themselves. But is it reason that, being so particular in my way of living, I should pretend to recommend myself to the public knowledge? And is it also reason that I should produce to the world, where art and handling have so much credit and authority, crude and simple effects of nature, and of a weak nature to boot? Is it not to build a wall without stone or brick, or some such thing, to write books without learning and without art? The fancies of music are carried on by art; mine by chance. I have this, at least, according to discipline, that never any man treated of a subject he better understood and knew than I what I have undertaken, and that in this I am the most understanding man alive : secondly, that never any man penetrated farther into his matter, nor better and more distinctly sifted the parts and sequences of it, nor ever more exactly and fully arrived at the end he proposed to himself. To perfect it, I need bring nothing but fidelity to the work ; and that is there, and the most pure and sincere that is anywhere to be found. I speak truth, not so much as I would, but as much as I dare ; and I dare a little the more, as I grow older ; for, methinks, custom allows to age more liberty of prating, and more indiscretion of talking of a man's self. That cannot fall out here, which I often see elsewhere, that the work and the artificer contradict one another : "Can a man of such sober conversation have written so foolish a book?" Or "Do so learned writings proceed from a man of so weak conversation?" He who talks at a very ordinary rate, and writes rare matter, 't is to say that his capacity is borrowed and not his own. A learned man is not learned in all things : but a sufficient man is sufficient throughout, even to ignorance itself ; here my book and I go hand in hand together. Elsewhere men may commend or censure the work, without reference to the workman ; here they cannot : who touches the one, touches the other. He who shall judge of it without knowing him, will more wrong himself than me ; he who does know him, gives me all the satisfaction I desire. I shall be happy beyond my desert, if I can obtain only thus much from the public approbation, as to make men of understanding perceive that I was capable of profiting by knowledge, had I had it ; and that I deserved to have been assisted by a better memory.

Be pleased here to excuse what I often repeat, that I very rarely repent, and that my conscience is satisfied with itself, not as the conscience of an angel, or that of a horse, but as the conscience of a man ; always adding this clause, not one of ceremony, but a true and real submission, that I speak inquiring and doubting, purely and simply referring myself to the common and accepted beliefs for the resolution. I do not teach, I only relate.

There is no vice that is absolutely a vice which does not offend, and that a sound judgment does not accuse ; for there is in it so manifest a deformity and inconvenience, that peradventure they are in the right who say that it is chiefly begotten by stupidity and ignorance : so hard is it to imagine that a man can know without abhorring it. Malice sucks up the greatest part of its own venom, and poisons itself. Vice leaves repentance in the soul, like an ulcer in the flesh, which is always scratching and lacerating itself : for reason effaces all other grief and sorrows, but it begets that of repentance, which is so much the more grievous, by reason it springs within, as the cold and heat of fevers are more sharp than those that only strike upon the outward skin. I hold for vices (but every one according to its proportion), not only those which reason and nature condemn, but those also which the opinion of men, though false and erroneous, have made such, if authorised by law and custom.

There is likewise no virtue which does not rejoice a well-descended nature : there is a kind of, I know not what, congratulation in well-doing that gives us an inward satisfaction, and a generous boldness that accompanies a good conscience : a soul daringly vicious may, peradventure, arm itself with security, but it cannot supply itself with this complacency and satisfaction. 'T is no little satisfaction to feel a man's self preserved from the contagion of so depraved an age, and to say to himself : " Whoever could penetrate into my soul would not there find me guilty either of the affliction or ruin of any one, or of revenge or envy, or any offence against the public laws, or of innovation or disturbance, or failure of my word ; and though the licence of the time permits and teaches every one so to do, yet have I not plundered any Frenchman's goods, or taken his money, and have lived upon what is my own, in war as well as in peace ; neither have I set any man to work without paying him his hire." These testimonies of a good conscience please, and this natural rejoicing is very beneficial to us, and the only reward that we can never fail of.

To ground the recompense of virtuous actions upon the approbation of others is too uncertain and unsafe a foundation, especially in so corrupt and ignorant an age as this, wherein the good opinion of the vulgar is injurious : upon whom do you rely to show you what is recommendable ? God defend me from being an honest man, according to the descriptions of honour I daily see every one make of himself :

Quæ fuerant vitia, mores sunt.

Some of my friends have at times schooled and scolded me with great sincerity and plainness, either of their own voluntary motion, or by me entreated to it as to an office, which to a well-composed soul surpasses not only in utility, but in kindness, all other offices of friendship : I have always received them with the most open arms, both of courtesy and acknowledgment ; but, to say the truth, I have often found so much false measure, both in their reproaches and praises, that I had not done much amiss, rather to have done ill, than to have done well according to their notions. We, who live private lives, not exposed to any other view than our own, ought chiefly to have settled a pattern within ourselves by which to try our actions ; and according to that, sometimes to encourage and sometimes to correct ourselves. I have my laws and my judicature to judge of myself, and apply myself more to these than to any other rules : I do, indeed, restrain my actions according to others ; but extend them not by any other rule than my own. You yourself only know if you are cowardly and cruel, loyal and devout : others see you not, and only guess at you by uncertain conjectures, and do not so much see your nature as your art ; rely not therefore upon their opinions, but stick to your own :

Tuo tibi judicio est utendum . . . Virtutis et vitiorum grave ipsius conscientiæ pondus est: quâ sublatâ, jacent omnia.

But the saying that repentance immediately follows the sin seems not to have respect to sin in its high estate, which is

lodged in us as in its own proper habitation. One may disown
and retract the vices that surprise us, and to which we are hurried by passions; but those which by a long habit are rooted
in a strong and vigorous will are not subject to contradiction.
Repentance is no other but a recanting of the will and an
opposition to our fancies, which lead us which way they
please. It makes this person disown his former virtue and
continency: —

> Quæ mens est hodie, cur eadem non puero fuit?
> Vel cur his animis incolumes non redeunt genæ?

'T is an exact life that maintains itself in due order in private. Every one may juggle his part, and represent an honest
man upon the stage: but within, and in his own bosom, where
all may do as they list, where all is concealed, to be regular,
— there's the point. The next degree is to be so in his house,
and in his ordinary actions, for which we are accountable to
none, and where there is no study nor artifice. And therefore
Bias, setting forth the excellent state of a private family, says:
"of which the master is the same within, by his own virtue
and temper, that he is abroad, for fear of the laws and report
of men." And it was a worthy saying of Julius Drusus, to the
masons who offered him, for three thousand crowns, to put his
house in such a posture that his neighbours should no longer
have the same inspection into it as before; "I will give you,"
said he, "six thousand to make it so that everybody may see
into every room." 'T is honourably recorded of Agesilaus, that
he used in his journeys always to take up his lodgings in temples, to the end that the people and the gods themselves might
pry into his most private actions. Such a one has been a
miracle to the world, in whom neither his wife nor servant has
ever seen anything so much as remarkable; few men have
been admired by their own domestics; no one was ever a
prophet, not merely in his own house, but in his own country,
says the experience of histories: 't is the same in things of
nought, and in this low example the image of a greater is to

be seen. In my country of Gascony, they look upon it as a drollery to see me in print; the further off I am read from my own home, the better I am esteemed. I purchase printers in Guienne; elsewhere they purchase me. Upon this it is that they lay their foundation who conceal themselves present and living, to obtain a name when they are dead and absent. I had rather have a great deal less in hand, and do not expose myself to the world upon any other account than my present share; when I leave it I quit the rest. See this functionary whom the people escort in state, with wonder and applause, to his very door; he puts off the pageant with his robe, and falls so much the lower by how much he was higher exalted: in himself within, all is tumult and degraded. And though all should be regular there, it will require a vivid and well-chosen judgment to perceive it in these low and private actions; to which may be added, that order is a dull, sombre virtue. To enter a breach, conduct an embassy, govern a people, are actions of renown; to reprehend, laugh, sell, pay, love, hate, and gently and justly converse with a man's own family and with himself; not to relax, not to give a man's self the lie, is more rare and hard, and less remarkable. By which means, retired lives, whatever is said to the contrary, undergo duties of as great or greater difficulty than the others do; and private men, says Aristotle, serve virtue more painfully and highly than those in authority do: we prepare ourselves for eminent occasions, more out of glory than conscience. The shortest way to arrive at glory, would be to do that for conscience which we do for glory: and the virtue of Alexander appears to me of much less vigour in his great theatre, than that of Socrates in his mean and obscure employment. I can easily conceive Socrates in the place of Alexander, but Alexander in that of Socrates, I cannot. Who shall ask the one what he can do, he will answer, "Subdue the world:" and who shall put the same question to the other, he will say, "Carry on human life conformably with its natural condition;" a much more general, weighty, and legitimate science than the other.

The virtue of the soul does not consist in flying high, but in walking orderly; its grandeur does not exercise itself in grandeur, but in mediocrity. As they who judge and try us within, make no great account of the lustre of our public actions, and see they are only streaks and rays of clear water springing from a slimy and muddy bottom: so, likewise, they who judge of us by this gallant outward appearance, in like manner conclude of our internal constitution; and cannot couple common faculties, and like their own, with the other faculties that astonish them, and are so far out of their sight. Therefore it is that we give such savage forms to demons: and who does not give Tamerlane great eyebrows, wide nostrils, a dreadful visage, and a prodigious stature, according to the imagination he has conceived by the report of his name? Had any one formerly brought me to Erasmus, I should hardly have believed but that all was adage and apothegm he spoke to his man or his hostess. We much more aptly imagine an artisan upon his close-stool, or upon his wife, than a great president venerable by his port and sufficiency: we fancy that they, from their high tribunals, will not abase themselves so much as to live. As vicious souls are often incited by some foreign impulse to do well, so are virtuous souls to do ill; they are therefore to be judged by their settled state, when they are at home, whenever that may be; and, at all events, when they are nearer repose, and in their native station.

Natural inclinations are much assisted and fortified by education; but they seldom alter and overcome their institution: a thousand natures of my time have escaped towards virtue or vice, through a quite contrary discipline: —

> Sic ubi, desuetæ silvis, in carcere clausæ
> Mansuevere feræ, et vultus posuere minaces,
> Atque hominem didicere pati, si torrida parvus
> Venit in ora cruor, redeunt rabiesque furorque,
> Admonitæque tument gustato sanguine fauces:
> Fervet, et a trepido vix abstinet ira magistro;

these original qualities are not to be rooted out; they may be covered and concealed. The Latin tongue is as it were natural to me; I understand it better than French; but I have not been used to speak it, nor hardly to write it, these forty years. And yet upon extreme and sudden emotions which I have fallen into twice or thrice in my life, and once seeing my father in perfect health fall upon me in a swoon, I have always uttered from the bottom of my heart my first words in Latin; nature deafened, and forcibly expressing itself, in spite of so long a discontinuation; and this example is said of many others.

They who in my time have attempted to correct the manners of the world by new opinions, reform seeming vices; but the essential vices they leave as they were, if indeed they do not augment them; and augmentation is therein to be feared; we defer all other well doing upon the account of these external reformations, of less cost and greater show, and thereby expiate good cheap, for the other natural, consubstantial, and intestine vices. Look a little into our experience: there is no man, if he listen to himself, who does not in himself discover a particular and governing form of his own, that jostles his education, and wrestles with the tempest of passions that are contrary to it. For my part, I seldom find myself agitated with surprises; I always find myself in my place, as heavy and unwieldy bodies do; if I am not at home, I am always near at hand; my dissipations do not transport me very far; there is nothing strange or extreme in the case; and yet I have sound and vigorous turns.

The true condemnation, and which touches the common practice of men, is that their very retirement itself is full of filth and corruption; the idea of their reformation composed, their repentance sick and faulty, very nearly as much as their sin. Some, either from having been linked to vice by a natural propension or long practice, cannot see its deformity. Others (of which constitution I am) do indeed feel the weight of vice, but they counterbalance it with pleasure, or some other occasion; and suffer and lend themselves to it for a certain price, but viciously and basely. Yet there might, haply, be imagined so vast a disproportion of measure, where with justice the pleasure might excuse the sin, as we say of utility; not only if accidental, and out of sin, as in thefts, but in the very exercise of sin, as in the enjoyment of women, where the temptation is violent, and 't is said, sometimes not to be overcome.

Being the other day at Armaignac, on the estate of a kinsman of mine, I there saw a peasant who was by every one nicknamed *the thief*. He thus related the story of his life: that, being born a beggar, and finding that he should not be able, so as to be clear of indigence, to get his living by the sweat of his brow, he resolved to turn thief, and by means of his strength of body had exercised this trade all the time of his youth in great security; for he ever made his harvest and vintage in other men's grounds, but a great way off, and in so great quantities, that it was not to be imagined one man could have carried away so much in one night upon his shoulders; and, moreover, he was careful equally to divide and distribute the mischief he did, that the loss was of less importance to every particular man. He is now grown old, and rich for a man of his condition, thanks to his trade, which he openly confesses to every one. And to make his peace with God, he says, that he is daily ready by good offices to make satisfaction to the successors of those he has robbed, and if he do not finish (for to do it all at once he is not able), he will then leave it in charge to his heirs to perform the rest, proportionably to the wrong he himself only knows he has done to each. By this description, true or false, this man looks upon theft as a dishonest action, and hates it, but less than poverty, and simply repents; but to the extent he has thus recompensed he repents not. This is not that habit which incorporates us into vice, and conforms even our understanding itself to it; nor is it that impetuous whirlwind that by gusts troubles and blinds our souls, and for the time precipitates us, judgment and all, into the power of vice.

I customarily do what I do thoroughly and make but one step on 't; I have rarely any movement that hides itself and steals away from my reason, and that does not proceed in the matter by the consent of all my faculties, without division or intestine sedition; my judgment is to have all the blame or all the praise; and the blame it once has, it has always; for almost from my infancy it has ever been one: the same inclination, the same turn, the same force; and as to universal opinions, I fixed myself from my childhood in the place where I resolved to stick. There are some sins that are impetuous, prompt, and sudden; let us set them aside: but in these other sins so often repeated, deliberated, and contrived, whether sins of complexion or sins of profession and vocation, I cannot conceive that they should have so long been settled in the same resolution, unless the reason and conscience of him who has them, be constant to have them; and the repentance he boasts to be inspired with on a sudden, is very hard for me to imagine or form. I follow not the opinion of the Pythagorean sect, "that men take up a new soul when they repair to the images of the gods to receive their oracles," unless he mean that it must needs be extrinsic, new, and lent for the time; our own showing so little sign of purification and cleanness, fit for such an office.

They act quite contrary to the stoical precepts, who do indeed command us to correct the imperfections and vices we know ourselves guilty of, but forbid us therefore to disturb the repose of our souls: these make us believe that they have great grief and remorse within: but of amendment, correction, or interruption, they make nothing appear. It cannot be a cure if the malady be not wholly discharged; if repentance were laid upon the scale of the balance, it would weigh down sin. I find no quality so easy to counterfeit as devotion, if men do not conform their manners and life to the profession; its essence is abstruse and occult; the appearances easy and ostentatious.

For my own part, I may desire in general to be other than

I am; I may condemn and dislike my whole form, and beg of Almighty God for an entire reformation, and that He will please to pardon my natural infirmity: but I ought not to call this repentance, methinks, no more than the being dissatisfied that I am not an angel or Cato. My actions are regular, and conformable to what I am and to my condition; I can do no better; and repentance does not properly touch things that are not in our power; sorrow does. I imagine an infinite number of natures more elevated and regular than mine; and yet I do not for all that improve my faculties, no more than my arm or will grow more strong and vigorous for conceiving those of another to be so. If to conceive and wish a nobler way of acting than that we have should produce a repentance of our own, we must then repent us of our most innocent actions, forasmuch as we may well suppose that in a more excellent nature they would have been carried on with greater dignity and perfection; and we would that ours were so. When I reflect upon the deportment of my youth, with that of my old age, I find that I have commonly behaved myself with equal order in both, according to what I understand: this is all that my resistance can do. I do not flatter myself; in the same circumstances I should do the same things. It is not a patch, but rather an universal tincture, with which I am stained. I know no repentance, superficial, half-way, and ceremonious; it must sting me all over before I can call it so, and must prick my bowels as deeply and universally as God sees into me.

As to business, many excellent opportunities have escaped me for want of good management; and yet my deliberations were sound enough, according to the occurrences presented to me: 'tis their way to choose always the easiest and safest course. I find that, in my former resolves, I have proceeded with discretion, according to my own rule, and according to the state of the subject proposed, and should do the same a thousand years hence in like occasions; I do not consider what it is now, but what it was then, when I deliberated on it: the force of all counsel consists in the time; occasions and things eternally shift and change. I have in my life committed some important errors, not for want of good understanding, but for want of good luck. There are secret, and not to be foreseen, parts in matters we have in hand, especially in the nature of men; mute conditions, that make no show, unknown sometimes even to the possessors themselves, that spring and start up by incidental occasions; if my prudence could not penetrate into nor foresee them, I blame it not: 'tis commissioned no further than its own limits; if the event be too hard for me, and take the side I have refused, there is no remedy; I do not blame myself, I accuse my fortune, and not my work; this cannot be called repentance.

Phocion, having given the Athenians an advice that was not followed, and the affair nevertheless succeeding contrary to his opinion, some one said to him, " Well, Phocion, art thou content that matters go so well?" " I am very well content," replied he, " that this has happened so well, but I do not repent that I counselled the other." When any of my friends address themselves to me for advice, I give it candidly and clearly, without sticking, as almost all other men do, at the hazard of the thing's falling out contrary to my opinion, and that I may be reproached for my counsel; I am very indifferent as to that, for the fault will be theirs for having consulted me, and I could not refuse them that office.

I, for my own part, can rarely blame anyone but myself for my oversights and misfortunes, for indeed I seldom solicit the advice of another, if not by honour of ceremony, or excepting where I stand in need of information, special science, or as to matter of fact. But in things wherein I stand in need of nothing but judgment, other men's reasons may serve to fortify my own, but have little power to dissuade me; I hear them all with civility and patience : but, to my recollection, I never made use of any but my own. With me, they are but flies and atoms, that confound and distract my will; I lay no great stress upon my opinions; but I lay as little upon those of others, and fortune rewards me accordingly : if I receive but little advice, I also give but little. I am seldom consulted, and still more seldom believed, and know no concern, either public or private, that has been mended or bettered by my advice. Even they whom fortune had in some sort tied to my direction, have more willingly suffered themselves to be governed by any other counsels than mine. And as a man who am as jealous of my repose as of my authority, I am better pleased that it should be so; in leaving me there, they humour what I profess, which is to settle and wholly contain myself within myself. I take a pleasure in being uninterested in other men's affairs, and disengaged from being their warranty, and responsible for what they do.

In all affairs that are past, be it how it will, I have very little regret; for this imagination puts me out of my pain, that they were so to fall out: they are in the great revolution of the world, and in the chain of stoical causes: your fancy cannot, by wish and imagination, move one tittle, but that the great current of things will not reverse both the past and the future.

As to the rest, I abominate that incidental repentance which old age brings along with it. He, who said of old, that he was obliged to his age for having weaned him from pleasure, was of another opinion than I am; I can never think myself beholden to impotency for any good it can do to me:

Nec tam aversa unquam videbitur ab opere suo providentia, ut debilitas inter optima inventa sit.

Our appetites are rare in old age; a profound satiety seizes us after the act; in this I see nothing of conscience; chagrin and weakness imprint in us a drowsy and rheumatic virtue. We must not suffer ourselves to be so wholly carried away by natural alterations as to suffer our judgments to be imposed upon by them. Youth and pleasure have not formerly so far prevailed with me, that I did not well enough discern the face of vice in pleasure; neither does the distaste that years have brought me, so far prevail with me now, that I cannot discern pleasure in vice. Now that I am no more in my flourishing age, I judge as well of these things as if I were. I, who narrowly and strictly examine it, find my reason the very same it was in my most licentious age, except, perhaps, that 't is weaker and more decayed by being grown older; and I find that the pleasure it refuses me upon the account of my bodily health, it would no more refuse now, in consideration of the health of my soul, than at any time heretofore. I do not repute it the more valiant for not being able to combat; my temptations are so broken and mortified, that they are not worth its opposition; holding but out my hands, I repel them. Should one present the old concupiscence before it, I fear it would have less power to resist it than heretofore; I do not discern that in itself it judges anything otherwise now, than it formerly did, nor that it has acquired any new light: wherefore, if there be convalescence, 't is an enchanted one. Miserable kind of remedy, to owe one's health to one's disease! 'T is not that our misfortune should perform this office, but the good fortune of our judgment. I am not to be made to do anything by persecutions and afflictions, but to curse them: that is for people who cannot be roused but by a whip. My reason is much more free in prosperity, and much more distracted, and put to 't to digest pains than pleasures: I see best in a clear sky; health admonishes me more cheerfully, and to better purpose, than sickness. I did all that in me lay to reform and regulate myself from pleasures, at a time when I had health and vigour to enjoy them; I should be ashamed and envious that the misery and misfortune of my old age should have credit over my good, healthful, sprightly, and vigorous years; and that men should estimate me, not by what I have been, but by what I have ceased to be.

In my opinion, 't is the happy living, and not (as Antisthenes said) the happy dying, in which human felicity consists. I have not made it my business to make a monstrous addition of a philosopher's tail to the head and body of a libertine; nor would I have this wretched remainder give the lie to the pleasant, sound, and long part of my life: I would present myself uniformly throughout. Were I to live my life over again, I should live it just as I have lived it; I neither complain of the past, nor do I fear the future; and if I am not much deceived, I am the same within that I am without. 'T is one main obligation I have to my fortune, that the succession of my bodily estate has been carried on according to the natural seasons; I have seen the grass, the blossom, and the fruit, and now see the withering; happily, however, because naturally. I bear the infirmities I have the better, because they came not till I had reason to expect them, and because also they make me with greater pleasure remember that long felicity of my past life. My wisdom may have been just the same in both ages; but it was more active, and of better grace whilst young and sprightly, than now it is when broken, peevish, and uneasy. I repudiate, then, these casual and painful reformations. God must touch our hearts; our consciences must amend of themselves, by the aid of our reason, and not by the decay of our appetites; pleasure is, in itself, neither pale nor discoloured, to be discerned by dim and decayed eyes.

We ought to love temperance for itself, and because God has commanded that and chastity; but that which we are reduced to by catarrhs, and for which I am indebted to the stone, is neither chastity nor temperance; a man cannot boast that he despises and resists pleasure, if he cannot see it, if he knows not what it is, and cannot discern its graces, its force, and most alluring beauties; I know both the one and the other, and may therefore the better say it. But, methinks, our souls in old age are subject to more troublesome maladies and imperfections than in youth; I said the same when young and when I was reproached with the want of a beard; and I say so now that my grey hairs give me some authority. We call the difficulty of our humours and the disrelish of present things wisdom; but, in truth, we do not so much forsake vices as we change them, and, in my opinion, for worse. Besides a foolish and feeble pride, an impertinent prating, froward and insociable humours, superstition, and a ridiculous desire of riches when we have lost the use of them, I find there more envy, injustice, and malice. Age imprints more wrinkles in the mind than it does on the face; and souls are never, or very rarely seen, that, in growing old, do not smell sour and musty. Man moves all together, both towards his perfection and decay. In observing the wisdom of Socrates, and many circumstances of his condemnation, I should dare to believe that he in some sort himself purposely, by collusion, contributed to it, seeing that, at the age of seventy years, he might fear to suffer the lofty motions of his mind to be cramped and his wonted lustre obscured. What strange metamorphoses do I see age every day make in many of my acquaintance! 'T is a potent malady, and that naturally and imperceptibly steals into us; a vast provision of study and great precaution are required to evade the imperfections it loads us with, or at least to weaken their progress. I find that, notwithstanding all my entrenchments, it gets foot by foot upon me: I make the best resistance I can, but I do not know to what at last it will reduce me. But fall out what will, I am content the world may know, when I am fallen, from what I fell.

SIR FRANCIS BACON (1561–1626)

OF STUDIES

(1597)

Studies serve for pastimes, for ornaments, and for abilities. Their chief use for pastime is in privateness and retiring; for ornament is in discourse, and for ability is in judgment. For expert men can execute, but learned men are fittest to judge or censure.

To spend too much time in them is sloth; to use them too much for ornament is affectation; to make judgment wholly by their rules is the humour of a scholar.

They perfect nature, and are perfected by experience.

Crafty men contemn them, simple men admire them, wise men use them: for they teach not their own use, but that is a wisdom without them and above them, won by observation.

Read not to contradict, nor to believe, but to weigh and consider.

Some books are to be tasted, others to be swallowed, and some few to be chewed and digested: that is, some books are to be read only in parts; others to be read, but cursorily, and some few to be read wholly, and with diligence and attention.

Reading maketh a full man, conference a ready man, and writing an exact man. And therefore if a man write little, he had need have a great memory; if he confer little, he had need have a present wit; and if he read little, he had need have much cunning, to seem to know that he doth not.

Histories make men wise, poets witty, the mathematics subtle, natural philosophy deep, moral grave, logic and rhetoric able to contend.

(1625)

Studies serve for delight, for ornament and for ability. Their chief use for delight is in privateness, and retiring; for ornament, is in discourse; and for ability, is in the judgment and disposition of business. For expert men can execute, and perhaps judge of particulars, one by one; but the general counsels, and the plots and marshalling of affairs, come best from those that are learned. To spend too much time in studies is sloth; to use them too much for ornament is affectation; to make judgment wholly by their rules is the humour of a scholar. They perfect nature, and are perfected by experience: for natural abilities are like natural plants, that need proyning by study; and studies themselves do give forth directions too much at large, except they be bounded in by experience. Crafty men contemn studies, simple men admire them, and wise men use them: for they teach not their own use; but that is a wisdom without them and above them, won by observation. Read not to contradict and confute; nor to believe and take for granted; nor to find talk and discourse; but to weigh and consider. Some books are to be tasted, others to be swallowed, and some few to be chewed and digested; that is, some books are to be read only in parts; others to be read, but not curiously; and some few to be read wholly, and with diligence and attention. Some books also may be read by deputy, and extracts made of them by others; but that would be only in the less important arguments, and the meaner sort of books; else distilled books are like common distilled waters, flashy things. Reading maketh a full man; conference a ready man; and writing an exact man. And therefore, if a man write little, he had need have a great memory; if he confer little, he had need have a present wit; and if he read little, he had need have much cunning, to seem to know that he doth not. Histories make men wise; poets witty; the mathematics subtile; natural philosophy deep; moral grave; logic and rhetoric able to contend. *Abeunt studia in mores.* Nay, there is no stond

or impediment in the wit, but may be wrought out by fit studies : like as diseases of the body may have appropriate exercises. Bowling is good for the stone and reins ; shooting for
the lungs and breast ; gentle walking for the stomach ; riding
for the head ; and the like. So if a man's wit be wandering,
let him study the mathematics ; for in demonstrations, if his
wit be called away never so little, he must begin again. If his
wit be not apt to distinguish or find differences, let him study
the schoolmen ; for they are *cymini sectores*. If he be not apt
to beat over matters, and to call up one thing to prove and
illustrate another, let him study the lawyers' cases. So every
defect of the mind may have a special receipt.

OF EMPIRE

(1612)

It is a miserable state of mind to have few things to desire
and many things to fear ; and yet that commonly is the case
of kings ; who, being at the highest, want matter of desire,
which makes their minds the more languishing ; and have
many representations of perils and shadows, which makes their
minds the less clear. And this is one reason also of that effect
which the Scripture speaketh of, *That the king's heart is inscrutable*. For multitude of jealousies, and lack of some predominant desire that should marshal and put in order all the
rest, maketh any man's heart hard to find or sound. Hence
cometh it likewise that princes many times make themselves
desires, and set their hearts upon toys : sometimes upon a building ; sometimes upon an order ; sometimes upon the advancing
of a person ; sometimes upon obtaining excellency in some art
or feat of the hand ; and such like things, which seem incredible to those that know not the principle, *That the mind of
man is more cheered and refreshed by profiting in small
things than by standing at a stay in great*. Therefore great
and fortunate conquerors in their first years turn melancholy

and superstitious in their latter; as did Alexander the Great, and in our memory Charles the Fifth, and many others. For he that is used to go forward, and findeth a stop, falleth out of his own favour. A true temper of government is a rare thing; for both temper and distemper consist of contraries. But it is one thing to mingle contraries, another to interchange them. The answer of Apollonius to Vespasian is full of excellent instruction. Vespasian asked him, *What was Nero's overthrow?* He answered: *Nero could touch and tune the harp well; but in government sometimes he used to wind the pins too high, and sometimes to let them down too low.* And certain it is that nothing destroyeth authority so much as the unequal and untimely interchange of pressing power and relaxing power. The wisdom of all these latter times in princes' affairs is rather fine deliveries and shiftings of dangers and mischiefs when they are near, than solid and grounded courses to keep them aloof. But let men beware how they neglect and suffer matter of trouble to be prepared; for no man can forbid the spark, nor tell whence it may come. The difficultness in princes' business are many times great; but the greatest difficulty is often in their own mind. For it is common with princes (saith Tacitus) to will contradictories: *Sunt plerumque regum voluntates vehementes, et inter se contrariæ.* For it is the solecism of power, to think to command the end, and yet not to endure the mean. Princes are like to the heavenly bodies, which cause good or evil times; and which have much veneration, but no rest. All precepts concerning kings are in effect comprehended in those two remembrances: *Memento quod es homo*, and *Memento quod es Deus* or *vice Dei:* the one to bridle their power, and the other their will.

(1625)

It is a miserable state of mind to have few things to desire and many things to fear; and yet that commonly is the case of kings; who, being at the highest, want matter of desire, which makes their minds more languishing; and have many representations of perils and shadows, which makes their minds the less clear. And this is one reason also of that effect which the Scripture speaketh of, *That the king's heart is inscrutable.* For multitude of jealousies, and lack of some predominant desire that should marshal and put in order all the rest, maketh any man's heart hard to find or sound. Hence it comes likewise that princes many times make themselves desires, and set their hearts upon toys: sometimes upon a building; sometimes upon erecting of an order; sometimes upon the advancing of a person; sometimes upon obtaining excellency in some art or feat of the hand; as Nero for playing on the harp, Domitian for certainty of the hand with the arrow, Commodus for playing at fence, Caracalla for driving chariots, and the like. This seemeth incredible unto those that know not the principle, *that the mind of man is more cheered and refreshed by profiting in small things than by standing at a stay in great.* We see also that kings that have been fortunate conquerors in their first years, it being not possible for them to go forward infinitely, but that they must have some check or arrest in their fortunes, turn in their latter years to be superstitious and melancholy; as did Alexander the Great, Diocletian, and in our memory Charles the Fifth, and others: for he that is used to go forward, and findeth a stop, falleth out of his own favour, and is not the thing he was.

To speak now of the true temper of empire: it is a thing rare, and hard to keep; for both temper and distemper consist of contraries. But it is one thing to mingle contraries, another to interchange them. The answer of Apollonius to Vespasian is full of excellent instruction. Vespasian asked him, *What was Nero's overthrow?* He answered, *Nero could touch and tune the harp well; but in government sometimes he used to wind the pins too high, sometimes to let them down too low.* And certain it is that nothing destroyeth authority so much as the unequal and untimely interchange of power pressed too far, and relaxed too much.

This is true, that the wisdom of all these latter times in

princes' affairs is rather fine deliveries and shiftings of dangers and mischiefs when they are near, than solid and grounded courses to keep them aloof. But this is but to try masteries with fortune. And let men beware how they neglect and suffer matter of trouble to be prepared; for no man can forbid the spark, nor tell whence it may come. The difficulties in princes' business are many and great; but the greatest difficulty is often in their own mind. For it is common with princes (saith Tacitus) to will contradictories: *Sunt plerumque regum voluntates vehementes, et inter se contrariæ.* For it is the solecism of power, to think to command the end, and yet not to endure the mean.

Kings have to deal with their neighbours, their wives, their children, their prelates or clergy, their nobles, their second-nobles or gentlemen, their merchants, their commons, and their men of war; and from all these arise dangers, if care and circumspection be not used.

First for their neighbours; there can no general rule be given (the occasions are so variable), save one, which ever holdeth; which is, that princes do keep due sentinel, that none of their neighbours do overgrow so (by increase of territory, by embracing of trade, by approaches, or the like) as they become more able to annoy them than they were. And this is generally the work of standing councils to foresee and to hinder it. During that triumvirate of kings, King Henry the Eighth of England, Francis the First King of France, and Charles the Fifth Emperor, there was such a watch kept, that none of the three could win a palm of ground, but the other two would straightways balance it, either by confederation, or, if need were, by a war; and would not in any wise take up peace at interest. And the like was done by that league (which Guicciardine saith was the security of Italy) made between Ferdinando King of Naples, Lorenzius Medices, and Ludovicus Sforza, potentates, the one of Florence, the other of Milan. Neither is the opinion of some of the schoolmen to be received, *that a war cannot justly be made but upon a precedent injury or provocation.* For there is no question but a just fear of an imminent danger, though there be no blow given, is a lawful cause of a war.

For their wives; there are cruel examples of them. Livia is infamed for the poisoning of her husband; Roxalana, Solyman's wife, was the destruction of that renowned prince Sultan Mustapha, and otherwise troubled his house and succession; Edward the Second of England his queen had the principal hand in the deposing and murther of her husband. This kind of danger is then to be feared chiefly, when the wives have plots for the raising of their own children, or else that they be advoutresses.

For their children; the tragedies likewise of dangers from them have been many. And generally, the entering of fathers into suspicion of their children hath been ever unfortunate. The destruction of Mustapha (that we named before) was so fatal to Solyman's line, as the succession of the Turks from Solyman until this day is suspected to be untrue, and of strange blood; for that Selymus the Second was thought to be supposititious. The destruction of Crispus, a young prince of rare towardness, by Constantinus the Great, his father, was in like manner fatal to his house; for both Constantinus and Constance, his sons, died violent deaths; and Constantius, his other son, did little better; who died indeed of sickness, but after that Julianus had taken arms against him. The destruction of Demetrius, son to Philip the Second of Macedon, turned upon the father, who died of repentance. And many like examples there are; but few or none where the fathers had good by such distrust; except it were where the sons were up in open arms against them; as was Selymus the First against Bajazet; and the three sons of Henry the Second, King of England.

For their prelates; when they are proud and great, there is also danger from them; as it was in the times of Anselmus and Thomas Becket, Archbishops of Canterbury; who with their crosiers did almost try it with the king's sword; and yet they had to deal with stout and haughty kings, William Rufus,

Henry the First, and Henry the Second. The danger is not from that state, but where it hath a dependence of foreign authority; or where the churchmen come in and are elected, not by the collation of the king, or particular patrons, but by the people.

For their nobles; to keep them at a distance, it is not amiss; but to depress them may make a king more absolute, but less safe, and less able to perform anything that he desires. I have noted it in my history of King Henry the Seventh of England, who depressed his nobility; whereupon it came to pass that his times were full of difficulties and troubles; for the nobility, though they continued loyal unto him, yet did they not co-operate with him in his business. So that in effect he was fain to do all things himself.

For their second-nobles; there is not much danger from them, being a body dispersed. They may sometimes discourse high, but that doth little hurt; besides, they are a counterpoise to the higher nobility, that they grow not too potent; and, lastly, being the most immediate in authority with the common people, they do best temper popular commotions.

For their merchants; they are *vena porta*; and if they flourish not, a kingdom may have good limbs, but will have empty veins, and nourish little. Taxes and imposts upon them do seldom good to the king's revenue; for that that he wins in the hundred he leeseth in the shire; the particular rates being increased, but the total bulk of trading rather decreased.

For their commons; there is little danger from them, except it be where they have great and potent heads; or where you meddle with the point of religion, or their customs, or means of life.

For their men of war; it is a dangerous state where they live and remain in a body, and are used to donatives; whereof we see examples in the janizaries, and pretorian bands of Rome: but trainings of men, and arming them in several places, and under several commanders, and without donatives, are things of defence, and no danger.

Princes are like to heavenly bodies, which cause good or evil times; and which have much veneration, but no rest. All precepts concerning kings are in effect comprehended in those two remembrances: *Memento quod es homo*, and *Memento quod es Deus*, or *vice Dei*: the one bridleth their power, and the other their will.

OF TRUTH

(1625)

What is truth? said jesting Pilate, and would not stay for an answer. Certainly there be that delight in giddiness, and count it a bondage to fix a belief; affecting free-will in thinking, as well as in acting. And though the sects of philosophers of that kind be gone, yet there remain certain discoursing wits which are of the same veins, though there be not so much blood in them as was in those of the ancients. But it is not only the difficulty and labour which men take in finding out of truth, nor again that when it is found it imposeth upon men's thoughts, that doth bring lies in favour; but a natural though corrupt love of the lie itself. One of the later school of the Grecians examineth the matter, and is at a stand to think what should be in it, that men should love lies, where neither they make for pleasure, as with poets, nor for advantage, as with the merchant, but for the lie's sake. But I cannot tell: this same truth is a naked and open day-light, that doth not shew the masques and mummeries and triumphs of the world half so stately and daintily as candle-lights. Truth may perhaps come to the price of a pearl, that sheweth best by day; but it will not rise to the price of a diamond or carbuncle, that sheweth best in varied lights. A mixture of a lie doth ever add pleasure. Doth any man doubt, that if there were taken out of men's minds vain opinions, flattering hopes, false valuations, imaginations as one would, and the like, but it would leave the minds of a number of men poor shrunken things, full of melancholy and indisposition, and unpleasing to themselves? One of the Fathers, in great severity, called poesy *vinum dæmonum*, because it filleth the imagination; and yet it is but with the shadow of a lie. But it is not the lie that passeth through the mind, but the lie that sinketh in and settleth in it, that doth the hurt, such as we spake of before. But howsoever these things are thus in men's depraved judgments and affections, yet truth, which only doth judge itself, teacheth that the inquiry of truth, which is the love-making or wooing of it, the knowledge of truth, which is the presence of it, and the belief of truth, which is the enjoying of it, is the sovereign good of human nature. The first creature of God, in the works of the days, was the light of the sense; the last was the light of reason; and his sabbath work ever since, is the illumination of his Spirit. First he breathed light upon the face of the matter or chaos; then he breathed light into the face of man; and still he breatheth and inspireth light into the face of his chosen. The poet that beautified the sect that was otherwise inferior to the rest, saith yet excellently well: *It is a pleasure to stand upon the shore, and to see ships tossed upon the sea; a pleasure to stand in the window of a castle, and to see a battle and the adventures thereof below: but no pleasure is comparable to the standing upon the vantage ground of Truth* (a hill not to be commanded, and where the air is always clear and serene), *and to see the errors, and wanderings, and mists, and tempests, in the vale below;* so always that this prospect be with pity, and not with swelling or pride. Certainly, it is heaven upon earth, to have a man's mind move in charity, rest in providence, and turn upon the poles of truth.

To pass from theological and philosophical truth to the truth of civil business: it will be acknowledged, even by those that practise it not, that clear and round dealing is the honour of man's nature; and that mixture of falsehood is like allay in coin of gold and silver, which may make the metal work the better, but it embaseth it. For these winding and crooked courses are the goings of the serpent; which goeth basely upon the belly, and not upon the feet. There is no vice that doth so cover a man with shame as to be found false and per-fidious. And therefore Montaigne saith prettily, when he in-quired the reason why the word of the lie should be such a disgrace and such an odious charge? Saith he, *If it be well weighed, to say that a man lieth is as much to say as that he is brave towards God and a coward towards men*. For a lie faces God, and shrinks from man. Surely the wicked-ness of falsehood and breach of faith cannot possibly be so highly expressed, as in that it shall be the last peal to call the judgments of God upon the generations of men; it being foretold, that when Christ cometh, *he shall not find faith upon the earth*.

OF DEATH

(1625)

Men fear Death as children fear to go in the dark; and as that natural fear in children is increased with tales, so is the other. Certainly, the contemplation of death, as the wages of sin and passage to another world, is holy and religious; but the fear of it, as a tribute due unto nature, is weak. Yet in religious meditations there is sometimes mixture of vanity and of superstition. You shall read in some of the friars' books of mortification, that a man should think with himself what the pain is if he have but his finger's end pressed or tortured, and thereby imagine what the pains of death are, when the whole body is corrupted and dissolved; when many times death passeth with less pain than the torture of a limb; for the most vital parts are not the quickest of sense. And by him that spake only as a philosopher and natural man, it was well said, *Pompa mortis magis terret quam mors ipsa*. Groans and convulsions, and a discoloured face, and friends weeping, and blacks, and obsequies, and the like, shew death terrible. It is worthy the observing, that there is no passion in the mind of man so weak, but it mates and masters the fear of death; and therefore death is no such terrible enemy when a man hath so many attendants about him that can win the combat of him. Revenge triumphs over death; love slights it; honour aspireth to it; grief flieth to it; fear pre-occupateth it; nay, we read, after Otho the Emperor had slain himself, pity (which is the tenderest of affections) provoked many to die, out of mere compassion to their sovereign, and as the truest sort of followers. Nay, Seneca adds niceness and satiety: *Cogita quamdiu eadem feceris; mori velle, non tantum fortis, aut miser, sed etiam fastidiosus potest.* A man would die, though he were neither valiant nor miserable, only upon a weariness to do the same thing so oft over and over. It is no less worthy to observe, how little alteration in good spirits the approaches of death make; for they appear to be the same men till the last instant. Augustus Cæsar died in a compliment: *Livia, conjugii nostri memor, vive et vale.* Tiberius in dissimulation, as Tacitus saith of him: *Iam Tiberium vires et corpus, non dissimulatio, deserebant.* Vespasian in a jest, sitting upon the stool: *Ut puto Deus fio.* Galba with a sentence, *Feri, si ex re sit populi Romani,* holding forth his neck. Septimius Severus in dispatch: *Adeste si quid mihi restat agendum.* And the like. Certainly the Stoics bestowed too much cost upon death, and by their great preparations made it appear more fearful. Better, saith he, *qui finem vitæ extremum inter munera ponat Naturæ.* It is as natural to die as to be born; and to a little infant, perhaps, the one is as painful as the other. He that dies in an earnest pursuit is like one that is wounded in hot blood; who, for the time, scarce feels the hurt; and therefore a mind fixed and bent upon somewhat that is good doth avert the dolours of death. But above all, believe it, the sweetest canticle is *Nunc dimittis;* when a man hath obtained worthy ends and expectations. Death hath this also, that it openeth the gate to good fame, and extinguisheth envy. *Extinctus amabitur idem.*

OF ADVERSITY

(1625)

It was an high speech of Seneca (after the manner of the Stoics) : *That the good things which belong to prosperity are to be wished ; but the good things that belong to adversity are to be admired. Bona rerum secundarum optabilia, adversarum mirabilia.* Certainly, if miracles be the command over nature, they appear most in adversity. It is yet a higher speech of his than the other (much too high for a heathen) : *It is true greatness to have in one the frailty of a man, and the security of a god. Vere magnum habere fragilitatem hominis, securitatem dei.* This would have done better in poesy, where transcendences are more allowed. And the poets indeed have been busy with it ; for it is in effect the thing which is figured in that strange fiction of the ancient poets, which seemeth not to be without mystery ; nay, and to have some approach to the state of a Christian : that *Hercules, when he went to unbind Prometheus* (by whom human nature is represented), *sailed the length of the great ocean in an earthen pot or pitcher* : lively describing Christian resolution, that saileth in the frail bark of the flesh thorough the waves of the world. But to speak in a mean. The virtue of prosperity is temperance ; the virtue of adversity is fortitude ; which in morals is the more heroical virtue. Prosperity is the blessing of the Old Testament ; adversity is the blessing of the New ; which carrieth the greater benediction, and the clearer revelation of God's favour. Yet even in the Old Testament, if you listen to David's harp, you shall hear as many hearse-like airs as carols ; and the pencil of the Holy Ghost hath laboured more in describing the afflictions of Job than the felicities of Salomon. Prosperity is not without many fears and distastes ; and adversity is not without comforts and hopes. We see in needleworks and embroideries, it is more pleasing to have a lively work upon a sad and solemn ground, than to have a dark and melancholy work upon a lightsome ground : judge therefore of the pleasure of the heart by the pleasure of the eye. Certainly virtue is like precious odours, most fragrant when they are incensed or crushed : for prosperity doth best discover vice ; but adversity doth best discover virtue.

OF ENVY

(1625)

There be none of the affections which have been noted to fascinate or bewitch, but love and envy. They both have vehement wishes ; they frame themselves readily into imaginations and suggestions ; and they come easily into the eye, especially upon the presence of the objects ; which are the points that conduce to fascination, if any such thing there be. We see likewise the Scripture calleth envy an *evil eye* ; and the astrologers call the evil influences of the stars *evil aspects* ; so that still there seemeth to be acknowledged, in the act of envy, an ejaculation or irradiation of the eye. Nay, some have been so curious as to note, that the times when the stroke or percussion of an envious eye doth most hurt, are when the party envied is beheld in glory or triumph ; for that sets an edge upon envy ; and besides, at such times the spirits of the person envied do come forth most into the outward parts, and so meet the blow.

But leaving these curiosities (though not unworthy to be thought on in fit place), we will handle, what persons are apt to envy others ; what persons are most subject to be envied themselves ; and what is the difference between public and private envy.

A man that hath no virtue in himself ever envieth virtue in others. For men's minds will either feed upon their own good or upon others' evil ; and who wanteth the one will prey upon the other ; and whoso is out of hope to attain to another's virtue will seek to come at even hand by depressing another's fortune.

A man that is busy and inquisitive is commonly envious.

For to know much of other men's matters cannot be because all that ado may concern his own estate; therefore it must needs be that he taketh a kind of play-pleasure in looking upon the fortunes of others. Neither can he that mindeth but his own business find much matter for envy. For envy is a gadding passion, and walketh the streets, and doth not keep home: *Non est curiosus, quin idem sit malevolus.*

Men of noble birth are noted to be envious towards new men when they rise. For the distance is altered; and it is like a deceit of the eye, that when others come on they think themselves go back.

Deformed persons, and eunuchs, and old men, and bastards, are envious. For he that cannot possibly mend his own case will do what he can to impair another's; except these defects light upon a very brave and heroical nature, which thinketh to make his natural wants part of his honour; in that it should be said, that an eunuch, or a lame man, did such great matters; affecting the honour of a miracle; as it was in Narses the eunuch, and Agesilaus and Tamberlanes, that were lame men.

The same is the case of men that rise after calamities and misfortunes. For they are as men fallen out with the times, and think other men's harms a redemption of their own sufferings.

They that desire to excel in too many matters, out of levity and vain-glory, are ever envious. For they cannot want work; it being impossible but many in some one of those things should surpass them. Which was the character of Adrian the Emperor, that mortally envied poets and painters and artificers in works wherein he had a vein to excel.

Lastly, near kinsfolks, and fellows in office, and those that have been bred together, are more apt to envy their equals when they are raised. For it doth upbraid unto them their own fortunes, and pointeth at them, and cometh oftener into their remembrance, and incurreth likewise more into the note of others; and envy ever redoubleth from speech and fame.

Cain's envy was the more vile and malignant towards his brother Abel, because when his sacrifice was better accepted there was nobody to look on. Thus much for those that are apt to envy.

Concerning those that are more or less subject to envy: First, persons of eminent virtue, when they are advanced, are less envied. For their fortune seemeth but due unto them; and no man envieth the payment of a debt, but rewards and liberality rather. Again, envy is ever joined with the comparing of a man's self; and where there is no comparison, no envy; and therefore kings are not envied but by kings. Nevertheless it is to be noted that unworthy persons are most envied at their first coming in, and afterwards overcome it better; whereas, contrariwise, persons of worth and merit are most envied when their fortune continueth long. For by that time, though their virtue be the same, yet it hath not the same lustre; for fresh men grow up that darken it.

Persons of noble blood are less envied in their rising; for it seemeth but right done to their birth. Besides, there seemeth not much added to their fortune; and envy is as the sunbeams, that beat hotter upon a bank or steep rising ground, than upon a flat. And for the same reason those that are advanced by degrees are less envied than those that are advanced suddenly and *per saltum*.

Those that have joined with their honour great travails, cares, or perils, are less subject to envy. For men think that they earn their honours hardly, and pity them sometimes; and pity ever healeth envy. Wherefore you shall observe that the more deep and sober sort of politic persons, in their greatness, are ever bemoaning themselves, what a life they lead; chanting a *quanta patimur*. Not that they feel it so, but only to abate the edge of envy. But this is to be understood of business that is laid upon men, and not such as they call unto themselves. For nothing increaseth envy more than an unnecessary and ambitious engrossing of business. And nothing doth extinguish envy more than for a great person to preserve all other inferior officers in their full rights and pre-eminences of their places. For by that means there be so many screens between him and envy.

Above all, those are most subject to envy, which carry the greatness of their fortunes in an insolent and proud manner; being never well but while they are shewing how great they are, either by outward pomp, or by triumphing over all opposition or competition; whereas wise men will rather do sacrifice to envy, in suffering themselves sometimes of purpose to be crossed and overborne in things that do not much concern them. Notwithstanding, so much is true, that the carriage of greatness in a plain and open manner (so it be without arrogancy and vain-glory) doth draw less envy than if it be in a more crafty and cunning fashion. For in that course a man doth but disavow fortune; and seemeth to be conscious of his own want in worth; and doth but teach others to envy him.

Lastly, to conclude this part; as we said in the beginning that the act of envy had somewhat in it of witchcraft, so there is no other cure of envy but the cure of witchcraft; and that is, to remove the *lot* (as they call it) and to lay it upon another. For which purpose, the wiser sort of great persons bring in ever upon the stage somebody upon whom to derive the envy that would come upon themselves; sometimes upon ministers and servants; sometimes upon colleagues and associates; and the like; and for that turn there are never wanting some persons of violent and undertaking natures, who, so they may have power and business, will take it at any cost.

Now to speak of public envy. There is yet some good in public envy, whereas in private there is none. For public envy is as an ostracism, that eclipseth men when they grow too great. And therefore it is a bridle also to great ones, to keep them within bounds.

This envy, being in the Latin word *invidia*, goeth in the modern languages by the name of *discontentment*; of which we shall speak in handling Sedition. It is a disease in a state like to infection. For as infection spreadeth upon that which is sound, and tainteth it; so when envy is gotten once into a state, it traduceth even the best actions thereof, and turneth them into an ill odour. And therefore there is little won by intermingling of plausible actions. For that doth argue but a weakness and fear of envy, which hurteth so much the more; as it is likewise usual in infections; which if you fear them, you call them upon you.

This public envy seemeth to beat chiefly upon principal officers or ministers, rather than upon kings and estates themselves. But this is a sure rule, that if the envy upon the minister be great, when the cause of it in him is small; or if the envy be general in a manner upon all the ministers of an estate; then the envy (though hidden) is truly upon the state itself. And so much of public envy or discontentment, and the difference thereof from private envy, which was handled in the first place.

We will add this in general touching the affection of envy, that of all other affections it is the most importune and continual. For of other affections there is occasion given but now and then; and therefore it was well said, *Invidia festos dies non agit:* for it is ever working upon some or other. And it is also noted that love and envy do make a man pine, which other affections do not, because they are not so continual. It is also the vilest affection, and the most depraved; for which cause it is the proper attribute of the devil, who is called *The envious man, that soweth tares amongst the wheat by night;* as it always cometh to pass, that envy worketh subtilly, and in the dark, and to the prejudice of good things, such as is the wheat.

OF TRAVEL

(1625)

Travel, in the younger sort, is a part of education; in the elder, a part of experience. He that travelleth into a country before he hath some entrance into the language, goeth to school, and not to travel. That young men travel under some tutor, or grave servant, I allow well; so that he be such a one that hath the language and hath been in the country before; whereby he may be able to tell them what things are worthy to be seen in the country where they go; what acquaintances they are to seek; what exercises or discipline the place yieldeth. For else young men shall go hooded, and look abroad little. It is a strange thing, that in sea-voyages, where there is nothing to be seen but sky and sea, men should make diaries; but in land-travel, wherein so much is to be observed, for the most part they omit it; as if chance were fitter to be registered than observation. Let diaries therefore be brought in use. The things to be seen and observed are: the courts of princes, specially when they give audience to ambassadors; the courts of justice, while they sit and hear causes; and so of consistories ecclesiastic; the churches and monasteries, with the monuments which are therein extant; the walls and fortifications of cities and towns, and so the havens and harbours; antiquities and ruins; libraries; colleges, disputations, and lectures, where any are; shipping and navies; houses and gardens of state and pleasure, near great cities; armories; arsenals; magazines; exchanges; bourses; warehouses; exercises of horsemanship, fencing, training of soldiers, and the like; comedies, such whereunto the better sort of persons do resort; treasuries of jewels and robes; cabinets and rarities; and, to conclude, whatsoever is memorable in the places where they go. After all which the tutors or servants ought to make diligent inquiry. As for triumphs, masques, feasts, weddings, funerals, capital executions, and such shows, men need not to be put in mind of them; yet are they not to be neglected. If you will have a young man to put his travel into a little room, and in short time to gather much, this you must do. First, as was said, he must have some entrance into the language, before he goeth. Then he must have such a servant or tutor as knoweth the country, as was likewise said. Let him carry with him also some card or book describing the country where he travelleth; which will be a good key to his enquiry. Let him keep also a diary. Let him not stay long in one city or town; more or less as the place deserveth, but not long; nay, when he stayeth in one city or town, let him change his lodging from one end and part of the town to another; which is a great adamant of acquaintance. Let him sequester himself from the company of his countrymen, and diet in such places where there is good company of the nation where he travelleth. Let him, upon his removes from one place to another, procure recommendation to some person of quality residing in the place whither he removeth; that he may use his favour in those things he desireth to see or know. Thus he may abridge his travel with much profit. As for the acquaintance which is to be sought in travel; that which is most of all profitable is acquaintance with the secretaries and employed men of ambassadors; for so in travelling in one country he shall suck the experience of many. Let him also see and visit eminent persons in all kinds, which are of great name abroad; that he may be able to tell how the life agreeth with the fame. For quarrels, they are with care and discretion to be avoided: they are commonly for mistresses, healths, place, and words. And let a man beware how he keepeth company with choleric and quarrelsome persons; for they will engage him into their own quarrels. When a traveller returneth home, let him not leave the countries where he hath travelled altogether behind him, but maintain a correspondence by letters with those of his acquaintance which are of most worth. And let his travel appear rather in his discourse than in his apparel or gesture; and in his discourse let him be rather advised in his answers than forward to tell stories; and let it appear that he doth not change his country manners for those of foreign parts, but only prick in some flowers of that he hath learned abroad into the customs of his own country.

OF FRIENDSHIP

(1625)

It had been hard for him that spake it to have put more truth and untruth together in a few words, than in that speech, *Whosoever is delighted in solitude is either a wild beast or a god.* For it is most true that a natural and secret hatred and aversation towards society in any man, hath somewhat of the savage beast; but it is most untrue that it should have any character at all of the divine nature; except it proceed, not out of a pleasure in solitude, but out of a love and desire to sequester a man's self for a higher conversation: such as is found to have been falsely and feignedly in some of the heathen; as Epimenides the Candian, Numa the Roman, Empedocles the Sicilian, and Apollonius of Tyana; and truly and really in divers of the ancient hermits and holy fathers of the church. But little do men perceive what solitude is, and how far it extendeth. For a crowd is not company, and faces are but a gallery of pictures, and talk but a tinkling cymbal, where there is no love. The Latin adage meeteth with it a little, *Magna civitas, magna solitudo*; because in a great town friends are scattered; so that there is not that fellowship, for the most part, which is in less neighbourhoods. But we may go further, and affirm most truly that it is a mere and miserable solitude to want true friends, without which the world is but a wilderness; and even in this sense also of solitude, whosoever in the frame of his nature and affections is unfit for friendship, he taketh it of the beast, and not from humanity.

A principal fruit of friendship is the ease and discharge of the fulness and swellings of the heart, which passions of all kinds do cause and induce. We know diseases of stoppings and suffocations are the most dangerous in the body; and it is not much otherwise in the mind: you may take sarza to open the liver, steel to open the spleen, flower of sulphur for the lungs, castoreum for the brain; but no receipt openeth the heart, but a true friend, to whom you may impart griefs, joys, fears, hopes, suspicions, counsels, and whatsoever lieth upon the heart to oppress it, in a kind of civil shrift or confession.

It is a strange thing to observe how high a rate great kings and monarchs do set upon this fruit of friendship whereof we speak : so great, as they purchase it many times at the hazard of their own safety and greatness. For princes, in regard of the distance of their fortune from that of their subjects and servants, cannot gather this fruit, except (to make themselves capable thereof) they raise some persons to be as it were companions and almost equals to themselves, which many times sorteth to inconvenience. The modern languages give unto such persons the name of favourites, or privadoes ; as if it were matter of grace, or conversation. But the Roman name attaineth the true use and cause thereof, naming them *participes curarum* ; for it is that which tieth the knot. And we see plainly that this hath been done, not by weak and passionate princes only, but by the wisest and most politic that ever reigned ; who have oftentimes joined to themselves some of their servants, whom both themselves have called friends, and allowed others likewise to call them in the same manner, using the word which is received between private men.

L. Sylla, when he commanded Rome, raised Pompey (after surnamed the Great) to that height, that Pompey vaunted himself for Sylla's overmatch. For when he had carried the consulship for a friend of his, against the pursuit of Sylla, and that Sylla did a little resent thereat, and began to speak great, Pompey turned upon him again, and in effect bade him be quiet ; *for that more men adored the sun rising than the sun setting.* With Julius Cæsar, Decimus Brutus had obtained that interest, as he set him down in his testament for heir in remainder after his nephew. And this was the man that had power with him to draw him forth to his death. For when Cæsar would have discharged the senate, in regard of some ill presages, and specially a dream of Calpurnia, this man lifted him gently by the arm out of his chair, telling him he hoped he would not dismiss the senate till his wife had dreamt a better dream. And it seemeth his favour was so great, as Antonius, in a letter which is recited *verbatim* in one of Cicero's Philippics, calleth him *venefica*, " witch " ; as if he had enchanted Cæsar. Augustus raised Agrippa (though of mean birth) to that height, as, when he consulted with Mæcenas about the marriage of his daughter Julia, Mæcenas took the liberty to tell him, *that he must either marry his daughter to Agrippa, or take away his life ; there was no third way, he had made him so great*. With Tiberius Cæsar, Sejanus had ascended to that height, as they two were termed and reckoned as a pair of friends. Tiberius in a letter to him saith, *Hæc pro amicitiâ nostrâ non occultavi* ; and the whole senate dedicated an altar to Friendship, as to a goddess, in respect of the great dearness of friendship between them two. The like or more was between Septimius Severus and Plautianus. For he forced his eldest son to marry the daughter of Plautianus ; and would often maintain Plautianus in doing affronts to his son ; and did write also in a letter to the senate by these words : *I love the man so well, as I wish he may over-live me*. Now if these princes had been as a Trajan, or a Marcus Aurelius, a man might have thought that this had proceeded of an abundant goodness of nature ; but being men so wise, for such strength and severity of mind, and so extreme lovers of themselves, as all these were, it proveth most plainly that they found their own felicity (though as great as ever happened to mortal men) but as an half piece, except they mought have a friend to make it entire : and yet, which is more, they were princes that had wives, sons, nephews ; and yet all these could not supply the comfort of friendship.

It is not to be forgotten, what Comineus observeth of his first master, Duke Charles the Hardy ; namely, that he would communicate his secrets with none, and least of all, those secrets which troubled him most. Whereupon he goeth on and saith that towards his latter time *that closeness did impair and a little perish his understanding.* Surely Comineus mought have made the same judgment also, if it had pleased him, of his second master, Lewis the Eleventh, whose closeness was indeed his tormentor. The parable of Pythagoras is dark, but true; *Cor ne edito,* " Eat not the heart." Certainly, if a man would give it a hard phrase, those that want friends to open themselves unto are cannibals of their own hearts. But one thing is most admirable (wherewith I will conclude this first fruit of friendship), which is, that this communicating of a man's self to his friend works two contrary effects; for it redoubleth joys, and cutteth griefs in halfs. For there is no man that imparteth his joys to his friend, but he joyeth the more; and no man that imparteth his griefs to his friend, but he grieveth the less. So that it is in truth of operation upon a man's mind, of like virtue as the alchymists use to attribute to their stone for man's body, that it worketh all contrary effects, but still to the good and benefit of nature. But yet, without praying in aid of alchymists, there is a manifest image of this in the ordinary course of nature. For in bodies, union strengtheneth and cherisheth any natural action; and on the other side weakeneth and dulleth any violent impression: and even so is it of minds.

The second fruit of friendship is healthful and sovereign for the understanding, as the first is for the affections. For friendship maketh indeed a fair day in the affections, from storm and tempests; but it maketh daylight in the understanding, out of darkness and confusion of thoughts. Neither is this to be understood only of faithful counsel, which a man receiveth from his friend; but before you come to that, certain it is that whosoever hath his mind fraught with many thoughts, his wits and understanding do clarify and break up, in the communicating and discoursing with another; he tosseth his thoughts more easily; he marshalleth them more orderly; he seeth how they look when they are turned into words; finally, he waxeth wiser than himself; and that more by an hour's discourse than by a day's meditation. It was well said by

Themistocles to the king of Persia, *that speech was like cloth of Arras, opened· and put abroad, whereby the imagery doth appear in figure ; whereas in thoughts they lie but as in packs.* Neither is this second fruit of friendship, in opening the understanding, restrained only to such friends as are able to give a man counsel (they indeed are best) ; but even without that, a man learneth of himself, and bringeth his own thoughts to light, and whetteth his wits as against a stone, which itself cuts not. In a word, a man were better relate himself to a statua or picture, than to suffer his thoughts to pass in smother.

Add now, to make this second fruit of friendship complete, that other point, which lieth more open and falleth within vulgar observation ; which is faithful counsel from a friend. Heraclitus saith well in one of his enigmas, *Dry light is ever the best.* And certain it is that the light that a man receiveth by counsel from another is drier and purer than that which cometh from his own understanding and judgment ; which is ever infused and drenched in his affections and customs. So as there is as much difference between the counsel that a friend giveth, and that a man giveth himself, as there is between the counsel of a friend and of a flatterer. For there is no such flatterer as is a man's self ; and there is no such remedy against flattery of a man's self as the liberty of a friend. Counsel is of two sorts ; the one concerning manners, the other concerning business. For the first, the best preservative to keep the mind in health is the faithful admonition of a friend. The calling of a man's self to a strict account is a medicine, sometime, too piercing and corrosive. Reading good books of morality is a little flat and dead. Observing our faults in others is sometimes improper for our case. But the best receipt (best, I say, to work, and best to take) is the admonition of a friend. It is a strange thing to behold what gross errors and extreme absurdities many (especially of the greater sort) do commit, for want of a friend to tell them of them, to the great damage both of their fame and fortune. For, as St. James saith, they are as men *that look sometimes into a glass, and presently forget their own shape and favour.* As for business, a man may think, if he will, that two eyes see no more than one ; or that a gamester seeth always more than a looker-on ; or that a man in anger is as wise as he that hath said over the four and twenty letters ; or that a musket may be shot off as well upon the arm as upon a rest ; and such other fond and high imaginations, to think himself all in all. But when all is done, the help of good counsel is that which setteth business straight. And if any man think that he will take counsel, but it shall be by pieces — asking counsel in one business of one man, and in another business of another man — it is well (that is to say, better perhaps than if he asked none at all) ; but he runneth two dangers ; one, that he shall not be faithfully counselled ; for it is a rare thing, except it be from a perfect and entire friend, to have counsel given, but such as shall be bowed and crooked to some ends which he hath that giveth it. The other, that he shall have counsel given, hurtful and unsafe (though with good meaning), and mixed partly of mischief and partly of remedy ; even as if you would call a physician that is thought good for the cure of the disease you complain of, but is unacquainted with your body ; and therefore may put you in way for a present cure, but overthroweth your health in some other kind ; and so cure the disease and kill the patient. But a friend that is wholly acquainted with a man's estate will beware, by furthering any present business, how he dasheth upon other inconvenience. And therefore rest not upon scattered counsels ; they will rather distract and mislead than settle and direct.

After these two noble fruits of friendship (peace in the affections, and support of the judgment) followeth the last fruit, which is like the pomegranate, full of many kernels ; I mean aid and bearing a part in all actions and occasions. Here the best way to represent to life the manifold use of friendship is to cast and see how many things there are which a man cannot do himself ; and then it will appear that it was a sparing speech of the ancients, to say, *that a friend is another himself ;* for that a friend is far more than himself. Men have their time, and die many times in desire of some things which they principally take to heart; the bestowing of a child, the finishing of a work, or the like. If a man have a true friend, he may rest almost secure that the care of those things will continue after him. So that a man hath as it were two lives in his desires. A man hath a body, and that body is confined to a place; but where friendship is, all offices of life are as it were granted to him and his deputy. For he may exercise them by his friend. How many things are there which a man cannot, with any face or comeliness, say or do himself! A man can scarce allege his own merits with modesty, much less extol them; a man cannot sometimes brook to supplicate or beg; and a number of the like. But all these things are graceful in a friend's mouth, which are blushing in a man's own. So again, a man's person hath many proper relations which he cannot put off. A man cannot speak to his son but as a father; to his wife but as a husband; to his enemy but upon terms: whereas a friend may speak as the case requires, and not as it sorteth with the person. But to enumerate these things were endless; I have given the rule, where a man cannot fitly play his own part; if he have not a friend, he may quit the stage.

OF PLANTATIONS

(1625)

Plantations are amongst ancient, primitive, and heroical works. When the world was young, it begat more children; but now it is old, it begets fewer: for I may justly account new plantations to be the children of former kingdoms. I like a plantation in a pure soil; that is, where people are not displanted to the end to plant in others. For else it is rather an extirpation than a plantation. Planting of countries is like planting of woods; for you must make account to leese almost twenty years profit, and expect your recompense in the end. For the principal thing that hath been the destruction of most plantations, hath been the base and hasty drawing of profit in the first years. It is true, speedy profit is not to be neglected, as far as may stand with the good of the plantation, but no further. It is a shameful and unblessed thing to take the scum of people, and wicked condemned men, to be the people with whom you plant: and not only so, but it spoileth the plantation; for they will ever live like rogues, and not fall to work, but be lazy, and do mischief, and spend victuals, and be quickly weary, and then certify over to their country to the discredit of the plantation. The people wherewith you plant ought to be gardeners, ploughmen, labourers, smiths, carpenters, joiners, fishermen, fowlers, with some few apothecaries, surgeons, cooks, and bakers. In a country of plantation, first look about, what kind of victual the country yields of itself to hand; as chestnuts, walnuts, pine-apples, olives, dates, plums, cherries, wild honey, and the like; and make use of them. Then consider what victual or esculent things there are, which grow speedily, and within the year; as parsnips, carrots, turnips, onions, radish, artichokes of Hierusalem, maize, and the like. For wheat, barley, and oats, they ask too much labour; but with pease and beans you may begin, both because they ask less labour, and because they serve for meat as well as for bread. And of rice likewise cometh a great increase, and it is a kind of meat. Above all, there ought to be brought store of biscuit, oat-meal, flour, meal, and the like, in the beginning, till bread may be had. For beasts or birds, take chiefly such as are least subject to diseases, and multiply fastest; as swine, goats, cocks, hens, turkeys, geese, house-doves, and the like. The victual in plantations ought to be expended almost as in a besieged town; that is, with certain allowance. And let the main part of the ground employed to gardens or corn be to a common stock; and to be laid in, and stored up, and then delivered out in proportion; besides some spots of ground that any particular person will manure for his own private. Consider likewise what commodities the soil where the plantation is doth naturally yield, that they may some way help to defray the charge of the plantation: so it be not, as was said, to the untimely prejudice of the main business, as it hath fared with tobacco in Virginia. Wood commonly aboundeth but too much; and therefore timber is fit to be one. If there be iron ore, and streams whereupon to set the mills, iron is a brave commodity where wood aboundeth. Making of bay-salt, if the climate be proper for it, would be put in experience. Growing silk likewise, if any be, is a likely commodity. Pitch and tar, where store of firs and pines are, will not fail. So drugs and sweet woods, where they are, cannot but yield great profit. Soap-ashes likewise, and other things that may be thought of. But moil not too much under ground; for the hope of mines is very uncertain, and useth to make the planters lazy in other things. For government, let it be in the hands of one, assisted with some counsel; and let them have commission to exercise martial laws, with some limitation. And above all, let men make that profit of being in the wilderness, as they have God always, and his service, before their eyes. Let not the government of the plantation depend upon too many counsellors and undertakers in the country that planteth, but upon a temperate number; and let those be rather noblemen and gentlemen than merchants; for they look ever to the present gain. Let there be freedoms from custom, till the plantation be of strength; and not only freedom from custom, but freedom to carry their commodities where they may make their best of them, except there be some special cause of caution. Cram not in people, by sending too fast company after company; but rather hearken how they waste, and send supplies proportionably; but so as the number may live well in the plantation, and not by surcharge be in penury. It hath been a great endangering to the health of some plantations, that they have built along the sea and rivers, in marish and unwholesome grounds. Therefore, though you begin there, to avoid carriage and other like discommodities, yet build still rather upwards from the streams than along. It concerneth likewise the health of the plantation that they have good store of salt with them, that they may use it in their victuals when it shall be necessary. If you plant where savages are, do not only entertain them with trifles and gingles; but use them justly and graciously, with sufficient guard nevertheless: and do not win their favour by helping them to invade their enemies, but for their defence it is not amiss. And send oft of them over to the country that plants, that they may see a better condition than their own, and commend it when they return. When the plantation grows to strength, then it is time to plant with women as well as with men; that the plantation may spread into generations, and not be ever pieced from without. It is the sinfullest thing in the world to forsake or destitute a plantation once in forwardness: for besides the dishonour, it is the guiltiness of blood of many commiserable persons.

OF GARDENS

(1625)

God Almighty first planted a garden. And indeed it is the purest of human pleasures. It is the greatest refreshment to the spirits of man; without which buildings and palaces are but gross handyworks: and a man shall ever see that when ages grow to civility and elegancy, men come to build stately sooner than to garden finely; as if gardening were the greater perfection. I do hold it, in the royal ordering of gardens, there ought to be gardens for all the months in the year; in which severally things of beauty may be then in season. For December and January, and the latter part of November, you must take such things as are green all winter: holly; ivy; bays; juniper; cypress-trees; yew; pine-apple-trees; fir-trees; rosemary; lavender; periwinkle, the white, the purple, and the blue; germander; flags; orange-trees; lemon-trees; and myrtles, if they be stoved; and sweet marjoram, warm set. There followeth, for the latter part of January and February, the mezereon-tree which then blossoms; crocus vernus, both the yellow and the grey; primroses; anemones; the early tulippa; hyacynthus orientalis; chamaïris; fritellaria. For March, there come violets, specially the single blue, which are the earliest;

the yellow daffodil ; the daisy ; the almond-tree in blossom ; the peach-tree in blossom; the cornelian-tree in blossom ; sweet-briar. In April follow the double white violet ; the wall-flower ; the stock-gilliflower ; the cowslip ; flower-de-lices, and lilies of all natures ; rosemary-flowers ; the tulippa ; the double piony ; the pale daffodil ; the French honeysuckle ; the cherry-tree in blossom ; the dammasin and plum-trees in blossom ; the white thorn in leaf ; the lilac-tree. In May and June come pinks of all sorts ; specially the blush-pink ; roses of all kinds, except the musk, which comes later ; honey-suckles ; strawberries ; bugloss ; columbine ; the French marigold ; flos Africanus ; cherry-tree in fruit ; ribes ; figs in fruit ; rasps ; vine flowers ; lavender in flowers ; the sweet satyrian, with the white flower ; herba muscaria ; lilium convallium ; the apple-tree in blossom. In July come gilliflowers of all varieties ; musk-roses ; the lime-tree in blossom ; early pears and plums in fruit ; genitings ; quadlins. In August come plums of all sorts in fruit ; pears ; apricocks ; berberries ; filberds ; musk-melons ; monks-hoods, of all colours. In September come grapes ; apples ; poppies of all colours ; peaches ; melocotones ; nectarines ; cornelians ; wardens ; quinces. In October and the beginning of November come services ; medlars ; bullises ; roses cut or removed to come late ; hollyoaks ; and such like. These particulars are for the climate of London ; but my meaning is perceived, that you may have *ver perpetuum*, as the place affords.

And because the breath of flowers is far sweeter in the air (where it comes and goes, like the warbling of music) than in the hand, therefore nothing is more fit for that delight, than to know what be the flowers and plants that do best perfume the air. Roses, damask and red, are fast flowers of their smells ; so that you may walk by a whole row of them, and find nothing of their sweetness ; yea, though it be in a morning's dew. Bays likewise yield no smell as they grow. Rosemary little ; nor sweet marjoram. That which above all others yields the sweetest smell in the air, is the violet, specially the white double violet, which comes twice a year ; about the middle of

April, and about Bartholomew-tide. Next to that is the musk-rose. Then the strawberry-leaves dying, which [yield] a most excellent cordial smell. Then the flower of the vines; it is a little dust, like the dust of a bent, which grows upon the cluster in the first coming forth. Then sweet-briar. Then wall-flowers, which are very delightful to be set under a parlour or lower chamber window. Then pinks and gilliflowers, specially the matted pink and clove gilliflower. Then the flowers of the lime-tree. Then the honeysuckles, so they be somewhat afar off. Of beanflowers I speak not, because they are field flowers. But those which perfume the air most delightfully, not passed by as the rest, but being trodden upon and crushed, are three; that is, burnet, wild thyme, and watermints. Therefore you are to set whole alleys of them, to have the pleasure when you walk or tread.

For gardens (speaking of those which are indeed prince-like, as we have done of buildings), the contents ought not well to be under thirty acres of ground, and to be divided into three parts: a green in the entrance; a heath or desert in the going forth; and the main garden in the midst; besides alleys on both sides. And I like well that four acres of ground be assigned to the green; six to the heath; four and four to either side; and twelve to the main garden. The green hath two pleasures: the one, because nothing is more pleasant to the eye than green grass kept finely shorn; the other, because it will give you a fair alley in the midst, by which you may go in front upon a stately hedge, which is to enclose the garden. But because the alley will be long, and, in great heat of the year or day, you ought not to buy the shade in the garden by going in the sun through the green, therefore you are, of either side the green, to plant a covert alley, upon carpenter's work, about twelve foot in height, by which you may go in shade into the garden. As for the making of knots or figures with divers coloured earths, that they may lie under the windows of the house on that side which the garden stands, they be but toys: you may see as good sights many times in tarts. The garden is best to be square, encompassed on all the four sides with a stately arched hedge. The arches to be upon pillars of carpenter's work, of some ten foot high and six foot broad; and the spaces between of the same dimension with the breadth of the arch. Over the arches let there be an entire hedge of some four foot high, framed also upon carpenter's work; and upon the upper hedge, over every arch, a little turret, with a belly, enough to receive a cage of birds; and over every space between the arches some other little figure, with broad plates of round coloured glass, gilt, for the sun to play upon. But this hedge I intend to be raised upon a bank, not steep, but gently slope, of some six foot, set all with flowers. Also I understand that this square of the garden should not be the whole breadth of the ground, but to leave on either side ground enough for diversity of side alleys; unto which the two covert alleys of the green may deliver you. But there must be no alleys with hedges at either end of this great enclosure: not at the hither end, for letting your prospect upon this fair hedge from the green; nor at the further end, for letting your prospect from the hedge through the arches upon the heath.

For the ordering of the ground within the great hedge, I leave it to variety of device; advising nevertheless that whatsoever form you cast it into, first, it be not too busy or full of work. Wherein I, for my part, do not like images cut out in juniper or other garden stuff: they be for children. Little low hedges, round, like welts, with some pretty pyramids, I like well; and in some places, fair columns upon frames of carpenter's work. I would also have the alleys spacious and fair. You may have closer alleys upon the side grounds, but none in the main garden. I wish also, in the very middle, a fair mount, with three ascents, and alleys, enough for four to walk abreast; which I would have to be perfect circles, without any bulwarks or embossments; and the whole amount to be thirty foot high; and some fine banqueting-house, with some chimneys neatly cast, and without too much glass.

For fountains, they are a great beauty and refreshment; but pools mar all, and make the garden unwholesome and full of flies and frogs. Fountains I intend to be of two natures: the one that sprinkleth or spouteth water; the other a fair receipt of water, of some thirty or forty foot square, but without fish, or slime, or mud. For the first, the ornaments of images gilt, or of marble, which are in use, do well: but the main matter is so to convey the water, as it never stay, either in the bowls or in the cistern; that the water be never by rest discoloured, green or red or the like, or gather any mossiness or putrefaction. Besides that, it is to be cleansed every day by the hand. Also some steps up to it, and some fine pavement about it, doth well. As for the other kind of fountain, which we may call a bathing pool, it may admit much curiosity and beauty, wherewith we will not trouble ourselves: as, that the bottom be finely paved, and with images; the sides likewise; and withal embellished with coloured glass, and such things of lustre; encompassed also with fine rails of low statuas. But the main point is the same which we mentioned in the former kind of fountain; which is, that the water be in perpetual motion, fed by a water higher than the pool, and delivered into it by fair spouts, and then discharged away under ground, by some equality of bores, that it stay little. And for fine devices, of arching water without spilling, and making it rise in several forms (of feathers, drinking glasses, canopies, and the like), they be pretty things to look on, but nothing to health and sweetness.

For the heath, which was the third part of our plot, I wish it to be framed, as much as may be, to a natural wildness. Trees I would have none in it, but some thickets made only of sweet-briar and honeysuckle, and some wild vine amongst; and the ground set with violets, strawberries, and primroses. For these are sweet, and prosper in the shade. And these to be in the heath, here and there, not in any order. I like also little heaps, in the nature of mole-hills (such as are in wild heaths), to be set, some with wild thyme, some with pinks, some with germander, that gives a good flower to the eye, some with periwinkle, some with violets, some with straw- berries, some with cowslips, some with daisies, some with red roses, some with lilium convallium, some with sweet-williams red, some with bear's-foot, and the like low flowers, being withal sweet and sightly. Part of which heaps are to be with standards of little bushes pricked upon their top, and part without. The standards to be roses, juniper, holly, berberries (but here and there, because of the smell of their blossom), red currants, gooseberry, rosemary, bays, sweet-briar, and such like. But these standards to be kept with cutting, that they grow not out of course.

For the side grounds, you are to fill them with variety of alleys, private, to give a full shade, some of them, whereso- ever the sun be. You are to frame some of them likewise for shelter, that when the wind blows sharp, you may walk as in a gallery. And those alleys must be likewise hedged at both ends, to keep out the wind; and these closer alleys must be ever finely gravelled, and no grass, because of going wet. In many of these alleys likewise, you are to set fruit-trees of all sorts; as well upon the walls as in ranges. And this would be generally observed, that the borders wherein you plant your fruit-trees be fair and large and low, and not steep; and set with fine flowers, but thin and sparingly, lest they deceive the trees. At the end of both the side grounds, I would have a mount of some pretty height, leaving the wall of the enclosure breast high, to look abroad into the fields.

For the main garden, I do not deny but there should be some fair alleys, ranged on both sides with fruit-trees; and some pretty tufts of fruit-trees, and arbours with seats, set in some decent order; but these to be by no means set too thick; but to leave the main garden so as it be not close, but the air open and free. For as for shade, I would have you rest upon the alleys of the side grounds, there to walk, if you be dis- posed, in the heat of the year or day; but to make account that the main garden is for the more temperate parts of the year; and, in the heat of summer, for the morning and the evening, or over-cast days.

For aviaries, I like them not, except they be of that largeness as they may be turfed, and have living plants and bushes set in them; that the birds may have more scope and natural nestling, and that no foulness appear in the floor of the aviary. So I have made a platform of a princely garden, partly by precept, partly by drawing, not a model, but some general lines of it; and in this I have spared for no cost. But it is nothing for great princes, that for the most part taking advice with workmen with no less cost set their things together, and sometimes add statuas, and such things, for state and magnificence, but nothing to the true pleasure of a garden.

ABRAHAM COWLEY (1618–1667)

THE DANGERS OF AN HONEST MAN IN MUCH COMPANY

(1668)

If twenty thousand naked Americans were not able to resist the assaults of but twenty well-armed Spaniards, I see little possibility for one honest man to defend himself against twenty thousand knaves, who are all furnished *cap-à-pie* with the defensive arms of worldly prudence, and the offensive, too, of craft and malice. He will find no less odds than this against him if he have much to do in human affairs. The only advice, therefore, which I can give him is, to be sure not to venture his person any longer in the open campaign, to retreat and entrench himself, to stop up all avenues, and draw up all bridges against so numerous an enemy. The truth of it is, that a man in much business must either make himself a knave, or else the world will make him a fool: and if the injury went no farther than the being laughed at, a wise man would content himself with the revenge of retaliation; but the case is much worse, for these civil cannibals too, as well as the wild ones, not only dance about such a taken stranger, but at last devour him. A sober man cannot get too soon out of drunken company; though they be never so kind and merry among themselves, 't is not unpleasant only, but dangerous to him. Do ye wonder that a virtuous man should love to be alone? It is hard for him to be otherwise; he is so, when he is among ten thousand; neither is the solitude so uncomfortable to be alone without any other creature, as it is to be alone in the midst of wild beasts. Man is to man all kind of beasts — a fawning dog, a roaring lion, a thieving fox, a robbing wolf, a dissembling crocodile, a treacherous decoy, and a rapacious vulture. The civilest, methinks, of all nations, are those whom we account the most barbarous; there is some moderation and good nature in the Toupinambaltians who eat no men but their enemies, whilst we learned and polite and Christian Europeans, like so many pikes and sharks, prey upon everything that we can swallow. It is the great boast of eloquence and philosophy, that they first congregated men dispersed, united them into societies, and built up the houses and the walls of cities. I wish they could unravel all they had woven; that we might have our woods and our innocence again instead of our castles and our policies. They have assembled many thousands of scattered people into one body: 't is true, they have done so, they have brought them together into cities to cozen, and into armies to murder, one another; they found them hunters and fishers of wild creatures, they have made them hunters and fishers of their brethren; they boast to have reduced them to a state of peace, when the truth is they have only taught them an art of war; they have framed, I must confess, wholesome laws for the restraint of vice, but they raised first that devil which now they conjure and cannot bind; though there were before no punishments for wickedness, yet there was less committed because there were no rewards for it. But the men who praise philosophy from this topic are much deceived; let oratory answer for itself, the tinkling, perhaps, of that may unite a swarm: it never was the work of philosophy to assemble multitudes, but to regulate only, and govern them when they were assembled, to make the best of an evil, and bring them, as much as is possible, to unity again. Avarice and ambition only were the first builders of towns, and founders of empire; they said, " Go to, let us build us a city and a tower whose top may reach unto heaven, and let us make us a name, lest we be scattered abroad upon the face of the earth." What was the beginning of Rome, the metropolis of all the world? What was it but a concourse of thieves, and a sanctuary of criminals? It was justly named by the augury of no less than twelve vultures, and the founder cemented his walls with the blood of his brother. Not unlike to this was the beginning even of the first town, too, in the world, and such is the original sin of most cities : their actual increase daily with their age and growth ; the more people, the more wicked all of them ; every one brings in his part to inflame the contagion, which becomes at last so universal and so strong, that no precepts can be sufficient preservatives, nor anything secure our safety, but flight from among the infected. We ought, in the choice of a situation, to regard above all things the healthfulness of the place, and the healthfulness of it for the mind rather than for the body. But suppose (which is hardly to be supposed) we had antidote enough against this poison ; nay, suppose, farther, we were always and at all pieces armed and provided both against the assaults of hostility and the mines of treachery, 't will yet be but an uncomfortable life to be ever in alarms ; though we were compassed round with fire to defend ourselves from wild beasts, the lodging would be unpleasant, because we must always be obliged to watch that fire, and to fear no less the defects of our guard than the diligences of our enemy. The sum of this is, that a virtuous man is in danger to be trod upon and destroyed in the crowd of his contraries ; nay, which is worse, to be changed and corrupted by them, and that 't is impossible to escape both these inconveniences without so much caution as will take away the whole quiet, that is, the happiness of his life. Ye see, then, what he may lose ; but, I pray, what can he get there ? *Quid Romæ faciam ? Mentiri nescio.* What should a man of truth and honesty do at Rome ? He can neither understand, nor speak the language of the place ; a naked man may swim in the sea, but 't is not the way to catch fish there ; they are likelier to devour him than he them, if he bring no nets and use no deceits. I think, therefore, it was wise and friendly advice which Martial gave to Fabian when he met him newly arrived at Rome.

> Honest and poor, faithful in word and thought;
> What has thee, Fabian, to the city brought?

Thou neither the buffoon nor bawd canst play,
Nor with false whispers the innocent betray :
Nor corrupt wives, nor from rich beldams get
A living by thy industry and sweat;
Nor with vain promises and projects cheat,
Nor bribe or flatter any of the great.
    But you 're a man of learning, prudent, just;
A man of courage, firm, and fit for trust.
    Why, you may stay, and live unenvied here;
But (faith) go back, and keep you where you were.

Nay, if nothing of all this were in the case, yet the very sight of uncleanness is loathsome to the cleanly ; the sight of folly and impiety vexatious to the wise and pious.

Lucretius, by his favour, though a good poet, was but an ill-natured man, when he said, " It was delightful to see other men in a great storm." And no less ill-natured should I think Democritus, who laughed at all the world, but that he retired himself so much out of it that we may perceive he took no great pleasure in that kind of mirth. I have been drawn twice or thrice by company to go to Bedlam, and have seen others very much delighted with the fantastical extravagancy of so many various madnesses, which upon me wrought so contrary an effect, that I always returned not only melancholy, but even sick with the sight. My compassion there was perhaps too tender, for I meet a thousand madmen abroad, without any perturbation, though, to weigh the matter justly, the total loss of reason is less deplorable than the total depravation of it. An exact judge of human blessings, of riches, honours, beauty, even of wit itself, should pity the abuse of them more than the want.

Briefly, though a wise man could pass never so securely through the great roads of human life, yet he will meet perpetually with so many objects and occasions of compassion, grief, shame, anger, hatred, indignation, and all passions but envy (for he will find nothing to deserve that) that he had better strike into some private path ; nay, go so far, if he could, out of the common way, *ut nec facta audiat Pelopidarum ;*

that he might not so much as hear of the actions of the sons of Adam. But whither shall we fly, then? Into the deserts, like the ancient hermits?

> *Quia terra patet fera regnat Erynnis.*
> *In facinus jurasse putes.*

One would think that all mankind had bound themselves by an oath to do all the wickedness they can; that they had all (as the Scripture speaks) sold themselves to sin: the difference only is, that some are a little more crafty (and but a little, God knows) in making of the bargain. I thought, when I went first to dwell in the country, that without doubt I should have met there with the simplicity of the old poetical golden age: I thought to have found no inhabitants there, but such as the shepherds of Sir Philip Sidney in Arcadia, or of Monsieur d'Urfé upon the banks of Lignon; and began to consider with myself, which way I might recommend no less to posterity the happiness and innocence of the men of Chertsey: but to confess the truth, I perceived quickly, by infallible demonstrations, that I was still in old England, and not in Arcadia, or La Forrest; that if I could not content myself with anything less than exact fidelity in human conversation, I had almost as good go back and seek for it in the Court, or the Exchange, or Westminster Hall. I ask again, then, whither shall we fly, or what shall we do? The world may so come in a man's way that he cannot choose but salute it; he must take heed, though, not to go a-whoring after it. If by any lawful vocation or just necessity men happen to be married to it, I can only give them St. Paul's advice: "Brethren, the time is short; it remains that they that have wives be as though they had none. But I would that all men were even as I myself."

In all cases they must be sure that they do *mundum ducere* and not *mundo nubere*. They must retain the superiority and headship over it: happy are they who can get out of the sight of this deceitful beauty, that they may not be led so much as into temptation ; who have not only quitted the metropolis, but can abstain from ever seeing the next market town of their country.

OF MYSELF

(1668)

It is a hard and nice subject for a man to write of himself ; it grates his own heart to say anything of disparagement and the reader's ears to hear anything of praise from him. There is no danger from me of offending him in this kind ; neither my mind, nor my body, nor my fortune allow me any materials for that vanity. It is sufficient for my own contentment that they have preserved me from being scandalous, or remarkable on the defective side. But besides that, I shall here speak of myself only in relation to the subject of these precedent discourses, and shall be likelier thereby to fall into the contempt than rise up to the estimation of most people. As far as my memory can return back into my past life, before I knew or was capable of guessing what the world, or glories, or business of it were, the natural affections of my soul gave me a secret bent of aversion from them, as some plants are said to turn away from others, by an antipathy imperceptible to themselves and inscrutable to man's understanding. Even when I was a very young boy at school, instead of running about on holidays and playing with my fellows, I was wont to steal from them and walk into the fields, either alone with a book, or with some one companion, if I could find any of the same temper. I was then, too, so much an enemy to all constraint, that my masters could never prevail on me, by any persuasions or encouragements, to learn without book the common rules of grammar, in which they dispensed with me alone, because they found I made a shift to do the usual exercise out of my own reading and observation. That I was then of the same mind as I am now (which I confess I wonder at myself) may appear by the latter end of an ode which I made when I was but thirteen years old, and which was then printed with many other verses. The beginning of it is boyish, but of this part which I here set down (if a very little were corrected) I should hardly now be much ashamed.

9

This only grant me, that my means may lie
Too low for envy, for contempt too high.
    Some honour I would have,
Not from great deeds, but good alone.
The unknown are better than ill known.
    Rumour can ope the grave;
Acquaintance I would have, but when 't depends
Not on the number, but the choice of friends.

10

Books should, not business, entertain the light,
And sleep, as undisturbed as death, the night.
    My house a cottage, more
Than palace, and should fitting be
For all my use, no luxury.
    My garden painted o'er
With Nature's hand, not Art's; and pleasures yield,
Horace might envy in his Sabine field.

11

Thus would I double my life's fading space,
For he that runs it well twice runs his race.
    And in this true delight,
These unbought sports, this happy state,
I would not fear, nor wish my fate,
    But boldly say each night,
To-morrow let my sun his beams display,
Or in clouds hide them; I have lived to-day.

You may see by it I was even then acquainted with the poets (for the conclusion is taken out of Horace), and perhaps it was the immature and immoderate love of them which stamped first, or rather engraved, these characters in me. They were like letters cut into the bark of a young tree, which with the tree still grow proportionably. But how this love came to be produced in me so early is a hard question. I believe I can tell the particular little chance that filled my head first with such chimes of verse as have never since left ringing there. For I remember when I began to read, and to take some pleasure in it, there was wont to lie in my mother's parlour (I know not by what accident, for she herself never in her life read any book but of devotion), but there was wont to lie Spenser's works; this I happened to fall upon, and was infinitely delighted with the stories of the knights, and giants, and monsters, and brave houses, which I found everywhere there (though my understanding had little to do with all this); and by degrees with the tinkling of the rhyme and dance of the numbers, so that I think I had read him all over before I was twelve years old, and was thus made a poet as immediately as a child is made an eunuch. With these affections of mind, and my heart wholly set upon letters, I went to the university, but was soon torn from thence by that violent public storm which would suffer nothing to stand where it did, but rooted up every plant, even from the princely cedars to me, the hyssop. Yet I had as good fortune as could have befallen me in such a tempest; for I was cast by it into the family of one of the best persons, and into the court of one of the best princesses of the world. Now though I was here engaged in ways most contrary to the original design of my life, that is, into much company, and no small business, and into a daily sight of greatness, both militant and triumphant (for that was the state then of the English and French Courts); yet all this was so far from altering my opinion, that it only added the confirmation of reason to that which was before but natural inclination. I saw plainly all the paint of that kind of life, the nearer I came to it; and that beauty which I did not fall in love with when, for aught I knew, it was real, was not like to bewitch or entice me when I saw that it was adulterate. I met with several great persons, whom I liked very well, but could not perceive that any part of their greatness was to be liked or desired, no more than I would be glad or content to be in a storm, though I saw many ships which rid safely and bravely in it. A storm would not agree with my stomach, if it did with my courage. Though I was in a crowd of as good company as could be found anywhere, though I was in business of great and honourable trust, though I eat at the best table, and enjoyed the best conveniences for present subsistence that ought to be desired by a man of my condition in banishment and public distresses; yet I could not abstain from renewing my old schoolboy's wish in a copy of verses to the same effect.

> Well then; I now do plainly see,
> This busy world and I shall ne'er agree, etc.

And I never then proposed to myself any other advantage from His Majesty's happy restoration, but the getting into some moderately convenient retreat in the country, which I thought in that case I might easily have compassed, as well as some others, with no greater probabilities or pretences, have arrived to extraordinary fortunes. But I had before written a shrewd prophecy against myself, and I think Apollo inspired me in the truth, though not in the elegance of it.

> Thou, neither great at court nor in the war,
> Nor at th' exchange shalt be, nor at the wrangling bar;
> Content thyself with the small barren praise,
> Which neglected verse does raise, etc.

However, by the failing of the forces which I had expected, I did not quit the design which I had resolved on; I cast myself into it *à corps perdu*, without making capitulations or taking counsel of fortune. But God laughs at a man who says to his soul, "Take thy ease": I met presently not only with many little encumbrances and impediments, but with so much sickness (a new misfortune to me) as would have spoiled the happiness of an emperor as well as mine. Yet I do neither repent nor alter my course. *Non ego perfidum dixi sacramentum.* Nothing shall separate me from a mistress which I have loved so long, and have now at last married, though she neither has brought me a rich portion, nor lived yet so quietly with me as I hoped from her.

—— Nec vos, dulcissima mundi
Nomina, vos Musæ, libertas, otia, libri,
Hortique sylvæque anima remanente relinquam.

Nor by me e'er shall you,
You of all names the sweetest, and the best,
You Muses, books, and liberty, and rest,
You gardens, fields, and woods forsaken be,
As long as life itself forsakes not me.

But this is a very petty ejaculation. Because I have concluded all the other chapters with a copy of verses, I will
maintain the humour to the last.

MARTIAL, BOOK 10, EPIGRAM 47

Vitam quæ faciunt beatiorem, etc.

Since, dearest friend, 't is your desire to see
A true receipt of happiness from me;
These are the chief ingredients, if not all:
Take an estate neither too great nor small,
Which *quantum sufficit* the doctors call.
Let this estate from parents' care descend:
The getting it too much of life does spend.
Take such a ground, whose gratitude may be
A fair encouragement for industry.
Let constant fires the winter's fury tame,
And let thy kitchen's be a vestal flame.
Thee to the town let never suit at law,
And rarely, very rarely, business draw.
Thy active mind in equal temper keep,
In undisturbéd peace, yet not in sleep.
Let exercise a vigorous health maintain,
Without which all the composition 's vain.
In the same weight prudence and innocence take,
Ana of each does the just mixture make.
But a few friendships wear, and let them be
By Nature and by Fortune fit for thee.
Instead of art and luxury in food,
Let mirth and freedom make thy table good.
If any cares into thy daytime creep,
At night, without wine's opium, let them sleep.

Let rest, which Nature does to darkness wed,
And not lust, recommend to thee thy bed.
Be satisfied, and pleased with what thou art;
Act cheerfully and well th' allotted part,
Enjoy the present hour, be thankful for the past,
And neither fear, nor wish th' approaches of the last.

MARTIAL, BOOK 10, EPIGRAM 96

Me, who have lived so long among the great,
You wonder to hear talk of a retreat:
And a retreat so distant, as may show
No thoughts of a return when once I go.
Give me a country, how remote so e'er,
Where happiness a moderate rate does bear,
Where poverty itself in plenty flows
And all the solid use of riches knows.
The ground about the house maintains it there,
The house maintains the ground about it here.
Here even hunger 's dear, and a full board
Devours the vital substance of the lord.
The land itself does there the feast bestow,
The land itself must here to market go.
Three or four suits one winter here does waste,
One suit does there three or four winters last.
Here every frugal man must oft be cold,
And little lukewarm fires are to you sold.
There fire 's an element as cheap and free
Almost as any of the other three.
Stay you then here, and live among the great,
Attend their sports, and at their tables eat.
When all the bounties here of men you score,
The place's bounty there shall give me more.

SEVENTEENTH CENTURY CHARACTERS

John Earle (1601–1665)

From *Microcosmographie* (1628)

A MERE YOUNG GENTLEMAN OF THE UNIVERSITY

Is one that comes there to wear a gown, and to say hereafter, he has been at the university. His father sent him
thither because he heard there were the best fencing and
dancing schools; from these he has his education, from his
tutor the oversight. The first element of his knowledge is to
be shown the colleges, and initiated in a tavern by the way,
which hereafter he will learn of himself. The two marks of
his seniority is the bare velvet of his gown and his proficiency
at tennis, where when he can once play a set, he is a fresh-
man no more. His study has commonly handsome shelves,
his books neat silk strings, which he shows to his father's
man, and is loth to untie or take down for fear of misplacing.
Upon foul days for recreation he retires thither, and looks
over the pretty book his tutor reads to him, which is commonly
some short history, or a piece of *Euphormio*; for which his
tutor gives him money to spend next day. His main loitering
is at the library, where he studies arms and books of honour,
and turns a gentleman-critic in pedigrees. Of all things he
endures not to be mistaken for a scholar, and hates a black
suit though it be of sattin. His companion is ordinarily some
stale fellow, that has been notorious for an ingle to gold
hatbands, whom he admires at first, afterward scorns. If he
have spirit or wit, he may light of better company, and may
learn some flashes of wit, which may do him knight's service

in the country hereafter. But he is now gone to the Inns-of-court, where he studies to forget what he learned before, his acquaintance and the fashion.

A CONTEMPLATIVE MAN

Is a scholar in this great university the World, and the same his book and study. He cloisters not his meditations in the narrow darkness of a room, but sends them abroad with his eyes, and his brain travels with his feet. He looks upon man from a high tower, and sees him trulier at this distance in his infirmities and poorness. He scorns to mix himself in men's actions, as he would to act upon a stage; but sits aloft on the scaffold a censuring spectator. Nature admits him as a partaker of her sports, and asks his approbation as it were of her own works and variety. He comes not in company, because he would not be solitary, but finds discourse enough with himself, and his own thoughts are his excellent playfellows. He looks not upon a thing as a yawning stranger at novelties; but his search is more mysterious and inward, and he spells Heaven out of earth. He knits his observations together, and makes a ladder of them all to climb to God. He is free from vice, because he has no occasion to employ it, and is above those ends that make men wicked. He has learnt all can here be taught him, and comes now to Heaven to see more.

JEAN LA BRUYÈRE (1645–1696)

From *Les Caractères* (1688–1694)

THE CHARACTER OF ARRIAS

Who, that goes into society, can help meeting with certain vain, fickle, familiar, and positive people who monopolise all conversation, and compel every one else to listen to them? They can be heard in the anteroom, and a person may boldly enter without fear of interrupting them; they continue their story without paying the smallest attention to any comers or goers, or to the rank and quality of their audience; they silence a man who begins to tell an anecdote, so that they may tell it themselves according to their fashion, which is the best; they heard it from Zamet, from Ruccellaï, or from Concini, whom they do not know, to whom they never spoke in their lives, and whom they would address as "Your Excellency," if ever they spoke to any one of them. They sometimes will go up to a man of the highest rank among those who are present, and whisper in his ear some circumstance which nobody else knows, and which they would not have divulged to others for the world; they conceal some names to disguise the anecdote they relate and to prevent the real persons being found out; you ask them to let you have these names, you urge them in vain. There are some things they must not tell, and some persons whom they cannot name; they have given their word of honour not to do so; it is a secret, a mystery of the greatest importance; moreover, you ask an impossibility. You might wish to learn something from them, but they know neither the facts nor the persons.

Arrias has read and seen everything, at least he would lead you to think so; he is a man of universal knowledge, or pretends to be, and would rather tell a falsehood than be silent or appear to ignore anything. Some person is talking at meal-time in the house of a man of rank of a northern court; he interrupts and prevents him telling what he knows; he goes hither and thither in that distant country as if he were a native of it; he discourses about the habits of its court, the native women, the laws and customs of the land; he tells many little stories which happened there, thinks them very entertaining, and is the first to laugh loudly at them. Somebody presumes to contradict him, and clearly proves to him that what he says is untrue. Arrias is not disconcerted; on the contrary, he grows angry at the interruption, and exclaims, "I aver and relate nothing but what I know on excellent authority; I had it from Sethon, the French ambassador at that court, who only a few days ago came back to Paris, and is a particular friend of mine; I asked him several questions, and he replied to them all without concealing anything." He continues his story with greater confidence than he began it, till one of the company informs him that the gentleman whom he has been contradicting was Sethon himself, but lately arrived from his embassy.

THE TATLER (1709–1711)

PROSPECTUS

No. 1. Tuesday, April 12, 1709

Quicquid agunt homines . . . nostri farrago libelli.

Though the other papers which are published for the use
of the good people of England have certainly very wholesome
effects, and are laudable in their particular kinds, yet they do
not seem to come up to the main design of such narrations,
which, I humbly presume, should be principally intended for
the use of politic persons, who are so public-spirited as to neglect their own affairs to look into transactions of state. Now
these gentlemen, for the most part, being men of strong zeal
and weak intellects, it is both a charitable and necessary work
to offer something, whereby such worthy and well-affected members of the commonwealth may be instructed, after their reading, what to think ; which shall be the end and purpose of this
my paper, wherein I shall from time to time report and consider all matters of what kind soever that shall occur to me,
and publish such my advices and reflections every Tuesday,
Thursday, and Saturday in the week, for the convenience of
the post. I have also resolved to have something which may
be of entertainment to the fair sex, in honour of whom I have
taken the title of this paper. I therefore earnestly desire all
persons, without distinction, to take it in for the present gratis,
and hereafter at the price of one penny, forbidding all hawkers
to take more for it at their peril. And I desire my readers to
consider, that I am at a very great charge for proper materials
for this work, as well as that, before I resolved upon it, I
had settled a correspondence in all parts of the known and

knowing world. And forasmuch as this globe is not trodden upon by mere drudges of business only, but that men of spirit and genius are justly to be esteemed as considerable agents in it, we shall not, upon a dearth of news, present you with musty foreign edicts, or dull proclamations, but shall divide our relation of the passages which occur in action or discourse throughout this town, as well as elsewhere, under such dates of places as may prepare you for the matter you are to expect, in the following manner:

All accounts of gallantry, pleasure, and entertainment, shall be under the article of White's Chocolate-house; poetry, under that of Will's Coffee-house; learning, under the title of Grecian; foreign and domestic news, you will have from St. James's Coffee-house; and what else I shall on any other subject offer, shall be dated from my own apartment.

I once more desire my reader to consider that as I cannot keep an ingenious man to go daily to Will's under twopence each day merely for his charges, to White's under sixpence, nor to the Grecian without allowing him some plain Spanish, to be as able as others at the learned table; and that a good observer cannot speak with even Kidney at St. James's without clean linen; I say, these considerations will, I hope, make all persons willing to comply with my humble request (when my gratis stock is exhausted) of a penny a piece; especially since they are sure of some proper amusement, and that it is impossible for me to want means to entertain them, having, besides the helps of my own parts, the power of divination, and that I can, by casting a figure, tell you all that will happen before it comes to pass.

But this last faculty I shall use very sparingly, and not speak of anything until it is passed, for fear of divulging matters which may offend our superiors. [STEELE]

ON DUELLING

No. 29. Thursday, June 16, 1709

White's Chocolate-house, June 14

Having a very solid respect for human nature, however it is distorted from its natural make by affectation, humour, custom, misfortune, or vice, I do apply myself to my friends to help me in raising arguments for preserving it in all its individuals, as long as it is permitted. To one of my letters on this subject, I have received the following answer:

Sir,

In answer to your question, why men of sense, virtue, and experience are seen still to comply with that ridiculous custom of duelling, I must desire you to reflect that custom has dished up in ruffs the wisest heads of our ancestors, and put the best of the present age into huge falbala periwigs. Men of sense would not impose such encumbrances on themselves, but be glad they might show their faces decently in public upon easier terms. If then such men appear reasonably slaves to the fashion, in what regards the figure of their persons, we ought not to wonder that they are at least so in what seems to touch their reputations. Besides, you can't be ignorant that dress and chivalry have been always encouraged by the ladies as the two principal branches of gallantry. It is to avoid being sneered at for his singularity, and from a desire to appear more agreeable to his mistress, that a wise, experienced, and polite man complies with the dress commonly received, and is prevailed upon to violate his reason and principles in hazarding his life and estate by a tilt, as well as suffering his pleasures to be constrained and soured by the constant apprehension of a quarrel. This is the more surprising, because men of the most delicate sense and principles have naturally in other cases a particular repugnance in accommodating themselves to the maxims of the world: but one may easily distinguish the man that is affected with beauetry and the reputation of a tilt from him who complies with both merely as they are imposed upon him by custom; for in the former you will remark an air of vanity and triumph, whereas when the latter appears in a long Duvillier full of powder, or has decided a quarrel by the sword, you may perceive in his face that he appeals to custom for an excuse. I think it may not be improper to inquire into the genealogy of this chimerical monster called a duel, which I take to be an illegitimate species of the ancient knight-errantry. By the laws of this whim, your heroic person, or man of gallantry, was indispensably obliged to starve in armour a certain number of years in the chase of monsters, encounter them at the peril of his life, and suffer great hardships in order to gain the affection of the fair lady, and qualify himself for assuming the *bel air*, that is, of a pretty fellow, or man of honour according to the fashion: but since the publishing of *Don Quixote* and extinction of the race of dragons, which Suetonius says happened in that of Wantley, the gallant and heroic spirits of these later times have been under the necessity of creating new chimerical monsters to entertain themselves with, by way of single combats, as the only proofs they are able to give their own sex, and the ladies, that they are in all points men of nice honour. But to do justice to the ancient and real monsters, I must observe that they never molested those who were not of a humour to hunt for them in the woods and deserts; whereas, on the contrary, our modern monsters are so familiarly admitted and entertained in all the courts and cities of Europe (except France) that one can scarce be in the most humanised society without risking one's life; the people of the best sort and the fine gentlemen of the age being so fond of them that they seldom appear in any public place without one. I have some further considerations upon this subject which, as you encourage me, shall be communicated to you by, Sir, a cousin but once removed from the best family of the Staffs, namely,

Sir,

Your humble Servant,

Kinsman and Friend,

Tim. Switch.

It is certain, Mr. Switch has hit upon the true source of this evil, and that it proceeds only from the force of custom that we contradict ourselves in half the particulars and occurrences of life. But such a tyranny in love, which the fair impose upon us, is a little too severe, that we must demonstrate our affection for them by no certain proof but hatred to one another, or come at them (only as one does to an estate) by survivorship. This way of application to gain a lady's heart is taking her as we do towns and castles, by distressing the place and letting none come near them without our pass. Were such a lover once to write the truth of his heart, and let her know his whole thoughts, he would appear indeed to have a passion for her; but it would hardly be called love. The billet-doux would run to this purpose:

Madame,

I have so tender a regard for you and your interests that I 'll knock any man in the head whom I observe to be of my mind, and like you. Mr. Truman the other day looked at you in so languishing a manner that I am resolved to run him through to-morrow morning: this, I think, he deserves for his guilt in admiring you, than which I cannot have a greater reason for murdering him, except it be that you also approve him. Whoever says he dies for you, I will make his words good, for I will kill him. I am,

Madame,

Your most obedient,

[STEELE] Most humble Servant.

HAPPY MARRIAGE

No. 95. November 17, 1709

Interea dulces pendent circum oscula nati; casta pudicitiam servat domus.

From my own Apartment, Nov. 16

There are several persons who have many pleasures and entertainments in their possession which they do not enjoy. It is therefore a kind and good office to acquaint them with their own happiness, and turn their attention to such instances of their good fortune which they are apt to overlook. Persons in the married state often want such a monitor, and pine away their days, by looking upon the same condition in anguish and murmur which carries with it in the opinion of others a complication of all the pleasures of life, and a retreat from its inquietudes.

I am led into this thought by a visit I made an old friend who was formerly my school-fellow. He came to town last week with his family for the winter, and yesterday morning sent me word his wife expected me to dinner. I am as it were at home at that house, and every member of it knows me for their well-wisher. I cannot indeed express the pleasure it is to be met by the children with so much joy as I am when I go thither: the boys and girls strive who shall come first when they think it is I that am knocking at the door; and that child which loses the race to me runs back again to tell the father it is Mr. Bickerstaff. This day I was led in by a pretty girl, that we all thought must have forgot me; for the family has been out of town these two years. Her knowing me again was a mighty subject with us, and took up our discourse at the first entrance. After which, they began to rally me upon a thousand little stories they heard in the country about my marriage to one of my neighbour's daughters: upon which the gentleman, my friend, said, "Nay, if Mr. Bickerstaff marries a child of any of his old companions, I hope mine shall have the preference; there's Mrs. Mary is now sixteen, and would make him as fine a widow as the best of them: but I know him too well; he is so enamoured with the very memory of those who flourished in our youth, that he will not so much as look upon the modern beauties. I remember, old gentleman, how often you went home in a day to refresh your countenance and dress when Teraminta reigned in your heart. As we came up in the coach, I repeated to my wife some of your verses on her." With such reflections on little passages which happened long ago, we passed our time during a cheerful and elegant meal. After dinner, his lady left the room, as did also the children. As soon as we were alone, he took me by the hand; "Well, my good friend," says he, "I am heartily glad to see thee; I was afraid you would never have seen all the company that dined with you to-day again. Do not you think the good woman of the house a little altered since you followed her from the play-house, to find out who she was, for me?" I perceived a tear fall down his cheek as he spoke, which moved me not a little. But to turn the discourse, said I, "She is not indeed quite that creature she was when she returned me the letter I carried from you; and told me, she hoped, as I was a gentleman, I would be employed no more to trouble her who had never offended me, but would be so much the gentleman's friend as to dissuade him from a pursuit which he could never succeed in. You may remember, I thought her in earnest, and you were forced to employ your cousin Will, who made his sister get acquainted with her for you. You cannot expect her to be forever fifteen." "Fifteen?" replied my good friend:

"ah! you little understand, you that have lived a bachelor, how great, how exquisite a pleasure there is in being really beloved! It is impossible that the most beauteous face in nature should raise in me such pleasing ideas as when I look upon that excellent woman. That fading in her countenance is chiefly caused by her watching with me in my fever. This was followed by a fit of sickness, which had like to have carried her off last winter. I tell you sincerely, I have so many obligations to her, that I cannot with any sort of moderation think of her present state of health. But as to what you say of fifteen, she gives me every day pleasures beyond what I ever knew in the possession of her beauty when I was in the vigour of youth. Every moment of her life brings me fresh instances of her complacency to my inclinations, and her prudence in regard to my fortune. Her face is to me much more beautiful than when I first saw it; there is no decay in any feature which I cannot trace from the very instant it was occasioned by some anxious concern for my welfare and interests. Thus at the same time, methinks, the love I conceived towards her for what she was, is heightened by my gratitude for what she is. The love of a wife is as much above the idle passion commonly called by that name, as the loud laughter of buffoons is inferior to the elegant mirth of gentlemen. Oh! she is an inestimable jewel. In her examination of her household affairs, she shows a certain fearfulness to find a fault, which makes her servants obey her like children; and the meanest we have has an ingenuous shame for an offence, not always to be seen in children in other families. I speak freely to you, my old friend; ever since her sickness, things that gave me the quickest joy before, turn now to a certain anxiety. As the children play in the next room, I know the poor things by their steps, and am considering what they must do, should they lose their mother in their tender years. The pleasure I used to take in telling my boy stories of the battles, and asking my girl questions about the disposal of her baby, and the gossiping of it, is turned into inward reflection and melancholy."

He would have gone on in this tender way, when the good lady entered, and with an inexpressible sweetness in her countenance told us, she had been searching her closet for something very good to treat such an old friend as I was. Her husband's eyes sparkled with pleasure at the cheerfulness of her countenance; and I saw all his fears vanish in an instant. The lady observing something in our looks which showed we had been more serious than ordinary, and seeing her husband receive her with great concern under a forced cheerfulness, immediately guessed at what we had been talking of; and applying herself to me, said, with a smile, "Mr. Bickerstaff, don't believe a word of what he tells you. I shall still live to have you for my second, as I have often promised you, unless he takes more care of himself than he has done since his coming to town. You must know, he tells me that he finds London is a much more healthy place than the country; for he sees several of his old acquaintance and school-fellows are here, young fellows with fair full-bottomed periwigs. I could scarce keep him this morning from going out open-breasted." My friend, who is always extremely delighted with her agreeable humour, made her sit down with us. She did it with that easiness which is peculiar to women of sense; and to keep up the good humour she had brought in with her, turned her raillery upon me. "Mr. Bickerstaff, you remember you followed me one night from the play-house; suppose you should carry me thither to-morrow night, and lead me into the front box." This put us into a long field of discourse about the beauties, who were mothers to the present, and shone in the boxes twenty years ago. I told her, I was glad she had transferred so many of her charms, and I did not question but her eldest daughter was within half-a-year of being a toast.

We were pleasing ourselves with this fantastical preferment of the young lady, when on a sudden we were alarmed with the noise of a drum, and immediately entered my little godson to give me a point of war. His mother, between laughing and chiding, would have put him out of the room; but I would not part with him so. I found, upon conversation with him, though he was a little noisy in his mirth, that the child had excellent parts, and was a great master of all the learning on the other side eight years old. I perceived him a very great historian in Æsop's Fables; but he frankly declared to me his mind, that he did not delight in that learning, because he did not believe they were true; for which reason, I found he had very much turned his studies, for about a twelve-month past, into the lives and adventures of Don Bellianis of Greece, Guy of Warwick, the Seven Champions, and other historians of that age. I could not but observe the satisfaction the father took in the forwardness of his son; and that these diversions might turn to some profit, I found the boy had made remarks, which might be of service to him during the course of his whole life. He would tell you the mismanagements of John Hickathrift, find fault with the passionate temper in Bevis of Southampton, and loved St. George for being the champion of England; and by this means had his thoughts insensibly moulded into the notions of discretion, virtue, and honour. I was extolling his accomplishments, when the mother told me, that the little girl who led me in this morning was in her way a better scholar than he. "Betty," says she, "deals chiefly in fairies and sprites; and sometimes in a winter night will terrify the maids with her accounts, until they are afraid to go up to bed."

I sat with them until it was very late, sometimes in merry, sometimes in serious discourse, with this particular pleasure, which gives the only true relish to all conversation, a sense that every one of us liked each other. I went home, considering the different conditions of a married life and that of a bachelor; and I must confess, it struck me with a secret concern to reflect that whenever I go off I shall leave no traces behind me. In this pensive mood I returned to my family; that is to say, to my maid, my dog, and my cat, who only can be the better or worse for what happens to me. [STEELE]

THE CLUB AT THE TRUMPET

No. 132.   February 11, 1710

Habeo senectuti magnam gratiam, quæ mihi sermonis aviditatem auxit, potionis et cibi sustulit.

Sheer Lane, February 10

After having applied my mind with more than ordinary attention to my studies, it is my usual custom to relax and unbend it in the conversation of such as are rather easy than shining companions. This I find particularly necessary for me before I retire to rest, in order to draw my slumbers upon me by degrees, and fall asleep insensibly. This is the particular use I make of a set of heavy honest men, with whom I have passed many hours, with much indolence, though not with great pleasure. Their conversation is a kind of preparative for sleep : it takes the mind down from its abstractions, leads it into the familiar traces of thought, and lulls it into that state of tranquillity, which is the condition of a thinking man when he is but half awake. After this, my reader will not be surprised to hear the account which I am about to give of a club of my own contemporaries, among whom I pass two or three hours every evening. This I look upon as taking my first nap before I go to bed. The truth of it is, I should think myself unjust to posterity, as well as to the society at the Trumpet, of which I am a member, did not I in some part of my writings give an account of the persons among whom I have passed almost a sixth part of my time for these last forty years. Our club consisted originally of fifteen ; but partly by the severity of the law in arbitrary times, and partly by the natural effects of old age, we are at present reduced to a third part of that number : in which, however, we have this consolation, that the best company is said to consist of five persons. I must confess, besides the aforementioned benefit which I meet with in the conversation of this select society, I am not the less pleased with the company, in that I find myself the greatest wit among them, and am heard as their oracle in all points of learning and difficulty.

Sir Jeoffrey Notch, who is the oldest of the club, has been in possession of the right-hand chair time out of mind, and is the only man among us that has the liberty of stirring the fire. This our foreman is a gentleman of an ancient family, that came to a great estate some years before he had discretion, and run it out in hounds, horses, and cock-fighting; for which reason he looks upon himself as an honest worthy gentleman who has had misfortunes in the world, and calls every thriving man a pitiful upstart.

Major Matchlock is the next senior, who served in the last civil wars, and has all the battles by heart. He does not think any action in Europe worth talking of since the fight of Marston Moor; and every night tells us of his having been knocked off his horse at the rising of the London apprentices; for which he is in great esteem among us.

Honest old Dick Reptile is the third of our society: he is a good-natured indolent man, who speaks little himself, but laughs at our jokes, and brings his young nephew along with him, a youth of eighteen years old, to show him good company, and give him a taste of the world. This young fellow sits generally silent; but whenever he opens his mouth, or laughs at anything that passes, he is constantly told by his uncle, after a jocular manner, "Ay, ay, Jack, you young men think us fools; but we old men know you are."

The greatest wit of our company, next to myself, is a bencher of the neighbouring inn, who in his youth frequented the ordinaries about Charing Cross, and pretends to have been intimate with Jack Ogle. He has about ten distichs of *Hudibras* without book, and never leaves the club till he has applied them all. If any modern wit be mentioned, or any town frolic spoken of, he shakes his head at the dulness of the present age, and tells us a story of Jack Ogle.

For my own part, I am esteemed among them, because they see I am something respected by others, though at the same time I understand by their behaviour, that I am considered by them as a man of a great deal of learning, but no knowledge of the world; insomuch that the Major sometimes, in the height of his military pride, calls me the philosopher: and Sir Jeoffrey, no longer ago than last night, upon a dispute what day of the month it was then in Holland, pulled his pipe out of his mouth, and cried, "What does the scholar say to it?"

Our club meets precisely at six o'clock in the evening; but I did not come last night until half an hour after seven, by which means I escaped the battle of Naseby, which the Major usually begins at about three-quarters after six; I found also, that my good friend the bencher had already spent three of his distichs, and only waiting an opportunity to hear a sermon spoken of, that he might introduce the couplet where "a stick" rhymes to "ecclesiastic." At my entrance into the room, they were naming a red petticoat and a cloak, by which I found that the bencher had been diverting them with a story of Jack Ogle.

I had no sooner taken my seat, but Sir Jeoffrey, to show his good-will towards me, gave me a pipe of his own tobacco, and stirred up the fire. I look upon it as a point of morality, to be obliged by those who endeavour to oblige me; and there-fore, in requital for his kindness, and to set the conversation a-going, I took the best occasion I could to put him upon tell-ing us the story of old Gantlett, which he always does with very particular concern. He traced up his descent on both sides for several generations, describing his diet and manner of life, with his several battles, and particularly that in which he fell. This Gantlett was a game-cock, upon whose head the knight in his youth had won five hundred pounds, and lost two thousand. This naturally set the Major upon the account of Edge-hill fight, and ended in a duel of Jack Ogle's.

Old Reptile was extremely attentive to all that was said, though it was the same he had heard every night for these twenty years, and, upon all occasions, winked upon his nephew to mind what passed.

This may suffice to give the world a taste of our innocent conversation, which we spun out until about ten of the clock, when my maid came with a lantern to light me home. I could not but reflect with myself, as I was going out, upon the talkative humour of old men, and the little figure which that part of life makes in one who cannot employ this natural propensity in discourses which would make him venerable. I must own, it makes me very melancholy in company, when I hear a young man begin a story; and have often observed, that one of a quarter of an hour long in a man of five-and-twenty, gathers circumstances every time he tells it, until it grows into a long Canterbury tale of two hours by that time he is threescore.

The only way of avoiding such a trifling and frivolous old age is to lay up in our way to it such stores of knowledge and observation as may make us useful and agreeable in our declining years. The mind of man in a long life will become a magazine of wisdom or folly, and will consequently discharge itself in something impertinent or improving. For which reason, as there is nothing more ridiculous than an old trifling story-teller, so there is nothing more venerable than one who has turned his experience to the entertainment and advantage of mankind.

In short, we who are in the last stage of life, and are apt to indulge ourselves in talk, ought to consider, if what we speak be worth being heard, and endeavour to make our discourse like that of Nestor, which Homer compares to the flowing of honey for its sweetness.

I am afraid I shall be thought guilty of this excess I am speaking of, when I cannot conclude without observing, that Milton certainly thought of this passage in Homer, when, in his description of an eloquent spirit, he says, "His tongue dropped manna." [Steele]

THE CHARACTER OF TOM FOLIO

No. 158. April 13, 1710

Faciunt næ intelligendo, ut nihil intelligant.

From my own Apartment, April 12

Tom Folio is a broker in learning, employed to get together good editions, and stock the libraries of great men. There is not a sale of books begins till Tom Folio is seen at the door. There is not an auction where his name is not heard, and that too in the very nick of time, in the critical moment, before the last decisive stroke of the hammer. There is not a subscription goes forward, in which Tom is not privy to the first rough draught of the proposals; nor a catalogue printed, that does not come to him wet from the press. He is an universal scholar, so far as the title-page of all authors, knows the manuscripts in which they were discovered, the editions through which they have passed, with the praises or censures which they have received from the several members of the learned world. He has a greater esteem for Aldus and Elzevir than for Virgil and Horace. If you talk of Herodotus, he breaks out into a panegyric upon Harry Stephans. He thinks he gives you an account of an author when he tells you the subject he treats of, the name of the editor, and the year in which it was printed. Or if you draw him into further particulars, he cries up the goodness of the paper, extolls the diligence of the corrector, and is transported with the beauty of the letter. This he looks upon to be sound learning and substantial criticism. As for those who talk of the fineness of style, and the justness of thought, or describe the brightness of any particular passages, nay, though they write themselves in the genius and spirit of the author they admire, Tom looks upon them as men of superficial learning and flashy parts.

I had yesterday morning a visit from this learned idiot (for that is the light in which I consider every pedant), when I discovered in him some little touches of the coxcomb which I had not before observed. Being very full of the figure which he makes in the republic of letters, and wonderfully satisfied with his great stock of knowledge, he gave me broad intimations that he did not "believe" in all points as his forefathers had done. He then communicated to me a thought of a certain author upon a passage of Virgil's account of the dead, which I made the subject of a late paper. This thought has taken very much among men of Tom's pitch and understanding, though universally exploded by all that know how to construe Virgil, or have any relish of antiquity. Not to trouble my reader with it, I found upon the whole that Tom did not believe a future state of rewards and punishments, because Æneas, at his leaving the empire of the dead, passed through the gate of ivory, and not through that of horn. Knowing that Tom had not sense enough to give up an opinion which he had once received, that he might avoid wrangling, I told him that Virgil possibly had his oversights as well as another author. "Ah! Mr. Bickerstaff," says he, "you would have another opinion of him if you would read him in Daniel Heinsius' edition. I have perused him myself several times in that edition," continued he; "and after the strictest and most malicious examination, could find but two faults in him: one of them is in the *Æneids*, where there are two commas instead of a parenthesis; and another in the third *Georgic*, where you may find a semicolon turned upside down." "Perhaps," said I, "these were not Virgil's faults, but those of the transcriber." "I do not design it," says Tom, "as a reflection on Virgil: on the contrary, I know that all the manuscripts reclaim against such a punctuation. Oh! Mr. Bickerstaff," says he, "what would a man give to see one simile of Virgil writ in his own hand?" I asked him which was the simile he meant, but was answered, "Any simile in Virgil." He then told me all the secret history in the commonwealth of learning: of modern pieces that had the names of ancient authors annexed to them; of all the books that were now writing or printing in the several parts of Europe; of many amendments which are made, and not yet published; and a thousand other particulars, which I would not have my memory burthened with for a Vatican.

At length, being fully persuaded that I thoroughly admired him and looked upon him as a prodigy of learning, he took his leave. I know several of Tom's class who are professed admirers of Tasso without understanding a word of Italian, and one in particular that carries a *Pastor Fido* in his pocket, in which I am sure he is acquainted with no other beauty but the clearness of the character.

There is another kind of pedant who, with all Tom Folio's impertinences, hath greater superstructures and embellishments of Greek and Latin, and is still more unsupportable than the other, in the same degree as he is more learned. Of this kind very often are editors, commentators, interpreters, scholiasts, and critics, and in short, all men of deep learning without common sense. These persons set a greater value on themselves for having found out the meaning of a passage in Greek, than upon the author for having written it; nay, will allow the passage itself not to have any beauty in it, at the same time that they would be considered as the greatest men of the age for having interpreted it. They will look with contempt upon the most beautiful poems that have been composed by any of their contemporaries; but will lock themselves up in their studies for a twelvemonth together to correct, publish, and expound such trifles of antiquity as a modern author would be contemned for. Men of the strictest morals, severest lives, and the gravest professions will write volumes upon an idle sonnet that is originally in Greek or Latin, give editions of the most immoral authors, and spin out whole pages upon the various readings of a lewd expression. All that can be said in excuse for them is that their works sufficiently show they have no taste of their authors, and that what they do in this kind is out of their great learning and not out of any levity or lasciviousness of temper.

A pedant of this nature is wonderfully well described in six lines of Boileau, with which I shall conclude his character:

Un Pédant enivré de sa vaine science,
Tout hérissé de Grec, tout bouffi d'arrogance,
Et qui, de mille auteurs retenus mot pour mot,
Dans sa tête entassés n'a souvent fait qu'un sot,
Croit qu'un livre fait tout, & que, sans Aristote,
La raison ne voit goutte, & le bon sens radote.

[ADDISON]

RECOLLECTIONS

No. 181. June 6, 1710

—— *Dies, ni fallor, adest, quem semper acerbum,*
Semper honoratum (sic di voluistis), habebo.

From my own Apartment, June 5

There are those among mankind who can enjoy no relish
of their being except the world is made acquainted with all
that relates to them, and think everything lost that passes
unobserved ; but others find a solid delight in stealing by the
crowd, and modelling their life after such a manner as is as
much above the approbation as the practice of the vulgar. Life
being too short to give instances great enough of true friendship or good-will, some sages have thought it pious to preserve
a certain reverence for the manes of their deceased friends,
and have withdrawn themselves from the rest of the world at
certain seasons, to commemorate in their own thoughts such
of their acquaintance who have gone before them out of this
life : and indeed, when we are advanced in years, there is not
a more pleasing entertainment than to recollect in a gloomy
moment the many we have parted with that have been dear
and agreeable to us, and to cast a melancholy thought or two
after those with whom, perhaps, we have indulged ourselves
in whole nights of mirth and jollity. With such inclinations
in my heart I went to my closet yesterday in the evening, and
resolved to be sorrowful ; upon which occasion I could not but
look with disdain upon myself, that though all the reasons

which I had to lament the loss of many of my friends are now as forcible as at the moment of their departure, yet did not my heart swell with the same sorrow which I felt at that time; but I could, without tears, reflect upon many pleasing adventures I have had with some who have long been blended with common earth. Though it is by the benefit of nature that length of time thus blots out the violence of afflictions; yet with tempers too much given to pleasure, it is almost necessary to revive the old places of grief in our memory, and ponder step by step on past life, to lead the mind into that sobriety of thought which poises the heart, and makes it beat with due time, without being quickened with desire, or retarded with despair, from its proper and equal motion. When we wind up a clock that is out of order, to make it go well for the future, we do not immediately set the hand to the present instant, but we make it strike the round of all its hours, before it can recover the regularity of its time. "Such," thought I, "shall be my method this evening; and since it is that day of the year which I dedicate to the memory of such in another life as I much delighted in when living, an hour or two shall be sacred to sorrow and their memory, while I run over all the melancholy circumstances of this kind which have occurred to me in my whole life."

The first sense of sorrow I ever knew was upon the death of my father, at which time I was not quite five years of age; but was rather amazed at what all the house meant than possessed with a real understanding why nobody was willing to play with me. I remember I went into the room where his body lay, and my mother sat weeping alone by it. I had my battledore in my hand, and fell a-beating the coffin, and calling "Papa"; for, I know not how, I had some slight idea that he was locked up there. My mother catched me in her arms, and transported beyond all patience of the silent grief she was before in, she almost smothered me in her embrace, and told me in a flood of tears, papa could not hear me, and would play with me no more, for they were going to put him under ground, whence he could never come to us again. She was a very beautiful woman, of a noble spirit, and there was a dignity in her grief amidst all the wildness of her transport which, methought, struck me with an instinct of sorrow, which, before I was sensible of what it was to grieve, seized my very soul, and has made pity the weakness of my heart ever since. The mind in infancy is, methinks, like the body in embryo, and receives impressions so forcible that they are as hard to be removed by reason as any mark with which a child is born is to be taken away by any future application. Hence it is that good-nature in me is no merit; but having been so frequently overwhelmed with her tears before I knew the cause of any affliction, or could draw defences from my own judgment, I imbibed commiseration, remorse, and an unmanly gentleness of mind, which has since ensnared me into ten thousand calamities, and from whence I can reap no advantage, except it be that in such a humour as I am now in, I can the better indulge myself in the softness of humanity, and enjoy that sweet anxiety which arises from the memory of past afflictions.

We that are very old are better able to remember things which befell us in our distant youth than the passages of later days. For this reason it is that the companions of my strong and vigorous years present themselves more immediately to me in this office of sorrow. Untimely or unhappy deaths are what we are most apt to lament, so little are we able to make it indifferent when a thing happens, though we know it must happen. Thus we groan under life, and bewail those who are relieved from it. Every object that returns to our imagination raises different passions according to the circumstance of their departure. Who can have lived in an army, and in a serious hour reflect upon the many gay and agreeable men that might long have flourished in the arts of peace, and not join with the imprecations of the fatherless and widow on the tyrant to whose ambition they fell sacrifices? But gallant men, who are cut off by the sword, move rather our veneration than our pity, and we gather relief enough from their own contempt of death, to make it no evil, which was approached with so much cheerfulness, and attended with so much honour. But when we turn our thoughts from the great parts of life on such occasions, and instead of lamenting those who stood ready to give death to those from whom they had the fortune to receive it; I say, when we let our thoughts wander from such noble objects, and consider the havoc which is made among the tender and the innocent, pity enters with an unmixed softness, and possesses all our souls at once.

Here (were there words to express such sentiments with proper tenderness) I should record the beauty, innocence, and untimely death of the first object my eyes ever beheld with love. The beauteous virgin! How ignorantly did she charm, how carelessly excel! O, Death! thou hast right to the bold, to the ambitious, to the high, and to the haughty; but why this cruelty to the humble, to the meek, to the undiscerning, to the thoughtless? Nor age, nor business, nor distress can erase the dear image from my imagination. In the same week, I saw her dressed for a ball, and in a shroud. How ill did the habit of Death become the pretty trifler! I still behold the smiling earth — A large train of disasters were coming on to my memory, when my servant knocked at my closet-door, and interrupted me with a letter, attended with a hamper of wine, of the same sort with that which is to be put to sale on Thursday next at Garraway's Coffee-house. Upon the receipt of it I sent for three of my friends. We are so intimate that we can be company in whatever state of mind we meet, and can entertain each other without expecting always to rejoice. The wine we found to be generous and warming, but with such a heat as moved us rather to be cheerful than frolicsome. It revived the spirits without firing the blood. We commended it till two of the clock this morning, and having to-day met a little before dinner, we found that, though we drank two bottles a man, we had much more reason to recollect than forget what had passed the night before. [STEELE]

FALSE REFINEMENTS IN STYLE

No. 230. September 28, 1710

From my own Apartment, Sept. 27

The following letter has laid before me many great and manifest evils in the world of letters which I had overlooked; but they open to me a very busy scene, and it will require no small care and application to amend errors which are become so universal. The affectation of politeness is exposed in this epistle with a great deal of wit and discernment; so that whatever discourses I may fall into hereafter upon the subjects the writer treats of, I shall at present lay the matter before the world without the least alteration from the words of my correspondent.

To Isaac Bickerstaff, Esq.

Sir,

There are some abuses among us of great consequence, the reformation of which is properly your province; though, as far as I have been conversant in your papers, you have not yet considered them. These are the deplorable ignorance that for some years hath reigned among our English writers, the great depravity of our taste, and the continual corruption of our style. I say nothing here of those who handle particular sciences, divinity, law, physic, and the like; I mean the traders in history and politics, and the *belles lettres*, together with those by whom books are not translated, but (as the common expressions are) *done* out of French, Latin, or other language, and made English. I cannot but observe to you that till of late years a Grub Street book was always bound in sheepskin, with suitable print and paper, the price never above a shilling, and taken off wholly by common tradesmen or country pedlars; but now they appear in all sizes and shapes, and in all places. They are handed about from lapfuls in every coffee-house to persons of quality; are shown in Westminster Hall and the Court of Requests. You may see them gilt, and in royal paper of five or six hundred pages, and rated accordingly. I would engage to furnish you with a catalogue of English books, published within the compass of seven years past, which at the first hand would cost you a hundred pounds, wherein you shall not be able to find ten lines together of common grammar or common sense.

These two evils, ignorance and want of taste, have produced a third; I mean the continual corruption of our English tongue, which, without some timely remedy, will suffer more by the false refinements of twenty years past than it hath been improved in the foregoing hundred. And this is what I design chiefly to enlarge upon, leaving the former evils to your animadversion.

But instead of giving you a list of the late refinements crept into our language, I here send you the copy of a letter I received some time ago from a most accomplished person in this way of writing; upon which I shall make some remarks. It is in these terms:

" Sir,

" I *cou'd n't* get the things you sent for all *about town* — I *thôt* to *ha'* come down myself, and then *I'd h' brot' um*; but I *ha' nt don 't*, and I believe I *can't d't*, *that 's pozz* — Tom begins to *gi 'mself* airs, because *he 's* going with the *plenipo's* — 'T is said the French King will *bamboozl'us agen*, which *causes many speculations*. The Jacks and others of that *kidney* are very *uppish*, and *alert upon 't*, as you may see by their *phizz's* — Will Hazzard has got the *hipps*, having lost *to the tune of* five hundr'd pound, *thô* he understands play very well, *nobody better*. He has promis't me upon *rep*, to leave off play; but you know 't is a weakness *he 's* too apt to *give into*, *thô* he has as much wit as any man, *nobody more*. He has lain *incog* ever since — The *mobb 's* very quiet with us now — I believe you *thôt I banter'd* you in my last, like a *country put* — I *shan't* leave town this month," etc.

This letter is in every point an admirable pattern of the present polite way of writing, nor is it less authority for being an epistle: you may gather every flower in it, with a thousand more of equal sweetness, from the books, pamphlets, and single papers offered us every day in the coffee-houses: and these are the beauties introduced to supply the want of wit, sense, humour, and learning, which formerly were looked upon as qualifications for a writer. If a man of wit, who died forty years ago, were to rise from the grave on purpose, how would he be able to read this letter? And after he had got through that difficulty, how would he be able to understand it? The first thing that strikes your eye, is the breaks at the end of almost every sentence, of which I know not the use, only that it is a refinement, and very frequently practised. Then you will observe the abbreviations and elisions, by which consonants of most obdurate sound are joined together, without one softening vowel to intervene; and all this only to make one syllable of two, directly contrary to the example of the Greeks and Romans, altogether of the Gothic strain, and a natural tendency towards relapsing into barbarity, which delights in monosyllables, and uniting of mute consonants, as it is observable in all the Northern languages. And this is still more visible in the next refinement, which consists in pronouncing the first syllable in a word that has many, and dismissing the rest; such as *phizz*, *hipps*, *mobb*, *pozz*, *rep*, and many more, when we are already overloaded with monosyllables, which are the disgrace of our language. Thus we cram one syllable, and cut off the rest, as the owl fattened her mice after she had bit off their legs to prevent them from running away; and if ours be the same reason for maiming our words, it will certainly answer the end, for I am sure no other nation will desire to borrow them. Some words are hitherto but fairly split, and therefore only in their way to perfection, as *incog* and *plenipo*: but in a short time 'tis to be hoped they will be further docked to *inc* and *plen*. This reflection has made me of late years very impatient for a peace, which I believe would save the lives of many brave words, as well as men. The war has introduced abundance of polysyllables, which will never be able to live many more campaigns: *speculations, operations, pre-liminaries, ambassadors, palisadoes, communication, circumvallation, battalions*: as numerous as they are, if they attack us too frequently in our coffee-houses, we shall certainly put them to flight, and cut off the rear.

The third refinement observable in the letter I send you consists in the choice of certain words, invented by some pretty fellows, such as *banter*, *bamboozle, country put*, and *kidney*, as it is there applied; some of which are now struggling for the vogue, and others are in possession of it. I have done my utmost for some years past to stop the progress of *mobb* and *banter*, but have been plainly borne down by numbers, and betrayed by those who promised to assist me.

In the last place, you are to take notice of certain choice phrases scattered through the letter, some of them tolerable enough, until they were worn to rags by servile imitators. You might easily find them, though they were not in a different print, and therefore I need not disturb them.

These are the false refinements in our style which you ought to correct: first, by argument and fair means; but if these fail, I think you are to make use of your authority as Censor, and by an annual *Index Expurgatorius* expunge all words and phrases that are offensive to good sense, and condemn those barbarous mutilations of vowels and syllables. In this last point the usual pretence is, that they spell as they speak: a noble standard for language! To depend upon the caprice of every coxcomb who, because words are the clothing of our thoughts, cuts them out and shapes them as he pleases, and changes them oftener than his dress! I believe all reasonable people would be content that such refiners were more sparing in their words, and liberal in their syllables: and upon this head I should be glad you would bestow some advice upon several young readers in our churches, who, coming up from the university full fraught with admiration of our town politeness, will needs correct the style of their prayer-books. In reading the Abso-lution, they are very careful to say *pardons* and *absolves*; and in the prayer for the royal family, it must be *endue'um, enrich'um, prosper'um*, and *bring'um*. Then in their sermons they use all the modern terms of art: *sham, banter, mobb, bubble, bully, cutting, shuffling*, and *palming*; all which, and many more of the like stamp, as I have heard them often in the pulpit from such young sophisters, so I have read them in some of those sermons that have made most noise of late. The design, it seems, is to avoid the dreadful imputation of pedantry; to show us that they know the town, understand men and manners, and have not been poring upon old unfashionable books in the university.

I should be glad to see you the instrument of introducing into our style that simplicity which is the best and truest ornament of most things in life, which the politer age always aimed at in their building and dress (*simplex munditiis*), as well as their productions of wit. It is manifest that all new affected modes of speech, whether borrowed from the court, the town, or the theatre, are the first perishing parts in any language; and, as I could prove by many hundred instances, have been so in ours. The writings of Hooker, who was a country clergyman, and of Parsons the Jesuit, both in the reign of Queen Elizabeth, are in a style that, with very few allowances, would not offend any present reader; much more clear and intelligible than those of Sir H. Wotton, Sir Rob. Naunton, Osborn, Daniel the historian, and several others who wrote later; but being men of the court, and affecting the phrases then in fashion, they are often either not to be understood, or appear perfectly ridiculous.

What remedies are to be applied to these evils, I have not room to consider, having, I fear, already taken up most of your paper. Besides, I think it is our office only to represent abuses, and yours to redress them. I am, with great respect,

Sir,

Your, &c.

[STEELE and SWIFT]

ON CONVERSATION

No. 244.   October 31, 1710

Quid voveat dulci nutricula majus alumno,
Qui sapere et fari possit quæ sentiat ? —

Will's Coffee-house, Oct. 30

It is no easy matter, when people are advancing in anything, to prevent their going too fast for want of patience. This happens in nothing more frequently than in the prosecution of studies. Hence it is, that we meet crowds who attempt to be eloquent before they can speak. They affect the flowers of rhetoric before they understand the parts of speech. In the ordinary conversation of this town, there are so many who can, as they call it, talk well, that there is not one in twenty that talks to be understood. This proceeds from an ambition to excel, or, as the term is, to shine, in company. The matter is not to make themselves understood, but admired. They come together with a certain emulation, rather than benevolence. When you fall among such companions, the safe way is to give yourself up, and let the orators declaim for your esteem, and trouble yourself no further. It is said that a poet must be born so ; but I think it may be much better said of an orator, especially when we talk of our town poets and orators ; but the town poets are full of rules and laws, the town orators go through thick and thin, and are, forsooth, persons of such eminent natural parts and knowledge of the world, that they despise all men as inexperienced scholastics who wait for an occasion before they speak, or who speak no more than is necessary. They had half persuaded me to go to the tavern the other night, but that a gentleman whispered me, " Prithee, Isaac, go with us ; there is Tom Varnish will be there, and he is a fellow that talks as well as any man in England."

I must confess, when a man expresses himself well upon any occasion, and his falling into an account of any subject arises from a desire to oblige the company, or from fulness of the circumstance itself, so that his speaking of it at large is occasioned only by the openness of a companion ; I say, in such a case as this, it is not only pardonable but agreeable, when a man takes the discourse to himself ; but when you see a fellow watch for opportunities for being copious, it is excessively troublesome. A man that stammers, if he has understanding, is to be attended with patience and good-nature; but he that speaks more than he need, has no right to such an indulgence. The man who has a defect in his speech takes pains to come to you, while a man of a weak capacity with fluency of speech triumphs in outrunning you. The stammerer strives to be fit for your company; the loquacious man endeavours to show you, you are not fit for his.

With thoughts of this kind do I always enter into that man's company who is recommended as a person that talks well; but if I were to choose the people with whom I would spend my hours of conversation, they should be certainly such as laboured no further than to make themselves readily and clearly apprehended, and would have patience and curiosity to understand me. To have good sense and the ability to express it are the most essential and necessary qualities in companions. When thoughts rise in us fit to utter, among familiar friends there needs but very little care in clothing them.

Urbanus is, I take it, a man one might live with whole years, and enjoy all the freedom and improvement imaginable, and yet be insensible of a contradiction to you in all the mistakes you can be guilty of. His great good-will to his friends has produced in him such a general deference in his discourse that if he differs from you in his sense of anything, he introduces his own thoughts by some agreeable circumlocution, or he has often observed such and such a circumstance that made him of another opinion. Again, where another would be apt to say, "This I am confident of; I may pretend to judge of this matter as well as anybody;" Urbanus says, " I am verily persuaded; I believe one may conclude." In a word, there is no man more clear in his thoughts and expressions than he is, or speaks with greater diffidence. You shall hardly find one man of any consideration, but you shall observe one of less consequence form himself after him. This happens to Urbanus; but the man who steals from him almost every sentiment he utters in a whole week, disguises the theft by carrying it with quite a different air. Umbratilis knows Urbanus's doubtful way of speaking proceeds from good-nature and good-breeding and not from uncertainty in his opinions. Umbratilis therefore has no more to do but repeat the thoughts of Urbanus in a positive manner, and appear to the undiscerning a wiser man than the person from whom he borrows : but those who know him can see the servant in the master's habit, and the more he struts, the less do his clothes appear his own.

In conversation the medium is neither to affect silence nor eloquence ; not to value our approbation, and to endeavour to excel us who are of your company, are equal injuries. The great enemies therefore to good company, and those who transgress most against the laws of equality (which is the life of it), are the clown, the wit, and the pedant. A clown, when he has sense, is conscious of his want of education, and with an awkward bluntness hopes to keep himself in countenance by overthrowing the use of all polite behaviour. He takes advantage of the restraint good-breeding lays upon others not to offend him, to trespass against them, and is under the man's own shelter while he intrudes upon him. The fellows of this class are very frequent in the repetition of the words " rough " and " manly." When these people happen to be by their fortunes of the rank of gentlemen, they defend their other absurdities by an impertinent courage ; and to help out the defect of their behaviour, add their being dangerous to their being disagreeable. This gentleman (though he displeases, professes to do so, and knowing that, dares still go on to do so) is not so painful a companion as he who will please you against your will, and resolves to be a wit.

This man, upon all occasions and whoever he falls in company with, talks in the same circle and in the same round of chat which he has learned at one of the tables of this coffeehouse. As poetry is in itself an elevation above ordinary and common sentiments, so there is no fop so near a madman in indifferent company as a poetical one. He is not apprehensive that the generality of the world are intent upon the business of their own fortune and profession, and have as little capacity as curiosity to enter into matters of ornament or speculation. I remember at a full table in the City one of these ubiquitary wits was entertaining the company with a soliloquy (for so I call it when a man talks to those who do not understand him) concerning wit and humour. An honest gentleman who sat next to me and was worth half a plum stared at him, and observing there was some sense, as he thought, mixed with his impertinence, whispered me, "Take my word for it, this fellow is more knave than fool." This was all my good friend's applause of the wittiest man of talk that I was ever present at, which wanted nothing to make it excellent but that there was no occasion for it.

The pedant is so obvious to ridicule that it would be to be one to offer to explain him. He is a gentleman so well known that there is none but those of his own class who do not laugh at and avoid him. Pedantry proceeds from much reading and little understanding. A pedant among men of learning and sense is like an ignorant servant giving an account of a polite conversation. You may find he has brought with him more than could have entered into his head without being there, but still that he is not a bit wiser than if he had not been there at all. [STEELE]

THE SPECTATOR (1711–1712)

THE CHARACTER OF MR. SPECTATOR

No. 1. Thursday, March 1, 1711

Non fumum ex fulgore, sed ex fumo dare lucem
Cogitat, ut speciosa dehinc miracula promat. — HOR.

I have observed that a reader seldom peruses a book with
pleasure till he knows whether the writer of it be a black or
a fair man, of a mild or choleric disposition, married or a
bachelor, with other particulars of the like nature, that conduce
very much to the right understanding of an author. To gratify
this curiosity, which is so natural in a reader, I design this
paper and my next as prefatory discourses to my following
writings, and shall give some account in them of the several
persons that are engaged in this work. As the chief trouble
of compiling, digesting, and correcting will fall to my share,
I must do myself the justice to open the work with my own
history.

I was born to a small hereditary estate, which, according to
the tradition of the village where it lies, was bounded by the
same hedges and ditches in William the Conqueror's time that
it is at present, and has been delivered down from father to
son, whole and entire, without the loss or acquisition of a
single field or meadow, during the space of six hundred years.
There runs a story in the family, that, when my mother was
gone with child of me about three months, she dreamed that
she was brought to bed of a judge. Whether this might
proceed from a law-suit which was then depending in the
family, or my father's being a justice of the peace, I cannot

determine ; for I am not so vain as to think it presaged any dignity that I should arrive at in my future life, though that was the interpretation which the neighbourhood put upon it. The gravity of my behaviour at my very first appearance in the world, and all the time that I sucked, seemed to favour my mother's dream ; for, as she has often told me, I threw away my rattle before I was two months old, and would not make use of my coral till they had taken away the bells from it.

As for the rest of my infancy, there being nothing in it remarkable, I shall pass over it in silence. I find that during my nonage, I had the reputation of a very sullen youth, but was always a favourite of my schoolmaster, who used to say "that my parts were solid, and would wear well." I had not been long at the university before I distinguished myself by a most profound silence ; for during the space of eight years, excepting in the public exercises of the college, I scarce uttered the quantity of a hundred words ; and indeed do not remember that I ever spoke three sentences together in my whole life. While I was in this learned body, I applied myself with so much diligence to my studies, that there are few very celebrated books, either in the learned or the modern tongues, which I am not acquainted with.

Upon the death of my father, I was resolved to travel into foreign countries, and therefore left the university with the character of an odd, unaccountable fellow, that had a great deal of learning, if I would but show it. An insatiable thirst after knowledge carried me into all the countries of Europe in which there was anything new or strange to be seen ; nay, to such a degree was my curiosity raised, that having read the controversies of some great men concerning the antiquities of Egypt, I made a voyage to Grand Cairo on purpose to take the measure of a pyramid ; and as soon as I had set myself right in that particular, returned to my native country with great satisfaction.

I have passed my latter years in this city, where I am frequently seen in most public places, though there are not above half-a-dozen of my select friends that know me; of whom my next paper shall give a more particular account. There is no place of general resort wherein I do not often make my appearance. Sometimes I am seen thrusting my head into a round of politicians at Will's, and listening with great attention to the narratives that are made in those little circular audiences. Sometimes I smoke a pipe at Child's, and whilst I seem attentive to nothing but the *Postman*, overhear the conversation of every table in the room. I appear on Sunday nights at St. James's coffee-house, and sometimes join the little committee of politics in the inner room, as one who comes there to hear and improve. My face is likewise very well known at the Grecian, the Cocoa-tree, and in the theaters both of Drury-lane and the Haymarket. I have been taken for a merchant upon the exchange for above these ten years, and sometimes pass for a Jew in the assembly of stock-jobbers at Jonathan's. In short, wherever I see a cluster of people, I always mix with them, though I never open my lips but in my own club.

Thus I live in the world rather as a Spectator of mankind than as one of the species, by which means I have made myself a speculative statesman, soldier, merchant, and artisan, without ever meddling with any practical part in life. I am very well versed in the theory of a husband, or a father, and can discern the errors in the economy, business, and diversions of others, better than those who are engaged in them; as standers-by discover blots, which are apt to escape those who are in the game. I never espoused any party with violence, and am resolved to observe a strict neutrality between the Whigs and Tories, unless I shall be forced to declare myself by the hostilities of either side. In short, I have acted in all the parts of my life as a looker-on, which is the character I intend to preserve in this paper.

I have given the reader just so much of my history and character as to let him see I am not altogether unqualified for the business I have undertaken. As for other particulars in my life and adventures, I shall insert them in following papers as I shall see occasion. In the mean time, when I consider how much I have seen, read, and heard, I begin to blame my own taciturnity; and since I have neither time nor inclination to communicate the fulness of my heart in speech, I am resolved to do it in writing, and to print myself out, if possible, before I die. I have been often told by my friends that it is pity so many useful discoveries which I have made, should be in the possession of a silent man. For this reason, therefore, I shall publish a sheetful of thoughts every morning for the benefit of my contemporaries; and if I can any way contribute to the diversion or improvement of the country in which I live, I shall leave it, when I am summoned out of it, with the secret satisfaction of thinking that I have not lived in vain.

There are three very material points which I have not spoken to in this paper, and which, for several important reasons, I must keep to myself, at least for some time : I mean, an account of my name, my age, and my lodgings. I must confess, I would gratify my reader in anything that is reasonable; but, as for these three particulars, though I am sensible they might tend very much to the embellishment of my paper, I cannot yet come to a resolution of communicating them to the public. They would indeed draw me out of that obscurity which I have enjoyed for many years, and expose me in public places to several salutes and civilities, which have been always very disagreeable to me; for the greatest pain I can suffer is the being talked to, and being stared at. It is for this reason likewise, that I keep my complexion and dress as very great secrets; though it is not impossible but I may make discoveries of both in the progress of the work I have undertaken.

After having been thus particular upon myself, I shall in to-morrow's paper give an account of those gentlemen who are concerned with me in this work; for, as I have before intimated, a plan of it is laid and concerted (as all other matters of importance are) in a club. However, as my friends have engaged me to stand in the front, those who have a mind to correspond with me, may direct their letters to the *Spectator*, at Mr. Buckley's, in Little Britain. For I must further acquaint the reader, that though our club meets only on Tuesdays and Thursdays, we have appointed a committee to sit every night, for the inspection of all such papers as may contribute to the advancement of the public weal. C [ADDISON]

THE SPECTATOR CLUB

No. 2. Friday, March 2, 1711

——Haec alii sex
Vel plures uno conclamant ore. — JUV.

The first of our society is a gentleman of Worcestershire, of ancient descent, a baronet, his name Sir Roger de Coverley. His great-grandfather was inventor of that famous country-dance which is called after him. All who know that shire are very well acquainted with the parts and merits of Sir Roger. He is a gentleman that is very singular in his behaviour, but his singularities proceed from his good sense, and are contradictions to the manners of the world only as he thinks the world is in the wrong. However, this humour creates him no enemies, for he does nothing with sourness or obstinacy; and his being unconfined to modes and forms makes him but the readier and more capable to please and oblige all who know him. When he is in town, he lives in Soho Square. It is said he keeps himself a bachelor by reason he was crossed in love by a perverse, beautiful widow of the next county to him. Before this disappointment, Sir Roger was what you call a fine gentleman; had often supped with my Lord Rochester and Sir George Etherege, fought a duel upon his first coming to town, and kicked Bully Dawson in a public coffee-house for calling him "youngster." But being ill-used by the above-mentioned widow, he was very serious for a year and a half; and though, his temper being naturally jovial, he at last got over it, he grew careless of himself, and never dressed afterwards.

He continues to wear a coat and doublet of the same cut that were in fashion at the time of his repulse, which, in his merry humours, he tells us, has been in and out twelve times since he first wore it. 'Tis said Sir Roger grew humble in his desires after he had forgot this cruel beauty, insomuch that it is reported he has frequently offended in point of chastity with beggars and gypsies; but this is looked upon by his friends rather as matter of raillery than truth. He is now in his fifty-sixth year, cheerful, gay, and hearty; keeps a good house in both town and country; a great lover of mankind; but there is such a mirthful cast in his behaviour that he is rather beloved than esteemed. His tenants grow rich, his servants look satisfied, all the young women profess love to him, and the young men are glad of his company. When he comes into a house, he calls the servants by their names, and talks all the way up-stairs to a visit. I must not omit that Sir Roger is a justice of the quorum; that he fills the chair at a quarter session with great abilities; and, three months ago, gained universal applause by explaining a passage in the Game Act.

The gentleman next in esteem and authority among us is another bachelor, who is a member of the Inner Temple; a man of great probity, wit, and understanding; but he has chosen his place of residence rather to obey the direction of an old humoursome father, than in pursuit of his own inclinations. He was placed there to study the laws of the land, and is the most learned of any of the house in those of the stage. Aristotle and Longinus are much better understood by him than Littleton or Coke. The father sends up, every post, questions relating to marriage-articles, leases, and tenures, in the neighbourhood; all which questions he agrees with an attorney to answer and take care of in the lump. He is studying the passions themselves, when he should be inquiring into the debates among men which arise from them. He knows the argument of each of the orations of Demosthenes and Tully, but not one case in the reports of our own courts. No one ever took him for a fool, but none, except his intimate friends, know he has a great deal of wit. This turn makes him at once both disinterested and agreeable; as few of his thoughts are drawn from business, they are most of them fit for conversation. His taste of books is a little too just for the age he lives in; he has read all, but approves of very few. His familiarity with the customs, manners, actions, and writings of the ancients makes him a very delicate observer of what occurs to him in the present world. He is an excellent critic, and the time of the play is his hour of business; exactly at five he passes through New Inn, crosses through Russell Court, and takes a turn at Will's till the play begins; he has his shoes rubbed and his periwig powdered at the barber's as you go into the Rose. It is for the good of the audience when he is at a play, for the actors have an ambition to please him.

The person of next consideration is Sir Andrew Freeport, a merchant of great eminence in the city of London. A person of indefatigable industry, strong reason, and great experience. His notions of trade are noble and generous, and (as every rich man has usually some sly way of jesting, which would make no great figure were he not a rich man) he calls the sea the British Common. He is acquainted with commerce in all its parts, and will tell you that it is a stupid and barbarous way to extend dominion by arms: for true power is to be got by arts and industry. He will often argue that if this part of our trade were well cultivated, we should gain from one nation; and if another, from another. I have heard him prove that diligence makes more lasting acquisitions than valour, and that sloth has ruined more nations than the sword. He abounds in several frugal maxims, among which the greatest favourite is, " A penny saved is a penny got." A general trader of good sense is pleasanter company than a general scholar; and Sir Andrew having a natural unaffected eloquence, the perspicuity of his discourse gives the same pleasure that wit would in another man. He has made his fortune himself; and says that England may be richer than other kingdoms, by as plain methods as he himself is richer than other men:

though at the same time I can say this of him, that there is not a point in the compass, but blows home a ship in which he is an owner.

Next to Sir Andrew in the club-room sits Captain Sentry, a gentleman of great courage, good understanding, but invincible modesty. He is one of those that deserve very well, but are very awkward at putting their talents within the observation of such as should take notice of them. He was some years a captain, and behaved himself with great gallantry in several engagements and at several sieges; but having a small estate of his own, and being next heir to Sir Roger, he has quitted a way of life in which no man can rise suitably to his merit, who is not something of a courtier as well as a soldier. I have heard him often lament that in a profession where merit is placed in so conspicuous a view, impudence should get the better of modesty. When he had talked to this purpose, I never heard him make a sour expression, but frankly confess that he left the world because he was not fit for it. A strict honesty, and an even regular behaviour, are in themselves obstacles to him that must press through crowds, who endeavour at the same end with himself, the favour of a commander. He will, however, in his way of talk excuse generals for not disposing according to men's desert, or inquiring into it; for, says he, that great man who has a mind to help me, has as many to break through to come at me, as I have to come at him: therefore he will conclude, that the man who would make a figure, especially in a military way, must get over all false modesty, and assist his patron against the importunity of other pretenders, by a proper assurance in his own vindication. He says it is a civil cowardice to be backward in asserting what you ought to expect, as it is a military fear to be slow in attacking when it is your duty. With this candour does the gentleman speak of himself and others. The same frankness runs through all his conversation. The military part of his life has furnished him with many adventures, in the relation of which he is very agreeable to the company; for he is never overbearing, though accustomed to command men in the utmost degree below him ; nor ever too obsequious, from a habit of obeying men highly above him.

But that our society may not appear a set of humorists, unacquainted with the gallantries and pleasures of the age, we have among us the gallant Will Honeycomb, a gentleman who, according to his years, should be in the decline of his life, but having ever been very careful of his person, and always had a very easy fortune, time has made but very little impression, either by wrinkles on his forehead, or traces in his brain. His person is well turned, of a good height. He is very ready at that sort of discourse with which men usually entertain women. He has all his life dressed very well, and remembers habits as others do men. He can smile when one speaks to him, and laughs easily. He knows the history of every mode, and can inform you from which of the French king's wenches our wives and daughters had this manner of curling their hair, that way of placing their hoods ; whose frailty was covered by such a sort of petticoat, and whose vanity to show her foot made that part of the dress so short in such a year. In a word, all his conversation and knowledge has been in the female world. As other men of his age will take notice to you what such a minister said upon such and such an occasion, he will tell you, when the Duke of Monmouth danced at court, such a woman was then smitten — another was taken with him at the head of his troop in the Park. In all these important relations, he has ever about the same time received a kind glance, or a blow of a fan from some celebrated beauty, mother of the present Lord Such-a-one. If you speak of a young commoner that said a lively thing in the house, he starts up, " He has good blood in his veins, Tom Mirabell begot him ; the rogue cheated me in that affair ; that young fellow's mother used me more like a dog than any woman I ever made advances to." This way of talking of his very much enlivens the conversation among us of a more sedate turn ; and I find there is not one of the company, but myself, who rarely speak at all, but speaks of him as of that sort of man, who is usually called a well-bred fine gentleman. To conclude his character, where women are not concerned, he is an honest, worthy man.

I cannot tell whether I am to account him whom I am next to speak of as one of our company, for he visits us but seldom; but when he does, it adds to every man else a new enjoyment of himself. He is a clergyman, a very philosophic man, of general learning, great sanctity of life, and the most exact good-breeding. He has the misfortune to be of a very weak constitution, and consequently cannot accept of such cares and business as preferments in his function would oblige him to; he is therefore among divines what a chamber-counsellor is among lawyers. The probity of his mind and the integrity of his life create him followers, as being eloquent or loud advances others. He seldom introduces the subject he speaks upon; but we are so far gone in years that he observes, when he is among us, an earnestness to have him fall on some divine topic, which he always treats with much authority, as one who has no interests in this world, as one who is hastening to the object of all his wishes, and conceives hope from his decays and infirmities. These are my ordinary companions. R [STEELE]

POPULAR SUPERSTITIONS

No. 7. Thursday, March 8, 1711

Somnia, terrores magicos, miracula, sagas,
Nocturnos lemures, portentaque Thessala rides? — HOR.

Going yesterday to dine with an old acquaintance, I had the misfortune to find his whole family very much dejected. Upon asking him the occasion of it, he told me that his wife had dreamed a very strange dream the night before, which they were afraid portended some misfortune to themselves or to their children. At her coming into the room, I observed a settled melancholy in her countenance, which I should have been troubled for, had I not heard from whence it proceeded. We were no sooner sat down, but after having looked upon me a little while, "My dear," says she, turning to her husband, "you may now see the stranger that was in the candle last night." Soon after this, as they began to talk of family affairs, a little boy at the lower end of the table told her that he was to go into join-hand on Thursday. "Thursday!" says she, "No, child, if it please God, you shall not begin upon Childer-mas-day; tell your writing-master that Friday will be soon enough." I was reflecting with myself on the oddness of her fancy, and wondering that anybody would establish it as a rule, to lose a day in every week. In the midst of these my musings, she desired me to reach her a little salt upon the point of my knife, which I did in such a trepidation and hurry of obedience, that I let it drop by the way; at which she immediately star-tled, and said it fell toward her. Upon this I looked very blank; and observing the concern of the whole table, began to consider myself, with some confusion, as a person that had brought a disaster upon the family. The lady, however, recov-ering herself after a little space, said to her husband with a sigh, "My dear, misfortunes never come single." My friend, I found, acted but an under-part at his table, and being a man of more good-nature than understanding, thinks himself obliged to fall in with all the passions and humours of his yoke-fellow. "Do not you remember, child," says she, "that the pigeon-house fell the very afternoon that our careless wench spilt the salt upon the table?" "Yes," says he, "my dear, and the next post brought us an account of the battle of Almanza." The reader may guess at the figure I made, after having done all this mischief. I dispatched my dinner as soon as I could, with my usual taciturnity; when, to my utter con-fusion, the lady seeing me quitting my knife and fork, and laying them across one another upon my plate, desired me that I would humour her so far as to take them out of that figure, and place them side by side. What the absurdity was which I had committed I did not know, but I suppose there was some traditionary superstition in it; and therefore, in obedience to the lady of the house, I disposed of my knife and fork in two parallel lines, which is the figure I shall always lay them in for the future, though I do not know any reason for it.

It is not difficult for a man to see that a person has conceived an aversion to him. For my own part, I quickly found, by the lady's looks, that she regarded me as a very odd kind of fellow, with an unfortunate aspect. For which reason I took my leave immediately after dinner, and withdrew to my own lodgings. Upon my return home, I fell into a profound contemplation on the evils that attend these superstitious follies of mankind; how they subject us to imaginary afflictions, and additional sorrows, that do not properly come within our lot. As if the natural calamities of life were not sufficient for it, we turn the most indifferent circumstances into misfortunes, and suffer as much from trifling accidents as from real evils. I have known the shooting of a star spoil a night's rest; and have seen a man in love grow pale, and lose his appetite, upon the plucking of a merry-thought. A screech-owl at midnight has alarmed a family more than a band of robbers; nay, the voice of a cricket hath struck more terror than the roaring of a lion. There is nothing so inconsiderable, which may not appear dreadful to an imagination that is filled with omens and prognostics. A rusty nail, or a crooked pin, shoot up into prodigies.

I remember I was once in a mixed assembly, that was full of noise and mirth, when on a sudden an old woman unluckily observed there were thirteen of us in company. This remark struck a panic terror into several who were present, insomuch that one or two of the ladies were going to leave the room; but a friend of mine taking notice that one of our female companions was big with child, affirmed there were fourteen in the room, and that, instead of portending one of the company should die, it plainly foretold one of them should be born. Had not my friend found out this expedient to break the omen, I question not but half the women in the company would have fallen sick that very night.

An old maid that is troubled with the vapours produces infinite disturbances of this kind among her friends and neighbours. I know a maiden aunt of a great family, who is one of these antiquated sybils, that forebodes and prophesies from one end of the year to the other. She is always seeing apparitions, and hearing death-watches; and was the other day almost frighted out of her wits by the great house-dog that howled in the stable, at a time when she lay ill with the tooth-ache. Such an extravagant cast of mind engages multitudes of people, not only in impertinent terrors, but in supernumerary duties of life; and arises from that fear and ignorance which are natural to the soul of man. The horror with which we entertain the thoughts of death (or indeed of any future evil), and the uncertainty of its approach, fill a melancholy mind with innumerable apprehensions and suspicions, and consequently dispose it to the observation of such groundless prodigies and predictions. For as it is the chief concern of wise men to retrench the evils of life by the reasonings of philosophy, it is the employment of fools to multiply them by the sentiments of superstition.

For my own part, I should be very much troubled were I endowed with this divining quality, though it should inform me truly of everything that can befall me. I would not anticipate the relish of any happiness, nor feel the weight of any misery, before it actually arrives.

I know but one way of fortifying my soul against these gloomy presages and terrors of mind, and that is, by securing to myself the friendship and protection of that Being, who disposes of events, and governs futurity. He sees, at one view, the whole thread of my existence, not only that part of it which I have already passed through, but that which runs forward into all the depths of eternity. When I lay me down to sleep, I recommend myself to his care; when I awake, I give myself up to his direction. Amidst all the evils that threaten me,

I will look up to him for help, and question not but he will
either avert them, or turn them to my advantage. Though I
know neither the time nor the manner of the death I am to
die, I am not at all solicitous about it; because I am sure that
he knows them both, and that he will not fail to comfort and
support me under them. C [ADDISON]

THE PURPOSE OF *THE SPECTATOR*

No. 10. Monday, March 12, 1711

Non aliter quam qui adverso vix flumine lembum
Remigiis subigit, si bracchia forte remisit,
Atque illum præceps prono rapit alveus amni. — VIRG.

It is with much satisfaction that I hear this great city inquiring day by day after these my papers, and receiving my
morning lectures with a becoming seriousness and attention.
My publisher tells me that there are already three thousand of
them distributed every day: so that if I allow twenty readers
to every paper, which I look upon as a modest computation,
I may reckon about threescore thousand disciples in London
and Westminster, who I hope will take care to distinguish
themselves from the thoughtless herd of their ignorant and
unattentive brethren. Since I have raised to myself so great
an audience, I shall spare no pains to make their instruction
agreeable, and their diversion useful. For which reasons I shall
endeavour to enliven morality with wit, and to temper wit with
morality, that my readers may, if possible, both ways find their
account in the speculation of the day. And to the end that
their virtue and discretion may not be short, transient, intermitting starts of thought, I have resolved to refresh their
memories from day to day, till I have recovered them out of
that desperate state of vice and folly into which the age is
fallen. The mind that lies fallow for a single day sprouts up
in follies that are only to be killed by a constant and assiduous
culture. It was said of Socrates that he brought philosophy

down from heaven, to inhabit among men; and I shall be ambitious to have it said of me, that I have brought philosophy out of closets and libraries, schools and colleges, to dwell in clubs and assemblies, at tea-tables and in coffee-houses.

I would therefore in a very particular manner recommend these my speculations to all well regulated families, that set apart an hour in every morning for tea and bread and butter; and would earnestly advise them for their good to order this paper to be punctually served up, and to be looked upon as a part of the tea-equipage.

Sir Francis Bacon observes that a well written book, compared with its rivals and antagonists, is like Moses's serpent, that immediately swallowed up and devoured those of the Egyptians. I shall not be so vain as to think that where the *Spectator* appears, the other public prints will vanish; but shall leave it to my reader's consideration, whether, is it not much better to be let into the knowledge of one's self, than to hear what passes in Muscovy or Poland; and to amuse ourselves with such writings as tend to the wearing out of ignorance, passion, and prejudice, than such as naturally conduce to inflame hatreds, and make enmities irreconcilable.

In the next place I would recommend this paper to the daily perusal of those gentlemen whom I cannot but consider as my good brothers and allies, I mean the fraternity of Spectators, who live in the world without having anything to do in it; and either by the affluence of their fortunes, or laziness of their dispositions, have no other business with the rest of mankind, but to look upon them. Under this class of men are comprehended all contemplative tradesmen, titular physicians, fellows of the Royal Society, Templars that are not given to be contentious, and statesmen that are out of business; in short, every one that considers the world as a theater, and desires to form a right judgment of those who are the actors on it.

There is another set of men that I must likewise lay a claim to, whom I have lately called the blanks of society, as being altogether unfurnished with ideas, till the business and

conversation of the day has supplied them. I have often considered these poor souls with an eye of great commiseration,
when I have heard them asking the first man they have met
with, whether there was any news stirring, and by that means
gathering together materials for thinking. These needy persons do not know what to talk of, till about twelve o'clock in
the morning; for by that time they are pretty good judges of
the weather, know which way the wind sits, and whether the
Dutch mail be come in. As they lie at the mercy of the first
man they meet, and are grave or impertinent all the day long,
according to the notions which they have imbibed in the morning, I would earnestly entreat them not to stir out of their
chambers till they have read this paper, and do promise them
that I will daily instill into them such sound and wholesome
sentiments, as shall have a good effect on their conversation
for the ensuing twelve hours.

But there are none to whom this paper will be more useful
than to the female world. I have often thought there has not
been sufficient pains taken in finding out proper employments
and diversions for the fair ones. Their amusements seem contrived for them, rather as they are women, than as they are
reasonable creatures; and are more adapted to the sex than to
the species. The toilet is their great scene of business, and
the right adjusting of their hair the principal employment
of their lives. The sorting of a suit of ribbons is reckoned
a very good morning's work; and if they make an excursion
to a mercer's or a toy-shop, so great a fatigue makes them
unfit for anything else all the day after. Their more serious
occupations are sewing and embroidery, and their greatest
drudgery the preparation of jellies and sweetmeats. This, I
say, is the state of ordinary women; though I know there are
multitudes of those of a more elevated life and conversation,
that move in an exalted sphere of knowledge and virtue, that
join all the beauties of the mind to the ornaments of dress,
and inspire a kind of awe and respect, as well as love, into
their male beholders. I hope to increase the number of these

by publishing this daily paper, which I shall always endeavour to make an innocent if not an improving entertainment, and by that means, at least, divert the minds of my female readers from greater trifles. At the same time, as I would fain give some finishing touches to those which are already the most beautiful pieces in human nature, I shall endeavour to point out all those imperfections that are the blemishes, as well as those virtues which are the embellishments, of the sex. In the meanwhile, I hope these my gentle readers, who have so much time on their hands, will not grudge throwing away a quarter of an hour in a day on this paper, since they may do it without any hinderance to business.

I know several of my friends and well-wishers are in great pain for me, lest I should not be able to keep up the spirit of a paper which I oblige myself to furnish every day; but to make them easy in this particular, I will promise them faithfully to give it over as soon as I grow dull. This I know will be matter of great raillery to the small wits, who will frequently put me in mind of my promise, desire me to keep my word, assure me that it is high time to give over, with many other little pleasantries of the like nature, which men of a little smart genius cannot forbear throwing out against their best friends, when they have such a handle given them of being witty. But let them remember that I do hereby enter my caveat against this piece of raillery. C [ADDISON]

ILL-NATURE IN SATIRE

No. 23. Tuesday, March 27, 1711

Sævit atrox Volscens, nec teli conspicit usquam
Auctorem, nec quo se ardens immittere possit. — VIRG.

There is nothing that more betrays a base ungenerous spirit than the giving of secret stabs to a man's reputation; lampoons and satires, that are written with wit and spirit, are like poisoned darts, which not only inflict a wound but make it incurable. For this reason I am very much troubled when I see the talents of humour and ridicule in the possession of an ill-natured man. There cannot be a greater gratification to a barbarous and inhuman wit, than to stir up sorrow in the heart of a private person, to raise uneasiness among near relations, and to expose whole families to derision, at the same time that he remains unseen and undiscovered. If, beside the accomplishments of being witty and ill-natured, a man is vicious into the bargain, he is one of the most mischievous creatures that can enter into a civil society. His satire will then chiefly fall upon those who ought to be the most exempt from it. Virtue, merit, and everything that is praiseworthy, will be made the subject of ridicule and buffoonery. It is impossible to enumerate the evils which arise from these arrows that fly in the dark ; and I know no other excuse that is or can be made for them, than that the wounds they give are only imaginary, and produce nothing more than a secret shame or sorrow in the mind of the suffering person. It must indeed be confessed, that a lampoon or satire do not carry in them robbery or murder ; but at the same time how many are there that would not rather lose a considerable sum of money, or even life itself, than be set up as a mark of infamy and derision ? And in this case a man should consider that an injury is not to be measured by the notions of him that gives, but of him that receives it.

Those who can put the best countenance upon the outrages of this nature which are offered them, are not without their secret anguish. I have often observed a passage in Socrates's behaviour at his death, in a light wherein none of the critics have considered it. That excellent man, entertaining his friends, a little before he drank the bowl of poison, with a discourse on the immortality of the soul, at his entering upon it says that he does not believe any, the most comic genius, can censure him for talking upon such a subject at such a time. This passage, I think, evidently glances upon Aristophanes, who wrote a comedy on purpose to ridicule the discourses of that divine philosopher. It has been observed by many writers, that

Socrates was so little moved at this piece of buffoonery, that he was several times present at its being acted upon the stage, and never expressed the least resentment of it. But with submission, I think the remark I have here made shows us, that this unworthy treatment made an impression upon his mind, though he had been too wise to discover it.

When Julius Cæsar was lampooned by Catullus, he invited him to a supper, and treated him with such a generous civility, that he made the poet his friend ever after. Cardinal Mazarine gave the same kind of treatment to the learned Quillet, who had reflected upon his eminence in a famous Latin poem. The cardinal sent for him, and, after some kind expostulations upon what he had written, assured him of his esteem, and dismissed him with a promise of the next good abbey that should fall, which he accordingly conferred upon him in a few months after. This had so good an effect upon the author, that he dedicated the second edition of his book to the cardinal, after having expunged the passages which had given him offense.

Sextus Quintus was not of so generous and forgiving a temper. Upon his being made pope, the statue of Pasquin was one night dressed in a very dirty shirt, with an excuse written under it, that he was forced to wear foul linen, because his laundress was made a princess. This was a reflection upon the pope's sister, who before the promotion of her brother, was in those mean circumstances that Pasquin represented her. As this pasquinade made a great noise in Rome, the pope offered a considerable sum of money to any person that should discover the author of it. The author, relying upon his holiness's generosity, as also on some private overtures which he had received from him, made the discovery himself; upon which the pope gave him the reward he had promised, but at the same time to disable the satirist for the future, ordered his tongue to be cut out, and both his hands to be chopped off. Aretine is too trite an instance. Every one knows that all the kings in Europe were his tributaries. Nay, there is a letter of his extant, in which he makes his boasts that he laid the Sophi of Persia under contribution.

Though, in the various examples which I have here drawn together, these several great men behaved themselves very differently toward the wits of the age who had reproached them; they all of them plainly showed that they were very sensible of their reproaches, and consequently that they received them as very great injuries. For my own part, I would never trust a man that I thought was capable of giving these secret wounds, and cannot but think that he would hurt the person whose reputation he thus assaults, in his body or in his fortune, could he do it with the same security. There is, indeed, something very barbarous and inhuman in the ordinary scribblers of lampoons. An innocent young lady shall be exposed for an unhappy feature; a father of a family turned to ridicule for some domestic calamity; a wife be made uneasy all her life for a misinterpreted word or action; nay, a good, a temperate, and a just man shall be put out of countenance by the representation of those qualities that should do him honour. So pernicious a thing is wit, when it is not tempered with virtue and humanity.

I have indeed heard of heedless, inconsiderate writers, that without any malice have sacrificed the reputation of their friends and acquaintance to a certain levity of temper, and a silly ambition of distinguishing themselves by a spirit of raillery and satire: as if it were not infinitely more honourable to be a good-natured man than a wit. Where there is this little petulant humour in an author, he is often very mischievous without designing to be so. For which reason, I always lay it down as a rule, that an indiscreet man is more hurtful than an ill-natured one; for, as the latter will only attack his enemies, and those he wishes ill to, the other injures indifferently both friends and foes. I cannot forbear on this occasion transcribing a fable out of Sir Roger l'Estrange, which accidentally lies before me. "A company of waggish boys were watching of frogs at the side of a pond, and still as any of 'em

put up their heads, they'd be pelting them down again with stones. ' Children,' says one of the frogs, ' you never consider, that though this may be play to you, 't is death to us.' "

As this week is in a manner set apart and dedicated to serious thoughts, I shall indulge myself in such speculations as may not be altogether unsuitable to the season ; and in the meantime, as the settling in ourselves a charitable frame of mind is a work very proper for the time, I have in this paper endeavoured to expose that particular breach of charity which has been generally overlooked by divines, because they are but few who can be guilty of it. C [ADDISON]

MEDITATIONS IN WESTMINSTER ABBEY

No. 26. Friday, March 30, 1711

Pallida mors aequo pulsat pede pauperum tabernas
Regumque turres. O beate Sesti,
Vitae summa brevis spem nos vetat incohare longam.
Jam te premet nox, fabulaeque manes,
Et domus exilis Plutonia ———. — HOR.

When I am in a serious humour, I very often walk by myself in Westminster Abbey : where the gloominess of the place, and the use to which it is applied, with the solemnity of the building, and the condition of the people who lie in it, are apt to fill the mind with a kind of melancholy, or rather thoughtfulness, that is not disagreeable. I yesterday passed a whole afternoon in the churchyard, the cloisters, and the church, amusing myself with the tombstones and inscriptions that I met with in those several regions of the dead. Most of them recorded nothing else of the buried person, but that he was born upon one day, and died upon another ; the whole history of his life being comprehended in those two circumstances that are common to all mankind. I could not but look upon these registers of existence, whether of brass or marble, as a kind of satire upon the departed persons ; who had left no other memorial of them, but that they were born, and that they died. They put me in mind of several persons mentioned in the battles of heroic poems, who have sounding names given them for no other reason but that they may be killed, and are celebrated for nothing but being knocked on the head.

Γλαῦκόν τε Μέδοντά τε Θερσίλοχόν τε. — Ηομ.
Glaucumque, Medontaque, Thersilochumque. — Virg.

The life of these men is finely described in holy writ by "the path of an arrow," which is immediately closed up and lost.

Upon my going into the church, I entertained myself with the digging of a grave; and saw in every shovel-full of it that was thrown up, the fragment of a bone or skull intermixed with a kind of fresh mouldering earth that some time or other had a place in the composition of a human body. Upon this I began to consider with myself what innumerable multitudes of people lay confused together under the pavement of that ancient cathedral; how men and women, friends and enemies, priests and soldiers, monks and prebendaries, were crumbled among one another, and blended together in the same common mass; how beauty, strength, and youth, with old age, weakness, and deformity, lay undistinguished in the same promiscuous heap of matter.

After having thus surveyed this great magazine of mortality, as it were, in the lump, I examined it more particularly by the accounts which I found on several of the monuments which are raised in every quarter of that ancient fabric. Some of them were covered with such extravagant epitaphs, that if it were possible for the dead person to be acquainted with them, he would blush at the praises which his friends have bestowed upon him. There are others so excessively modest that they deliver the character of the person departed in Greek or Hebrew, and by that means are not understood once in a twelvemonth. In the poetical quarter, I found there were poets who had no monuments, and monuments which had no poets. I observed, indeed, that the present war has filled the church with many of these uninhabited monuments, which had been erected to the memory of persons whose bodies were perhaps buried in the plains of Blenheim, or in the bosom of the ocean.

I could not but be very much delighted with several modern epitaphs, which are written with great elegance of expression and justness of thought, and therefore do honour to the living as well as to the dead. As a foreigner is very apt to conceive an idea of the ignorance or politeness of a nation from the turn of their public monuments and inscriptions, they should be submitted to the perusal of men of learning and genius before they are put in execution. Sir Cloudesly Shovel's monument has very often given me great offense. Instead of the brave, rough English admiral, which was the distinguishing character of that plain, gallant man, he is represented on his tomb by the figure of a beau, dressed in a long periwig, and reposing himself upon velvet cushions, under a canopy of state. The inscription is answerable to the monument; for instead of celebrating the many remarkable actions he had performed in the service of his country, it acquaints us only with the manner of his death, in which it was impossible for him to reap any honour. The Dutch, whom we are apt to despise for want of genius, show an infinitely greater taste of antiquity and politeness in their buildings and works of this nature than what we meet with in those of our own country. The monuments of their admirals, which have been erected at the public expense, represent them like themselves, and are adorned with rostral crowns and naval ornaments, with beautiful festoons of sea-weed, shells, and coral.

But to return to our subject. I have left the repository of our English kings for the contemplation of another day, when I shall find my mind disposed for so serious an amusement. I know that entertainments of this nature are apt to raise dark and dismal thoughts in timorous minds and gloomy imaginations; but for my own part, though I am always serious, I do not know what it is to be melancholy; and can therefore take a view of nature in her deep and solemn scenes with the same pleasure as in her most gay and delightful ones. By this means I can improve myself with those objects which others consider with terror. When I look upon the tombs of the great, every emotion of envy dies within me; when I read the epitaphs of the beautiful, every inordinate desire goes out; when I meet with the grief of parents upon a tombstone, my heart melts with compassion; when I see the tomb of the parents themselves, I consider the vanity of grieving for those whom we must quickly follow. When I see kings lying by those who deposed them, when I consider rival wits placed side by side, or the holy men that divided the world with their contests and disputes, I reflect with sorrow and astonishment on the little competitions, factions, and debates of mankind. When I read the several dates of the tombs, of some that died yesterday, and some six hundred years ago, I consider that great day when we shall all of us be contemporaries, and make our appearance together. C [ADDISON]

COFFEE–HOUSE COMPANY

No. 49. Thursday, April 26, 1711

——— *Hominem pagina nostra sapit.* — MART.

It is very natural for a man who is not turned for mirthful meetings of men, or assemblies of the fair sex, to delight in that sort of conversation which we find in coffee-houses. Here a man of my temper is in his element; for if he cannot talk, he can still be more agreeable to his company, as well as pleased in himself, in being only a hearer. It is a secret known but to few, yet of no small use in the conduct of life, that when you fall into a man's conversation, the first thing you should consider is, whether he has a greater inclination to hear you, or that you should hear him. The latter is the more general desire, and I know very able flatterers that never speak a word in praise of the persons from whom they obtain daily favours, but still practice a skillful attention to whatever is uttered by those with whom they converse. We are very curious to observe the behaviour of great men and their clients; but the same passions and interests move men in lower spheres; and I (that have nothing else to do but make observations) see in every parish, street, lane, and alley of this populous city, a little potentate that has his court and his flatterers, who lay snares for his affection and favour by the same arts that are practiced upon men in higher stations.

In the place I most usually frequent, men differ rather in the time of day in which they make a figure, than in any real greatness above one another. I, who am at the coffee-house at six in a morning, know that my friend Beaver, the haberdasher, has a levee of more undissembled friends and admirers than most of the courtiers or generals of Great Britain. Every man about him has, perhaps, a newspaper in his hand; but none can pretend to guess what step will be taken in any one court of Europe, till Mr. Beaver has thrown down his pipe, and declares what measures the allies must enter into upon this new posture of affairs. Our coffee-house is near one of the inns of court, and Beaver has the audience and admiration of his neighbours from six till within a quarter of eight, at which time he is interrupted by the students of the house; some of whom are ready dressed for Westminster at eight in a morning, with faces as busy as if they were retained in every cause there; and others come in their nightgowns to saunter away their time, as if they never designed to go thither. I do not know that I meet, in any of my walks, objects which move both my spleen and laughter so effectually as those young fellows at the Grecian, Squire's, Searle's, and all other coffee-houses adjacent to the law, who rise early for no other purpose but to publish their laziness. One would think these young virtuosos take a gay cap and slippers, with a scarf and parti-coloured gown, to be ensigns of dignity; for the vain things approach each other with an air, which shows they regard one another for their vestments. I have observed that the superiority among these proceeds from an opinion of gallantry and fashion. The gentleman in the strawberry sash, who presides so much over the rest, has, it seems, subscribed to every opera this last winter, and is supposed to receive favours from one of the actresses.

When the day grows too busy for these gentlemen to enjoy any longer the pleasures of their dishabille with any manner of confidence, they give place to men who have business or good sense in their faces, and come to the coffee-house either to transact affairs, or enjoy conversation. The persons to whose behaviour and discourse I have most regard, are such as are between these two sorts of men; such as have not spirits too active to be happy and well pleased in a private condition, nor complexions too warm to make them neglect the duties and relations of life. Of these sort of men consist the worthier part of mankind; of these are all good fathers, generous brothers, sincere friends, and faithful subjects. Their entertainments are derived rather from reason than imagination: which is the cause that there is no impatience or instability in their speech or action. You see in their countenances they are at home, and in quiet possession of the present instant as it passes, without desiring to quicken it by gratifying any passion, or prosecuting any new design. These are the men formed for society, and those little communities which we express by the word neighbourhoods.

The coffee-house is the place of rendezvous to all that live near it, who are thus turned to relish calm and ordinary life. Eubulus presides over the middle hours of the day, when this assembly of men meet together. He enjoys a great fortune handsomely, without launching into expense; and exerts many noble and useful qualities, without appearing in any public employment. His wisdom and knowledge are serviceable to all that think fit to make use of them; and he does the office of a counsel, a judge, an executor, and a friend, to all his acquaintance, not only without the profits which attend such offices, but also without the deference and homage which are usually paid to them. The giving of thanks is displeasing to him. The greatest gratitude you can show him is to let him see that you are the better man for his services; and that you are as ready to oblige others, as he is to oblige you.

In the private exigencies of his friends, he lends at legal value considerable sums which he might highly increase by rolling in the public stocks. He does not consider in whose hands his money will improve most, but where it will do most good.

Eubulus has so great an authority in his little diurnal audience, that when he shakes his head at any piece of public news, they all of them appear dejected; and on the contrary, go home to their dinners with a good stomach and cheerful aspect when Eubulus seems to intimate that things go well. Nay, their veneration toward him is so great, that when they are in other company they speak and act after him; are wise in his sentences and are no sooner sat down at their own tables, but they hope or fear, rejoice or despond, as they saw him do at the coffee-house. In a word, every man is Eubulus as soon as his back is turned.

Having here given an account of the several reigns that succeed each other from day-break till dinner-time, I shall mention the monarchs of the afternoon on another occasion, and shut up the whole series of them with the history of Tom the Tyrant; who, as the first minister of the coffee-house, takes the government upon him between the hours of eleven and twelve at night, and gives his orders in the most arbitrary manner to the servants below him, as to the disposition of liquors, coal, and cinders. R [STEELE]

THE JOURNAL OF THE INDIAN KINGS

No. 50. Friday, April 27, 1711

Nunquam aliud natura, aliud sapientia dicit. — Juv.

When the four Indian kings were in this country about a twelvemonth ago, I often mixed with the rabble, and followed them a whole day together, being wonderfully struck with the sight of everything that is new or uncommon. I have since their departure employed a friend to make many inquiries of their landlord the upholsterer, relating to their manners and conversation, as also concerning the remarks which they made in this country; for next to the forming a right notion of such strangers, I should be desirous of learning what ideas they have conceived of us.

The upholsterer finding my friend very inquisitive about these his lodgers, brought him some time since a little bundle of papers, which he assured him were written by King Sa Ga Yean Qua Rash Tow, and, as he supposes, left behind by some mistake. These papers are now translated, and contain abundance of very odd observations, which I find this little fraternity of kings made during their stay in the isle of Great Britain. I shall present my reader with a short specimen of them in this paper, and may perhaps communicate more to him hereafter. In the article of London are the following words, which without doubt are meant of the church of St. Paul:

On the most rising part of the town there stands a huge house, big enough to contain the whole nation of which I am king. Our good brother E Tow O Koam, King of the Rivers, is of opinion it was made by the hands of that great God to whom it is consecrated. The kings of Granajah and of the Six Nations believe that it was created with the earth, and produced on the same day with the sun and moon. But for my own part, by the best information that I could get of this matter, I am apt to think that this prodigious pile was fashioned into the shape it now bears by several tools and instruments of which they have a wonderful variety in this country. It was probably at first a huge misshapen rock that grew upon the top of the hill, which the natives of the country (after having cut it into a kind of regular figure) bored and hollowed with incredible pains and industry, till they had wrought in it all those beautiful vaults and caverns into which it is divided at this day. As soon as this rock was thus curiously scooped to their liking, a prodigious number of hands must have been employed in chipping the outside of it, which is now as smooth as the surface of a pebble; and is in several places hewn out into pillars that stand like the trunks of so many trees bound about the top with garlands of leaves. It is probable that when this great work was begun, which must have been many hundred years ago, there was some religion among this people; for they give it the name of a temple, and have a tradition that it was designed for men to pay their devotions in. And indeed there are several reasons which make us think that the natives of this country had formerly among them some sort of worship, for they set apart every seventh day as sacred; but upon my going into one of these holy houses on that day, I could not observe any circumstance of devotion in their behaviour. There was indeed a man in black, who was mounted above the rest, and seemed to utter something with a great deal of vehemence; but as for those underneath him, instead of paying their worship to the deity of the place, they were most of them bowing and curtseying to one another, and a considerable number of them fast asleep.

The queen of the country appointed two men to attend us, that had enough of our language to make themselves understood in some few particulars. But we soon perceived that these two were great enemies to one another, and did not always agree in the same story. We could make shift to gather out of one of them, that this island was very much infested with a monstrous kind of animals, in the shape of men, called whigs; and he often told us that he hoped we should meet with none of them in our way, for that if we did, they would be apt to knock us down for being kings.

Our other interpreter used to talk very much of a kind of animal called a tory, that was as great a monster as the whig, and would treat us as ill for being foreigners. These two creatures, it seems, are born with a secret antipathy to one another, and engage when they meet as naturally as the elephant and the rhinoceros. But as we saw none of either of these species, we are apt to think that our guides deceived us with misrepresentations and fictions, and amused us with an account of such monsters as are not really in their country.

These particulars we made a shift to pick out from the discourse of our interpreters, which we put together as well as we could, being able to understand but here and there a word of what they said, and afterward making up the meaning of it among ourselves. The men of the country are very cunning and ingenious in handicraft works, but withal so very idle, that we often saw young, lusty, raw-boned fellows carried up and down the streets in little covered rooms, by a couple of porters who are hired for that service. Their dress is likewise very barbarous, for they almost strangle themselves about the neck, and bind their bodies with many ligatures, that we are apt to think are the occasion of several distempers among them which our country is entirely free from. Instead of those beautiful feathers with which we adorn our heads, they often buy up a monstrous bush of hair, which covers their heads and falls down in a large fleece below the middle of their backs, with which they walk up and down the streets, and are as proud of it as if it was of their own growth.

We were invited to one of their public diversions, where we hoped to have seen the great men of their country running down a stag, or pitching a bar, that we might have discovered who were the persons of the greatest abilities among them; but instead of that, they conveyed us into a huge room lighted up with abundance of candles, where this lazy people sat still above three hours to see several feats of ingenuity performed by others, who it seems were paid for it.

As for the women of the country, not being able to talk with them, we could only make our remarks upon them at a distance. They let the hair of their heads grow to a great length; but as the men make a great show with heads of hair that are none of their own, the women, who they say have very fine heads of hair, tie it up in a knot, and cover it from being seen. The women look like angels, and would be more beautiful than the sun, were it not for little black spots that are apt to break out in their faces, and sometimes rise in very odd figures. I have observed that those little blemishes wear off very soon; but when they disappear in one part of the face, they are very apt to break out in another, insomuch that I have seen a spot upon the forehead in the afternoon, which was upon the chin in the morning.

The author then proceeds to show the absurdity of breeches and petticoats, with many other curious observations which I shall reserve for another occasion. I cannot, however, conclude this paper without taking notice that amidst these wild remarks there now and then appears something very reasonable. I cannot likewise forbear observing that we are all guilty in some measure of the same narrow way of thinking which we meet with in this abstract of the Indian journal, when we fancy the customs, dresses, and manners of other countries are ridiculous and extravagant, if they do not resemble those of our own. C [ADDISON]

THE EDUCATION OF GIRLS

No. 66. Wednesday, May 16, 1711

Motus doceri gaudet Ionicos
Matura virgo, et fingitur artibus
Jam nunc et incestos amores
De tenero mediatur ungui. — Hor.

The two following letters are upon a subject of very great importance, though expressed without any air of gravity.

To the Spectator

Sir,

I take the freedom of asking your advice in behalf of a young country kinswoman of mine who is lately come to town, and under my care for her education. She is very pretty, but you can't imagine how unformed a creature it is. She comes to my hands just as nature left her, half finished, and without any acquired improvements. When I look on her I often think of the Belle Sauvage mentioned in one of your papers. Dear Mr. Spectator, help me to make her comprehend the visible graces of speech, and the dumb eloquence of motion; for she is at present a perfect stranger to both. She knows no way to express herself but by her tongue, and that always to signify her meaning. Her eyes serve her yet only to see with, and she is utterly a foreigner to the language of looks and glances. In this I fancy you could help her better than anybody. I have bestowed two months in teaching her to sigh when she is not concerned, and to smile when she is not pleased, and am ashamed to own she makes little or no improvement. Then she is no more able now to walk, than she was to go at a year old. By walking, you will easily know I mean that regular but easy motion which gives our persons so irresistible a grace, as if we moved to music, and is a kind of disengaged figure, or, if I may so speak, recitative dancing. But the want of this I cannot blame in her, for I find she has no ear, and means nothing by walking but to change her place. I could pardon too her blushing, if she knew how to carry herself in it, and if it did not manifestly injure her complexion.

They tell me you are a person who have seen the world, and are a judge of fine breeding; which makes me ambitious of some instructions from you for her improvement: which when you have favored me with, I shall farther advise with you about the disposal of this fair forester in marriage: for I will make it no secret to you, that her person and education are to be her fortune.

I am, Sir,
Your very humble servant,
Celimene.

Sir,

Being employed by Celimene to make up and send to you her letter, I make bold to recommend the case therein mentioned to your consideration, because she and I happen to differ a little in our notions. I, who am a rough man, am afraid the young girl is in a fair way to be spoiled; therefore, pray, Mr. Spectator, let us have your opinion of this fine thing called fine breeding; for I am afraid it differs too much from that plain thing called good breeding.

Your most humble servant.

The general mistake among us in the educating our children is, that in our daughters we take care of their persons and neglect their minds; in our sons we are so intent upon adorning their minds, that we wholly neglect their bodies. It is from this that you shall see a young lady celebrated and admired in all the assemblies about town, when her elder brother is afraid to come into a room. From this ill management it arises, that we frequently observe a man's life is half spent, before he is taken notice of, and a woman in the prime of her years is out of fashion and neglected. The boy I shall consider upon some other occasion, and at present stick to the girl: and I am the more inclined to this, because I have several letters which complain to me that my female readers have not understood me for some days last past, and take themselves to be unconcerned in the present turn of my writings. When a girl is safely brought from her nurse, before she is capable of forming one simple notion of anything in life, she is delivered to the hands of her dancing-master; and with a collar round her neck, the pretty, wild thing is taught a fantastical gravity of behaviour, and forced to a particular way of holding her head, heaving her breast, and moving with her whole body; and all this under pain of never having a husband, if she steps, looks, or moves awry. This gives the young lady wonderful workings of imagination, what is to pass between her and this husband, that she is every moment told of, and for whom she seems to be educated. Thus her fancy is engaged to turn all her endeavours to the ornament of her person, as what must determine her good and ill in this life:

and she naturally thinks, if she is tall enough, she is wise enough for anything for which her education makes her think she is designed. To make her an agreeable person is the main purpose of her parents; to that is all their cost, to that all their care directed; and from this general folly of parents we owe our present numerous race of coquettes. These reflections puzzle me, when I think of giving my advice on the subject of managing the wild thing mentioned in the letter of my correspondent. But sure there is a middle way to be followed; the management of a young lady's person is not to be overlooked, but the erudition of her mind is much more to be regarded. According as this is managed, you will see the mind follow the appetites of the body, or the body express the virtues of the mind.

Cleomira dances with all the elegance of motion imaginable; but her eyes are so chastised with the simplicity and innocence of her thoughts, that she raises in her beholders admiration and good-will, but no loose hope or wild imagination. The true art in this case is, to make the mind and body improve together; and, if possible, to make gesture follow thought, and not let thought be employed upon gesture. R [STEELE]

SIR ROGER DE COVERLEY AT HOME

No. 106. Monday, July 2, 1711

———— *Hinc tibi copia*
Manabit ad plenum benigno
Ruris honorum opulenta cornu. —— HOR.

Having often received an invitation from my friend Sir Roger de Coverley to pass away a month with him in the country, I last week accompanied him thither, and am settled with him for some time at his country-house, where I intend to form several of my ensuing speculations. Sir Roger, who is very well acquainted with my humour, lets me rise and go to bed when I please, dine at his own table or in my chamber as I think fit, sit still and say nothing without bidding me be merry. When the gentlemen of the country come to see him, he only shows me at a distance. As I have been walking in his fields I have observed them stealing a sight of me over a hedge, and have heard the knight desiring them not to let me see them, for that I hated to be stared at.

I am the more at ease in Sir Roger's family, because it consists of sober and staid persons; for as the knight is the best master in the world, he seldom changes his servants; and as he is beloved by all about him, his servants never care for leaving him; by this means his domestics are all in years, and grown old with their master. You would take his valet-de-chambre for his brother, his butler is gray-headed, his groom is one of the gravest men that I have ever seen, and his coachman has the looks of a privy-councillor. You see the goodness of the master even in the old house-dog, and in a gray pad that is kept in the stable with great care and tenderness, out of regard to his past services, though he has been useless for several years.

I could not but observe with a great deal of pleasure the joy that appeared in the countenances of these ancient domestics upon my friend's arrival at his country seat. Some of them could not refrain from tears at the sight of their old master; every one of them pressed forward to do something for him, and seemed discouraged if they were not employed. At the same time the good old knight, with a mixture of the father and the master of the family, tempered the inquiries after his own affairs with several kind questions relating to themselves. This humanity and good-nature engages everybody to him, so that when he is pleasant upon any of them, all his family are in good humour, and none so much as the person whom he diverts himself with; on the contrary, if he coughs, or betrays any infirmity of old age, it is easy for a stander-by to observe a secret concern in the looks of all his servants.

My worthy friend has put me under the particular care of his butler, who is a very prudent man, and, as well as the rest of his fellow-servants, wonderfully desirous of pleasing me, because they have often heard their master talk of me as of his particular friend.

My chief companion, when Sir Roger is diverting himself in the woods or the fields, is a very venerable man who is ever with Sir Roger, and has lived at his house in the nature of a chaplain above thirty years. This gentleman is a person of good sense and some learning, of a very regular life and obliging conversation; he heartily loves Sir Roger, and knows that he is very much in the old knight's esteem, so that he lives in the family rather as a relation than a dependent.

I have observed in several of my papers, that my friend Sir Roger, amidst all his good qualities, is something of a humorist; and that his virtues, as well as imperfections, are as it were tinged by a certain extravagance, which makes them particularly *his*, and distinguishes them from those of other men. This cast of mind, as it is generally very innocent in itself, so it renders his conversation highly agreeable, and more delightful than the same degree of sense and virtue would appear in their common and ordinary colours. As I was walking with him last night, he asked me how I liked the good man whom I have just now mentioned, and without staying for my answer, told me that he was afraid of being insulted with Latin and Greek at his own table; for which reason he desired a particular friend of his at the university to find him out a clergyman rather of plain sense than much learning, of a good aspect, a clear voice, a sociable temper, and, if possible, a man that understood a little of backgammon. "My friend," says Sir Roger, "found me out this gentleman, who, beside the endowments required of him, is, they tell me, a good scholar, though he does not show it. I have given him the patronage of the parish; and because I know his value, have settled upon him a good annuity for life. If he outlives me, he shall find that he was higher in my esteem than perhaps he thinks he is. He has now been with me thirty years; and though he does not know I have taken notice of it, has never in all that time asked anything of me for himself, though he is every day soliciting me for something in behalf of one or other of my tenants his parishioners. There has not been a lawsuit in the parish since he has lived among them; if any dispute arises, they apply themselves to him for the decision: if they do not acquiesce in his judgment, which I think never happened above once, or twice at most, they appeal to me. At his first settling with me, I made him a present of all the good sermons which have been printed in English, and only begged of him that every Sunday he would pronounce one of them in the pulpit. Accordingly, he has digested them into such a series, that they follow one another naturally, and make a continued system of practical divinity."

As Sir Roger was going on in his story, the gentleman we were talking of came up to us; and upon the knight's asking him who preached to-morrow (for it was Saturday night), told us the bishop of St. Asaph in the morning, and Dr. South in the afternoon. He then showed us his list of preachers for the whole year, where I saw with a great deal of pleasure Archbishop Tillotson, Bishop Saunderson, Dr. Barrow, Dr. Calamy, with several living authors who have published discourses of practical divinity. I no sooner saw this venerable man in the pulpit, but I very much approved of my friend's insisting upon the qualifications of a good aspect and a clear voice; for I was so charmed with the gracefulness of his figure and delivery, as well as with the discourses he pronounced, that I think I never passed any time more to my satisfaction. A sermon repeated after this manner is like the composition of a poet in the mouth of a graceful actor.

I could heartily wish that more of our country clergy would follow this example; and instead of wasting their spirits in laborious compositions of their own, would endeavour after a handsome elocution, and all those other talents that are proper to enforce what has been penned by great masters. This would not only be more easy to themselves, but more edifying to the people. L [ADDISON]

THE CHARACTER OF WILL WIMBLE

No. 108. Wednesday, July 4, 1711

Gratis anhelans, multa agendo nihil agens. — PHÆD.

As I was yesterday morning walking with Sir Roger before his house, a country fellow brought him a huge fish, which, he told him, Mr. William Wimble had caught that very morning; and that he presented it with his service to him, and intended to come and dine with him. At the same time he delivered a letter, which my friend read to me as soon as the messenger left him.

Sir Roger,

I desire you to accept of a jack, which is the best I have caught this season. I intend to come and stay with you a week, and see how the perch bite in the Black River. I observed with some concern, the last time I saw you upon the bowling-green, that your whip wanted a lash to it; I will bring half a dozen with me that I twisted last week, which I hope will serve you all the time you are in the country. I have not been out of the saddle for six days last past, having been at Eton with Sir John's eldest son. He takes to his learning hugely.

I am, Sir, your humble servant,
Will Wimble.

This extraordinary letter, and message that accompanied it, made me very curious to know the character and quality of the gentleman who sent them; which I found to be as follows: — Will Wimble is younger brother to a baronet, and descended of the ancient family of the Wimbles. He is now between forty and fifty; but being bred to no business and born to no estate, he generally lives with his elder brother as superintendent of his game. He hunts a pack of dogs better than any man in the country, and is very famous for finding out a hare. He is extremely well versed in all the little handicrafts of an idle man. He makes a May-fly to a miracle: and furnishes the whole country with angle-rods. As he is a good-natured, officious fellow, and very much esteemed upon account of his family, he is a welcome guest at every house, and keeps up a good correspondence among all the gentlemen about him. He carries a tulip root in his pocket from one to another, or exchanges a puppy between a couple of friends that live perhaps in the opposite sides of the county. Will is a particular favourite of all the young heirs, whom he frequently obliges with a net that he has weaved, or a setting-dog that he has made himself. He now and then presents a pair of garters of his own knitting to their mothers and sisters ; and raises a great deal of mirth among them, by inquiring as often as he meets them " how they wear ? " These gentleman-like manufactures and obliging little humours make Will the darling of the country.

Sir Roger was proceeding in the character of him, when he saw him make up to us with two or three hazel twigs in his hand that he had cut in Sir Roger's woods, as he came through them in his way to the house. I was very much pleased to observe on one side the hearty and sincere welcome with which Sir Roger received him, and on the other, the secret joy which his guest discovered at the sight of the good old knight. After the first salutes were over, Will desired Sir Roger to lend him one of his servants to carry a set of shuttlecocks he had with him in a little box, to a lady that lived about a mile off, to whom it seems he had promised such a present for above this half-year. Sir Roger's back was no sooner turned, but honest Will began to tell me of a large cock pheasant that he had sprung in one of the neighbouring woods, with two or three other adventures of the same nature. Odd and uncommon characters are the game that I look for and most delight in ; for which reason I was as much pleased with the novelty of the person that talked to me, as he could be for his life with the springing of a pheasant, and therefore listened to him with more than ordinary attention.

In the midst of his discourse the bell rang to dinner, where the gentleman I have been speaking of had the pleasure of seeing the huge jack he had caught served up for the first dish in a most sumptuous manner. Upon our sitting down to it he gave us a long account how he had hooked it, played with it, foiled it, and at length drew it out upon the bank — with several other particulars that lasted all the first course. A dish of wild fowl that came afterward furnished conversation for the rest of the dinner, which concluded with a late invention of Will's for improving the quail-pipe.

Upon withdrawing into my room after dinner, I was secretly touched with compassion towards the honest gentleman that had dined with us ; and could not but consider with a great deal of concern, how so good a heart and such busy hands were wholly employed in trifles ; that so much humanity should be so little beneficial to others, and so much industry so little advantageous to himself. The same temper of mind and application to affairs might have recommended him to the public esteem, and have raised his fortune in another station of life. What good to his country or himself might not a trader or merchant have done with such useful though ordinary qualifications ?

Will Wimble's is the case of many a younger brother of a great family, who had rather see their children starve like gentlemen, than thrive in a trade or profession that is beneath their quality. This humour fills several parts of Europe with pride and beggary. It is the happiness of a trading nation like ours, that the younger sons, though incapable of any liberal art or profession, may be placed in such a way of life as may perhaps enable them to vie with the best of their family. Accordingly we find several citizens that were launched into the world with narrow fortunes, rising by an honest industry to greater estates than those of their elder brothers. It is not improbable but Will was formerly tried at divinity, law, or physic, and that, finding his genius did not lie in that way, his parents gave him up at length to his own inventions. But certainly, however improper he might have been for studies of a higher nature, he was perfectly well turned for the occupations of trade and commerce. As I think this is a point which cannot be too much inculcated, I shall desire my reader to compare what I have here written with what I have said in my twenty-first speculation. L [ADDISON]

THE STORY OF EUDOXUS AND LEONTINE

No. 123.   Saturday, July 21, 1711

Doctrina sed vim promovet insitam
Rectique cultus pectora roborant :
Utcunque defecere mores,
Dedecorant bene nata culpæ. — HOR.

As I was yesterday taking the air with my friend Sir Roger, we were met by a fresh-coloured, ruddy young man who rode by us full speed, with a couple of servants behind him. Upon my inquiry who he was, Sir Roger told me that he was a young gentleman of a considerable estate, who had been educated by a tender mother that lived not many miles from the place where we were. She is a very good lady, says my friend, but took so much care of her son's health, that she has made him good for nothing. She quickly found that reading was bad for his eyes, and that writing made his head ache. He was let loose among the woods as soon as he was able to ride on horseback, or to carry a gun upon his shoulder. To be brief, I found, by my friend's account of him, that he had got a great stock of health, and nothing else ; and that if it were a man's business only to live, there would not be a more accomplished young fellow in the whole county.

The truth of it is, since my residing in these parts, I have seen and heard innumerable instances of young heirs and elder brothers, who, either from their own reflecting upon the estates they are born to, and therefore thinking all other accomplishments unnecessary, or from hearing these notions frequently inculcated to them by the flattery of their servants and domestics, or from the same foolish thought prevailing in those who have the care of their education, are of no manner of use but to keep up their families, and transmit their lands and houses in a line to posterity.

This makes me often think on a story I have heard of two friends, which I shall give my reader at large, under feigned names. The moral of it may, I hope, be useful, though there are some circumstances which make it rather appear like a novel, than a true story.

Eudoxus and Leontine began the world with small estates. They were both of them men of good sense and great virtue. They prosecuted their studies together in their earlier years, and entered into such a friendship as lasted to the end of their lives. Eudoxus, at his first setting out in the world, threw himself into a court, where by his natural endowments and his acquired abilities, he made his way from one post to another, till at length he had raised a very considerable fortune. Leontine, on the contrary, sought all opportunities of improving his mind by study, conversation, and travel. He was not only acquainted with all the sciences, but with the most eminent professors of them throughout Europe. He knew perfectly well the interests of its princes, with the customs and fashions of their courts, and could scarce meet with the name of an extraordinary person in the Gazette whom he had not either talked to or seen. In short, he had so well mixed and digested his knowledge of men and books, that he made one of the most accomplished persons of his age. During the whole course of his studies and travels he kept up a punctual correspondence with Eudoxus, who often made himself acceptable to the principal men about court, by the intelligence which he received from Leontine. When they were both turned of forty (an age in which, according to Mr. Cowley, "there is no dallying with life"), they determined, pursuant to the resolution they had taken in the beginning of their lives, to retire, and pass the remainder of their days in the country. In order to this, they both of them married much about the same time. Leontine, with his own and his wife's fortune, bought a farm of three hundred a year, which lay within the neighbourhood of his friend Eudoxus, who had purchased an estate of as many thousands. They were both of them fathers about the same time, Eudoxus having a son born to him, and Leontine a daughter; but to the unspeakable grief of the latter, his young wife (in whom all his happiness was wrapt up) died in a few days after the birth of her daughter. His affliction would have been insupportable, had not he been comforted by the daily visits and conversations of his friend. As they were one day talking together with their usual intimacy, Leontine, considering how incapable he was of giving his daughter a proper education in his own house, and Eudoxus reflecting on the ordinary behaviour of a son who knows himself to be the heir of a great estate, they both agreed upon an exchange of children, namely, that the boy should be bred up with Leontine as his son, and that the girl should live with Eudoxus as his daughter, till they were each of them arrived at years of discretion. The wife of Eudoxus, knowing that her son could not be so advantageously brought up as under the care of Leontine, and considering at the same time that he would be perpetually under her own eye, was by degrees prevailed upon to fall in with the project. She therefore took Leonilla, for that was the name of the girl, and educated her as her own daughter. The two friends on each side had wrought themselves to such an habitual tenderness for the children who were under their direction, that each of them had the real passion of a father, where the title was but imaginary. Florio, the name of the young heir that lived with Leontine, though he had all the duty and affection imaginable for his supposed parent, was taught to rejoice at the sight of Eudoxus, who visited his friend very frequently, and was dictated by his natural affection, as well as by the rules of prudence, to make himself esteemed and beloved by Florio. The boy was now old enough to know his supposed father's circumstances, and that therefore he was to make his way in the world by his own industry. This consideration grew stronger in him every day, and produced so good an effect, that he applied himself with more than ordinary attention to the pursuit of everything which Leontine recommended to him. His natural abilities, which were very good, assisted by the directions of so excellent a counselor, enabled him to make a quicker progress than ordinary through all the parts of his education.

Before he was twenty years of age, having finished his studies and exercises with great applause, he was removed from the university to the inns of court, where there are very few that make themselves considerable proficients in the studies of the place, who know they shall arrive at great estates without them. This was not Florio's case; he found that three hundred a year was but a poor estate for Leontine and himself to live upon, so that he studied without intermission till he gained a very good insight into the constitution and laws of his country.

I should have told my reader that, while Florio lived at the house of his foster-father, he was always an acceptable guest in the family of Eudoxus, where he became acquainted with Leonilla from her infancy. His acquaintance with her by degrees grew into love, which in a mind trained up in all the sentiments of honour and virtue became a very uneasy passion. He despaired of gaining an heiress of so great a fortune and would rather have died than attempted it by any indirect methods. Leonilla, who was a woman of the greatest beauty, joined with the greatest modesty, entertained at the same time a secret passion for Florio, but conducted herself with so much prudence that she never gave him the least intimation of it. Florio was now engaged in all those arts and improvements that are proper to raise a man's private fortune and give him a figure in his country, but secretly tormented with that passion which burns with the greatest fury in a virtuous and noble heart, when he received a sudden summons from Leontine to repair to him into the country the next day: for it seems Eudoxus was so filled with the report of his son's reputation, that he could no longer withhold making himself known to him. The morning after his arrival at the house of his supposed father, Leontine told him that Eudoxus had something of great importance to communicate to him; upon which the good man embraced him, and wept. Florio was no sooner arrived at the great house that stood in his neighbourhood, but Eudoxus took him by the hand, after the first salutes were over, and conducted him into his closet. He there opened to

him the whole secret of his parentage and education, concluding after this manner: "I have no other way left of acknowledging my gratitude to Leontine, than by marrying you to his
daughter. He shall not lose the pleasure of being your father
by the discovery I have made to you. Leonilla, too, shall be
still my daughter: her filial piety, though misplaced, has been
so exemplary that it deserves the greatest reward I can confer
upon it. You shall have the pleasure of seeing a great estate
fall to you, which you would have lost the relish of had you
known yourself born to it. Continue only to deserve it in the
same manner you did before you were possessed of it. I have
left your mother in the next room. Her heart yearns towards
you. She is making the same discoveries to Leonilla which I
have made to yourself." Florio was so overwhelmed with this
profusion of happiness that he was not able to make a reply,
but threw himself down at his father's feet, and, amidst a flood
of tears, kissed and embraced his knees, asking his blessing,
and expressing in dumb show those sentiments of love, duty,
and gratitude, that were too big for utterance. To conclude,
the happy pair were married, and half Eudoxus's estate settled
upon them. Leontine and Eudoxus passed the remainder of
their lives together, and received in the dutiful and affectionate
behaviour of Florio and Leonilla the just recompense, as well
as the natural effects, of that care which they had bestowed
upon them in their education. L [ADDISON]

THE VISION OF MIRZA

No. 159. Saturday, September 1, 1711

———*Omnem, quae nunc obducta tuenti*
Mortales hebetat visus tibi, et humida circum
Caligat, nubem eripiam ———. — VIRG.

When I was at Grand Cairo, I picked up several oriental
manuscripts, which I have still by me. Among others I met
with one entitled, *The Visions of Mirza*, which I have read

over with great pleasure. I intend to give it to the public when I have no other entertainment for them; and shall begin with the first vision, which I have translated word for word as follows:

On the fifth day of the moon, which according to the custom of my fore-fathers I always keep holy, after having washed myself, and offered up my morning devotions, I ascended the high hills of Bagdad, in order to pass the rest of the day in meditation and prayer. As I was here airing myself on the tops of the mountains, I fell into a profound contemplation on the van-ity of human life; and passing from one thought to another, "Surely," said I, "man is but a shadow, and life a dream." While I was thus musing, I cast my eyes towards the summit of a rock that was not far from me, where I discovered one in the habit of a shepherd, with a little musical instrument in his hand. As I looked upon him he applied it to his lips, and began to play upon it. The sound of it was exceeding sweet, and wrought into a va-riety of tunes that were inexpressibly melodious, and altogether different from anything I had ever heard. They put me in mind of those heavenly airs that are played to the departed souls of good men upon their first ar-rival in Paradise, to wear out the impressions of the last agonies, and qualify them for the pleasures of that happy place. My heart melted away in secret raptures.

I had been often told that the rock before me was the haunt of a genius; and that several had been entertained with music who had passed by it, but never heard that the musician had before made himself visible. When he had raised my thoughts by those transporting airs which he played, to taste the pleasures of his conversation, as I looked upon him like one astonished, he beckoned to me, and by the waving of his hand directed me to approach the place where he sat. I drew near with that reverence which is due to a superior nature; and as my heart was entirely subdued by the captivating strains I had heard, I fell down at his feet and wept. The genius smiled upon me with a look of compassion and affability that familiarized him to my imagination, and at once dispelled all the fears and apprehensions with which I approached him. He lifted me from the ground, and taking me by the hand, "Mirza," said he, "I have heard thee in thy soliloquies; follow me."

He then led me to the highest pinnacle of the rock, and placing me on the top of it — "Cast thy eyes eastward," said he, "and tell me what thou seest." "I see," said I, "a huge valley, and a prodigious tide of water roll-ing through it." — "The valley that thou seest," said he, "is the Vale of Misery, and the tide of water that thou seest is part of the great tide of eter-nity." — "What is the reason," said I, "that the tide I see rises out of a

thick mist at one end, and again loses itself in a thick mist at the other?"
—"What thou seest," said he, "is that portion of eternity which is called
time, measured out by the sun, and reaching from the beginning of the
world to its consummation." "Examine now," said he, "this sea that is
bounded with darkness at both ends, and tell me what thou discoverest in
it."—"I see a bridge," said I, "standing in the midst of the tide."—
"The bridge thou seest," said he, "is human life; consider it attentively."
Upon a more leisurely survey of it, I found that it consisted of threescore
and ten entire arches, with several broken arches, which, added to those that
were entire, made up the number about a hundred. As I was counting the
arches, the genius told me that this bridge consisted at first of a thousand
arches: but that a great flood swept away the rest, and left the bridge in the
ruinous condition I now beheld it. "But tell me further," said he, "what
thou discoverest on it."—"I see multitudes of people passing over it,"
said I, "and a black cloud hanging on each end of it." As I looked more
attentively, I saw several of the passengers dropping through the bridge
into the great tide that flowed underneath it: and, upon farther examination, perceived there were innumerable trap-doors that lay concealed
in the bridge, which the passengers no sooner trod upon, but they fell
through them into the tide, and immediately disappeared. These hidden
pitfalls were set very thick at the entrance of the bridge, so that throngs
of people no sooner broke through the cloud, but many of them fell into
them. They grew thinner toward the middle, but multiplied and lay closer
together toward the end of the arches that were entire.

There were indeed some persons, but their number was very small, that
continued a kind of hobbling march on the broken arches, but fell through
one after another, being quite tired and spent with so long a walk.

I passed some time in the contemplation of this wonderful structure, and
the great variety of objects which it presented. My heart was filled with a
deep melancholy to see several dropping unexpectedly in the midst of mirth
and jollity, and catching at everything that stood by them to save themselves.
Some were looking up toward the heavens in a thoughtful posture, and in
the midst of a speculation stumbled and fell out of sight. Multitudes were
very busy in the pursuit of bubbles that glittered in their eyes and danced
before them; but often when they thought themselves within the reach of
them, their footing failed, and down they sank. In this confusion of objects, I observed some with scimitars in their hands, and others with urinals,
who ran to and fro upon the bridge, thrusting several persons on trap-doors
which did not seem to lie in their way, and which they might have escaped
had they not been thus forced upon them.

The genius seeing me indulge myself in this melancholy prospect, told
me I had dwelt long enough upon it. "Take thine eyes off the bridge,"
said he, "and tell me if thou yet seest anything thou dost not comprehend."

Upon looking up, " What mean," said I, " those great flights of birds that are perpetually hovering about the bridge, and settling upon it from time to time? I see vultures, harpies, ravens, cormorants, and among many other feathered creatures several little winged boys, that perch in great numbers upon the middle arches." — " These," said the genius, " are Envy, Avarice, Superstition, Despair, Love, with the like cares and passions that infest human life."

I here fetched a deep sigh. " Alas," said I, " man was made in vain! how is he given away to misery and mortality! tortured in life, and swallowed up in death!" The genius, being moved with compassion toward me, bid me quit so uncomfortable a prospect. " Look no more," said he, " on man in the first stage of his existence, in his setting out for eternity; but cast thine eye on that thick mist into which the tide bears the several generations of mortals that fall into it." I directed my sight as I was ordered, and (whether or no the good genius strengthened it with any supernatural force, or dissipated part of the mist that was before too thick for the eye to penetrate) I saw the valley opening at the farther end, and spreading forth into an immense ocean, that had a huge rock of adamant running through the midst of it, and dividing it into two equal parts. The clouds still rested on one half of it, insomuch that I could discover nothing in it: but the other appeared to me a vast ocean planted with innumerable islands, that were covered with fruits and flowers, and interwoven with a thousand little shining seas that ran among them. I could see persons dressed in glorious habits, with garlands upon their heads, passing among the trees, lying down by the sides of fountains, or resting on beds of flowers; and could hear a confused harmony of singing birds, falling waters, human voices, and musical instruments. Gladness grew in me upon the discovery of so delightful a scene. I wished for the wings of an eagle, that I might fly away to those happy seats: but the genius told me there was no passage to them, except through the gates of death that I saw opening every moment upon the bridge. " The islands," said he, " that lie so fresh and green before thee, and with which the whole face of the ocean appears spotted as far as thou canst see, are more in number than the sands on the sea-shore; there are myriads of islands behind those which thou here discoverest, reaching further than thine eye, or even thine imagination can extend itself. These are the mansions of good men after death, who, according to the degree and kinds of virtue in which they excelled, are distributed among these several islands; which abound with pleasures of different kinds and degrees, suitable to the relishes and perfections of those who are settled in them; every island is a paradise accommodated to its respective inhabitants. Are not these, O Mirza, habitations worth contending for? Does life appear miserable, that gives thee opportunities of earning such a reward? Is death to be feared, that will convey thee to so happy an existence? Think not man was made in vain, who has such an eternity reserved for him." I gazed with inexpressible pleasure on these happy islands. "At length," said I, "show me now, I beseech thee, the secrets that lie hid under those dark clouds which cover the ocean on the other side of the rock of adamant." The genius making me no answer, I turned about to address myself to him a second time, but I found that he had left me: I then turned again to the vision which I had been so long contemplating; but instead of the rolling tide, the arched bridge, and the happy islands, I saw nothing but the long, hollow valley of Bagdad, with oxen, sheep, and camels, grazing upon the sides of it.

The End of the First Vision of Mirza.

C [ADDISON]

A COQUETTE'S HEART

No. 281. Tuesday, January 22, 1712

Pectoribus inhians spirantia consulit exta. — VIRG.

Having already given an account of the dissection of the beau's head, with the several discoveries made on that occasion; I shall here, according to my promise, enter upon the dissection of a coquette's heart, and communicate to the public such particularities as we observed in that curious piece of anatomy.

I should perhaps have waived this undertaking, had not I been put in mind of my promise by several of my unknown correspondents, who are very importunate with me to make an example of the coquette, as I have already done of the beau. It is therefore in compliance with the request of my friends, that I have looked over the minutes of my former dream, in order to give the public an exact relation of it, which I shall enter upon without further preface.

Our operator, before he engaged in this visionary dissection, told us that there was nothing in his art more difficult than to lay open the heart of a coquette, by reason of the many labyrinths and recesses which are to be found in it, and which do not appear in the heart of any other animal.

He desired us first of all to observe the pericardium, or outward case of the heart, which we did very attentively; and by the help of our glasses discerned in it millions of little scars, which seemed to have been occasioned by the points of innumerable darts and arrows, that from time to time had glanced upon the outward coat; though we could not discover the smallest orifice, by which any of them had entered and pierced the inward substance.

Every smatterer in anatomy knows that this pericardium, or case of the heart, contains in it a thin reddish liquor, supposed to be bred from the vapours which exhale out of the heart, and being stopped here, are condensed into this watery substance. Upon examining this liquor, we found that it had in it all the qualities of that spirit which is made use of in the thermometer, to show the change of weather.

Nor must I here omit an experiment one of the company assured us he himself had made with this liquor, which he found in great quantity about the heart of a coquette whom he had formerly dissected. He affirmed to us that he had actually inclosed it in a small tube made after the manner of a weather-glass; but that instead of acquainting him with the variations of the atmosphere, it showed him the qualities of those persons who entered the room where it stood. He affirmed also that it rose at the approach of a plume of feathers, an embroidered coat, or a pair of fringed gloves; and that it fell as soon as an ill-shaped periwig, a clumsy pair of shoes, or an unfashionable coat came into his house. Nay, he proceeded so far as to assure us that upon his laughing aloud when he stood by it, the liquor mounted very sensibly, and immediately sunk again upon his looking serious. In short, he told us that he knew very well, by this invention, whenever he had a man of sense or a coxcomb in his room.

Having cleared away the pericardium, or the case, and liquor above-mentioned, we came to the heart itself. The outward surface of it was extremely slippery, and the mucro, or point, so very cold withal, that upon endeavouring to take hold of it, it glided through the fingers like a smooth piece of ice.

The fibers were turned and twisted in a more intricate and perplexed manner than they are usually found in other hearts; insomuch that the whole heart was wound up together in a Gordian knot, and must have had very irregular and unequal motions, while it was employed in its vital function.

One thing we thought very observable, namely, that upon examining all the vessels which came into it, or issued out of it, we could not discover any communication that it had with the tongue.

We could not but take notice likewise, that several of those little nerves in the heart which are affected by the sentiments of love, hatred, and other passions, did not descend to this before us from the brain, but from the muscles which lie about the eye.

Upon weighing the heart in my hand, I found it to be extremely light, and consequently very hollow, which I did not wonder at, when, upon looking into the inside of it, I saw multitudes of cells and cavities, running one within another, as our historians describe the apartments of Rosamond's bower. Several of these little hollows were stuffed with innumerable sorts of trifles, which I shall forbear giving any particular account of, and shall therefore only take notice of what lay first and uppermost, which upon our unfolding it, and applying our microscope to it, appeared to be a flame-coloured hood.

We were informed that the lady of this heart, when living, received the addresses of several who made love to her, and did not only give each of them encouragement, but made every one she conversed with believe that she regarded him with an eye of kindness; for which reason we expected to have seen the impressions of multitudes of faces among the several plaits and foldings of the heart; but to our great surprise not a single print of this nature discovered itself till we came into the very core and center of it. We there observed a little figure, which, upon applying our glasses to it, appeared dressed in a very fantastic manner. The more I looked upon it, the more I thought I had seen the face before, but could not possibly recollect either the place or time ; when at length, one of the company, who had examined this figure more nicely than the rest, showed us plainly by the make of its face, and the several turns of its features, that the little idol that was thus lodged in the very middle of the heart was the deceased beau, whose head I gave some account of in my last Tuesday's paper.

As soon as we had finished our dissection, we resolved to make an experiment of the heart, not being able to determine among ourselves the nature of its substance, which differed in so many particulars from that of the heart in other females. Accordingly we laid it in a pan of burning coals, when we observed in it a certain salamandrine quality, that made it capable of living in the midst of fire and flame, without being consumed, or so much as singed.

As we were admiring this strange phenomenon, and standing round the heart in a circle, it gave a most prodigious sigh, or rather crack, and dispersed all at once in smoke and vapour. This imaginary noise, which, methought, was louder than the burst of a cannon, produced such a violent shake in my brain, that it dissipated the fumes of sleep and left me in an instant broad awake. L [ADDISON]

CLARINDA'S JOURNAL

No. 323. Tuesday, March 11, 1712

———— *Modo vir, modo femina* ————. — OVID.

The journal with which I presented my reader on Tuesday last, has brought me in several letters with account of many private lives cast into that form. I have the *Rake's Journal*, the *Sot's Journal*, the *Whoremaster's Journal*, and among several others, a very curious piece, entitled *The Journal of a Mohock*. By these instances, I find that the intention of my last Tuesday's paper has been mistaken by many of my readers. I did not design so much to expose vice, as idleness, and aimed at those persons who pass away their time rather in trifle and impertinence, than in crimes and immoralities. Offenses of this latter kind are not to be dallied with, or treated in so ludicrous a manner. In short, my journal only holds up folly to the light, and shows the disagreeableness of such actions as are indifferent in themselves, and blamable only as they proceed from creatures endowed with reason.

My following correspondent, who calls herself Clarinda, is such a journalist as I require. She seems by her letter to be placed in a modish state of indifference between vice and virtue, and to be susceptible of either, were there proper pains taken with her. Had her journal been filled with gallantries, or such occurrences as had shown her wholly divested of her natural innocence, notwithstanding it might have been more pleasing to the generality of readers, I should not have published it : but as it is only the picture of a life filled with a fashionable kind of gayety and laziness, I shall set down five days of it, as I have received it from the hand of my fair correspondent.

Dear Mr. Spectator,

You having set your readers an exercise in one of your last week's papers, I have performed mine according to your orders, and herewith send it you inclosed. You must know, Mr. Spectator, that I am a maiden lady of a good fortune, who have had several good matches offered me for these ten years last past, and have at present warm applications made to me by " A Very Pretty Fellow." As I am at my own disposal, I come up to town every winter, and pass my time in it after the manner you will find in the following journal, which I began to write upon the very day after your *Spectator* upon that subject.

"*Tuesday* night. Could not go to sleep till one in the morning for thinking of my journal.

"*Wednesday*. From eight till ten. Drank two dishes of chocolate in bed, and fell asleep after them.

"From ten to eleven. Ate a slice of bread and butter, drank a dish of bohea, and read the *Spectator*.

"From eleven to one. At my toilette, tried a new head. Gave orders for Veny to be combed and washed. Mem. I look best in blue.

"From one till half an hour after two. Drove to the 'Change. Cheapened a couple of fans.

"Till four. At dinner. Mem. Mr. Froth passed by in his new liveries.

"From four to six. Dressed; paid a visit to old Lady Blithe and her sister, having before heard they were gone out of town that day.

"From six to eleven. At basset. Mem. Never set again upon the ace of diamonds.

"*Thursday*. From eleven at night to eight in the morning. Dreamed that I punted to Mr. Froth.

"From eight to ten. Chocolate. Read two acts in *Aurengzebe* a-bed.

"From ten to eleven. Tea-table. Sent to borrow Lady Faddle's Cupid for Veny. Read the play-bills. Received a letter from Mr. Froth. Mem. Locked it up in my strong box.

"Rest of the morning. Fontange, the tire-woman, her account of my lady Blithe's wash. Broke a tooth in my little tortoise-shell comb. Sent Frank to know how my Lady Hectic rested after her monkey's leaping out at window. Looked pale. Fontange tells me my glass is not true. Dressed by three.

"From three to four. Dinner cold before I sat down.

"From four to eleven. Saw company. Mr. Froth's opinion of Milton. His account of the Mohocks. His fancy of a pincushion. Picture in the lid of his snuff-box. Old Lady Faddle promises me her woman to cut my hair. Lost five guineas at crimp.

"Twelve o'clock at night. Went to bed.

"*Friday*. Eight in the morning. A-bed. Read over all Mr. Froth's letters. Cupid and Veny.

"Ten o'clock. Stayed within all day, not at home.

"From ten to twelve. In conference with my mantuamaker. Sorted a suit of ribbons. Broke my blue china cup.

"From twelve to one. Shut myself up in my chamber, practiced Lady Betty Modley's skuttle.

"One in the afternoon. Called for my flowered handkerchief. Worked half a violet leaf in it. Eyes ached and head out of order. Threw by my work, and read over the remaining part of *Aurengzebe*.

"From three to four. Dined.

"From four to twelve. Changed my mind, dressed, went abroad, and played at crimp till midnight. Found Mrs. Spitely at home. Conversation. Mrs. Brilliant's necklace false stones. Old Lady Loveday going to be married to a young fellow that is not worth a groat. Miss Prue gone into the country. Tom Townley has red hair. Mem. Mrs. Spitely whispered in my ear that she had something to tell me about Mr. Froth; I am sure it is not true.

"Between twelve and one. Dreamed that Mr. Froth lay at my feet, and called me Indamora.

"*Saturday*. Rose at eight o'clock in the morning. Sat down to my toilette.

" From eight to nine. Shifted a patch for half an hour before I could determine it. Fixed it above my left eyebrow.

" From nine to twelve. Drank my tea and dressed.

" From twelve to two. At chapel. A great deal of good company. Mem. The third air in the new opera. Lady Blithe dressed frightfully.

" From three to four. Dined. Miss Kitty called upon me to go to the opera before I was risen from table.

" From dinner to six. Drank tea. Turned off a footman for being rude to Veny.

" Six o'clock. Went to the opera. I did not see Mr. Froth till the beginning of the second act. Mr. Froth talked to a gentleman in a black wig. Bowed to a lady in the front box. Mr. Froth and his friend clapped Nicolini in the third act. Mr. Froth cried out ' Ancora.' Mr. Froth led me to my chair. I think he squeezed my hand.

" Eleven at night. Went to bed. Melancholy dreams. Methought Nicolini said he was Mr. Froth.

" *Sunday*. Indisposed.

" *Monday*. Eight o'clock. Waked by Miss Kitty. *Aurengzebe* lay upon the chair by me. Kitty repeated without book the eight best lines in the play. Went in our mobs to the dumb man, according to appointment. Told me that my lover's name began with a G. Mem. The conjurer was within a letter of Mr. Froth's name, etc."

Upon looking back into this my journal, I find that I am at a loss to know whether I pass my time well or ill; and indeed never thought of considering how I did it before I perused your speculation upon that subject. I scarce find a single action in these five days that I can thoroughly approve of, except in the working upon the violet leaf, which I am resolved to finish the first day I am at leisure. As for Mr. Froth and Veny, I did not think they took up so much of my time and thoughts as I find they do upon my journal. The latter of them I will turn off, if you insist upon it; and if Mr. Froth does not bring matters to a conclusion very suddenly, I will not let my life run away in a dream.

Your humble Servant,
Clarinda.

To resume one of the morals of my first paper, and to confirm Clarinda in her good inclinations, I would have her consider what a pretty figure she would make among posterity, were the history of her whole life published like these five days of it. I shall conclude my paper with an epitaph written by an uncertain author on Sir Philip Sidney's sister, a lady who seems to have been of a temper very much different from that of Clarinda. The last thought of it is so very noble, that I dare say my reader will pardon me the quotation.

ON THE COUNTESS DOWAGER OF PEMBROKE

> Underneath this marble hearse
> Lies the subject of all verse,
> Sidney's sister, Pembroke's mother;
> Death, ere thou hast kill'd another,
> Fair and learn'd, and good as she,
> Time shall throw a dart at thee.   L

[ADDISON]

CHEERFULNESS

No. 381. Saturday, May 17, 1712

Aequam memento rebus in arduis
Servare mentem, non secus in bonis,
Ab insolenti temperatam
Laetitia, moriture Deli. — HOR.

I have always preferred cheerfulness to mirth. The latter I consider as an act, the former as a habit of the mind. Mirth is short and transient, cheerfulness fixed and permanent. Those are often raised into the greatest transports of mirth, who are subject to the greatest depressions of melancholy. On the contrary, cheerfulness, though it does not give the mind such an exquisite gladness, prevents us from falling into any depths of sorrow. Mirth is like a flash of lightning, that breaks through a gloom of clouds and glitters for a moment; cheerfulness keeps up a kind of daylight in the mind, and fills it with a steady and perpetual serenity.

Men of austere principles look upon mirth as too wanton and dissolute for a state of probation, and as filled with a certain triumph and insolence of heart that is inconsistent with a life which is every moment obnoxious to the greatest

dangers. Writers of this complexion have observed that the
Sacred Person who was the great pattern of perfection was
never seen to laugh.

Cheerfulness of mind is not liable to any of these exceptions; it is of a serious and composed nature; it does not
throw the mind into a condition improper for the present
state of humanity, and is very conspicuous in the characters
of those who are looked upon as the greatest philosophers
among the heathens, as well as among those who have been
deservedly esteemed as saints and holy men among Christians.

If we consider cheerfulness in three lights, with regard to
ourselves, to those we converse with, and to the great Author
of our being, it will not a little recommend itself on each of
these accounts. The man who is possessed of this excellent
frame of mind is not only easy in his thoughts, but a perfect
master of all the powers and faculties of his soul. His imagination is always clear, and his judgment undisturbed; his
temper is even and unruffled, whether in action or in solitude.
He comes with relish to all those goods which nature has provided for him, tastes all the pleasures of the creation which
are poured about him, and does not feel the full weight of
those accidental evils which may befall him.

If we consider him in relation to the persons whom he
converses with, it naturally produces love and good-will towards
him. A cheerful mind is not only disposed to be affable and
obliging, but raises the same good humour in those who come
within its influence. A man finds himself pleased, he does
not know why, with the cheerfulness of his companion. It is
like a sudden sunshine that awakens a secret delight in the
mind, without her attending to it. The heart rejoices of its
own accord, and naturally flows out into friendship and benevolence toward the person who has so kindly an effect upon it.

When I consider this cheerful state of mind in its third
relation, I cannot but look upon it as a constant habitual gratitude to the great Author of nature. An inward cheerfulness
is an implicit praise and thanksgiving to Providence under all

its dispensations. It is a kind of acquiescence in the state wherein we are placed, and a secret approbation of the Divine Will in his conduct toward man.

There are but two things which, in my opinion, can reasonably deprive us of this cheerfulness of heart. The first of these is the sense of guilt. A man who lives in a state of vice and impenitence can have no title to that evenness and tranquillity of mind which is the health of the soul, and the natural effect of virtue and innocence. Cheerfulness in an ill man deserves a harder name than language can furnish us with, and is many degrees beyond what we commonly call folly or madness.

Atheism, by which I mean a disbelief of a Supreme Being, and consequently of a future state, under whatsoever titles it shelters itself, may likewise very reasonably deprive a man of this cheerfulness of temper. There is something so particularly gloomy and offensive to human nature in the prospect of non-existence, that I cannot but wonder, with many excellent writers, how it is possible for a man to outlive the expectation of it. For my own part, I think the being of a God is so little to be doubted, that it is almost the only truth we are sure of ; and such a truth as we meet with in every object, in every occurrence, and in every thought. If we look into the characters of this tribe of infidels, we generally find they are made up of pride, spleen, and cavil. It is indeed no wonder that men who are uneasy to themselves should be so to the rest of the world ; and how is it possible for a man to be otherwise than uneasy in himself, who is in danger every moment of losing his entire existence, and dropping into nothing ?

The vicious man and atheist have therefore no pretense to cheerfulness, and would act very unreasonably should they endeavour after it. It is impossible for any one to live in good-humour, and enjoy his present existence, who is apprehensive either of torment or of annihilation, of being miserable, or of not being at all.

After having mentioned these two great principles, which are destructive of cheerfulness in their own nature, as well as in right reason, I cannot think of any other that ought to banish this happy temper from a virtuous mind. Pain and sickness, shame and reproach, poverty and old age, nay death itself, considering the shortness of their duration, and the advantage we may reap from them, do not deserve the name of evils. A good mind may bear up under them with fortitude, with indolence, and with cheerfulness of heart. The tossing of a tempest does not discompose him, which he is sure will bring him to a joyful harbour.

A man who uses his best endeavours to live according to the dictates of virtue and right reason, has two perpetual sources of cheerfulness, in the consideration of his own nature, and of that Being on whom he has a dependence. If he looks into himself, he cannot but rejoice in that existence which is so lately bestowed upon him, and which after millions of ages will be still new and still in its beginning. How many self-congratulations naturally arise in the mind, when it reflects on this its entrance into eternity, when it takes a view of those improvable faculties, which in a few years, and even at its first setting out, have made so considerable a progress, and which will still be receiving an increase of perfection, and consequently an increase of happiness. The consciousness of such a being spreads a perpetual diffusion of joy through the soul of a virtuous man, and makes him look upon himself every moment as more happy than he knows how to conceive.

The second source of cheerfulness to a good mind is its consideration of that Being on whom we have our dependence, and in whom, though we behold him as yet but in the first faint discoveries of his perfections, we see everything that we can imagine, as great, glorious, or amiable. We find ourselves everywhere upheld by his goodness, and surrounded with an immensity of love and mercy. In short, we depend upon a Being whose power qualifies him to make us happy by an infinity of means, whose goodness and truth engage him to

make those happy who desire it of him, and whose unchange-
ableness will secure us in this happiness to all eternity.

Such considerations, which every one should perpetually
cherish in his thoughts, will banish from us all that secret
heaviness of heart which unthinking men are subject to when
they lie under no real affliction, all that anguish which we may
feel from any evil that actually oppresses us, to which I may
likewise add those little cracklings of mirth and folly that are
apter to betray virtue than support it; and establish in us such
an even and cheerful temper, as makes us pleasing to ourselves, to those with whom we converse, and to Him whom
we were made to please. I [ADDISON]

LITERARY TASTE

No. 409. Thursday, June 19, 1712

——— *Musæo contingens cuncta lepore.* — LUCR.

Gratian very often recommends "the fine taste" as the
utmost perfection of an accomplished man. As this word
arises very often in conversation, I shall endeavour to give
some account of it, and to lay down rules how we may know
whether we are possessed of it, and how we may acquire that
fine taste of writing which is so much talked of among the
polite world.

Most languages make use of this metaphor, to express that
faculty of the mind which distinguishes all the most concealed
faults and nicest perfections in writing. We may be sure this
metaphor would not have been so general in all tongues, had
there not been a very great conformity between that mental
taste, which is the subject of this paper, and that sensitive
taste, which gives us a relish of every different flavour that
affects the palate. Accordingly we find there are as many
degrees of refinement in the intellectual faculty as in the sense
which is marked out by this common denomination.

I knew a person who possessed the one in so great a perfection, that, after having tasted ten different kinds of tea, he would distinguish, without seeing the colour of it, the particular sort which was offered him; and not only so, but any two sorts of them that were mixed together in an equal proportion; nay, he has carried the experiment so far, as, upon tasting the composition of three different sorts, to name the parcels from whence the three several ingredients were taken. A man of a fine taste in writing will discern, after the same manner, not only the general beauties and imperfections of an author, but discover the several ways of thinking and expressing himself, which diversify him from all other authors, with the several foreign infusions of thought and language, and the particular authors from whom they were borrowed.

After having thus far explained what is generally meant by a fine taste in writing, and shown the propriety of the metaphor which is used on this occasion, I think I may define it to be " that faculty of the soul, which discerns the beauties of an author with pleasure, and the imperfections with dislike." If a man would know whether he is possessed of this faculty, I would have him read over the celebrated works of antiquity, which have stood the test of so many different ages and countries, or those works among the moderns which have the sanction of the politer part of our contemporaries. If, upon the perusal of such writings, he does not find himself delighted in an extraordinary manner, or if, upon reading the admired passages in such authors, he finds a coldness and indifference in his thoughts, he ought to conclude, not (as is too usual among tasteless readers) that the author wants those perfections which have been admired in him, but that he himself wants the faculty of discovering them.

He should, in the second place, be very careful to observe whether he tastes the distinguishing perfections, or, if I may be allowed to call them so, the specific qualities of the author whom he peruses; whether he is particularly pleased with Livy for his manner of telling a story, with Sallust for his entering into those internal principles of action which arise from the characters and manners of the persons he describes, or with Tacitus for displaying those outward motives of safety and interest which give birth to the whole series of transactions which he relates.

He may likewise consider how differently he is affected by the same thought which presents itself in a great writer, from what he is when he finds it delivered by a person of an ordinary genius; for there is as much difference in apprehending a thought clothed in Cicero's language, and that of a common author, as in seeing an object by the light of a taper, or by the light of the sun.

It is very difficult to lay down rules for the acquirement of such a taste as that I am here speaking of. The faculty must, in some degree, be born with us; and it very often happens that those who have other qualities in perfection are wholly void of this. One of the most eminent mathematicians of the age has assured me that the greatest pleasure he took in reading Virgil was in examining Æneas's voyage by the map; as I question not but many a modern compiler of history would be delighted with little more in that divine author than the bare matters of fact.

But, notwithstanding this faculty must in some measure be born with us, there are several methods for cultivating and improving it, and without which it will be very uncertain, and of little use to the person that possesses it. The most natural method for this purpose is to be conversant among the writings of the most polite authors. A man who has any relish for fine writing either discovers new beauties, or receives stronger impressions, from the masterly strokes of a great author, every time he peruses him; beside that he naturally wears himself into the same manner of speaking and thinking.

Conversation with men of a polite genius is another method for improving our natural taste. It is impossible for a man of the greatest parts to consider anything in its whole extent, and in all its variety of lights. Every man, beside those general observations which are to be made upon an author, forms several reflections that are peculiar to his own manner of thinking; so that conversation will naturally furnish us with hints which we did not attend to, and make us enjoy other men's parts and reflections as well as our own. This is the best reason I can give for the observation which several have made, that men of great genius in the same way of writing seldom rise up singly, but at certain periods of time appear together, and in a body; as they did at Rome in the reign of Augustus, and in Greece about the age of Socrates. I cannot think that Corneille, Racine, Molière, Boileau, La Fontaine, Bruyère, Bossu, or the Daciers, would have written so well as they have done, had they not been friends and contemporaries.

It is likewise necessary for a man who would form to himself a finished taste of good writing to be well versed in the works of the best critics, both ancient and modern. I must confess that I could wish there were authors of this kind, who beside the mechanical rules, which a man of very little taste may discourse upon, would enter into the very spirit and soul of fine writing, and show us the several sources of that pleasure which rises in the mind upon the perusal of a noble work. Thus, although in poetry it be absolutely necessary that the unities of time, place, and action, with other points of the same nature, should be thoroughly explained and understood, there is still something more essential to the art, something that elevates and astonishes the fancy, and gives a greatness of mind to the reader, which few of the critics beside Longinus have considered.

Our general taste in England is for epigram, turns of wit, and forced conceits, which have no manner of influence either for the bettering or enlarging the mind of him who reads them, and have been carefully avoided by the greatest writers both among the ancients and moderns. I have endeavoured, in several of my speculations, to banish this Gothic taste which has taken possession among us. I entertained the town for a week together with an essay upon wit, in which I endeavoured to detect several of those false kinds which have been admired in the different ages of the world, and at the same time to show wherein the nature of true wit consists. I afterward gave an instance of the great force which lies in a natural simplicity of thought to affect the mind of the reader, from such vulgar pieces as have little else beside this single qualification to recommend them. I have likewise examined the works of the greatest poet which our nation, or perhaps any other has produced, and particularized most of those rational and manly beauties which give a value to that divine work. I shall next Saturday enter upon an essay on " The Pleasures of the Imagination," which, though it shall consider that subject at large, will perhaps suggest to the reader what it is that gives a beauty to many passages of the finest writers both in prose and verse. As an undertaking of this nature is entirely new, I question not but it will be received with candour. O [ADDISON]

ON RAILLERY

No. 422. Friday, July 4, 1712

Haec . . . scripsi . . . non otii abundantia sed amoris erga te. — TULL. EPIS.

I do not know anything which gives greater disturbance to conversation than the false notion some people have of raillery. It ought, certainly, to be the first point to be aimed at in society, to gain the good-will of those with whom you converse ; the way to that is to show you are well inclined toward them. What then can be more absurd than to set up for being extremely sharp and biting, as the term is, in your expressions to your familiars ? A man who has no good quality but courage is in a very ill way toward making an agreeable figure in the world, because that which he has superior to other people cannot be exerted without raising himself an enemy. Your gentleman of a satirical vein is in the like condition. To say a thing which perplexes the heart of him you speak to, or brings blushes into his face, is a degree of murder; and it is, I think, an unpardonable offense to show a man you do not care whether he is pleased or displeased. But won't you then take a jest? — Yes: but pray let it be a jest. It is no jest to put me, who am so unhappy as to have an utter aversion to speaking to more than one man at a time, under a necessity to explain myself in much company, and reducing me to shame and derision, except I perform what my infirmity of silence disables me to do.

Calisthenes has great wit, accompanied with that quality without which a man can have no wit at all — a sound judgment. This gentleman rallies the best of any man I know; for he forms his ridicule upon a circumstance which you are, in your heart, not unwilling to grant him; to wit, that you are guilty of an excess in something which is in itself laudable. He very well understands what you would be, and needs not fear your anger for declaring you are a little too much that thing. The generous will bear being reproached as lavish, and the valiant rash, without being provoked to resentment against their monitor. What has been said to be a mark of a good writer will fall in with the character of a good companion. The good writer makes his reader better pleased with himself, and the agreeable man makes his friends enjoy themselves, rather than him, while he is in their company. Calisthenes does this with inimitable pleasantry. He whispered a friend the other day, so as to be overheard by a young officer who gave symptoms of cocking upon the company, "That gentleman has very much of the air of a general officer." The youth immediately put on a composed behaviour, and behaved himself suitably to the conceptions he believed the company had of him. It is to be allowed that Calisthenes will make a man run into impertinent relations to his own advantage, and express the satisfaction he has in his own dear self, till he is very ridiculous; but in this case the man is made a fool by his own consent, and not exposed as such whether he will or no. I take it, therefore, that to make raillery agreeable, a man must either not know he is rallied, or think never the worse of himself if he sees he is.

Acetus is of a quite contrary genius, and is more generally admired than Calisthenes, but not with justice. Acetus has no regard to the modesty or weakness of the person he rallies; but if his quality or humility gives him any superiority to the man he would fall upon, he has no mercy in making the onset. He can be pleased to see his best friend out of countenance, while the laugh is loud in his own applause. His raillery always puts the company into little divisions and separate interests, while that of Calisthenes cements it, and makes every man not only better pleased with himself, but also with all the rest in the conversation.

To rally well, it is absolutely necessary that kindness must run through all you say; and you must ever preserve the character of a friend to support your pretensions to be free with a man. Acetus ought to be banished human society, because he raises his mirth upon giving pain to the person upon whom he is pleasant. Nothing but the malevolence which is too general toward those who excel could make his company tolerated; but they with whom he converses are sure to see some man sacrificed wherever he is admitted; and all the credit he has for wit, is owing to the gratification it gives to other men's ill-nature.

Minutius has a wit that conciliates a man's love, at the same time that it is exerted against his faults. He has an art in keeping the person he rallies in countenance, by insinuating that he himself is guilty of the same imperfection. This he does with so much address that he seems rather to bewail himself, than fall upon his friend.

It is really monstrous to see how unaccountably it prevails among men to take the liberty of displeasing each other. One would think sometimes that the contention is who shall be most disagreeable. Allusions to past follies, hints which revive what a man has a mind to forget forever, and deserves that all the rest of the world should, are commonly brought forth

even in company of men of distinction. They do not thrust
with the skill of fencers, but cut up with the barbarity of
butchers. It is, methinks, below the character of men of
humanity and good-manners to be capable of mirth while there
is any one of the company in pain and disorder. They who
have the true taste of conversation enjoy themselves in a communication of each other's excellencies, and not in a triumph
over their imperfections. Fortius would have been reckoned
a wit if there had never been a fool in the world ; he wants
not foils to be a beauty, but has that natural pleasure in observing perfection in others, that his own faults are overlooked,
out of gratitude, by all his acquaintance.

After these several characters of men who succeed or fail
in raillery, it may not be amiss to reflect a little further what
one takes to be the most agreeable kind of it ; and that to
me appears when the satire is directed against vice, with an
air of contempt of the fault, but no ill-will to the criminal.
Mr. Congreve's Doris is a masterpiece in this kind. It is the
character of a woman utterly abandoned ; but her impudence,
by the finest piece of raillery, is made only generosity :

> Peculiar therefore is her way,
>   Whether by nature taught,
> I shall not undertake to say,
>   Or by experience bought ;
>
> But who o'ernight obtain'd her grace
>   She can next day disown,
> And stare upon the strange man's face,
>   As one she ne'er had known.
>
> So well she can the truth disguise,
>   Such artful wonder frame,
> The lover or distrusts his eyes,
>   Or thinks 't was all a dream.
>
> Some censure this as lewd or low,
>   Who are to bounty blind ;
> But to forget what we bestow
>   Bespeaks a noble mind.

[STEELE]

T

ON GARDENS

No. 477. Saturday, September 6, 1712

―――― *An me ludit amabilis*
Insania ? Audire et videor pios
Errare per lucos amœnæ
Quos et aquæ subeunt et auræ. — Hor.

Sir,

Having lately read your essay on "The Pleasures of the Imagination," I was so taken with your thoughts upon some of our English gardens that I cannot forbear troubling you with a letter upon that subject. I am one, you must know, who am looked upon as a humorist in gardening. I have several acres about my house, which I call my garden, and which a skillful gardener would not know what to call. It is a confusion of kitchen and parterre, orchard and flower garden, which lie so mixed and interwoven with one another that if a foreigner who had seen nothing of our country should be conveyed into my garden at his first landing, he would look upon it as a natural wilderness, and one of the uncultivated parts of our country. My flowers grow up in several parts of the garden in the greatest luxuriancy and profusion. I am so far from being fond of any particular one, by reason of its rarity, that if I meet with any one in a field which pleases me, I give it a place in my garden. By this means, when a stranger walks with me, he is surprised to see several large spots of ground covered with ten thousand different colours, and has often singled out flowers that he might have met with under a common hedge, in a field, or in a meadow, as some of the greatest beauties of the place. The only method I observe in this particular is to range in the same quarter the products of the same season, that they may make their appearance together, and compose a picture of the greatest variety. There is the same irregularity in my plantations, which run into as great a wildness as their natures will permit. I take in none that do not naturally rejoice in the soil ; and am pleased, when I am walking in a labyrinth of my own raising, not to know whether the next tree I shall meet with is an apple or an oak, an elm or a pear-tree. My kitchen has likewise its particular quarters assigned it ; for beside the wholesome luxury which that place abounds with, I have always thought a kitchen-garden a more pleasant sight than the finest orangery, or arti-ficial green-house. I love to see everything in its perfection ; and am more pleased to survey my rows of coleworts and cabbages, with a thousand nameless pot-herbs, springing up in their full fragrancy and verdure, than to see the tender plants of foreign countries kept alive by artificial heats, or withering in an air and soil that are not adapted to them. I must not omit that there is a fountain rising in the upper part of my garden, which forms a little wandering rill, and administers to the pleasure as well as the plenty of the place. I have so con-ducted it that it visits most of my plantations : and have taken particular care to let it run in the same manner as it would do in an open field, so that it generally passes through banks of violets and primroses, plats of willow, or other plants, that seem to be of its own producing. There is another circum-stance in which I am very particular, or, as my neighbours call me, very whimsical : as my garden invites into it all the birds of the country, by offering them the conveniency of springs and shades, solitude and shelter, I do not suffer any one to destroy their nests in the spring, or drive them from their usual haunts in fruit-time ; I value my garden more for being full of blackbirds than cherries, and very frankly give them fruit for their songs. By this means, I have always the music of the season in its perfection, and am highly delighted to see the jay or the thrush hopping about my walks, and shooting before my eye across the several little glades and alleys that I pass through. I think there are as many kinds of gardening as of poetry : your makers of parterres and flower-gardens are epigrammatists and sonneteers in this art ; contrivers of bowers and grottoes, treillages and cascades, are romance writers. Wise and London are our heroic poets ; and if, as a critic, I may single out any passage of their works to commend, I shall take notice of that part in the upper garden at Kensington, which was at first nothing but a gravel-pit. It must have been a fine genius for gardening that could have thought of forming such an unsightly hollow into so beautiful an area, and to have hit the eye with so uncommon and agreeable a scene as that which it is now wrought into. To give this particular spot of ground the greater effect, they have made a very pleasing contrast; for, as on one side of the walk you see this hollow basin, with its several little plantations, lying so conveniently under the eye of the beholder, on the other side of it there appears a seeming mount, made up of trees, rising one higher than another, in proportion as they approach the center. A spectator, who has not heard this account of it, would think this circular mount was not only a real one, but that it had been actually scooped out of that hollow space which I have before mentioned. I never yet met with any one who has walked in this garden, who was not struck with that part of it which I have here mentioned. As for myself, you will find, by the account which I have already given you, that my compositions in gardening are altogether after the Pindaric manner, and run into the beautiful wildness of nature, without affecting the nicer elegances of art. What I am now going to mention will perhaps deserve your attention more than anything I have yet said. I find that, in the discourse which I spoke of at the beginning of my letter, you are against filling an English garden with evergreens; and indeed I am so far of your opinion, that I can by no means think the verdure of an evergreen comparable to that which shoots out annually, and clothes our trees in the summer season. But I have often wondered that those who are like myself, and love to live in gardens, have never thought of contriving a winter garden, which should consist of such trees only as never cast their leaves. We have very often little snatches of sunshine and fair weather in the most uncomfortable parts of the year, and have frequently several days in November and January that are as agreeable as any in the finest months. At such times, therefore, I think there could not be a greater pleasure than to walk in such a winter garden as I have proposed. In the summer season the whole country blooms, and is a kind of garden ; for which reason we are not so sensible of those beauties that at this time may be everywhere met with ; but when nature is in her desolation, and presents us with nothing but bleak and barren prospects, there is something unspeakably cheerful in a spot of ground which is covered with trees that smile amidst all the rigours of winter, and give us a view of the most gay season in the midst of that which is the most dead and melancholy. I have so far indulged myself in this thought that I have set apart a whole acre of ground for the executing of it. The walls are covered with ivy instead of vines. The laurel, the horn-beam, and the holly, with many other trees and plants of the same nature, grow so thick in it that you cannot imagine a more lively scene. The glowing redness of the berries with which they are hung at this time vies with the verdure of their leaves, and are apt to inspire the heart of the beholder with that vernal delight which you have somewhere taken notice of in your former papers. It is very pleasant, at the same time, to see the several kinds of birds retiring into this little green spot, and enjoying themselves among the branches and foliage, when my great garden, which I have before mentioned to you, does not afford a single leaf for their shelter.

You must know, Sir, that I look upon the pleasure which we take in a garden as one of the most innocent delights in human life. A garden was the habitation of our first parents before the fall. It is naturally apt to fill the mind with calmness and tranquillity, and to lay all its turbulent passions at rest. It gives us a great insight into the contrivance and wisdom of Providence, and suggests innumerable subjects for meditation. I cannot but think the very complacency and satisfaction which a man takes in these works of nature to be a laudable, if not a virtuous, habit of mind. For all which reasons, I hope you will pardon the length of my present letter.

I am, Sir, etc.

C [ADDISON]

THE RAMBLER (1750–1752)

SAMUEL JOHNSON (1709–1784)

THE FOLLY OF ANTICIPATING MISFORTUNES

No. 29. Tuesday, June 26, 1750

Prudens futuri temporis exitum
Caliginosa nocte premit deus,
Ridetque si mortalis ultra
Fas trepidet ————. — HOR.

There is nothing recommended with greater frequency among the gayer poets of antiquity than the secure possession of the present hour, and the dismission of all the cares which intrude upon our quiet, or hinder, by importunate perturbations, the enjoyment of those delights which our condition happens to set before us.

The ancient poets are, indeed, by no means unexceptionable teachers of morality; their precepts are to be always considered as the sallies of a genius, intent rather upon giving pleasure than instruction, eager to take every advantage of insinuation, and, provided the passions can be engaged on its side, very little solicitous about the suffrage of reason.

The darkness and uncertainty through which the heathens were compelled to wander in the pursuit of happiness may, indeed, be alleged as an excuse for many of their seducing invitations to immediate enjoyment, which the moderns, by whom they have been imitated, have not to plead. It is no wonder that such as had no promise of another state should eagerly turn their thoughts upon the improvement of that which was before them ; but surely those who are acquainted with the hopes and fears of eternity, might think it necessary to put some restraint upon their imagination, and reflect that by echoing the songs of the ancient bacchanals, and transmitting the maxims of past debauchery, they not only prove that they want invention, but virtue, and submit to the servility of imitation only to copy that of which the writer, if he was to live now, would often be ashamed.

Yet as the errors and follies of a great genius are seldom without some radiations of understanding, by which meaner minds may be enlightened, the incitements to pleasure are, in those authors, generally mingled with such reflections upon life as well deserve to be considered distinctly from the purposes for which they are produced, and to be treasured up as the settled conclusions of extensive observation, acute sagacity, and mature experience.

It is not without true judgment, that on these occasions they often warn their readers against inquiries into futurity, and solicitude about events which lie hid in causes yet unactive, and which time has not brought forward into the view of reason. An idle and thoughtless resignation to chance, without any struggle against calamity, or endeavour after advantage, is indeed below the dignity of a reasonable being, in whose power Providence has put a great part even of his present happiness ; but it shows an equal ignorance of our proper sphere, to harass our thoughts with conjectures about things not yet in being. How can we regulate events of which we yet know not whether they will ever happen ? And why should we think, with painful anxiety, about that on which our thoughts can have no influence ?

It is a maxim commonly received, that a wise man is never surprised ; and, perhaps, this exemption from astonishment may be imagined to proceed from such a prospect into futurity, as gave previous intimation of those evils which often fall unexpected upon others that have less foresight. But the truth is, that things to come, except when they approach very nearly, are equally hidden from men of all degrees of understanding ; and if a wise man is not amazed at sudden occurrences, it is not that he has thought more, but less upon futurity. He never considered things not yet existing as the proper objects of his attention ; he never indulged dreams till he was deceived by their phantoms, nor ever realized nonentities to his mind. He is not surprised because he is not disappointed, and he escapes disappointment because he never forms any expectations.

The concern about things to come, that is so justly censured, is not the result of those general reflections on the variableness of fortune, the uncertainty of life, and the universal insecurity of all human acquisitions, which must always be suggested by the view of the world ; but such a desponding anticipation of misfortune, as fixes the mind upon scenes of gloom and melancholy, and makes fear predominate in every imagination.

Anxiety of this kind is nearly of the same nature with jealousy in love, and suspicion in the general commerce of life ; a temper which keeps the man always in alarms, disposes him to judge of every thing in a manner that least favours his own quiet, fills him with perpetual stratagems of counteraction, wears him out in schemes to obviate evils which never threatened him, and at length, perhaps, contributes to the production of those mischiefs of which it had raised such dreadful apprehensions.

It has been usual in all ages for moralists to repress the swellings of vain hope, by representations of the innumerable casualties to which life is subject, and by instances of the unexpected defeat of the wisest schemes of policy, and sudden subversions of the highest eminences of greatness. It has, perhaps, not been equally observed, that all these examples afford the proper antidote to fear as well as to hope, and may be applied with no less efficacy as consolations to the timorous, than as restraints to the proud.

Evil is uncertain in the same degree as good, and for the reason that we ought not to hope too securely, we ought not to fear with too much dejection. The state of the world is continually changing, and none can tell the result of the next vicissitude. Whatever is afloat in the stream of time, may, when it is very near us, be driven away by an accidental blast, which shall happen to cross the general course of the current. The sudden accidents by which the powerful are depressed may fall upon those whose malice we fear; and the greatness by which we expect to be overborne may become another proof of the false flatteries of fortune. Our enemies may become weak, or we grow strong before our encounter, or we may advance against each other without ever meeting. There are, indeed, natural evils which we can flatter ourselves with no hopes of escaping, and with little of delaying; but of the ills which are apprehended from human malignity, or the opposition of rival interests, we may always alleviate the terror by considering that our persecutors are weak and ignorant, and mortal like ourselves.

The misfortunes which arise from the concurrence of unhappy incidents should never be suffered to disturb us before they happen; because, if the breast be once laid open to the dread of mere possibilities of misery, life must be given a prey to dismal solicitude, and quiet must be lost forever.

It is remarked by old Cornaro that it is absurd to be afraid of the natural dissolution of the body, because it must certainly happen, and can, by no caution or artifice, be avoided. Whether this sentiment be entirely just, I shall not examine; but certainly if it be improper to fear events which must happen, it is yet more evidently contrary to right reason to fear those which may never happen, and which, if they should come upon us, we cannot resist.

As we ought not to give way to fear, any more than indulgence to hope, because the objects both of fear and hope are yet uncertain, so we ought not to trust the representations of one more than of the other, because they are both equally fallacious; as hope enlarges happiness, fear aggravates calamity. It is generally allowed, that no man ever found the happiness of possession proportionate to that expectation which incited his desire, and invigorated his pursuit; nor has any man found the evils of life so formidable in reality as they were described to him by his own imagination; every species of distress brings with it some peculiar supports, some unforeseen means of resisting, or power of enduring. Taylor justly blames some pious persons, who indulge their fancies too much, set themselves, by the force of imagination, in the place of the ancient martyrs and confessors, and question the validity of their own faith because they shrink at the thoughts of flames and tortures. "It is," says he, "sufficient that you are able to encounter the temptations which now assault you; when God sends trials, he may send strength."

All fear is in itself painful; and when it conduces not to safety is painful without use. Every consideration, therefore, by which groundless terrors may be removed, adds something to human happiness. It is likewise not unworthy of remark, that in proportion as our cares are employed upon the future they are abstracted from the present, from the only time which we can call our own, and of which if we neglect the apparent duties, to make provision against visionary attacks, we shall certainly counteract our own purpose; for he, doubtless, mistakes his true interest, who thinks that he can increase his safety when he impairs his virtue.

THE MISERY OF A FASHIONABLE LADY IN THE COUNTRY

No. 42.   Saturday, August 11, 1750

Mihi tarda fluunt ingrataque tempora. — HOR.

To THE RAMBLER

Mr. Rambler,

I am no great admirer of grave writings, and therefore very frequently lay your papers aside before I have read them through; yet I cannot but confess that, by slow degrees, you have raised my opinion of your understanding, and that, though I believe it will be long before I can be prevailed upon to regard you with much kindness, you have, however, more of my

esteem than those whom I sometimes make happy with opportunities to fill my tea-pot, or pick up my fan. I shall therefore
choose you for the confident of my distresses, and ask your
counsel with regard to the means of conquering or escaping
them, though I never expect from you any of that softness and
pliancy which constitutes the perfection of a companion for
the ladies : as, in the place where I now am, I have recourse
to the mastiff for protection, though I have no intention of
making him a lapdog.

My mamma is a very fine lady, who has more numerous and
more frequent assemblies at our house than any other person
in the same quarter of the town. I was bred from my earliest
infancy to a perpetual tumult of pleasure, and remember to
have heard of little else than messages, visits, playhouses, and
balls ; of the awkwardness of one woman, and the coquetry of
another ; the charming convenience of some rising fashion, the
difficulty of playing a new game, the incidents of a masquerade, and the dresses of a court-night. I knew before I was
ten years old all the rules of paying and receiving visits, and
to how much civility every one of my acquaintance was entitled :
and was able to return, with the proper degree of reserve or
vivacity, the stated and established answer to every compliment ;
so that I was very soon celebrated as a wit and a beauty, and
had heard before I was thirteen all that is ever said to a young
lady. My mother was generous to so uncommon a degree as
to be pleased with my advance into life, and allowed me, without envy or reproof, to enjoy the same happiness with herself ;
though most women about her own age were very angry to
see young girls so forward, and many fine gentlemen told her
how cruel it was to throw new claims upon mankind, and to
tyrannize over them at the same time with her own charms
and those of her daughter.

I have now lived two-and-twenty years, and have passed of
each year nine months in town, and three at Richmond ; so
that my time has been spent uniformly in the same company
and the same amusements, except as fashion has introduced

new diversions, or the revolutions of the gay world have afforded new successions of wits and beaux. However, my mother is so good an economist of pleasure that I have no spare hours upon my hands; for every morning brings some new appointment, and every night is hurried away by the necessity of making our appearance at different places, and of being with one lady at the opera, and with another at the card-table.

When the time came of settling our scheme of felicity for the summer, it was determined that I should pay a visit to a rich aunt in a remote county. As you know, the chief conversation of all tea-tables, in the spring, arises from a communication of the manner in which time is to be passed till winter, it was a great relief to the barrenness of our topics to relate the pleasures that were in store for me, to describe my uncle's seat, with the park and gardens, the charming walks and beautiful waterfalls; and everyone told me how much she envied me, and what satisfaction she had once enjoyed in a situation of the same kind.

As we are all credulous in our own favour, and willing to imagine some latent satisfaction in any thing which we have not experienced, I will confess to you, without restraint, that I had suffered my head to be filled with expectations of some nameless pleasure in a rural life, and that I hoped for the happy hour that should set me free from noise, and flutter, and ceremony, dismiss me to the peaceful shade, and lull me in content and tranquillity. To solace myself under the misery of delay, I sometimes heard a studious lady of my acquaintance read pastorals, I was delighted with scarce any talk but of leaving the town, and never went to bed without dreaming of groves, and meadows, and frisking lambs.

At length I had all my clothes in a trunk, and saw the coach at the door; I sprung in with ecstasy, quarreled with my maid for being too long in taking leave of the other servants, and rejoiced as the ground grew less which lay between me and the completion of my wishes. A few days brought me to a large old house, encompassed on three sides with woody hills, and looking from the front on a gentle river, the sight of which renewed all my expectations of pleasure, and gave me some regret for having lived so long without the enjoyment which these delightful scenes were now to afford me. My aunt came out to receive me, but in a dress so far removed from the present fashion that I could scarcely look upon her without laughter, which would have been no kind requital for the trouble which she had taken to make herself fine against my arrival. The night and the next morning were driven along with inquiries about our family; my aunt then explained our pedigree, and told me stories of my great grandfather's bravery in the civil wars; nor was it less than three days before I could persuade her to leave me to myself.

At last economy prevailed; she went in the usual manner about her own affairs, and I was at liberty to range in the wilderness, and sit by the cascade. The novelty of the objects about me pleased me for a while, but after a few days they were new no longer, and I soon began to perceive that the country was not my element; that shades, and flowers, and lawns, and waters had very soon exhausted all their power of pleasing, and that I had not in myself any fund of satisfaction with which I could supply the loss of my customary amusements. I unhappily told my aunt, in the first warmth of our embraces, that I had leave to stay with her ten weeks. Six only are yet gone, and how shall I live through the remaining four? I go out and return; I pluck a flower, and throw it away; I catch an insect, and when I have examined its colours, set it at liberty; I fling a pebble into the water, and see one circle spread after another. When it chances to rain I walk in the great hall, and watch the minute-hand upon the dial, or play with a litter of kittens which the cat happens to have brought in a lucky time.

My aunt is afraid I shall grow melancholy, and therefore encourages the neighbouring gentry to visit us. They came at first with great eagerness to see the fine lady from London, but when we met we had no common topic on which we could converse; they had no curiosity after plays, operas, or music;

and I find as little satisfaction from their accounts of the quarrels or alliances of families, whose names, when once I can escape, I shall never hear. The women have now seen me, know how my gown is made, and are satisfied; the men are generally afraid of me, and say little, because they think themselves not at liberty to talk rudely.

Thus am I condemned to solitude; the day moves slowly forward, and I see the dawn with uneasiness, because I consider that night is at a great distance. I have tried to sleep by a brook, but find its murmurs ineffectual; so that I am forced to be awake at least twelve hours, without visits, without cards, without laughter, and without flattery. I walk because I am disgusted with sitting still, and sit down because I am weary with walking. I have no motive to action, nor any object of love, or hate, or fear, or inclination. I cannot dress with spirit, for I have neither rival nor admirer. I cannot dance without a partner, nor be kind, or cruel, without a lover.

Such is the life of Euphelia, and such it is likely to continue for a month to come. I have not yet declared against existence, nor called upon the destinies to cut my thread; but I have sincerely resolved not to condemn myself to such another summer, nor too hastily to flatter myself with happiness. Yet I have heard, Mr. Rambler, of those who never thought themselves so much at ease as in solitude, and cannot but suspect it to be some way or other my own fault, that, without great pain, either of mind or body, I am thus weary of myself: that the current of youth stagnates, and that I am languishing in a dead calm for want of some external impulse. I shall therefore think you a benefactor to our sex, if you will teach me the art of living alone; for I am confident that a thousand and a thousand and a thousand ladies, who affect to talk with ecstasies of the pleasures of the country, are, in reality, like me, longing for the winter, and wishing to be delivered from themselves by company and diversion.

I am, Sir, yours,

Euphelia.

THE CITIZEN OF THE WORLD (1760–1761)

Oliver Goldsmith (1728–1774)

THE CHINESE PHILOSOPHER IN ENGLAND

Letter I

To Mr. * * * *, Merchant in London

Amsterdam

Sir,

Yours of the 13th instant, covering two bills, one on Messrs. R. and D., value £478,10 s., and the other on Mr. * * * *, value £285, duly came to hand, the former of which met with honour, but the other has been trifled with, and I am afraid will be returned protested.

The bearer of this is my friend, therefore let him be yours. He is a native of Honan in China, and one who did me signal services when he was a mandarine, and I a factor at Canton. By frequently conversing with the English there, he has learned the language, though he is entirely a stranger to their manners and customs. I am told he is a philosopher, I am sure he is an honest man ; that to you will be his best recommendation, next to the consideration of his being the friend of, Sir,

Yours, &c.

FIRST IMPRESSIONS OF ENGLAND

Letter II

Lond. From Lien Chi Altangi to * * * *, Merchant in Amsterdam

Friend of my Heart,

May the wings of peace rest upon thy dwelling, and the shield of conscience preserve thee from vice and misery : for all thy favours accept my gratitude and esteem, the only tributes a poor philosophic wanderer can return; sure fortune is resolved to make me unhappy, when she gives others a power of testifying their friendship by actions, and leaves me only words to express the sincerity of mine.

I am perfectly sensible of the delicacy with which you endeavour to lessen your own merit and my obligations. By calling your late instances of friendship only a return for former favours, you would induce me to impute to your justice what I owe to your generosity.

The services I did you at Canton, justice, humanity, and my office bade me perform; those you have done me since my arrival at Amsterdam, no laws obliged you to, no justice required, even half your favours would have been greater than my most sanguine expectations.

The sum of money therefore which you privately conveyed into my baggage, when I was leaving Holland, and which I was ignorant of till my arrival in London, I must beg leave to return. You have been bred a merchant, and I a scholar; you consequently love money better than I. You can find pleasure in superfluity, I am perfectly content with what is sufficient; take therefore what is yours, it may give you some pleasure, even though you have no occasion to use it; my happiness it cannot improve, for I have already all that I want.

My passage by sea from Rotterdam to England was more painful to me than all the journies I ever made on land. I have traversed the immeasurable wilds of Mogul Tartary; felt all the rigours of Siberian skies; I have had my repose an hundred times disturbed by invading savages, and have seen without shrinking the desert sands rise like a troubled ocean all around me; against these calamities I was armed with resolution; but in my passage to England, though nothing occurred that gave the mariners any uneasiness, to one who was never at sea before, all was a subject of astonishment and terror. To find the land disappear, to see our ship mount the waves swift as an arrow from the Tartar bow, to hear the wind howling through the cordage, to feel a sickness which depresses even the spirits of the brave; these were unexpected distresses, and consequently assaulted me unprepared to receive them.

You men of Europe think nothing of a voyage by sea. With us of China, a man who has been from sight of land is regarded upon his return with admiration. I have known some provinces where there is not even a name for the ocean. What a strange people therefore am I got amongst, who have founded an empire on this unstable element, who build cities upon billows that rise higher than the mountains of Tipartala, and make the deep more formidable than the wildest tempest.

Such accounts as these, I must confess, were my first motives for seeing England. These induced me to undertake a journey of seven hundred painful days, in order to examine its opulence, buildings, arts, sciences, and manufactures on the spot. Judge then my disappointment on entering London, to see no signs of that opulence so much talked of abroad; wherever I turn, I am presented with a gloomy solemnity in the houses, the streets, and the inhabitants; none of that beautiful gilding which makes a principal ornament in Chinese architecture. The streets of Nankin are sometimes strewed with gold leaf; very different are those of London: in the midst of their pavements, a great lazy puddle moves muddily along; heavy laden machines with wheels of unwieldy thickness crowd up every passage; so that a stranger, instead of finding time for observation, is often happy if he has time to escape from being crushed to pieces.

The houses borrow very few ornaments from architecture; their chief decoration seems to be a paltry piece of painting, hung out at their doors or windows, at once a proof of their indigence and vanity. Their vanity, in each having one of those pictures exposed to public view; and their indigence, in being unable to get them better painted. In this respect, the fancy of their painters is also deplorable. Could you believe it? I have seen five black lions and three blue boars in less than the circuit of half a mile; and yet you know that animals of these colours are no where to be found except in the wild imaginations of Europe.

From these circumstances in their buildings, and from the dismal looks of the inhabitants, I am induced to conclude that the nation is actually poor; and that like the Persians, they make a splendid figure every where but at home. The proverb of Xixofou is, that a man's riches may be seen in his eyes; if we judge of the English by this rule, there is not a poorer nation under the sun.

I have been here but two days, so will not be hasty in my decisions; such letters as I shall write to Fipsihi in Moscow, I beg you'll endeavour to forward with all diligence; I shall send them open, in order that you may take copies or translations, as you are equally versed in the Dutch and Chinese languages. Dear friend, think of my absence with regret, as I sincerely regret yours; even while I write, I lament our separation. Farewell.

NATIONAL CHARACTERISTICS

Letter IV

From Lien Chi Altangi, to the care of Fipsihi, resident in Moscow; to be forwarded by the Russian caravan to Fum Hoam, first President of the Ceremonial Academy at Pekin in China

The English seem as silent as the Japanese, yet vainer than the inhabitants of Siam. Upon my arrival I attributed that reserve to modesty, which I now find has its origin in pride. Condescend to address them first, and you are sure of their acquaintance; stoop to flattery, and you conciliate their friendship and esteem. They bear hunger, cold, fatigue, and all the miseries of life without shrinking; danger only calls forth their fortitude; they even exult in calamity; but contempt is what they cannot bear. An Englishman fears contempt more than death; he often flies to death as a refuge from its pressure; and dies when he fancies the world has ceased to esteem him.

Pride seems the source not only of their national vices, but of their national virtues also. An Englishman is taught to love his king as his friend, but to acknowledge no other master than the laws which himself has contributed to enact. He despises those nations, who, that one may be free, are all content to be slaves; who first lift a tyrant into terror, and then shrink under his power as if delegated from heaven. Liberty is echoed in all their assemblies, and thousands might be found ready to offer up their lives for the sound, though perhaps not one of all the number understands its meaning. The lowest mechanic however looks upon it as his duty to be a watchful guardian of his country's freedom, and often uses a language that might seem haughty, even in the mouth of the great emperor who traces his ancestry to the moon.

A few days ago, passing by one of their prisons, I could not avoid stopping, in order to listen to a dialogue which I thought might afford me some entertainment. The conversation was carried on between a debtor through the grate of his prison, a porter, who had stopped to rest his burden, and a soldier at the window. The subject was upon a threatened invasion from France, and each seemed extremely anxious to rescue his country from the impending danger. "For my part," cries the prisoner, "the greatest of my apprehensions is for our freedom; if the French should conquer, what would become of English liberty? My dear friends, liberty is the Englishman's prerogative; we must preserve that at the expense of our lives, of that the French shall never deprive us; it is not to be expected that men who are slaves themselves would preserve our freedom should they happen to conquer." "Ay, slaves," cries the porter, "they are all slaves, fit only to carry burdens every one of them. Before I would stoop to slavery, may this be my poison (and he held the goblet in his hand) may this be my poison — but I would sooner list for a soldier."

The soldier taking the goblet from his friend, with much awe fervently cried out, "It is not so much our liberties as our religion that would suffer by such a change. Ay, our religion, my lads. May the Devil sink me into flames (such was the solemnity of his adjuration), if the French should come over, but our religion would be utterly undone." So saying, instead of a libation, he applied the goblet to his lips, and confirmed his sentiments with a ceremony of the most persevering devotion.

In short, every man here pretends to be a politician; even the fair sex are sometimes found to mix the severity of national altercation with the blandishments of love, and often become conquerors by more weapons of destruction than their eyes.

This universal passion for politics is gratified by Daily Gazettes, as with us at China. But, as in ours the emperor endeavours to instruct his people, in theirs the people endeavour to instruct the administration. You must not, however, imagine that they who compile these papers have any actual knowledge of the politics, or the government of a state; they only collect their materials from the oracle of some coffee-house, which oracle has himself gathered them the night before from a beau at a gaming-table, who has pillaged his knowledge from a great man's porter, who has had his information from the great man's gentleman, who has invented the whole story for his own amusement the night preceding.

The English in general seem fonder of gaining the esteem than the love of those they converse with: this gives a formality to their amusements; their gayest conversations have something too wise for innocent relaxation; though in company you are seldom disgusted with the absurdity of a fool, you are seldom lifted into rapture by those strokes of vivacity which give instant, though not permanent pleasure.

What they want, however, in gaiety, they make up in politeness. You smile at hearing me praise the English for their politeness: you who have heard very different accounts from the missionaries at Pekin, who have seen such a different behaviour in their merchants and seamen at home. But I must still repeat it, the English seem more polite than any of their neighbours; their great art in this respect lies in endeavouring, while they oblige, to lessen the force of the favour. Other countries are fond of obliging a stranger; but seem desirous that he should be sensible of the obligation. The English confer their kindness with an appearance of indifference, and give away benefits with an air as if they despised them.

Walking a few days ago between an English and Frenchman into the suburbs of the city, we were overtaken by a heavy shower of rain. I was unprepared; but they had each large coats, which defended them from what seemed to me a perfect inundation. The Englishman seeing me shrink from the weather, accosted me thus: "Psha, man, what dost shrink at? Here, take this coat; I don't want it; I find it no way useful to me; I had as lief be without it." The Frenchman began to shew his politeness in turn. "My dear friend," cries he, "why won't you oblige me by making use of my coat; you see how well it defends me from the rain; I should not choose to part with it to others, but to such a friend as you, I could even part with my skin to do him service."

From such minute instances as these, most reverend Fum Hoam, I am sensible your sagacity will collect instruction. The volume of nature is the book of knowledge; and he becomes most wise who makes the most judicious selection. Farewell.

THE CHARACTER OF BEAU TIBBS

Letter LIV

From Lien Chi Altangi, to Fum Hoam, first President of the Ceremonial Academy at Pekin, in China

Though naturally pensive, yet I am fond of gay company, and take every opportunity of thus dismissing the mind from duty. From this motive I am often found in the centre of a crowd; and wherever pleasure is to be sold, am always a purchaser. In those places, without being remarked by any, I join in whatever goes forward, work my passions into a similitude of frivolous earnestness, shout as they shout, and condemn as they happen to disapprove. A mind thus sunk for a while below its natural standard is qualified for stronger flights, as those first retire who would spring forward with greater vigour.

Attracted by the serenity of the evening, my friend and I lately went to gaze upon the company in one of the public walks near the city. Here we sauntered together for some time, either praising the beauty of such as were handsome, or the dresses of such as had nothing else to recommend them. We had gone thus deliberately forward for some time, when stopping on a sudden, my friend caught me by the elbow, and led me out of the public walk; I could perceive by the quickness of his pace, and by his frequently looking behind, that he was attempting to avoid somebody who followed; we now turned to the right, then to the left; as we went forward he still went faster, but in vain; the person whom he attempted to escape hunted us through every doubling, and gained upon us each moment; so that at last we fairly stood still, resolving to face what we could not avoid.

Our pursuer soon came up, and joined us with all the familiarity of an old acquaintance. "My dear Drybone," cries he, shaking my friend's hand, "where have you been hiding this half a century? Positively I had fancied you were gone down to cultivate matrimony and your estate in the country." During the reply, I had an opportunity of surveying the appearance of our new companion; his hat was pinched up with peculiar smartness; his looks were pale, thin, and sharp; round his neck he wore a broad black ribbon, and in his bosom a buckle studded with glass; his coat was trimmed with tarnished twist; he wore by his side a sword with a black hilt, and his stockings of silk, though newly washed, were grown yellow by long service. I was so much engaged with the peculiarity of his dress that I attended only to the latter part of my friend's reply, in which he complimented Mr. Tibbs on the taste of his clothes, and the bloom in his countenance: "Psha, psha, Will," cried the figure, "no more of that if you love me, you know I hate flattery, on my soul I do; and yet to be sure an intimacy with the great

will improve one's appearance, and a course of venison will
fatten; and yet faith I despise the great as much as you do;
but there are a great many damn'd honest fellows among them;
and we must not quarrel with one half, because the other wants
weeding. If they were all such as my Lord Muddler, one of
the most good-natured creatures that ever squeezed a lemon, I
should myself be among the number of their admirers. I was
yesterday to dine at the Duchess of Piccadilly's, my lord was
there. 'Ned,' says he to me, 'Ned,' says he, 'I'll hold gold to
silver I can tell where you were poaching last night.' 'Poaching, my lord,' says I; 'faith you have missed already; for I
staid at home, and let the girls poach for me. That's my
way; I take a fine woman as some animals do their prey;
stand still, and swoop, they fall into my mouth.'"

"Ah, Tibbs, thou art an happy fellow," cried my companion,
with looks of infinite pity, "I hope your fortune is as much
improved as your understanding in such company?" "Improved," replied the other; "You shall know, — but let it go
no further, — a great secret — five hundred a year to begin
with. — My lord's word of honour for it — His lordship took
me down in his own chariot yesterday, and we had a tete-a-tete
dinner in the country; where we talked of nothing else." "I
fancy you forget, sir," cried I, "you told us but this moment
of your dining yesterday in town!" "Did I say so," replied
he coolly, "to be sure if I said so it was so — dined in town;
egad now I do remember, I did dine in town; but I dined in
the country too; for you must know, my boys, I eat two dinners. By the bye, I am grown as nice as the devil in my eating. I'll tell you a pleasant affair about that: We were a select
party of us to dine at Lady Grogram's, an affected piece, but
let it go no further; a secret: well, there happened to be no
asafœtida in the sauce to a turkey, upon which, says I, I'll
hold a thousand guineas, and say done first, that — But, dear
Drybone, you are an honest creature, lend me half-a-crown for
a minute or two, or so, just till — But hearkee, ask me for it
the next time we meet, or it may be twenty to one but I forget
to pay you."

When he left us, our conversation naturally turned upon so extraordinary a character. " His very dress," cries my friend, " is not less extraordinary than his conduct. If you meet him this day you find him in rags, if the next in embroidery. With those persons of distinction, of whom he talks so familiarly, he has scarcely a coffee-house acquaintance. However, both for the interests of society, and perhaps for his own, heaven has made him poor, and while all the world perceive his wants, he fancies them concealed from every eye. An agreeable companion because he understands flattery, and all must be pleased with the first part of his conversation, though all are sure of its ending with a demand on their purse. While his youth countenances the levity of his conduct, he may thus earn a precarious subsistence, but when age comes on, the gravity of which is incompatible with buffoonery, then will he find himself forsaken by all. Condemned in the decline of life to hang upon some rich family whom he once despised, there to undergo all the ingenuity of studied contempt, to be employed only as a spy upon the servants, or a bugbear to frighten the children into obedience." Adieu.

THE CHARACTER OF BEAU TIBBS (CONTINUED)

Letter LV

To the same

I am apt to fancy I have contracted a new acquaintance whom it will be no easy matter to shake off. My little beau yesterday overtook me again in one of the public walks, and slapping me on the shoulder, saluted me with an air of the most perfect familiarity. His dress was the same as usual, except that he had more powder in his hair, wore a dirtier shirt, a pair of temple spectacles, and his hat under his arm.

As I knew him to be an harmless amusing little thing, I could not return his smiles with any degree of severity; so we walked forward on terms of the utmost intimacy, and in a few minutes discussed all the usual topics preliminary to particular conversation.

The oddities that marked his character, however, soon began to appear ; he bowed to several well-dressed persons, who, by their manner of returning the compliment, appeared perfect strangers. At intervals he drew out a pocket-book, seeming to take memorandums before all the company, with much importance and assiduity. In this manner he led me through the length of the whole walk, fretting at his absurdities, and fancying myself laughed at not less than him by every spectator.

When we were got to the end of our procession, "Blast me," cries he, with an air of vivacity, "I never saw the park so thin in my life before ; there 's no company at all to-day. Not a single face to be seen." " No company," interrupted I peevishly ; " no company where there is such a crowd ; why man, there 's too much. What are the thousands that have been laughing at us but company ! " " Lard, my dear," returned he, with the utmost good-humour, "you seem immensely chagrined ; but blast me, when the world laughs at me, I laugh at all the world, and so we are even. My Lord Trip, Bill Squash the Creolian, and I, sometimes make a party at being ridiculous ; and so we say and do a thousand things for the joke sake. But I see you are grave, and if you are for a fine grave sentimental companion, you shall dine with me and my wife to-day, I must insist on 't ; I 'll introduce you to Mrs. Tibbs, a lady of as elegant qualifications as any in nature ; she was bred, but that 's between ourselves, under the inspection of the Countess of All-night. A charming body of voice, but no more of that, she will give us a song. You shall see my little girl too, Carolina Wilhelma Amelia Tibbs, a sweet pretty creature ; I design her for my Lord Drumstick's eldest son, but that 's in friendship, let it go no further ; she 's but six years old, and yet she walks a minuet, and plays on the guitar immensely already. I intend she shall be as perfect as possible in every accomplishment. In the first place I 'll make her a scholar ; I 'll teach her Greek myself, and learn that language purposely to instruct her ; but let that be a secret."

Thus saying, without waiting for a reply, he took me by the

arm, and hauled me along. We passed through many dark alleys and winding ways; for, from some motives to me unknown, he seemed to have a particular aversion to every frequented street; at last, however, we got to the door of a dismal looking house in the outlets of the town, where he informed me he chose to reside for the benefit of the air.

We entered the lower door, which ever seemed to lie most hospitably open; and I began to ascend an old and creaking stair-case, when, as he mounted to show me the way, he demanded, whether I delighted in prospects, to which answering in the affirmative, "Then," says he, "I shall show you one of the most charming in the world out of my windows; we shall see the ships sailing, and the whole country for twenty miles round, tip top, quite high. My Lord Swamp would give ten thousand guineas for such a one; but as I sometimes pleasantly tell him, I always love to keep my prospects at home, that my friends may see me the oftener."

By this time we were arrived as high as the stairs would permit us to ascend, till we came to what he was facetiously pleased to call the first floor down the chimney; and knocking at the door, a voice from within demanded, who's there? My conductor answered that it was him. But this not satisfying the querist, the voice again repeated the demand: to which he answered louder than before; and now the door was opened by an old woman with cautious reluctance.

When we were got in, he welcomed me to his house with great ceremony, and turning to the old woman, asked where was her lady? "Good troth," replied she, in a peculiar dialect, "she's washing your two shirts at the next door, because they have taken an oath against lending out the tub any longer." "My two shirts," cries he in a tone that faltered with confusion, "what does the idiot mean!" "I ken what I mean well enough," replied the other, "she's washing your twa shirts at the next door, because ——" "Fire and fury, no more of thy stupid explanations," cried he, —"Go and inform her we have got company. Were that Scotch hag to be for ever in the family, she would never learn politeness, nor forget that absurd poisonous accent of hers, or testify the smallest specimen of breeding or high life; and yet it is very surprising too, as I had her from a parliament-man, a friend of mine, from the highlands, one of the politest men in the world; but that's a secret."

We waited some time for Mrs. Tibbs's arrival, during which interval I had a full opportunity of surveying the chamber and all its furniture; which consisted of four chairs with old wrought bottoms, that he assured me were his wife's embroidery; a square table that had been once japanned, a cradle in one corner, a lumbering cabinet in the other; a broken shepherdess, and a mandarine without a head were stuck over the chimney; and round the walls several paltry, unframed pictures, which he observed were all his own drawing: "What do you think, sir, of that head in a corner, done in the manner of Grisoni? There's the true keeping in it; it's my own face, and though there happens to be no likeness, a countess offered me an hundred for its fellow; I refused her, for, hang it, that would be mechanical, you know."

The wife at last made her appearance, at once a slattern and a coquette; much emaciated, but still carrying the remains of beauty. She made twenty apologies for being seen in such odious dishabille, but hoped to be excused, as she had staid out all night at the gardens with the countess, who was excessively fond of the "horns." "And, indeed, my dear," added she, turning to her husband, "his lordship drank your health in a bumper." "Poor Jack," cries he, "a dear good-natured creature, I know he loves me; but I hope, my dear, you have given orders for dinner; you need make no great preparations neither, there are but three of us, something elegant, and little will do; a turbot, an ortolan, or a —— " "Or what do you think, my dear," interrupts the wife, "of a nice pretty bit of ox-cheek, piping hot, and dressed with a little of my own sauce —— " "The very thing," replies he, "it will eat best with some smart bottled beer; but be sure to let's have the sauce his grace was so fond of. I hate your immense loads of meat, that is country all over; extreme disgusting to those who are in the least acquainted with high life."

By this time my curiosity began to abate, and my appetite to increase; the company of fools may at first make us smile, but at last never fails of rendering us melancholy; I therefore pretended to recollect a prior engagement, and after having shown my respect to the house, according to the fashion of the English, by giving the old servant a piece of money at the door, I took my leave; Mr. Tibbs assuring me that dinner, if I staid, would be ready at least in less than two hours.

A VISIT TO A LONDON SILK MERCHANT

Letter LXXVII

From Lien Chi Altangi, to Fum Hoam, first President of the Ceremonial Academy, at Pekin, in China

The shops of London are as well furnished as those of Pekin. Those of London have a picture hung at their door, informing the passengers what they have to sell, as those at Pekin have a board to assure the buyer that they have no intentions to cheat him.

I was this morning to buy silk for a night-cap; immediately upon entering the mercer's shop, the master and his two men, with wigs plastered with powder, appeared to ask my commands. They were certainly the civilest people alive; if I but looked, they flew to the place where I cast my eye; every motion of mine sent them running round the whole shop for my satisfaction. I informed them that I wanted what was good, and they showed me not less than forty pieces, and each was better than the former; the prettiest pattern in nature, and the fittest in the world for night-caps. "My very good friend," said I to the mercer, "you must not pretend to instruct me in silks, I know these in particular to be no better than your mere flimsy Bungees." "That may be," cried the mercer, who I afterwards found had never contradicted a man in his life, "I can't pretend to say but they may; but I can assure you, my Lady Trail has had a sacque from this piece this very morning." "But friend," said I, "though my lady has chosen a sacque from it, I see no necessity that I should wear it for a night-cap." "That may be," returned he again, "yet what becomes a pretty lady, will at any time look well on a handsome gentleman." This short compliment was thrown in so very seasonably upon my ugly face, that even though I disliked the silk, I desired him to cut me off the pattern of a night-cap.

While this business was consigned to his journeyman, the master himself took down some pieces of silk still finer than any I had yet seen, and spreading them before me, "There," cries he, "there's beauty, my Lord Snakeskin has bespoke the fellow to this for the birth-night this very morning; it would look charmingly in waistcoats." "But I don't want a waistcoat," replied I. "Not want a waistcoat," returned the mercer, "then I would advise you to buy one; when waistcoats are wanted, you may depend upon it they will come dear. Always buy before you want, and you are sure to be well used, as they say in Cheapside." There was so much justice in his advice, that I could not refuse taking it; besides, the silk, which was really a good one, increased the temptation, so I gave orders for that too.

As I was waiting to have my bargains measured and cut, which, I know not how, they executed but slowly; during the interval, the mercer entertained me with the modern manner of some of the nobility receiving company in their morning gowns. "Perhaps, sir," adds he, "you have a mind to see what kind of silk is universally worn." Without waiting for my reply, he spreads a piece before me, which might be reckoned beautiful even in China. "If the nobility," continues he, "were to know I sold this to any under a Right Honourable, I should certainly lose their custom; you see, my Lord, it is at once rich, tasty, and quite the thing." "I am no Lord," interrupted I. — "I beg pardon," cried he, "but be pleased to remember, when you intend buying a morning gown, that you had an offer from me of something worth money. Conscience, sir, conscience is my way of dealing; you may buy a morning gown now, or you may stay till they become dearer and less fashionable, but it is not my business to advise." In short, most reverend Fum, he persuaded me to buy a morning gown also, and would probably have persuaded me to have bought half the goods in his shop, if I had stayed long enough, or was furnished with sufficient money.

Upon returning home, I could not help reflecting with some astonishment, how this very man with such a confined education and capacity, was yet capable of turning me as he thought proper, and moulding me to his inclinations! I knew he was only answering his own purposes, even while he attempted to appear solicitous about mine; yet by a voluntary infatuation, a sort of passion compounded of vanity and good nature, I walked into the snare with my eyes open, and put myself to future pain in order to give him immediate pleasure. The wisdom of the ignorant somewhat resembles the instinct of animals; it is diffused in but a very narrow sphere, but within that circle it acts with vigour, uniformity, and success. Adieu.

CHARLES LAMB (1775–1834)

A BACHELOR'S COMPLAINT OF THE BEHAVIOUR OF MARRIED PEOPLE

Reflector No. 4, 1811–1812; *London Magazine*, September, 1822

As a single man, I have spent a good deal of my time in noting down the infirmities of Married People, to console myself for those superior pleasures, which they tell me I have lost by remaining as I am.

I cannot say that the quarrels of men and their wives ever made any great impression upon me, or had much tendency to strengthen me in those anti-social resolutions, which I took up long ago upon more substantial considerations. What oftenest offends me at the houses of married persons where I visit, is an error of quite a different description; — it is that they are too loving.

Not too loving neither: that does not explain my meaning. Besides, why should that offend me? The very act of separating themselves from the rest of the world, to have the fuller enjoyment of each other's society, implies that they prefer one another to all the world.

But what I complain of is that they carry this preference so undisguisedly, they perk it up in the faces of us single people so shamelessly, you cannot be in their company a moment without being made to feel, by some indirect hint or open avowal, that *you* are not the object of this preference. Now there are some things which give no offence, while implied or taken for granted merely; but expressed, there is much offence in them. If a man were to accost the first homely-featured or plain-dressed young woman of his acquaintance, and tell her bluntly, that she was not handsome or rich enough for him,

and he could not marry her, he would deserve to be kicked for
his ill manners; yet no less is implied in the fact that having
access and opportunity of putting the question to her, he has
never yet thought fit to do it. The young woman understands
this as clearly as if it were put into words; but no reasonable
young woman would think of making this a ground of a quarrel. Just as little right have a married couple to tell me by
speeches and looks that are scarce less plain than speeches, that
I am not the happy man, — the lady's choice. It is enough
that I know that I am not: I do not want this perpetual
reminding.

The display of superior knowledge or riches may be made
sufficiently mortifying; but these admit of a palliative. The
knowledge which is brought out to insult me may accidentally
improve me; and in the rich man's houses and pictures, his
parks and gardens, I have a temporary usufruct at least. But
the display of married happiness has none of these palliatives:
it is throughout pure, unrecompensed, unqualified insult.

Marriage by its best title is a monopoly, and not of the least
invidious sort. It is the cunning of most possessors of any
exclusive privilege to keep their advantage as much out of sight
as possible, that their less favoured neighbours, seeing little of
the benefit, may the less be disposed to question the right.
But these married monopolists thrust the most obnoxious part
of their patent into our faces.

Nothing is to me more distasteful than that entire complacency and satisfaction which beam in the countenances of a
new-married couple, — in that of the lady particularly: it tells
you that her lot is disposed of in this world; that *you* can
have no hopes of her. It is true, I have none; nor wishes
either, perhaps: but this is one of those truths which ought,
as I said before, to be taken for granted, not expressed.

The excessive airs which those people give themselves,
founded on the ignorance of us unmarried people, would be
more offensive if they were less irrational. We will allow them
to understand the mysteries belonging to their own craft better

than we who have not had the happiness to be made free of the company : but their arrogance is not content within these limits. If a single person presume to offer his opinion in their presence, though upon the most indifferent subject, he is immediately silenced as an incompetent person. Nay, a young married lady of my acquaintance who, the best of the jest was, had not changed her condition above a fortnight before, in a question on which I had the misfortune to differ from her, respecting the properest mode of breeding oysters for the London market, had the assurance to ask with a sneer, how such an old Bachelor as I could pretend to know anything about such matters.

But what I have spoken of hitherto is nothing to the airs which these creatures give themselves when they come, as they generally do, to have children. When I consider how little of a rarity children are, — that every street and blind alley swarms with them, — that the poorest people commonly have them in most abundance, — that there are few marriages that are not blest with at least one of these bargains, — how often they turn out ill, and defeat the fond hopes of their parents, taking to vicious courses, which end in poverty, disgrace, the gallows, &c. — I cannot for my life tell what cause for pride there can possibly be in having them. If they were young phœnixes, indeed, that were born but one in a year, there might be a pretext. But when they are so common ——

I do not advert to the insolent merit which they assume with their husbands on these occasions. Let them look to that. But why *we*, who are not their natural-born subjects, should be expected to bring our spices, myrrh, and incense, — our tribute and homage of admiration, — I do not see.

" Like as the arrows in the hand of the giant, even so are the young children : " so says the excellent office in our Prayer-book appointed for the churching of women. " Happy is the man that hath his quiver full of them." So say I; but then don't let him discharge his quiver upon us that are weaponless ; — let them be arrows, but not to gall and stick us. I have generally observed that these arrows are double-headed : they have two forks, to be sure to hit with one or the other. As for instance, where you come into a house which is full of children, if you happen to take no notice of them (you are thinking of something else, perhaps, and turn a deaf ear to their innocent caresses), you are set down as untractable, morose, a hater of children. On the other hand, if you find them more than usually engaging, — if you are taken with their pretty manners, and set about in earnest to romp and play with them, some pretext or other is sure to be found for sending them out of the room : they are too noisy or boisterous, or Mr. ———— does not like children. With one or other of these forks the arrow is sure to hit you.

I could forgive their jealousy, and dispense with toying with their brats, if it gives them any pain ; but I think it unreasonable to be called upon to *love* them, where I see no occasion, — to love a whole family, perhaps, eight, nine, or ten, indiscriminately, — to love all the pretty dears, because children are so engaging.

I know there is a proverb, " Love me, love my dog : " that is not always so very practicable, particularly if the dog be set upon you to tease you or snap at you in sport. But a dog, or a lesser thing, — any inanimate substance, as a keepsake, a watch or a ring, a tree, or the place where we last parted when my friend went away upon a long absence, I can make shift to love, because I love him, and anything that reminds me of him ; provided it be in its nature indifferent, and apt to receive whatever hue fancy can give it. But children have a real character and an essential being of themselves : they are amiable or unamiable *per se* ; I must love or hate them as I see cause for either in their qualities. A child's nature is too serious a thing to admit of its being regarded as a mere appendage to another being, and to be loved or hated accordingly : they stand with me upon their own stock, as much as men and women do. O ! but you will say, sure it is an attractive age, — there is something in the tender years of infancy that of itself charms us. That is the very reason why I am more nice about them. I know that a sweet child is the sweetest thing in nature, not even excepting the delicate creatures which bear them ; but the prettier the kind of a thing is, the more desirable it is that it should be pretty of its kind. One daisy differs not much from another in glory ; but a violet should look and smell the daintiest. — I was always rather squeamish in my women and children.

But this is not the worst: one must be admitted into their familiarity at least, before they can complain of inattention. It implies visits, and some kind of intercourse. But if the husband be a man with whom you have lived on a friendly footing before marriage, — if you did not come in on the wife's side, — if you did not sneak into the house in her train, but were an old friend in fast habits of intimacy before their courtship was so much as thought on, — look about you — your tenure is precarious — before a twelvemonth shall roll over your head, you shall find your old friend gradually grow cool and altered towards you, and at last seek opportunities of breaking with you. I have scarce a married friend of my acquaintance upon whose firm faith I can rely, whose friendship did not commence *after the period of his marriage*. With some limitations they can endure that: but that the good man should have dared to enter into a solemn league of friendship in which they were not consulted, though it happened before they knew him, — before they that are now man and wife ever met, — this is intolerable to them. Every long friendship, every old authentic intimacy, must be brought into their office to be new stamped with their currency, as a sovereign Prince calls in the good old money that was coined in some reign before he was born or thought of, to be new marked and minted with the stamp of his authority, before he will let it pass current in the world. You may guess what luck generally befalls such a rusty piece of metal as I am in these *new mintings*.

Innumerable are the ways which they take to insult and worm you out of their husband's confidence. Laughing at all you say with a kind of wonder, as if you were a queer kind of fellow that said good things, *but an oddity*, is one of the ways; — they have a particular kind of stare for the purpose; — till at last the husband, who used to defer to your judgment, and would pass over some excrescences of understanding and manner for the sake of a general vein of observation (not quite vulgar) which he perceived in you, begins to suspect whether you are not altogether a humorist, — a fellow well enough to have consorted with in his bachelor days, but not quite so proper to be introduced to ladies. This may be called the staring way; and is that which has oftenest been put in practice against me.

Then there is the exaggerating way, or the way of irony: that is, where they find you an object of especial regard with their husband, who is not so easily to be shaken from the lasting attachment founded on esteem which he has conceived towards you; by never-qualified exaggerations to cry up all that you say or do, till the good man, who understands well enough that it is all done in compliment to him, grows weary of the debt of gratitude which is due to so much candour, and by relaxing a little on his part, and taking down a peg or two in his enthusiasm, sinks at length to that kindly level of moderate esteem, — that " decent affection and complacent kindness " towards you, where she herself can join in sympathy with him without much stretch and violence to her sincerity.

Another way (for the ways they have to accomplish so desirable a purpose are infinite) is, with a kind of innocent simplicity, continually to mistake what it was which first made their husband.fond of you. If an esteem for something excellent in your moral character was that which riveted the chain which she is to break, upon any imaginary discovery of a want of poignancy in your conversation, she will cry, " I thought, my dear, you described your friend, Mr. ⸺ as a great wit." If, on the other hand, it was for some supposed charm in your conversation that he first grew to like you, and was content for this to overlook some trifling irregularities in your moral deportment, upon the first notice of any of these she as readily exclaims, " This, my dear, is your good Mr. ———." One good lady whom I took the liberty of expostulating with for not showing me quite so much respect as I thought due to her husband's old friend, had the candour to confess to me that she had often heard Mr. ——— speak of me before marriage, and that she had conceived a great desire to be acquainted with me, but that the sight of me had very much disappointed her expectations ; for from her husband's representations of me, she had formed a notion that she was to see a fine, tall, officer-like looking man (I use her very words) ; the very reverse of which proved to be the truth. This was candid ; and I had the civility not to ask her in return, how she came to pitch upon a standard of personal accomplishments for her husband's friends which differed so much from his own ; for my friend's dimensions as near as possible approximate to mine ; he standing five feet five in his shoes, in which I have the advantage of him by about half an inch ; and he no more than myself exhibiting any indications of a martial character in his air or countenance.

These are some of the mortifications which I have encountered in the absurd attempt to visit at their houses. To enumerate them all would be a vain endeavour : I shall therefore just glance at the very common impropriety of which married ladies are guilty, — of treating us as if we were their husbands, and *vice versâ*. I mean, when they use us with familiarity, and their husbands with ceremony. Testacea, for instance, kept me the other night two or three hours beyond my usual time of supping, while she was fretting because Mr. ——— did not come home, till the oysters were all spoiled, rather than she would be guilty of the impoliteness of touching one in his absence. This was reversing the point of good manners : for ceremony is an invention to take off the uneasy feeling which we derive from knowing ourselves to be less the object of love and esteem with a fellow-creature than some other person is. It endeavours to make up, by superior attentions in little points, for that invidious preference which it is forced to deny in the greater. Had Testacea kept the oysters back for me, and withstood her husband's importunities to go to supper, she would have acted according to the strict rules of propriety. I know no ceremony that ladies are bound to observe to their husbands, beyond the point of a modest behaviour and decorum : therefore I must protest against the vicarious gluttony of Cerasia, who at her own table sent away a dish of Morellas, which I was applying to with great good will, to her husband at the other end of the table, and recommended a plate of less extraordinary gooseberries to my unwedded palate in their stead. Neither can I excuse the wanton affront of ———.

But I am weary of stringing up all my married acquaintance by Roman denominations. Let them amend and change their manners, or I promise to record the full-length English of their names, to the terror of all such desperate offenders in future.

VALENTINE'S DAY

Examiner, February 14 and 15, 1819; *Indicator*, February 14, 1821

Hail to thy returning festival, old Bishop Valentine ! Great is thy name in the rubric, thou venerable Archflamen of Hymen ! Immortal Go-between ! who and what manner of person art thou ? Art thou but a *name*, typifying the restless principle which impels poor humans to seek perfection in union ? or wert thou indeed a mortal prelate, with thy tippet and thy rochet, thy apron on, and decent lawn sleeves ? Mysterious personage ! like unto thee, assuredly, there is no other mitred father in the calendar ; not Jerome, nor Ambrose, nor Cyril ; nor the consigner of undipt infants to eternal torments, Austin, whom all mothers hate ; nor he who hated all mothers,

Origen; nor Bishop Bull, nor Archbishop Parker, nor Whit-gift. Thou comest attended with thousands and ten thousands of little Loves, and the air is

Brush'd with the hiss of rustling wings.

Singing Cupids are thy choristers and thy precentors; and instead of the crosier, the mystical arrow is borne before thee.

In other words, this is the day on which those charming little missives, ycleped Valentines, cross and intercross each other at every street and turning. The weary and all forspent twopenny postman sinks beneath a load of delicate embarrass-ments, not his own. It is scarcely credible to what an extent this ephemeral courtship is carried on in this loving town, to the great enrichment of porters, and detriment of knockers and bell-wires. In these little visual interpretations, no emblem is so common as the *heart*, — that little three-cornered expo-nent of all our hopes and fears, — the bestuck and bleeding heart; it is twisted and tortured into more allegories and affec-tations than an opera hat. What authority we have in history or mythology for placing the headquarters and metropolis of God Cupid in this anatomical seat rather than in any other, is not very clear; but we have got it, and it will serve as well as any other. Else we might easily imagine, upon some other system which might have prevailed for any thing which our pathology knows to the contrary, a lover addressing his mis-tress, in perfect simplicity of feeling, "Madam, my *liver* and fortune are entirely at your disposal"; or putting a delicate question, "Amanda, have you a *midriff* to bestow?" But custom has settled these things, and awarded the seat of sentiment to the aforesaid triangle, while its less fortunate neighbours wait at animal and anatomical distance.

Not many sounds in life, and I include all urban and all rural sounds, exceed in interest a *knock at the door*. It "gives a very echo to the throne where Hope is seated." But its issues seldom answer to this oracle within. It is so seldom that just the person we want to see comes. But of all the

clamorous visitations the welcomest in expectation is the sound
that ushers in, or seems to usher in, a Valentine. As the
raven himself was hoarse that announced the fatal entrance
of Duncan, so the knock of the postman on this day is light,
airy, confident, and befitting one that bringeth good tidings.
It is less mechanical than on other days ; you will say, "That
is not the post I am sure." Visions of Love, of Cupids, of
Hymens ! — delightful eternal common-places, which "having
been will always be"; which no school-boy nor school-man
can write away ; having your irreversible throne in the fancy
and affections — what are your transports, when the happy
maiden, opening with careful finger, careful not to break the
emblematic seal, bursts upon the sight of some well-designed
allegory, some type, some youthful fancy, not without verses —

> Lovers all,
> A madrigal,

or some such device, not over abundant in sense — young
Love disclaims it, — and not quite silly — something between
wind and water, a chorus where the sheep might almost
join the shepherd, as they did, or as I apprehend they did,
in Arcadia.

All Valentines are not foolish ; and I shall not easily forget
thine, my kind friend (if I may have leave to call you so)
E. B. — E. B. lived opposite a young maiden, whom he had
often seen, unseen, from his parlour window in C — e Street.
She was all joyousness and innocence, and just of an age to
enjoy receiving a Valentine, and just of a temper to bear the
disappointment of missing one with good humour. E. B. is an
artist of no common powers ; in the fancy parts of designing,
perhaps inferior to none ; his name is known at the bottom of
many a well-executed vignette in the way of his profession, but
no further ; for E. B. is modest, and the world meets nobody
half-way. E. B. meditated how he could repay this young
maiden for many a favour which she had done him unknown ;
for when a kindly face greets us, though but passing by, and

never knows us again, nor we it, we should feel it as an obligation ; and E. B. did. This good artist set himself at work to please the damsel. It was just before Valentine's day three years since. He wrought, unseen and unsuspected, a wondrous work. We need not say it was on the finest gilt paper with borders — full, not of common hearts and heartless allegory, but all the prettiest stories of love from Ovid, and older poets than Ovid (for E. B. is a scholar). There was Pyramus and Thisbe, and be sure Dido was not forgot, nor Hero and Leander, and swans more than sang in Cayster, with mottos and fanciful devices, such as beseemed, — a work in short of magic. Iris dipt the woof. This on Valentine's eve he commended to the all-swallowing indiscriminate orifice — (O ignoble trust !) — of the common post ; but the humble medium did its duty, and from his watchful stand, the next morning, he saw the cheerful messenger knock, and by and by the precious charge delivered. He saw, unseen, the happy girl unfold the Valentine, dance about, clap her hands, as one after one the pretty emblems unfolded themselves. She danced about, not with light love, or foolish expectations, for she had no lover ; or, if she had, none she knew that could have created those bright images which delighted her. It was more like some fairy present ; a God-send, as our familiarly pious ancestors termed a benefit received, where the benefactor was unknown. It would do her no harm. It would do her good for ever after. It is good to love the unknown. I only give this as a specimen of E. B. and his modest way of doing a concealed kindness.

Good-morrow to my Valentine, sings poor Ophelia ; and no better wish, but with better auspices, we wish to all faithful lovers, who are not too wise to despise old legends, but are content to rank themselves humble diocesans of old Bishop Valentine, and his true church.

CHRIST'S HOSPITAL FIVE AND THIRTY YEARS AGO

London Magazine, November, 1820

In Mr. Lamb's *Works*, published a year or two since, I
find a magnificent eulogy on my old school, such as it was, or
now appears to him to have been, between the years 1782 and
1789. It happens, very oddly, that my own standing at Christ's
was nearly corresponding with his; and, with all gratitude to
him for his enthusiasm for the cloisters, I think he has contrived to bring together whatever can be said in praise of them,
dropping all the other side of the argument most ingeniously.

I remember L. at school; and can well recollect that he had
some peculiar advantages, which I and others of his school-
fellows had not. His friends lived in town, and were near at
hand; and he had the privilege of going to see them, almost
as often as he wished, through some invidious distinction,
which was denied to us. The present worthy sub-treasurer to
the Inner Temple can explain how that happened. He had
his tea and hot rolls in a morning, while we were battening
upon our quarter of a penny loaf — our *crug* — moistened with
attenuated small beer, in wooden piggins, smacking of the
pitched leathern jack it was poured from. Our Monday's milk
porritch, blue and tasteless, and the pease soup of Saturday,
coarse and choking, were enriched for him with a slice of
" extraordinary bread and butter," from the hot-loaf of the
Temple. The Wednesday's mess of millet, somewhat less
repugnant — (we had three banyan to four meat days in the
week) — was endeared to his palate with a lump of double-
refined, and a smack of ginger (to make it go down the more
glibly) or the fragrant cinnamon. In lieu of our *half-pickled*
Sundays, or *quite fresh* boiled beef on Thursdays (strong as
caro equina), with detestable marigolds floating in the pail to
poison the broth — our scanty mutton crags on Fridays — and
rather more savoury, but grudging, portions of the same flesh,
rotten-roasted or rare, on the Tuesdays (the only dish which
excited our appetites, and disappointed our stomachs, in almost

equal proportion) — he had his hot plate of roast veal, or the more tempting griskin (exotics unknown to our palates), cooked in the paternal kitchen (a great thing), and brought him daily by his maid or aunt! I remember the good old relative (in whom love forbade pride) squatting down upon some odd stone in a by-nook of the cloisters, disclosing the viands (of higher regale than those cates which the ravens ministered to the Tishbite); and the contending passions of L. at the unfolding. There was love for the bringer; shame for the thing brought, and the manner of its bringing; sympathy for those who were too many to share in it; and, at top of all, hunger (eldest, strongest of the passions!) predominant, breaking down the stony fences of shame, and awkwardness, and a troubling over-consciousness.

I was a poor friendless boy. My parents, and those who should care for me, were far away. Those few acquaintances of theirs, which they could reckon upon being kind to me in the great city, after a little forced notice, which they had the grace to take of me on my first arrival in town, soon grew tired of my holiday visits. They seemed to them to recur too often, though I thought them few enough; and, one after another, they all failed me, and I felt myself alone among six hundred playmates.

O the cruelty of separating a poor lad from his early homestead! The yearnings which I used to have towards it in those unfledged years! How, in my dreams, would my native town (far in the west) come back, with its church, and trees, and faces! How I would wake weeping, and in the anguish of my heart exclaim upon sweet Calne in Wiltshire!

To this late hour of my life, I trace impressions left by the recollection of those friendless holidays. The long warm days of summer never return but they bring with them a gloom from the haunting memory of those *whole-day-leaves*, when, by some strange arrangement, we were turned out, for the live-long day, upon our own hands, whether we had friends to go to, or none. I remember those bathing excursions to the New River, which L. recalls with such relish, better, I think, than he can — for he was a home-seeking lad, and did not much care for such water-pastimes : — How merrily we would sally forth into the fields ; and strip under the first warmth of the sun ; and wanton like young dace in the streams ; getting us appetites for noon, which those of us that were penniless (our scanty morning crust long since exhausted) had not the means of allaying — while the cattle, and the birds, and the fishes, were at feed about us, and we had nothing to satisfy our cravings — the very beauty of the day, and the exercise of the pastime, and the sense of liberty, setting a keener edge upon them ! — How faint and languid finally we would return, towards nightfall, to our desired morsel, half-rejoicing, half-reluctant, that the hours of our uneasy liberty had expired !

It was worse in the days of winter, to go prowling about the streets objectless — shivering at cold windows of print-shops, to extract a little amusement ; or haply, as a last resort, in the hope of a little novelty, to pay a fifty-times repeated visit (where our individual faces should be as well known to the warden as those of his own charges) to the Lions in the Tower — to whose levée, by courtesy immemorial, we had a prescriptive title to admission.

L.'s governor (so we called the patron who presented us to the foundation) lived in a manner under his paternal roof. Any complaint which he had to make was sure of being attended to. This was understood at Christ's, and was an effectual screen to him against the severity of masters, or worse tyranny of the monitors. The oppressions of these young brutes are heart-sickening to call to recollection. I have been called out of my bed, and *waked for the purpose*, in the coldest winter nights — and this not once, but night after night — in my shirt, to receive the discipline of a leathern thong, with eleven other sufferers, because it pleased my callow overseer, when there has been any talking heard after we were gone to bed, to make the six last beds in the dormitory, where the youngest children of us slept, answerable for an offence they neither dared to commit, nor had the power to hinder. — The same execrable tyranny drove the younger part of us from the fires, when our feet were perishing with snow; and under the cruelest penalties, forbade the indulgence of a drink of water, when we lay in sleepless summer nights, fevered with the season, and the day's sports.

There was one H———, who, I learned, in after days, was seen expiating some maturer offence in the hulks. (Do I flatter myself in fancying that this might be the planter of that name, who suffered —— at Nevis, I think, or St. Kitts, —— some few years since? My friend Tobin was the benevolent instrument of bringing him to the gallows.) This petty Nero actually branded a boy, who had offended him, with a red-hot iron; and nearly starved forty of us, with exacting contributions, to the one half of our bread, to pamper a young ass, which, incredible as it may seem, with the connivance of the nurse's daughter (a young flame of his) he had contrived to smuggle in, and keep upon the leads of the *ward*, as they called our dormitories. This game went on for better than a week, till the foolish beast, not able to fare well but he must cry roast meat — happier than Caligula's minion, could he have kept his own counsel — but, foolisher, alas! than any of his species in the fables — waxing fat, and kicking, in the fulness of bread, one unlucky minute would needs proclaim his good fortune to the world below; and, laying out his simple throat, blew such a ram's horn blast, as (toppling down the walls of his own Jericho) set concealment any longer at defiance. The client was dismissed, with certain attentions, to Smithfield; but I never understood that the patron underwent any censure on the occasion. This was in the stewardship of L.'s admired Perry.

Under the same *facile* administration, can L. have forgotten the cool impunity with which the nurses used to carry away openly, in open platters, for their own tables, one out of two of every hot joint, which the careful matron had been seeing scrupulously weighed out for our dinners? These things were daily practised in that magnificent apartment, which L. (grown connoisseur since, we presume) praises so highly for the grand paintings "by Verrio, and others," with which it is "hung round and adorned." But the sight of sleek, well-fed blue-coat boys in pictures was, at that time, I believe, little consolatory to him, or us, the living ones, who saw the better part of our provisions carried away before our faces by harpies; and ourselves reduced (with the Trojan in the hall of Dido)

> To feed our mind with idle portraiture.

L. has recorded the repugnance of the school to *gags*, or the fat of fresh beef boiled; and sets it down to some superstition. But these unctuous morsels are never grateful to young palates (children are universally fat-haters) and in strong, coarse, boiled meats, *unsalted*, are detestable. A *gag-eater* in our time was equivalent to a *goul*, and held in equal detestation. —— suffered under the imputation.

> —— 'Twas said,
> He ate strange flesh.

He was observed, after dinner, carefully to gather up the remnants left at his table (not many, nor very choice fragments, you may credit me) — and, in an especial manner, these disreputable morsels, which he would convey away, and secretly stow in the settle that stood at his bed-side. None saw when he ate them. It was rumoured that he privately devoured them in the night. He was watched, but no traces of such midnight practices were discoverable. Some reported that, on leave-days, he had been seen to carry out of the bounds a large blue check handkerchief, full of something. This then must be the accursed thing. Conjecture next was at work to imagine how he could dispose of it. Some said he sold it to the beggars. This belief generally prevailed. He went about moping. None spake to him. No one would play with him. He was excommunicated; put out of the pale of the school. He was too powerful a boy to be beaten, but he underwent every mode of that negative punishment, which is more grievous than many stripes. Still he persevered. At length he was observed by two of his school-fellows, who were determined to get at the secret, and had traced him one leave-day for that purpose, to enter a large worn-out building, such as there exist specimens of in Chancery Lane, which are let out to various scales of pauperism with open door, and a common staircase. After him they silently slunk in, and followed by stealth up four flights, and saw him tap at a poor wicket, which was opened by an aged woman, meanly clad. Suspicion was now ripened into certainty. The informers had secured their victim. They had him in their toils. Accusation was formally preferred, and retribution most signal was looked for. Mr. Hathaway, the then steward (for this happened a little after my time), with that patient sagacity which tempered all his conduct, determined to investigate the matter, before he proceeded to sentence. The result was that the supposed mendicants, the receivers or purchasers of the mysterious scraps, turned out to be the parents of ——, an honest couple come to decay, — whom this seasonable supply had, in all probability, saved from mendicancy; and that this young stork, at the expense of his own good name, had all this while been only feeding the old birds! — The governors on this occasion, much to their honour, voted a present relief to the family of ——, and presented him with a silver medal. The lesson which the steward read upon RASH JUDGMENT, on the occasion of publicly delivering the medal to ——, I believe, would not be lost upon his auditory. — I had left school then, but I well remember ——. He was a tall, shambling youth, with a cast in his eye, not at all calculated to conciliate hostile prejudices. I have since seen him carrying a baker's basket. I think I heard he did not do quite so well by himself, as he had done by the old folks.

I was a hypochondriac lad; and the sight of a boy in fetters, upon the day of my first putting on the blue clothes, was not exactly fitted to assuage the natural terrors of initiation. I was of tender years, barely turned of seven; and had only read of such things in books, or seen them but in dreams. I was told he had *run away*. This was the punishment for the first offence. — As a novice I was soon after taken to see the dungeons. These were little, square, Bedlam cells, where a boy could just lie at his length upon straw and a blanket — a mattress, I think, was afterwards substituted — with a peep of light, let in askance, from a prison-orifice at top, barely enough to read by. Here the poor boy was locked in by himself all day, without sight of any but the porter who brought him his bread and water — who *might not speak to him*; — or of the beadle, who came twice a week to call him out to receive his periodical chastisement, which was almost welcome, because it separated him for a brief interval from solitude : — and here he was shut up by himself *of nights*, out of the reach of any sound, to suffer whatever horrors the weak nerves, and superstition incident to his time of life, might subject him to.[1] This was the penalty for the second offence. — Wouldst thou like, reader, to see what became of him in the next degree?

The culprit, who had been a third time an offender, and whose expulsion was at this time deemed irreversible, was brought forth, as at some solemn *auto da fe*, arrayed in uncouth and most appalling attire — all trace of his late " watchet weeds " carefully effaced, he was exposed in a jacket, resembling those which London lamplighters formerly delighted in, with a cap of the same. The effect of this divestiture was such as the ingenious devisers of it could have anticipated. With his pale and frighted features, it was as if some of those disfigurements in Dante had seized upon him. In this disguisement he was brought into the hall (*L's favourite state-room*), where awaited him the whole number of his schoolfellows, whose joint lessons and sports he was thenceforth to share no more ; the awful presence of the steward, to be seen for the

[1] One or two instances of lunacy, or attempted suicide, accordingly, at length convinced the governors of the impolicy of this part of the sentence, and the midnight torture to the spirits was dispensed with. — This fancy of dungeons for children was a sprout of Howard's brain ; for which (saving the reverence due to Holy Paul), methinks, I could willingly spit upon his statue.

last time ; of the executioner beadle, clad in his state robe for the occasion ; and of two faces more, of direr import, because never but in these extremities visible. These were governors ; two of whom, by choice, or charter, were always accustomed to officiate at these *Ultima Supplicia* ; not to mitigate (so at least we understood it), but to enforce the uttermost stripe. Old Bamber Gascoigne, and Peter Aubert, I remember, were colleagues on one occasion, when the beadle turning rather pale, a glass of brandy was ordered to prepare him for the mysteries. The scourging was, after the old Roman fashion, long and stately. The lictor accompanied the criminal quite round the hall. We were generally too faint with attending to the previous disgusting circumstances, to make accurate report with our eyes of the degree of corporal suffering inflicted. Report, of course, gave out the back knotty and livid. After scourging, he was made over, in his *San Benito*, to his friends, if he had any (but commonly such poor runagates were friendless), or to his parish officer, who, to enhance the effect of the scene, had his station allotted to him on the outside of the hall gate.

These solemn pageantries were not played off so often as to spoil the general mirth of the community. We had plenty of exercise and recreation *after* school hours ; and, for myself, I must confess, that I was never happier, than *in* them. The Upper and Lower Grammar Schools were held in the same room ; and an imaginary line only divided their bounds. Their character was as different as that of the inhabitants on the two sides of the Pyrenees. The Rev. James Boyer was the Upper Master ; but the Rev. Matthew Field presided over that portion of the apartment of which I had the good fortune to be a member. We lived a life as careless as birds. We talked and did just what we pleased, and nobody molested us. We carried an accidence, or a grammar, for form ; but, for any trouble it gave us, we might take two years in getting through the verbs deponent, and another two in forgetting all that we had learned about them. There was now and then the formality of saying a lesson, but if you had not learned it, a brush across the shoulders (just enough to disturb a fly) was the sole remonstrance. Field never used the rod; and in truth he wielded the cane with no great good will — holding it "like a dancer." It looked in his hands rather like an emblem than an instrument of authority; and an emblem, too, he was ashamed of. He was a good easy man, that did not care to ruffle his own peace, nor perhaps set any great consideration upon the value of juvenile time. He came among us, now and then, but often stayed away whole days from us; and when he came, it made no difference to us — he had his private room to retire to, the short time he stayed, to be out of the sound of our noise. Our mirth and uproar went on. We had classics of our own, without being beholden to "insolent Greece or haughty Rome," that passed current among us — *Peter Wilkins* — *The Adventures of the Hon. Capt. Robert Boyle* — *The Fortunate Blue Coat Boy* — and the like. Or we cultivated a turn for mechanic or scientific operation; making little sun-dials of paper; or weaving those ingenious parentheses, called *cat-cradles*; or making dry peas to dance upon the end of a tin pipe; or studying the art military over that laudable game "French and English," and a hundred other such devices to pass away the time — mixing the useful with the agreeable — as would have made the souls of Rousseau and John Locke chuckle to have seen us.

Matthew Field belonged to that class of modest divines who affect to mix in equal proportion the *gentleman,* the *scholar,* and the *Christian*; but, I know not how, the first ingredient is generally found to be the predominating dose in the composition. He was engaged in gay parties, or with his courtly bow at some episcopal levée, when he should have been attending upon us. He had for many years the classical charge of a hundred children, during the four or five first years of their education; and his very highest form seldom proceeded further than two or three of the introductory fables of Phædrus. How things were suffered to go on thus, I cannot guess. Boyer, who was the proper person to have remedied these abuses, always affected, perhaps felt, a delicacy in interfering in a province not strictly his own. I have not been without my suspicions that he was not altogether displeased at the contrast we presented to his end of the school. We were a sort of Helots to his young Spartans. He would sometimes, with ironic deference, send to borrow a rod of the Under Master, and then, with Sardonic grin, observe to one of his upper boys, "how neat and fresh the twigs looked." While his pale students were battering their brains over Xenophon and Plato, with a silence as deep as that enjoined by the Samite, we were enjoying ourselves at our ease in our little Goshen. We saw a little into the secrets of his discipline, and the prospect did but the more reconcile us to our lot. His thunders rolled innocuous for us; his storms came near, but never touched us; contrary to Gideon's miracle, while all around were drenched, our fleece was dry.[1] His boys turned out the better scholars; we, I suspect, have the advantage in temper. His pupils cannot speak of him without something of terror allaying their gratitude; the remembrance of Field comes back with all the soothing images of indolence, and summer slumbers, and work like play, and innocent idleness, and Elysian exemptions, and life itself a "playing holiday."

Though sufficiently removed from the jurisdiction of Boyer, we were near enough (as I have said) to understand a little of his system. We occasionally heard sounds of the *Ululantes*, and caught glances of Tartarus. B. was a rabid pedant. His English style was cramped to barbarism. His Easter anthems (for his duty obliged him to those periodical flights) were grating as scrannel pipes.[2] — He would laugh, ay, and heartily,

---

[1] Cowley.

[2] In this and everything B. was the antipodes of his coadjutor. While the former was digging his brains for crude anthems, worth a pig-nut, F. would be recreating his gentlemanly fancy in the more flowery walks of the Muses. A little dramatic effusion of his, under the name of *Vertumnus and Pomona*, is not yet forgotten by the chroniclers of that sort of literature. It was accepted by Garrick, but the town did not give it their sanction. — B. used to say of it, in a way of half-compliment, half-irony, that it was *too classical for representation.*

but then it must be at Flaccus's quibble about *Rex* —— or at the *tristis severitas in vultu*, or *inspicere in patinas*, of Terence — thin jests, which at their first broaching could hardly have had *vis* enough to move a Roman muscle. — He had two wigs, both pedantic, but of differing omen. The one serene, smiling, fresh powdered, betokening a mild day. The other, an old discoloured, unkempt, angry caxon, denoting frequent and bloody execution. Woe to the school, when he made his morning appearance in his *passy*, or *passionate wig*. No comet expounded surer. — J. B. had a heavy hand. I have known him double his knotty fist at a poor trembling child (the maternal milk hardly dry upon its lips) with a " Sirrah, do you presume to set your wits at me ? " — Nothing was more common than to see him make a headlong entry into the schoolroom, from his inner recess, or library, and, with turbulent eye, singling out a lad, roar out, " Od's my life, Sirrah " (his favourite adjuration), " I have a great mind to whip you," — then, with as sudden a retracting impulse, fling back into his lair — and, after a cooling lapse of some minutes (during which all but the culprit had totally forgotten the context) drive headlong out again, piecing out his imperfect sense, as if it had been some Devil's Litany, with the expletory yell — " *and I* WILL *too*." — In his gentler moods, when the *rabidus furor* was assuaged, he had resort to an ingenious method, peculiar, for what I have heard, to himself, of whipping the boy, and reading the Debates, at the same time ; a paragraph, and a lash between ; which in those times, when parliamentary oratory was most at a height and flourishing in these realms, was not calculated to impress the patient with a veneration for the diffuser graces of rhetoric.

Once, and but once, the uplifted rod was known to fall ineffectual from his hand — when droll squinting W—— having been caught putting the inside of the master's desk to a use for which the architect had clearly not designed it, to justify himself, with great simplicity averred that *he did not know that the thing had been forewarned*. This exquisite irrecognition of any law antecedent to the *oral* or *declaratory* struck so irresistibly upon the fancy of all who heard it (the pedagogue himself not excepted) that remission was unavoidable.

L. has given credit to B.'s great merits as an instructor. Coleridge, in his literary life, has pronounced a more intelligible and ample encomium on them. The author of the *Country Spectator* doubts not to compare him with the ablest teachers of antiquity. Perhaps we cannot dismiss him better than with the pious ejaculation of C. — when he heard that his old master was on his death-bed — " Poor J. B. ! — may all his faults be forgiven ; and may he be wafted to bliss by little cherub boys, all head and wings, with no *bottoms* to reproach his sublunary infirmities."

Under him were many good and sound scholars bred. — First Grecian of my time was Lancelot Pepys Stevens, kindest of boys and men, since Co-grammar-master (and inseparable companion) with Dr. T———e. What an edifying spectacle did this brace of friends present to those who remembered the anti-socialities of their predecessors ! — You never met the one by chance in the street without a wonder, which was quickly dissipated by the almost immediate sub-appearance of the other. Generally arm in arm, these kindly coadjutors lightened for each other the toilsome duties of their profession, and when, in advanced age, one found it convenient to retire, the other was not long in discovering that it suited him to lay down the fasces also. Oh, it is pleasant, as it is rare, to find the same arm linked in yours at forty, which at thirteen helped it to turn over the *Cicero De Amicitia*, or some tale of Antique Friendship, which the young heart even then was burning to anticipate ! — Co-Grecian with S. was Th———, who has since executed with ability various diplomatic functions at the Northern courts. Th——— was a tall, dark, saturnine youth, sparing of speech, with raven locks. — Thomas Fanshaw Middleton followed him (now Bishop of Calcutta) a scholar and a gentleman in his teens. He has the reputation of an excellent critic ; and is author (besides the *Country Spectator*) of a *Treatise on the Greek Article,* against Sharpe — M. is said to bear his mitre high in India, where the *regni novitas* (I dare say) sufficiently justifies the bearing. A humility quite as primitive as that of Jewel or Hooker might not be exactly fitted to impress the minds of those Anglo-Asiatic diocesans with a reverence for home institutions, and the church which those fathers watered. The manners of M. at school, though firm, were mild, and unassuming. — Next to M. (if not senior to him) was Richards, author of the *Aboriginal Britons,* the most spirited of the Oxford Prize Poems ; a pale, studious Grecian. — Then followed poor S———, ill-fated M———! of these the Muse is silent.

> Finding some of Edward's race
> Unhappy, pass their annals by.

Come back into memory, like as thou wert in the dayspring of thy fancies, with hope like a fiery column before thee — the dark pillar not yet turned — Samuel Taylor Coleridge — Logician, Metaphysician, Bard ! — How have I seen the casual passer through the Cloisters stand still, entranced with admiration (while he weighed the disproportion between the *speech* and the *garb* of the young Mirandula), to hear thee unfold, in thy deep and sweet intonations, the mysteries of Jamblichus, or Plotinus (for even in those years thou waxedst not pale at such philosophic draughts), or reciting Homer in his Greek, or Pindar — while the walls of the old Grey Friars re-echoed to the accents of the *inspired charity-boy* ! — Many were the " wit-combats " (to dally awhile with the words of old Fuller) between him and C. V. Le G———, " which two I behold like a Spanish great gallion, and an English man-of-war ; Master Coleridge, like the former, was built far higher in learning, solid, but slow in his performances. C. V. L., with the English man-of-war, lesser in bulk, but lighter in sailing, could turn with all tides, tack about, and take advantage of all winds, by the quickness of his wit and invention."

Nor shalt thou, their compeer, be quickly forgotten, Allen, with the cordial smile, and still more cordial laugh, with which thou wert wont to make the old Cloisters shake, in thy cognition of some poignant jest of theirs; or the anticipation of some more material, and, peradventure, practical one, of thine own. Extinct are those smiles, with that beautiful countenance, with which (for thou wert the *Nireus formosus* of the school), in the days of thy maturer waggery, thou didst disarm the wrath of infuriated town-damsel, who, incensed by provoking pinch, turning tigress-like round, suddenly converted by thy angel-look, exchanged the half-formed terrible " *bl*——," for a gentler greeting — " *bless thy handsome face !* "

Next follow two, who ought to be now alive, and the friends of Elia — the junior Le G——— and F——— ; who impelled, the former by a roving temper, the latter by too quick a sense of neglect — ill capable of enduring the slights poor Sizars are sometimes subject to in our seats of learning — exchanged their Alma Mater for the camp; perishing, one by climate, and one on the plains of Salamanca : — Le G——— sanguine, volatile, sweet-natured; F——— dogged, faithful, anticipative of insult, warm-hearted, with something of the old Roman height about him.

Fine, frank-hearted Fr———, the present master of Hertford, with Marmaduke T———, mildest of Missionaries — and both my good friends still — close the catalogue of Grecians in my time.

THE TWO RACES OF MEN

London Magazine, December, 1820

The human species, according to the best theory I can form of it, is composed of two distinct races, *the men who borrow*, and *the men who lend*. To these two original diversities may be reduced all those impertinent classifications of Gothic and Celtic tribes, white men, black men, red men. All the dwellers upon earth, " Parthians, and Medes, and Elamites," flock hither, and do naturally fall in with one or other of these primary distinctions. The infinite superiority of the former, which I choose to designate as the *great race*, is discernible in their figure, port, and a certain instinctive sovereignty. The latter are born degraded. " He shall serve his brethren." There is something in the air of one of this cast, lean and suspicious ; contrasting with the open, trusting, generous manner of the other.

Observe who have been the greatest borrowers of all ages — Alcibiades — Falstaff — Sir Richard Steele — our late incomparable Brinsley — what a family likeness in all four !

What a careless, even deportment hath your borrower ! what rosy gills ! what a beautiful reliance on Providence doth he manifest, — taking no more thought than lilies ! What contempt for money, — accounting it (yours and mine especially) no better than dross ! What a liberal confounding of those pedantic distinctions of *meum* and *tuum* ! or rather, what a noble simplification of language (beyond Tooke), resolving these supposed opposites into one clear, intelligible pronoun adjective ! — What near approaches doth he make to the primitive *community*, — to the extent of one-half of the principle at least ! —

He is the true taxer who " calleth all the world up to be taxed " ; and the distance is as vast between him and *one of us*, as subsisted betwixt the Augustan Majesty and the poorest obolary Jew that paid it tribute-pittance at Jerusalem ! — His exactions, too, have such a cheerful, voluntary air ! So far removed from your sour parochial or state-gatherers, — those inkhorn varlets, who carry their want of welcome in their faces ! He cometh to you with a smile, and troubleth you with no receipt ; confining himself to no set season. Every day is his Candlemas, or his Feast of Holy Michael. He applieth the *lene tormentum* of a pleasant look to your purse, — which to that gentle warmth expands her silken leaves, as naturally as the cloak of the traveller, for which sun and wind contended ! He is the true Propontic which never ebbeth ! The sea which taketh handsomely at each man's hand. In vain the victim, whom he delighteth to honour, struggles with destiny ; he is in the net. Lend therefore cheerfully, O man ordained to lend — that thou lose not in the end, with thy worldly penny, the reversion promised. Combine not preposterously in thine own person the penalties of Lazarus and of Dives!—but, when thou seest the proper authority coming, meet it smilingly, as it were half-way. Come, a handsome sacrifice ! See how light *he* makes of it ! Strain not courtesies with a noble enemy.)

Reflections like the foregoing were forced upon my mind by the death of my old friend, Ralph Bigod, Esq., who departed this life on Wednesday evening; dying, as he had lived, without much trouble. He boasted himself a descendant from mighty ancestors of that name, who heretofore held ducal dignities in this realm. In his actions and sentiments he belied not the stock to which he pretended. Early in life he found himself invested with ample revenues ; which, with that noble disinter-estedness which I have noticed as inherent in men of the *great race*, he took almost immediate measures entirely to dissipate and bring to nothing : for there is something revolting in the idea of a king holding a private purse ; and the thoughts of Bigod were all regal. Thus furnished, by the very act of disfurnishment ; getting rid of the cumbersome luggage of riches, more apt (as one sings)

> To slacken virtue, and abate her edge,
> Than prompt her to do aught may merit praise,

he set forth, like some Alexander, upon his great enterprise, "borrowing and to borrow !"

In his periegesis, or triumphant progress throughout this island, it has been calculated that he laid a tithe part of the inhabitants under contribution. I reject this estimate as greatly exaggerated :— but having had the honour of accompanying my friend, divers times, in his perambulations about this vast city, I own I was greatly struck at first with the prodigious number of faces we met, who claimed a sort of respectful ac quaintance with us. He was one day so obliging as to explain the phenomenon. It seems, these were his tributaries ; feeders of his exchequer; gentlemen, his good friends (as he was pleased to express himself), to whom he had occasionally been beholden for a loan. Their multitudes did no way disconcert him. He rather took a pride in numbering them; and, with Comus, seemed pleased to be "stocked with so fair a herd."

With such sources, it was a wonder how he contrived to keep his treasury always empty. He did it by force of an aphorism, which he had often in his mouth, that "money kept longer than three days stinks." So he made use of it while it was fresh. A good part he drank away (for he was an excellent toss-pot), some he gave away, the rest he threw away, literally tossing and hurling it violently from him — as boys do burrs, or as if it had been infectious, — into ponds or ditches, or deep holes, — inscrutable cavities of the earth; — or he would bury it (where he would never seek it again) by a river's side under some bank, which (he would facetiously observe) paid no interest — but out away from him it must go peremptorily, as Hagar's offspring into the wilderness, while it was sweet. He never missed it. The streams were perennial which fed his fisc. When new supplies became necessary, the first person that had the felicity to fall in with him, friend or stranger, was sure to contribute to the deficiency. For Bigod had an *undeniable* way with him. He had a cheerful, open exterior, a quick jovial eye, a bald forehead, just touched with grey (*cana fides*). He anticipated no excuse, and found none. And, waiving for a while my theory as to the *great race*, I would put it to the most untheorising reader, who may at times have disposable coin in his pocket, whether it is not more repugnant to the kindliness of his nature to refuse such a one as I am describing, than to say *no* to a poor petitionary rogue (your bastard borrower), who, by his mumping visnomy, tells you that he expects nothing better; and, therefore, whose preconceived notions and expectations you do in reality so much less shock in the refusal.

When I think of this man; his fiery glow of heart; his swell of feeling; how magnificent, how *ideal* he was; how great at the midnight hour; and when I compare with him the companions with whom I have associated since, I grudge the saving of a few idle ducats, and think that I am fallen into the society of *lenders*, and *little men*.

To one like Elia, whose treasures are rather cased in leather covers than closed in iron coffers, there is a class of alienators more formidable than that which I have touched upon; I mean your *borrowers of books* — those mutilators of collections, spoilers of the symmetry of shelves, and creators of odd volumes. There is Comberbatch, matchless in his depredations!

That foul gap in the bottom shelf facing you, like a great eye-tooth knocked out — (you are now with me in my little back study in Bloomsbury, reader!) — with the huge Switzer-like tomes on each side (like the Guildhall giants, in their reformed posture, guardant of nothing) once held the tallest of my folios, *Opera Bonaventuræ*, choice and massy divinity, to which its two supporters (school divinity also, but of a lesser calibre, — Bellarmine, and Holy Thomas), showed but as dwarfs, — itself an Ascapart! — *that* Comberbatch abstracted upon the faith of a theory he holds, which is more easy, I confess, for me to suffer by than to refute, namely, that "the title to property in a book (my Bonaventure, for instance), is in exact ratio to the claimant's powers of understanding and appreciating the same." Should he go on acting upon this theory, which of our shelves is safe?

The slight vacuum in the left hand case — two shelves from the ceiling — scarcely distinguishable but by the quick eye of a loser —— was whilom the commodious resting-place of Brown on Urn Burial. C. will hardly allege that he knows more about that treatise than I do, who introduced it to him, and was indeed the first (of the moderns) to discover its beauties — but so have I known a foolish lover to praise his mistress in the presence of a rival more qualified to carry her off than himself. — Just below, Dodsley's dramas want their fourth volume, where *Vittoria Corombona* is! The remainder nine are as distasteful as Priam's refuse sons, when the Fates *borrowed* Hector. Here

stood the *Anatomy of Melancholy*, in sober state. — There loi-
tered *The Complete Angler*; quiet as in life, by some stream
side. — In yonder nook, *John Buncle*, a widower-volume, with
" eyes closed," mourns his ravished mate.

One justice I must do my friend, that if he sometimes, like
the sea, sweeps away a treasure, at another time, sea-like, he
throws up as rich an equivalent to match it. I have a small
under-collection of this nature (my friend's gatherings in his
various calls), picked up, he has forgotten at what odd places,
and deposited with as little memory at mine. I take in these
orphans, the twice-deserted. These proselytes of the gate are
welcome as the true Hebrews. There they stand in conjunction ; natives, and naturalised. The latter seemed as little disposed to inquire out their true lineage as I am. — I charge no
warehouse-room for these deodands, nor shall ever put myself
to the ungentlemanly trouble of advertising a sale of them to
pay expenses.

To lose a volume to C. carries some sense and meaning in
it. You are sure that he will make one hearty meal on your
viands, if he can give no account of the platter after it. But
what moved thee, wayward, spiteful K., to be so importunate
to carry off with thee, in spite of tears and adjurations to thee
to forbear, the *Letters* of that princely woman, the thrice noble
Margaret Newcastle ? — knowing at the time, and knowing that
I knew also, thou most assuredly wouldst never turn over one
leaf of the illustrious folio : — what but the mere spirit of
contradiction, and childish love of getting the better of thy
friend ? — Then, worst cut of all ! to transport it with thee
to the Gallican land —

> Unworthy land to harbour such a sweetness,
> A virtue in which all ennobling thoughts dwelt,
> Pure thoughts, kind thoughts, high thoughts, her sex's wonder !

— hadst thou not thy play-books, and books of jests and fancies, about thee, to keep thee merry, even as thou keepest all
companies with thy quips and mirthful tales ? — Child of the

Green-room, it was unkindly done of thee. Thy wife, too, that part-French, better-part Englishwoman! — that *she* could fix upon no other treatise to bear away in kindly token of remembering us, than the works of Fulke Greville, Lord Brook — of which no Frenchman, nor woman of France, Italy, or England, was ever by nature constituted to comprehend a tittle! *Was there not Zimmerman on Solitude?*

Reader, if haply thou art blessed with a moderate collection, be shy of showing it; or if thy heart overfloweth to lend them, lend thy books; but let it be to such a one as S. T. C. — he will return them (generally anticipating the time appointed) with usury; enriched with annotations, tripling their value. I have had experience. Many are these precious MSS. of his — (in *matter* oftentimes, and almost in *quantity* not infrequently, vying with the originals) — in no very clerkly hand — legible in my Daniel; in old Burton; in Sir Thomas Browne; and those abstruser cogitations of the Greville, now, alas! wandering in Pagan lands — I counsel thee, shut not thy heart, nor thy library, against S. T. C.

IMPERFECT SYMPATHIES

London Magazine, August, 1821

I am of a constitution so general, that it consorts and sympathiseth with all things; I have no antipathy, or rather idiosyncrasy in anything. Those national repugnances do not touch me, nor do I behold with prejudice the French, Italian, Spaniard, or Dutch. — *Religio Medici*

That the author of the *Religio Medici*, mounted upon the airy stilts of abstraction, conversant about notional and conjectural essences; in whose categories of Being the possible took the upper hand of the actual; should have overlooked the impertinent individualities of such poor concretions as mankind, is not much to be admired. It is rather to be wondered at, that in the genus of animals he should have condescended to distinguish that species at all. For myself — earth-bound and fettered to the scene of my activities, —

Standing on earth, not rapt above the sky,

I confess that I do feel the differences of mankind, national or individual, to an unhealthy excess. I can look with no indifferent eye upon things or persons. Whatever is, is to me a matter of taste or distaste; or when once it becomes indifferent, it begins to be disrelishing. I am, in plainer words, a bundle of prejudices — made up of likings and dislikings — the veriest thrall to sympathies, apathies, antipathies. In a certain sense, I hope it may be said of me that I am a lover of my species. I can feel for all indifferently, but I cannot feel towards all equally. The more purely-English word that expresses sympathy will better explain my meaning. I can be a friend to a worthy man, who upon another account cannot be my mate or *fellow*. I cannot *like* all people alike.[1]

I have been trying all my life to like Scotchmen, and am obliged to desist from the experiment in despair. They cannot like me — and in truth, I never knew one of that nation who attempted to do it. There is something more plain and ingenuous in their mode of proceeding. We know one another at first sight. There is an order of imperfect intellects (under which mine must be content to rank) which in its constitution

[1] I would be understood as confining myself to the subject of *imperfect sympathies*. To nations or classes of men there can be no direct *antipathy*. There may be individuals born and constellated so opposite to another individual nature, that the same sphere cannot hold them. I have met with my moral antipodes, and can believe the story of two persons meeting (who never saw one another before in their lives) and instantly fighting.

> ———We by proof find there should be
> 'Twixt man and man such an antipathy,
> That though he can show no just reason why
> For any former wrong or injury,
> Can neither find a blemish in his fame,
> Nor aught in face or feature justly blame,
> Can challenge or accuse him of no evil,
> Yet notwithstanding hates him as a devil.

The lines are from old Heywood's *Hierarchie of Angels*, and he subjoins a curious story in confirmation, of a Spaniard who attempted to assassinate a King Ferdinand of Spain, and being put to the rack could give no other reason for the deed but an inveterate antipathy which he had taken to the first sight of the King.

> ———The cause which to that act compell'd him
> Was, he ne'er loved him since he first beheld him.

is essentially anti-Caledonian. The owners of the sort of faculties I allude to have minds rather suggestive than comprehen-
sive. They have no pretences to much clearness or precision
in their ideas, or in their manner of expressing them. Their
intellectual wardrobe (to confess fairly) has few whole pieces
in it. They are content with fragments and scattered pieces of
Truth. She presents no full front to them — a feature or side-
face at the most. Hints and glimpses, germs and crude essays
at a system, is the utmost they pretend to. They beat up a
little game peradventure — and leave it to knottier heads, more
robust constitutions, to run it down. The light that lights them
is not steady and polar, but mutable and shifting : waxing, and
again waning. Their conversation is accordingly. They will
throw out a random word in or out of season, and be content
to let it pass for what it is worth. They cannot speak always
as if they were upon their oath — but must be understood,
speaking or writing, with some abatement. They seldom wait
to mature a proposition, but e'en bring it to market in the
green ear. They delight to impart their defective discoveries
as they arise, without waiting for their full development. They
are no systematisers, and would but err more by attempting it.
Their minds, as I said before, are suggestive merely. The
brain of a true Caledonian (if I am not mistaken) is constituted upon quite a different plan. His Minerva is born in
panoply. You are never admitted to see his ideas in their
growth — if, indeed, they do grow, and are not rather put
together upon principles of clockwork. You never catch his
mind in an undress. He never hints or suggests any thing, but
unlades his stock of ideas in perfect order and completeness.
He brings his total wealth into company, and gravely unpacks
it. His riches are always about him. He never stoops to catch
a glittering something in your presence, to share it with you,
before he quite knows whether it be true touch or not. You
cannot cry *halves* to any thing that he finds. He does not
find, but bring. You never witness his first apprehension of
a thing. His understanding is always at its meridian — you

never see the first dawn, the early streaks. — He has no falterings of self-suspicion. Surmises, guesses, misgivings, half-intuitions, semi-consciousnesses, partial illuminations, dim instincts, embryo conceptions, have no place in his brain, or vocabulary. The twilight of dubiety never falls upon him. Is he orthodox — he has no doubts. Is he an infidel — he has none either. Between the affirmative and the negative there is no border-land with him. You cannot hover with him upon the confines of truth, or wander in the maze of a probable argument. He always keeps the path. You cannot make excursions with him — for he sets you right. His taste never fluctuates. His morality never abates. He cannot compromise, or understand middle actions. There can be but a right and a wrong. His conversation is as a book. His affirmations have the sanctity of an oath. You must speak upon the square with him. He stops a metaphor like a suspected person in an enemy's country. "A healthy book!" — said one of his countrymen to me, who had ventured to give that appellation to *John Buncle*, — "did I catch rightly what you said? I have heard of a man in health, and of a healthy state of body, but I do not see how that epithet can be properly applied to a book." Above all, you must beware of indirect expressions before a Caledonian. Clap an extinguisher upon your irony, if you are unhappily blest with a vein of it. Remember you are upon your oath. I have a print of a graceful female after Leonardo da Vinci, which I was showing off to Mr. ———. After he had examined it minutely, I ventured to ask him how he liked MY BEAUTY (a foolish name it goes by among my friends) — when he very gravely assured me that "he had considerable respect for my character and talents" (so he was pleased to say), "but had not given himself much thought about the degree of my personal pretensions." The misconception staggered me, but did not seem much to disconcert him. — Persons of this nation are particularly fond of affirming a truth — which nobody doubts. They do not so properly affirm, as annunciate it. They do indeed appear to have such a love of truth (as if, like virtue, it were valuable for itself) that all truth becomes equally valuable, whether the proposition that contains it be new or old, disputed, or such as is impossible to become a subject of disputation. I was present not long since at a party of North Britons, where a son of Burns was expected; and happened to drop a silly expression (in my South British way), that I wished it were the father instead of the son — when four of them started up at once to inform me that "that was impossible, because he was dead." An impracticable wish, it seems, was more than they could conceive. Swift has hit off this part of their character, namely their love of truth, in his biting way, but with an illiberality that necessarily confines the passages to the margin.[1] The tediousness of these people is certainly provoking. I wonder if they ever tire one another! — In my early life I had a passionate fondness for the poetry of Burns. I have sometimes foolishly hoped to ingratiate myself with his countrymen by expressing it. But I have always found that a true Scot resents your admiration of his compatriot, even more than he would your contempt of him. The latter he imputes to your "imperfect acquaintance with many of the words which he uses"; and the same objection makes it a presumption in you to suppose that you can admire him. — Thomson they seem to have forgotten. Smollett they have neither forgotten nor forgiven for his delineation of Rory and his companion, upon their first introduction to our metropolis. — Speak of Smollett as a great genius, and they will retort upon you Hume's *History* compared with *his* Continuation of it. What if the historian had continued *Humphrey Clinker*?

---

[1] There are some people who think they sufficiently acquit themselves and entertain their company, with relating facts of no consequence, not at all out of the road of such common incidents as happen every day; and this I have observed more frequently among the Scots than any other nation, who are very careful not to omit the minutest circumstances of time or place; which kind of discourse, if it were not a little relieved by the uncouth terms and phrases, as well as accent and gesture peculiar to that country, would be hardly tolerable. — *Hints towards an Essay on Conversation.*

I have, in the abstract, no disrespect for Jews. They are a piece of stubborn antiquity, compared with which Stonehenge is in its nonage. They date beyond the pyramids. But I should not care to be in habits of familiar intercourse with any of that nation. I confess that I have not the nerves to enter their synagogues. Old prejudices cling about me. I cannot shake off the story of Hugh of Lincoln. Centuries of injury, contempt, and hate, on the one side, — of cloaked revenge, dissimulation, and hate, on the other, between our and their fathers, must, and ought to affect the blood of the children. I cannot believe it can run clear and kindly yet; or that a few fine words, such as candour, liberality, the light of a nineteenth century, can close up the breaches of so deadly a disunion. A Hebrew is nowhere congenial to me. He is least distasteful on 'Change — for the mercantile spirit levels all distinctions, as all are beauties in the dark. I boldly confess that I do not relish the approximation of Jew and Christian, which has become so fashionable. The reciprocal endearments have, to me, something hypocritical and unnatural in them. I do not like to see the Church and Synagogue kissing and congeeing in awkward postures of an affected civility. If *they* are converted, why do they not come over to us altogether? Why keep up a form of separation, when the life of it is fled? If they can sit with us at table, why do they keck at our cookery? I do not understand these half convertites. Jews christianising — Christians judaising — puzzle me. I like fish or flesh. A moderate Jew is a more confounding piece of anomaly than a wet Quaker. The spirit of the synagogue is essentially *separative*. B—— would have been more in keeping if he had abided by the faith of his forefathers. There is a fine scorn in his face, which nature meant to be of — Christians. The Hebrew spirit is strong in him, in spite of his proselytism. He cannot conquer the Shibboleth. How it breaks out, when he sings, "The Children of Israel passed through the Red Sea!" The auditors, for the moment, are as Egyptians to him, and he rides over

our necks in triumph. There is no mistaking him. — B——
has a strong expression of sense in his countenance, and it is
confirmed by his singing. The foundation of his vocal excellence is sense. He sings with understanding, as Kemble delivered dialogue. He would sing the Commandments, and
give an appropriate character to each prohibition. His nation,
in general, have not over-sensible countenances. How should
they? — but you seldom see a silly expression among them.
Gain, and the pursuit of gain, sharpen a man's visage. I
never heard of an idiot being born among them. — Some
admire the Jewish female physiognomy. I admire it — but
with trembling. Jael had those full dark inscrutable eyes.

In the Negro countenance you will often meet with strong
traits of benignity. I have felt yearnings of tenderness towards
some of these faces — or rather masks — that have looked out
kindly upon one in casual encounters in the streets and high-
ways. I love what Fuller beautifully calls — these "images of
God cut in ebony." But I should not like to associate with
them, to share my meals and my good-nights with them —
because they are black.

I love Quaker ways, and Quaker worship. I venerate the
Quaker principles. It does me good for the rest of the day
when I meet any of their people in my path. When I am
ruffled or disturbed by any occurrence, the sight, or quiet
voice of a Quaker, acts upon me as a ventilator, lightening
the air, and taking off a load from the bosom. But I cannot
like the Quakers (as Desdemona would say) "to live with
them." I am all over sophisticated — with humours, fancies,
craving hourly sympathy. I must have books, pictures, theatres, chit-chat, scandal, jokes, ambiguities, and a thousand
whim-whams, which their simpler taste can do without. I
should starve at their primitive banquet. My appetites are too
high for the salads which (according to Evelyn) Eve dressed
for the angel, my gusto too excited

To sit a guest with Daniel at his pulse.

The indirect answers which Quakers are often found to return to a question put to them may be explained, I think, without the vulgar assumption that they are more given to evasion and equivocating than other people. They naturally look to their words more carefully, and are more cautious of committing themselves. They have a peculiar character to keep up on this head. They stand in a manner upon their veracity. A Quaker is by law exempted from taking an oath. The custom of resorting to an oath in extreme cases, sanctified as it is by all religious antiquity, is apt (it must be confessed) to introduce into the laxer sort of minds the notion of two kinds of truth—the one applicable to the solemn affairs of justice, and the other to the common proceedings of daily intercourse. As truth bound upon the conscience by an oath can be but truth, so in the common affirmations of the shop and the market-place a latitude is expected, and conceded upon questions wanting this solemn covenant. Something less than truth satisfies. It is common to hear a person say, "You do not expect me to speak as if I were upon my oath." Hence a great deal of incorrectness and inadvertency, short of falsehood, creeps into ordinary conversation ; and a kind of secondary or laic-truth is tolerated, where clergy-truth—oath-truth, by the nature of the circumstances, is not required. A Quaker knows none of this distinction. His simple affirmation being received, upon the most sacred occasions, without any further test, stamps a value upon the words which he is to use upon the most indifferent topics of life. He looks to them, naturally, with more severity. You can have of him no more than his word. He knows, if he is caught tripping in a casual expression, he forfeits, for himself, at least, his claim to the invidious exemption. He knows that his syllables are weighed—and how far a consciousness of this particular watchfulness, exerted against a person, has a tendency to produce indirect answers, and a diverting of the question by honest means might be illustrated, and the practice justified, by a more sacred example than is proper to be adduced upon this occasion. The admirable presence of mind, which is notorious in Quakers upon all contingencies, might be traced to this imposed self-watchfulness — if it did not seem rather an humble and secular scion of that old stock of religious constancy, which never bent or faltered in the Primitive Friends, or gave way to the winds of persecution, to the violence of judge or accuser, under trials and racking examinations. "You will never be the wiser, if I sit here answering your questions till midnight," said one of those upright Justices to Penn, who had been putting law-cases with a puzzling subtlety. "Thereafter as the answers may be," retorted the Quaker. The astonishing composure of this people is sometimes ludicrously displayed in lighter instances. — I was travelling in a stage coach with three male Quakers, buttoned up in the straitest non-conformity of their sect. We stopped to bait at Andover, where a meal, partly tea apparatus, partly supper, was set before us. My friends confined themselves to the tea-table. I in my way took supper. When the landlady brought in the bill, the eldest of my companions discovered that she had charged for both meals. This was resisted. Mine hostess was very clamorous and positive. Some mild arguments were used on the part of the Quakers, for which the heated mind of the good lady seemed by no means a fit recipient. The guard came in with his usual peremptory notice. The Quakers pulled out their money, and formally tendered it — so much for tea — I, in humble imitation, tendering mine — for the supper which I had taken. She would not relax in her demand. So they all three quietly put up their silver, as did myself, and marched out of the room, the eldest and gravest going first, with myself closing up the rear, who thought I could not do better than follow the example of such grave and warrantable personages. We got in. The steps went up. The coach drove off. The murmurs of mine hostess, not very indistinctly or ambiguously pronounced, became after a time inaudible — and now my conscience, which the whimsical scene had for a while suspended, beginning to give some twitches, I waited, in the hope that some justification would be offered by these serious persons for the seeming injustice of their conduct. To my great surprise, not a syllable was dropped on the subject. They sat as mute as at a meeting. At length the eldest of them broke silence, by inquiring of his next neighbour, " Hast thee heard how indigos go at the India House ? " and the question operated as a soporific on my moral feeling as far as Exeter.

DREAM-CHILDREN; A REVERIE

London Magazine, January, 1822

Children love to listen to stories about their elders, when *they* were children; to stretch their imagination to the conception of a traditionary great-uncle or grandame, whom they never saw. It was in this spirit that my little ones crept about me the other evening to hear about their great-grandmother Field, who lived in a great house in Norfolk (a hundred times bigger than that in which they and papa lived) which had been the scene — so at least it was generally believed in that part of the country — of the tragic incidents which they had lately become familiar with from the ballad of the Children in the Wood. Certain it is that the whole story of the children and their cruel uncle was to be seen fairly carved out in wood upon the chimney-piece of the great hall, the whole story down to the Robin Redbreasts, till a foolish rich person pulled it down to set up a marble one of modern invention in its stead, with no story upon it. Here Alice put out one of her dear mother's looks, too tender to be called upbraiding. Then I went on to say, how religious and how good their great-grandmother Field was, how beloved and respected by every body, though she was not indeed the mistress of this great house, but had only the charge of it (and yet in some respects she might be said to be the mistress of it too) committed to her by the owner, who preferred living in a newer and more fashionable mansion which he had purchased somewhere in the adjoining county ; but still she lived in it in a manner as if it had been her own, and kept up the dignity of the great house in a sort while she lived, which afterwards came to decay, and was nearly pulled down, and all its old ornaments stripped and carried away to the owner's other house, where they were set up, and looked as awkward as if some one were to carry away the old tombs they had seen lately at the Abbey, and stick them up in Lady C.'s tawdry gilt drawing-room. Here John smiled, as much as to say, "that would be foolish indeed." And then I told how, when she came to die, her funeral was attended by a concourse of all the poor, and some of the gentry too, of the neighbourhood for many miles round, to show their respect for her memory, because she had been such a good and religious woman ; so good indeed that she knew all the Psaltery by heart, ay, and a great part of the Testament besides. Here little Alice spread her hands. Then I told what a tall, upright, graceful person their great-grandmother Field once was ; and how in her youth she was esteemed the best dancer — here Alice's little right foot played an involuntary movement, till upon my looking grave, it desisted — the best dancer, I was saying, in the county, till a cruel disease, called a cancer, came, and bowed her down with pain ; but it could never bend her good spirits, or make them stoop, but they were still upright, because she was so good and religious. Then I told how she was used to sleep by herself in a lone chamber of the great lone house ; and how she believed that an apparition of two infants was to be seen at midnight gliding up and down the great staircase near where she slept, but she said "those innocents would do her no harm " ; and how frightened I used to be, though in those days I had my maid to sleep with me, because I was never half so good or religious as she — and yet I never saw the infants. Here John expanded all his eyebrows and tried to look courageous. Then I told how good she was to all her grand-children, having us to the great house in the holydays, where I in particular used to spend many hours by myself, in gazing upon the old busts

of the Twelve Cæsars, that had been Emperors of Rome, till
the old marble heads would seem to live again, or I to be
turned into marble with them; how I never could be tired
with roaming about that huge mansion, with its vast empty
rooms, with their worn-out hangings, fluttering tapestry, and
carved oaken panels, with the gilding almost rubbed out —
sometimes in the spacious old-fashioned gardens, which I had
almost to myself, unless when now and then a solitary gardening man would cross me — and how the nectarines and
peaches hung upon the walls, without my ever offering to
pluck them, because they were forbidden fruit, unless now
and then, — and because I had more pleasure in strolling
about among the old melancholy-looking yew trees, or the
firs, and picking up the red berries, and the fir apples, which
were good for nothing but to look at — or in lying about upon
the fresh grass, with all the fine garden smells around me —
or basking in the orangery, till I could almost fancy myself
ripening too along with the oranges and the limes in that
grateful warmth — or in watching the dace that darted to and
fro in the fish-pond, at the bottom of the garden, with here
and there a great sulky pike hanging midway down the water
in silent state, as if it mocked at their impertinent friskings,
— I had more pleasure in these busy-idle diversions than in
all the sweet flavours of peaches, nectarines, oranges, and such
like common baits of children. Here John slily deposited back
upon the plate a bunch of grapes, which, not unobserved by
Alice, he had meditated dividing with her, and both seemed
willing to relinquish them for the present as irrelevant. Then
in somewhat a more heightened tone, I told how, though
their great-grandmother Field loved all her grand-children, yet
in an especial manner she might be said to love their uncle,
John L———, because he was so handsome and spirited a
youth, and a king to the rest of us; and, instead of moping
about in solitary corners, like some of us, he would mount
the most mettlesome horse he could get, when but an imp no
bigger than themselves, and make it carry him half over the

county in a morning, and join the hunters when there were any out — and yet he loved the old great house and gardens too, but had too much spirit to be always pent up within their boundaries — and how their uncle grew up to man's estate as brave as he was handsome, to the admiration of every body, but of their great-grandmother Field most especially; and how he used to carry me upon his back when I was a lame-footed boy — for he was a good bit older than me — many a mile when I could not walk for pain; — and how in after life he became lame-footed too, and I did not always (I fear) make allowances enough for him when he was impatient, and in pain, nor remember sufficiently how considerate he had been to me when I was lame-footed; and how when he died, though he had not been dead an hour, it seemed as if he had died a great while ago, such a distance there is betwixt life and death; and how I bore his death as I thought pretty well at first, but afterwards it haunted and haunted me; and though I did not cry or take it to heart as some do, and as I think he would have done if I had died, yet I missed him all day long, and knew not till then how much I had loved him. I missed his kindness, and I missed his crossness, and wished him to be alive again, to be quarrelling with him (for we quarrelled sometimes), rather than not have him again, and was as un-easy without him, as he their poor uncle must have been when the doctor took off his limb. Here the children fell a crying, and asked if their little mourning which they had on was not for uncle John, and they looked up, and prayed me not to go on about their uncle, but to tell them some stories about their pretty dead mother. Then I told how for seven long years, in hope sometimes, sometimes in despair, yet persisting ever, I courted the fair Alice W——n; and, as much as children could understand, I explained to them what coyness, and diffi-culty, and denial meant in maidens — when suddenly, turning to Alice, the soul of the first Alice looked out at her eyes with such a reality of re-presentment, that I became in doubt which of them stood there before me, or whose that bright

hair was; and while I stood gazing, both the children gradually grew fainter to my view, receding, and still receding till
nothing at last but two mournful features were seen in the
uttermost distance, which, without speech, strangely impressed
upon me the effects of speech; "We are not of Alice, nor of
thee, nor are we children at all. The children of Alice call
Bartrum father. We are nothing; less than nothing, and
dreams. We are only what might have been, and must wait
upon the tedious shores of Lethe millions of ages before we
have existence, and a name" — and immediately awaking, I
found myself quietly seated in my bachelor armchair, where
I had fallen asleep, with the faithful Bridget unchanged by
my side — but John L. (or James Elia) was gone for ever.

THE PRAISE OF CHIMNEY–SWEEPERS

London Magazine, May, 1822

I like to meet a sweep — understand me — not a grown
sweeper — old chimney-sweepers are by no means attractive
— but one of those tender novices, blooming through their
first nigritude, the maternal washings not quite effaced from
the cheek — such as come forth with the dawn, or somewhat
earlier, with their little professional notes sounding like the
peep peep of a young sparrow; or liker to the matin lark should
I pronounce them, in their aerial ascents not seldom anticipating
the sun-rise?

I have a kindly yearning toward these dim specks — poor
blots — innocent blacknesses —

I reverence these young Africans of our own growth —
these almost clergy imps, who sport their cloth without assumption; and from their little pulpits (the tops of chimneys),
in the nipping air of a December morning, preach a lesson of
patience to mankind.

When a child, what a mysterious pleasure it was to witness
their operation! to see a chit no bigger than one's-self enter,

one knew not by what process, into what seemed the *fauces Averni* — to pursue him in imagination, as he went sounding on through so many dark stifling caverns, horrid shades! — to shudder with the idea that " now, surely, he must be lost for ever!" — to revive at hearing his feeble shout of discovered day-light — and then (O fulness of delight) running out of doors, to come just in time to see the sable phenomenon emerge in safety, the brandished weapon of his art victorious like some flag waved over a conquered citadel! I seem to remember having been told that a bad sweep was once left in a stack with his brush, to indicate which way the wind blew. It was an awful spectacle certainly; not much unlike the old stage direction in *Macbeth*, where the " Apparition of a child crowned, with a tree in his hand, rises."

Reader, if thou meetest one of these small gentry in thy early rambles, it is good to give him a penny. It is better to give him two-pence. If it be starving weather, and to the proper troubles of his hard occupation, a pair of kibed heels (no unusual accompaniment) be superadded, the demand on thy humanity will surely rise to a tester.

There is a composition, the ground-work of which I have understood to be the sweet wood 'yclept sassafras. This wood boiled down to a kind of tea, and tempered with an infusion of milk and sugar, hath to some tastes a delicacy beyond the China luxury. I know not how thy palate may relish it; for myself, with every deference to the judicious Mr. Read, who hath time out of mind kept open a shop (the only one he avers in London) for the vending of this " wholesome and pleasant beverage," on the south side of Fleet Street, as thou approachest Bridge Street — *the only Salopian house*, — I have never yet ventured to dip my own particular lip in a basin of his commended ingredients — a cautious premonition to the olfactories constantly whispering to me that my stomach must infallibly, with all due courtesy, decline it. Yet I have seen palates, otherwise not uninstructed in dietetical elegances, sup it up with avidity.

I know not by what particular conformation of the organ it happens, but I have always found that this composition is surprisingly gratifying to the palate of a young chimney-sweeper — whether the oily particles (sassafras is slightly oleaginous) do attenuate and soften the fuliginous concretions, which are sometimes found (in dissections) to adhere to the roof of the mouth in these unfledged practitioners; or whether Nature, sensible that she had mingled too much of bitter wood in the lot of these raw victims, caused to grow out of the earth her sassafras for a sweet lenitive — but so it is, that no possible taste or odour to the senses of a young chimney-sweeper can convey a delicate excitement comparable to this mixture. Being penniless, they will yet hang their black heads over the ascending steam, to gratify one sense if possible, seemingly no less pleased than those domestic animals — cats — when they purr over a new-found sprig of valerian. There is something more in these sympathies than philosophy can inculcate.

Now albeit Mr. Read boasteth, not without reason, that his is the *only Salopian house*; yet be it known to thee, reader — if thou art one who keepest what are called good hours, thou art haply ignorant of the fact — he hath a race of industrious imitators, who from stalls, and under open sky, dispense the same savoury mess to humbler customers, at that dead time of the dawn, when (as extremes meet) the rake, reeling home from his midnight cups, and the hard-handed artisan leaving his bed to resume the premature labours of the day, jostle, not unfrequently to the manifest disconcerting of the former, for the honours of the pavement. It is the time when, in summer, between the expired and the not yet relumined kitchen-fires, the kennels of our fair metropolis give forth their least satisfactory odours. The rake, who wisheth to dissipate his o'er-night vapours in more grateful coffee, curses the ungenial fume, as he passeth; but the artisan stops to taste, and blesses the fragrant breakfast.

This is *Saloop* — the precocious herb-woman's darling — the delight of the early gardener, who transports his smoking cabbages by break of day from Hammersmith to Covent Garden's famed piazzas — the delight, and, oh I fear, too often the envy, of the unpennied sweep. Him shouldest thou haply encounter, with his dim visage pendent over the grateful steam, regale him with a sumptuous basin (it will cost thee but three half-pennies) and a slice of delicate bread and butter (an added halfpenny) — so may thy culinary fires, eased of the o'er-charged secretions from thy worse-placed hospitalities, curl up a lighter volume to the welkin — so may the descending soot never taint thy costly well-ingredienced soups — nor the odious cry, quick-reaching from street to street, of the *fired chimney*, invite the rattling engines from ten adjacent parishes, to disturb for a casual scintillation thy peace and pocket!

I am by nature extremely susceptible of street affronts; the jeers and taunts of the populace; the low-bred triumph they display over the casual trip, or splashed stocking, of a gentleman. Yet can I endure the jocularity of a young sweep with something more than forgiveness. — In the last winter but one, pacing along Cheapside with my accustomed precipitation when I walk westward, a treacherous slide brought me upon my back in an instant. I scrambled up with pain and shame enough — yet outwardly trying to face it down, as if nothing had happened — when the roguish grin of one of these young wits encountered me. There he stood, pointing me out with his dusky finger to the mob, and to a poor woman (I suppose his mother) in particular, till the tears for the exquisiteness of the fun (so he thought it) worked themselves out at the corners of his poor red eyes, red from many a previous weeping, and soot-inflamed, yet twinkling through all with such a joy, snatched out of desolation, that Hogarth — but Hogarth has got him already (how could he miss him?) in the *March to Finchley*, grinning at the pie-man — there he stood, as he stands in the picture, irremovable, as if the jest was to last for ever — with such a maximum of glee, and minimum of mischief, in his mirth — for the grin of a genuine sweep hath absolutely no malice in it — that I could have been content, if the honour of a gentleman might endure it, to have remained his butt and his mockery till midnight.

I am by theory obdurate to the seductiveness of what are called a fine set of teeth. Every pair of rosy lips (the ladies must pardon me) is a casket, presumably holding such jewels; but, methinks, they should take leave to " air " them as frugally as possible. The fine lady, or fine gentleman, who show me their teeth, show me bones. Yet must I confess, that from the mouth of a true sweep a display (even to ostentation) of those white and shining ossifications strikes me as an agreeable anomaly in manners, and an allowable piece of foppery. It is, as when

A sable cloud
Turns forth her silver lining on the night.

It is like some remnant of gentry not quite extinct; a badge of better days; a hint of nobility: — and, doubtless, under the obscuring darkness and double night of their forlorn disguisement, oftentimes lurketh good blood, and gentle conditions, derived from lost ancestry, and a lapsed pedigree. The premature apprenticements of these tender victims give but too much encouragement, I fear, to clandestine, and almost infantile abductions; the seeds of civility and true courtesy, so often discernible in these young grafts (not otherwise to be accounted for) plainly hint at some forced adoptions; many noble Rachels mourning for their children, even in our days, countenance the fact; the tales of fairy-spiriting may shadow a lamentable verity, and the recovery of the young Montagu be but a solitary instance of good fortune, out of many irreparable and hopeless *defiliations*.

In one of the state-beds at Arundel Castle, a few years since — under a ducal canopy — (that seat of the Howards is an object of curiosity to visitors chiefly for its beds, in which the late duke was especially a connoisseur) — encircled with curtains of delicatest crimson, with starry coronets inwoven — folded between a pair of sheets whiter and softer than the lap where Venus lulled Ascanius — was discovered by chance, after all methods of search had failed, at noon-day, fast asleep, a lost chimney-sweeper. The little creature, having somehow confounded his passage among the intricacies of those lordly chimneys, by some unknown aperture had alighted upon this magnificent chamber ; and, tired with his tedious explorations, was unable to resist the delicious invitement to repose, which he there saw exhibited ; so, creeping between the sheets very quietly, laid his black head upon the pillow, and slept like a young Howard.

Such is the account given to the visitors at the Castle. — But I cannot help seeming to perceive a confirmation of what I have just hinted at in this story. A high instinct was at work in the case, or I am mistaken. Is it probable that a poor child of that description, with whatever weariness he might be visited, would have ventured, under such a penalty as he would be taught to expect, to uncover the sheets of a Duke's bed, and deliberately to lay himself down between them, when the rug, or the carpet, presented an obvious couch, still far above his pretensions — is this probable, I would ask, if the great power of nature, which I contend for, had not been manifested within him, prompting to the adventure ? Doubtless this young nobleman (for such my mind misgives me that he must be) was allured by some memory, not amounting to full consciousness, of his condition in infancy, when he was used to be lapt by his mother, or his nurse, in just such sheets as he there found, into which he was but now creeping back as into his proper *incunabula*, and resting-place. — By no other theory, than by this sentiment of a pre-existent state (as I may call it), can I explain a deed so venturous, and, indeed, upon any other system, so indecorous, in this tender, but unseasonable, sleeper.

My pleasant friend JEM WHITE was so impressed with a belief of metamorphoses like this frequently taking place, that in some sort to reverse the wrongs of fortune in these poor changelings, he instituted an annual feast of chimney-sweepers, at which it was his pleasure to officiate as host and waiter. It

was a solemn supper held in Smithfield, upon the yearly
return of the fair of St. Bartholomew. Cards were issued a
week before to the master-sweeps in and about the metropolis, confining the invitation to their younger fry. Now and
then an elderly stripling would get in among us, and be good-
naturedly winked at; but our main body were infantry. One
unfortunate wight, indeed, who relying upon his dusky suit,
had intruded himself into our party, but by tokens was provi-
dentially discovered in time to be no chimney-sweeper (all is
not soot which looks so), was quoited out of the presence with
universal indignation, as not having on the wedding garment;
but in general the greatest harmony prevailed. The place
chosen was a convenient spot among the pens, at the north
side of the fair, not so far distant as to be impervious to the
agreeable hubbub of that vanity; but remote enough not to be
obvious to the interruption of every gaping spectator in it.
The guests assembled about seven. In those little temporary
parlours three tables were spread with napery, not so fine as
substantial, and at every board a comely hostess presided with
her pan of hissing sausages. The nostrils of the young rogues
dilated at the savour. JAMES WHITE, as head waiter, had
charge of the first table; and myself, with our trusty companion BIGOD, ordinarily ministered to the other two. There was
clambering and jostling, you may be sure, who should get at
the first table — for Rochester in his maddest days could not
have done the humours of the scene with more spirit than
my friend. After some general expression of thanks for the
honour the company had done him, his inaugural ceremony
was to clasp the greasy waist of old dame Ursula (the fattest
of the three), that stood frying and fretting, half-blessing, half-
cursing "the gentleman," and imprint upon her chaste lips a
tender salute, whereat the universal host would set up a shout
that tore the concave, while hundreds of grinning teeth startled
the night with their brightness. O it was a pleasure to see
the sable younkers lick in the unctuous meat, with *his* more
unctuous sayings — how he would fit the tit-bits to the puny

mouths, reserving the lengthier links for the seniors — how he would intercept a morsel even in the jaws of some young desperado, declaring it " must to the pan again to be browned, for it was not fit for a gentleman's eating " — how he would recommend this slice of white bread, or that piece of kissing-crust, to a tender juvenile, advising them all to have a care of cracking their teeth, which were their best patrimony, — how genteelly he would deal about the small ale, as if it were wine, naming the brewer, and protesting, if it were not good he should lose their custom ; with a special recommendation to wipe the lip before drinking. Then we had our toasts — " The King," — the " Cloth," — which, whether they understood or not, was equally diverting and flattering ; — and for a crowning sentiment, which never failed, " May the Brush supersede the Laurel ! " All these, and fifty other fancies, which were rather felt than comprehended by his guests, would he utter, standing upon tables, and prefacing every sentiment with a " Gentlemen, give me leave to propose so and so," which was a prodigious comfort to those young orphans ; every now and then stuffing into his mouth (for it did not do to be squeamish on these occasions) indiscriminate pieces of those reeking sausages, which pleased them mightily, and was the savouriest part, you may believe, of the entertainment.

> Golden lads and lasses must,
> As chimney-sweepers, come to dust —

JAMES WHITE is extinct, and with him these suppers have long ceased. He carried away with him half the fun of the world when he died — of my world at least. His old clients look for him among the pens ; and, missing him, reproach the altered feast of St. Bartholomew, and the glory of Smithfield departed for ever.

DETACHED THOUGHTS ON BOOKS AND READING

London Magazine, July, 1822

To mind the inside of a book is to entertain one's self with the forced product of another man's brain. Now I think a man of quality and breeding may be much amused with the natural sprouts of his own. — *Lord Foppington in the Relapse*

An ingenious acquaintance of my own was so much struck with this bright sally of his Lordship, that he has left off reading altogether, to the great improvement of his originality. At the hazard of losing some credit on this head, I must confess that I dedicate no inconsiderable portion of my time to other people's thoughts. I dream away my life in others' speculations. I love to lose myself in other men's minds. When I am not walking, I am reading; I cannot sit and think. Books think for me.

I have no repugnances. Shaftesbury is not too genteel for me, nor *Jonathan Wild* too low. I can read anything which I call a *book*. There are things in that shape which I cannot allow for such.

In this catalogue of *books which are no books — biblia a-biblia* — I reckon Court Calendars, Directories, Pocket Books, Draught Boards, bound and lettered on the back, Scientific Treatises, Almanacks, Statutes at Large; the works of Hume, Gibbon, Robertson, Beattie, Soame Jenyns, and, generally, all those volumes which " no gentleman's library should be without ": the Histories of Flavius Josephus (that learned Jew), and Paley's *Moral Philosophy*. With these exceptions, I can read almost anything. I bless my stars for a taste so catholic, so unexcluding.

I confess that **it** moves my spleen to see these *things in books' clothing* perched upon shelves, like false saints, usurpers of true shrines, intruders into the sanctuary, thrusting out the legitimate occupants. To reach down a well-bound semblance of a volume, and hope it is some kind-hearted playbook, then, opening what " seem its leaves," to come bolt upon a withering Population Essay. To expect a Steele, or a Farquhar, and find — Adam Smith. To view a well-arranged assortment of blockheaded Encyclopædias (Anglicanas or Metropolitanas) set out in an array of Russia, or Morocco, when a tithe of that good leather would comfortably re-clothe my shivering folios ; would renovate Paracelsus himself, and enable old Raymund Lully to look like himself again in the world. I never see these impostors, but I long to strip them, to warm my ragged veterans in their spoils.

To be strong-backed and neat-bound is the desideratum of a volume. Magnificence comes after. This, when it can be afforded, is not to be lavished upon all kinds of books indiscriminately. I would not dress a set of Magazines, for instance, in full suit. The dishabille, or half-binding (with Russia backs ever) is *our* costume. A Shakspeare, or a Milton (unless the first editions), it were mere foppery to trick out in gay apparel. The possession of them confers no distinction. The exterior of them (the things themselves being so common), strange to say, raises no sweet emotions, no tickling sense of property in the owner. Thomson's *Seasons*, again, looks best (I maintain it) a little torn, and dog's-eared. How beautiful to a genuine lover of reading are the sullied leaves, and wornout appearance, nay, the very odour (beyond Russia), if we would not forget kind feelings in fastidiousness, of an old " Circulating Library " *Tom Jones*, or *Vicar of Wakefield* ! How they speak of the thousand thumbs, that have turned over their pages with delight ! — of the lone sempstress, whom they may have cheered (milliner, or harder-working mantua-maker) after her long day's needle-toil, running far into midnight, when she has snatched an hour, ill-spared from sleep, to steep her cares, as in some Lethean cup, in spelling out their enchanting contents ! Who would have them a whit less soiled ? What better condition could we desire to see them in ?

In some respects the better a book is, the less it demands from binding. Fielding, Smollet, Sterne, and all that class of perpetually self-reproductive volumes — Great Nature's Stereotypes —

we see them individually perish with less regret, because we know the copies of them to be "eterne." But where a book is at once both good and rare — where the individual is almost the species, and when *that* perishes,

> We know not where is that Promethean torch
> That can its light relumine —

such a book, for instance, as the *Life of the Duke of New-castle*, by his Duchess — no casket is rich enough, no casing sufficiently durable, to honour and keep safe such a jewel.

Not only rare volumes of this description, which seem hopeless ever to be reprinted ; but old editions of writers, such as Sir Philip Sydney, Bishop Taylor, Milton in his prose-works, Fuller — of whom we *have* reprints, yet the books themselves, though they go about, and are talked of here and there, we know, have not endenizened themselves (nor possibly ever will) in the national heart, so as to become stock books — it is good to possess these in durable and costly covers. I do not care for a First Folio of Shakspeare. I rather prefer the common editions of Rowe and Tonson without notes, and with *plates*, which, being so execrably bad, serve as maps, or modest remembrancers, to the text; and without pretending to any supposable emulation with it, are so much better than the Shakspeare gallery *engravings*, which *did*. I have a community of feeling with my countrymen about his Plays, and I like those editions of him best which have been oftenest tumbled about and handled. — On the contrary, I cannot read Beaumont and Fletcher but in Folio. The Octavo editions are painful to look at. I have no sympathy with them. If they were as much read as the current editions of the other poet, I should prefer them in that shape to the older one. I do not know a more heartless sight than the reprint of the *Anatomy of Melancholy*. What need was there of unearthing the bones of that fantastic old great man, to expose them in a winding-sheet of the newest fashion to modern censure ? what hapless stationer could dream of Burton ever becoming popular ? — The wretched

Malone could not do worse, when he bribed the sexton of Stratford church to let him white-wash the painted effigy of old Shakspeare, which stood there, in rude but lively fashion depicted, to the very colour of the cheek, the eye, the eyebrow, hair, the very dress he used to wear — the only authentic testimony we had, however imperfect, of these curious parts and parcels of him. They covered him over with a coat of white paint. By ——, if I had been a justice of peace for Warwickshire, I would have clapt both commentator and sexton fast in the stocks, for a pair of meddling sacrilegious varlets.

I think I see them at their work — these sapient trouble-tombs.

Shall I be thought fantastical, if I confess, that the names of some of our poets sound sweeter, and have a finer relish to the ear — to mine, at least — than that of Milton or of Shakspeare? It may be that the latter are more staled and rung upon in common discourse. The sweetest names, and which carry a perfume in the mention, are Kit Marlowe, Drayton, Drummond of Hawthornden, and Cowley.

Much depends upon *when* and *where* you read a book. In the five or six impatient minutes, before the dinner is quite ready, who would think of taking up the *Fairy Queen* for a stop-gap, or a volume of Bishop Andrewes' sermons?

Milton almost requires a solemn service of music to be played before you enter upon him. But he brings his music, to which, who listens, had need bring docile thoughts, and purged ears.

Winter evenings — the world shut out — with less of ceremony the gentle Shakspeare enters. At such a season, the *Tempest*, or his own *Winter's Tale* —

These two poets you cannot avoid reading aloud — to yourself, or (as it chances) to some single person listening. More than one — and it degenerates into an audience.

Books of quick interest, that hurry on for incidents, are for the eye to glide over only. It will not do to read them out. I could never listen to even the better kind of modern novels without extreme irksomeness.

A newspaper, read out, is intolerable. In some of the Bank offices it is the custom (to save so much individual time) for one of the clerks — who is the best scholar — to commence upon the *Times*, or the *Chronicle*, and recite its entire contents aloud *pro bono publico*. With every advantage of lungs and elocution, the effect is singularly vapid. In barbers' shops and public-houses a fellow will get up, and spell out a paragraph which he communicates as some discovery. Another follows with *his* selection. So the entire journal transpires at length by piece-meal. Seldom-readers are slow readers, and without this expedient no one in the company would probably ever travel through the contents of a whole paper.

Newspapers always excite curiosity. No one ever lays one down without a feeling of disappointment.

What an eternal time that gentleman in black, at Nando's, keeps the paper! I am sick of hearing the waiter bawling out incessantly, "the *Chronicle* is in hand, Sir."

Coming in to an inn at night — having ordered your supper — what can be more delightful than to find lying in the window-seat, left there time out of mind by the carelessness of some former guest — two or three numbers of the old *Town and Country Magazine*, with its amusing *tête-à-tête* pictures — "The Royal Lover and Lady G———;" "The Melting Platonic and the Old Beau," — and such like antiquated scandal? Would you exchange it — at that time, and in that place — for a better book?

Poor Tobin, who latterly fell blind, did not regret it so much for the weightier kinds of reading — the *Paradise Lost*, or *Comus*, he could have *read* to him — but he missed the pleasure of skimming over with his own eye a magazine, or a light pamphlet.

I should not care to be caught in the serious avenues of some cathedral alone and reading *Candide*.

I do not remember a more whimsical surprise than having been once detected — by a familiar damsel — reclined at my ease upon the grass, on Primrose Hill (her Cythera), reading —

Pamela. There was nothing in the book to make a man seriously ashamed at the exposure ; but as she seated herself down by me, and seemed determined to read in company, I could have wished it had been — any other book. We read on very sociably for a few pages ; and, not finding the author much to her taste, she got up, and — went away. Gentle casuist, I leave it to thee to conjecture, whether the blush (for there was one between us) was the property of the nymph or the swain in this dilemma. From me you shall never get the secret.

I am not much a friend to out-of-doors reading. I cannot settle my spirits to it. I knew a Unitarian minister, who was generally to be seen upon Snow Hill (as yet Skinner's Street *was not*), between the hours of ten and eleven in the morning, studying a volume of Lardner. I own this to have been a strain of abstraction beyond my reach. I used to admire how he sidled along, keeping clear of secular contacts. An illiterate encounter with a porter's knot, or a bread basket, would have quickly put to flight all the theology I am master of, and have left me worse than indifferent to the five points.

There is a class of street-readers whom I can never contemplate without affection — the poor gentry, who, not having wherewithal to buy or hire a book, filch a little learning at the open stalls — the owner, with his hard eye, casting envious looks at them all the while, and thinking when they will have done. Venturing tenderly, page after page, expecting every moment when he shall interpose his interdict, and yet unable to deny themselves the gratification, they " snatch a fearful joy." Martin B——, in this way, by daily fragments, got through two volumes of *Clarissa*, when the stall-keeper damped his laudable ambition, by asking him (it was in his younger days) whether he meant to purchase the work. M. declares that under no circumstance in his life did he ever peruse a book with half the satisfaction which he took in those uneasy snatches. A quaint poetess of our day has moralised upon this subject in two very touching but homely stanzas.

I saw a boy with eager eye
Open a book upon a stall,
And read, as he 'd devour it all ;
Which when the stall-man did espy,
Soon to the boy I heard him call,
" You, Sir, you never buy a book,
Therefore in one you shall not look."
The boy pass'd slowly on, and with a sigh
He wish'd he never had been taught to read,
Then of the old churl's books he should have had no need.

Of sufferings the poor have many,
Which never can the rich annoy :
I soon perceiv'd another boy,
Who look'd as if he 'd not had any
Food, for that day at least — enjoy
The sight of cold meat in a tavern larder.
This boy's case, then thought I, is surely harder,
Thus hungry, longing, thus without a penny,
Beholding choice of dainty-dressed meat :
No wonder if he wish he ne'er had learn'd to eat.

MODERN GALLANTRY

London Magazine, November, 1822

In comparing modern with ancient manners, we are pleased to compliment ourselves upon the point of gallantry ; a certain obsequiousness, or deferential respect, which we are supposed to pay to females, as females.

I shall believe that this principle actuates our conduct, when I can forget that in the nineteenth century of the era from which we date our civility, we are but just beginning to leave off the very frequent practice of whipping females in public, in common with the coarsest male offenders.

I shall believe it to be influential, when I can shut my eyes to the fact that in England women are still occasionally — hanged.

I shall believe in it, when actresses are no longer subject to be hissed off a stage by gentlemen.

I shall believe in it, when Dorimant hands a fish-wife across the kennel; or assists the apple-woman to pick up her wandering fruit, which some unlucky dray has just dissipated.

I shall believe in it, when the Dorimants in humbler life, who would be thought in their way notable adepts in this refinement, shall act upon it in places where they are not known, or think themselves not observed — when I shall see the traveller for some rich tradesman part with his admired box-coat, to spread it over the defenceless shoulders of the poor woman who is passing to her parish on the roof of the same stage-coach with him, drenched in the rain — when I shall no longer see a woman standing up in the pit of a London theatre, till she is sick and faint with the exertion, with men about her, seated at their ease, and jeering at her distress; till one, that seems to have more manners or con-science than the rest, significantly declares "she should be welcome to his seat, if she were a little younger and hand-somer." Place this dapper warehouseman, or that rider, in a circle of their own female acquaintance, and you shall confess you have not seen a politer-bred man in Lothbury.

Lastly, I shall begin to believe that there is some such principle influencing our conduct, when more than one-half of the drudgery and coarse servitude of the world shall cease to be performed by women.

Until that day comes, I shall never believe this boasted point to be anything more than a conventional fiction; a pageant got up between the sexes, in a certain rank, and at a certain time of life, in which both find their account equally.

I shall be even disposed to rank it among the salutary fictions of life, when in polite circles I shall see the same attentions paid to age as to youth, to homely features as to handsome, to coarse complexions as to clear — to the woman, as she is a woman, not as she is a beauty, a fortune, or a title.

I shall believe it to be something more than a name, when a well-dressed gentleman in a well-dressed company can advert to the topic of *female old age* without exciting, and intending to excite, a sneer : — when the phrases "antiquated virginity," and such a one has "overstood her market," pronounced in good company, shall raise immediate offence in man, or woman, that shall hear them spoken.

Joseph Paice, of Bread Street Hill, merchant, and one of the Directors of the South-Sea Company — the same to whom Edwards, the Shakspeare commentator, has addressed a fine sonnet — was the only pattern of consistent gallantry I have met with. He took me under his shelter at an early age, and bestowed some pains upon me. I owe to his precepts and example whatever there is of the man of business (and that is not much) in my composition. It was not his fault that I did not profit more. Though bred a Presbyterian, and brought up a merchant, he was the finest gentleman of his time. He had not *one* system of attention to females in the drawing-room, and *another* in the shop, or at the stall. I do not mean that he made no distinction. But he never lost sight of sex, or overlooked it in the casualties of a disadvantageous situation. I have seen him stand bare-headed — smile if you please — to a poor servant girl, while she has been inquiring of him the way to some street — in such a posture of unforced civility, as neither to embarrass her in the acceptance, nor himself in the offer, of it. He was no dangler, in the common acceptation of the word, after women : but he reverenced and upheld, in every form in which it came before him, *womanhood*. I have seen him — nay, smile not — tenderly escorting a market-woman, whom he had encountered in a shower, exalting his umbrella over her poor basket of fruit, that it might receive no damage, with as much carefulness as if she had been a Countess. To the reverend form of Female Eld he would yield the wall (though it were to an ancient beggar-woman) with more ceremony than we can afford to show our grandams. He was the Preux Chevalier of Age ; the Sir Calidore, or Sir Tristan, to those who have no Calidores or Tristans to defend them. The roses, that had long faded thence, still bloomed for him in those withered and yellow cheeks.

He was never married, but in his youth he paid his addresses to the beautiful Susan Winstanley — old Winstanley's daughter of Clapton — who dying in the early days of their courtship, confirmed in him the resolution of perpetual bachelorship. It was during their short courtship, he told me, that he had been one day treating his mistress with a profusion of civil speeches — the common gallantries — to which kind of thing she had hitherto manifested no repugnance — but in this instance with no effect. He could not obtain from her a decent acknowledgment in return. She rather seemed to resent his compliments. He could not set it down to caprice, for the lady had always shown herself above that littleness. When he ventured on the following day, finding her a little better humoured, to expostulate with her on her coldness of yesterday, she confessed, with her usual frankness, that she had no sort of dislike to his attentions; that she could even endure some high-flown compliments; that a young woman placed in her situation had a right to expect all sort of civil things said to her; that she hoped she could digest a dose of adulation, short of insincerity, with as little injury to her humility as most young women: but that — a little before he had commenced his compliments — she had overheard him by accident, in rather rough language, rating a young woman, who had not brought home his cravats quite to the appointed time, and she thought to herself, " As I am Miss Susan Winstanley, and a young lady — a reputed beauty, and known to be a fortune, — I can have my choice of the finest speeches from the mouth of this very fine gentleman who is courting me — but if I had been poor Mary Such-a-one (*naming the milliner*), — and had failed of bringing home the cravats to the appointed hour — though perhaps I had sat up half the night to forward them — what sort of compliments should I have received then ? And my woman's pride came to my assistance; and I thought that if it were only to do *me* honour, a female, like myself, might have received handsomer usage: and I was determined not to accept any fine speeches, to the compromise of that sex, the belonging to which was after all my strongest claim and title to them."

I think the lady discovered both generosity, and a just way of thinking, in this rebuke which she gave her lover; and I have sometimes imagined that the uncommon strain of courtesy, which through life regulated the actions and behaviour of my friend towards all of womankind indiscriminately, owed its happy origin to this seasonable lesson from the lips of his lamented mistress.

I wish the whole female world would entertain the same notion of these things that Miss Winstanley showed. Then we should see something of the spirit of consistent gallantry; and no longer witness the anomaly of the same man — a pattern of true politeness to a wife — of cold contempt, or rudeness, to a sister — the idolater of his female mistress — the disparager and despiser of his no less female aunt, or unfortunate — still female — maiden cousin. Just so much respect as a woman derogates from her own sex, in whatever condition placed — her handmaid, or dependent — she deserves to have diminished from herself on that score; and probably will feel the diminution, when youth, and beauty, and advantages, not inseparable from sex, shall lose of their attraction. What a woman should demand of a man in courtship, or after it, is first — respect for her as she is a woman; — and next to that — to be respected by him above all other women. But let her stand upon her female character as upon a foundation; and let the attentions, incident to individual preference, be so many pretty additaments and ornaments — as many, and as fanciful, as you please — to that main structure. Let her first lesson be — with sweet Susan Winstanley — to *reverence her sex*.

OLD CHINA

London Magazine, March, 1823

I have an almost feminine partiality for old china. When I go to see any great house, I inquire for the china-closet, and next for the picture-gallery. I cannot defend the order of preference, but by saying that we have all some taste or other, of too ancient a date to admit of our remembering distinctly that it was an acquired one. I can call to mind the first play, and the first exhibition, that I was taken to; but I am not conscious of a time when china jars and saucers were introduced into my imagination.

I had no repugnance then — why should I now have? — to those little, lawless, azure-tinctured grotesques, that under the notion of men and women, float about, uncircumscribed by any element, in that world before perspective — a china tea-cup.

I like to see my old friends — whom distance cannot diminish — figuring up in the air (so they appear to our optics), yet on *terra firma* still — for so we must in courtesy interpret that speck of deeper blue, which the decorous artist, to prevent absurdity, had made to spring up beneath their sandals.

I love the men with women's faces, and the women, if possible, with still more womanish expressions.

Here is a young and courtly Mandarin, handing tea to a lady from a salver — two miles off. See how distance seems to set off respect! And here the same lady, or another—for likeness is identity on tea-cups — is stepping into a little fairy boat, moored on the hither side of this calm garden river, with a dainty mincing foot, which in a right angle of incidence (as angles go in our world) must infallibly land her in the midst of a flowery mead — a furlong off on the other side of the same strange stream!

Farther on — if far or near can be predicated of their world — see horses, trees, pagodas, dancing the hays.

Here — a cow and rabbit couchant, and co-extensive — so objects show, seen through the lucid atmosphere of fine Cathay.

I was pointing out to my cousin last evening, over our Hyson, (which we are old fashioned enough to drink unmixed still of an afternoon) some of these *speciosa miracula* upon a set of extraordinary old blue china (a recent purchase) which we were now for the first time using; and could not help remarking how favourable circumstances had been to us of late years, that we could afford to please the eye sometimes with trifles of this sort — when a passing sentiment seemed to over-shade the brows of my companion. I am quick at detecting these summer clouds in Bridget.

"I wish the good old times would come again," she said, "when we were not quite so rich. I do not mean that I want to be poor; but there was a middle state" — so she was pleased to ramble on, — "in which I am sure we were a great deal happier. A purchase is but a purchase, now that you have money enough and to spare. Formerly it used to be a triumph. When we coveted a cheap luxury (and, O! how much ado I had to get you to consent in those times!) — we were used to have a debate two or three days before, and to weigh the *for* and *against*, and think what we might spare it out of, and what saving we could hit upon, that should be an equivalent. A thing was worth buying then, when we felt the money that we paid for it.

"Do you remember the brown suit, which you made to hang upon you, till all your friends cried shame upon you, it grew so thread-bare — and all because of that folio Beaumont and Fletcher, which you dragged home late at night from Barker's in Covent Garden? Do you remember how we eyed it for weeks before we could make up our minds to the purchase, and had not come to a determination till it was near ten o'clock of the Saturday night, when you set off from Islington, fearing you should be too late — and when the old bookseller with some grumbling opened his shop, and by the twinkling taper (for he was setting bedwards) lighted out the relic from his dusty treasures — and when you lugged it home, wishing it were twice as cumbersome — and when you presented it to me — and when

we were exploring the perfectness of it (*collating* you called it)
— and while I was repairing some of the loose leaves with
paste, which your impatience would not suffer to be left till
daybreak — was there no pleasure in being a poor man ? or can
those neat black clothes which you wear now, and are so careful to keep brushed, since we have become rich and finical,
give you half the honest vanity, with which you flaunted it about
in that overworn suit — your old corbeau — for four or five
weeks longer than you should have done, to pacify your conscience for the mighty sum of fifteen — or sixteen shillings was
it? — a great affair we thought it then — which you had lavished
on the old folio. Now you can afford to buy any book that
pleases you, but I do not see that you ever bring me home any
nice old purchases now.

" When you came home with twenty apologies for laying out
a less number of shillings upon that print after Lionardo, which
we christened the *Lady Blanch* ; when you looked at the purchase, and thought of the money — and thought of the money,
and looked again at the picture — was there no pleasure in being
a poor man ? Now, you have nothing to do but to walk into
Colnaghi's, and buy a wilderness of Lionardos. Yet do you ?

" Then, do you remember our pleasant walks to Enfield, and
Potter's Bar, and Waltham, when we had a holyday — holydays, and all other fun, are gone, now we are rich — and the
little hand-basket in which I used to deposit our day's fare of
savoury cold lamb and salad — and how you would pry about
at noon-tide for some decent house, where we might go in, and
produce our store — only paying for the ale that you must call
for — and speculate upon the looks of the landlady, and whether
she was likely to allow us a table-cloth — and wish for such
another honest hostess, as Izaak Walton has described many a
one on the pleasant banks of the Lea, when he went a fishing
— and sometimes they would prove obliging enough, and sometimes they would look grudgingly upon us — but we had cheerful looks still for one another, and would eat our plain food
savourily, scarcely grudging Piscator his Trout Hall ? Now, when

we go out a day's pleasuring, which is seldom moreover, we *ride* part of the way — and go into a fine inn, and order the best of dinners, never debating the expense — which, after all, never has half the relish of those chance country snaps, when we were at the mercy of uncertain usage, and a precarious welcome.

"You are too proud to see a play anywhere now but in the pit. Do you remember where it was we used to sit, when we saw the *Battle of Hexham*, and the *Surrender of Calais*, and Bannister and Mrs. Bland in the *Children in the Wood* — when we squeezed out our shillings a-piece to sit three or four times in a season in the one-shilling gallery — where you felt all the time that you ought not to have brought me — and more strongly I felt obligation to you for having brought me — and the pleasure was the better for a little shame — and when the curtain drew up, what cared we for our place in the house, or what mattered it where we were sitting, when our thoughts were with Rosalind in Arden, or with Viola at the Court of Illyria? You used to say that the Gallery was the best place of all for enjoying a play socially — that the relish of such exhibitions must be in proportion to the infrequency of going — that the company we met there, not being in general readers of plays, were obliged to attend the more, and did attend, to what was going on on the stage — because a word lost would have been a chasm, which it was impossible for them to fill up. With such reflections we consoled our pride then — and I appeal to you, whether, as a woman, I met generally with less attention and accommodation than I have done since in more expensive situations in the house? The getting in, indeed, and the crowding up those inconvenient staircases was bad enough, — but there was still a law of civility to women recognised to quite as great an extent as we ever found in the other passages — and how a little difficulty overcome heightened the snug seat, and the play, afterwards! Now we can only pay our money and walk in. You cannot see, you say, in the galleries now. I am sure we saw, and heard too, well enough then — but sight, and all, I think, is gone with our poverty.

"There was pleasure in eating strawberries, before they became quite common — in the first dish of peas, while they were yet dear — to have them for a nice supper, a treat. What treat can we have now? If we were to treat ourselves now — that is, to have dainties a little above our means, it would be selfish and wicked. It is the very little more that we allow ourselves beyond what the actual poor can get at, that makes what I call a treat — when two people living together, as we have done, now and then indulge themselves in a cheap luxury, which both like; while each apologises, and is willing to take both halves of the blame to his single share. I see no harm in people making much of themselves in that sense of the word. It may give them a hint how to make much of others. But now — what I mean by the word — we never do make much of ourselves. None but the poor can do it. I do not mean the veriest poor of all, but persons as we were, just above poverty.

"I know what you were going to say, that it is mighty pleasant at the end of the year to make all meet, — and much ado we used to have every Thirty-first Night of December to account for our exceedings — many a long face did you make over your puzzled accounts, and in contriving to make it out how we had spent so much — or that we had not spent so much — or that it was impossible we should spend so much next year — and still we found our slender capital decreasing — but then, betwixt ways, and projects, and compromises of one sort or another, and talk of curtailing this charge, and doing without that for the future — and the hope that youth brings, and laughing spirits (in which you were never poor till now) we pocketed up our loss, and in conclusion, with 'lusty brimmers' (as you used to quote it out of *hearty cheerful Mr. Cotton*, as you called him), we used to welcome in the 'coming guest.' Now we have no reckoning at all at the end of the old year — no flattering promises about the new year doing better for us."

Bridget is so sparing of her speech on most occasions that when she gets into a rhetorical vein, I am careful how I interrupt it. I could not help, however, smiling at the phantom of wealth which her dear imagination had conjured up out of a clear income of a poor — hundred pounds a year. "It is true we were happier when we were poorer, but we were also younger, my cousin. I am afraid we must put up with the excess, for if we were to shake the superflux into the sea, we should not much mend ourselves. That we had much to struggle with, as we grew up together, we have reason to be most thankful. It strengthened, and knit our compact closer. We could never have been what we have been to each other, if we had always had the sufficiency which you now complain of. The resisting power — those natural dilations of the youthful spirit, which circumstances cannot straiten — with us are long since passed away. Competence to age is supplementary youth ; a sorry supplement, indeed, but I fear the best that is to be had. We must ride where we formerly walked : live better, and lie softer — and shall be wise to do so — than we had means to do in those good old days you speak of. Yet could those days return — could you and I once more walk our thirty miles a-day — could Bannister and Mrs. Bland again be young, and you and I be young to see them — could the good old one-shilling gallery days return — they are dreams, my cousin, now — but could you and I at this moment, instead of this quiet argument, by our well-carpeted fire-side, sitting on this luxurious sofa — be once more struggling up those inconvenient staircases, pushed about, and squeezed, and elbowed by the poorest rabble of poor gallery scramblers — could I once more hear those anxious shrieks of yours — and the delicious *Thank God, we are safe*, which always followed when the topmost stair, conquered, let in the first light of the whole cheerful theatre down beneath us — I know not the fathom line that ever touched a descent so deep as I would be willing to bury more wealth in than Crœsus had, or the great Jew R —— is supposed to have, to purchase it. And now do just look at that merry little Chinese waiter holding an umbrella, big enough for a bed-tester, over the head of that pretty insipid half-Madonaish chit of a lady in that very blue summer house."

POOR RELATIONS

London Magazine, May, 1823

A Poor Relation — is the most irrelevant thing in nature, — a piece of impertinent correspondency, — an odious approximation, — a haunting conscience, — a preposterous shadow, lengthening in the noontide of our prosperity, — an unwelcome remembrancer, — a perpetually recurring mortification, — a drain on your purse, — a more intolerable dun upon your pride, — a drawback upon success, — a rebuke to your rising, — a stain in your blood, — a blot on your 'scutcheon, — a rent in your garment, — a death's head at your banquet, — Agathocles' pot, — a Mordecai in your gate, — a Lazarus at your door, — a lion in your path, — a frog in your chamber, — a fly in your ointment, — a mote in your eye, — a triumph to your enemy, an apology to your friends, — the one thing not needful, — the hail in harvest, — the ounce of sour in a pound of sweet.

He is known by his knock. Your heart telleth you "That is Mr. ——." A rap, between familiarity and respect; that demands, and, at the same time, seems to despair of, entertainment. He entereth smiling and — embarrassed. He holdeth out his hand to you to shake, and — draweth it back again. He casually looketh in about dinner-time — when the table is full. He offereth to go away, seeing you have company — but is induced to stay. He filleth a chair, and your visitor's two children are accommodated at a side table. He never cometh upon open days, when your wife says with some complacency, "My dear, perhaps Mr. —— will drop in to-day." He remembereth birthdays — and professeth he is fortunate to have stumbled upon one. He declareth against fish, the turbot being small — yet suffereth himself to be importuned into a slice against his first resolution. He sticketh by the port — yet will be prevailed upon to empty the remainder glass of claret, if a stranger press it upon him. He is a puzzle to the servants, who are fearful of being too obsequious, or not civil enough, to him. The guests think "they have seen him before." Everyone speculateth upon his condition; and the most part take him to be — a tide waiter. He calleth you by your Christian name, to imply that his other is the same with your own. He is too familiar by half, yet you wish he had less diffidence. With half the familiarity he might pass for a casual dependent; with more boldness he would be in no danger of being taken for what he is. He is too humble for a friend, yet taketh on him more state than befits a client. He is a worse guest than a country tenant, inasmuch as he bringeth up no rent — yet 't is odds, from his garb and demeanour, that your guests take him for one. He is asked to make one at the whist table; refuseth on the score of poverty, and — resents being left out. When the company break up he proffereth to go for a coach — and lets the servant go. He recollects your grandfather; and will thrust in some mean and quite unimportant anecdote of — the family. He knew it when it was not quite so flourishing as "he is blest in seeing it now." He reviveth past situations to institute what he calleth — favourable comparisons. With a reflecting sort of congratulation, he will inquire the price of your furniture; and insults you with a special commendation of your window-curtains. He is of opinion that the urn is the more elegant shape, but, after all, there was something more comfortable about the old tea-kettle — which you must remember. He dare say you must find a great convenience in having a carriage of your own, and appealeth to your lady if it is not so. Inquireth if you have had your arms done on vellum yet; and did not know, till lately, that such-and-such had been the crest of the family. His memory is unseasonable; his compliments perverse; his talk a trouble; his stay pertinacious; and when he goeth away, you dismiss his chair into a corner, as precipitately as possible, and feel fairly rid of two nuisances.

There is a worse evil under the sun, and that is — a female Poor Relation. You may do something with the other; you may pass him off tolerably well; but your indigent she-relative is hopeless. "He is an old humourist," you may say, "and affects to go threadbare. His circumstances are better than folks would take them to be. You are fond of having a Character at your table, and truly he is one." But in the indications of female poverty there can be no disguise. No woman dresses below herself from caprice. The truth must out without shuffling. "She is plainly related to the L——s; or what does she at their house?" She is, in all probability, your wife's cousin. Nine times out of ten, at least, this is the case. Her garb is something between a gentlewoman and a beggar, yet the former evidently predominates. She is most provokingly humble, and ostentatiously sensible to her inferiority. He may require to be repressed sometimes — *aliquando sufflaminandus erat* — but there is no raising her. You send her soup at dinner, and she begs to be helped — after the gentlemen. Mr. —— requests the honour of taking wine with her; she hesitates between Port and Madeira, and chooses the former — because he does. She calls the servant *Sir*; and insists on not troubling him to hold her plate. The housekeeper patronises her. The children's governess takes upon her to correct her, when she has mistaken the piano for a harpsichord.

Richard Amlet, Esq., in the play, is a notable instance of the disadvantages to which this chimerical notion of *affinity constituting a claim to acquaintance* may subject the spirit of a gentleman. A little foolish blood is all that is betwixt him and a lady of great estate. His stars are perpetually crossed by the malignant maternity of an old woman, who persists in calling him "her son Dick." But she has wherewithal in the end to recompense his indignities, and float him again upon the brilliant surface, under which it had been her seeming business and pleasure all along to sink him. All men, besides, are not of Dick's temperament. I knew an Amlet in real life, who, wanting Dick's buoyancy, sank indeed. Poor W—— was of my own standing at Christ's, a fine classic, and a youth of promise. If he had a blemish, it was too much

pride; but its quality was inoffensive; it was not of that sort
which hardens the heart, and serves to keep inferiors at a distance; it only sought to ward off derogation from itself. It
was the principle of self-respect carried as far as it could go,
without infringing upon that respect which he would have
every one else equally maintain for himself. He would have
you to think alike with him on this topic. Many a quarrel
have I had with him, when we were rather older boys, and
our tallness made us more obnoxious to observation in the
blue clothes, because I would not thread the alleys and blind
ways of the town with him to elude notice, when we have
been out together on a holiday in the streets of this sneering
and prying metropolis. W—— went, sore with these notions,
to Oxford, where the dignity and sweetness of a scholar's life,
meeting with the alloy of a humble introduction, wrought in
him a passionate devotion to the place, with a profound aversion from the society. The servitor's gown (worse than his
school array) clung to him with Nessian venom. He thought
himself ridiculous in a garb under which Latimer must have
walked erect; and in which Hooker, in his young days, possibly
flaunted in a vein of no discommendable vanity. In the depths
of college shades, or in his lonely chamber, the poor student
shrunk from observation. He found shelter among books,
which insult not; and studies, that ask no questions of a
youth's finances. He was lord of his library, and seldom
cared for looking out beyond his domains. The healing influence of studious pursuits was upon him, to soothe and to
abstract. He was almost a healthy man; when the wayward-
ness of his fate broke out against him with a second and
worse malignity. The father of W—— had hitherto exercised
the humble profession of house-painter at N——, near Oxford. A supposed interest with some of the heads of colleges
had now induced him to take up his abode in that city, with
the hope of being employed upon some public works which
were talked of. From that moment, I read in the countenance
of the young man the determination which at length tore him

from academical pursuits for ever. To a person unacquainted with our Universities, the distance between the gownsmen and the townsmen, as they are called — the trading part of the latter especially — is carried to an excess that would appear harsh and incredible. The temperament of W——'s father was diametrically the reverse of his own. Old W—— was a little, busy, cringing tradesman, who, with his son upon his arm, would stand bowing and scraping, cap in hand, to anything that wore the semblance of a gown — insensible to the winks and opener remonstrances of the young man, to whose chamber-fellow, or equal in standing, perhaps, he was thus obsequiously and gratuitously ducking. Such a state of things could not last. W—— must change the air of Oxford or be suffocated. He chose the former; and let the sturdy moralist, who strains the point of the filial duties as high as they can bear, censure the dereliction; he cannot estimate the struggle. I stood with W——, the last afternoon I ever saw him, under the eaves of his paternal dwelling. It was in the fine lane leading from the High Street to the back of —— college, where W—— kept his rooms. He seemed thoughtful, and more reconciled. I ventured to rally him — finding him in a better mood — upon a representation of the Artist Evangelist, which the old man, whose affairs were beginning to flourish, had caused to be set up in a splendid sort of frame over his really handsome shop, either as a token of prosperity, or badge of gratitude to his saint. W—— looked up at the Luke, and, like Satan, " knew his mounted sign — and fled." A letter on his father's table the next morning announced that he had accepted a commission in a regiment about to embark for Portugal. He was among the first who perished before the walls of St. Sebastian.

I do not know how, upon a subject which I began with treating half seriously, I should have fallen upon a recital so eminently painful; but this theme of poor relationship is replete with so much matter for tragic as well as comic associations, that it is difficult to keep the account distinct without blending.

The earliest impressions which I received on this matter are certainly not attended with anything painful, or very humiliating, in the recalling. At my father's table (no very splendid one) was to be found, every Saturday, the mysterious figure of an aged gentleman, clothed in neat black, of a sad yet comely appearance. His deportment was of the essence of gravity; his words few or none; and I was not to make a noise in his presence. I had little inclination to have done so — for my cue was to admire in silence. A particular elbow chair was appropriated to him, which was in no case to be violated. A peculiar sort of sweet pudding, which appeared on no other occasion, distinguished the days of his coming. I used to think him a prodigiously rich man. All I could make out of him was that he and my father had been schoolfellows a world ago at Lincoln, and that he came from the Mint. The Mint I knew to be a place where all the money was coined — and I thought he was the owner of all that money. Awful ideas of the Tower twined themselves about his presence. He seemed above human infirmities and passions. A sort of melancholy grandeur invested him. From some inexplicable doom I fancied him obliged to go about in an eternal suit of mourning; a captive — a stately being, let out of the Tower on Saturdays. Often have I wondered at the temerity of my father, who, in spite of an habitual general respect which we all in common manifested towards him, would venture now and then to stand up against him in some argument, touching their youthful days. The houses of the ancient city of Lincoln are divided (as most of my readers know) between the dwellers on the hill, and in the valley. This marked distinction formed an obvious division between the boys who lived above (however brought together in a common school) and the boys whose paternal residence was on the plain; a sufficient cause of hostility in the code of these young Grotiuses. My father had been a leading Mountaineer; and would still maintain the general superiority, in skill and hardihood, of the *Above Boys* (his own faction) over the *Below Boys* (so were they called), of which party his contemporary had been a chieftain. Many and hot were the skirmishes on this topic — the only one upon which the old gentleman was ever brought out — and bad blood bred; even sometimes almost to the recommencement (so I expected) of actual hostilities. But my father, who scorned to insist upon advantages, generally contrived to turn the conversation upon some adroit by-commendation of the old Minster; in the general preference of which, before all other cathedrals in the island, the dweller on the hill, and the plain-born, could meet on a conciliating level, and lay down their less important differences. Once only I saw the old gentleman really ruffled, and I remembered with anguish the thought that came over me: "Perhaps he will never come here again." He had been pressed to take another plate of the viand, which I have already mentioned as the indispensable concomitant of his visits. He had refused with a resistance amounting to rigour — when my aunt, an old Lincolnian, but who had something of this in common with my cousin Bridget, that she would sometimes press civility out of season — uttered the following memorable application — "Do take another slice, Mr. Billet, for you do not get pudding every day." The old gentleman said nothing at the time — but he took occasion in the course of the evening, when some argument had intervened between them, to utter with an emphasis which chilled the company, and which chills me now as I write it — "Woman, you are superannuated." John Billet did not survive long, after the digesting of this affront; but he survived long enough to assure me that peace was actually restored! and, if I remember aright, another pudding was discreetly substituted in the place of that which had occasioned the offence. He died at the Mint (anno 1781) where he had long held, what he accounted, a comfortable independence; and with five pounds, fourteen shillings, and a penny, which were found in his escrutoire after his decease, left the world, blessing God that he had enough to bury him, and that he had never been obliged to any man for a sixpence. This was — a Poor Relation.

THE SUPERANNUATED MAN

London Magazine, May, 1825

Sera tamen respexit libertas. — VIRGIL
A Clerk I was in London gay. — O'KEEFE

If peradventure, Reader, it has been thy lot to waste the golden years of thy life — thy shining youth — in the irksome confinement of an office; to have thy prison days prolonged through middle age down to decrepitude and silver hairs, without hope of release or respite; to have lived to forget that there are such things as holidays, or to remember them but as the prerogatives of childhood; then, and then only, will you be able to appreciate my deliverance.

It is now six and thirty years since I took my seat at the desk in Mincing Lane. Melancholy was the transition at fourteen from the abundant playtime, and the frequently intervening vacations of school days, to the eight, nine, and sometimes ten hours' a-day attendance at a counting-house. But time partially reconciles us to anything. I gradually became content — doggedly contented, as wild animals in cages.

It is true I had my Sundays to myself; but Sundays, admirable as the institution of them is for purposes of worship, are for that very reason the very worst adapted for days of unbending and recreation. In particular, there is a gloom for me attendant upon a city Sunday, a weight in the air. I miss the cheerful cries of London, the music, and the ballad-singers — the buzz and stirring murmur of the streets. Those eternal bells depress me. The closed shops repel me. Prints, pictures, all the glittering and endless succession of knacks and gewgaws, and ostentatiously displayed wares of tradesmen, which make a week-day saunter through the less busy parts of the metropolis so delightful — are shut out. No book-stalls deliciously to idle over — No busy faces to recreate the idle man who contemplates them ever passing by — the very face of business a charm by contrast to his temporary relaxation from it. Nothing to be seen but unhappy countenances —

or half-happy at best — of emancipated 'prentices and little tradesfolks, with here and there a servant maid that has got leave to go out, who, slaving all the week, with the habit has lost almost the capacity of enjoying a free hour ; and livelily expressing the hollowness of a day's pleasuring. The very strollers in the fields on that day look anything but comfortable.

But besides Sundays I had a day at Easter, and a day at Christmas, with a full week in the summer to go and air myself in my native fields of Hertfordshire. This last was a great indulgence ; and the prospect of its recurrence, I believe, alone kept me up through the year, and made my durance tolerable. But when the week came round, did the glittering phantom of the distance keep touch with me ? or rather was it not a series of seven uneasy days, spent in restless pursuit of pleasure, and a wearisome anxiety to find out how to make the most of them ? Where was the quiet, where the promised rest ? Before I had a taste of it, it was vanished. I was at the desk again, counting upon the fifty-one tedious weeks that must intervene before such another snatch would come. Still the prospect of its coming threw something of an illumination upon the darker side of my captivity. Without it, as I have said, I could scarcely have sustained my thraldom.

Independently of the rigours of attendance, I have ever been haunted with a sense (perhaps a mere caprice) of incapacity for business. This, during my latter years, had increased to such a degree, that it was visible in all the lines of my countenance. My health and my good spirits flagged. I had perpetually a dread of some crisis, to which I should be found unequal. Besides my daylight servitude, I served over again all night in my sleep, and would awake with terrors of imaginary false entries, errors in my accounts, and the like. I was fifty years of age, and no prospect of emancipation presented itself. I had grown to my desk, as it were : and the wood had entered into my soul.

My fellows in the office would sometimes rally me upon the trouble legible in my countenance ; but I did not know that it had raised the suspicions of any of my employers, when on the 5th of last month, a day ever to be remembered by me, L——, the junior partner in the firm, calling me on one side, directly taxed me with my bad looks, and frankly inquired the cause of them. So taxed, I honestly made confession of my infirmity, and added that I was afraid I should eventually be obliged to resign his service. He spoke some words of course to hearten me, and there the matter rested. A whole week I remained labouring under the impression that I had acted imprudently in my disclosure; that I had foolishly given a handle against myself, and had been anticipating my own dismissal. A week passed in this manner, the most anxious one, I verily believe, in my whole life, when on the evening of the 12th of April, just as I was about quitting my desk to go home (it might be about eight o'clock) I received an awful summons to attend the presence of the whole assembled firm in the formidable back parlour. I thought now my time is surely come, I have done for myself, I am going to be told that they have no longer occasion for me. L——, I could see, smiled at the terror I was in, which was a little relief to me, — when to my utter astonishment B——, the eldest partner, began a formal harangue to me on the length of my services, my very meritorious conduct during the whole of the time (the deuce, thought I, how did he find out that? I protest I never had the confidence to think as much). He went on to descant on the expediency of retiring at a certain time of life (how my heart panted!), and asking me a few questions as to the amount of my own property, of which I have a little, ended with a proposal, to which his three partners nodded a grave assent, that I should accept from the house, which I had served so well, a pension for life to the amount of two-thirds of my accustomed salary — a magnificent offer! I do not know what I answered between surprise and gratitude, but it was understood that I accepted their proposal, and I was told that I was free from that hour to leave their service. I stammered out a bow, and at just ten minutes after eight I went

home — for ever. This noble benefit — gratitude forbids me
to conceal their names — I owe to the kindness of the
most munificent firm in the world — the house of Boldero,
Merryweather, Bosanquet, and Lacy.

Esto perpetua !

For the first day or two I felt stunned, overwhelmed. I
could only apprehend my felicity; I was too confused to
taste it sincerely. I wandered about, thinking I was happy,
and knowing that I was not. I was in the condition of a
prisoner in the Old Bastile, suddenly let loose after a forty
years' confinement. I could scarce trust myself with myself.
It was like passing out of Time into Eternity — for it is a sort
of Eternity for a man to have his Time all to himself. It
seemed to me that I had more time on my hands than I could
ever manage. From a poor man, poor in Time, I was suddenly lifted up into a vast revenue; I could see no end of
my possessions; I wanted some steward, or judicious bailiff, to
manage my estates in Time for me. And here let me caution
persons grown old in active business, not lightly, nor without
weighing their own resources, to forego their customary employment all at once, for there may be danger in it. I feel it
by myself, but I know that my resources are sufficient; and
now that those first giddy raptures have subsided, I have a
quiet home-feeling of the blessedness of my condition. I am
in no hurry. Having all holidays, I am as though I had none.
If Time hung heavy upon me, I could walk it away; but I
do *not* walk all day long, as I used to do in those old transient holidays, thirty miles a day, to make the most of them.
If Time were troublesome, I could read it away, but I do *not*
read in that violent measure, with which, having no Time my
own but candlelight Time, I used to weary out my head and
eye-sight in by-gone winters. I walk, read, or scribble (as now)
just when the fit seizes me. I no longer hunt after pleasure;
I let it come to me. I am like the man

—— that's born, and has his years come to him,
In some green desert.

"Years," you will say; "what is this superannuated simpleton calculating upon? He has already told us he is past fifty."

I have indeed lived nominally fifty years, but deduct out of them the hours which I have lived to other people, and not to myself, and you will find me still a young fellow. For *that* is the only true Time, which a man can properly call his own, that which he has all to himself; the rest, though in some sense he may be said to live it, is other people's time, not his. The remnant of my poor days, long or short, is at least multiplied for me threefold. My ten next years, if I stretch so far, will be as long as any preceding thirty. 'T is a fair rule-of-three sum.

Among the strange fantasies which beset me at the commencement of my freedom, and of which all traces are not yet gone, one was that a vast tract of time had intervened since I quitted the Counting-House. I could not conceive of it as an affair of yesterday. The partners, and the clerks with whom I had for so many years, and for so many hours in each day of the year been closely associated — being suddenly removed from them — they seemed as dead to me. There is a fine passage, which may serve to illustrate this fancy, in a Tragedy by Sir Robert Howard, speaking of a friend's death:

> —— 'T was but just now he went away;
> I have not since had time to shed a tear;
> And yet the distance does the same appear
> As if he had been a thousand years from me.
> Time takes no measure in Eternity.

To dissipate this awkward feeling, I have been fain to go among them once or twice since; to visit my old desk-fellows — my co-brethren of the quill — that I had left below in the state militant. Not all the kindness with which they received me could quite restore to me that pleasant familiarity which I had heretofore enjoyed among them. We cracked some of our old jokes, but methought they went off but faintly. My old desk, the peg where I hung my hat, were appropriated to another. I knew it must be, but I could not take it kindly. D——l take

me if I did not feel some remorse — beast, if I had not, —
at quitting my old compeers, the faithful partners of my toils
for six and thirty years, that smoothed for me with their jokes
and conundrums the ruggedness of my professional road. Had
it been so rugged then after all? or was I a coward simply?
Well, it is too late to repent; and I also know that these suggestions are a common fallacy of the mind on such occasions.
But my heart smote me. I had violently broken the bands betwixt us. It was at least not courteous. I shall be some time
before I get quite reconciled to the separation. Farewell, old
cronies, yet not for long, for again and again I will come among
ye, if I shall have your leave. Farewell, Ch——, dry, sarcastic,
and friendly! Do——, mild, slow to move, and gentlemanly!
Pl——, officious to do, and to volunteer, good services! — and
thou, thou dreary pile, fit mansion for a Gresham or a Whittington of old, stately House of Merchants; with thy laby-
rinthine passages, and light-excluding, pent-up offices, where
candles for one half the year supplied the place of the sun's
light; unhealthy contributor to my weal, stern fosterer of my
living, farewell! In thee remain, and not in the obscure collection of some wandering bookseller, my "works"! There let
them rest, as I do from my labours, piled on thy massy shelves,
more MSS. in folio than ever Aquinas left, and full as useful!
My mantle I bequeath among ye.

A fortnight has passed since the date of my first communication. At that period I was approaching to tranquillity, but had
not reached it. I boasted of a calm indeed, but it was compara-
tive only. Something of the first flutter was left; an unsettling
sense of novelty; the dazzle to weak eyes of unaccustomed
light. I missed my old chains, forsooth, as if they had been
some necessary part of my apparel. I was a poor Carthusian,
from strict cellular discipline suddenly by some revolution returned upon the world. I am now as if I had never been other
than my own master. It is natural to me to go where I please,
to do what I please. I find myself at eleven o'clock in the day
in Bond Street, and it seems to me that I have been sauntering

there at that very hour for years past. I digress into Soho, to explore a book-stall. Methinks I have been thirty years a collector. There is nothing strange nor new in it. I find myself before a fine picture in the morning. Was it ever otherwise? What is become of Fish Street Hill? Where is Fenchurch Street? Stones of old Mincing Lane which I have worn with my daily pilgrimage for six and thirty years, to the footsteps of what toil-worn clerk are your everlasting flints now vocal? I indent the gayer flags of Pall Mall. It is 'Change time, and I am strangely among the Elgin marbles. It was no hyperbole when I ventured to compare the change in my condition to a passing into another world. Time stands still in a manner to me. I have lost all distinction of season. I do not know the day of the week, or of the month. Each day used to be individually felt by me in its reference to the foreign post days; in its distance from, or propinquity to the next Sunday. I had my Wednesday feelings, my Saturday nights' sensations. The genius of each day was upon me distinctly during the whole of it, affecting my appetite, spirits, &c. The phantom of the next day, with the dreary five to follow, sate as a load upon my poor Sabbath recreations. What charm has washed the Ethiop white? What is gone of Black Monday? All days are the same. Sunday itself — that unfortunate failure of a holiday as it too often proved, what with my sense of its fugitiveness, and over-care to get the greatest quantity of pleasure out of it — is melted down into a week day. I can spare to go to church now, without grudging the huge cantle which it used to seem to cut out of the holiday. I have Time for everything. I can visit a sick friend. I can interrupt the man of much occupation when he is busiest. I can insult over him with an invitation to take a day's pleasure with me to Windsor this fine May-morning. It is Lucretian pleasure to behold the poor drudges, whom I have left behind in the world, carking and caring; like horses in a mill, drudging on in the same eternal round — and what is it all for? A man can never have too much Time to himself, nor too little to do. Had I a little son, I would christen him

NOTHING-TO-DO; he should do nothing. Man, I verily believe, is out of his element as long as he is operative. I am altogether for the life contemplative. Will no kindly earthquake come and swallow up those accursed cotton mills? Take me that lumber of a desk there, and bowl it down

As low as to the fiends.

I am no longer * * * * * *, clerk to the firm of, &c. I am Retired Leisure. I am to be met with in trim gardens. I am already come to be known by my vacant face and careless gesture, perambulating at no fixed pace nor with any settled purpose. I walk about; not to and from. They tell me, a certain *cum dignitate* air, that has been buried so long with my other good parts, has begun to shoot forth in my person. I grow into gentility perceptibly. When I take up a newspaper it is to read the state of the opera. *Opus operatum est.* I have done all that I came into this world to do. I have worked task-work, and have the rest of the day to myself.

JAMES HENRY LEIGH HUNT (1784–1859)

AUTUMNAL COMMENCEMENT OF FIRES

Indicator, October 20, 1819

How pleasant it is to have fires again! We have not time to regret summer, when the cold fogs begin to force upon us the necessity of a new kind of warmth; — a warmth not so fine as sunshine, but as manners go, more sociable. The English get together over their fires as the Italians do in their summer shade. We do not enjoy our sunshine as we ought; our climate seems to render us almost unaware that the weather is fine, when it really becomes so; but for the same reason we make as much of our winter as the anti-social habits that have grown upon us from other causes will allow. And for a similar reason, the southern European is unprepared for a cold day. The houses in many parts of Italy are summer houses, unprepared for winter; so that when a fit of cold weather comes, the dismayed inhabitant, walking and shivering about with a little brazier in his hands, presents an awkward image of insufficiency and perplexity. A few of our fogs, shutting up the sight of every thing out of doors and making the trees and the eaves of the houses drip like rain, would admonish him to get warm in good earnest. If "the web of our life" is always to be "of a mingled yarn," a good warm hearth-rug is not the worst part of the manufacture.

Here we are then again, with our fire before us and our books on each side. What shall we do? Shall we take out a Life of somebody, or a Theocritus, or Petrarch, or Ariosto, or Montaigne, or Marcus Aurelius, or Molière, or Shakespeare who includes them all? Or shall we *read* an engraving from Poussin or Raphael? Or shall we sit with tilted chairs, planting our wrists upon our knees and toasting the up-turned palms of our hands, while we discourse of manners and man's heart and hopes, with at least a sincerity, a good intention, and good-nature that shall warrant what we say with the sincere, the good-intentioned, and the good-natured?

Ah — take care. You see what that old-looking saucer is, with a handle to it? It is a venerable piece of earthenware, which may have been worth to an Athenian, about two-pence; but to an author, is worth a great deal more than ever he could — deny for it. And yet he would deny it too. It will fetch his imagination more than ever it fetched potter or penny-maker. Its little shallow circle overflows with the milk and honey of a thousand pleasant associations. This is one of the uses of having mantle-pieces. You may often see on no very rich mantle-piece a representative body of all the elements physical and intellectual — a shell for the sea, a stuffed bird or some feathers for the air, a curious piece of mineral for the earth, a glass of water with some flowers in it for the visible process of creation, — a cast from sculpture for the mind of man; — and underneath all, is the bright and ever-springing fire, running up through them heavenwards, like hope through materiality. We like to have any little curiosity of the mantle-piece kind within our reach and inspection. For the same reason, we like a small study, where we are almost in contact with our books. We like to feel them about us — to be in the arms of our mistress Philosophy, rather than see her from a distance. To have a huge apartment for a study is like lying in the great bed at Ware, or being snug on a milestone upon Hounslow Heath. It is space and physical activity, not repose and concentration. It is fit only for grandeur and ostentation, — for those who have secretaries, and are to be approached like gods in a temple. The Archbishop of Toledo, no doubt, wrote his homilies in a room ninety feet long. The Marquis Marialva must have been approached through whole ranks of glittering authors, standing at due distance. But Ariosto, whose mind could fly out of its nest over all nature, wrote over the house he built, "*parva, sed apta mihi*" — small, but suited to me. However, it is to be observed that he could not afford a large. He was a Duodenarian, in that respect, like ourselves. We do not know how our ideas of a study might expand with our walls. Montaigne, who was Montaigne " of that ilk " and lord of a great chateau, had a study " of sixteen paces in diameter, with three noble and free prospects." He congratulates himself, at the same time, on its circular figure, evidently from a feeling allied to the one in favour of smallness. "The figure of my study," says he, "is round, and has no more flat (bare) wall than what is taken up by my table and my chairs ; so that the remaining parts of the circle present me with a view of all my books at once, set upon five degrees of shelves round about me." (Cotton's *Montaigne*, B. 3, ch. 3.)

A great prospect we hold to be a very disputable advantage, upon the same reasoning as before ; but we like to have some green boughs about our windows, and to fancy ourselves as much as possible in the country, when we are not there. Milton expressed a wish with regard to his study extremely suitable to our present purpose. He would have the lamp in it *seen* ; thus letting others into a share of his enjoyments by the imagination of them.

> And let my lamp at midnight hour
> Be *seen* in some high lonely tower,
> Where I may oft outwatch the Bear
> With thrice-great Hermes ; or unsphere
> The Spirit of Plato, to unfold
> What world or what vast regions hold
> The immortal mind, that hath forsook
> Her mansion in this fleshly nook.

There is a fine passionate burst of enthusiasm on the subject of a study in Fletcher's play of the *Elder Brother*, Act 1, Scene 2 :

> Sordid and dunghill minds, composed of earth,
> In that gross elements fix all their happiness :
> But purer spirits, purged and refined,
> Shake off that clog of human frailty. Give me
> Leave to enjoy myself. That place that does

Contain my books, the best companions, is
To me a glorious court, where hourly I
Converse with the old sages and philosophers;
And sometimes for variety I confer
With kings and emperors, and weigh their counsels;
Calling their victories, if unjustly got,
Unto a strict account; and in my fancy,
Deface their ill-placed statues. Can I then
Part with such constant pleasures, to embrace
Uncertain vanities? No, be it your care
To augment a heap of wealth: it shall be mine
To increase in knowledge. Lights there for my study.

GETTING UP ON COLD MORNINGS

Indicator, January 19, 1820

An Italian author — Giulio Cordara, a Jesuit — has written a poem upon insects, which he begins by insisting that those troublesome and abominable little animals were created for our annoyance, and that they were certainly not inhabitants of Paradise. We of the North may dispute this piece of theology; but on the other hand, it is as clear as the snow cn the house-tops that Adam was not under the necessity of shaving; and that when Eve walked out of her delicious bower, she did not step upon ice three inches thick.

Some people say it is a very easy thing to get up of a cold morning. You have only, they tell you, to take the resolution; and the thing is done. This may be very true; just as a boy at school has only to take a flogging, and the thing is over. But we have not at all made up our minds upon it; and we find it a very pleasant exercise to discuss the matter, candidly, before we get up. This at least is not idling, though it may be lying. It affords an excellent answer to those who ask how lying in bed can be indulged in by a reasoning being, — a rational creature. How? Why with the argument calmly at work in one's head, and the clothes over one's shoulder. Oh — it is a fine way of spending a sensible, impartial half-hour.

If these people would be more charitable, they would get on with their argument better. But they are apt to reason so ill, and to assert so dogmatically, that one could wish to have them stand round one's bed of a bitter morning, and *lie* before their faces. They ought to hear both sides of the bed, the inside and out. If they cannot entertain themselves with their own thoughts for half an hour or so, it is not the fault of those who can.

Candid enquiries into one's decumbency, besides the greater or less privileges to be allowed a man in proportion to his ability of keeping early hours, the work given his faculties, &c., will at least concede their due merits to such representations as the following. In the first place, says the injured but calm appealer, I have been warm all night, and find my system in a state perfectly suitable to a warm-blooded animal. To get out of this state into the cold, besides the inharmonious and uncritical abruptness of the transition, is so unnatural to such a creature that the poets, refining upon the tortures of the damned, make one of their greatest agonies consist in being suddenly transported from heat to cold, — from fire to ice. They are " haled " out of their " beds," says Milton, by " harpy-footed furies," — fellows who come to call them. — On my first movement towards the anticipation of getting up, I find that such parts of the sheets and bolster as are exposed to the air of the room are stone cold. On opening my eyes, the first thing that meets them is my own breath rolling forth, as if in the open air, like smoke out of a chimney. Think of this symptom. Then I turn my eyes sideways and see the window all frozen over. Think of that. Then the servant comes in. " It is very cold this morning, is it not ? " — " Very cold, Sir." — " Very cold indeed, is n't it ? " — " Very cold indeed, Sir." — " More than usually so, is n't it, even for this weather ? " (Here the servant's wit and good nature are put to a considerable test, and the enquirer lies on thorns for the answer.) "Why, Sir —— I think it *is*." (Good creature! There is not a better or more truth-telling servant going.) " I must rise, however — get me some warm water." — Here comes a fine interval between the departure of the servant and the arrival of the hot water; during which, of course, it is of "no use" to get up. The hot water comes. "Is it quite hot?" — "Yes, Sir." — "Perhaps too hot for shaving: I must wait a little?" — "No, Sir; it will just do." (There is an over-nice propriety sometimes, an officious zeal of virtue, a little troublesome.) "Oh — the shirt — you must air my clean shirt; — linen gets very damp this weather." — "Yes, Sir." Here another delicious five minutes. A knock at the door. "Oh, the shirt — very well. My stockings — I think the stockings had better be aired too." — "Very well, Sir." — Here another interval. At length everything is ready, except myself. I now, continues our incumbent (a happy word, by the by, for a country vicar) — I now cannot help thinking a good deal — who can? — upon the unnecessary and villainous custom of shaving: it is a thing so unmanly (here I nestle closer) — so effeminate (here I recoil from an unlucky step into the colder part of the bed). — No wonder that the Queen of France took part with the rebels against that degenerate King, her husband, who first affronted her smooth visage with a face like her own. The Emperor Julian never showed the luxuriency of his genius to better advantage than in reviving the flowing beard. Look at Cardinal Bembo's picture — at Michael Angelo's — at Titian's — at Shakespeare's — at Fletcher's — at Spenser's — at Chaucer's — at Alfred's — at Plato's — I could name a great man for every tick of my watch. — Look at the Turks, a grave and otiose people. — Think of Haroun Al Raschid and Bed-ridden Hassan. — Think of Wortley Montague, the worthy son of his mother, above the prejudice of his time. — Look at the Persian gentlemen, whom one is ashamed of meeting about the suburbs, their dress and appearance are so much finer than our own. — Lastly, think of the razor itself — how totally opposed to every sensation of bed — how cold, how edgy, how hard! how utterly different from anything like the warm and circling amplitude, which

> Sweetly recommends itself
> Unto our gentle senses.

Add to this, benumbed fingers, which may help you to cut
yourself, a quivering body, a frozen towel, and an ewer full of
ice, and he that says there is nothing to oppose in all this, only
shows that he has no merit in opposing it.

Thomson, the poet, who exclaims in his *Seasons* —

Falsely luxurious! Will not man awake?

used to lie in bed till noon, because he said he had no motive
in getting up. He could imagine the good of rising; but then
he could also imagine the good of lying still; and his excla-
mation, it must be allowed, was made upon summer-time, not
winter. We must proportion the argument to the individual
character. A money-getter may be drawn out of his bed by
three and fourpence; but this will not suffice for a student.
A proud man may say "What shall I think of myself, if I
don't get up?" but the more humble one will be content to
waive this prodigious notion of himself, out of respect to his
kindly bed. The mechanical man shall get up without any ado
at all; and so shall the barometer. An ingenious lier in bed
will find hard matter of discussion even on the score of health
and longevity. He will ask us for our proofs and precedents
of the ill effects of lying later in cold weather; and sophisticate
much on the advantages of an even temperature of body; of
the natural propensity (pretty universal) to have one's way;
and of the animals that roll themselves up, and sleep all the
winter. As to longevity, he will ask whether the longest is of
necessity the best; and whether Holborn is the handsomest
street in London.

THE OLD GENTLEMAN

Indicator, February 2, 1820

Our Old Gentleman, in order to be exclusively himself, must
be either a widower or a bachelor. Suppose the former. We
do not mention his precise age, which would be invidious; —
nor whether he wears his own hair or a wig; which would be

wanting in universality. If a wig, it is a compromise between the more modern scratch and the departed glory of the toupee. If his own hair, it is white, in spite of his favourite grandson, who used to get on the chair behind him, and pull the silver hairs out, ten years ago. If he is bald at top, the hairdresser, hovering and breathing about him like a second youth, takes care to give the bald place as much powder as the covered; in order that he may convey to the sensorium within a pleasing indistinctness of idea respecting the exact limits of skin and hair. He is very clean and neat; and in warm weather, is proud of opening his waistcoat half way down, and letting so much of his frill be seen, in order to show his hardiness as well as taste. His watch and shirt-buttons are of the best; and he does not care if he has two rings on a finger. If his watch ever failed him at the club or coffee-house, he would take a walk every day to the nearest clock of good character, purely to keep it right. He has a cane at home, but seldom uses it, on finding it out of fashion with his elderly juniors. He has a small cocked hat for gala days, which he lifts higher from his head than the round one, when bowed to. In his pockets are two handkerchiefs (one for the neck at nighttime), his spectacles, and his pocket-book. The pocket-book, among other things, contains a receipt for a cough, and some verses cut out of an odd sheet of an old magazine, on the lovely Duchess of A., beginning—

When beauteous Mira walks the plain.

He intends this for a common-place book which he keeps, consisting of passages in verse and prose cut out of newspapers and magazines, and pasted in columns; some of them rather gay. His principal other books are Shakespeare's *Plays* and Milton's *Paradise Lost*; the *Spectator*, the *History of England*; the works of Lady M. W. Montague, Pope, and Churchill; Middleton's *Geography*, *The Gentleman's Magazine*; Sir John Sinclair on Longevity; several plays with portraits in character; *Account of Elizabeth Canning*, *Memoirs of George*

Ann Bellamy, Poetical Amusements at Bath-Easton, Blair's *Works, Elegant Extracts*; Junius as originally published; a few pamphlets on the American War and Lord George Gordon, &c. and one on the French Revolution. In his sitting rooms are some engravings from Hogarth and Sir Joshua; an engraved portrait of the Marquis of Granby; ditto of M. le Comte de Grasse surrendering to Admiral Rodney; a humorous piece after Penny; and a portrait of himself, painted by Sir Joshua. His wife's portrait is in his chamber, looking upon his bed. She is a little girl, stepping forward with a smile and a pointed toe, as if going to dance. He lost her when she was sixty.

The Old Gentleman is an early riser, because he intends to live at least twenty years longer. He continues to take tea for breakfast, in spite of what is said against its nervous effects; having been satisfied on that point some years ago by Dr. Johnson's criticism on Hanway, and a great liking for tea previously. His china cups and saucers have been broken since his wife's death, all but one, which is religiously kept for his use. He passes his morning in walking or riding, looking in at auctions, looking after his India bonds or some such money securities, furthering some subscription set on foot by his excellent friend Sir John, or cheapening a new old print for his portfolio. He also hears of the newspapers; not caring to see them till after dinner at the coffee-house. He may also cheapen a fish or so; the fishmonger soliciting his doubting eye as he passes, with a profound bow of recognition. He eats a pear before dinner.

His dinner at the coffee-house is served up to him at the accustomed hour, in the old accustomed way, and by the accustomed waiter. If William did not bring it, the fish would be sure to be stale, and the flesh new. He eats no tart; or if he ventures on a little, takes cheese with it. You might as soon attempt to persuade him out of his senses, as that cheese is not good for digestion. He takes port; and if he has drunk more than usual, and in a more private place, may be induced

by some respectful inquiries respecting the old style of music,
to sing a song composed by Mr. Oswald or Mr. Lampe,
such as —

> Chloe, by that borrowed kiss,

or

> Come, gentle god of soft repose;

or his wife's favourite ballad beginning —

> At Upton on the Hill
> There lived a happy pair.

Of course, no such exploit can take place in the coffee-room;
but he will canvass the theory of that matter there with you,
or discuss the weather, or the markets, or the theatres, or
the merits of "my Lord North" or "my Lord Rockingham";
for he rarely says simply, lord; it is generally "my lord,"
trippingly and genteelly off the tongue. If alone after dinner,
his great delight is the newspaper; which he prepares to read
by wiping his spectacles, carefully adjusting them on his eyes,
and drawing the candle close to him, so as to stand sideways
betwixt his ocular aim and the small type. He then holds the
paper at arm's length, and dropping his eyelids half down and
his mouth half open, takes cognizance of the day's information. If he leaves off, it is only when the door is opened by
a new-comer, or when he suspects somebody is over-anxious
to get the paper out of his hand. On these occasions, he
gives an important hem! or so; and resumes.

In the evening, our Old Gentleman is fond of going to
the theatre, or of having a game of cards. If he enjoys the
latter at his own house or lodgings, he likes to play with some
friends whom he has known for many years; but an elderly
stranger may be introduced, if quiet and scientific; and the
privilege is extended to younger men of letters; who, if ill
players, are good losers. Not that he is a miser; but to win
money at cards is like proving his victory by getting the baggage; and to win of a younger man is a substitute for his
not being able to beat him at rackets. He breaks up early,
whether at home or abroad.

At the theatre, he likes a front row in the pit. He comes early, if he can do so without getting into a squeeze, and sits patiently waiting for the drawing up of the curtain, with his hands placidly lying one over the other on the top of his stick. He generously admires some of the best performers, but thinks them far inferior to Garrick, Woodward, and Clive. During splendid scenes, he is anxious that the little boy should see.

He has been induced to look in at Vauxhall again, but likes it still less than he did years back, and cannot bear it in comparison with Ranelagh. He thinks everything looks poor, flaring, and jaded. "Ah!" says he, with a sort of triumphant sigh, "Ranelagh was a noble place! Such taste, such elegance, such beauty! There was the Duchess of A., the finest woman in England, Sir; and Mrs. L., a mighty fine creature; and Lady Susan what's her name, that had that unfortunate affair with Sir Charles. Sir, they came swimming by you like the swans."

The Old Gentleman is very particular in having his slippers ready for him at the fire, when he comes home. He is also extremely choice in his snuff, and delights to get a fresh boxful in Tavistock Street, in his way to the theatre. His box is a curiosity from India. He calls favourite young ladies by their Christian names, however slightly acquainted with them; and has a privilege also of saluting all brides, mothers, and indeed every species of lady on the least holiday occasion. If the husband, for instance, has met with a piece of luck, he instantly moves forward, and gravely kisses the wife on the cheek. The wife then says, "My niece, Sir, from the country"; and he kisses the niece. The niece, seeing her cousin biting her lips at the joke, says, "My cousin Harriet, Sir"; and he kisses the cousin. He never recollects such weather, except during the Great Frost, or when he rode down with Jack Skrimshire to Newmarket. He grows young again in his little grandchildren, especially the one which he thinks most like himself; which is the handsomest. Yet he likes best perhaps the one most resembling his wife; and will sit with him on his lap, holding his hand in silence, for a quarter of an hour together. He plays most tricks with the former, and makes him sneeze. He asks little boys in general who was the father of Zebedee's children. If his grandsons are at school, he often goes to see them; and makes them blush by telling the master or the upper-scholars, that they are fine boys, and of a precocious genius. He is much struck when an old acquaintance dies, but adds that he lived too fast; and that poor Bob was a sad dog in his youth; "a very sad dog, Sir, mightily set upon a short life and a merry one."

When he gets very old indeed, he will sit for whole evenings, and say little or nothing; but informs you that there is Mrs. Jones (the housekeeper) — " *She'll* talk."

DEATHS OF LITTLE CHILDREN

Indicator, April 5, 1820

A Grecian philosopher being asked why he wept for the death of his son, since the sorrow was in vain, replied, " I weep on that account." And his answer became his wisdom. It is only for sophists to pretend that we, whose eyes contain the fountains of tears, need never give way to them. It would be unwise not to do so on some occasions. Sorrow unlocks them in her balmy moods. The first bursts may be bitter and overwhelming; but the soil on which they pour would be worse without them. They refresh the fever of the soul, — the dry misery, which parches the countenance into furrows, and renders us liable to our most terrible " flesh-quakes."

There are sorrows, it is true, so great that to give them some of the ordinary vents is to run a hazard of being overthrown. These we must rather strengthen ourselves to resist, or bow quietly and dryly down in order to let them pass over us, as the traveller does the wind of the desert. But where we feel that tears would relieve us, it is false philosophy to deny ourselves at least that first refreshment; and it is always false consolation to tell people that because they cannot help a thing, they are not to mind it. The true way is to let them grapple with the unavoidable sorrow, and try to win it into gentleness by a reasonable yielding. There are griefs so gentle in their very nature that it would be worse than false heroism to refuse them a tear. Of this kind are the deaths of infants. Particular circumstances may render it more or less advisable to indulge in grief for the loss of a little child; but in general, parents should be no more advised to repress their first tears on such an occasion, than to repress their smiles towards a child surviving, or to indulge in any other sympathy. It is an appeal to the same gentle tenderness; and such appeals are never made in vain. The end of them is an acquittal from the harsher bonds of affliction, — from the tying down of the spirit to one melancholy idea.

It is the nature of tears of this kind, however strongly they may gush forth, to run into quiet waters at last. We cannot easily, for the whole course of our lives, think with pain of any good and kind person whom we have lost. It is the divine nature of their qualities to conquer pain and death itself; to turn the memory of them into pleasure; to survive with a placid aspect in our imaginations. We are writing, at this moment, just opposite a spot which contains the grave of one inexpressibly dear to us. We see from our window the trees about it, and the church-spire. The green fields lie around. The clouds are travelling overhead, alternately taking away the sunshine and restoring it. The vernal winds, piping of the flowery summer-time, are nevertheless calling to mind the far distant and dangerous ocean, which the heart that lies in that grave had many reasons to think of. And yet the sight of this spot does not give us pain. So far from it, it is the existence of that grave which doubles every charm of the spot; which links the pleasures of our childhood and manhood together; which puts a hushing tenderness in the winds, and a patient joy upon the landscape; which seems to unite heaven and earth, mortality and immortality, the grass of the tomb and the grass of the green field, and gives a more maternal aspect to the whole kindness of nature. It does not hinder gaiety itself. Happiness was what its tenant, through all her troubles, would have diffused. To diffuse happiness, and to enjoy it, is not only carrying on her wishes, but realizing her hopes ; and gaiety, freed from its only pollutions, malignity and want of sympathy, is but a child playing about the knees of its mother.

The remembered innocence and endearments of a child stand us in stead of virtues that have died older. Children have not exercised the voluntary offices of friendship ; they have not chosen to be kind and good to us ; nor stood by us, from conscious will, in the hour of adversity. But they have shared their pleasures and pains with us as well as they could : the interchange of good offices between us has, of necessity, been less mingled with the troubles of the world ; the sorrow arising from their death is the only one which we can associate with their memories. These are happy thoughts that cannot die. Our loss may always render them pensive ; but they will not always be painful. It is a part of the benignity of Nature, that pain does not survive like pleasure, at any time, much less where the cause of it is an innocent one. The smile will remain reflected by memory, as the moon reflects the light upon us when the sun has gone into heaven.

When writers like ourselves quarrel with earthly pain (we mean writers of the same intentions, without implying, of course, anything about abilities or otherwise) they are misunderstood if they are supposed to quarrel with pains of every sort. This would be idle and effeminate. They do not pretend, indeed, that humanity might not wish, if it could, to be entirely free from pain ; for it endeavours at all times to turn pain into pleasure, or at least to set off the one with the other ; to make the former a zest, and the latter a refreshment. The most unaffected dignity of suffering does this ; and if wise, acknowledges it. The greatest benevolence towards others, the most unselfish relish of their pleasures, even at its own expense, does but look to increasing the general stock of happiness, though content, if it could, to have its identity swallowed up in that splendid contemplation. We are far from meaning that this is to be called selfishness. We are far, indeed, from thinking so, or of so confounding words. But neither is it to be called pain, when most unselfish, if disinterestedness be truly understood. The pain that is in it softens into pleasure, as the darker hue of the rainbow melts into the brighter. Yet even if a harsher line is to be drawn between the pain and pleasure of the most unselfish mind (and ill health, for instance, may draw it), we should not quarrel with it, if it contributed to the general mass of comfort, and were of a nature which general kindliness could not avoid. Made as we are, there are certain pains, without which it would be difficult to conceive certain great and overbalancing pleasures. We may conceive it possible for beings to be made entirely happy; but in our composition, something of pain seems to be a necessary ingredient, in order that the materials may turn to as fine account as possible; though our clay, in the course of ages and experience, may be refined more and more. We may get rid of the worst earth, though not of earth itself.

Now the liability to the loss of children — or rather what renders us sensible of it, the occasional loss itself — seems to be one of these necessary bitters thrown into the cup of humanity. We do not mean that everyone must lose one of his children, in order to enjoy the rest; or that every individual loss afflicts us in the same proportion. We allude to the deaths of infants in general. These might be as few as we could render them. But if none at all ever took place, we should regard every little child as a man or woman secured; and it will easily be conceived, what a world of endearing cares and hopes this security would endanger. The very idea of infancy would lose its continuity with us. Girls and boys would be future men and women, not present children. They would have attained their full growth in our imaginations, and might as well have been men and women at once. On the other hand, those who have lost an infant are never, as it were, without an infant child. They are the only persons who, in one sense, retain it always, and they furnish their neighbours with the same idea.[1] The other children grow up to manhood and womanhood, and suffer all the changes of mortality. This one alone is rendered an immortal child. Death has arrested it with his kindly harshness, and blessed it into an eternal image of youth and innocence.

Of such as these are the pleasantest shapes that visit our fancy and our hopes. They are the ever-smiling emblems of joy; the prettiest pages that wait upon imagination. Lastly, "of these are the kingdom of heaven." Wherever there is a province of that benevolent and all-accessible empire, whether on earth or elsewhere, such are the gentle spirits that must inhabit it. To such simplicity, or the resemblance of it, must they come. Such must be the ready confidence of their hearts, and creativeness of their fancy. And so ignorant must they be of the "knowledge of good and evil," losing their discernment of that self-created trouble, by enjoying the garden before them, and not being ashamed of what is kindly and innocent.

SHAKING HANDS

Indicator, July 12, 1820

Among the first things which we remember noticing in the manners of people were two errors in the custom of shaking hands. Some, we observed, grasped everybody's hand alike, —with an equal fervour of grip. You would have thought that Jenkins was the best friend they had in the world; but on succeeding to the squeeze, though a slight acquaintance, you found it equally flattering to yourself; and on the appearance of somebody else (whose name, it turned out, the operator

---

[1] "I sighed," says old Captain Bolton, "when I envied you the two bonnie children, but I sigh not now to call either the monk or the soldier mine own." — *Monastery*, vol. iii. p. 341.

had forgotten) the crush was no less complimentary : — the face was as earnest and beaming, the "glad to see you" as syllabical and sincere, and the shake as close, as long, and as rejoicing, as if the semi-unknown was a friend come home from the Desarts.

On the other hand, there would be a gentleman now and then as coy of his hand as if he were a prude, or had a whit-low. It was in vain that your pretensions did not go beyond the "civil salute" of the ordinary shake ; or that being intro-duced to him in a friendly manner and expected to shake hands with the rest of the company, you could not in decency omit his. His fingers, half coming out, and half retreating, seemed to think that you were going to do them a mischief ; and when you got hold of them, the whole shake was on your side : the other hand did but proudly or pensively ac-quiesce — there was no knowing which ; you had to sustain it, as you might a lady's in handing her to a seat ; and it was an equal perplexity to know how to shake or to let it go. The one seemed a violence done to the patient ; the other an awkward responsibility brought upon yourself. You did not know, all the evening, whether you were not an object of dis-like to the person ; till on the party's breaking up, you saw him behave like an equally ill-used gentleman to all who practised the same unthinking civility.

Both these errors, we think, might as well be avoided : but of the two we must say we prefer the former. If it does not look so much like particular sincerity, it looks more like general kindness ; and if those two virtues are to be separated (which they assuredly need not be, if considered without spleen) the world can better afford to dispense with an un-pleasant truth than a gratuitous humanity. Besides, it is more difficult to make sure of the one, than to practise the other ; and kindness itself is the best of all truths. As long as we are sure of that, we are sure of something, and of something pleasant. It is always the best end, if not in every instance the most logical means.

This manual shyness is sometimes attributed to modesty, but never, we suspect, with justice, unless it be that sort of modesty whose fear of committing itself is grounded in pride. Want of address is a better reason, but this particular instance of it would be grounded in the same feeling. It always implies a habit either of pride or mistrust. We have met with two really kind men, who evinced this soreness of hand. Neither of them, perhaps, thought himself inferior to anybody about him, and both had good reason to think highly of themselves; but both had been sanguine men contradicted in their early hopes. There was a plot to meet the hand of one of them with a fish-slice, in order to show him the disadvantage to which he put his friends by that flat mode of salutation; but the conspirator had not the courage to do it. Whether he heard of the intention, we know not; but shortly afterwards he took very kindly to a shake. The other was the only man of a warm set of politicians who remained true to his first love of mankind. He was impatient at the change of his companions and at the folly and inattention of the rest; but though his manner became cold, his consistency still remained warm; and this gave him a right to be as strange as he pleased.

WILLIAM HAZLITT (1778–1830)

ON READING OLD BOOKS

London Magazine, February, 1821

I hate to read new books. There are twenty or thirty volumes that I have read over and over again, and these are the only ones that I have any desire ever to read at all. It was a long time before I could bring myself to sit down to the *Tales of My Landlord*, but now that author's works have made a considerable addition to my scanty library. I am told that some of Lady Morgan's are good, and have been recommended to look into *Anastasius*; but I have not yet ventured upon that task. A lady, the other day, could not refrain from expressing her surprise to a friend, who said he had been reading *Delphine*: — she asked, — If it had not been published some time back? Women judge of books as they do of fashions or complexions, which are admired only " in their newest gloss." That is not my way. I am not one of those who trouble the circulating libraries much, or pester the booksellers for mail-coach copies of standard periodical publications. I cannot say that I am greatly addicted to black-letter, but I profess myself well versed in the marble bindings of Andrew Millar, in the middle of the last century; nor does my taste revolt at Thurlow's *State Papers*, in Russia leather; or an ample impression of Sir William Temple's *Essays*, with a portrait after Sir Godfrey Kneller in front. I do not think altogether the worse of a book for having survived the author a generation or two. I have more confidence in the dead than the living. Contemporary writers may generally be divided into two classes — one's friends or one's foes. Of the first we are compelled to think too well, and of the last we are disposed to think too ill, to receive much genuine pleasure from the perusal, or to judge fairly of the merits of either. One candidate for literary fame, who happens to be of our acquaintance, writes finely, and like a man of genius; but unfortunately has a foolish face, which spoils a delicate passage; another inspires us with the highest respect for his personal talents and character, but does not quite come up to our expectations in print. All these contradictions and petty details interrupt the calm current of our reflections. If you want to know what any of the authors were who lived before our time, and are still objects of anxious inquiry, you have only to look into their works. But the dust and smoke and noise of modern literature have nothing in common with the pure, silent air of immortality.

When I take up a work that I have read before (the oftener the better), I know what I have to expect. The satisfaction is not lessened by being anticipated. When the entertainment is altogether new, I sit down to it as I should to a strange dish — turn and pick out a bit here and there, and am in doubt what to think of the composition. There is a want of confidence and security to second appetite. New-fangled books are also like made-dishes in this respect, that they are generally little else than hashes and *rifaccimentos* of what has been served up entire and in a more natural state at other times. Besides, in thus turning to a well-known author, there is not only an assurance that my time will not be thrown away, or my palate nauseated with the most insipid or vilest trash, but I shake hands with, and look an old, tried, and valued friend in the face, compare notes, and chat the hours away. It is true, we form dear friendships with such ideal guests — dearer, alas! and more lasting, than those with our most intimate acquaintance. In reading a book which is an old favourite with me (say the first novel I ever read) I not only have the pleasure of imagination and of a critical relish of the work, but the pleasures of memory added to it. It recalls the same feelings and associations which I had in first reading it, and which I can never have again in any other way. Standard productions of this kind are links in the chain of our conscious being. They bind together the different scattered divisions of our personal identity. They are landmarks and guides in our journey through life. They are pegs and loops on which we can hang up, or from which we can take down, at pleasure, the wardrobe of a moral imagination, the relics of our best affections, the tokens and records of our happiest hours. They are "for thoughts and for remembrance!" They are like Fortunatus's Wishing Cap — they give us the best riches — those of Fancy; and transport us, not over half the globe, but (which is better) over half our lives, at a word's notice!

My father Shandy solaced himself with Bruscambille. Give me for this purpose a volume of *Peregrine Pickle* or *Tom Jones*. Open either of them anywhere — at the Memoirs of Lady Vane, or the adventures at the masquerade with Lady Bellaston, or the disputes between Thwackum and Square, or the escape of Molly Seagrim, or the incident of Sophia and her muff, or the edifying prolixity of her aunt's lecture — and there I find the same delightful, busy, bustling scene as ever, and feel myself the same as when I was first introduced into the midst of it. Nay, sometimes the sight of an odd volume of these good old English authors on a stall, or the name lettered on the back among others on the shelves of a library, answers the purpose, revives the whole train of ideas, and sets "the puppets dallying." Twenty years are struck off the list, and I am a child again. A sage philosopher, who was not a very wise man, said that he should like very well to be young again, if he could take his experience along with him. This ingenious person did not seem to be aware, by the gravity of his remark, that the great advantage of being young is to be without this weight of experience, which he would fain place upon the shoulders of youth, and which never comes too late with years. Oh! what a privilege to be able to let this hump, like Christian's burthen, drop from off one's back, and transport oneself, by the help of a little musty duodecimo, to the time when "ignorance was bliss," and when we first got a peep at the raree-show of the world, through the glass of fiction — gazing at mankind, as we do at wild beasts in a menagerie, through the bars of their cages — or at curiosities in a museum, that we must not touch! For myself, not only are the old ideas of the contents of the work brought back to my mind in all their vividness, but the old associations of the faces and persons of those I then knew, as they were in their lifetime — the place where I sat to read the volume, the day when I got it, the feeling of the air, the fields, the sky — return, and all my early impressions with them. This is better to me — those places, those times, those persons, and those feelings that come across me as I retrace the story and devour the page, are to me better far than the wet sheets of the last new novel from the Ballantyne press, to say nothing of the Minerva press in Leadenhall Street. It is like visiting the scenes of early youth. I think of the time "when I was in my father's house, and my path ran down with butter and honey" — when I was a little, thoughtless child, and had no other wish or care but to con my daily task, and be happy! *Tom Jones*, I remember, was the first work that broke the spell. It came down in numbers once a fortnight, in Cooke's pocket-edition, embellished with cuts. I had hitherto read only in school-books, and a tiresome ecclesiastical history (with the exception of Mrs. Radcliffe's *Romance of the Forest*): but this had a different relish with it — "sweet in the mouth," though not "bitter in the belly." It smacked of the world I lived in, and in which I was to live — and showed me groups, "gay creatures" not "of the element," but of the earth; not "living in the clouds," but travelling the same road that I did; — some that had passed on before me, and others that might soon overtake me. My heart had palpitated at the thoughts of a boarding-school ball, or gala-day at Midsummer or Christmas: but the world I had found out in Cooke's edition of the *British Novelists* was to me a dance through life, a perpetual gala-day. The sixpenny numbers of this work regularly contrived to leave off just in the middle of a sentence, and in the nick of a story, where Tom Jones discovers Square behind the blanket; or where Parson Adams, in the inextricable confusion of events, very undesignedly gets to bed to Mrs. Slip-slop. Let me caution the reader against this impression of *Joseph Andrews*; for there is a picture of Fanny in it which he should not set his heart on, lest he should never meet with anything like it; or if he should, it would, perhaps, be better for him that he had not. It was just like —— —— ! With what eagerness I used to look forward to the next number, and open the prints! Ah! never again shall I feel the enthusiastic delight with which I gazed at the figures, and anticipated the story and adventures of Major Bath and Commodore Trunnion, of Trim and my Uncle Toby, of Don Quixote and Sancho and Dapple, of Gil Blas and Dame Lorenza Sephora, of Laura and the fair Lucretia, whose lips open and shut like buds of roses. To what nameless ideas did they give rise — with what airy delights I filled up the outlines, as I hung in silence over the page! Let me still recall them, that they may breathe fresh life into me, and that I may live that birthday of thought and romantic pleasure over again! Talk of the *ideal*! This is the only true ideal — the heavenly tints of Fancy reflected in the bubbles that float upon the spring-tide of human life.

> O Memory! shield me from the world's poor strife,
> And give those scenes thine everlasting life!

The paradox with which I set out is, I hope, less startling than it was; the reader will, by this time, have been let into my secret. Much about the same time, or I believe rather earlier, I took a particular satisfaction in reading Chubb's *Tracts*, and I often think I will get them again to wade through. There is a high gusto of polemical divinity in them; and you fancy that you hear a club of shoemakers at Salisbury debating a disputable text from one of St. Paul's Epistles in a workmanlike style, with equal shrewdness and pertinacity.

I cannot say much for my metaphysical studies, into which I launched shortly after with great ardour, so as to make a toil of a pleasure. I was presently entangled in the briars and thorns of subtle distinctions — of "fate, free-will, fore-knowledge absolute," though I cannot add that "in their wandering mazes I found no end"; for I did arrive at some very satisfactory and potent conclusions; nor will I go so far, however ungrateful the subject might seem, as to exclaim with Marlowe's Faustus — "Would I had never seen Wittenberg, never read book" — that is, never studied such authors as Hartley, Hume, Berkeley, etc. Locke's *Essay on the Human Understanding* is, however, a work from which I never derived either pleasure or profit; and Hobbes, dry and powerful as he is, I did not read till long afterwards. I read a few poets, which did not much hit my taste — for I would have the reader understand, I am deficient in the faculty of imagination; but I fell early upon French romances and philosophy, and devoured them tooth-and-nail. Many a dainty repast have I made of the *New Eloise*; — the description of the kiss; the excursion on the water; the letter of St. Preux, recalling the time of their first loves; and the account of Julia's death; these I read over and over again with unspeakable delight and wonder. Some years after, when I met with this work again, I found I had lost nearly my whole relish for it (except some few parts), and was, I remember, very much mortified with the change in my taste, which I sought to attribute to the smallness and gilt edges of the edition I had bought, and its being perfumed with rose-leaves. Nothing could exceed the gravity, the solemnity with which I carried home and read the Dedication to the *Social Contract*, with some other pieces of the same author, which I had picked up at a stall in a coarse leathern cover. Of the *Confessions* I have spoken elsewhere, and may repeat what I have said — "Sweet is the dew of their memory, and pleasant the balm of their recollection!" Their beauties are not "scattered like stray-gifts o'er the earth," but sown thick on the page, rich and rare. I wish I had never read the *Emilius*, or read it with implicit faith. I had no occasion to pamper my natural aversion to affectation or pretence, by romantic and artificial means. I had better have formed myself on the model of Sir Fopling Flutter. There is a class of persons whose virtues and most shining qualities sink in, and are concealed by, an absorbent ground of modesty and reserve ; and such a one I do, without vanity, profess myself.[1] Now these are the very persons who are likely to attach themselves to the character of Emilius, and of whom it is sure to be the bane. This dull, phlegmatic, retiring humour is not in a fair way to be corrected, but confirmed and rendered desperate, by being in that work held up as an object of imitation, as an example of simplicity and magnanimity — by coming upon us with all the recommendations of novelty, surprise, and superiority to the prejudices of the world — by being stuck upon a pedestal, made amiable, dazzling, a *leurre de dupe* ! The reliance on solid worth which it inculcates, the preference of sober truth to gaudy tinsel, hangs like a mill-stone round the neck of the imagination — " a load to sink a navy " — impedes our progress, and blocks up every prospect in life. A man, to get on, to be successful, conspicuous, applauded, should not retire upon the centre of his conscious resources, but be always at the circumference of appearances. He must envelop himself in a halo of mystery — he must ride in an equipage of opinion — he must walk with a train of self-conceit following him — he must not strip himself to a buff-jerkin, to the doublet and hose of his real merits, but must surround himself with a *cortège* of prejudices, like the signs of the Zodiac — he must seem anything but what he is, and then he may pass for anything he pleases. The world love to be amused by hollow professions, to be deceived by flattering appearances, to live in a state of

[1] Nearly the same sentiment was wittily and happily expressed by a friend, who had some lottery puffs, which he had been employed to write, returned on his hands for their too great severity of thought and classical terseness of style, and who observed on that occasion that " Modest merit never can succeed ! "

hallucination; and can forgive everything but the plain, down-right, simple, honest truth — such as we see it chalked out in the character of Emilius. To return from this digression, which is a little out of place here.

Books have in a great measure lost their power over me; nor can I revive the same interest in them as formerly. I perceive when a thing is good, rather than feel it. It is true,

Marcian Colonna is a dainty book;

and the reading of Mr. Keats's *Eve of St. Agnes* lately made me regret that I was not young again. The beautiful and tender images there conjured up, "come like shadows — so depart." The "tiger-moth's wings," which he has spread over his rich poetic blazonry, just flit across my fancy; the gorgeous twilight window which he has painted over again in his verse, to me "blushes" almost in vain "with blood of queens and kings." I know how I should have felt at one time in read-ing such passages; and that is all. The sharp luscious flavour, the fine *aroma* is fled, and nothing but the stalk, the bran, the husk of literature is left. If any one were to ask me what I read now, I might answer with my Lord Hamlet in the play — "Words, words, words." — "What is the matter?" — "*Nothing*!" — They have scarce a meaning. But it was not always so. There was a time when to my thinking, every word was a flower or a pearl, like those which dropped from the mouth of the little peasant-girl in the Fairy tale, or like those that fall from the great preacher in the Caledonian Chapel! I drank of the stream of knowledge that tempted, but did not mock my lips, as of the river of life, freely. How eagerly I slaked my thirst of German sentiment, "as the hart that panteth for the water-springs"; how I bathed and rev-elled, and added my floods of tears to Goethe's *Sorrows of Werter*, and to Schiller's *Robbers* —

Giving my stock of more to that which had too much!

I read and assented with all my soul to Coleridge's fine Sonnet, beginning —

> Schiller! that hour I would have wish'd to die,
> If through the shuddering midnight I had sent,
> From the dark dungeon of the tow'r time-rent,
> That fearful voice, a famish'd father's cry!

I believe I may date my insight into the mysteries of poetry from the commencement of my acquaintance with the Authors of the *Lyrical Ballads*; at least, my discrimination of the higher sorts — not my predilection for such writers as Goldsmith or Pope : nor do I imagine they will say I got my liking for the Novelists, or the comic writers — for the characters of Valentine, Tattle, or Miss Prue — from them. If so, I must have got from them what they never had themselves. In points where poetic diction and conception are concerned, I may be at a loss, and liable to be imposed upon : but in forming an estimate of passages relating to common life and manners, I cannot think I am a plagiarist from any man. I there " know my cue without a prompter." I may say of such studies, *Intus et in cute*. I am just able to admire those literal touches of observation and description which persons of loftier pretensions overlook and despise. I think I comprehend something of the characteristic part of Shakespeare ; and in him indeed all is characteristic, even the nonsense and poetry. I believe it was the celebrated Sir Humphry Davy who used to say that Shakespeare was rather a metaphysician than a poet. At any rate, it was not ill said. I wish that I had sooner known the dramatic writers contemporary with Shakespeare ; for in looking them over about a year ago, I almost revived my old passion for reading, and my old delight in books, though they were very nearly new to me. The Periodical Essayists I read long ago. The *Spectator* I liked extremely : but the *Tatler* took my fancy most. I read the others soon after, the *Rambler*, the

Adventurer, the *World*, the *Connoisseur*. I was not sorry to get to the end of them, and have no desire to go regularly through them again. I consider myself a thorough adept in Richardson. I like the longest of his novels best, and think no part of them tedious; nor should I ask to have anything better to do than to read them from beginning to end, to take them up when I chose, and lay them down when I was tired, in some old family mansion in the country, till every word and syllable relating to the bright Clarissa, the divine Clementina, the beautiful Pamela, "with every trick and line of their sweet favour," were once more "graven in my heart's table."[1] I have a sneaking kindness for Mackenzie's *Julia de Roubigné* — for the deserted mansion, and straggling gilliflowers on the mouldering garden-wall; and still more for his *Man of Feeling*; not that it is better, nor so good; but at the time I read it, I sometimes thought of the heroine, Miss Walton, and of Miss —— together, and "that ligament, fine as it was, was never broken!" — One of the poets that I have always read with most pleasure, and can wander about in for ever with a sort of voluptuous indolence, is Spenser; and I like Chaucer even better. The only writer among the Italians I can pretend to any knowledge of is Boccaccio, and of him I cannot express half my admiration. His story of the Hawk I could read and think of from day to day, just as I would look at a picture of Titian's!

I remember, as long ago as the year 1798, going to a neighbouring town (Shrewsbury, where Farquhar has laid the plot of his *Recruiting Officer*) and bringing home with me,

---

[1] During the peace of Amiens, a young English officer, of the name of Lovelace, was presented at Buonaparte's levee. Instead of the usual question, "Where have you served, Sir?" the First Consul immediately addressed him, "I perceive your name, Sir, is the same as that of the hero of Richardson's Romance!" Here was a Consul. The young man's uncle, who was called Lovelace, told me this anecdote while we were stopping together at Calais. I had also been thinking that his was the same name as that of the hero of Richardson's Romance. This is one of my reasons for liking Buonaparte.

"at one proud swoop," a copy of Milton's *Paradise Lost*, and another of Burke's *Reflections on the French Revolution* — both which I have still; and I still recollect, when I see the covers, the pleasure with which I dipped into them as I returned with my double prize. I was set up for one while. That time is past "with all its giddy raptures": but I am still anxious to preserve its memory, "embalmed with odours." — With respect to the first of these works, I would be permitted to remark here in passing that it is a sufficient answer to the German criticism which has since been started against the character of Satan (viz., that it is not one of disgusting deformity, or pure, defecated malice), to say that Milton has there drawn, not the abstract principle of evil, not a devil incarnate, but a fallen angel. This is the Scriptural account, and the poet has followed it. We may safely retain such passages as that well-known one —

> —— His form had not yet lost
> All her original brightness; nor appear'd
> Less than archangel ruin'd; and the excess
> Of glory obscur'd —

for the theory, which is opposed to them, "falls flat upon the grunsel edge, and shames its worshippers." Let us hear no more, then, of this monkish cant, and bigoted outcry for the restoration of the horns and tail of the devil! — Again, as to the other work, Burke's *Reflections*, I took a particular pride and pleasure in it, and read it to myself and others for months afterwards. I had reason for my prejudice in favour of this author. To understand an adversary is some praise: to admire him is more. I thought I did both: I knew I did one. From the first time I ever cast my eyes on anything of Burke's (which was an extract from his "Letter to a Noble Lord" in a three-times-a-week paper, the *St. James's Chronicle*, in 1796), I said to myself, "This is true eloquence: this is a man pouring out his mind on paper." All other style seemed to me pedantic and impertinent. Dr. Johnson's was walking on stilts; and even Junius's (who was at that time a favourite

with me), with all his terseness, shrunk up into little anti-
thetic points and well-trimmed sentences. But Burke's style
was forked and playful as the lightning, crested like the serpent. He delivered plain things on a plain ground; but when
he rose, there was no end of his flights and circumgyrations
— and in this very Letter, "he, like an eagle in a dove-cot,
fluttered *his* Volscians," (the Duke of Bedford and the Earl
of Lauderdale) "in Corioli." I did not care for his doctrines.
I was then, and am still, proof against their contagion; but I
admired the author, and was considered as not a very staunch
partisan of the opposite side, though I thought myself that an
abstract proposition was one thing — a masterly transition, a
brilliant metaphor, another. I conceived, too, that he might
be wrong in his main argument, and yet deliver fifty truths in
arriving at a false conclusion. I remember Coleridge assuring
me, as a poetical and political set-off to my sceptical admiration, that Wordsworth had written an Essay on Marriage,
which, for manly thought and nervous expression, he deemed
incomparably superior. As I had not, at that time, seen any
specimens of Mr. Wordsworth's prose style, I could not express my doubts on the subject. If there are greater prose-
writers than Burke, they either lie out of my course of study,
or are beyond my sphere of comprehension. I am too old to
be a convert to a new mythology of genius. The niches are
occupied, the tables are full. If such is still my admiration of
this man's misapplied powers, what must it have been at a
time when I myself was in vain trying, year after year, to
write a single essay, nay, a single page or sentence; when I
regarded the wonders of his pen with the longing eyes of one
who was dumb and a changeling; and when to be able to convey the slightest conception of my meaning to others in words,
was the height of an almost hopeless ambition ! But I never
measured others' excellences by my own defects : though a
sense of my own incapacity, and of the steep, impassable
ascent from me to them, made me regard them with greater
awe and fondness. I have thus run through most of my early

studies and favourite authors, some of whom I have since criticised more at large. Whether those observations will survive me, I neither know nor do I much care : but to the works themselves, "worthy of all acceptation," and to the feelings they have always excited in me since I could distinguish a meaning in language, nothing shall ever prevent me from looking back with gratitude and triumph. To have lived in the cultivation of an intimacy with such works, and to have familiarly relished such names, is not to have lived quite in vain.

There are other authors whom I have never read, and yet whom I have frequently had a great desire to read, from some circumstance relating to them. Among these is Lord Clarendon's *History of the Grand Rebellion*, after which I have a hankering, from hearing it spoken of by good judges — from my interest in the events, and knowledge of the characters from other sources, and from having seen fine portraits of most of them. I like to read a well-penned character, and Clarendon is said to have been a master in his way. I should like to read Froissart's *Chronicles*, Holinshed and Stowe, and Fuller's *Worthies*. I intend, whenever I can, to read Beaumont and Fletcher all through. There are fifty-two of their plays, and I have only read a dozen or fourteen of them. *A Wife for a Month* and *Thierry and Theodoret* are, I am told, delicious, and I can believe it. I should like to read the speeches in Thucydides, and Guicciardini's *History of Florence*, and *Don Quixote* in the original. I have often thought of reading the *Loves of Persiles and Sigismunda*, and the *Galatea* of the same author. But I somehow reserve them like "another Yarrow." I should also like to read the last new novel (if I could be sure it was so) of the author of *Waverley* : — no one would be more glad than I to find it the best!

ON GOING A JOURNEY

New Monthly Magazine, 1822

[One of the pleasantest things in the world is going a journey; but I like to go by myself.] I can enjoy society in a room; but out of doors, nature is company enough for me. I am then never less alone then when alone.

> The fields his study, nature was his book.

I cannot see the wit of walking and talking at the same time. When I am in the country, I wish to vegetate like the country. I am not for criticising hedge-rows and black cattle. I go out of town in order to forget the town and all that is in it. There are those who for this purpose go to watering-places, and carry the metropolis with them. I like more elbow-room, and fewer incumbrances. I like solitude, when I give myself up to it, for the sake of solitude; nor do I ask for

> —— a friend in my retreat,
> Whom I may whisper, solitude is sweet.

The soul of a journey is liberty, perfect liberty, to think, feel, do, just as one pleases. We go a journey chiefly to be free of all impediments and of all inconveniences; to leave ourselves behind, much more to get rid of others. It is because I want a little breathing-space to muse on indifferent matters, where Contemplation

> May plume her feathers and let grow her wings,
> That in the various bustle of resort
> Were all too ruffled, and sometimes impair'd,

that I absent myself from the town for a while, without feeling at a loss the moment I am left by myself. Instead of a friend in a post-chaise or in a Tilbury, to exchange good things with, and vary the same stale topics over again, for once let me have a truce with impertinence. [Give me the clear blue sky over my head, and the green turf beneath my feet, a winding road before me, and a three hours' march to dinner — and

then to thinking! It is hard if I cannot start some game
on these lone heaths. I laugh, I run, I leap, I sing for joy.
From the point of yonder rolling cloud, I plunge into my
past being, and revel there, as the sun-burnt Indian plunges
headlong into the wave that wafts him to his native shore.
Then long-forgotten things, like "sunken wrack and sumless
treasures," burst upon my eager sight, and I begin to feel,
think, and be myself again. Instead of an awkward silence,
broken by attempts at wit or dull commonplaces, mine is that
undisturbed silence of the heart which alone is perfect eloquence. No one likes puns, alliterations, antitheses, argument,
and analysis better than I do; but I sometimes had rather be
without them. "Leave, oh, leave me to my repose!" I have
just now other business in hand, which would seem idle to you,
but is with me "very stuff o' the conscience." Is not this wild
rose sweet without a comment? Does not this daisy leap to
my heart set in its coat of emerald? Yet if I were to explain
to you the circumstance that has so endeared it to me, you
would only smile. Had I not better then keep it to myself,
and let it serve me to brood over, from here to yonder craggy
point, and from thence onward to the far-distant horizon? I
should be but bad company all that way, and therefore prefer
being alone. I have heard it said that you may, when the
moody fit comes on, walk or ride on by yourself, and indulge
your reveries. But this looks like a breach of manners, a neglect of others, and you are thinking all the time that you
ought to rejoin your party. "Out upon such half-faced fellowship," say I. I like to be either entirely to myself, or entirely
at the disposal of others; to talk or be silent, to walk or sit
still, to be sociable or solitary. I was pleased with an observation of Mr. Cobbett's, that "he thought it a bad French custom to drink our wine with our meals, and that an Englishman
ought to do only one thing at a time." So I cannot talk and
think, or indulge in melancholy musing and lively conversation
by fits and starts. "Let me have a companion of my way,"
says Sterne, "were it but to remark how the shadows lengthen

as the sun declines." It is beautifully said; but in my opinion, this continual comparing of notes interferes with the involuntary impression of things upon the mind, and hurts the sentiment. If you only hint what you feel in a kind of dumb show, it is insipid: if you have to explain it, it is making a toil of a pleasure. You cannot read the book of nature without being perpetually put to the trouble of translating it for the benefit of others. I am for the synthetical method on a journey in preference to the analytical. I am content to lay in a stock of ideas then, and to examine and anatomise them afterwards. I want to see my vague notions float like the down of the thistle before the breeze, and not to have them entangled in the briars and thorns of controversy. For once, I like to have it all my own way; and this is impossible unless you are alone, or in such company as I do not covet. I have no objection to argue a point with any one for twenty miles of measured road, but not for pleasure. If you remark the scent of a bean-field crossing the road, perhaps your fellow-traveller has no smell. If you point to a distant object, perhaps he is short-sighted, and has to take out his glass to look at it. There is a feeling in the air, a tone in the colour of a cloud which hits your fancy, but the effect of which you are unable to account for. There is then no sympathy, but an uneasy craving after it, and a dissatisfaction which pursues you on the way, and in the end probably produces ill-humour. Now I never quarrel with myself, and take all my own conclusions for granted till I find it necessary to defend them against objections. It is not merely that you may not be of accord on the objects and circumstances that present themselves before you — these may recall a number of objects, and lead to associations too delicate and refined to be possibly communicated to others. Yet these I love to cherish, and sometimes still fondly clutch them, when I can escape from the throng to do so. To give way to our feelings before company seems extravagance or affectation; and, on the other hand, to have to unravel this mystery of our being at every turn, and to make others take an equal interest in it (otherwise the end is not answered) is a task to which few are competent. We must "give it an understanding, but no tongue." My old friend Coleridge, however, could do both. He could go on in the most delightful explanatory way over hill and dale a summer's day, and convert a landscape into a didactic poem or a Pindaric ode. "He talked far above singing." If I could so clothe my ideas in sounding and flowing words, I might perhaps wish to have some one with me to admire the swelling theme; or I could be more content, were it possible for me still to hear his echoing voice in the woods of All-Foxden. They had "that fine madness in them which our first poets had"; and if they could have been caught by some rare instrument, would have breathed such strains as the following : —

—— Here be woods as green
As any, air likewise as fresh and sweet
As when smooth Zephyrus plays on the fleet
Face of the curled streams, with flow'rs as many
As the young spring gives, and as choice as any;
Here be all new delights, cool streams and wells;
Arbours o'ergrown with woodbines, caves and dells;
Choose where thou wilt, while I sit by and sing,
Or gather rushes, to make many a ring
For thy long fingers; tell thee tales of love;
How the pale Phœbe, hunting in a grove,
First saw the boy Endymion, from whose eyes
She took eternal fire that never dies;
How she convey'd him softly in a sleep,
His temples bound with poppy, to the steep
Head of old Latmos, where she stoops each night,
Gilding the mountain with her brother's light,
To kiss her sweetest.[1]

Had I words and images at command like these, I would attempt to wake the thoughts that lie slumbering on golden ridges in the evening clouds : but at the sight of nature my fancy, poor as it is, droops and closes up its leaves, like flowers at sunset. I can make nothing out on the spot : — I must have time to collect myself. —

[1] Fletcher's *Faithful Shepherdess*.

In general, a good thing spoils out-of-door prospects : it should be reserved for Table-talk. Lamb is for this reason, I take it, the worst company in the world out of doors ; because he is the best within. I grant there is one subject on which it is pleasant to talk on a journey ; and that is, what one shall have for supper when we get to our inn at night. The open air improves this sort of conversation or friendly altercation, by setting a keener edge on appetite. Every mile of the road heightens the flavour of the viands we expect at the end of it. How fine it is to enter some old town, walled and turreted, just at the approach of nightfall, or to come to some straggling village, with the lights streaming through the surrounding gloom ; and then, after inquiring for the best entertainment that the place affords, to "take one's ease at one's inn!" These eventful moments in our lives' history are too precious, too full of solid, heartfelt happiness to be frittered and dribbled away in imperfect sympathy. I would have them all to myself, and drain them to the last drop : they will do to talk of or to write about afterwards. What a delicate speculation it is, after drinking whole goblets of tea,

> The cups that cheer, but not inebriate,

and letting the fumes ascend into the brain, to sit considering what we shall have for supper — eggs and a rasher, a rabbit smothered in onions, or an excellent veal cutlet! Sancho in such a situation once fixed upon cow-heel ; and his choice, though he could not help it, is not to be disparaged. Then in the intervals of pictured scenery and Shandean contemplation, to catch the preparation and the stir in the kitchen. *Procul, O procul este profani!* These hours are sacred to silence and to musing, to be treasured up in the memory, and to feed the source of smiling thoughts hereafter. I would not waste them in idle talk ; or if I must have the integrity of fancy broken in upon, I would rather it were by a stranger than a friend. A stranger takes his hue and character from the time and place ; he is a part of the furniture and

costume of an inn. If he is a Quaker, or from the West
Riding of Yorkshire, so much the better. I do not even try
to sympathise with him, and he breaks no squares. I associate nothing with my travelling companion but present objects
and passing events. In his ignorance of me and my affairs,
I in a manner forget myself. But a friend reminds one of
other things, rips up old grievances, and destroys the abstraction of the scene. He comes in ungraciously between us and
our imaginary character. Something is dropped in the course
of conversation that gives a hint of your profession and pursuits; or from having someone with you that knows the less
sublime portions of your history, it seems that other people
do. You are no longer a citizen of the world; but your "unhoused free condition is put into circumscription and confine."
The *incognito* of an inn is one of its striking privileges —
"lord of one's self, uncumbered with a name." Oh! it is
great to shake off the trammels of the world and of public
opinion — to lose our importunate, tormenting, everlasting
personal identity in the elements of nature, and become the
creature of the moment, clear of all ties — to hold to the universe only by a dish of sweetbreads, and to owe nothing but
the score of the evening — and no longer seeking for applause
and meeting with contempt, to be known by no other title
than *the Gentleman in the parlour*! One may take one's
choice of all characters in this romantic state of uncertainty
as to one's real pretensions, and become indefinitely respectable and negatively right-worshipful. We baffle prejudice and
disappoint conjecture; and from being so to others, begin to
be objects of curiosity and wonder even to ourselves. We are
no more those hackneyed commonplaces that we appear in
the world: an inn restores us to the level of nature, and quits
scores with society! I have certainly spent some enviable
hours at inns — sometimes when I have been left entirely to
myself, and have tried to solve some metaphysical problem,
as once at Witham Common, where I found out the proof
that likeness is not a case of the association of ideas — at

other times, when there have been pictures in the room, as at St. Neot's (I think it was), where I first met with Gribelin's engravings of the Cartoons, into which I entered at once, and at a little inn on the borders of Wales, where there happened to be hanging some of Westall's drawings, which I compared triumphantly (for a theory that I had, not for the admired artist) with the figure of a girl who had ferried me over the Severn, standing up in a boat between me and the twilight — at other times I might mention luxuriating in books, with a peculiar interest in this way, as I remember sitting up half the night to read *Paul and Virginia*, which I picked up at an inn at Bridgewater, after being drenched in the rain all day; and at the same place I got through two volumes of Madame D'Arblay's *Camilla*. It was on the 10th of April, 1798, that I sat down to a volume of the *New Eloise*, at the inn at Llangollen, over a bottle of sherry and a cold chicken. The letter I chose was that in which St. Preux describes his feelings as he first caught a glimpse from the heights of the Jura of the Pays de Vaud, which I had brought with me as a *bon bouche* to crown the evening with. It was my birthday, and I had for the first time come from a place in the neighbourhood to visit this delightful spot. The road to Llangollen turns off between Chirk and Wrexham; and on passing a certain point, you come all at once upon the valley, which opens like an amphitheatre, broad, barren hills rising in majestic state on either side, with "green upland swells that echo to the bleat of flocks" below, and the river Dee babbling over its stony bed in the midst of them. The valley at this time "glittered green with sunny showers," and a budding ash-tree dipped its tender branches in the chiding stream. How proud, how glad I was to walk along the high road that overlooks the delicious prospect, repeating the lines which I have just quoted from Mr. Coleridge's poems! But besides the prospect which opened beneath my feet, another also opened to my inward sight, a heavenly vision, on which were written, in letters large as Hope could make them, these four words, LIBERTY,

GENIUS, LOVE, VIRTUE; which have since faded into the light of common day, or mock my idle gaze.

The beautiful is vanished, and returns not.

Still I would return some time or other to this enchanted spot; but I would return to it alone. What other self could I find to share that influx of thoughts, of regret, and delight, the fragments of which I could hardly conjure up to myself, so much have they been broken and defaced! I could stand on some tall rock, and overlook the precipice of years that separates me from what I then was. I was at that time going shortly to visit the poet whom I have above named. Where is he now? Not only I myself have changed; the world, which was then new to me, has become old and incorrigible. Yet will I turn to thee in thought, O sylvan Dee, in joy, in youth and gladness as thou then wert; and thou shalt always be to me the river of Paradise, where I will drink of the waters of life freely!

There is hardly anything that shows the short-sightedness or capriciousness of the imagination more than travelling does. With change of place we change our ideas; nay, our opinions and feelings. We can by an effort indeed transport ourselves to old and long-forgotten scenes, and then the picture of the mind revives again; but we forget those that we have just left. It seems that we can think but of one place at a time. The canvas of the fancy is but of a certain extent, and if we paint one set of objects upon it, they immediately efface every other. We cannot enlarge our conceptions, we only shift our point of view. The landscape bares its bosom to the enraptured eye, we take our fill of it, and seem as if we could form no other image of beauty or grandeur. We pass on, and think no more of it: the horizon that shuts it from our sight also blots it from our memory like a dream. In travelling through a wild, barren country, I can form no idea of a woody and cultivated one. It appears to me that all the world must be barren, like what I see of it. In the country we forget the town, and in town we despise the country. "Beyond Hyde Park," says Sir Fopling Flutter, "all is a desert." All that part of the map that we do not see before us is blank. The world in our conceit of it is not much bigger than a nutshell. It is not one prospect expanded into another, county joined to county, kingdom to kingdom, lands to seas, making an image voluminous and vast; — the mind can form no larger idea of space than the eye can take in at a single glance. The rest is a name written in a map, a calculation of arithmetic. For instance, what is the true signification of that immense mass of territory and population, known by the name of China to us? An inch of pasteboard on a wooden globe, of no more account than a China orange! Things near us are seen of the size of life: things at a distance are diminished to the size of the understanding. We measure the universe by ourselves, and even comprehend the texture of our own being only piecemeal. In this way, however, we remember an infinity of things and places. The mind is like a mechanical instrument that plays a great variety of tunes, but it must play them in succession. One idea recalls another, but it at the same time excludes all others. In trying to renew old recollections, we cannot as it were unfold the whole web of our existence; we must pick out the single threads. So in coming to a place where we have formerly lived, and with which we have intimate associations, every one must have found that the feeling grows more vivid the nearer we approach the spot, from the mere anticipation of the actual impression: we remember circumstances, feelings, persons, faces, names that we had not thought of for years; but for the time all the rest of the world is forgotten! — To return to the question I have quitted above.

I have no objection to go to see ruins, aqueducts, pictures, in company with a friend or a party, but rather the contrary, for the former reason reversed. They are intelligible matters, and will bear talking about. The sentiment here is not tacit, but communicable and overt. Salisbury Plain is barren of criticism, but Stonehenge will bear a discussion antiquarian, picturesque, and philosophical. In setting out on a party of pleasure, the first consideration always is where we shall go to : in taking a solitary ramble, the question is what we shall meet with by the way. " The mind is its own place " ; nor are we anxious to arrive at the end of our journey. I can myself do the honours indifferently well to works of art and curiosity. I once took a party to Oxford with no mean *éclat* — showed them that seat of the Muses at a distance,

> With glistering spires and pinnacles adorn'd —

descanted on the learned air that breathes from the grassy quadrangles and stone walls of halls and cottages — was at home in the Bodleian ; and at Blenheim quite superseded the powdered Cicerone that attended us, and that pointed in vain with his wand to commonplace beauties in matchless pictures. As another exception to the above reasoning, I should not feel confident in venturing on a journey in a foreign country without a companion. I should want at intervals to hear the sound of my own language. There is an involuntary antipathy in the mind of an Englishman to foreign manners and notions that requires the assistance of social sympathy to carry it off. As the distance from home increases, this relief, which was at first a luxury, becomes a passion and an appetite. A person would almost feel stifled to find himself in the deserts of Arabia without friends and countrymen : there must be allowed to be something in the view of Athens or old Rome that claims the utterance of speech ; and I own that the Pyramids are too mighty for any single contemplation. In such situations, so opposite to all one's ordinary train of ideas, one seems a species by one's-self, a limb torn off from society, unless one can meet with instant fellowship and support. Yet I did not feel this want or craving very pressing once, when I first set my foot on the laughing shores of France. Calais was peopled with novelty and delight. The confused, busy murmur of the place was like oil and wine poured into my ears ; nor did the Mariners' Hymn, which was sung from the top of an old crazy vessel in the harbour, as the sun went down, send an alien sound into my soul. I only breathed the air of general humanity. I walked over " the vine-covered hills and gay regions of France," erect and satisfied ; for the image of man was not cast down and chained to the foot of arbitrary thrones : I was at no loss for language, for that of all the great schools of painting was open to me. The whole is vanished like a shade. Pictures, heroes, glory, freedom, all are fled : nothing remains but the Bourbons and the French people ! — There is undoubtedly a sensation in travelling into foreign parts that is to be had nowhere else : but it is more pleasing at the time than lasting. It is too remote from our habitual associations to be a common topic of discourse or reference, and, like a dream or another state of existence, does not piece into our daily modes of life. It is an animated but a momentary hallucination. It demands an effort to exchange our actual for our ideal identity ; and to feel the pulse of our old transports revive very keenly, we must " jump " all our present comforts and connexions. Our romantic and itinerant character is not to be domesticated. Dr. Johnson remarked how little foreign travel added to the facilities of conversation in those who had been abroad. In fact, the time we have spent there is both delightful, and, in one sense, instructive ; but it appears to be cut out of our substantial, downright existence, and never to join kindly on to it. We are not the same, but another, and perhaps more enviable individual, all the time we are out of our own country. We are lost to ourselves, as well as our friends. So the poet somewhat quaintly sings,

> Out of my country and myself I go.

Those who wish to forget painful thoughts, do well to absent themselves for a while from the ties and objects that recall them : but we can be said only to fulfil our destiny in the place that gave us birth. I should on this account like well enough to spend the whole of my life in travelling abroad, if I could anywhere borrow another life to spend afterwards at home !

ON THE FEELING OF IMMORTALITY IN YOUTH

Monthly Magazine, March, 1827

"Life is a pure flame, and we live by an invisible sun within us."—
SIR THOMAS BROWN

No young man believes he shall ever die. It was a saying of my brother's, and a fine one. There is a feeling of Eternity in youth, which makes us amends for everything. To be young is to be as one of the Immortal Gods. One half of time indeed is flown — the other half remains in store for us with all its countless treasures; for there is no line drawn, and we see no limit to our hopes and wishes. We make the coming age our own. ——

The vast, the unbounded prospect lies before us.

Death, old age, are words without a meaning, that pass by us like the idle air which we regard not. Others may have undergone, or may still be liable to them — we "bear a charmed life," which laughs to scorn all such sickly fancies. As in setting out on a delightful journey, we strain our eager gaze forward —

Bidding the lovely scenes at distance hail, —

and see no end to the landscape, new objects presenting themselves as we advance; so, in the commencement of life, we set no bounds to our inclinations, nor to the unrestricted opportunities of gratifying them. We have as yet found no obstacle, no disposition to flag; and it seems that we can go on so for ever. We look round in a new world, full of life, and motion, and ceaseless progress; and feel in ourselves all the vigour and spirit to keep pace with it, and do not foresee from any present symptoms how we shall be left behind in the natural course of things, decline into old age, and drop into the grave. It is the simplicity, and as it were *abstractedness* of our feelings in youth, that (so to speak) identifies us with nature, and (our experience being slight and our passions strong) deludes us into a belief of being immortal like it. Our short-lived connection with existence, we fondly flatter ourselves, is an indissoluble and lasting union — a honey-moon that knows neither coldness, jar, nor separation. As infants smile and sleep, we are rocked in the cradle of our wayward fancies, and lulled into security by the roar of the universe around us — we quaff the cup of life with eager haste without draining it, instead of which it only overflows the more — objects press around us, filling the mind with their magnitude and with the throng of desires that wait upon them, so that we have no room for the thoughts of death. From that plenitude of our being, we cannot change all at once to dust and ashes, we cannot imagine "this sensible, warm motion, to become a kneaded clod" — we are too much dazzled by the brightness of the waking dream around us to look into the darkness of the tomb. We no more see our end than our beginning: the one is lost in oblivion and vacancy, as the other is hid from us by the crowd and hurry of approaching events. Or the grim shadow is seen lingering in the horizon, which we are doomed never to overtake, or whose last, faint, glimmering outline touches upon Heaven and translates us to the skies! Nor would the hold that life has taken of us permit us to detach our thoughts from present objects and pursuits, even if we would. What is there more opposed to health, than sickness; to strength and beauty, than decay and dissolution; to the active search of knowledge than mere oblivion? Or is there none of the usual advantage to bar the approach of Death, and mock his idle threats; Hope supplies their place, and draws a veil over the abrupt termination of all our cherished schemes. While the spirit of youth remains unimpaired, ere the "wine of life is drank up" we are like people intoxicated or in a fever, who are hurried away by the violence of their own sensations: it is only as present objects begin to pall upon the sense, as we have been disappointed in our favourite pursuits, cut off from our closest ties, that passion loosens its hold upon the breast, that we by degrees become weaned from the world, and allow ourselves to contemplate, " as in a glass, darkly," the possibility of parting with it for good. The example of others, the voice of experience, has no effect upon us whatever. Casualties we must avoid : the slow and deliberate advances of age we can play at *hide-and-seek* with. We think ourselves too lusty and too nimble for that blear-eyed decrepid old gentleman to catch us. Like the foolish fat scullion, in Sterne, when she hears that Master Bobby is dead, our only reflection is — " So am not I ! " The idea of death, instead of staggering our confidence, rather seems to strengthen and enhance our possession and our enjoyment of life. Others may fall around us like leaves, or be mowed down like flowers by the scythe of Time : these are but tropes and figures to the unreflecting ears and overweening presumption of youth. It is not till we see the flowers of Love, Hope, and Joy, withering around us, and our own pleasures cut up by the roots, that we bring the moral home to ourselves, that we abate something of the wanton extravagance of our pretensions, or that the emptiness and dreariness of the prospect before us reconciles us to the stillness of the grave !

> Life ! thou strange thing, that hast a power to feel
> Thou art, and to perceive that others are.[1]

Well might the poet begin his indignant invective against an art, whose professed object is its destruction, with this animated apostrophe to life. Life is indeed a strange gift, and its privileges are most miraculous. Nor is it singular that when the splendid boon is first granted us, our gratitude, our admiration, and our delight should prevent us from reflecting on our own nothingness, or from thinking it will ever be recalled. Our first and strongest impressions are taken from the mighty scene that is opened to us, and we very innocently transfer its durability as well as magnificence to ourselves. So newly found, we cannot make up our minds to parting with it yet and at least put off that consideration to an indefinite term.

[1] Fawcett's *Art of War*, a poem, 1794.

Like a clown at a fair, we are full of amazement and rapture, and have no thoughts of going home, or that it will soon be night. We know our existence only from external objects, and we measure it by them. We can never be satisfied with gazing; and nature will still want us to look on and applaud. Otherwise, the sumptuous entertainment, " the feast of reason and the flow of soul," to which they were invited seems little better than a mockery and a cruel insult. We do not go from a play till the scene is ended, and the lights are ready to be extinguished. But the fair face of things still shines on; shall we be called away, before the curtain falls, or ere we have scarce had a glimpse of what is going on ? Like children, our step-mother Nature holds us up to see the raree-show of the universe; and then, as if life were a burthen to support, lets us instantly down again. Yet in that short interval, what " brave sublunary things " does not the spectacle unfold; like a bubble, at one minute reflecting the universe, and the next, shook to air ! — To see the golden sun and the azure sky, the outstretched ocean, to walk upon the green earth, and to be lord of a thousand creatures, to look down giddy precipices or over distant flowery vales, to see the world spread out under one's finger in a map, to bring the stars near, to view the smallest insects in a microscope, to read history, and witness the revolutions of empires and the succession of generations, to hear of the glory of Sidon and Tyre, of Babylon and Susa, as of a faded pageant, and to say all these were, and are now nothing, to think that we exist in such a point of time, and in such a corner of space, to be at once spectators and a part of the moving scene, to watch the return of the seasons, of spring and autumn, to hear

> —— The stockdove plain amid the forest deep,
> That drowsy rustles to the sighing gale ——

to traverse desert wildernesses, to listen to the midnight choir, to visit lighted halls, or plunge into the dungeon's gloom, or sit in crowded theatres and see life itself mocked, to feel heat

and cold, pleasure and pain, right and wrong, truth and falsehood, to study the works of art and refine the sense of beauty
to agony, to worship fame and to dream of immortality, to
have read Shakspeare and belong to the same species as
Sir Isaac Newton ; to be and to do all this, and then in a
moment to be nothing, to have it all snatched from one like
a juggler's ball or a phantasmagoria ; there is something revolting and incredible to sense in the transition, and no wonder
that, aided by youth and warm blood, and the flush of enthusiasm, the mind contrives for a long time to reject it with
disdain and loathing as a monstrous and improbable fiction,
like a monkey on a house-top, that is loath, amidst its fine
discoveries and specious antics, to be tumbled head-long into
the street, and crushed to atoms, the sport and laughter of
the multitude !

The change, from the commencement to the close of life,
appears like a fable, after it has taken place ; how should we
treat it otherwise than as a chimera before it has come to pass?
There are some things that happened so long ago, places or
persons we have formerly seen, of which such dim traces remain, we hardly know whether it was sleeping or waking they
occurred ; they are like dreams within the dream of life, a mist,
a film before the eye of memory, which, as we try to recall
them more distinctly, elude our notice altogether. It is but
natural that the long interval that we thus look back upon,
should have appeared long and endless in prospect. There are
others so distinct and fresh, they seem but of yesterday—their
very vividness might be deemed a pledge of their permanence.
Then, however far back our impressions may go, we find others
still older (for our years are multiplied in youth) ; descriptions
of scenes that we had read, and people before our time, Priam
and the Trojan war ; and even then, Nestor was old and dwelt
delighted on his youth, and spoke of the race of heroes that
were no more ; — what wonder that, seeing this long line of
being pictured in our minds, and reviving as it were in us, we
should give ourselves involuntary credit for an indeterminate

period of existence? In the Cathedral at Peterborough there is a monument to Mary, Queen of Scots, at which I used to gaze when a boy, while the events of the period, all that had happened since, passed in review before me. If all this mass of feeling and imagination could be crowded into a moment's compass, what might not the whole of life be supposed to contain? We are heirs of the past; we count upon the future as our natural reversion. Besides, there are some of our early impressions so exquisitely tempered, it appears that they must always last — nothing can add to or take away from their sweetness and purity — the first breath of spring, the hyacinth dipped in the dew, the mild lustre of the evening-star, the rainbow after a storm — while we have the full enjoyment of these, we must be young; and what can ever alter us in this respect? Truth, friendship, love, books, are also proof against the canker of time; and while we live but for them, we can never grow old. We take out a new lease of existence from the objects on which we set our affections, and become abstracted, impassive, immortal in them. We cannot conceive how certain sentiments should ever decay or grow cold in our breasts; and, consequently, to maintain them in their first youthful glow and vigour, the flame of life must continue to burn as bright as ever, or rather, they are the fuel that feed the sacred lamp, that kindle "the purple light of love," and spread a golden cloud around our heads! Again, we not only flourish and survive in our affections (in which we will not listen to the possibility of a change, any more than we foresee the wrinkles on the brow of a mistress), but we have a farther guarantee against the thoughts of death in our favourite studies and pursuits, and in their continual advance. Art we know is long; life, we feel, should be so too. We see no end of the difficulties we have to encounter: perfection is slow of attainment, and we must have time to accomplish it in. Rubens complained that when he had just learnt his art, he was snatched away from it: we trust we shall be more fortunate! A wrinkle in an old head takes whole days to finish it properly : but to catch "the Raphael grace, the Guido air," no limit should be put to our endeavours. What a prospect for the future ! What a task we have entered upon ! and shall we be arrested in the middle of it ? We do not reckon our time thus employed lost, or our pains thrown away, or our progress slow — we do not droop or grow tired, but "gain new vigour at our endless task"; — and shall Time grudge us the opportunity to finish what we have auspiciously begun, and have formed a sort of compact with nature to achieve ? The fame of the great names we look up to is also imperishable; and shall not we, who contemplate it with such intense yearnings, imbibe a portion of ethereal fire, the *divinæ particula auræ*, which nothing can extinguish ? I remember to have looked at a print of Rembrandt for hours together, without being conscious of the flight of time, trying to resolve it into its component parts, to connect its strong and sharp gradations, to learn the secret of its reflected lights, and found neither satiety nor pause in the prosecution of my studies. The print over which I was poring would last long enough; why should the idea in my mind, which was finer, more impalpable, perish before it ? At this, I redoubled the ardour of my pursuit, and by the very subtlety and refinement of my inquiries, seemed to bespeak for them an exemption from corruption and the rude grasp of Death.[1]

Objects, on our first acquaintance with them, have that singleness and integrity of impression that it seems as if nothing could destroy or obliterate them, so firmly are they stamped and rivetted on the brain. We repose on them with a sort of voluptuous indolence, in full faith and boundless confidence. We are absorbed in the present moment, or return to the same point — idling away a great deal of time in youth, thinking we have enough and to spare. There is often a local feeling in the air, which is as fixed as if it were of marble;

---

[1] Is it not this that frequently keeps artists alive so long, *viz.* the constant occupation of their minds with vivid images, with little of the *wear-and-tear* of the body?

we loiter in dim cloisters, losing ourselves in thought and in their glimmering arches; a winding road before us seems as long as the journey of life, and as full of events. Time and experience dissipate this illusion; and by reducing them to detail, circumscribe the limits of our expectations. It is only as the pageant of life passes by and the masques turn their backs upon us, that we see through the deception, or believe that the train will have an end. In many cases, the slow progress and monotonous texture of our lives, before we mingle with the world and are embroiled in its affairs, has a tendency to aid the same feeling. We have a difficulty, when left to ourselves, and without the resource of books or some more lively pursuit, to "beguile the slow and creeping hours of time," and argue that if it moves on always at this tedious snail's-pace, it can never come to an end. We are willing to skip over certain portions of it that separate us from favourite objects, that irritate ourselves at the unnecessary delay. The young are prodigal of life from a superabundance of it; the old are tenacious on the same score, because they have little left, and cannot enjoy even what remains of it.

For my part, I set out in life with the French Revolution, and that event had considerable influence on my early feelings, as on those of others. Youth was then doubly such. It was the dawn of a new era, a new impulse had been given to men's minds, and the sun of Liberty rose upon the sun of Life in the same day, and both were proud to run their race together. Little did I dream, while my first hopes and wishes went hand in hand with those of the human race, that long before my eyes should close, that dawn would be overcast, and set once more in the night of despotism — "total eclipse!" Happy that I did not. I felt for years, and during the best part of my existence, *heart-whole* in that cause, and triumphed in the triumphs over the enemies of man! At that time, while the fairest aspirations of the human mind seemed about to be realized, ere the image of man was defaced and his breast mangled in scorn, philosophy took a higher, poetry could afford a deeper range. At that time, to read the *Robbers*, was indeed delicious, and to hear

> From the dungeon of the tower time-rent,
> That fearful voice, a famish'd father's cry,

could be borne only amidst the fulness of hope, the crash of the fall of the strongholds of power, and the exulting sounds of the march of human freedom. What feelings the death-scene in *Don Carlos* sent into the soul! In that headlong career of lofty enthusiasm, and the joyous opening of the prospects of the world and our own, the thought of death crossing it smote doubly cold upon the mind; there was a stifling sense of oppression and confinement, an impatience of our present knowledge, a desire to grasp the whole of our existence in one strong embrace, to sound the mystery of life and death, and in order to put an end to the agony of doubt and dread, to burst through our prison-house, and confront the King of Terrors in his grisly palace! . . . As I was writing out this passage, my miniature-picture when a child lay on the mantle-piece, and I took it out of the case to look at it. I could perceive few traces of myself in it; but there was the same placid brow, the dimpled mouth, the same timid, inquisitive glance as ever. But its careless smile did not seem to reproach me with having become a recreant to the senti-ments that were then sown in my mind, or with having writ-ten a sentence that could call up a blush in this image of ingenuous youth!

"That time is past with all its giddy raptures." Since the future was barred to my progress, I have turned for consola-tion to the past, gathering up the fragments of my early recol-lections, and putting them into a form that might live. It is thus, that when we find our personal and substantial identity vanishing from us, we strive to gain a reflected and substituted one in our thoughts: we do not like to perish wholly, and wish to bequeath our names at least to posterity. As long as we can keep alive our cherished thoughts and nearest interests

in the minds of others, we do not appear to have retired altogether from the stage, we still occupy a place in the estimation
of mankind, exercise a powerful influence over them, and it is
only our bodies that are trampled into dust or dispersed to air.
Our darling speculations still find favour and encouragement,
and we make as good a figure in the eyes of our descendants,
nay, perhaps, a better than we did in our life-time. This is
one point gained; the demands of our self-love are so far satisfied. Besides, if by the proofs of intellectual superiority we
survive ourselves in this world, by exemplary virtue or unblem-
ished faith we are taught to ensure an interest in another and
a higher state of being, and to anticipate at the same time the
applauses of men and angels.

> Even from the tomb the voice of nature cries;
> Even in our ashes live their wonted fires.

As we advance in life, we acquire a keener sense of the value
of time. Nothing else, indeed, seems of any consequence; and
we become misers in this respect. We try to arrest its few
last tottering steps, and to make it linger on the brink of the
grave. We can never leave off wondering how that which has
ever been should cease to be, and would still live on, that we
may wonder at our own shadow, and when "all the life of life
is flown," dwell on the retrospect of the past. This is accompanied by a mechanical tenaciousness of whatever we possess,
by a distrust and a sense of fallacious hollowness in all we
see. Instead of the full, pulpy feeling of youth, everything is
flat and insipid. The world is a painted witch, that puts us
off with false shews and tempting appearances. The ease, the
jocund gaiety, the unsuspecting security of youth are fled: nor
can we, without flying in the face of common sense,

> From the last dregs of life, hope to receive
> What its first sprightly runnings could not give.

If we can slip out of the world without notice or mischance,
can tamper with bodily infirmity, and frame our minds to the

becoming composure of *still-life*, before we sink into total insensibility, it is as much as we ought to expect. We do not in the regular course of nature die all at once: we have mouldered away gradually long before; faculty after faculty, attachment after attachment, we are torn from ourselves piece-meal while living; year after year takes something from us; and death only consigns the last remnant of what we were to the grave. The revulsion is not so great, and a quiet *euthanasia* is a winding-up of the plot, that is not out of reason or nature.

That we should thus in a manner outlive ourselves, and dwindle imperceptibly into nothing, is not surprising, when even in our prime the strongest impressions leave so little traces of themselves behind, and the last object is driven out by the succeeding one. How little effect is produced on us at any time by the books we have read, the scenes we have witnessed, the sufferings we have gone through! Think only of the variety of feelings we experience in reading an interesting romance, or being present at a fine play — what beauty, what sublimity, what soothing, what heart-rending emotions! You would suppose these would last for ever, or at least subdue the mind to a correspondent tone and harmony — while we turn over the page, while the scene is passing before us, it seems as if nothing could ever after shake our resolution, that " treason domestic, foreign levy, nothing could touch us farther ! " The first splash of mud we get, on entering the street, the first pettifogging shop-keeper that cheats us out of twopence, and the whole vanishes clean out of our remembrance, and we become the idle prey of the most petty and annoying circumstances. The mind soars by an effort to the grand and lofty: it is at home in the grovelling, the disagreeable, and the little. This happens in the height and heyday of our existence, when novelty gives a stronger impulse to the blood and takes a faster hold of the brain, (I have known the impression on coming out of a gallery of pictures then last half a day) — as we grow old, we become more feeble and querulous, every object " reverbs its own hollowness," and both worlds are not enough to satisfy the peevish importunity and extravagant presumption of our desires! There are a few superior, happy beings, who are born with a temper exempt from every trifling annoyance. This spirit sits serene and smiling as in its native skies, and a divine harmony (whether heard or not) plays around them. This is to be at peace. Without this, it is in vain to fly into deserts, or to build a hermitage on the top of rocks, if regret and ill-humour follow us there: and with this, it is needless to make the experiment. The only true retirement is that of the heart; the only true leisure is the repose of the passions. To such persons it makes little difference whether they are young or old; and they die as they have lived, with graceful resignation.

WILLIAM MAKEPEACE THACKERAY
(1811–1863)

TUNBRIDGE TOYS

Cornhill Magazine, September, 1860

I wonder whether those little silver pencil-cases with a movable almanack at the butt-end are still favourite implements with boys, and whether pedlars still hawk them about the country? Are there pedlars and hawkers still, or are rustics and children grown too sharp to deal with them? Those pencil-cases, as far as my memory serves me, were not of much use. The screw, upon which the movable almanack turned, was constantly getting loose. The 1 of the table would work from its moorings, under Tuesday or Wednesday, as the case might be, and you would find, on examination, that Th. or W. was the 23½ of the month (which was absurd on the face of the thing), and in a word your cherished pencil-case an utterly unreliable time-keeper. Nor was this a matter of wonder. Consider the position of a pencil-case in a boy's pocket. You had hardbake in it; marbles, kept in your purse when the money was all gone; your mother's purse, knitted so fondly and supplied with a little bit of gold, long since — prodigal little son! — scattered amongst the swine — I mean amongst brandy-balls, open tarts, three-cornered puffs, and similar abominations. You had a top and string; a knife; a piece of cobbler's wax; two or three bullets; a "Little Warbler"; and I, for my part, remember, for a considerable period, a brass-barrelled pocket-pistol (which would fire beautifully, for with it I shot off a button from Butt Major's jacket); — with all these things, and ever so many more, clinking and rattling in your pockets, and your hands, of course, keeping them in perpetual movement, how could

333

you expect your movable almanack not to be twisted out of
its place now and again — your pencil-case to be bent — your
liquorice water not to leak out of your bottle over the cobbler's
wax, your bull's-eyes not to ram up the lock and barrel of your
pistol, and so forth?

In the month of June, thirty-seven years ago, I bought one
of those pencil-cases from a boy whom I shall call Hawker,
and who was in my form. Is he dead? Is he a millionaire?
Is he a bankrupt now? He was an immense screw at school,
and I believe to this day that the value of the thing for which
I owed and eventually paid three-and-sixpence, was in reality
not one-and-nine.

I certainly enjoyed the case at first a good deal, and amused
myself with twiddling round the movable calendar. But this
pleasure wore off. The jewel, as I said, was not paid for, and
Hawker, a large and violent boy, was exceedingly unpleasant
as a creditor. His constant remark was, " When are you going
to pay me that three-and-sixpence? What sneaks your relations must be! They come to see you. You go out to them
on Saturdays and Sundays, and they never give you anything!
Don't tell *me*, you little humbug!" and so forth. The truth
is that my relations were respectable; but my parents were
making a tour in Scotland; and my friends in London, whom
I used to go and see, were most kind to me, certainly, but
somehow never tipped me. That term, of May to August
1823, passed in agonies, then, in consequence of my debt to
Hawker. What was the pleasure of a calendar pencil-case in
comparison with the doubt and torture of mind occasioned
by the sense of the debt, and the constant reproach in that
fellow's scowling eyes and gloomy coarse reminders? How
was I to pay off such a debt out of sixpence a week? ludicrous! Why did not some one come to see me, and tip me?
Ah! my dear sir, if you have any little friends at school, go
and see them, and do the natural thing by them. You won't
miss the sovereign. You don't know what a blessing it will be
to them. Don't fancy they are too old — try 'em. And they

will remember you, and bless you in future days; and their gratitude shall accompany your dreary after life; and they shall meet you kindly when thanks for kindness are scant. Oh mercy! shall I ever forget that sovereign you gave me, Captain Bob? or the agonies of being in debt to Hawker? In that very term, a relation of mine was going to India. I actually was fetched from school in order to take leave of him. I am afraid I told Hawker of this circumstance. I own I speculated upon my friend's giving me a pound. A pound? Pooh! A relation going to India, and deeply affected at parting from his darling kinsman, might give five pounds to the dear fellow! . . . There was Hawker when I came back — of course there he was. As he looked in my scared face, his turned livid with rage. He muttered curses, terrible from the lips of so young a boy. My relation, about to cross the ocean to fill a lucrative appointment, asked me with much interest about my progress at school, heard me construe a passage of Eutropius, the pleasing Latin work on which I was then engaged; gave me a God bless you, and sent me back to school; upon my word of honour, without so much as a half-crown! It is all very well, my dear sir, to say that boys contract habits of expecting tips from their parents' friends, that they become avaricious, and so forth. Avaricious! fudge! Boys contract habits of tart and toffee eating, which they do not carry into after life. On the contrary, I wish I *did* like 'em. What raptures of pleasure one could have now for five shillings, if one could but pick it off the pastry-cook's tray! No. If you have any little friends at school, out with your half-crowns, my friend, and impart to those little ones the little fleeting joys of their age.

Well, then. At the beginning of August 1823, Bartlemytide holidays came, and I was to go to my parents, who were at Tunbridge Wells. My place in the coach was taken by my tutor's servants — "Bolt-in-Tun," Fleet Street, seven o'clock in the morning, was the word. My tutor, the Reverend Edward P——, to whom I hereby present my best compliments, had a parting interview with me: gave me my little account for my governor : the remaining part of the coach-hire ; five shillings for my own expenses ; and some five-and-twenty shillings on an old account which had been overpaid, and was to be restored to my family.

Away I ran and paid Hawker his three-and-six. Ouf ! what a weight it was off my mind ! (He was a Norfolk boy, and used to go home from Mrs. Nelson's " Bell Inn," Aldgate — but that is not to the point.) The next morning, of course, we were an hour before the time. I and another boy shared a hackney-coach, two-and-six ; porter for putting luggage on coach, threepence. I had no more money of my own left. Rasherwell, my companion, went into the " Bolt-in-Tun " coffee-room, and had a good breakfast. I could n't : because, though I had five-and-twenty shillings of my parents' money, I had none of my own, you see.

I certainly intended to go without breakfast, and still remember how strongly I had that resolution in my mind. But there was that hour to wait. A beautiful August morning — I am very hungry. There is Rasherwell " tucking " away in the coffee-room. I pace the street, as sadly almost as if I had been coming to school, not going thence. I turn into a court by mere chance — I vow it was by mere chance — and there I see a coffee-shop with a placard in the window. " Coffee, Twopence. Round of buttered toast, Twopence." And here am I hungry, penniless, with five-and-twenty shillings of my parents' money in my pocket.

What would you have done ? You see I had had my money, and spent it in that pencil-case affair. The five-and-twenty shillings were a trust — by me to be handed over.

But then would my parents wish their only child to be actually without breakfast ? Having this money and being so hungry, so *very* hungry, might n't I take ever so little ? Might n't I at home eat as much as I chose ?

Well, I went into the coffee-shop, and spent fourpence. I remember the taste of the coffee and toast to this day — a peculiar, muddy, not-sweet-enough, most fragrant coffee — a rich, rancid, yet not-buttered-enough, delicious toast. The waiter had nothing. At any rate, fourpence, I know, was the sum I spent. And the hunger appeased, I got on the coach a guilty being.

At the last stage, — what is its name? I have forgotten in seven-and-thirty years, — there is an inn with a little green and trees before it; and by the trees there is an open carriage. It is our carriage. Yes, there are Prince and Blucher, the horses; and my parents in the carriage. Oh! how I had been counting the days until this one came! Oh! how happy had I been to see them yesterday! But there was that fourpence. All the journey down the toast had choked me, and the coffee poisoned me.

I was in such a state of remorse about the fourpence that I forgot the maternal joy and caresses, the tender paternal voice. I pulled out the twenty-four shillings and eightpence with a trembling hand.

"Here's your money," I gasped out, "which Mr. P—— owes you, all but fourpence. I owed three-and-sixpence to Hawker out of my money for a pencil-case, and I had none left, and I took fourpence of yours, and had some coffee at a shop."

I suppose I must have been choking whilst uttering this confession.

"My dear boy," says the governor, "why didn't you go and breakfast at the hotel?"

"He must be starved," says my mother.

I had confessed; I had been a prodigal; I had been taken back to my parents' arms again. It was not a very great crime as yet, or a very long career of prodigality; but don't we know that a boy who takes a pin which is not his own, will take a thousand pounds when occasion serves, bring his parents' grey heads with sorrow to the grave, and carry his own to the gallows? Witness the career of Dick Idle, upon whom our friend Mr. Sala has been discoursing. Dick only began by playing pitch-and-toss on a tombstone: playing fair, for what we know: and even for that sin he was promptly caned by the beadle. The bamboo was ineffectual to cane that reprobate's bad courses out of him. From pitch-and-toss he proceeded to manslaughter if necessary : to highway robbery ; to Tyburn and the rope there. Ah! Heaven be thanked, my parents' heads are still above the grass, and mine still out of the noose.

As I look up from my desk, I see Tunbridge Wells Common and the rocks, the strange familiar place which I remember forty years ago. Boys saunter over the green with stumps and cricket-bats. Other boys gallop by on the riding-master's hacks. I protest it is " Cramp, Riding Master," as it used to be in the reign of George IV, and that Centaur Cramp must be at least a hundred years old. Yonder comes a footman with a bundle of novels from the library. Are they as good as *our* novels? Oh! how delightful they were! Shades of Valancour, awful ghost of Manfroni, how I shudder at your appearance! Sweet image of Thaddeus of Warsaw, how often has this almost infantile hand tried to depict you in a Polish cap and richly embroidered tights! And as for Corinthian Tom in light blue pantaloons and hessians, and Jerry Hawthorn from the country, can all the fashion, can all the splendour of real life which these eyes have subsequently beheld, can all the wit I have heard or read in later times, compare with your fashion, with your brilliancy, with your delightful grace, and sparkling vivacious rattle?

Who knows? They *may* have kept those very books at the library still — at the well-remembered library on the Pantiles, where they sell that delightful, useful Tunbridge ware. I will go and see. I wend my way to the Pantiles, the queer little old-world Pantiles, where, a hundred years since, so much good company came to take its pleasure. Is it possible, that in the past century, gentlefolks of the first rank (as I read lately in a lecture on George II in the *Cornhill Magazine*) assembled here and entertained each other with gaming, dancing, fiddling, and tea? There are fiddlers, harpers, and trumpeters performing at this moment in a weak little old balcony, but where is the fine company? Where are the earls, duchesses, bishops, and magnificent embroidered gamesters? A half-dozen of children and their nurses are listening to the musicians; an old lady or two in a poke bonnet passes; and for the rest, I see but an uninteresting population of native tradesmen. As for the library, its window is full of pictures of burly theologians, and their works, sermons, apologues, and so forth. Can I go in and ask the young ladies at the counter for *Manfroni, or the One-handed Monk,* and *Life in London, or the Adventures of Corinthian Tom, Jeremiah Hawthorn, Esquire, and their friend Bob Logic* ? — absurd. I turn away abashed from the casement — from the Pantiles — no longer Pantiles — but Parade. I stroll over the Common and survey the beautiful purple hills around, twinkling with a thousand bright villas, which have sprung up over this charming ground since first I saw it. What an admirable scene of peace and plenty! What a delicious air breathes over the heath, blows the cloud-shadows across it, and murmurs through the full-clad trees! Can the world show a land fairer, richer, more cheerful? I see a portion of it when I look up from the window at which I write. But fair scene, green woods, bright terraces gleaming in sunshine, and purple clouds swollen with summer rain — nay, the very pages over which my head bends — disappear from before my eyes. They are looking backwards, back into forty years off, into a dark room, into a little house hard by on the Common here, in the Bartlemytide holidays. The parents have gone to town for two days: the house is all his own, his own and a grim old maid-servant's, and a little boy is seated at night in the lonely drawing-room, poring over *Manfroni, or the One-handed Monk,* so frightened that he scarcely dares to turn round.

ON BEING FOUND OUT

Cornhill Magazine, May, 1861

At the close (let us say) of Queen Anne's reign, when I was a boy at a private and preparatory school for young gentlemen, I remember the wiseacre of a master ordering us all, one night, to march into a little garden at the back of the house, and thence to proceed one by one into a tool- or hen-house (I was but a tender little thing just put into short clothes, and can't exactly say whether the house was for tools or hens), and in that house to put our hands into a sack which stood on a bench, a candle burning beside it. I put my hand into the sack. My hand came out quite black. I went and joined the other boys in the schoolroom; and all their hands were black too.

By reason of my tender age (and there are some critics who, I hope, will be satisfied by my acknowledging that I am a hundred and fifty-six next birthday) I could not understand what was the meaning of this night excursion — this candle, this tool-house, this bag of soot. I think we little boys were taken out of our sleep to be brought to the ordeal. We came, then, and showed our little hands to the master; washed them or not — most probably, I should say, not — and so went bewildered back to bed.

Something had been stolen in the school that day; and Mr. Wiseacre having read in a book of an ingenious method of finding out a thief by making him put his hand into a sack (which, if guilty, the rogue would shirk from doing), all we boys were subjected to the trial. Goodness knows what the lost object was, or who stole it. We all had black hands to show to the master. And the thief, whoever he was, was not Found Out that time.

I wonder if the rascal is alive — an elderly scoundrel he must be by this time; and a hoary old hypocrite, to whom an old schoolfellow presents his kindest regards — parenthetically remarking what a dreadful place that private school was : cold, chilblains, bad dinners, not enough victuals, and caning awful! — Are you alive still, I say, you nameless villain, who escaped discovery on that day of crime? I hope you have escaped often since, old sinner. Ah, what a lucky thing it is, for you and me, my man, that we are *not* found out in all our pecca-dilloes; and that our backs can slip away from the master and the cane!

Just consider what life would be, if every rogue was found
out, and flogged *coram populo*! What a butchery, what an
indecency, what an endless swishing of the rod! Don't cry
out about my misanthropy. My good friend Mealymouth, I
will trouble you to tell me, do you go to church? When there,
do you say, or do you not, that you are a miserable sinner?
and saying so, do you believe or disbelieve it? If you are a
M. S., don't you deserve correction, and aren't you grateful
if you are to be let off? I say, again, what a blessed thing it
is that we are not all found out!

Just picture to yourself everybody who does wrong being
found out, and punished accordingly. Fancy all the boys in
all the school being whipped; and then the assistants, and
then the head master (Doctor Badford let us call him). Fancy
the provost-marshal being tied up, having previously superin-
tended the correction of the whole army. After the young
gentlemen have had their turn for the faulty exercises, fancy
Doctor Lincolnsinn being taken up for certain faults in *his*
Essay and Review. After the clergyman has cried his peccavi,
suppose we hoist up a Bishop, and give him a couple of dozen!
(I see my Lord Bishop of Double-Gloucester sitting in a very
uneasy posture on his right reverend bench.) After we have
cast off the Bishop, what are we to say to the Minister who
appointed him? My Lord Cinqwarden, it is painful to have
to use personal correction to a boy of your age; but really . . .
Siste tandem, carnifex! The butchery is too horrible. The
hand drops powerless, appalled at the quantity of birch which
it must cut and brandish. I am glad we are not all found out,
I say again; and protest, my dear brethren, against our having
our deserts.

To fancy all men found out and punished is bad enough;
but imagine all women found out in the distinguished social
circle in which you and I have the honour to move. Is it not
a mercy that so many of these fair criminals remain unpunished
and undiscovered? There is Mrs. Longbow, who is for ever
practising, and who shoots poisoned arrows, too; when you

meet her you don't call her liar, and charge her with the wickedness she has done, and is doing. There is Mrs. Painter, who passes for a most respectable woman, and a model in society. There is no use in saying what you really know regarding her and her goings on. There is Diana Hunter — what a little haughty prude it is; and yet *we* know stories about her which are not altogether edifying. I say it is best, for the sake of the good, that the bad should not all be found out. You don't want your children to know the history of that lady in the next box, who is so handsome, and whom they admire so. Ah me! what would life be if we were all found out, and punished for all our faults? Jack Ketch would be in permanence; and then who would hang Jack Ketch?

They talk of murderers being pretty certainly found out. Psha! I have heard an authority awfully competent vow and declare that scores and hundreds of murders are committed, and nobody is the wiser. That terrible man mentioned one or two ways of committing murder, which he maintained were quite common, and were scarcely ever found out. A man, for instance, comes home to his wife, and . . . but I pause — I know that this Magazine has a very large circulation. Hundreds and hundreds of thousands — why not say a million of people at once? — well, say a million read it. And amongst these countless readers, I might be teaching some monster how to make away with his wife without being found out, some fiend of a woman how to destroy her dear husband. I will *not* then tell this easy and simple way of murder, as communicated to me by a most respectable party in the confidence of private intercourse. Suppose some gentle reader were to try this most simple and easy receipt — it seems to me almost infallible — and come to grief in consequence, and be found out and hanged? Should I ever pardon myself for having been the means of doing injury to a single one of our esteemed subscribers? The prescription whereof I speak — that is to say whereof I *don't* speak — shall be buried in this bosom. No, I am a humane man. I am not one of your Bluebeards to go and say to my wife, "My dear! I am going away for a few days to Brighton. Here are all the keys of the house. You may open every door and closet, except the one at the end of the oak-room opposite the fireplace, with the little bronze Shakspeare on the mantelpiece (or what not)." I don't say this to a woman — unless, to be sure, I want to get rid of her — because, after such a caution, I know she'll peep into the closet. I say nothing about the closet at all. I keep the key in my pocket, and a being whom I love, but who, as I know, has many weaknesses, out of harm's way. You toss up your head, dear angel, drub on the ground with your lovely little feet, on the table with your sweet rosy fingers, and cry, "Oh, sneerer! You don't know the depth of woman's feeling, the lofty scorn of all deceit, the entire absence of mean curiosity in the sex, or never, never would you libel us so!" Ah, Delia! dear dear Delia! It is because I fancy I *do* know something about you (not all, mind — no, no; no man knows that) — Ah, my bride, my ringdove, my rose, my poppet — choose, in fact, whatever name you like — bulbul of my grove, fountain of my desert, sunshine of my darkling life, and joy of my dungeoned existence, it is because I *do* know a little about you that I conclude to say nothing of that private closet, and keep my key in my pocket. You take away that closet-key then, and the house-key. You lock Delia in. You keep her out of harm's way and gadding, and so she never *can* be found out.

And yet by little strange accidents and coincidences how we are being found out every day. You remember that old story of the Abbé Kakatoes, who told the company at supper one night how the first confession he ever received was — from a murderer let us say. Presently enters to supper the Marquis de Croquemitaine. "Palsambleu, abbé!" says the brilliant Marquis, taking a pinch of snuff, "are you here? Gentlemen and ladies! I was the abbé's first penitent, and I made him a confession which I promise you astonished him."

To be sure how queerly things are found out! Here is an instance. Only the other day I was writing in these *Roundabout*

Papers about a certain man, whom I facetiously called Baggs, and who had abused me to my friends, who of course told me. Shortly after that paper was published another friend — Sacks let us call him — scowls fiercely at me as I am sitting in perfect good-humour at the club, and passes on without speaking. A cut. A quarrel. Sacks thinks it is about him that I was writing : whereas, upon my honour and conscience, I never had him once in my mind, and was pointing my moral from quite another man. But don't you see, by this wrath of the guilty-conscienced Sacks, that he had been abusing me too ? He has owned himself guilty, never having been accused. He has winced when nobody thought of hitting him. I did but put the cap out, and madly butting and chafing, behold my friend rushes to put his head into it ! Never mind, Sacks, you are found out; but I bear you no malice, my man.

And yet to be found out, I know from my own experience, must be painful and odious, and cruelly mortifying to the inward vanity. Suppose I am a poltroon, let us say. With fierce moustache, loud talk, plentiful oaths, and an immense stick, I keep up nevertheless a character for courage. I swear fearfully at cabmen and women ; brandish my bludgeon, and perhaps knock down a little man or two with it : brag of the images which I break at the shooting-gallery, and pass amongst my friends for a whiskery fire-eater, afraid of neither man nor dragon. Ah me ! Suppose some brisk little chap steps up and gives me a caning in St. James's Street, with all the heads of my friends looking out of all the club windows. My reputation is gone. I frighten no man more. My nose is pulled by whipper-snappers, who jump up on a chair to reach it. I am found out. And in the days of my triumphs, when people were yet afraid of me, and were taken in by my swagger, I always knew that I was a lily-liver, and expected that I should be found out some day.

That certainty of being found out must haunt and depress many a bold braggadocio spirit. Let us say it is a clergyman, who can pump copious floods of tears out of his own eyes and those of his audience. He thinks to himself, "I am but a poor swindling chattering rogue. My bills are unpaid. I have jilted several women whom I have promised to marry. I don't know whether I believe what I preach, and I know I have stolen the very sermon over which I have been snivelling. Have they found me out?" says he, as his head drops down on the cushion.

Then your writer, poet, historian, novelist, or what not? The *Beacon* says that "Jones's work is one of the first order." The *Lamp* declares that "Jones's tragedy surpasses every work since the days of Him of Avon." The *Comet* asserts that "J.'s *Life of Goody Two-shoes* is a κτῆμα ἐς ἀεὶ, a noble and enduring monument to the fame of that admirable Englishwoman," and so forth. But then Jones knows that he has lent the critic of the *Beacon* five pounds; that his publisher has a half-share in the *Lamp*; and that the *Comet* comes repeatedly to dine with him. It is all very well. Jones is immortal until he is found out; and then down comes the extinguisher, and the immortal is dead and buried. The idea (*dies iræ!*) of discovery must haunt many a man, and make him uneasy, as the trumpets are puffing in his triumph. Brown, who has a higher place than he deserves, cowers before Smith, who has found him out. What is a chorus of critics shouting "Bravo"? — a public clapping hands and flinging garlands? Brown knows that Smith has found him out. Puff, trumpets! Wave, banners! Huzza, boys, for the immortal Brown! "This is all very well," B. thinks (bowing the while, smiling, laying his hand to his heart); "but there stands Smith at the window: *he* has measured me; and some day the others will find me out too." It is a very curious sensation to sit by a man who has found you out, and who you know has found you out; or, *vice versâ*, to sit with a man whom *you* have found out. His talent? Bah! His virtue? We know a little story or two about his virtue, and he knows we know it. We are thinking over friend Robinson's antecedents, as we grin, bow, and talk; and we are both humbugs together. Robinson a good fellow, is he? You know how he behaved to Hicks? A good-natured man, is he? Pray do you remember that little story of Mrs. Robinson's black eye? How men have to work, to talk, to smile, to go to bed, and try to sleep, with this dread of being found out on their consciences! Bardolph, who has robbed a church, and Nym, who has taken a purse, go to their usual haunts, and smoke their pipes with their companions. Mr. Detective Bulls-eye appears, and says, "Oh, Bardolph, I want you about that there pyx business!" Mr. Bardolph knocks the ashes out of his pipe, puts out his hands to the little steel cuffs, and walks away quite meekly. He is found out. He must go. "Good-bye, Doll Tearsheet! Good-bye, Mrs. Quickly, ma'am!" The other gentlemen and ladies *de la société* look on and exchange mute adieux with the departing friends. And an assured time will come when the other gentlemen and ladies will be found out too.

What a wonderful and beautiful provision of nature it has been that, for the most part, our womankind are not endowed with the faculty of finding us out! *They* don't doubt, and probe, and weigh, and take your measure. Lay down this paper, my benevolent friend and reader, go into your drawing-room now, and utter a joke ever so old, and I wager sixpence the ladies there will all begin to laugh. Go to Brown's house, and tell Mrs. Brown and the young ladies what you think of him, and see what a welcome you will get! In like manner, let him come to your house, and tell *your* good lady his candid opinion of you, and fancy how she will receive him! Would you have your wife and children know you exactly for what you are, and esteem you precisely at your worth? If so, my friend, you will live in a dreary house, and you will have but a chilly fireside. Do you suppose the people round it don't see your homely face as under a glamour, and, as it were, with a halo of love round it? You don't fancy you *are*, as you seem to them? No such thing, my man. Put away that monstrous conceit, and be thankful that *they* have not found you out.

DE FINIBUS

Cornhill Magazine, August, 1862

When Swift was in love with Stella, and despatching her a letter from London thrice a month, by the Irish packet, you may remember how he would begin Letter No. xxiii, we will say, on the very day when xxii had been sent away, stealing out of the coffee-house or the assembly so as to be able to prattle with his dear; "never letting go her kind hand, as it were," as some commentator or other has said in speaking of the Dean and his amour. When Mr. Johnson, walking to Dodsley's, and touching the posts in Pall Mall as he walked, forgot to pat the head of one of them, he went back and imposed his hands on it, — impelled I know not by what superstition. I have this I hope not dangerous mania too. As soon as a piece of work is out of hand, and before going to sleep, I like to begin another; it may be to write only half-a-dozen lines: but that is something towards Number the Next. The printer's boy has not yet reached Green Arbour Court with the copy. Those people who were alive half-an-hour since, Pendennis, Clive Newcome, and (what do you call him? what was the name of the last hero? I remember now!) Philip Firmin, have hardly drunk their glass of wine, and the mammas have only this minute got the children's cloaks on, and have been bowed out of my premises — and here I come back to the study again: *tamen usque recurro.* How lonely it looks now all these people are gone! My dear good friends, some folk are utterly tired of you, and say, "What a poverty of friends the man has! He is always asking us to meet those Pendennises, Newcomes, and so forth. Why does he not introduce us to some new characters? Why is he not thrilling like Twostars, learned and profound like Threestars, exquisitely humorous and human like Fourstars? Why, finally, is he not somebody else?" My good people, it is not only impossible to please you all, but it is absurd to try. The dish which one man devours, another dislikes. Is the dinner of to-day not to your taste? Let us hope to-morrow's entertainment will be more agreeable. . . . I resume my original subject. What an odd, pleasant, humorous, melancholy feeling it is to sit in the study alone and quiet, now all these people are gone who have been boarding and lodging with me for twenty months! They have interrupted my rest: they have plagued me at all sorts of minutes: they have thrust themselves upon me when I was ill, or wished to be idle, and I have growled out a " Be hanged to you, can't you leave me alone now?" Once or twice they have prevented my going out to dinner. Many and many a time they have prevented my coming home, because I knew they were there waiting in the study, and a plague take them, and I have left home and family, and gone to dine at the Club, and told nobody where I went. They have bored me, those people. They have plagued me at all sorts of uncomfortable hours. They have made such a disturbance in my mind and house, that sometimes I have hardly known what was going on in my family and scarcely have heard what my neighbour said to me. They are gone at last, and you would expect me to be at ease? Far from it. I should almost be glad if Woolcomb would walk in and talk to me; or Twysden reappear, take his place in that chair opposite me, and begin one of his tremendous stories.

Madmen, you know, see visions, hold conversations with, even draw the likeness of, people invisible to you and me. Is this making of people out of fancy madness? and are novel-writers at all entitled to strait-waistcoats? I often forget people's names in life; and in my own stories contritely own that I make dreadful blunders regarding them; but I declare, my dear sir, with respect to the personages introduced into your humble servant's fables, I know the people utterly — I know the sound of their voices. A gentleman came in to see me the other day, who was so like the picture of Philip Firmin in Mr. Walker's charming drawings in the *Cornhill Magazine* that he was quite a curiosity to me. The same eyes, beard, shoulders, just as you have seen them from month to month. Well, he is not like the Philip Firmin in my mind. Asleep, asleep in the grave, lies the bold, the generous, the reckless, the tender-hearted creature whom I have made to pass through those adventures which have just been brought to an end. It is years since I heard the laughter ringing, or saw the bright blue eyes. When I knew him both were young. I become young as I think of him. And this morning he was alive again in this room, ready to laugh, to fight, to weep. As I write, do you know, it is the grey of evening; the house is quiet; everybody is out; the room is getting a little dark, and I look rather wistfully up from the paper with perhaps ever so little fancy that HE MAY COME IN. —— No? No movement. No grey shade, growing more palpable, out of which at last look the well-known eyes. No, the printer came and took him away with the last page of the proofs. And with the printer's boy did the whole cortège of ghosts flit away, invisible! Ha! stay! what is this? Angels and ministers of grace! The door opens, and a dark form — enters, bearing a black — a black suit of clothes. It is John. He says it is time to dress for dinner.

.   .   .   .

Every man who has had his German tutor, and has been coached through the famous *Faust* of Goethe (thou wert my instructor, good old Weissenborn, and these eyes beheld the great master himself in dear little Weimar town!) has read those charming verses which are prefixed to the drama, in which the poet reverts to the time when his work was first composed, and recalls the friends now departed, who once listened to his song. The dear shadows rise up around him, he says; he lives in the past again. It is to-day which appears vague and visionary. We humbler writers cannot create Fausts, or raise up monumental works that shall endure for all ages; but our books are diaries, in which our own feelings must of necessity be set down. As we look to the page written last month, or ten years ago, we remember the day and its events; the child ill, mayhap, in the adjoining room, and the doubts and fears which racked the brain as it still pursued its work; the dear old friend who read the commencement of the tale, and whose gentle hand shall be laid in ours no more. I own for my part that, in reading pages which this hand penned formerly, I often lose sight of the text under my eyes. It is not the words I see; but that past day; that bygone page of life's history; that tragedy, comedy it may be, which our little home-company was enacting; that merry-making which we shared; that funeral which we followed; that bitter bitter grief which we buried.

And, such being the state of my mind, I pray gentle readers to deal kindly with their humble servant's manifold shortcomings, blunders, and slips of memory. As sure as I read a page of my own composition, I find a fault or two, half-a-dozen. Jones is called Brown. Brown, who is dead, is brought to life. Aghast, and months after the number was printed, I saw that I had called Philip Firmin, Clive Newcome. Now Clive Newcome is the hero of another story by the reader's most obedient writer. The two men are as different in my mind's eye, as — as Lord Palmerston and Mr. Disraeli let us say. But there is that blunder at page 990, line 76, volume 84 of the *Cornhill Magazine*, and it is past mending; and I wish in my life I had made no worse blunders or errors than that which is hereby acknowledged.

Another Finis written. Another mile-stone passed on this journey from birth to the next world! Sure it is a subject for solemn cogitation. Shall we continue this story-telling business and be voluble to the end of our age! Will it not be presently time, O prattler, to hold your tongue, and let younger people speak! I have a friend, a painter, who, like other persons who shall be nameless, is growing old. He has never painted with such laborious finish as his works now show. This master is still the most humble and diligent of scholars. Of Art, his mistress, he is always an eager, reverent pupil. In his calling, in yours, in mine, industry and humility will help and comfort us. A word with you. In a pretty large experience I have not found the men who write books superior in wit or learning to those who don't write at all. In regard of mere information, non-writers must often be superior to writers. You don't expect a lawyer in full practice to be conversant with all kinds of literature; he is too busy with his law; and so a writer is commonly too busy with his own books to be able to bestow attention on the works of other people. After a day's work (in which I have been depicting, let us say, the agonies of Louisa on parting with the Captain, or the atrocious behaviour of the wicked Marquis to Lady Emily) I march to the Club, proposing to improve my mind and keep myself "posted up," as the Americans phrase it, in the literature of the day. And what happens? Given a walk after luncheon, a pleasing book, and a most comfortable arm-chair by the fire, and you know the rest. A doze ensues. Pleasing book drops suddenly, is picked up once with an air of some confusion, is laid presently softly in lap: head falls on comfortable arm-chair cushion: eyes close: soft nasal music is heard. Am I telling Club secrets? Of afternoons, after lunch, I say, scores of sensible fogies have a doze. Perhaps I have fallen asleep over that very book to which " Finis " has just been written. "And if the writer sleeps, what happens to the readers?" says Jones, coming down upon me with his lightning wit. What? you *did* sleep over it? And a very good thing too. These eyes have more than once seen a friend dozing over pages which this hand has written. There is a vignette somewhere in one of my books of a friend so caught napping with *Pendennis*, or *The Newcomes*, in his lap; and if a writer can give you a sweet, soothing, harmless sleep, has he not done you a kindness? So is the author who excites and interests you worthy of your thanks and benedictions. I am troubled with fever and ague, that seize me at odd intervals and prostrate me for a day. There is cold fit, for which, I am thankful to say, hot brandy-and-water is prescribed; and this induces hot fit, and so on. In one or two of these fits I have read novels with the most fearful contentment of mind. Once on the Mississippi, it was my dearly beloved *Jacob Faithful*: once, at Frankfort O. M., the delightful *Vingt Ans Après* of Monsieur Dumas: once, at Tunbridge Wells, the thrilling *Woman in White*: and these books gave me amusement from morning till sunset. I remember those ague fits with a great deal of pleasure and gratitude. Think of a whole day in bed, and a good novel for a companion! No cares: no remorse about idleness: no visitors: and the Woman in White or the Chevalier d'Artagnan to tell me stories from dawn to night! "Please, ma'am, my master's compliments, and can he have the third volume?" (This message was sent to an astonished friend and neighbour who lent me, volume by volume, the *W. in W.*) How do you like your novels? I like mine strong, "hot with," and no mistake: no love-making: no observations about society: little dialogue, except where the characters are bullying each other: plenty of fighting: and a villain in the cupboard, who is to suffer tortures just before Finis. I don't like your melancholy Finis. I never read the history of a consumptive heroine twice. If I might give a short hint to an impartial writer (as the *Examiner* used to say in old days), it would be to act, *not* à la mode le pays de Pole (I think that was the phraseology) but *always* to give quarter. In the story of Philip, just come to an end, I have the permission of the author to state that he was going to drown the two villains of the piece — a certain Doctor F——— and a certain Mr. T. H——— on board the *President*, or some other tragic ship — but you see I relented. I pictured to myself Firmin's ghastly face amid the crowd of shuddering people on that reeling deck in the lonely ocean and thought, "Thou ghastly lying wretch, thou shalt not be drowned; thou shalt have a fever only; a knowledge of thy danger; and a chance — ever so small a chance — of repentance." I wonder whether he *did* repent when he found himself in the yellow-fever, in

Virginia? The probability is he fancied that his son had injured him very much, and forgave him on his death-bed. Do you imagine there is a great deal of genuine right-down remorse in the world? Don't people rather find excuses which make their minds easy; endeavour to prove to themselves that they have been lamentably belied and misunderstood; and try and forgive the persecutors who *will* present that bill when it is due; and not bear malice against the cruel ruffian who takes them to the police-office for stealing the spoons? Years ago I had a quarrel with a certain well-known person (I believed a statement regarding him which his friends imparted to me, and which turned out to be quite incorrect). To his dying day that quarrel was never quite made up. I said to his brother, "Why is your brother's soul still dark against me? It is I who ought to be angry and unforgiving: for I was in the wrong." In the region which they now inhabit (for Finis has been set to the volumes of the lives of both here below), if they take any cognisance of our squabbles, and tittle-tattles, and gossips on earth here, I hope they admit that my little error was not of a nature unpardonable. If you have never committed a worse, my good sir, surely the score against you will not be heavy. Ha, *dilectissimi fratres*! It is in regard of sins *not* found out that we may say or sing (in an undertone in a most penitent and lugubrious minor key), "Miserere nobis miseris peccatoribus."

Among the sins of commission which novel-writers not seldom perpetrate, is the sin of grandiloquence, or tall-talking, against which, for my part, I will offer up a special *libera me*. This is the sin of schoolmasters, governesses, critics, sermoners, and instructors of young or old people. Nay (for I am making a clean breast, and liberating my soul), perhaps of all the novel-spinners now extant, the present speaker is the most addicted to preaching. Does he not stop perpetually in his story and begin to preach to you? When he ought to be engaged with business, is he not for ever taking the Muse by the sleeve, and plaguing her with some of his cynical sermons? I cry *peccavi* loudly and heartily. I tell you I would like to be able to write a story which should show no egotism whatever — in which there should be no reflections, no cynicism, no vulgarity (and so forth), but an incident in every other page, a villain, a battle, a mystery in every chapter. I should like to be able to feed a reader so spicily as to leave him hungering and thirsting for more at the end of every monthly meal.

Alexandre Dumas describes himself, when inventing the plan of a work, as lying silent on his back for two whole days on the deck of a yacht in a Mediterranean port. At the end of the two days he arose and called for dinner. In those two days he had built his plot. He had moulded a mighty clay, to be cast presently in perennial brass. The chapters, the characters, the incidents, the combinations were all arranged in the artist's brain ere he set a pen to paper. My Pegasus won't fly, so as to let me survey the field below me. He has no wings, he is blind of one eye certainly; he is restive, stubborn, slow; crops a hedge when he ought to be galloping, or gallops when he ought to be quiet. He never will show off when I want him. Sometimes he goes at a pace which surprises me. Sometimes, when I most wish him to make the running, the brute turns restive, and I am obliged to let him take his own time. I wonder do other novel-writers experience this fatalism? They *must* go a certain way, in spite of themselves. I have been surprised at the observations made by some of my characters. It seems as if an occult Power was moving the pen. The personage does or says something, and I ask, How the dickens did he come to think of that? Every man has remarked in dreams, the vast dramatic power which is sometimes evinced; I won't say the surprising power, for nothing does surprise you in dreams. But those strange characters you meet make instant observations of which you never can have thought previously. In like manner, the imagination foretells things. We spake anon of the inflated style of some writers. What also if there is an *afflated* style, — when a writer is like a Pythoness on her oracle tripod, and mighty words,

words which he cannot help, come blowing, and bellowing, and whistling, and moaning through the speaking pipes of his bodily organ? I have told you it was a very queer shock to me the other day when, with a letter of introduction in his hand, the artist's (not my) Philip Firmin walked into this room, and sat down in the chair opposite. In the novel of *Pendennis*, written ten years ago, there is an account of a certain Costigan, whom I had invented (as I suppose authors invent their personages out of scraps, heel-taps, odds and ends of characters). I was smoking in a tavern parlour one night — and this Costigan came into the room alive — the very man : — the most remarkable resemblance of the printed sketches of the man, of the rude drawings in which I had depicted him. He had the same little coat, the same battered hat, cocked on one eye, the same twinkle in that eye. " Sir," said I, knowing him to be an old friend whom I had met in unknown regions, " sir," I said, " may I offer you a glass of brandy-and-water ? " " *Bedad, ye may*," says he, " *and I'll sing ye a song tu*." Of course he spoke with an Irish brogue. Of course he had been in the army. In ten minutes he pulled out an Army Agent's account, whereon his name was written. A few months after we read of him in a police-court. How had I come to know him, to divine him ? Nothing shall convince me that I have not seen that man in the world of spirits. In the world of spirits and water I know I did : but that is a mere quibble of words. I was not surprised when he spoke in an Irish brogue. I had had cognisance of him before somehow. Who has not felt that little shock which arises when a person, a place, some words in a book (there is always a collocation) present themselves to you, and you know that you have before met the same person, words, scene, and so forth ?

They used to call the good Sir Walter the " Wizard of the North." What if some writer should appear who can write so *enchantingly* that he shall be able to call into actual life the people whom he invents ? What if Mignon, and Margaret, and Goetz von Berlichingen are alive now (though I don't say they are visible), and Dugald Dalgetty and Ivanhoe were to step in at that open window by the little garden yonder? Suppose Uncas and our noble old Leather-stocking were to glide silently in? Suppose Athos, Porthos, and Aramis should enter with a noiseless swagger, curling their moustaches? And dearest Amelia Booth, on Uncle Toby's arm; and Tittlebat Titmouse, with his hair dyed green; and all the Crummles company of comedians, with the Gil Blas troop; and Sir Roger de Coverley; and the greatest of all crazy gentlemen, the Knight of La Mancha, with his blessed squire? I say to you, I look rather wistfully towards the window, musing upon these people. Were any of them to enter, I think I should not be very much frightened. Dear old friends, what pleasant hours I have had with them! We do not see each other very often, but when we do, we are ever happy to meet. I had a capital half-hour with Jacob Faithful last night; when the last sheet was corrected, when "Finis," had been written, and the printer's boy, with the copy, was safe in Green Arbour Court.

So you are gone, little printer's boy, with the last scratches and corrections on the proof, and a fine flourish by way of Finis at the story's end. The last corrections? I say those last corrections seem never to be finished. A plague upon the weeds! Every day, when I walk in my own little literary garden-plot, I spy some, and should like to have a spud, and root them out. Those idle words, neighbour, are past remedy. That turning back to the old pages produces anything but elation of mind. Would you not pay a pretty fine to be able to cancel some of them? Oh, the sad old pages, the dull old pages! Oh, the cares, the *ennui*, the squabbles, the repetitions, the old conversations over and over again. But now and again a kind thought is recalled, and now and again a dear memory. Yet a few chapters more, and then the last: after which, behold Finis itself come to an end, and the Infinite begun.

ROBERT LOUIS STEVENSON (1850–1894)

WALKING TOURS

Cornhill Magazine, June, 1876

It must not be imagined that a walking tour, as some would have us fancy, is merely a better or worse way of seeing the country. There are many ways of seeing landscape quite as good ; and none more vivid, in spite of canting dilettantes, than from a railway train. But landscape on a walking tour is quite accessory. He who is indeed of the brotherhood does not voyage in quest of the picturesque, but of certain jolly humours — of the hope and spirit with which the march begins at morning, and the peace and spiritual repletion of the evening's rest. He cannot tell whether he puts his knapsack on, or takes it off, with more delight. The excitement of the departure puts him in key for that of the arrival. Whatever he does is not only a reward in itself, but will be further rewarded in the sequel ; and so pleasure leads on to pleasure in an endless chain. It is this that so few can understand ; they will either be always lounging or always at five miles an hour ; they do not play off the one against the other, prepare all day for the evening, and all evening for the next day. And, above all, it is here that your overwalker fails of comprehension. His heart rises against those who drink their curaçoa in liqueur glasses, when he himself can swill it in a brown john. He will not believe that the flavour is more delicate in the smaller dose. He will not believe that to walk this unconscionable distance is merely to stupefy and brutalise himself, and come to his inn, at night, with a sort of frost on his five wits, and a starless night of darkness in his spirit. Not for him the mild luminous evening of the temperate walker ! He has nothing left of man but a physical need for bedtime and a double night-cap; and even his pipe, if he be a smoker, will be savourless and disenchanted. It is the fate of such an one to take twice as much trouble as is needed to obtain happiness, and miss the happiness in the end; he is the man of the proverb, in short, who goes further and fares worse.

Now, to be properly enjoyed, a walking tour should be gone upon alone. If you go in a company, or even in pairs, it is no longer a walking tour in anything but name; it is something else and more in the nature of a picnic. A walking tour should be gone upon alone, because freedom is of the essence; because you should be able to stop and go on, and follow this way or that, as the freak takes you; and because you must have your own pace, and neither trot alongside a champion walker, nor mince in time with a girl. And then you must be open to all impressions and let your thoughts take colour from what you see. You should be as a pipe for any wind to play upon. "I cannot see the wit," says Hazlitt, "of walking and talking at the same time. When I am in the country, I wish to vegetate like the country," — which is the gist of all that can be said upon the matter. There should be no cackle of voices at your elbow, to jar on the meditative silence of the morning. And so long as a man is reasoning he cannot surrender himself to that fine intoxication that comes of much motion in the open air, that begins in a sort of dazzle and sluggishness of the brain, and ends in a peace that passes comprehension.

During the first day or so of any tour there are moments of bitterness, when the traveller feels more than coldly towards his knapsack, when he is half in a mind to throw it bodily over the hedge and, like Christian on a similar occasion, "give three leaps and go on singing." And yet it soon acquires a property of easiness. It becomes magnetic; the spirit of the journey enters into it. And no sooner have you passed the straps over your shoulder than the lees of sleep are cleared from you, you pull yourself together with a shake, and fall at once into your stride. And surely, of all possible moods, this, in which a man takes the road, is the best. Of course, if he *will* keep thinking of his anxieties, if he *will* open the merchant Abudah's chest and walk arm in arm with the hag — why, wherever he is, and whether he walk fast or slow, the chances are that he will not be happy. And so much the more shame to himself! There are perhaps thirty men setting forth at that same hour, and I would lay a large wager there is not another dull face among the thirty. It would be a fine thing to follow, in a coat of darkness, one after another of these wayfarers, some summer morning, for the first few miles upon the road. This one, who walks fast, with a keen look in his eyes, is all concentrated in his own mind; he is up at his loom, weaving and weaving, to set the landscape to words. This one peers about, as he goes, among the grasses; he waits by the canal to watch the dragon-flies; he leans on the gate of the pasture, and cannot look enough upon the complacent kine. And here comes another, talking, laughing, and gesticulating to himself. His face changes from time to time, as indignation flashes from his eyes or anger clouds his forehead. He is composing articles, delivering orations, and conducting the most impassioned interviews, by the way. A little farther on, and it is as like as not he will begin to sing. And well for him, supposing him to be no great master in that art, if he stumble across no stolid peasant at a corner; for on such an occasion, I scarcely know which is the more troubled, or whether it is worse to suffer the confusion of your troubadour, or the unfeigned alarm of your clown. A sedentary population, accustomed, besides, to the strange mechanical bearing of the common tramp, can in no wise explain to itself the gaiety of these passers-by. I knew one man who was arrested as a runaway lunatic, because, although a full-grown person with a red beard, he skipped as he went like a child. And you would be astonished if I were to tell you all the grave and learned heads who have confessed to me that, when on walking tours, they sang — and sang very ill — and had a pair of red ears when, as described above, the inauspicious peasant plumped into their arms from round a corner. And here, lest you should think I am exaggerating, is Hazlitt's own confession, from his essay *On Going a Journey*, which is so good that there should be a tax levied on all who have not read it:

"Give me the clear blue sky over my head," says he, "and the green turf beneath my feet, a winding road before me, and a three hours' march to dinner — and then to thinking! It is hard if I cannot start some game on these lone heaths. I laugh, I run, I leap, I sing for joy."

Bravo! After that adventure of my friend with the policeman, you would not have cared, would you, to publish that in the first person? But we have no bravery nowadays, and, even in books, must all pretend to be as dull and foolish as our neighbours. It was not so with Hazlitt. And notice how learned he is (as, indeed, throughout the essay) in the theory of walking tours. He is none of your athletic men in purple stockings, who walk their fifty miles a day: three hours' march is his ideal. And then he must have a winding road, the epicure!

Yet there is one thing I object to in these words of his, one thing in the great master's practice that seems to me not wholly wise. I do not approve of that leaping and running. Both of these hurry the respiration; they both shake up the brain out of its glorious open-air confusion; and they both break the pace. Uneven walking is not so agreeable to the body, and it distracts and irritates the mind. Whereas, when once you have fallen into an equable stride, it requires no conscious thought from you to keep it up, and yet it prevents you from thinking earnestly of anything else. Like knitting, like the work of a copying clerk, it gradually neutralises and sets to sleep the serious activity of the mind. We can think of this or that, lightly and laughingly, as a child thinks, or as we think in a morning doze; we can make puns or puzzle out acrostics, and trifle in a thousand ways with words and rhymes;

but when it comes to honest work, when we come to gather ourselves together for an effort, we may sound the trumpet as loud and long as we please ; the great barons of the mind will not rally to the standard, but sit, each one, at home, warming his hands over his own fire and brooding on his own private thought !

In the course of a day's walk, you see, there is much variance in the mood. From the exhilaration of the start, to the happy phlegm of the arrival, the change is certainly great. As the day goes on, the traveller moves from the one extreme towards the other. He becomes more and more incorporated with the material landscape, and the open-air drunkenness grows upon him with great strides, until he posts along the road, and sees everything about him, as in a cheerful dream. The first is certainly brighter, but the second stage is the more peaceful. A man does not make so many articles towards the end, nor does he laugh aloud ; but the purely animal pleasures, the sense of physical wellbeing, the delight of every inhalation, of every time the muscles tighten down the thigh, console him for the absence of the others, and bring him to his destination still content.

Nor must I forget to say a word on bivouacs. You come to a milestone on a hill, or some place where deep ways meet under trees ; and off goes the knapsack, and down you sit to smoke a pipe in the shade. You sink into yourself, and the birds come round and look at you ; and your smoke dissipates upon the afternoon under the blue dome of heaven ; and the sun lies warm upon your feet, and the cool air visits your neck and turns aside your open shirt. If you are not happy, you must have an evil conscience. You may dally as long as you like by the roadside. It is almost as if the millennium were arrived, when we shall throw our clocks and watches over the house-top, and remember time and seasons no more. Not to keep hours for a lifetime is, I was going to say, to live for ever. You have no idea, unless you have tried it, how endlessly long is a summer's day, that you measure out only by hunger, and bring to an end only when you are drowsy. I know a village where there are hardly any clocks, where no one knows more of the days of the week than by a sort of instinct for the *fête* on Sundays, and where only one person can tell you the day of the month, and she is generally wrong; and if people were aware how slow Time journeyed in that village, and what armfuls of spare hours he gives, over and above the bargain, to its wise inhabitants, I believe there would be a stampede out of London, Liverpool, Paris, and a variety of large towns, where the clocks lose their heads, and shake the hours out each one faster than the other, as though they were all in a wager. And all these foolish pilgrims would each bring his own misery along with him, in a watch-pocket! It is to be noticed, there were no clocks and watches in the much-vaunted days before the flood. It follows, of course, there were no appointments, and punctuality was not yet thought upon. "Though ye take from a covetous man all his treasure," says Milton, "he has yet one jewel left; ye cannot deprive him of his covetousness." And so I would say of a modern man of business, you may do what you will for him, put him in Eden, give him the elixir of life — he has still a flaw at heart, he still has his business habits. Now, there is no time when business habits are more mitigated than on a walking tour. And so during these halts, as I say, you will feel almost free.

But it is at night, and after dinner, that the best hour comes. There are no such pipes to be smoked as those that follow a good day's march; the flavour of the tobacco is a thing to be remembered, it is so dry and aromatic, so full and so fine. If you wind up the evening with grog, you will own there was never such grog; at every sip a jocund tranquillity spreads about your limbs, and sits easily in your heart. If you read a book — and you will never do so save by fits and starts — you find the language strangely racy and harmonious; words take a new meaning; single sentences possess the ear for half an hour together; and the writer endears himself to you, at every page, by the nicest coincidence of sentiment. It seems as if

it were a book you had written yourself in a dream. To all
we have read on such occasions we look back with special
favour. " It was on the 10th of April, 1798," says Hazlitt,
with amorous precision, " that I sat down to a volume of the
new *Héloïse*, at the Inn at Llangollen, over a bottle of sherry
and a cold chicken." I should wish to quote more, for though
we are mighty fine fellows nowadays, we cannot write like
Hazlitt. And, talking of that, a volume of Hazlitt's essays
would be a capital pocket-book on such a journey ; so would
a volume of Heine's songs ; and for *Tristram Shandy* I can
pledge a fair experience.

If the evening be fine and warm, there is nothing better in
life than to lounge before the inn door in the sunset, or lean
over the parapet of the bridge, to watch the weeds and the
quick fishes. It is then, if ever, that you taste joviality to the
full significance of that audacious word. Your muscles are so
agreeably slack, you feel so clean and so strong and so idle,
that whether you move or sit still, whatever you do is done
with pride and a kingly sort of pleasure. You fall in talk with
any one, wise or foolish, drunk or sober. And it seems as if a
hot walk purged you, more than of anything else, of all narrowness and pride, and left curiosity to play its part freely, as in a
child or a man of science. You lay aside all your own hobbies,
to watch provincial humours develop themselves before you,
now as a laughable farce, and now grave and beautiful like
an old tale.

Or perhaps you are left to your own company for the night,
and surly weather imprisons you by the fire. You may remember how Burns, numbering past pleasures, dwells upon the
hours when he has been " happy thinking." It is a phrase
that may well perplex a poor modern, girt about on every side
by clocks and chimes, and haunted, even at night, by flaming
dial-plates. For we are all so busy, and have so many far-off
projects to realise, and castles in the fire to turn into solid,
habitable mansions on a gravel soil, that we can find no time
for pleasure trips into the Land of Thought and among the

Hills of Vanity. Changed times, indeed, when we must sit all night, beside the fire, with folded hands; and a changed world for most of us, when we find we can pass the hours without discontent, and be happy thinking. We are in such haste to be doing, to be writing, to be gathering gear, to make our voice audible a moment in the derisive silence of eternity, that we forget that one thing, of which these are but the parts — namely to live. We fall in love, we drink hard, we run to and fro upon the earth like frightened sheep. And now you are to ask yourself if, when all is done, you would not have been better to sit by the fire at home, and be happy thinking. To sit still and contemplate, — to remember the faces of women without desire, to be pleased by the great deeds of men without envy, to be everything and everywhere in sympathy, and yet content to remain where and what you are — is not this to know both wisdom and virtue, and to dwell with happiness? After all, it is not they who carry flags, but they who look upon it from a private chamber, who have the fun of the procession. And once you are at that, you are in the very humour of all social heresy. It is no time for shuffling, or for big, empty words. If you ask yourself what you mean by fame, riches, or learning, the answer is far to seek; and you go back into that kingdom of light imaginations, which seem so vain in the eyes of Philistines perspiring after wealth, and so momentous to those who are stricken with the disproportions of the world, and, in the face of the gigantic stars, cannot stop to split differences between two degrees of the infinitesimally small, such as a tobacco pipe or the Roman Empire, a million of money or a fiddlestick's end.

You lean from the window, your last pipe reeking whitely into the darkness, your body full of delicious pains, your mind enthroned in the seventh circle of content; when suddenly the mood changes, the weather-cock goes about, and you ask yourself one question more: whether, for the interval, you have been the wisest philosopher or the most egregious of donkeys? Human experience is not yet able to reply; but at least you have had a fine moment, and looked down upon all the kingdoms of the earth. And whether it was wise or foolish, to-morrow's travel will carry you, body and mind, into some different parish of the infinite.

ON FALLING IN LOVE

Cornhill Magazine, February, 1877

" Lord, what fools these mortals be ! "

There is only one event in life which really astonishes a man and startles him out of his prepared opinions. Everything else befalls him very much as he expected. Event succeeds to event, with an agreeable variety indeed, but with little that is either startling or intense ; they form together no more than a sort of background, or running accompaniment to the man's own reflections ; and he falls naturally into a cool, curious, and smiling habit of mind, and builds himself up in a conception of life which expects to-morrow to be after the pattern of to-day and yesterday. He may be accustomed to the vagaries of his friends and acquaintances under the influence of love. He may sometimes look forward to it for himself with an incomprehensible expectation. But it is a subject in which neither intuition nor the behaviour of others will help the philosopher to the truth. There is probably nothing rightly thought or rightly written on this matter of love that is not a piece of the person's experience. I remember an anecdote of a well-known French theorist, who was debating a point eagerly in his *cénacle*. It was objected against him that he had never experienced love. Whereupon he arose, left the society, and made it a point not to return to it until he considered that he had supplied the defect. " Now," he remarked, on entering, " now I am in a position to continue the discussion." Perhaps he had not penetrated very deeply into the subject after all ; but the story indicates right thinking, and may serve as an apologue to readers of this essay.

When at last the scales fall from his eyes, it is not without something of the nature of dismay that the man finds himself in such changed conditions. He has to deal with commanding emotions instead of the easy dislikes and preferences in which he has hitherto passed his days; and he recognises capabilities for pain and pleasure of which he had not yet suspected the existence. Falling in love is the one illogical adventure, the one thing of which we are tempted to think as supernatural, in our trite and reasonable world. The effect is out of all proportion with the cause. Two persons, neither of them, it may be, very amiable or very beautiful, meet, speak a little, and look a little into each other's eyes. That has been done a dozen or so of times in the experience of either with no great result. But on this occasion all is different. They fall at once into that state in which another person becomes to us the very gist and centrepoint of God's creation, and demolishes our laborious theories with a smile; in which our ideas are so bound up with the one master-thought that even the trivial cares of our own person become so many acts of devotion, and the love of life itself is translated into a wish to remain in the same world with so precious and desirable a fellow-creature. And all the while their acquaintances look on in stupor, and ask each other, with almost passionate emphasis, what so-and-so can see in that woman, or such-an-one in that man? I am sure, gentlemen, I cannot tell you. For my part, I cannot think what the women mean. It might be very well, if the Apollo Belvedere should suddenly glow all over into life, and step forward from the pedestal with that godlike air of his. But of the misbegotten changelings who call themselves men, and prate intolerably over dinner-tables, I never saw one who seemed worthy to inspire love — no, nor read of any, except Leonardo da Vinci, and perhaps Goethe in his youth. About women I entertain a somewhat different opinion; but there, I have the misfortune to be a man.

There are many matters in which you may waylay Destiny, and bid him stand and deliver. Hard work, high thinking, adventurous excitement, and a great deal more that forms a part of this or the other person's spiritual bill of fare, are within the reach of almost any one who can dare a little and be patient. But it is by no means in the way of every one to fall in love. You know the difficulty Shakespeare was put into when Queen Elizabeth asked him to show Falstaff in love. I do not believe that Henry Fielding was ever in love. Scott, if it were not for a passage or two in *Rob Roy*, would give me very much the same effect. These are great names and (what is more to the purpose) strong, healthy, highstrung, and generous natures, of whom the reverse might have been expected. As for the innumerable army of anæmic and tailorish persons who occupy the face of this planet with so much pro-priety, it is palpably absurd to imagine them in any such situation as a love-affair. A wet rag goes safely by the fire; and if a man is blind, he cannot expect to be much impressed by romantic scenery. Apart from all this, many lovable people miss each other in the world, or meet under some unfavourable star. There is the nice and critical moment of declaration to be got over. From timidity or lack of opportunity a good half of possible love cases never get so far, and at least another quarter do there cease and determine. A very adroit person, to be sure, manages to prepare the way and out with his declaration in the nick of time. And then there is a fine solid sort of man, who goes on from snub to snub; and if he has to declare forty times, will continue imperturbably declar-ing, amid the astonished consideration of men and angels, until he has a favourable answer. I daresay, if one were a woman, one would like to marry a man who was capable of doing this, but not quite one who had done so. It is just a little bit abject, and somehow just a little bit gross; and marriages in which one of the parties has been thus battered into consent scarcely form agreeable subjects for meditation. Love should run out to meet love with open arms. Indeed, the ideal story is that of two people who go into love step for step, with a fluttered consciousness, like a pair of children venturing together into a dark room. From the first moment when they see each other, with a pang of curiosity, through stage after stage of growing pleasure and embarrassment, they can read the expression of their own trouble in each other's eyes. There is here no declaration properly so called; the feeling is so plainly shared, that as soon as the man knows what it is in his own heart, he is sure of what it is in the woman's.

This simple accident of falling in love is as beneficial as it is astonishing. It arrests the petrifying influence of years, disproves cold-blooded and cynical conclusions, and awakens dormant sensibilities. Hitherto the man had found it a good policy to disbelieve the existence of any enjoyment which was out of his reach; and thus he turned his back upon the strong, sunny parts of nature, and accustomed himself to look exclusively on what was common and dull. He accepted a prose ideal, let himself go blind of many sympathies by disuse; and if he were young and witty, or beautiful, wilfully forewent these advantages. He joined himself to the following of what, in the old mythology of love, was prettily called *nonchaloir*; and in an odd mixture of feelings, a fling of self-respect, a preference for selfish liberty, and a great dash of that fear with which honest people regard serious interests, kept himself back from the straightforward course of life among certain selected activities. And now, all of a sudden, he is unhorsed, like St. Paul, from his infidel affectation. His heart, which has been ticking accurate seconds for the last year, gives a bound and begins to beat high and irregularly in his breast. It seems as if he had never heard or felt or seen until that moment; and by the report of his memory, he must have lived his past life between sleep or waking, or with the preoccupied attention of a brown study. He is practically incommoded by the generosity of his feelings, smiles much when he is alone, and develops a habit of looking rather blankly upon the moon and stars. But it is not at all within the province of a prose essayist to give a picture of this hyperbolical frame of mind; and the thing has been done already, and that to admiration. In *Adelaide*, in Tennyson's *Maud*, and in some of Heine's songs, you get the absolute expression of this midsummer spirit. Romeo and Juliet were very much in love; although they tell me some German critics are of a different opinion, probably the same who would have us think Mercutio a dull fellow. Poor Antony was in love, and no mistake. That lay figure Marius, in *Les Misérables*, is also a genuine case in his own way, and worth observation. A good many of George Sand's people are thoroughly in love; and so are a good many of George Meredith's. Altogether, there is plenty to read on the subject. If the root of the matter be in him, and if he has the requisite chords to set in vibration, a young man may occasionally enter, with the key of art, into that land of Beulah which is upon the borders of Heaven and within sight of the City of Love. There let him sit awhile to hatch delightful hopes and perilous illusions.

One thing that accompanies the passion in its first blush is certainly difficult to explain. It comes (I do not quite see how) that from having a very supreme sense of pleasure in all parts of life — in lying down to sleep, in waking, in motion, in breathing, in continuing to be — the lover begins to regard his happiness as beneficial for the rest of the world and highly meritorious in himself. Our race has never been able contentedly to suppose that the noise of its wars, conducted by a few young gentlemen in a corner of an inconsiderable star, does not re-echo among the courts of Heaven with quite a formidable effect. In much the same taste, when people find a great to-do in their own breasts, they imagine it must have some influence in their neighbourhood. The presence of the two lovers is so enchanting to each other that it seems as if it must be the best thing possible for everybody else. They are half inclined to fancy it is because of them and their love that the sky is blue and the sun shines. And certainly the weather is usually fine while people are courting. . . . In point of fact, although the happy man feels very kindly towards others of his own sex, there is apt to be something too much of the magnifico in his demeanour. If people grow presuming and self-important over such matters as a dukedom or the Holy See, they will scarcely support the dizziest elevation in life without some suspicion of a strut; and the dizziest elevation is to love and be loved in return. Consequently, accepted lovers are a trifle condescending in their address to other men. An overweening sense of the passion and importance of life hardly conduces to simplicity of manner. To women, they feel very nobly, very purely, and very generously, as if they were so many Joan-of-Arc's; but this does not come out in their behaviour; and they treat them to Grandisonian airs marked with a suspicion of fatuity. I am not quite certain that women do not like this sort of thing; but really, after having bemused myself over *Daniel Deronda*, I have given up trying to understand what they like.

If it did nothing else, this sublime and ridiculous superstition, that the pleasure of the pair is somehow blessed to others, and everybody is made happier in their happiness, would serve at least to keep love generous and great-hearted. Nor is it quite a baseless superstition after all. Other lovers are hugely interested. They strike the nicest balance between pity and approval, when they see people aping the greatness of their own sentiments. It is an understood thing in the play that while the young gentlefolk are courting on the terrace, a rough flirtation is being carried on, and a light, trivial sort of love is growing up, between the footman and the singing chambermaid. As people are generally cast for the leading parts in their own imaginations, the reader can apply the parallel to real life without much chance of going wrong. In short, they are quite sure this other love-affair is not so deep-seated as their own, but they like dearly to see it going forward. And love, considered as a spectacle, must have attractions for many who are not of the confraternity. The sentimental old maid is a commonplace of the novelists; and he must be rather a poor sort of human being, to be sure, who can look on at this pretty madness without indulgence and sympathy. For nature commends itself to people with a most insinuating art; the busiest is now and again arrested by a great sunset; and you may be as pacific or as cold-blooded as you will, but you cannot help some emotion when you read of well-disputed battles, or meet a pair of lovers in the lane.

Certainly, whatever it may be with regard to the world at large, this idea of beneficent pleasure is true as between the sweethearts. To do good and communicate is the lover's grand intention. It is the happiness of the other that makes his own most intense gratification. It is not possible to disentangle the different emotions, the pride, humility, pity, and passion, which are excited by a look of happy love or an unexpected caress. To make one's self beautiful, to dress the hair, to excel in talk, to do anything and all things that puff out the character and attributes and make them imposing in the eyes of others, is not only to magnify one's self, but to offer the most delicate homage at the same time. And it is in this latter intention that they are done by lovers; for the essence of love is kindness; and indeed it may be best defined as passionate kindness: kindness, so to speak, run mad and become importunate and violent. Vanity in a merely personal sense exists no longer. The lover takes a perilous pleasure in privately displaying his weak points and having them, one after another, accepted and condoned. He wishes to be assured that he is not loved for this or that good quality, but for himself, or something as like himself as he can contrive to set forward. For, although it may have been a very difficult thing to paint the marriage of Cana, or write the fourth act of *Antony and Cleopatra*, there is a more difficult piece of art before every one in this world who cares to set about explaining his own character to others. Words and acts are easily wrenched from their true significance; and they are all the language we have to come and go upon. A pitiful job we make of it, as a rule. For better or worse, people mistake our meaning and take our emotions at a wrong valuation. And generally we rest pretty content with our failures; we are content to be misapprehended by cackling flirts; but when once a man is moonstruck with this affection of love, he makes it a point of honour to clear such dubieties away. He cannot have the Best of her Sex misled upon a point of this importance; and his pride revolts at being loved in a mistake.

He discovers a great reluctance to return on former periods of his life. To all that has not been shared with her, rights and duties, bygone fortunes and dispositions, he can look back only by a difficult and repugnant effort of the will. That he should have wasted some years in ignorance of what alone was really important, that he may have entertained the thought of other women with any show of complacency, is a burthen almost too heavy for his self-respect. But it is the thought of another past that rankles in his spirit like a poisoned wound. That he himself made a fashion of being alive in the bald, beggarly days before a certain meeting, is deplorable enough in all good conscience. But that She should have permitted herself the same liberty seems inconsistent with a Divine providence.

A great many people run down jealousy, on the score that it is an artificial feeling, as well as practically inconvenient. This is scarcely fair; for the feeling on which it merely attends, like an ill-humoured courtier, is itself artificial in exactly the same sense and to the same degree. I suppose what is meant by that objection is that jealousy has not always been a character of man; formed no part of that very modest kit of sentiments with which he is supposed to have begun the world; but waited to make its appearance in better days and among richer natures. And this is equally true of love, and friendship, and love of country, and delight in what they call the beauties of nature, and most other things worth having. Love, in particular, will not endure any historical scrutiny: to all who have fallen across it, it is one of the most incontestable facts in the world; but if you begin to ask what it was in other periods and countries, in Greece for instance, the strangest doubts begin to spring up, and everything seems so vague and changing that a dream is logical in comparison. Jealousy, at any rate, is one of the consequences of love; you may like it or not, at pleasure; but there it is.

It is not exactly jealousy, however, that we feel when we reflect on the past of those we love. A bundle of letters found after years of happy union creates no sense of insecurity in the present; and yet it will pain a man sharply. The two people entertain no vulgar doubt of each other: but this preëxistence of both occurs to the mind as something indelicate. To be altogether right, they should have had twin birth together, at the same moment with the feeling that unites them. Then indeed it would be simple and perfect and without reserve or afterthought. Then they would understand each other with a fulness impossible otherwise. There would be no barrier between them of associations that cannot be imparted. They would be led into none of those comparisons that send the blood back to the heart. And they would know that there had been no time lost, and they had been together as much as was possible. For besides terror for the separation that must follow some time or other in the future, men feel anger, and something like remorse, when they think of that other separation which endured until they met. Some one has written that love makes people believe in immortality, because there seems not to be room enough in life for so great a tenderness, and it is inconceivable that the most masterful of our emotions should have no more than the spare moments of a few years. Indeed, it seems strange; but if we call to mind analogies, we can hardly regard it as impossible.

"The blind bow-boy," who smiles upon us from the end of terraces in old Dutch gardens, laughingly hails his bird-bolts among a fleeting generation. But for as fast as ever he shoots, the game dissolves and disappears into eternity from under his falling arrows; this one is gone ere he is struck; the other has but time to make one gesture and give one passionate cry; and they are all the things of a moment. When the generation is gone, when the play is over, when the thirty years' panorama has been withdrawn in tatters from the stage of the world, we may ask what has become of these great, weighty, and undying loves, and the sweethearts who despised mortal conditions in a fine credulity; and they can only show us a few songs in a bygone taste, a few actions worth remembering, and a few children who have retained some happy stamp from the disposition of their parents.

THE LANTERN-BEARERS[1]

Scribner's Magazine, February, 1888

I

These boys congregated every autumn about a certain easterly fisher-village, where they tasted in a high degree the glory of existence. The place was created seemingly on purpose for the diversion of young gentlemen. A street or two of houses, mostly red and many of them tiled; a number of fine trees clustered about the manse and the kirkyard, and turning the chief street into a shady alley; many little gardens more than usually bright with flowers; nets a-drying, and fisher-wives scolding in the backward parts; a smell of fish, a genial smell of seaweed; whiffs of blowing sand at the street-corners; shops with golf-balls and bottled lollipops; another shop with penny pickwicks (that remarkable cigar) and the *London Journal*, dear to me for its startling pictures, and a few novels, dear for their suggestive names: such, as well as memory serves me, were the ingredients of the town. These, you are to conceive posted on a spit between two sandy bays, and sparsely flanked with villas — enough for the boys to lodge in with their subsidiary parents, not enough (not yet enough) to cocknify the scene: a haven in the rocks in front: in front of that, a file of gray islets: to the left, endless links and sand wreaths, a wilderness of hiding-holes, alive with popping rabbits and soaring gulls: to the right, a range of seaward crags, one rugged brow beyond

[1] From *Across the Plains*. Charles Scribner's Sons. Reprinted by permission.

another; the ruins of a mighty and ancient fortress on the brink of one; coves between — now charmed into sunshine quiet, now whistling with wind and clamorous with bursting surges; the dens and sheltered hollows redolent of thyme and southernwood, the air at the cliff's edge brisk and clean and pungent of the sea — in front of all, the Bass Rock, tilted seaward like a doubtful bather, the surf ringing it with white, the solan-geese hanging round its summit like a great and glittering smoke. This choice piece of seaboard was sacred, besides, to the wrecker; and the Bass, in the eye of fancy, still flew the colours of King James; and in the ear of fancy the arches of Tantallon still rang with horseshoe iron, and echoed to the commands of Bell-the-Cat.

There was nothing to mar your days, if you were a boy summering in that part, but the embarrassment of pleasure. You might golf if you wanted; but I seem to have been better employed. You might secrete yourself in the Lady's Walk, a certain sunless dingle of elders, all mossed over by the damp as green as grass, and dotted here and there by the streamside with roofless walls, the cold homes of anchorites. To fit themselves for life, and with a special eye to acquire the art of smoking, it was even common for the boys to harbour there; and you might have seen a single penny pickwick, honestly shared in lengths with a blunt knife, bestrew the glen with these apprentices. Again, you might join our fishing parties, where we sat perched as thick as solan-geese, a covey of little anglers, boy and girl, angling over each other's heads, to the much entanglement of lines and loss of podleys and consequent shrill recrimination — shrill as the geese themselves. Indeed, had that been all, you might have done this often; but though fishing be a fine pastime, the podley is scarce to be regarded as a dainty for the table; and it was a point of honour that a boy should eat all that he had taken. Or again, you might climb the Law, where the whale's jawbone stood landmark in the buzzing wind, and behold the face of many counties, and the smoke and spires of many towns, and the sails of distant ships. You might bathe, now in the flaws of fine weather, that we pathetically call our summer, now in a gale of wind, with the sand scourging your bare hide, your clothes thrashing abroad from underneath their guardian stone, the froth of the great breakers casting you headlong ere it had drowned your knees. Or you might explore the tidal rocks, above all in the ebb of springs, when the very roots of the hills were for the nonce discovered; following my leader from one group to another, groping in slippery tangle for the wreck of ships, wading in pools after the abominable creatures of the sea, and ever with an eye cast backward on the march of the tide and the menaced line of your retreat. And then you might go Crusoeing, a word that covers all extempore eating in the open air: digging perhaps a house under the margin of the links, kindling a fire of the sea-ware, and cooking apples there — if they were truly apples, for I sometimes suppose the merchant must have played us off with some inferior and quite local fruit, capable of resolving, in the neighbourhood of fire, into mere sand and smoke and iodine; or perhaps pushing to Tantallon, you might lunch on sandwiches and visions in the grassy court, while the wind hummed in the crumbling turrets; or clambering along the coast, eat geans (the worst, I must suppose, in Christendom) from an adventurous gean tree that had taken root under a cliff, where it was shaken with an ague of east wind, and silvered after gales with salt, and grew so foreign among its bleak surroundings that to eat of its produce was an adventure in itself.

There are mingled some dismal memories with so many that were joyous. Of the fisher-wife, for instance, who had cut her throat at Canty Bay; and of how I ran with the other children to the top of the Quadrant, and beheld a posse of silent people escorting a cart, and on the cart, bound in a chair, her throat bandaged, and the bandage all bloody — horror! — the fisher-wife herself, who continued thenceforth to hag-ride my thoughts, and even to-day (as I recall the scene) darkens daylight. She was lodged in the little old jail in the chief street; but whether or no she died there, with a wise terror of the worst, I never inquired. She had been tippling; it was but a dingy tragedy; and it seems strange and hard that, after all these years, the poor crazy sinner should be still pilloried on her cart in the scrap-book of my memory. Nor shall I readily forget a certain house in the Quadrant where a visitor died, and a dark old woman continued to dwell alone with the dead body; nor how this old woman conceived a hatred to myself and one of my cousins, and in the dread hour of the dusk, as we were clambering on the garden-walls, opened a window in that house of mortality and cursed us in a shrill voice and with a marrowy choice of language. It was a pair of very colourless urchins that fled down the lane from this remarkable experience! But I recall with a more doubtful sentiment, compounded out of fear and exultation, the coil of equinoctial tempests; trumpeting squalls, scouring flaws of rain; the boats with their reefed lugsails scudding for the harbour mouth, where danger lay, for it was hard to make when the wind had any east in it; the wives clustered with blowing shawls at the pier-head, where (if fate was against them) they might see boat and husband and sons — their whole wealth and their whole family — engulfed under their eyes; and (what I saw but once) a troop of neighbours forcing such an unfortunate homeward, and she squalling and battling in their midst, a figure scarcely human, a tragic Maenad.

These are things that I recall with interest; but what my memory dwells upon the most, I have been all this while withholding. It was a sport peculiar to the place, and indeed to a week or so of our two months' holiday there. Maybe it still flourishes in its native spot; for boys and their pastimes are swayed by periodic forces inscrutable to man; so that tops and marbles reappear in their due season, regular like the sun and moon; and the harmless art of knucklebones has seen the fall of the Roman empire and the rise of the United States. It may still flourish in its native spot, but nowhere else, I am persuaded; for I tried myself to introduce it on Tweedside, and was defeated lamentably; its charm being quite local, like a country wine that cannot be exported.

The idle manner of it was this: —

Toward the end of September, when school-time was drawing near and the nights were already black, we would begin to sally from our respective villas, each equipped with a tin bull's-eye lantern. The thing was so well known that it had worn a rut in the commerce of Great Britain; and the grocers, about the due time, began to garnish their windows with our particular brand of luminary. We wore them buckled to the waist upon a cricket belt, and over them, such was the rigour of the game, a buttoned top-coat. They smelled noisomely of blistered tin; they never burned aright, though they would always burn our fingers; their use was naught; the pleasure of them merely fanciful; and yet a boy with a bull's-eye under his top-coat asked for nothing more. The fishermen used lanterns about their boats, and it was from them, I suppose, that we had got the hint; but theirs were not bull's-eyes, nor did we ever play at being fishermen. The police carried them at their belts, and we had plainly copied them in that; yet we did not pretend to be policemen. Burglars, indeed, we may have had some haunting thoughts of; and we had certainly an eye to past ages when lanterns were more common, and to certain story-books in which we had found them to figure very largely. But take it for all in all, the pleasure of the thing was substantive; and to be a boy with a bull's-eye under his top-coat was good enough for us.

When two of these asses met, there would be an anxious " Have you got your lantern?" and a gratified "Yes!" That was the shibboleth, and very needful too; for, as it was the rule to keep our glory contained, none could recognize a lantern-bearer, unless (like the pole-cat) by the smell. Four or five would sometimes climb into the belly of a ten-man lugger, with nothing but the thwarts above them — for the cabin was usually locked, or choose out some hollow of the links where the wind might whistle overhead. There the coats would be unbuttoned and the bull's-eyes discovered; and in the chequering glimmer, under the huge windy hall of the night, and cheered by a rich steam of toasting tinware, these fortunate young gentlemen would crouch together in the cold sand of the links or on the scaly bilges of the fishing-boat, and delight themselves with inappropriate talk. Woe is me that I may not give some specimens — some of their foresights of life, or deep inquiries into the rudiments of man and nature, these were so fiery and so innocent, they were so richly silly, so romantically young. But the talk, at any rate, was but a condiment; and these gatherings themselves only accidents in the career of the lantern-bearer. The essence of this bliss was to walk by yourself in the black night; the slide shut, the top-coat buttoned; not a ray escaping, whether to conduct your footsteps or to make your glory public: a mere pillar of darkness in the dark; and all the while, deep down in the privacy of your fool's heart, to know you had a bull's-eye at your belt, and to exult and sing over the knowledge.

II

It is said that a poet has died young in the breast of the most stolid. It may be contended, rather, that this (somewhat minor) bard in almost every case survives, and is the spice of life to his possessor. Justice is not done to the versatility and unplumbed childishness of man's imagination. His life from without may seem but a rude mound of mud; there will be some golden chamber at the heart of it, in which he dwells delighted; and for as dark as his pathway seems to the observer, he will have some kind of a bull's-eye at his belt.

It would be hard to pick out a career more cheerless than that of Dancer, the miser, as he figures in the *Old Bailey Reports*, a prey to the most sordid persecutions, the butt of his neighbourhood, betrayed by his hired man, his house beleaguered by the impish school-boy, and he himself grinding and fuming and impotently fleeing to the law against these pin-pricks. You marvel at first that any one should willingly prolong a life so destitute of charm and dignity; and then you call to memory that had he chosen, had he ceased to be a miser, he could have been freed at once from these trials, and might have built himself a castle and gone escorted by a squadron. For the love of more recondite joys, which we cannot estimate, which, it may be, we should envy, the man had willingly foregone both comfort and consideration. " His mind to him a kingdom was "; and sure enough, digging into that mind, which seems at first a dust-heap, we unearth some priceless jewels. For Dancer must have had the love of power and the disdain of using it, a noble character in itself; disdain of many pleasures, a chief part of what is commonly called wisdom; disdain of the inevitable end, that finest trait of mankind; scorn of men's opinions, another element of virtue; and at the back of all, a conscience just like yours and mine, whining like a cur, swindling like a thimble-rigger, but still pointing (there or thereabout) to some conventional standard. Here were a cabinet portrait to which Hawthorne perhaps had done justice; and yet not Hawthorne either, for he was mildly minded, and it lay not in him to create for us that throb of the miser's pulse, his fretful energy of gusto, his vast arms of ambition clutching in he knows not what: insatiable, insane, a god with a muck-rake. Thus, at least, looking in the bosom of the miser, consideration detects the poet in the full tide of life, with more, indeed, of the poetic fire than usually goes to epics; and tracing that mean man about his cold hearth, and to and fro in his discomfortable house, spies within him a blazing bonfire of delight. And so with others, who do not live by bread alone, but by some cherished and perhaps fantastic pleasure; who are meat salesmen to the external eye, and possibly to themselves are Shakespeares, Napoleons, or Beethovens; who have not one virtue to rub against another in the field of active life, and yet perhaps, in the life of contemplation, sit with the saints. We see them on the street, and we can count their buttons; but heaven knows in what they pride themselves! heaven knows where they have set their treasure!

There is one fable that touches very near the quick of life : the fable of the monk who passed into the woods, heard a bird break into song, hearkened for a trill or two, and found himself on his return a stranger at his convent gates ; for he had been absent fifty years, and of all his comrades there survived but one to recognise him. It is not only in the woods that this enchanter carols, though perhaps he is native there. He sings in the most doleful places. The miser hears him and chuckles, and the days are moments. With no more apparatus than an ill-smelling lantern I have evoked him on the naked links. All life that is not merely mechanical is spun out of two strands : seeking for that bird and hearing him. And it is just this that makes life so hard to value, and the delight of each so incommunicable. And just a knowledge of this, and a remembrance of those fortunate hours in which the bird has sung to us, that fills us with such wonder when we turn the pages of the realist. There, to be sure, we find a picture of life in so far as it consists of mud and of old iron, cheap desires and cheap fears, that which we are ashamed to remember and that which we are careless whether we forget ; but of the note of that time-devouring nightingale we hear no news.

The case of these writers of romance is most obscure. They have been boys and youths ; they have lingered outside the window of the beloved, who was then most probably writing to some one else ; they have sat before a sheet of paper, and felt themselves mere continents of congested poetry, not one line of which would flow ; they have walked alone in the woods, they have walked in cities under the countless lamps ; they have been to sea, they have hated, they have feared, they have longed to knife a man, and maybe done it ; the wild taste of life has stung their palate. Or, if you deny them all the rest, one pleasure at least they have tasted to the full — their books are there to prove it — the keen pleasure of successful literary composition. And yet they fill the globe with volumes, whose cleverness inspires me with despairing admiration, and whose consistent falsity to all I care to call existence, with despairing wrath. If I had no better hope than to continue to revolve among the dreary and petty businesses, and to be moved by the paltry hopes and fears with which they surround and animate their heroes, I declare I would die now. But there has never an hour of mine gone quite so dully yet; if it were spent waiting at a railway junction, I would have some scattering thoughts, I could count some grains of memory, compared to which the whole of one of these romances seems but dross.

These writers would retort (if I take them properly) that this was very true; that it was the same with themselves and other persons of (what they call) the artistic temperament; that in this we were exceptional, and should apparently be ashamed of ourselves; but that our works must deal exclusively with (what they call) the average man, who was a prodigious dull fellow, and quite dead to all but the paltriest considerations. I accept the issue. We can only know others by ourselves. The artistic temperament (a plague on the expression!) does not make us different from our fellow-men, or it would make us incapable of writing novels; and the average man (a murrain on the word!) is just like you and me, or he would not be average. It was Whitman who stamped a kind of Birmingham sacredness upon the latter phrase; but Whitman knew very well, and showed very nobly, that the average man was full of joys and full of a poetry of his own. And this harping on life's dulness and man's meanness is a loud profession of incompetence; it is one of two things: the cry of the blind eye, *I cannot see*, or the complaint of the dumb tongue, *I cannot utter*. To draw a life without delights is to prove I have not realized it. To picture a man without some sort of poetry — well, it goes near to prove my case, for it shows an author may have little enough. To see Dancer only as a dirty, old, small-minded, impotently fuming man, in a dirty house, besieged by Harrow boys, and probably beset by small attorneys, is to show myself as keen an observer as . . . the Harrow boys. But these young gentlemen (with a more becoming modesty) were content to pluck Dancer by the coat-tails; they did not suppose they had surprised his secret or could put him living in a book: and it is there my error would have lain. Or say that in the same romance — I continue to call these books romances, in the hope of giving pain — say that in the same romance, which now begins really to take shape, I should leave to speak of Dancer, and follow instead the Harrow boys; and say that I came on some such business as that of my lantern-bearers on the links; and described the boys as very cold, spat upon by flurries of rain, and drearily surrounded, all of which they were; and their talk as silly and indecent, which it certainly was. I might upon these lines, and had I Zola's genius, turn out, in a page or so, a gem of literary art, render the lantern-light with the touches of a master, and lay on the indecency with the ungrudging hand of love; and when all was done, what a triumph would my picture be of shallowness and dulness! how it would have missed the point! how it would have belied the boys! To the ear of the stenographer, the talk is merely silly and indecent; but ask the boys themselves, and they are discussing (as it is highly proper they should) the possibilities of existence. To the eye of the observer they are wet and cold and drearily surrounded; but ask themselves, and they are in the heaven of a recondite pleasure, the ground of which is an ill-smelling lantern.

III

For, to repeat, the ground of a man's joy is often hard to hit. It may hinge at times upon a mere accessory, like the lantern; it may reside, like Dancer's, in the mysterious inwards of psychology. It may consist with perpetual failure, and find exercise in the continued chase. It has so little bond with externals (such as the observer scribbles in his note-book) that it may even touch them not; and the man's true life, for which he consents to live, lie altogether in the field of fancy. The clergyman, in his spare hours, may be winning battles, the farmer sailing ships, the banker reaping triumph in the arts:

all leading another life, plying another trade from that they
chose; like the poet's housebuilder, who, after all is cased
in stone,

> By his fireside, as impotent fancy prompts,
> Rebuilds it to his liking.

In such a case the poetry runs underground. The observer
(poor soul, with his documents!) is all abroad. For to look at
the man is but to court deception. We shall see the trunk
from which he draws his nourishment; but he himself is above
and abroad in the green dome of foliage, hummed through by
winds and nested in by nightingales. And the true realism
were that of the poets, to climb up after him like a squirrel,
and catch some glimpse of the heaven for which he lives.
And the true realism, always and everywhere, is that of the
poets: to find out where joy resides and give it a voice far
beyond singing.

For to miss the joy is to miss all. In the joy of the actors
lies the sense of any action. That is the explanation, that the
excuse. To one who has not the secret of the lanterns, the
scene upon the links is meaningless. And hence the haunting
and truly spectral unreality of realistic books. Hence, when
we read the English realists, the incredulous wonder with
which we observe the hero's constancy under the submerging
tide of dulness, and how he bears up with his jibbing sweet-
heart, and endures the chatter of idiot girls, and stands by his
whole unfeatured wilderness of an existence, instead of seeking relief in drink or foreign travel. Hence, in the French,
in that meat-market of middle-aged sensuality, the disgusted
surprise with which we see the hero drift sidelong, and practically quite untempted, into every description of misconduct
and dishonour. In each, we miss the personal poetry, the
enchanted atmosphere, that rainbow work of fancy that clothes
what is naked and seems to ennoble what is base; in each,
life falls dead like dough, instead of soaring away like a bal-
loon into the colours of the sunset; each is true, each inconceivable; for no man lives in the external truth, among salts

and acids, but in the warm, phantasmagoric chamber of his brain, with the painted windows and the storied walls.

Of this falsity we have had a recent example from a man who knows far better — Tolstoi's *Powers of Darkness*. Here is a piece full of force and truth, yet quite untrue. For before Mikita was led into so dire a situation he was tempted, and temptations are beautiful at least in part; and a work which dwells on the ugliness of crime and gives no hint of any loveliness in the temptation, sins against the modesty of life, and even when a Tolstoi writes it, sinks to melodrama. The peasants are not understood; they saw their life in fairer colours; even the deaf girl was clothed in poetry for Mikita, or he had never fallen. And so, once again, even an Old Bailey melodrama, without some brightness of poetry and lustre of existence, falls into the inconceivable and ranks with fairy tales.

IV

In nobler books we are moved with something like the emotions of life; and this emotion is very variously provoked. We are so moved when Levine labours in the field, when André sinks beyond emotion, when Richard Feverel and Lucy Desborough meet beside the river, when Antony, "not cowardly, puts off his helmet," when Kent has infinite pity on the dying Lear, when, in Dostoieffsky's *Despised and Rejected*, the uncomplaining hero drains his cup of suffering and virtue. These are notes that please the great heart of man. Not only love, and the fields, and the bright face of danger, but sacrifice and death and unmerited suffering humbly supported, touch in us the vein of the poetic. We love to think of them, we long to try them, we are humbly hopeful that we may prove heroes also.

We have heard, perhaps, too much of lesser matters. Here is the door, here is the open air. *Itur in antiquam silvam.*

BIBLIOGRAPHICAL NOTE

I. GENERAL WORKS ON THE ENGLISH FAMILIAR ESSAY

The only book treating the whole development of the English essay in anything like a detailed way is Hugh Walker's recently published *English Essay and Essayists* (The Channels of English Literature, E. P. Dutton & Co., 1915). Though rather a series of portraits of individual essayists than a real history of the genre, Professor Walker's volume contains much suggestive commentary, as well as many of the essential facts. Shorter general accounts, valuable more for suggestions than for detailed information, are Edmund Gosse's in the eleventh edition of the Encyclopædia Britannica, and J. H. Lobban's in *English Essays* (The Warwick Library, London, 1902). Useful articles on the principal English essayists, accompanied by bibliographies, will be found in the *Dictionary of National Biography*.

II. MONTAIGNE AND THE BEGINNINGS OF THE ESSAY IN ENGLAND

1. *Texts*. The texts necessary for the study of the essay in this period are, with a few exceptions, easily accessible. French editions of Montaigne's *Essais* abound; perhaps the best, pending the completion of the magnificent Édition Municipale of M. Fortunat Strowski, are those of Dézeimeris and Barkhausen (for the *Essais* of 1580) and of Motheau and Jouaust (for the *Essais* of 1588 and 1595). Of the English translations, Florio's is obtainable in the Tudor Translations (3 vols., 1893) with an introduction by George Saintsbury, in the Temple Classics (6 vols., 1897), and in Everyman's Library (3 vols.); Cotton's (as revised by William and W. C. Hazlitt) in Bohn's Popular Library (3 vols., 1913). The student interested in Montaigne's sources and models will find in certain chapters of Sir Thomas Elyot's *Governour* (in Everyman's Library) very good examples of sixteenth-century *leçons morales*. Accessible also in Everyman's Library are selections from Plutarch's *Moralia*, in the early seventeenth-century rendering of Philemon Holland.—— The standard edition of

Bacon's *Essays* is that of James Spedding in Vol. VI of *The Works of Francis Bacon*, collected and edited by Spedding, Ellis, and Heath (new edition, London, 1890). The basis of this edition, as of nearly all modern reprints, is the third, or 1625, text of the *Essays*; the editor, however, gives in an Appendix the two earlier texts of 1597 and 1612, thus furnishing all the necessary material for a critical study of Bacon's development as an essayist. The same material, in a somewhat more scholarly and usable form, is also accessible in Edward Arber's *Harmony of the Essays, etc. of Francis Bacon* (English Reprints, Constable, Westminster, 1895). Of the innumerable other editions of Bacon, that of Mary Augusta Scott (Charles Scribner's Sons, 1908) deserves particular mention for its full and helpful explanatory notes. —— Cowley's *Essays* are reprinted from the folio of 1668 by A. R. Waller in the Cambridge English Classics (Cambridge, 1906). A good inexpensive edition is that of Alfred B. Gough (*The Essays and other Prose Writings*, Oxford Press, 1915). —— There are no complete modern editions of Temple. "An Essay upon the Ancient and Modern Learning" and "Of Poetry" are accessible in J. E. Spingarn's *Critical Essays of the Seventeenth Century* (Vol. III, Oxford, 1909); for the others, the reader must go to some one of the various collected editions of Temple's *Works* published between his death and the early nineteenth century. —— Of the less prominent or influential essayists of this period, Cornwallis, Robert Johnson, Clarendon, Collier, and Buckingham are obtainable only in early editions; Felltham's *Resolves* can be read in a reprint by Oliphant Smeaton (Temple Classics), and Sir Thomas Browne's *Religio Medici*, in numerous modern editions, the most valuable perhaps being that by W. A. Greenhill (The Macmillan Company, 1881), and the least expensive perhaps that in the Temple Classics (1896). —— A good selection of English "characters" is given by Henry Morley in *Character Writings of the Seventeenth Century* (The Carisbrooke Library, London, 1891). Of La Bruyère, the best French edition is that in the Grands Écrivains series (ed. G. Servois, Paris, 1865); the best English translation, that of Van Laun (London, 1885).

2. *Studies.* There exists no adequate single account of the early history of the English essay. Certain pages in the *Cambridge History of English Literature* (particularly Vol. IV, chap. xvi, and Vol. VIII, chap. xvi) furnish a few facts, but for more detailed information one must have recourse to special monographs and articles. Only the most notable of these can be mentioned here. For all that relates to Montaigne and the origins of the essay the authoritative work is M. Pierre Villey's *Les Sources et l'évolution des Essais de Montaigne* (2 vols., Hachette, Paris, 1908). The main results of this study, together with much illustrative material, are presented in

briefer compass in the same writer's *Montaigne : textes choisis et com-
mentés* (Plon-Nourrit, Paris, n.d.). Other studies by Villey concern Montaigne's influence in England. See especially " Montaigne en Angleterre,"
in *Revue des deux mondes* (1913), pp. 115–150, and " Montaigne a-t-il eu
quelque influence sur François Bacon," in *Revue de la Renaissance*, t. XII
(1911), 121–158, 185–203 ; t. XIII (1912), 21–46, 61–82 — the latter containing by far the best exposition of Bacon's development as an essayist
that has yet appeared. The chapter on Montaigne in A. H. Upham's *The
French Influence in English Literature from the Accession of Elizabeth
to the Restoration* (New York, 1908), while for the most part superseded
by Villey's later work, nevertheless deserves to be consulted for its treatment of Montaigne's influence on Cornwallis, Browne, and other minor
writers. Of value also are W. L. MacDonald's *Beginnings of the English
Essay* (Toronto, 1914), Joseph Texte's " La descendance de Montaigne :
Sir Thomas Browne," in *Études de littérature européenne* (Paris, 1898),
Charles Lamb's " The Genteel Style in Writing " (on Sir William Temple),
in *Last Essays of Elia*, and Professor E. C. Baldwin's studies of the development of character-writing (see *Publications of the Modern Language
Association*, Vols. XVIII and XIX).

III. THE PERIODICAL ESSAY OF THE EIGHTEENTH
CENTURY

1. *Texts*. *The British Essayists* of A. Chalmers (1803, and various
later editions) contains reprints of the following eighteenth-century periodicals : *Tatler*, *Spectator*, *Guardian*, *Rambler*, *Adventurer*, *World*,
Connoisseur, *Idler*, *Mirror*, *Lounger*, *Observer*, and *Looker-on* — in a
word, of nearly all the more important or influential collections. Many
essays not appearing in these papers may be found in Nathan Drake's
*The Gleaner : a series of Periodical Essays ; selected and arranged from
scarce or neglected volumes* (4 vols., London, 1811). Of the periodicals
which preceded the *Tatler*, such as the *Athenian Mercury* and Defoe's
Review, there are unfortunately no modern reprints. —— The best texts of
the more important essay-papers are to be found, not in the general collections mentioned above, but in separate editions. The standard edition
of the *Tatler* — an edition by no means critical, however — is that of
G. A. Aitken (4 vols., London, 1898–1899). *The Spectator* has been ad-
mirably edited, with respect to both text and commentary, by G. Gregory
Smith (8 vols., London, 1897–1898 ; practically the same work is reprinted
in four volumes in Everyman's Library). Fielding's essays are accessible

in his *Works* (ed. Leslie Stephen, Vol. VI, London, 1882), and a critical edition of his *Covent-Garden Journal* has recently been announced by the Yale University Press. Goldsmith's *Citizen of the World* may be read in an excellent but inexpensive reprint by Austin Dobson (2 vols., the Temple Classics, 1900). The same series contains also his *Bee and other Essays*. —— Of the numerous volumes of selections of eighteenth-century essays two only need be mentioned, for the excellence of their editing: Austin Dobson's *Steele: Selections from the Tatler, Spectator and Guardian* (Oxford, 1885; 2d edition, 1896), and Wendell and Greenough's *Selections from the Writings of Joseph Addison* (Ginn and Company, Boston, 1905).

2. *Studies.* Historical study of the eighteenth-century periodical essay may be said to have begun with Nathan Drake, whose *Essays . . . illustrative of the Tatler, Spectator, and Guardian*, and *Essays . . . illustrative of the Rambler, Adventurer, and Idler* were published in 1805 and 1809–1810 respectively. Despite their early date, these works are still valuable sources of information, particularly of a bibliographical sort, on the eighteenth-century periodicals. They need, however, to be supplemented by more recent studies, such as A. Beljame's section on the early periodicals in his *Le Public et les Hommes de lettres en Angleterre au dix-huitième siècle* (Paris, 1881), Leslie Stephen's article on Addison in the *Dictionary of National Biography* (1885), G. A. Aitken's account of the *Tatler* and *Spectator* in his *Life of Richard Steele* (1889; see especially Vol. I, pp. 239–258 and 309–321), Lawrence Lewis's *The Advertisements of the Spectator* (1909; valuable for the understanding it gives of some of the material conditions amid which the eighteenth-century essay took form), and Harold V. Routh's very suggestive study of Addison and Steele in the *Cambridge History of English Literature* (Vol. IX, chap. ii, 1913). Readers in search of appreciative comment on the eighteenth-century essayists will naturally turn to the lives of Addison by Dr. Johnson and Macaulay, to Thackeray's *English Humourists of the Eighteenth Century*, and to Hazlitt's finely discriminating lecture " On the Periodical Essayists " in his *English Comic Writers*.

IV. THE NEW MAGAZINE ESSAY OF THE NINETEENTH CENTURY

1. *Texts.* The serious student of the nineteenth-century essay will find it indispensable to go directly to the magazines in which the work of most of the essayists of this period originally appeared. The greater number of these are accessible in any large library. For ordinary purposes, however, the more recent collected editions are sufficient and possibly preferable. Such are E. V. Lucas's edition of *The Works of Charles and Mary Lamb* (7 vols., Methuen & Co., London, 1903–1905), Alfred Ainger's edition of the *Essays of Elia* (Macmillan & Co., London, 1883), *The Collected Works of William Hazlitt*, edited by A. R. Waller and Arnold Glover (13 vols., J. M. Dent, London, 1902–1906), *The Collected Writings of Thomas De Quincey*, edited by David Masson (14 vols., London, 1889), the Biographical edition of Thackeray (13 vols., Harper & Brothers, New York, 1898–1899), and the Thistle edition of Stevenson (27 vols., Charles Scribner's Sons, New York). No complete edition of Leigh Hunt has yet appeared; a helpful guide to his widely scattered writings is Alexander Ireland's *List of the Writings of William Hazlitt and Leigh Hunt*, etc. (John Russell Smith, London, 1868); and a fairly representative selection of his essays, with a good introduction, is obtainable in the World's Classics (Oxford Press). Other selections from his work are contained in *The Indicator and The Companion* (2 vols., Henry Colburn, London, 1834), and in *Men, Women, and Books* and *Table-Talk* (both published by Smith, Elder & Co., London). —— Inexpensive reprints of the principal essay collections of the nineteenth century may be had in the old Bohn Library (George Bell & Sons), Everyman's Library (E. P. Dutton & Company), the World's Classics (Oxford Press), and the Temple Classics (E. P. Dutton & Company).

2. *Studies.* In addition to the chapters on the essayists of the nineteenth century in Walker's *English Essay and Essayists*, the reader may be referred to Oliver Elton's *A Survey of English Literature, 1780–1830* (London, 1912), and to C. T. Winchester's *A Group of English Essayists of the Early Nineteenth Century* (The Macmillan Company, 1910). Both of these works deal with the period during which the new essay was taking form, and present more or less satisfactory studies of Lamb, Hazlitt, Hunt, De Quincey, and " Christopher North." So far there has been no serious extended treatment of the essay in the middle and later years of the century. —— A full list of the critical articles which the essayists of this period have inspired would greatly exceed the limits of this note. The following are perhaps the most helpful and suggestive: Hazlitt's papers on Lamb

and Hunt in *The Spirit of the Age*, Walter Pater's essay on Lamb in *Appreciations*, W. E. Henley's study of Hazlitt (printed as an introduction to the Waller-Glover edition), Sir Walter Raleigh's *Robert Louis Stevenson* (1895), and Leslie Stephen's article on the same writer in his *Studies of a Biographer* (Vol. IV, 1902). The lives of Lamb, Hazlitt, De Quincey, and Thackeray in the English Men of Letters series should also be consulted, as should Cosmo Monkhouse's *Leigh Hunt* (Great Writers, 1893) and Graham Balfour's *Life of Robert Louis Stevenson* (2 vols., 1901). In the *Letters* of Lamb and Stevenson and in Hunt's *Autobiography* may be found excellent commentary on the work of those writers as essayists.

NOTES

MICHEL DE MONTAIGNE

With the exception of " The Author to the Reader," which is given in Florio's version, the texts of Montaigne in the present collection are based upon Charles Cotton's translation of 1685 as revised successively by William Hazlitt and William Carew Hazlitt (Reeves and Turner, London, 1902). Whatever advantages there might have been from a historical point of view in reproducing either Florio's rendering or the original text of Cotton are more than offset by the superior accuracy and intelligibility of the Hazlitt revision.

THE AUTHOR TO THE READER

Montaigne's preface to the first edition of his *Essais* (1580).

PAGE 1.

1. **those nations :** the savages of the New World, who were thought by many of Montaigne's contemporaries to possess virtues sadly lacking in civilized Europeans. Montaigne himself seems to have shared this view, at least in part, and in general manifested a keen interest in the newly discovered barbarians. See his essays entitled " Of Custom," " Of Cannibals," and " Of Coaches," and, on the whole subject of the attitude of sixteenth-century Frenchmen to the American natives, the very interesting recent work of Gilbert Chinard, *L'Exotisme américain dans la littérature française au XVIᵉ siècle* (Paris, 1911).

OF SORROW

The essay " De la tristesse " first appeared as Chapter II of Book I in the edition of 1580. The date of its composition is fixed by Villey (*Les Sources et l'évolution des Essais de Montaigne*, I, 337) at about 1572; it belongs, therefore, to the earliest period of Montaigne's literary career, of which it is thoroughly typical.

PAGE 2.

1. **the Stoics :** a school of ancient philosophers, founded by Zeno about 308 B.C. In general, they taught that the highest virtue consists in firmness,

resolution, and an insensibility to joy and sorrow. At the time of the composition of this essay Montaigne's own thinking was largely colored by Stoic doctrines.

2. **Psammitichus:** or Psammenitus; the story is told by Herodotus (iii, 14), but Montaigne may have read it in one of the numerous contemporary collections of moral " examples."

PAGE 3.

3. **the ancient painter:** this " example," like the last, Montaigne probably borrowed from some sixteenth-century compilation. Ancient authorities for the story were Cicero (*Orator* xxii) and Pliny (*Historia Naturalis* xxxv, 10).

4. **the sacrifice of Iphigenia:** an allusion to the famous Greek legend in which Agamemnon, at the suggestion of the Delphic oracle, prepared to offer his daughter as a sacrifice to appease the wrath of Artemis.

5. **Diriguisse malis:** Ovid, *Metamorphoses* vi, 303: " petrified by her misfortunes."

6. **Et via vix tandem voci laxata dolore est:** Virgil, *Æneid* xi, 151: " and at length and with difficulty a way is opened by grief for speech."

PAGE 4.

7. **Chi puo dir com' egli arde, è in picciol fuoco:** Petrarch, *Sonetti* I, cxviii :

> He that can say how he doth fry,
> In petty-gentle flames doth lie. — Florio's translation.

8. **Innamoratos:** Florio translates simply " lovers."

9. **Misero quod omneis, etc.:** Catullus 51, 5–12 : " And this steals all my senses from me. For as soon as I see thee, Lesbia, I have not a word that I can say, for very frenzy. My tongue is numbed; a fine flame flows in and through my limbs; my ears, too, are filled with ringing, and my eyes are mantled in double darkness."

10. **Curæ leves loquuntur, ingentes stupent:** Seneca, *Hippolytus*, l. 607: " Light griefs speak; heavy sorrows remain silent."

PAGE 5.

11. **Ut me conspexit venientem, etc.:** Virgil, *Æneid* iii, 306: " As she saw me approaching and beheld with surprise the Trojan arms about me, frightened with so great a marvel, she fainted at the very sight: the warmth of life forsook her limbs, she sank down, and after a long time with difficulty she spoke."

12. **the examples of the Roman lady, etc.:** it is unnecessary to indicate for these anecdotes their sources in ancient literature, for Montaigne

probably took them already collected from one of the most popular compilations of the sixteenth century, the *Officina* of Ravisius Textor.

13. **Pope Leo X :** the pontificate of Leo X extended from 1513 to 1521. The source of the "example" was probably Guicciardini's (1483–1540) *Storia d'Italia*, a history much admired and quoted by Montaigne.

OF REPENTANCE

This essay was first published, under the title of "Du repentir," in the *Essais* of 1588, where it formed Chapter II of Book III. In composition it must have been later than 1580, though its exact date is impossible to determine. It has all the distinguishing qualities of the essays of Montaigne's last period. See the Introduction to the present volume, pp. xv–xvi.

PAGE 6.

1. **Demades :** quoted in Plutarch's *Life of Demosthenes.*

PAGE 8.

2. **Malice sucks up, etc. :** a translation of Seneca, *Epistolæ* 81.

PAGE 9.

3. **Quæ fuerant vitia, mores sunt :** Seneca, *Epistolæ* 39: "What were formerly vices are now fashions."

4. **Tuo tibi judicio est utendum, etc. :** see Cicero, *De Natura Deorum* iii, 35: "You must use your own judgment . . . The weight of the very conscience of vice and virtues is heavy : take that away, and all is down" (Florio's translation).

PAGE 10.

5. **Quæ mens est hodie, etc. :** Horace, *Odes* iv, 10, 7: "Why had I not the same inclination, when I was young, that I have to-day, or why, when I am so disposed, does not my bloom return to me?"

6. **Bias :** an early Greek philosopher (fl. sixth century B.C.), one of the "Seven Sages." The apothegm quoted by Montaigne is recorded by Plutarch in his *Banquet of the Seven Sages.*

7. **Julius Drusus :** a Roman politician (d. cir. 109 B.C.); his real name was Marcus Livius Drusus.

8. **Agesilaus :** King of Sparta from 399 to 361 B.C. For this anecdote see Plutarch, *Life of Agesilaus.*

PAGE 11.

9. **Gascony . . . Guienne :** Gascony and Guienne formed in the sixteenth century a single "government."

10. **private men, says Aristotle :** in his *Nicomachean Ethics* x, 7.

PAGE 12.

11. **Tamerlane**: a corruption of Timur-Leng ("Timur the Lame"), the name of a Tartar monarch who between about 1370 and 1405 conquered Persia, central Asia, and a large part of India, and made preparations for an invasion of China. The story of his deeds, told and retold in numerous popular histories, made a profound impression on the imagination of western Europe in the sixteenth century. In England, a year before this essay was published, Marlowe devoted to Tamerlane's career the first of his great tragedies. See also Bacon's essay " Of Envy," above, p. 36.

12. **Erasmus**: the great representative of humanism in northern Europe, born at Rotterdam probably in 1466, died at Basel in 1536. In the sixteenth century Erasmus's reputation rested to a very large extent upon his *Adagia* (1600), a collection of " sentences " and " apothegms " from ancient writers ; it is to the fame of this work that Montaigne's remark applies.

13. **Sic ubi, desuetæ silvis, in carcere clausæ, etc.**: Lucan, *Pharsalia*, iv, 237 : " So when wild beasts, grown unaccustomed to the woods and shut up in cages, grow tame and lay aside their threatening look, and learn to put up with man, if but a drop of blood comes to their parched mouths, their ravenous fury returns and their throats swell, reminded by the taste of blood ; their fury rages and scarcely stops short of the trembling keeper."

PAGE 14.

14. **Armaignac**: a district in southeastern Gascony not far distant from Montaigne's estates.

PAGE 15.

15. **the Pythagorean sect**: the followers of Pythagoras (cir. 582–cir. 500 B.C.), a Greek philosopher.

PAGE 16.

16. **Cato**: Marcus Porcius Cato, commonly known as " The Censor," a Roman statesman and writer (234–149 B.C.). Montaigne's allusion refers to the severity of morals for which he was noted.

PAGE 17.

17. **Phocion**: an Athenian statesman and general (cir. 402–317 B.C.). The anecdote which Montaigne tells of him he probably found in Plutarch's collection of apothegms.

PAGE 18.

18. **He, who said of old**: Sophocles. The " sentence " is quoted from Cicero, *De Senectute* 14.

19. **Nec tam aversa, etc.:** Quintilian, *Institutio oratoria*, v, 12: "Nor will Providence ever be seen so hostile to her own work that impotence should be included among the best things."

PAGE 19.

20. **Antisthenes:** a Greek philosopher (cir. 444–after 371 B.C.). The saying quoted by Montaigne is to be found in Diogenes Laertius, *Life of Antisthenes*.

SIR FRANCIS BACON

The text of Bacon is that of *The Works of Francis Bacon*, edited by Spedding, Ellis, and Heath. It has been collated throughout, however, with the original text of the same versions as printed by Arber in his *Harmony of the Essays* (1895).

OF STUDIES

As a means of illustrating the development of Bacon's methods of composition, this essay is given both in the original version of 1597 and in the final revision of 1625. In the former it occupied first place and bore the title "Of Study"; in the latter it was printed as No. 50.

PAGE 23.

1. **Abeunt studia in mores:** Ovid, *Heroides*, xv, 83: "Studies have an influence and operation upon the manners of those that are conversant in them" (Bacon's paraphrase in *The Advancement of Learning*, Bk. I).

PAGE 24.

2. **the schoolmen:** the philosophers of the medieval universities, a prominent feature of whose method was a reliance on fine distinctions between terms. Bacon was one of the leaders of the general revolt against their philosophy which took place at the end of the sixteenth century.

3. **cymini sectores:** literally dividers of cumin-seed; hair-splitters.

OF EMPIRE

The essay "Of Empire" appeared first in a manuscript version of the *Essays* written between 1607 and 1612; it was first printed (as No. 9) in the edition of 1612; it was reprinted, with numerous additions, as No. 19 in the edition of 1625. It is given here in the versions of 1612 and 1625. A comparison of the two texts will enable the reader to verify the statements made in the Introduction regarding the evolution of Bacon's conception and practice of the essay.

1. **That the king's heart is inscrutable:** see Proverbs xxv, 3.

PAGE 25.

2. **Alexander the Great and . . . Charles the Fifth :** Alexander (356–323 B.C.) was disappointed at being turned back from India by the refusal of his soldiers to go on. Charles the Fifth (1500–1558), Emperor of the Holy Roman Empire, abdicated his crown in favor of his son Philip (1556) and spent the remainder of his life in the vicinity of a secluded Spanish monastery.

3. **temper and distemper :** in the old physiology "temper" meant a proper mixture or balance of elements in the body ; "distemper," a departure from a proper mixture and a consequent disturbance.

4. **The answer of Apollonius :** Apollonius of Tyana (cir. 4 B.C.–cir. 97 A.D.) was a late Greek philosopher with supposed magical powers. His reply to Vespasian (Roman emperor, 70–79 A.D.) is reported by Philostratus in his life of Apollonius, v, 28.

5. **saith Tacitus, etc. :** "The desires of kings are mostly vehement, and inconsistent with one another." The author of the "sentence" was not Tacitus but Sallust (*Bellum Jugurthinum*, 113).

6. **solecism of power :** "solecism" here signifies inconsistency or incongruity.

7. **Memento quod es homo, etc. :** "Remember that you are man ; remember that you are God, or the lieutenant of God."

PAGE 26.

8. **Nero . . . Domitian . . . Commodus . . . Caracalla :** all Roman emperors. Nero reigned from 54 to 68 A.D.; Domitian, from 81 to 96; Commodus, from 180 to 192; and Caracalla, from 211 to 217.

9. **Diocletian :** Roman emperor from 284 to 305 A.D. He spent the later part of his life, after his abdication in 305, on his estates in Dalmatia.

PAGE 27.

10. **that triumvirate of kings :** the first reigned from 1509 to 1547; the second, from 1515 to 1547; and the third, from 1519 to 1556.

11. **Guicciardine :** Francesco Guicciardini (1483–1540), a Florentine historian, whose *Storia d'Italia* ("History of Italy") was one of the most important and widely read works of the Italian Renaissance.

12. **Ferdinando King of Naples :** Ferdinand II (1469–1496).

13. **Lorenzius Medices :** Lorenzo de' Medici (cir. 1449–1492), surnamed "The Magnificent," a Florentine statesman and patron of letters, the virtual ruler of his city from 1478 to his death.

14. **Ludovicus Sforza :** Lodovico Sforza (d. cir. 1510), Duke of Milan.

Page 28.

15. **Livia**: see Tacitus, *Annals*, iv, 3.

16. **infamed**: defamed.

17. **Roxalana**: the murder of Prince Mustapha through the instigation of Roxalana, one of his father's wives, took place in 1553. It was a favorite incident with Elizabethan dramatists, entering into no less than five plays between 1581 and 1638. See Wann, "The Oriental in Elizabethan Drama," in *Modern Philology*, xii (1915), 434–435.

18. **Edward the Second of England his queen**: Edward II (reigned 1307–1327) was deposed as a result of an uprising led by his queen, Isabella of France, and was murdered in prison. — The form of the possessive used in this phrase was the common form with proper names until well into the seventeenth century.

19. **advoutresses**: adulteresses.

20. **Solyman**: Solyman I, who ruled over the Ottoman Turks from 1520 to 1566.

21. **Selymus the Second**: Solyman's son, Sultan from 1566 to 1574.

22. **The destruction of Crispus**: A.D. 326. Constantine was Roman emperor from 306 to 337; his sons died respectively in 340, 350, and 361.

23. **Philip the Second**: King of Macedon from 359 to 336 B.C., the father of Alexander the Great.

24. **Selymus the First**: Sultan of the Ottoman Turks from 1512, when he dethroned his father, Bajazet II (1447–1512), to his death in 1520.

25. **the three sons of Henry the Second**: the three sons were Henry and Geoffrey, both of whom died before their father in 1183 and 1186 respectively, and Richard, who succeeded his father in 1189 as Richard I.

26. **Anselmus and Thomas Becket**: the former was Archbishop of Canterbury from 1093 to 1109, during the reigns of William II (1087–1100) and of Henry I (1100–1135); the latter, from 1162 to 1170, during the reign of Henry II (1154–1189). Both Anselm and Becket were defenders of Church privilege against the claims of royal power. Bacon's attitude toward them is typical of the Protestant and monarchical views dominant in England in the sixteenth and seventeenth centuries.

Page 29.

27. **collation**: gift, applied to the bestowal of a benefice upon a clergyman.

28. **I have noted it in my history of King Henry the Seventh**: see *The Works of Francis Bacon*, ed. Spedding, Ellis, and Heath, vi (1890), 242. Bacon's *History* was finished in 1621 and published the following year.

29. **vena porta**: literally "gate veins." The meaning is perhaps explained by the following sentence from *The History of Henry the Seventh* (quoted by M. A. Scott, *The Essays of Francis Bacon*, p. 89): "he could not endure to have trade sick, nor any obstruction to continue in the gate-vein which disperseth the blood." The term belongs to the medical vocabulary of Bacon's time.

30. **leeseth**: a regular form, much in use in the sixteenth century, later entirely superseded by "lose," which is in part derived from the same root.

31. **donatives**: gifts.

32. **janizaries**: Turkish troops forming the life-guard of the Sultan.

33. **pretorian bands**: the body-guard of the Roman emperors.

OF TRUTH

First printed (as No. 1) in the edition of 1625.

PAGE 30.

1. **What is truth?** John xviii, 38.

2. **sects of philosophers**: the Sceptics, a group of ancient philosophers who denied the possibility of human knowledge. One of the most celebrated representatives of the school was Pyrrho (360?–270? B.C.), from whose name the sceptical attitude was often known as Pyrrhonism.

3. **discoursing**: the word may mean here either argumentative or discursive, that is, unsettled, roving. The sentence in which it stands has been interpreted, probably without any justification, as an allusion to Montaigne.

4. **One of the later school of the Grecians**: Lucian of Samosata (second century A.D.), who discusses the question in his dialogue *Philopseudes*.

PAGE 31.

5. **vinum dæmonum**: devils' wine.

6. **The poet . . . saith yet excellently well**: Lucretius (cir. 96–55 B.C.), whose great poem, *De Rerum Natura*, was written to expound the philosophy of Epicurus. The passage quoted by Bacon is a paraphase of the beginning of Book II.

7. **round dealing**: direct, plain, straightforward treatment.

8. **allay**: an old form of "alloy."

9. **embaseth**: destroys the purity of the metal by introducing alloy.

PAGE 32.

10. **And therefore Montaigne saith prettily**: *Essais*, ii, 18. Montaigne is here quoting and commenting upon a passage from Plutarch's *Life of Lysander*.

11. **he shall not find faith upon the earth**: see Luke xviii, 8.

Of Death

Written by 1607–1612; printed as No. 2 in both 1612 and 1625. The 1625 text, which is reproduced here, differs in a few unimportant details from that of 1612.

1. **the friars' books of mortification:** books of devotion intended to facilitate the subduing of the bodily appetites.

2. **Pompa mortis, etc.:** "The shows of death are more fearful than death itself." Quoted freely from Seneca, *Epistolæ* iii, 3, 14.

3. **Groans and convulsions, etc.:** this sentence may have been suggested to Bacon by the following passage from Montaigne's essay "Que philosopher c'est apprendre à mourir" (i, 20), as translated by Florio: "I verily believe these fearful looks and astonishing countenances wherewith we encompass it are those that more amaze and terrify us than death: a new form of life; the outcries of mothers; the wailing of women and children; the visitation of dismayed and swooning friends; the assistance of a number of pale-looking, distracted, and whining servants; a dark chamber; tapers burning round about; our couch beset round with physicians and preachers; and to conclude, nothing but horror and astonishment on every side of us: are we not already dead and buried?"

4. **mates:** weakens, overpowers.

PAGE 33.

5. **pre-occupateth:** anticipates.

6. **Otho the Emperor:** Roman emperor, January–April, 69 A.D.

7. **niceness:** the word may mean either luxury or fastidiousness.

8. **Cogita quamdiu, etc.:** Seneca, *Epistolæ* iii, 1: "Think how frequently you do the same things; one may wish to die, not so much because he is brave or miserable as because he is weary of living."

9. **Livia, conjugii, etc.:** Suetonius, *Augustus*, 99: "Livia, in remembrance of our married life, live on; farewell." This and the quotations that follow reflect a very characteristic element in Bacon's culture — his fondness for the Roman historians.

10. **Iam Tiberium, etc.:** Tacitus, *Annals*, vi, 50: "Tiberius's strength and manhood were now leaving him, but not his love of dissimulation."

11. **Ut puto Deus fio:** Suetonius, *Vespasian*, 23: "I suppose that I am becoming a god."

12. **Feri, si ex re, etc.:** Tacitus, *Historia* i, 41: "Strike, if it be for the good of the Roman people."

13. **Adeste si quid, etc.:** Dion Cassius, lxxvi, 17: "Make haste, if anything remains for me to do."

14. **qui finem vitæ, etc.**: "Who counts the end of life as one of Nature's gifts." An inaccurate quotation from Juvenal, *Satires*, x, 358.

15. **the sweetest canticle is Nunc dimittis**: the song of Simeon: "Lord, now lettest thy servant depart in peace." See Luke ii, 29–32.

16. **Extinctus amabitur idem**: Horace, *Epistolæ* II, i, 14: "The same one, dead, will be loved."

OF ADVERSITY

First printed (as No. 5) in the edition of 1625. If, as appears likely, Bacon in writing this essay was thinking of his own period of adversity following his conviction and disgrace on the charge of corruption, its date of composition must have been after 1621.

PAGE 34.

1. **Seneca**: the two quotations are from *Epistolæ* VII, iv, 29 and VI, i, 12 respectively.

2. **transcendences**: elevated sentiments and expressions.

3. **Prometheus**: according to the Greek myth, Prometheus, for the crime of giving mankind fire, was bound by Zeus to a rock on Mt. Caucasus, where he was the prey of a huge vulture. He was released by Hercules.

OF ENVY

First printed (as No. 9) in the edition of 1625.

PAGE 35.

1. **an ejaculation or irradiation of the eye**: "ejaculation" here means the emission of rays having a magic influence.

2. **curiosities**: niceties.

3. **to come at even hand**: to make himself even.

PAGE 36.

4. **play-pleasure**: the pleasure one takes in looking at a play.

5. **Non est curiosus, etc.**: "No one is curious without being also malevolent."

6. **Narses**: a Byzantine general (cir. 478–cir. 573 A.D.).

7. **Agesilaus**: see note 8 to page 10.

8. **Tamberlanes**: see note 11 to page 12.

9. **Adrian the Emperor**: Publius Ælius Hadrianus, Roman emperor from 117 to 138 A.D.

10. **incurreth**: here used in the etymological sense of running into or toward.

PAGE 37.

11. **per saltum:** at a bound.

12. **quanta patimur:** how much we suffer.

PAGE 38.

13. **derive:** to turn the course of, divert.

PAGE 39.

14. **plausible:** worthy of applause.

15. **estates:** states, bodies politic.

16. **Invidia festos dies non agit:** " Envy takes no holidays."

17. **The envious man, that soweth tares, etc.:** probably a reminiscence of Matthew xiii, 25.

OF TRAVEL

First printed (as No. 18) in the edition of 1625.

PAGE 40.

1. **allow:** approve.

2. **bourses:** stock exchanges. The word is derived from (Fr.) *bourse*, a purse.

3. **triumphs, masques:** see Bacon's essay on this subject.

PAGE 41.

4. **a great adamant of acquaintance:** adamant here means loadstone or magnet.

OF FRIENDSHIP

An essay " Of Friendship " appeared in the 1612 edition of Bacon's *Essays*. It was entirely rewritten, however, for the collection of 1625, in which it appeared as No. 27. The latter text is printed here.

PAGE 42.

1. **Whosoever is delighted in solitude, etc.:** Aristotle, *Politics* i, 2, 14.

2. **aversation:** aversion.

3. **Epimenides, etc.:** Epimenides (seventh century B.C.), a Cretan poet and prophet. Numa, the legendary second king of Rome. Empedocles (cir. 490–430 B.C.), a Sicilian philosopher and poet. On Apollonius see note 4 to page 25.

4. **Magna civitas, magna solitudo:** " A great city is a great solitude." Bacon probably quoted the phrase from Erasmus's *Adagia*. See Introduction, p. xii, and note 12 to page 12.

5. **sarza, etc.:** names of medicines in familiar use in Bacon's time. Sarza is modern sarsaparilla; castoreum, a secretion of the beaver.

PAGE 43.

6. **privadoes :** private friends (Spanish).

7. **participes curarum :** sharers of sorrows or cares.

8. **L. Sylla, etc. :** of the "examples" cited in this paragraph, the anecdote of Sylla and Pompey came from Plutarch's *Life of Pompey* ; that of
Cæsar and Brutus, from the same writer's *Life of Cæsar* ; the characterization of Brutus from Cicero's *Philippics* (xiii, 11) ; the remark of Mæcenas,
from Dion Cassius' *Roman History* (lvi, 6) ; the account of Tiberius's friendship with Sejanus, from Tacitus's *Annals* (lv, 40) ; and the story of Severus
and Plautianus, from Dion Cassius (lxxv, 15). Sylla or Sulla (138–78 B.C.)
and Pompey (106–48 B.C.) were Roman generals of the later days of the
Republic, at first friends, but later rivals. By "against the pursuit of Sylla"
Bacon means that Sylla was supporting another candidate. Augustus
(63 B.C.–14 A.D.), Tiberius Cæsar (42 B.C.–37 A.D.), and Septimius Severus
(146–211 A.D.) were Roman emperors. Maecenas (d. 8 B.C.) was a statesman of the reign of Augustus ; he is perhaps best known as the patron
of Virgil and Horace. Agrippa (63–12 B.C.) was the leading statesman of
the same reign ; he married Augustus's daughter Julia as his third wife.
Sejanus (d. 31 A.D.) was the chief minister of Tiberius. His career was
made familiar to Bacon's contemporaries by a tragedy of Ben Jonson.
Plautianus was praetorian prefect during the reign of Septimius Severus.

PAGE 44.

9. **Hæc pro amicitiâ nostrâ non occultavi :** "I have told you this in
consideration of our friendship."

10. **mought :** an old form of "might."

PAGE 45.

11. **Comineus :** Philip de Commines, a French historian of the fifteenth
century (cir. 1447–1511). His *Memoires* narrated the more important
events of the reign of Louis XI, especially his wars with Charles the Bold
of Burgundy.

12. **Pythagoras :** Greek philosopher (cir. 582–cir. 500 B.C.). The saying
attributed to him here is quoted in Plutarch's essay *Of the Education
of Children*.

13. **It was well said by Themistocles :** see Plutarch's *Life of Themistocles*.

PAGE 46.

14. **Heraclitus :** Greek philosopher (cir. 535–cir. 475 B.C.).

15. **St. James saith :** James i, 23, 24.

PAGE 47.

16. **the four and twenty letters :** in Bacon's day *i* and *j*, and *u* and *v*
were not differentiated, except to a certain extent typographically.

Of Plantations

First published (as No. 33) in the edition of 1625. The subject of "plantations," or colonies, was provoking much discussion in England at the time; and Bacon's own interest in it had more than a speculative basis. He was an "adventurer," or stockholder, in the London or South Virginia Company, chartered in 1609, and he took a lively interest in the projects for planting English colonies in the north of Ireland. Many of the practical directions for the conduct of plantations which he gives in the essay may well have been suggested to him by his observation of these contemporary enterprises.

Page 48.

1. **leese**: lose.

Page 49.

2. **It is a shameful and unblessed thing to take the scum of people**: as was done, for example, in the early attempts to colonize Virginia, of which perhaps Bacon was thinking.

3. **artichokes of Hierusalem**: a plant with an edible root introduced from South America by the Italians, who called it *girasole articiocco*, or "sunflower artichoke." The connection with Jerusalem was evidently due to English misunderstanding of the Italian name.

4. **his own private**: his own private use or business.

Page 50.

5. **as it hath fared with tobacco in Virginia**: as the English text of this passage stands, it seems natural to make the phrase "as it hath fared with tobacco in Virginia" modify "to the untimely prejudice of the main business." This interpretation, moreover, has the support of the known facts concerning the early cultivation of tobacco in Virginia. Gardiner (*History of England . . . 1603–1642* (ed. 1901), III, 158–159) thus describes the situation which resulted from its introduction in 1616: "Everyone was in haste to grow rich, and everyone forgot that tobacco would not prove a substitute for bread. Every inch of ground which had been cleared was devoted to tobacco. The very streets of Jamestown were dug up to make room for the precious leaf. Men had no time to speak of anything but tobacco. The church, the bridge, the palisades, were allowed to fall into decay, whilst every available hand was engaged upon the crop which was preparing for exportation. The natural result followed. Starvation once more stared the settlers in the face." The Latin translation of the *Essays*, however, part of which at least was done under Bacon's supervision, places the phrase in question after "charge of plantation" and before "so it be not, as was said, etc." — an arrangement which completely alters the sense.

6. **put in experience** : proved by actual test.

7. **moil** : labor, drudge.

8. **undertakers** : projectors.

9. **marish** : marshy.

PAGE 51.

10. **gingles** : an old spelling of "jingles."

OF GARDENS

First printed (as No. 46) in the edition of 1625.

1. **lavender** : the reader who is curious to know the modern botanical names of the plants and flowers mentioned by Bacon will find them carefully distinguished in the edition of the *Essays* by Mary Augusta Scott (Scribner's, 1908).

2. **stoved** : kept warm in a house by artificial heat.

PAGE 52.

3. **ver perpetuum** : perpetual spring.

4. **fast flowers of their smells** : flowers tenacious of their smells.

PAGE 53.

5. **Bartholomew-tide** : St. Bartholomew's Day, August 24.

6. **which [yield]** : the original has here "which a most excellent cordial smell." The emendation given in the text is supported by the Latin translation of the essay, which reads "quae habitum emittunt plane cardiacum." Spedding in his standard edition of the *Essays* follows the edition of 1639 and prints "with a most excellent cordial smell."

7. **the dust of a bent** : "dust" here means pollen; a "bent" is a kind of grass.

8. **heath or desert** : a part of the garden left more or less uncultivated.

PAGE 54.

9. **letting your prospect** : shutting off your view — "let" in the old sense of hinder.

10. **welts** : borders, fringes.

PAGE 55.

11. **statuas** : statues (Lat.).

PAGE 56.

12. **and no grass, because of going wet** : because it conduces to wetness.

13. **some fair alleys, ranged on both sides with fruit-trees** : the original edition sets off the phrase "ranged on both sides" with commas, thereby

confusing the interpretation of the sentence. Spedding reads " some fair alleys ranged on both sides, with fruit-trees "; but the punctuation given in the text would seem more reasonable.

ABRAHAM COWLEY

The Dangers of an Honest Man in Much Company

This essay was No. 8 in *Several Discourses by Way of Essays, in Verse and Prose*, first printed in the folio edition of Cowley's works issued in 1668. Like all the other essays it concluded with a bit of verse, which is here omitted.

Page 58.

1. **twenty thousand naked Americans** : perhaps an allusion to the massacre of Cholula in Mexico during the expedition of Cortes (1519). See Prescott, *History of the Conquest of Mexico*, Bk. III, chap. vii.

2. **cap-à-pie** : from head to foot, completely.

Page 59.

3. **the Toupinambaltians** : a savage tribe of Brazil, celebrated for its " natural virtues " by seventeenth-century writers of voyages. See Chinard, *L'Amérique et le rêve exotique dans la littérature française au XVIIe et au XVIIIe siècle* (Paris, 1913), chap. i.

4. **cozen** : cheat.

5. **Go to, let us build us a city** : see Genesis xi, 4.

6. **the beginning of Rome** : Cowley in this sentence alludes to two incidents in the founding of Rome as related in Livy (I, vii, viii). Before the construction of the new city was very far advanced, the question of its name occasioned a quarrel between Romulus and his brother Remus. They decided to leave it to an augury of vultures. When Romulus won, Remus in derision leaped over the newly erected wall; whereupon Romulus slew him. Later Romulus, in order to people his city, made it a place of refuge for the criminals and outlaws of the surrounding country.

Page 60.

7. **the first town . . . in the world** : the city of Enoch built by Cain after his murder of Abel. See Genesis iv, 17.

8. **Quid Romæ faciam? Mentiri nescio** : Juvenal, *Satires* iii, 41 : " What should I do at Rome? I know not how to lie."

9. **advice which Martial gave to Fabian** : *Epigrams*, iv, 5.

PAGE 61.

10. **Lucretius:** *De Rerum Natura* ii, 1.

11. **Democritus:** Greek philosopher (born cir. 460 B.C.), traditionally known as the "laughing philosopher."

12. **Bedlam:** this form represents the popular English pronunciation of Bethlehem. From the fourteenth century the Hospital of St. Mary of Bethlehem in London (incorporated in 1547) was the principal lunatic asylum in England. The word "bedlam," originally applied to this hospital, came in time to signify a lunatic asylum in general, and later still any scene of madness. Cowley is using it probably in the first sense.

13. **ut nec facta audiat Pelopidarum:** quoted by Cicero, *Ad Familiares* vii, 30. With the substitution of "sons of Adam" for "sons of Pelops" the phrase is translated in the next clause.

PAGE 62.

14. **Quia terra patet, etc.:** Ovid, *Metamorphoses* i, 241–242: "Wherever earth extends, a wild fury reigns; you would think that men had sworn allegiance to crime."

15. **the shepherds of Sir Philip Sidney:** an allusion to Sidney's pastoral romance *Arcadia* (printed in 1590, but written before 1586), a work still in general circulation in Cowley's day.

16. **Monsieur d'Urfé:** Honoré d'Urfé (1567–1625), a French writer, author of the pastoral romance *l'Astrée* (1610), one of the most celebrated works of fiction of the seventeenth century. Lignon and La Forrest are names of places in the story.

17. **Chertsey:** a small town on the Thames west of London, where Cowley was living when he wrote this essay.

18. **St. Paul's advice:** 1 Corinthians vii, 29.

19. **mundum ducere and not mundo nubere:** marry the world as a husband, and not be wedded to the world as a wife.

OF MYSELF

The last, or No. 11, of Cowley's *Several Discourses*.

PAGE 64.

1. **Horace might envy in his Sabine field:** Horace's country place referred to in many of his *Odes*.

2. **the conclusion is taken out of Horace:** *Odes* III, xxix, 41 ff.

PAGE 65.

3. **I went to the university:** Cowley became a scholar of Trinity College, Cambridge, in 1637. He received his B.A. in 1639, was elected minor fellow

in 1640, and took his M.A. degree in 1642. In the winter of 1643–1644 he was ejected from his college by the Puritans.

4. **I was cast . . . into the family of one of the best persons :** after leaving college Cowley became a member of the household of Jermyn, afterwards Earl of St. Albans. In 1646 he accompanied the queen, Henrietta Maria, to France, where he was employed on various diplomatic missions by the exiled English court.

PAGE 66.

5. **the failing of the forces which I had expected :** for several years after the Restoration Cowley was unable to secure any aid from the government of Charles II in recognition of his services. Finally, however, through the influence of the Earl of St. Albans and the Duke of Buckingham, he was given a lease of land in Surrey.

6. **à corps perdu :** without reflection or hope of return.

7. **Non ego perfidum dixi sacramentum :** Horace, *Odes* II, xvii, 9–10 : " I have not sworn a perjured oath."

PAGE 67.

8. **Nec vos, dulcissima mundi :** the editors have been unable to discover the source of this quotation.

9. **quantum sufficit :** a sufficient quantity.

SEVENTEENTH CENTURY CHARACTERS
JOHN EARLE

Earle's "characters" were first printed in 1628 under the title of *Microcosmographie, or a Piece of the World Discovered in Essays and Characters*. There were many later editions. The present text is taken from Arber's reprint of the editio princeps in English Reprints (1869).

A MERE YOUNG GENTLEMAN OF THE UNIVERSITY
No. 23 in the edition of 1628.

PAGE 69.

1. **neat silk strings :** strings were used in the seventeenth century, as earlier, to hold the covers of books shut.

2. **a piece of Euphormio :** *Euphormionis Satyricon*, a satirical novel written in Latin prose by John Barclay (1582–1621), a Scotchman who lived and wrote for the most part on the Continent.

3. **he studies arms and books of honour :** books of heraldry and etiquette.

4. **an ingle to gold hatbands :** a flatterer of the rich.

PAGE 70.

5. **Inns-of-court**: see note 4 to page 83.

A CONTEMPLATIVE MAN

No. 44 in the edition of 1628.

JEAN LA BRUYÈRE
THE CHARACTER OF ARRIAS

A part of the chapter "De la Société et de la Conversation" in La Bruyère's *Les Caractères ou les mœurs de ce siècle*. The reflections forming the first paragraph appeared originally in the fourth edition of *Les Caractères* (1689); the portrait of Arrias was added in the eighth edition (1694). The translation reproduced here is that of Henri Van Laun (*The "Characters" of Jean La Bruyère newly rendered into English*. London, John C. Nimmo (1885), pp. 103–105).

PAGE 71.

1. **Zamet . . . Ruccellaï . . . Concini**: three Italians, favorites of Marie de Medicis (La Bruyère's note).

2. **than . . . appear to ignore anything**: a careless translation; the original has "que de . . . paraître ignorer quelque chose."

THE TATLER

The text of the *Tatler* presented in this collection is based on the edition of G. A. Aitken (4 vols., London, 1898–1899), corrected where necessary by reference to the original sheets and the early octavo reprints. A critical edition of the *Tatler* is still a desideratum.

PROSPECTUS

This announcement was printed in italic type before Nos. 1, 2, and 3 of the original issue of the *Tatler*—the "*gratis* stock" referred to in the text.

PAGE 73.

1. Motto: Juvenal, *Sat.* i, 85, 86: "What mankind does shall my collections fill."

In the original sheets Nos. 2–40 of the *Tatler* had the same motto as No. 1; in the early collected editions these numbers appeared without mottoes. From No. 41 on, various mottoes were used, with frequent recurrence of *Quicquid agunt homines* and frequent omission of a motto altogether. In neither the *Tatler* nor the *Spectator* were the mottoes translated —a fact which Thackeray overlooked in writing the imaginary *Spectator* paper in *Henry Esmond* (Bk. III, chap. iii). Most of the translations of mottoes given in these notes are taken from *The Mottoes of the Spectators, Tatlers, and Guardians, translated into English.* Second edition, 1737. While the versions in this book are not as a rule literal, nor always even accurate, they have perhaps the merit of being contemporary, or nearly contemporary, renderings.

2. **the convenience of the post**: the mail for the country left London on these days.

PAGE 74.

3. **White's Chocolate-house, etc.**: the names of celebrated taverns in early eighteenth-century London. White's was situated in St. James Street, in the neighborhood of the Court, and therefore in the center of fashionable life; Will's (so called from the original proprietor, William Urwin), in Russell Street near the Drury Lane and Covent Garden theaters; the Grecian (a resort of lawyers and scholars), in Devereux Court, off the Strand; and the St. James (a favorite meeting place of Whig politicians), in St. James Street.

4. **some plain Spanish**: wine.

5. **Kidney**: the head waiter at the St. James Coffee-house, the object of many bantering allusions in the *Tatler* and the *Spectator*. See, in the former, Nos. 10, 26, 69, and, in the latter, No. 24.

ON DUELLING

Only the first part of this number of the *Tatler* — the "news" from White's — is given in the text. In the original the satire on duelling is followed by an essay, dated "From my own Apartment, June 14," on critics, and by a budget of foreign news, dated "St. James's Coffee-house, June 15."

PAGE 75.

1. **that ridiculous custom of duelling**: this paper belongs to a series of essays, begun early in the *Tatler*, in which Steele attempted to picture the absurdities of the duel. The others are Nos. 25, 26, 28, 31, 38, and 39.

2. **huge falbala periwigs**: the periwig, also called the furbelow, was the dress wig of the period. It was made with plaits, and its length provoked not a little satire. Thus in *Tatler* 180 was printed a mock advertisement of "a stage coach to set out every evening for Mr. Tiptoe's dancing-school," to which was appended the note that "dancing shoes, not exceeding four inches height in the heel, and periwigs not exceeding three foot in length, are carried in the coach box *gratis.*"

3. **beauetry:** so in the original. Chalmers in the *British Essayists* reprint, followed by Aitken, emends to "beauty," which is clearly wrong. The word is a simple formation from "beau" on the model of "coquetry" from "coquette"; its use in the early eighteenth century is attested by other passages.

4. **a long Duvillier:** a furbelow; named from a famous French wigmaker.

PAGE 76.

5. **Don Quixote:** Cervantes' (1547–1616) novel satirizing the extravagances of the Spanish romances of chivalry. The first part was published in 1605, the second in 1615. It was well known in England in the early eighteenth century, at least three translations having appeared since 1612.

6. **Wantley:** the Dragon of Wantley is the subject of a ballad of the seventeenth century, which celebrates his overthrow at the hands of Moor of Moor Hall, Yorkshire. Cf. Percy's *Reliques*, Ser. III, Bk. III, No. 13. The reference to Suetonius is manifestly jocose.

7. **except France:** where duelling was forbidden.

HAPPY MARRIAGE

PAGE 77.

1. Motto: Virgil, *Georgics* ii, 523–524:

> Meantime, his children hang upon his lips,
> His faithful bed is crowned with chaste delights.

PAGE 78.

2. **Mrs. Mary:** in the seventeenth and eighteenth centuries " Mrs." was regularly prefixed to the name of an unmarried lady or girl.

PAGE 79.

3. **baby:** doll, a common usage.

4. **gossiping:** christening.

PAGE 80.

5. **a point of war:** a martial tune. Cf. *2 Henry IV*, IV, i, 52.

PAGE 81.

6. **Don Bellianis of Greece:** the first of these heroes belonged to a Spanish romance of the sixteenth century, translated into English in 1598 as *The Honour of Chivalry. Set downe in the most Famous Historie of . . . Prince Don Bellianis*, and reprinted frequently in the next two hundred years. The adventures of Guy of Warwick formed the subject of a romance popular in England from at least the thirteenth century; the

story could still be read in 1709 in as many as five versions, all the work of the preceding thirty years (see *Publications of the Modern Language Association*, XXX (1915), 165–187). The " Seven Champions " were St. George of England, St. Denis of France, St. James of Spain, St. Anthony of Italy, St. Andrew of Scotland, St. Patrick of Ireland, and St. David of Wales. Their story, as told by Richard Johnson in a romance first published in 1596, remained exceedingly popular with children and country people until well into the eighteenth century. John Hickathrift, or Hickerthrift, was one of numerous popular English heroes who rose from poverty to greatness by their bodily prowess. Bevis of Southampton was the chief personage of a medieval romance similar to *Guy of Warwick* in character and of about the same date; it, too, circulated in versions of the late seventeenth century. Summaries of most of these stories, together with reproductions of the crude woodcuts which adorned the editions in which Mr. Bickerstaff's young friend probably read them, will be found in John Ashton's *Chap-books of the Eighteenth Century* (London, 1882).

7. **sprites :** spirits.

The Club at the Trumpet

PAGE 82.

1. Motto: Cicero, *De Senectute* 46: " I hold myself obliged to old age, which has improved my desire after knowledge and taken it away from eating and drinking."

2. **the Trumpet :** this tavern was located in Shire Lane, near Temple Bar, on the site of the present Law Courts.

PAGE 83.

3. **the last civil wars :** the Great Rebellion of 1642–1649. The actions mentioned on this and the next two pages all occurred during this struggle : Marston Moor in 1644, the rising of the London apprentices in 1647, Naseby in 1645, and Edgehill, the first battle of the war, in 1642.

4. **a bencher of the neighbouring inn :** the Inns of Court comprise four groups of buildings — the Inner Temple, the Middle Temple, Lincoln's Inn, and Gray's Inn — all situated near the central part of London, and belonging to legal societies which have the exclusive right of admitting persons to practice at the bar. A " bencher " is a senior member of one of these societies.

5. **Jack Ogle :** a famous character about town in the time of Charles II, well known as a gambler and duelist.

6. **Hudibras :** a satirical poem on the Puritans, written by Samuel Butler (1612–1680), and published in three parts between 1663 and 1678. It was

written in octosyllabic couplets, many of which on account of their pointed sense and unexpected rimes have become familiar quotations. For an example see the next note.

PAGE 84.

7. **the couplet where "a stick" rhymes to "ecclesiastic"**: *Hudibras* I, i, 11–12:

> And Pulpit, Drum Ecclesiastick,
> Was beat with fist, instead of a Stick.

8. **red petticoat**: the story of Jack alluded to here is to the effect that once, while he was a trooper in the Guards, having pawned his own coat, he was compelled to appear on parade in his landlady's red petticoat.

PAGE 85.

9. **Nestor**: the oldest of the Greek chieftains engaged in the siege of Troy. Cf. *Iliad* i, 249.

10. **"His tongue dropped manna"**: *Paradise Lost*, ii, 112–113.

THE CHARACTER OF TOM FOLIO

PAGE 86.

1. Motto: Terence, *Andria*, Prologue, 17: "While they endeavour to show their learning, they make it appear that they understand nothing."

2. **Aldus and Elzevir, Harry Stephans**: printers famous for their editions of the classics. Aldus Manutius (cir. 1450–1515) was the founder of the celebrated Aldine press at Venice. Elzevir was the name of a family of Dutch printers whose greatest activity fell between about 1625 and 1650. Harry Stephans (*Fr.* Henri Estienne) was the name of two French printers of the sixteenth century — Henri Estienne (1470–1520), the founder of the family, and his grandson, Henri Estienne II (1528–1598). The allusion here is probably to Henri Estienne II, who was a classical scholar and editor as well as a printer.

3. **flashy**: without substance, trashy.

PAGE 87.

4. **a late paper**: *Tatler* 154.

5. **Æneas**: Cf. *Æneid* vi, 893 ff.

6. **Daniel Heinsius' edition**: Heinsius (1580–1655) was a celebrated Dutch classical scholar of the seventeenth century. His edition of Virgil was published in 1636.

PAGE 88.

7. **Tasso**: an Italian poet of the sixteenth century (1544–1595), the author of *Jerusalem Delivered*, one of the great epic poems of the Renaissance.

8. **Pastor Fido:** an Italian pastoral drama by Guarini (1537–1612).

9. **the character:** the type.

10. **sonnet:** even as late as the early eighteenth century the term "sonnet" was frequently used to designate any short lyrical poem, especially one dealing with love.

11. **various readings:** the pedantry of editors of the classics was a favorite topic of satire with Addison. In *Spectator* 470 he ridicules at length the practice of printing after the text of a poem the different readings, good and bad, of all the manuscripts in which it was found.

12. **six lines of Boileau:** *Satires* iv, 5–10: "a pedant drunk with his vain knowledge, bristling with Greek and puffed up with arrogance; who out of a thousand authors remembered word for word and heaped up in his brain has often made only nonsense; who believes that a book does everything, and that without Aristotle Reason itself cannot see, and Good Sense wanders."

RECOLLECTIONS

PAGE 89.

1. Motto: Virgil, *Æneid* v, 49:

> And now the rising day renews the year,
> (A day forever sad, forever dear).

PAGE 90.

2. **battledore:** an instrument resembling a racket used in the game of battledore and shuttlecock.

PAGE 92.

3. **wine, of the same sort with that which is to be put to sale on Thursday next at Garraway's Coffee-house:** a bit of puffing on Steele's part. The sale was formally announced among the advertisements in the same issue.

FALSE REFINEMENTS IN STYLE

PAGE 93.

1. **a Grub Street book:** a worthless, commercial production; so called from a street in London (now Milton Street) formerly "much inhabited by writers of small histories, dictionaries, and temporary poems" (Dr. Johnson).

2. **Westminster Hall:** the building, near the site of the present Parliament Houses, in which the Law Courts sat.

3. **the Court of Requests:** a court of equity intended for the trial of small civil cases.

PAGE 94.

4. **the Jacks :** Jacobites, the supporters of the exiled Stuarts.

5. **altogether of the Gothic strain :** " Gothic," originally applied to the productions of the Middle Ages, had come by the beginning of the eighteenth century to have the general meaning of " barbarous," " rude," " unpolished."

6. **phizz, etc. :** while the origin of most of these words is evident from the context in which they are used in the letter, one or two perhaps require a word of explanation. " Hipps " is an abbreviation of " hypochondria "; " mobb " of Latin *mobile vulgus* through *mobile* (which was used in the same sense during the seventeenth century); " plenipo " (on page 95), of " plenipotentiary."

PAGE 95.

7. **The war has introduced abundance of polysyllables :** Swift's meaning in this sentence is not altogether clear. " The war " can refer only to the War of the Spanish Succession (1701–1713); yet an examination of the passages cited in the Oxford Dictionary shows that of the eight words he mentions as introduced by " the war," five — the last five — were in use in England considerably earlier.

8. **banter, bamboozle, etc. :** in spite of Swift's efforts at least three of these words — " banter," " bamboozle," and " mobb " — have survived in modern English speech. A " country put " was a lout or bumpkin. " Kidney " was slang for temperament or nature.

9. **your authority as Censor :** see *Tatler* 162.

10. **Index Expurgatorius :** an allusion to the lists of books which Catholics are forbidden to read, issued at frequent intervals since the sixteenth century.

11. **sham, etc. :** of the words in this list not explained above, and no longer in common use, " sham " meant a trick or hoax; " bubble," to delude or cheat; " bully," a blustering " gallant," or perhaps the protector of a prostitute; " palming," playing a trick or cheating.

PAGE 96.

12. **simplex munditiis :** " of simple elegance." The phrase occurs in Horace, *Odes* I, v, 5.

13. **Hooker :** Richard Hooker (cir. 1553-1600), author of *The Laws of Ecclesiastical Polity*, an elaborate and eloquent justification of the Church of England.

14. **Parsons the Jesuit :** Robert Parsons (1546–1610), an English Catholic sent in 1580 by the Pope to attempt the conversion of England to the Church of Rome. His chief literary work was *A Christian Directory*.

15. **Wotton:** Sir Henry Wotton (1568–1639) was English ambassador at Venice and the author of a number of poems and miscellaneous treatises.

16. **Naunton:** Sir Robert Naunton (1563–1635) is best known as the writer of *Fragmenta Regalia*, a series of descriptions of the chief personages at the court of Queen Elizabeth.

17. **Osborn:** probably Francis Osborne (1593–1659); his chief work was *Advice to a Son* (1656, 1658).

18. **Daniel:** Samuel Daniel (1562–1619), an Elizabethan poet and historian, the author of *A History of England*.

ON CONVERSATION

1. Motto: Horace, *Epistles* I, iv, 8–9:

> What could a nurse for her dear child wish more
> Than that he might be sober whilst he lives,
> And able to express what he conceives.

PAGE 99.

2. **the pedant:** compare Addison's definition of pedantry, pp. 86–89, above.

3. **ubiquitary:** omnipresent.

THE SPECTATOR

The present text of the *Spectator* follows, except for details of spelling and punctuation, Professor Gregory Smith's reprint of the first collected edition of 1712–1715 (London, 1897–1898; Everyman's Library, 1907).

THE CHARACTER OF MR. SPECTATOR

PAGE 101.

1. Motto: Horace, *Ars Poetica* 143–144:

> He strikes out light from smoke, not smoke from light,
> New scenes of wonder opening to the sight.

2. **black or a fair man:** a man of dark or light complexion.

PAGE 103.

3. **Will's, etc.:** the location of some of these coffee-houses is given above (note 3 to page 74). Of the others, Child's was in St. Paul's Churchyard; the Cocoa-tree (a Tory house), in St. James Street; and Jonathan's (according to the *Tatler* " the general mart for stock-jobbers ") in 'Change Alley, Cornhill.

4. **the Postman:** one of the principal newspapers of the day, published on Tuesdays, Thursdays, and Saturdays.

5. **politics**: politicians.

6. **blots**: in backgammon the exposure of a piece or "man" so that it is liable to be taken or forfeited is called a blot.

Page 105.

7. **Mr. Buckley's**: Samuel Buckley was the first publisher of the *Spectator*. His address was "the Dolphin in Little Britain."

The Spectator Club

1. Motto: Juvenal, *Satires* vii, 166–167: "But six others or more cry out with one voice."

2. **my Lord Rochester**: John Wilmot, Earl of Rochester (1647–1680), a poet and man of fashion in the time of Charles II. Pepys said of him in his *Diary* (Feb. 17, 1669) that it was "to the King's everlasting shame to have so idle a rogue his companion."

3. **Sir George Etherege**: a comic dramatist of the Restoration period (cir. 1635–1691), a companion of Rochester in many wild escapades. In 1676 both men were obliged to leave England on account of a brawl.

4. **Bully Dawson**: a celebrated London sharper, contemporary with Etherege and Rochester.

Page 106.

5. **a justice of the quorum**: one of the justices of peace of a county, whose presence was necessary to constitute a court.

6. **a quarter session**: a local county court meeting every quarter.

7. **Inner Temple**: see note 4 to page 83.

8. **Aristotle and Longinus**: two ancient Greek critics whose reputation was especially high during the period of neoclassicism. Longinus (210–273 A.D.) was the reputed author of a treatise *On the Sublime*. Aristotle's (384–322 B.C.) critical work was the *Poetics*, an essay treating principally of the laws of drama.

9. **Littleton or Coke**: Sir Thomas Littleton (1402–1481), an English jurist, was the author of a work on land tenures which, with the commentary by Sir Edward Coke (1552–1634), was long the authority on the English law of real property.

Page 109.

10. **Duke of Monmouth**: an illegitimate son of Charles II, much admired in English society for his fine manners and elegant dancing. In 1685 he attempted a rebellion against his uncle James II, but was defeated and executed.

Popular Superstitions

1. Motto: Horace, *Epistles* II, ii, 208–209:

> At magic miracles, hobgoblins, dreams,
> And the portents of Thessaly dost laugh?

2. **join-hand**: writing in which the letters are joined in words — the second stage which an eighteenth-century boy went through in learning to write.

3. **Childermas-day**: the popular term for the festival of the Holy Innocents (December 28), a day on which, according to a common superstition, "it was impossible to have good luck" in any undertaking. The allusion to Thursday, March 8, as "Childermas-day," and Mr. Spectator's reflection on the losing of "a day in every week," have puzzled several editors. Both remarks become clear, however, if one remembers that "Childermas-day" also signified "the day of the week throughout the year answering to the day in which the feast of the Holy Innocents is solemnized" (Dr. Johnson), and that in 1710 (reckoning the year, according to the old style still in use in the early eighteenth century, as extending to March 25) the feast fell on Thursday.

4. **the battle of Almanza**: a battle in the War of the Spanish Succession, in which the English under Lord Galway were defeated by the French and Spaniards. It was fought April 25, 1707.

5. **merry-thought**: the wishbone.

6. **death-watches**: a popular name for certain insects which make a noise like the ticking of a watch — supposed to portend death.

The Purpose of the Spectator

1. Motto: Virgil, *Georgics* i, 201–203:

> So the boat's crew against the current row,
> But if they slack their hands or cease to strive,
> Down with the flood with headlong haste they drive.

2. **My publisher tells me**: "The circulation of the *Spectator*," says Professor Gregory Smith in his note on this passage, "is said to have risen from 3000 to 4000, to 20,000, and even to 30,000 copies. Ten thousand copies probably represented the average issue during the closing months of the daily issue." These figures, whatever their source, are curiously out of

harmony with the evidence as to circulation presented by the essays themselves. After his statement in No. 10, Addison said no more about the sale
of the *Spectator* until No. 262 (Dec. 31, 1711), when he remarked that the
demand for his papers had "increased every month since their first appearance in the world." On July 31 of the next year, speaking of the Stamp
Tax of a halfpenny on each half-sheet which was to go into effect the next
day, and anticipating a falling-off in circulation, he declared that he would
be pleased if his country received five or six pounds a day by his labors.
Now five or six pounds a day in taxes implies a daily circulation of no
more than 2800 copies — surely a modest enough expectation if the circulation before the Stamp Tax was imposed was really as large as Professor
Smith supposes. Even these hopes, however, proved to be too high. In
the last number of the daily issue (No. 555, Dec. 6, 1712) Steele reckoned
that the tax on each half-sheet had netted the Stamp Office on the average something above twenty pounds a week — a sum implying an average
daily circulation of perhaps a little over 1600. As he stated also that at first
the tax had reduced the sale to "less than half the number that was usually
printed before this tax was laid," we are forced to conclude that at no time
could the daily circulation of the *Spectator* have been very much over 3200.
This was somewhat above the circulation enjoyed in 1710 by the official
newspaper, *The London Gazette*. See *The Nation*, July 8, 1915, p. 70.

3. **It was said of Socrates:** Cicero, *Tusculanæ Quæstiones* v, 10.

PAGE 115.

4. **Sir Francis Bacon observes:** *Advancement of Learning*, ii, Introduction, §14.

5. **fellows of the Royal Society:** the Royal Society for the advancement
of mathematics and the natural sciences was incorporated in 1662 after an
informal existence of several years. Its president in 1711 was Sir Isaac
Newton. Addison and Steele in their advocacy of a general literary culture
found much to ridicule in the specialization which was characteristic of
members of the Society. "They seem," Steele wrote in *Tatler* 236, "to
be in a confederacy against men of polite genius, noble thought, and dif-
fusive learning, and choose into their assemblies such as have no pretence
to wisdom but want of wit, or to natural knowledge but ignorance of everything else. I have made observations in this matter so long that when I
meet with a young fellow that is an humble admirer of these sciences, but
more dull than the rest of the company, I conclude him to be a Fellow of
the Royal Society."

6. **Templars:** barristers who were members of the Middle or Inner
Temple. See note 4 to page 83.

Ill-nature in Satire

Page 117.

1. Motto: Virgil, *Æneid* ix, 420–421:

> Fierce Volscens foams with rage, and gazing round
> Descried not him who gave the fatal wound,
> Nor knew to fix revenge ——

Page 118.

2. **a passage in Socrates's behaviour at his death**: see Plato's *Phædo*.

3. **Aristophanes**: the greatest Greek writer of comedy (cir. 450–cir. 380 B.C.). He attacked Socrates in *The Clouds*.

Page 119.

4. **Catullus**: Roman lyric poet (cir. 87–cir. 54 B.C.). For the passage alluded to in the text see *Carmina* xxix.

5. **Cardinal Mazarine**: French statesman and ecclesiastic (1602–1661), the successor of Richelieu as prime minister. The *Callipædia* of Claude Quillet, in which the Cardinal's Sicilian birth was made the subject of a jest, appeared in 1655.

6. **Sextus Quintus**: Sixtus V, Pope from 1585 to 1590.

7. **Pasquin**: an Italian of the late fifteenth century, variously described as a tailor, a cobbler, and a barber. His name was applied to a statue near the Braschi Palace in Rome, on which the populace were wont to affix lampoons, or "pasquinades."

8. **Aretine**: Pietro Aretino (1492–1556), a famous and influential Italian satirist, commonly known as the "Scourge of Princes."

Page 120.

9. **a fable out of Sir Roger l'Estrange**: l'Estrange (1616–1704) published in 1692 a translation of Æsop's *Fables*, which was frequently reprinted, and remained for a long time the most widely read version. A fourth edition appeared in 1704.

Meditations in Westminster Abbey

Page 121.

1. Motto: Horace, *Odes* I, iv, 13 ff.:

> Intruding death, with equal freedom, greets
>   The low-built huts and stately gates
> Of lofty palaces and royal seats.
> Be wise, O Sestius! to prolong forbear,
>   Since life is short, thy hopes and care;
> The fabled shades and gloomy state draw near.

PAGE 122.

    2. **Homer:** *Iliad* xvii, 216.

    3. **Virgil:** *Æneid* vi, 483.

    4. **in holy writ:** The Wisdom of Solomon v, 12–13.

PAGE 123.

    5. **Blenheim:** an English victory in the War of the Spanish Succession (1701–1713), won August 13, 1704. Addison celebrated it at the time in his poem *The Campaign* (1705).

    6. **Sir Cloudesly Shovel:** an English admiral (cir. 1650–1707). He met his death by drowning when his ship was wrecked off the Scilly Islands.

COFFEE-HOUSE COMPANY

PAGE 124.

    1. **Motto:** Martial, *Epigrams* X, iv, 10: " Our book most strongly savors of the man."

    2. **coffee-houses:** for an extended description of the London coffee-houses of the early eighteenth century, see Ashton, *Social Life in the Reign of Queen Anne*, chaps. xviii, xix.

PAGE 125.

    3. **Westminster:** where the Law Courts were situated.

    4. **coffee-houses adjacent to the law:** near the Inns of Court.

PAGE 127.

    5. **Tom the Tyrant:** the head waiter at White's Coffee-house.

THE JOURNAL OF THE INDIAN KINGS

According to Swift the ultimate source of this paper was a hint given by him to Steele. In the *Journal to Stella* on April 28 he wrote: " The *Spectator* is written by Steele with Addison's help; 't is often very pretty. Yesterday it was made of a noble hint I gave him long ago for his *Tatlers*, about an Indian supposed to write his travels into England. I repent he ever had it. I intended to have written a book on that subject. I believe he has spent it all in one paper, and all the under hints there are mine too." The essay belongs to a large group of similar satires, of which the best known in English is Goldsmith's *Letters from a Citizen of the World*. For a partial list see Wendell and Greenough, *Selections from the Writings of Joseph Addison*, p. 306 (Ginn and Company, Boston, 1905).

PAGE 128.

    1. **Motto:** Juvenal, *Satires* xiv, 321: " Nature and Wisdom always say the same."

2. **the four Indian kings**: in April 1710 four (or, according to some reports, five) Iroquois chieftains paid a visit to England. Their ostensible purpose was to urge Queen Anne to drive the French out of Canada; in reality their visit was a scheme of the English colonial authorities to impress them with the greatness of England. During their stay in London they received a good deal of attention: their portraits were painted and engraved; their alleged speech before the queen was circulated in pamphlet form; ballads were written about them; and Steele introduced an account of them into the *Tatler* (No. 171, May 13, 1710).

3. **the Six Nations**: the "Six Nations," or Iroquois Confederacy, were formed out of the earlier "Five Nations" by the accession of the Tuscaroras. As this event did not take place until some time between 1712 and 1722 (*Handbook of American Indians*, Part II, pp. 846–847), it is difficult to see how Addison came by the name in 1711.

THE EDUCATION OF GIRLS

PAGE 131.

1. Motto: Horace, *Odes* III, vi, 21–24:

> The blooming virgin, ripe for man,
> A thousand wanton airs displays;
> Trained to the dance, her well-wrought limbs she moves,
> And sates her wishing soul with loose incestuous loves.

2. **The two following letters**: according to Henry Morley, these letters were written by John Hughes (1677–1720), a critic and miscellaneous writer and an occasional contributor to the *Spectator*.

3. **the Belle Sauvage**: see *Spectator* 28.

SIR ROGER DE COVERLEY AT HOME

PAGE 133.

1. Motto: Horace, *Odes* I, xvii, 14–16:

> Here to thee shall Plenty flow,
> And all her riches show,
> To raise the honours of the quiet plain.

PAGE 136.

2. **the bishop of St. Asaph**: the allusion may be either to William Beveridge (1637–1708) or to William Fleetwood (1656–1723), probably to the former.

3. **Dr. South**: Robert South (1633–1716), one of the most admired English preachers of the time.

4. **Archbishop Tillotson:** John Tillotson (1630–1694), Archbishop of Canterbury from 1691 to his death.

5. **Dr. Barrow:** Isaac Barrow (1630–1677).

6. **Dr. Calamy:** Benjamin Calamy (1642–1686).

THE CHARACTER OF WILL WIMBLE

PAGE 137.

1. Motto: Phædrus, *Fables* II, v, 3: "Puffing hard, and making much to-do about nothing."

2. **the character . . . of the gentleman:** "The passage following," write Professors Wendell and Greenough (*Selections from the Writings of Joseph Addison*, p. 313) "makes this paper especially interesting in the development of character writing in England. It shows the formal character embedded in what is almost a scene from a novel; furthermore, it shows the character differing from the earlier work of Overbury, Earle, and others, in that the person here has a name, and that the characterization of him, though not in direct discourse, is really put into the mouth of one of the other persons in the story." See Introduction, pp. xxxi–xxxii.

3. **May-fly:** here of course an artificial fly made in imitation of the May-fly.

THE STORY OF EUDOXUS AND LEONTINE

PAGE 140.

1. Motto: Horace, *Odes* IV, iv, 33–36:

> Yet the best blood by learning is refined,
> And virtue arms the solid mind;
> Whilst vice will stain the noblest race,
> And the paternal stamp efface.

PAGE 141.

2. **according to Mr. Cowley:** Addison was thinking of the following sentence of Cowley's essay on "The Danger of Procrastination": "But there is no fooling with life, when it is once turned beyond forty."

THE VISION OF MIRZA

PAGE 144.

1. Motto: Virgil, *Æneid* ii, 604–606:

> —— While I dissolve
> The mists and films that mortal eyes involve,
> Purge from your sight the dross ——

2. **Grand Cairo:** see *Spectator* 1.

A Coquette's Heart

PAGE 148.

1. Motto: Virgil, *Æneid* iv, 64: " He anxiously the panting entrails views."

2. **the dissection of the beau's head:** see *Spectator* 275.

PAGE 149.

3. **mucro:** the top or sharp point of anything.

PAGE 150.

4. **a Gordian knot:** here any closely or intricately tied knot. The cutting of the original Gordian knot (so called from Gordius, king of Phrygia, who tied it) was one of the exploits of Alexander the Great most celebrated in legend.

PAGE 151.

5. **salamandrine:** having the qualities of a salamander, which, according to popular belief, was supposed to live in fire.

Clarinda's Journal

1. Motto: Ovid, *Metamorphoses* iv, 280: " One while a man, another while a woman."

2. **The journal with which I presented my reader:** the journal of a citizen. See *Spectator* 317.

3. **Mohock:** " One of a class of aristocratic ruffians who infested the streets of London in the early years of the eighteenth century" (New English Dictionary). They seem to have been especially active in 1712. See Ashton, *Social Life in the Reign of Queen Anne*, chap. xxxvii, and *Spectator* 324, in which a correspondent describes the usages of the Mohock Club.

PAGE 152.

4. **an exercise:** an allusion to Addison's words in *Spectator* 317: " I would . . . recommend to every one of my readers the keeping a journal of their lives for one week and setting down punctually their whole series of employments during that space of time."

5. **a new head:** a new method of hairdressing.

PAGE 153.

6. **basset:** an obsolete game of cards, resembling faro, popular in the early eighteenth century.

7. **punted:** a term in basset, meaning " laid a stake against the bank."

8. **Aurengzebe:** the title of one of Dryden's "heroic dramas" (published 1676).

9. **tire-woman**: a lady's maid.

10. **crimp**: an obsolete game of cards.

11. **Cupid and Veny**: familiar names for lapdogs. Veny = Venus.

12. **skuttle**: a mincing, affected method of walking.

13. **Indamora**: the name of a captive queen in Dryden's *Aurengzebe*.

PAGE 154.

14. **Nicolini**: Nicolino Grimaldi (1673–1726), an Italian opera singer who came to England in 1708 and was immensely popular with English society.

15. **mobs**: the word may signify either a type of loosely fitting cap much worn at the time, or negligé attire in general. The latter meaning appears in the following phrase from *Spectator* 302: "wrapping gowns and dirty linen, with all that huddled economy of dress which passes under the general name of a mob."

16. **dumb man**: Duncan Campbell (1680?–1730), a dumb astrologer and fortune teller much in demand in the early eighteenth century. He is the subject of one of Defoe's pamphlets.

PAGE 155.

17. **an uncertain author**: probably William Browne (1591–1643?), best known as a writer of pastoral poetry. The lines have, however, been attributed to Ben Jonson.

CHEERFULNESS

1. Motto: Horace, *Odes* II, iii, 1–4:

> An even mind in every state,
> Amidst the frowns and smiles of fate,
>   Dear mortal Delius always show.
> Let not too much of cloudy fear,
> Nor too intemperate joys appear,
>   Or to contract or to extend thy brow.

LITERARY TASTE

PAGE 159.

1. Motto: Lucretius, *De Rerum Natura* i, 933:

> —— To hit
> Each subject with the best address and wit.

2. **Gratian**: Baltasar Gracián (d. 1658), a Spanish Jesuit, the author of an important and influential treatise on style.

3. **sensitive**: pertaining to the senses as opposed to the mind.

Page 160.

4. **Livy**: Titus Livius (59 B.C.–17 A.D.), the historian of the early days of Rome.

5. **Sallust**: Roman historian (86–34 B.C.); his two chief works dealt with the conspiracy of Catiline and the Jugurthine War.

Page 161.

6. **Tacitus**: Roman historian (cir. 55–cir. 117 A.D.).

Page 162.

7. **Corneille, etc.**: all of these writers were Frenchmen of the age of Louis XIV. Corneille (1606–1684) and Racine (1639–1699) were writers of tragedy; Molière (1622–1673) was the most eminent of French comic dramatists; La Fontaine (1621–1695) was the greatest of French fabulists; La Bruyère (1645–1696) was an essayist and social critic; Boileau (1636–1711), Le Bossu (1631–1680), and the Daciers — André (1651–1722) and his wife Anne (1654–1720) — were literary critics.

8. **Longinus**: Diogenes Cassius Longinus (cir. 210–273 A.D.), a Greek writer and statesman, to whom has been attributed one of the best-known critical works of antiquity, a treatise *On the Sublime*.

9. **forced conceits**: extravagantly ingenious or far-fetched comparisons and illustrations. Antipathy to "conceits" was one of the distinguishing marks of the "classical" movement in English poetry. Cf. *Spectator* 62, in which Addison contrasts "mixed wit," or conceit, with "that beautiful simplicity which we so much admire in the compositions of the ancients."

10. **Gothic**: on this word see note 5 to page 94.

11. **I entertained the town for a week**: May 7 to May 12, 1711. See *Spectator* 58–63.

Page 163.

12. **I have . . . examined the works of the greatest poet**: Addison's papers on Milton appeared in the *Spectator* on Saturdays from No. 267 to No. 369.

13. **an essay on The Pleasures of the Imagination**: see Nos. 411–421.

On Raillery

1. Motto: Cicero, *Epistolæ ad Familiares* vii, 1 : "I have writ this, not through the abundance of leisure, but of love towards thee."

Page 164.

2. **Calisthenes**: the original of this "character" has been supposed to be Addison.

Page 166.

3. **Mr. Congreve's " Doris " :** William Congreve (1670–1729), though he wrote some society verse of the type quoted by Steele, is best known as a comic dramatist, the author of four of the most brilliantly witty comedies of the Restoration school.

On Gardens

Page 167.

1. Motto : Horace, *Odes* III, iv, 5–8 :

> —— Or airy frenzies cheat
> My mind well pleased with the deceit!
> I seem to hear, I seem to move,
> And wander through the happy grove,
> Where smooth springs flow, and murmuring breeze
> Does wanton through the waving trees.

2. **your thoughts upon some of our English gardens :** see *Spectator* 414.

3. **kitchen and parterre :** kitchen-garden (or vegetable garden) and flower garden.

Page 168.

4. **plats of willow :** plots or patches.

5. **treillages :** trellises.

6. **Wise and London :** a celebrated firm of London gardeners, largely responsible for the vogue in England of the formal Dutch garden, against which the present essay was one of the earliest protests.

Page 169.

7. **the Pindaric manner :** in the manner of Pindar (cir. 522–443 B.C.), the Greek lyric poet. What his "manner" was conceived to be in the early eighteenth century appears in the following sentence from *Spectator* 160 (by Addison): " Pindar was a great genius of the first class, who was hurried on by a natural fire and impetuosity to vast conceptions of things, and noble sallies of imagination."

Page 170.

8. **that vernal delight which you have somewhere taken notice of :** see *Spectator* 393.

THE RAMBLER

The text of the *Rambler* given here is based upon the last edition revised by Johnson, as reprinted by Chalmers in *British Essayists* (1803).

THE FOLLY OF ANTICIPATING MISFORTUNES

PAGE 171.

1. Motto: Horace, *Odes* III, xxix, 29–32:

> But God has wisely hid from human sight
>   The dark decrees of future fate,
> And sown their seeds in depth of night;
>   He laughs at all the giddy turns of state,
>   When mortals search too soon, and fear too late. — Dryden.

PAGE 174.

2. **old Cornaro:** Luigi Cornaro, an Italian writer on health, the author of a treatise on temperance and sobriety (1588).

PAGE 175.

3. **Taylor:** Jeremy Taylor (1613–1667), an eloquent English divine and religious writer; his chief works are *Holy Living* and *Holy Dying*.

THE MISERY OF A FASHIONABLE LADY IN THE COUNTRY

1. Motto: Horace, *Epistles* I, i, 23: "How heavily my time revolves along."

PAGE 178.

2. **At last economy prevailed:** "economy" is used here in the sense of domestic management.

THE CITIZEN OF THE WORLD

Goldsmith's Chinese letters were originally published in the *Public Ledger*, a newspaper edited by John Newbery, between January 24, 1760, and August 14, 1761. They were reissued in book form in 1762. The present text is that of the third edition (1774).

THE CHINESE PHILOSOPHER IN ENGLAND

PAGE 180.

1. **a factor at Canton:** a commercial agent.

FIRST IMPRESSIONS OF ENGLAND

PAGE 182.

1. **a paltry piece of painting:** signs were still largely used in the middle of the eighteenth century to designate houses.

THE CHARACTER OF BEAU TIBBS

PAGE 192.

1. **mandarine :** a toy representing a grotesque seated figure in Chinese costume.

A VISIT TO A LONDON SILK MERCHANT

PAGE 194.

1. **as they say in Cheapside :** a phrase equivalent to " as they say among us merchants." Cheapside is a street in the City, or business section of London.

CHARLES LAMB

Of the essays included in this selection, " Detached Thoughts," " Old China," " Poor Relations," and " The Superannuated Man " were first collected in the *Last Essays of Elia* (1833); all the others were included in the *Essays of Elia* (1823).

A BACHELOR'S COMPLAINT OF THE BEHAVIOUR OF MARRIED PEOPLE

PAGE 198.

1. **free of the company :** having the rights and privileges of membership in the guild.

2. **bring our spices, myrrh, and incense :** probably an allusion to the gifts of the Magi to the infant Jesus; see Matthew ii, 11.

3. **" Like as the arrows," etc. :** see Psalm cxxvii, 4–5.

PAGE 199.

4. **per se :** of themselves, because of their own individuality.

PAGE 200.

5. **One daisy differs not much, etc. :** probably a recollection of 1 Corinthians xv, 41.

PAGE 201.

6. **humorist :** an eccentric person.

7. **" decent affection and complacent kindness " :** from *Douglas*, I, i, 43, a tragedy by John Home (1722–1808).

PAGE 203.

8. **Morellas :** cultivated dark cherries, named after a town in Spain.

VALENTINE'S DAY

1. **Archflamen :** a flamen was a Roman priest devoted to the service of a particular god.

2. **tippet, rochet**: ecclesiastical garments, the former a kind of cape, the latter a close-fitting vestment of linen.

3. **Jerome**: Saint Jerome (d. 420), one of the fathers of the Latin church, translated the Vulgate version of the Bible from Hebrew into Latin.

4. **Ambrose**: Saint Ambrose (d. 397), Bishop of Milan and one of the fathers of the Latin church.

5. **Cyril**: Saint Cyril (d. 444), Archbishop of Alexandria and noted controversial theologian.

6. **Austin**: Saint Augustine (354–430), the most famous of the church fathers; he taught that unbaptized infants were damned.

PAGE 204.

7. **Origen**: (d. 253), one of the Greek fathers of the church and a prolific theological writer; the reason for Lamb's statement that he "hated all mothers" is not apparent.

8. **Bishop Bull, etc.**: George Bull (1634–1710), Bishop of St. David's.

9. **Archbishop Parker**: Matthew Parker (1504–1575), Archbishop of Canterbury.

10. **Whitgift**: John Whitgift (1530?–1604), Archbishop of Canterbury.

11. **"Brush'd with the hiss of rustling wings"**: *Paradise Lost*, i, 768.

12. **"gives a very echo to the throne where Hope is seated"**: see *Twelfth Night*, II, iv, 21–22.

PAGE 205.

13. **the raven himself was hoarse, etc.**: see *Macbeth*, I, v, 39–40.

14. **"having been will always be"**: see Wordsworth's *Ode on the Intimations of Immortality*, ll. 182–183.

15. **E. B.**: Edward Burney (1760–1848), an illustrator and the brother of Frances Burney, the novelist.

PAGE 206.

16. **Ovid**: Publius Ovidius Naso (43 B.C.–17 or 18 A.D.), one of the great Roman poets of the Augustan age; his subjects were usually amatory or mythological.

17. **Pyramus and Thisbe**: a pair of devoted and unfortunate lovers, whose story is told in Ovid's *Metamorphoses*.

18. **Dido**: the beautiful queen of Carthage, loved by Æneas, but later abandoned by him. Her story is told in part in Ovid's *Heroides* as well as in Book IV of the *Æneid*.

19. **Hero and Leander**: the beautiful priestess of Venus and her gallant lover, the central figures of a tragic love story told in Latin by Ovid and in English by Marlowe and Chapman.

20. **Cayster:** a river abounding in swans; see *Iliad* ii, 459 ff. (in Bryant's translation, 566 ff.).

21. **Iris:** in Greek mythology the messenger of the gods or the personification of the rainbow. "Iris dipt the woof" is in *Paradise Lost*, xi, 244.

22. **Good-morrow to my Valentine, sings poor Ophelia:** see *Hamlet*, IV, v, 46–51.

Christ's Hospital Five-and-Thirty Years Ago

Page 207.

1. **Christ's Hospital:** a famous charity school for boys, founded in 1552 by Edward VI in the buildings formerly belonging to the dissolved order of Grey Friars.

2. **eulogy on my old school:** *Recollections of Christ's Hospital*, first published in the *Gentleman's Magazine* (1813) and reprinted with some changes in Lamb's *Works* (1818).

3. **I remember L. at school:** in this essay Lamb is not purely autobiographical, but purposely confuses Coleridge's experiences with his own.

4. **crug:** still current slang in Christ's Hospital.

5. **piggins:** small wooden pails.

6. **pitched leathern jack:** a leather jug or bottle, covered with pitch to prevent leakage.

7. **banyan days:** vegetarian days.

8. **double-refined:** sugar.

9. **caro equina:** horseflesh.

10. **crags:** necks.

Page 208.

11. **griskin:** the lean part of a loin of pork.

12. **good old relative:** Lamb's aunt, Sarah Lamb (d. 1797).

13. **the Tishbite:** Elijah (see 1 Kings xvii).

14. **Calne in Wiltshire:** Lamb is here writing as Coleridge, who actually came from Ottery St. Mary, Devonshire.

Page 209.

15. **Lions in the Tower:** the lions, formerly one of the sights of the Tower of London, were transferred to the Zoölogical Gardens in 1831.

Page 210.

16. **H——, etc.:** in Lamb's *Key* H's name is given as Hodges; Nevis and St. Kitts are islands in the West Indies; James Webb Tobin, the grandson of a rich sugar planter, died at Nevis in 1814.

17. **Nero:** a Roman emperor (54–68) whose name has become a synonym for a wantonly cruel tyrant.

18. **leads:** the roof, covered with sheets of lead.

19. **Caligula's minion:** a horse which the mad Roman emperor, Caligula (37–41), fed on gilded oats and made chief consul.

20. **waxing fat, and kicking:** see Deuteronomy xxxii, 15.

21. **ram's horn blast . . . Jericho:** see Joshua vi.

22. **Smithfield:** where there was a horse and cattle market.

23. **Perry:** John Perry, mentioned in the *Recollections*, was steward from 1761 to 1785.

PAGE 211.

24. **grand paintings "by Verrio":** the picture especially referred to represents James II receiving the members of Christ's Hospital; Verrio (1634–1707) was an Italian historical painter.

25. **harpies:** the creatures, part bird and part woman, who carried away or defiled the feast of the Trojans; see *Æneid* iii, 225 ff.

26. **Trojan in the hall of Dido:** Æneas tried to gain comfort by gazing on the Trojan scenes depicted in the temple being erected by Dido; "*Animum pictura pascit inani*" — *Æneid* i, 464.

27. **goul:** usually spelled "ghoul"; an evil spirit that preys upon corpses.

28. "—— 'T was said
    He ate strange flesh": see *Antony and Cleopatra*, I, iv, 67–68.

29. **the accursed thing:** see Joshua vii, 13.

PAGE 212.

30. **young stork:** it was once believed that young storks fed and tended the parent birds.

PAGE 213.

31. **auto da fe:** execution of heretics by the Inquisition; the phrase literally means "act of faith."

32. **"watchet weeds":** blue clothes; the outer dress of the Christ's Hospital boys is a blue coat reaching to the heels, from which they have the name "Blue-coat Boys."

33. **disfigurements in Dante:** see, for example, Canto 28 of the *Inferno*, where Dante describes the horrible mutilations and disfigurements by which the guilty are punished.

34. **Howard:** John Howard (1726–1790), the English prison reformer.

PAGE 214.

35. **Ultima Supplicia:** extreme punishments.

36. **lictor:** the officer attending the highest Roman magistrates and executing sentence upon criminals.

37. **San Benito:** the robe worn by the victim of an *auto da fé*.

38. **inhabitants on the two sides of the Pyrenees:** the proverbially gay French and grave Spaniards.

PAGE 215.

39. **"like a dancer":** see *Antony and Cleopatra*, III, xi, 35–36.

40. **"insolent Greece or haughty Rome":** from Ben Jonson's (1573?–1637) *To the Memory of My Beloved, Master William Shakespeare*, l. 39.

41. **Peter Wilkins, etc.:** the first two are stories of travel and marvelous experiences; the last, the story of the rise of a Blue-coat boy through a rich marriage.

42. **Rousseau and John Locke:** Jean Jacques Rousseau (1712–1778) in *Émile*, and John Locke (1632–1704) in *Some Thoughts concerning Education*, advocated educational methods that should force the child less and take more account of his natural inclinations.

43. **Phædrus:** a writer of Latin fables in verse (first century A.D.).

PAGE 216.

44. **Helots to his young Spartans:** Spartan parents exhibited to their sons drunken serfs (Helots) as deterrent examples.

45. **Xenophon:** (cir. 430–after 357 B.C.), the Greek essayist and historian, author of the *Anabasis*.

46. **Plato:** (cir. 429–347 B.C.), the Greek philosopher, disciple of Socrates and teacher of Aristotle.

47. **the Samite:** Pythagoras of Samos (sixth century B.C.), whose pupils were not to speak of his teachings until after they had listened for five years.

48. **Goshen:** the home of the Israelites in Egypt. It was exempted from the plague of flies; see Genesis xlvii and Exodus viii, 22.

49. **Gideon's miracle:** see Judges vi, 37–38. Lamb's reference to Cowley in the note is to stanza 7 of the latter's *Complaint*.

50. **"playing holiday":** see *1 Henry IV*, I, ii, 227.

51. **Ululantes:** howling sufferers. — **Tartarus:** the infernal regions; see *Æneid* vi, 548 ff.

52. **scrannel pipes:**

> —— Their lean and flashy songs
> Grate on their scrannel pipes of wretched straw.
>
> Milton, *Lycidas*, 123–124

53. **Garrick:** David Garrick (1717–1779), probably the greatest English actor-manager, whose death "eclipsed the gayety of nations."

PAGE 217.

54. **Flaccus's quibble, etc.**: Horace, *Satires* I, vii, 34–35 — a play upon *rex* as King, a personal name, and as king, a monarch. — **tristis severitas in vultu**: gloomy severity in his face (*Andria* V, ii, 16). — **inspicere in patinas**: look into your saucepans (*Adelphœ* III, iii, 74–75). — **vis**: force. The jests really are so thin as not to deserve extended commentary.

55. **comet expounded**: the appearance of a comet was formerly believed to forebode great disasters.

56. **rabidus furor**: mad rage.

57. **forewarned**: expressly forbidden.

PAGE 218.

58. **Coleridge, in his literary life**: *Biographia Literaria*, chap. i.

59. **author of the Country Spectator**: Thomas Fanshaw Middleton; see the next paragraph of the essay.

60. **First Grecian**: the Grecians were the two picked students who each year were given scholarships to Cambridge on the understanding that they should enter the Church.

61. **Dr. T——e**: Arthur William Trollope, who succeeded Boyer as Upper Grammar Master.

62. **fasces**: the bundle of rods bound about an ax and borne before Roman magistrates as the symbol of authority.

63. **Cicero De Amicitia**: Cicero's essay *On Friendship*.

64. **Th——**: Sir Edward Thornton, minister to Sweden, Denmark, and later to Portugal.

PAGE 219.

65. **regni novitas**: infancy of power; see *Æneid* I, 563. Middleton was the first Bishop of Calcutta.

66. **Jewel**: John Jewel (1522–1571), Bishop of Salisbury and author of *Apologia pro Ecclesia Anglicana*.

67. **Hooker**: see note 13 to page 96.

68. **poor S——, ill-fated M——**: according to Lamb's *Key*, Scott, who died in a madhouse, and Maunde, who was expelled from school.

69. **Finding some of Edward's race, etc.**: Matthew Prior's (1664–1721) *Carmen Sæculare* for 1700, stanza 8, has "Finding some of Stuart's race," etc. Lamb changes to Edward, as Christ's Hospital was founded by Edward VI.

70. **fiery column . . . dark pillar**: an allusion to *Exodus* xiii, 21–22.

71. **Mirandula**: Giovanni Pico della Mirandola (1463–1494), a brilliant scholar and philosopher of the Italian Renaissance.

72. **Jamblichus . . . Plotinus:** Neoplatonic philosophers of the third and fourth centuries A.D.

73. **Pindar:** (cir. 522–443 B.C.), the greatest Greek lyric poet.

74. **C. V. Le G——:** Charles Valentine Le Grice in Lamb's *Key*.

75. **words of old Fuller:** an adaptation of the famous passage in Fuller's *Worthies* concerning Shakespeare and Ben Jonson.

PAGE 220.

76. **Nireus formosus:** handsome Nireus, the handsomest of the Greeks in the war against Troy; see *Iliad* ii, 673.

77. **junior Le G——:** Samuel Le Grice, who died in the West Indies.

78. **F——:** according to the *Key*, "[Joseph] Favell; left Cambridge, ashamed of his father, who was a house-painter there." A fuller account of him is given as W—— in "Poor Relations," pp. 266–268.

79. **Fr——:** Frederick William Franklin, master of the Hertford branch of Christ's from 1801 to 1827.

80. **T——:** Marmaduke Thompson, to whom Lamb dedicated his *Rosamund Gray*.

THE TWO RACES OF MEN

1. **Parthians, and Medes, and Elamites:** see Acts ii, 9.

PAGE 221.

2. **"He shall serve his brethren":** see Genesis ix, 25.

3. **one of this cast, lean and suspicious:** probably an allusion to Cæsar's characterization of Cassius; see *Julius Cæsar*, I, ii, 192 ff.

4. **Alcibiades:** the celebrated Athenian general and politician, haughty and extravagant; Lamb probably had in mind the figure in *Timon of Athens*.

5. **Falstaff:** see *Henry IV*, *passim*.

6. **Sir Richard Steele:** Sir Richard Steele (1672–1729), the essayist and dramatist, an equally reckless borrower and generous spender.

7. **Brinsley:** Richard Brinsley Sheridan (1751–1816), the dramatist, lived notoriously beyond his means.

8. **no more thought than lilies:** see Matthew vi, 28–29.

9. **meum and tuum:** mine and yours.

10. **simplification of language (beyond Tooke):** as proposed by John Horne Tooke (1736–1812), an English politician and philologist, in his *Diversions of Purley*.

11. **"calleth all the world up to be taxed":** adapted from Luke ii, 1: "there went out a decree . . . that all the world should be taxed."

12. **obolary:** impoverished; an obolus was a very small silver coin.

13. **Candlemas . . . Feast of Holy Michael**: Candlemas (February 2) is a Scotch and Michaelmas (September 29) an English quarter-day, on which payments, particularly of rent, are due.

14. **lene tormentum**: a gentle stimulus; see Horace *Odes* III, xxi, 13.

15. **cloak . . . for which sun and wind contended**: in one of the fables of Æsop.

16. **true Propontic**: probably an allusion to *Othello*, III, iii, 453–456.

PAGE 222.

17. **the reversion promised**: " He that hath pity upon the poor lendeth unto the Lord; and that which he hath given will he pay him again." — Proverbs xix, 17.

18. **penalties of Lazarus and of Dives**: see Luke xvi, 19–26.

19. **Ralph Bigod**: really John Fenwick, a friend of Lamb's of whom little is known. He is again mentioned in " Chimney-Sweepers."

20. **To slacken virtue, etc.**: *Paradise Regained*, ii, 455–456.

21. **like some Alexander . . . " borrowing and to borrow "**: an alteration of Revelations vi, 2 — " conquering and to conquer " — and an application to Alexander the Great, who is said to have wept because he had no more worlds to conquer.

22. **periegesis**: properly a description of a place or region; here used in the sense of a journey about, a tour.

PAGE 223.

23. **" stocked with so fair a herd "**: see Milton's *Comus*, 152.

24. **Hagar's offspring**: see Genesis xxi, 9–21.

25. **cana fides**: hoary honor; see *Æneid* i, 292.

26. **mumping visnomy**: sullen countenance.

PAGE 224.

27. **Comberbatch**: Coleridge, who had once enlisted in the dragoons under the name Silas Tomkyn Comberbach.

28. **Switzer-like**: enormous; from the gigantic Swiss Guards formerly in the French service.

29. **Guildhall giants**: the colossal wooden figures known as " Gog and Magog " in the council hall of the City of London.

30. **Bonaventura**: Saint Bonaventura (1221–1274), an Italian scholastic philosopher.

31. **Bellarmine**: Roberto Bellarmino (1542–1621), an Italian cardinal and Jesuit theologian and controversialist.

32. **Holy Thomas**: Saint Thomas Aquinas (cir. 1225–1274), an Italian theologian and one of the greatest of the scholastic philosophers.

33. **Ascapart:** the giant overcome by Sir Bevis of Southampton, the hero of romance.

34. **Brown on Urn Burial:** Sir Thomas Browne (1605–1682). His best-known works are *Religio Medici* and *Hydriotaphia, or Urn-Burial*. He is famed for freshness and ingenuity of mind and for stately eloquence of style. See the motto and first paragraph of " Imperfect Sympathies."

35. **Dodsley's dramas:** Robert Dodsley's *Select Collection of Old Plays* (1744). It first made generally accessible many plays of the Elizabethan period.

36. **Vittoria Corombona:** the central figure of *The White Devil*, a tragedy by John Webster (1580?–1625?).

37. **Priam's refuse sons:** nine of Priam's fifty sons remained after Achilles had slain Hector. See *Iliad* xxiv.

PAGE 225.

38. **Anatomy of Melancholy:** by Robert Burton (1577–1640). It is an infinitely learned treatise on (1) the causes and symptoms of melancholy, (2) its cure, and (3) on erotic and religious melancholy. It is one of the curiosities of English literature and a great mine of quotations.

39. **Complete Angler:** by Izaak Walton (1593–1683). It consists largely of dialogues between Piscator (Angler), Venator (Hunter), and Auceps (Falconer), in which the superior charms of angling are made clear. The work is interspersed with charming lyrics. To the fifth edition Charles Cotton (1630–1687) added a continuation on fly-fishing. It is largely in the form of a dialogue between Piscator, Jr. and Viator (Traveller), who proves to be Venator of the first part. A favorite haunt of Piscator is Trout Hall, " an honest ale-house."

40. **John Buncle:** *The Life of John Buncle, Esq.* by Thomas Amory (1691?–1788), an eccentric writer. John Buncle is married seven times.

41. **deodands:** a deodand is in legal terminology a personal article which, having caused the death of someone, is sold, and the proceeds of which are distributed in charity, that is, given to God.

42. **K.:** James Kenney (1780–1849), a playwright, then living at Versailles.

43. **thrice noble Margaret Newcastle:** besides the *Letters*, Margaret (1624?–1674), wife of the first Duke of Newcastle, wrote *The Life of the Thrice Noble, High, and Puissant Prince, William Cavendish, Duke, Marquis, and Earl of Newcastle*. Both she and her husband were distinguished for their almost fantastic devotion to each other.

44. **Unworthy land, etc.:** these lines were probably invented by Lamb, though the phrase " thy sex's wonder " occurs in Cyril Tourneur's (cir. 1575–1626) *The Atheist's Tragedy*, which Lamb knew well.

PAGE 226.

45. **Fulke Greville, Lord Brook:** (1554–1628), the friend and biographer of Sir Philip Sidney, and the author of many poems and some closet tragedies.

46. **Zimmerman on Solitude:** by Johann Georg von Zimmermann (1728–1795), a Swiss philosophical writer.

IMPERFECT SYMPATHIES

1. Motto: from *Religio Medici*, Pt. II, sect. i; see note 34 to page 224.
2. **Standing on earth, etc.:**

> Standing on earth, not rapt above the pole.
>
> *Paradise Lost*, vii, 23

PAGE 227.

3. **Heywood's Hierarchie of Angels:** the passage is from Book IV, *The Dominations*. Thomas Heywood (died cir. 1650) is best known as a dramatist, though he was also a poet and translator.

PAGE 228.

4. **Minerva . . . in panoply:** Minerva, the goddess of wisdom, sprang fully armed from the head of Jupiter.

5. **true touch:** a reference to the touchstone, by which the purity of gold was tested.

PAGE 229.

6. **John Buncle:** see note 40 to page 225.

7. **print . . . after Leonardo da Vinci:** the picture referred to is the *Virgin of the Rocks*. Leonardo da Vinci (1452–1519) was a famous Italian artist and scientist — the painter of the *Mona Lisa*.

PAGE 230.

8. **Thomson . . . Smollett . . . Rory . . . Hume's History:** James Thomson, the poet of *The Seasons*, and Tobias Smollett, the novelist, were both Scotchmen. The delineation of Rory is in *Roderick Random*, chap. xiii. Smollett wrote a continuation of the *History of England* by David Hume, also a Scotchman.

PAGE 231.

9. **Stonehenge:** a celebrated English prehistoric monument formed of gigantic stones set up on Salisbury Plain.

10. **Hugh of Lincoln:** a Lincoln child who, according to tradition, was the victim of a ritual murder by the Jews. See Chaucer's *Prioress's Tale* for a similar story.

11. **congeeing:** bowing.

12. **keck:** retch, suffer vomiting qualms.

13. **B——:** John Braham (1774?–1856), a great tenor, abandoned Judaism for Christianity.

PAGE 232.

14. **Kemble:** John Philip Kemble (1757–1823), the tragedian, brother of Charles Kemble and Mrs. Siddons.

15. **Jael:** the slayer of Sisera, the enemy of Israel, who had taken refuge in her tent; see Judges iv, 17–22.

16. **"to live with them":** see *Othello*, I, iii, 249.

17. **salads ... Evelyn ... for the angel:** John Evelyn (1620–1706), best known for his *Diary*. The reference here is to his *Acetaria: a Discourse of Sallets*.

18. **To sit a guest with Daniel at his pulse:** see *Paradise Regained*, ii, 278.

PAGE 233.

19. **a more sacred example:** an allusion, probably, to the practice of Jesus when Jewish casuists sought to entrap him.

PAGE 234.

20. **Penn:** William Penn (1644–1718), the founder of Pennsylvania.

DREAM-CHILDREN; A REVERIE

This essay was probably begun very soon after the death of Lamb's brother John on October 26, 1821 — an event which in large measure occasioned the paper and colored its mood.

PAGE 235.

1. **great-grandmother Field:** Lamb's grandmother, Mary Field, who died of cancer in 1792, had been for more than fifty years housekeeper at Blakesware, a countryseat, not in Norfolk but in Hertfordshire. It is, of course, the same place as the subject of the essay "Blakesmoor, in H——shire."

PAGE 238.

2. **seven long years ... I courted the fair Alice W——n:** according to the *Key* the name Alice W——n was "feigned"; in all probability the seven years of courtship was also — in duration, at least — a fiction. Apparently, as a youth, Lamb became tenderly attached to a young Hertfordshire girl, Ann Simmons, — the Anna of his early sonnets and the Alice W——n of the Elia essays, — but by the time he reached the age of

twenty-one his passion for her had died. About the memory of her, however, Lamb continued to gather sentimental longings and fond imaginings.
Ann Simmons married a Mr. Bartrum, a pawnbroker of London.

PAGE 239.

3. **Lethe**: see *Æneid* vi, 748–751, which tells how spirits, after a long
period of probation, drink of Lethe, that they may again be willing to
return to mortal bodies.

THE PRAISE OF CHIMNEY-SWEEPERS

1. **nigritude**: blackness.

PAGE 240.

2. **fauces Averni**: jaws of hell; see *Æneid* vi, 201.

3. **stage direction in Macbeth**: *Macbeth*, IV, i.

4. **kibed**: chapped, cracked with cold.

5. **tester**: a sixpence.

PAGE 241.

6. **fuliginous concretions**: deposits of soot.

PAGE 242.

7. **Hogarth**: William Hogarth (1697–1764), a celebrated English painter
and engraver. His subjects are usually some phase of "town" life, and
his treatment is comic and satiric.

PAGE 243.

8. **"air" them**: probably an allusion to *Cymbeline*, II, iv, 96.

9. **A sable cloud, etc.**: see Milton's *Comus*, 223–224.

10. **Rachels mourning for their children**: see Jeremiah xxxi, 15.

11. **recovery of the young Montagu**: Edward Wortley Montagu, the son
of Lady Mary Wortley Montagu, in one of his runnings away from school
became a chimney sweep.

12. **defiliations**: losses of children.

13. **Howards**: Howard is the surname of the dukes of Norfolk, who,
in the English peerage, rank next after princes of the royal blood.

14. **Venus lulled Ascanius**: see *Æneid* i, 643–722.

PAGE 244.

15. **incunabula**: the literal meaning is "swaddling clothes."

16. **Jem White**: James White (1775–1820), a schoolfellow of Lamb's at
Christ's and the author of a Shakespearean parody or imitation, *Original
Letters, etc. of Sir John Falstaff.*

Page 245.

17. **fair of St. Bartholomew:** formerly held in Smithfield, a locality in London, on September 3. It existed from 1133 to 1855.

18. **not having on the wedding garment:** see Matthew xxii, 11–13.

19. **Bigod:** see "Two Races of Men," pp. 222–224, and note 19 to page 222.

20. **Rochester:** John Wilmot (1647–1680), second Earl of Rochester, a wild companion of Charles II.

21. **universal host would set up, etc.:** see *Paradise Lost*, i, 541–542.

Page 246.

22. **Golden lads and lasses must, etc.:** see *Cymbeline*, IV, ii, 262–263.

Detached Thoughts on Books and Reading

Page 247.

1. **the Relapse:** a comedy by Sir John Vanbrugh (1664–1726).

2. **Shaftesbury:** the third Earl of Shaftesbury (1671–1713), the author of *Characteristics*. Lamb, in "The Genteel Style in Writing," speaks of his "inflated finical rhapsodies."

3. **Jonathan Wild:** *The Life of Jonathan Wild the Great*, by Fielding, is an account of the life of a notorious thief and scoundrel.

4. **biblia a-biblia:** Greek for the preceding "books which are no books."

5. **Hume . . . Jenyns:** David Hume (1711–1776), essayist, skeptical philosopher, and historian of England; Edward Gibbon (1737–1794), historian of Rome; William Robertson (1721–1793), historian; James Beattie (1735–1803), essayist and poet of *The Minstrel*; Soame Jenyns (1704–1787), miscellaneous writer, whose best-known work is *A Free Enquiry into the Nature and Origin of Evil.*

6. **Flavius Josephus:** (37–cir. 95) author of *Jewish Antiquities* and *The History of the Jewish War.*

7. **Paley's Moral Philosophy:** by William Paley (1743–1805), an English theologian and philosopher; it was for a long time the standard work on the subject in English.

Page 248.

8. **Population Essay:** Thomas Robert Malthus (1766–1834) promulgated the "Malthusian Doctrine" in his *Essay on the Principle of Population* (1798); this publication called forth a number of "population essays."

9. **Steele . . . Farquhar . . . Adam Smith:** Sir Richard Steele (1672–1729), comic dramatist and originator of the *Tatler*; George Farquhar (1678–1707), a writer of clever though frequently coarse comedies; Adam

Smith (1723–1790), the political economist. His *Inquiry into the Nature and Causes of the Wealth of Nations* (1776) practically founded the modern science of political economy.

10. **Paracelsus . . . Lully**: Philippus Aureolus Paracelsus (1493–1541) was a celebrated Swiss-German physician and alchemist; Raymond Lully (cir. 1235–1315) was a Spanish alchemist and scholastic philosopher.

11. **Thomson's Seasons**: the poems *The Seasons* and *The Castle of Indolence* by James Thomson (1700–1748) in both form and matter largely continue the tradition of Milton and of Spenser instead of observing the dominant conventions of so-called classicism in English poetry.

12. **Tom Jones**: the greatest novel of Henry Fielding (1707–1754); his others are *Joseph Andrews* and *Amelia*. Fielding began *Joseph Andrews* as a parody on Richardson's *Pamela*, in order to express his disgust with the latter's sentimentality and specious morality. His own novels are marred by coarse passages, but they are unsurpassed in the presentation of life and character and in wise and genial humor.

13. **Vicar of Wakefield**: the delightfully tender and humorous novel by Oliver Goldsmith (1728–1774).

14. **Smollett**: Tobias George Smollett (1721–1771) wrote *Roderick Random*, *Peregrine Pickle*, *Ferdinand, Count Fathom*, *Sir Launcelot Greaves*, and *Humphrey Clinker*. These novels are, as a whole, marked by broad comedy, coarseness of feeling, and bustling action.

15. **Sterne**: Laurence Sterne (1713–1768) was a sentimentalist and whimsical humorist. His chief works are the novels — if they may be called such — *Tristram Shandy* and *A Sentimental Journey through France and Italy*. In addition he wrote the *Sermons of Mr. Yorick*.

PAGE 249.

16. **copies . . . "eterne"**: see *Macbeth*, III, ii, 38.

17. **We know not where, etc.**: see *Othello*, V, ii, 12–13.

18. **Life of the Duke of Newcastle**: see note 43 to page 225.

19. **Sir Philip Sydney**: (1554–1586), poet, romancer, and chivalrous gentleman; author of the sonnet sequence *Astrophel and Stella*, the pastoral romance *Arcadia*, and the critical essay the *Defence of Poesie*.

20. **Bishop Taylor**: see note 3 to page 175.

21. **Fuller**: Thomas Fuller (1608–1661), divine, antiquary, and voluminous writer. His best-known work is the *History of the Worthies of England*, a mine of antiquarian and biographical material. Fuller's style made him one of Lamb's favorite authors.

22. **first folio of Shakspeare**: the first collective edition of Shakespeare's plays, published in 1623.

23. **Beaumont and Fletcher:** Francis Beaumont (1584–1616) and John Fletcher (1579–1625) from about 1607 to 1614–1616 lived in the closest personal and professional intimacy and jointly produced a number of plays. Fletcher, particularly after Beaumont's death, wrote a large number independently or in collaboration with other dramatists; in one or two plays he probably collaborated with Shakespeare before the latter's retirement. Most of the plays in which Fletcher had a hand are loosely grouped as Beaumont and Fletcher's. Both Beaumont and Fletcher wrote poetry other than plays.

24. **Anatomy of Melancholy:** see note 38 to page 225.

PAGE 250.

25. **Malone:** Edmund Malone (1741–1812), Shakespearean critic and editor.

26. **Kit Marlowe . . . Cowley:** Christopher Marlowe (1564–1593), poet, and the greatest of Shakespeare's English predecessors as dramatist. Michael Drayton (1563–1631), a writer of English patriotic and love poems. William Drummond of Hawthornden (1585–1649), a Scotch poet; he also published *Notes of Ben Jonson's Conversations*. Abraham Cowley (1618–1667), poet and essayist.

27. **Bishop Andrewes:** Lancelot Andrewes (1555–1626), Bishop of Winchester, and one of the translators of the King James version of the Bible.

PAGE 251.

28. **pro bono publico:** for the general good.

29. **Nando's:** a London coffee-house, near which Lamb once lived.

30. **Candide:** by (François Marie Arouet) Voltaire (1694–1778). It is a romance satirizing philosophical optimism; it is not at all the book of a devout churchgoer and in passages is highly indecent.

31. **Cythera:** a Grecian island sacred to Venus.

PAGE 252.

32. **Pamela:** Richardson's *Pamela, or Virtue Rewarded* is the story of a servant girl who resists her master's attacks upon her virtue and is at last rewarded by marriage to him.

33. **Lardner:** Nathaniel Lardner (1684–1768), a nonconformist theologian.

34. **the five points:** the cardinal tenets of Calvinistic doctrine — Original Sin, Predestination, Irresistible Grace, Particular Redemption, and the Final Perseverance of the Saints.

35. **"snatch a fearful joy":** Thomas Gray (1716–1771), *Ode on a Distant Prospect of Eton College*, 40.

36. **Martin B——:** Martin Burney, a friend of the Lambs, to whom Lamb dedicated the prose part of his *Works* in 1818.

37. **Clarissa**: *Clarissa Harlowe*, Richardson's greatest novel.

38. **A quaint poetess**: Lamb's sister, Mary. The poem is in *Poetry for Children* (1809) by Charles and Mary Lamb.

MODERN GALLANTRY

PAGE 254.

1. **Dorimant**: a man of fashion in the Restoration comedy, *The Man of Mode*, by Sir George Etherege (1635?–1691).

2. **poor woman . . . passing to her parish**: on her way to the almshouse.

PAGE 255.

3. **Eld**: old age.

4. **Preux Chevalier**: gallant knight.

5. **Sir Calidore**: the hero of Book VI of the *Faerie Queene* and the pattern of courtesy.

6. **Sir Tristan**: one of the most famous heroes of the romances of chivalry; see, for example, Malory, Book VIII.

OLD CHINA

PAGE 258.

1. **terra firma**: solid earth.

2. **the hays**: an old English dance.

3. **couchant**: here used in the heraldic sense — lying with the body resting on the legs and the head raised.

4. **Cathay**: a poetical name for China.

PAGE 259.

5. **Hyson**: a fragrant green tea.

6. **cousin . . . Bridget**: Lamb's sister, Mary. In the *Essays of Elia* Lamb always speaks of his sister as his "cousin Bridget."

7. **speciosa miracula**: shining wonders; Horace, *Ars Poetica* 144.

8. **Beaumont and Fletcher**: see note 23 to page 249.

PAGE 260.

9. **corbeau**: dark green, almost black.

10. **Lionardo . . . Lady Blanch**: on Leonardo see note 7 to page 229. The *Lady Blanch* is usually called *Modesty and Vanity*.

11. **Izaak Walton . . . Piscator . . . Trout Hall**: see note 39 to page 225.

PAGE 261.

12. **Battle of Hexham . . . Surrender of Calais**: comedies by George Colman the Younger (1762–1836).

13. **Bannister . . . Mrs. Bland**: John Bannister (1760–1836), a noted comedian; Mrs. Bland (1769–1838), a popular actress and singer.

14. **the Children in the Wood**: a "pathetic afterpiece" by Thomas Morton (1764–1838). In another play he invented Mrs. Grundy.

15. **Rosalind**: in *As You Like It*; Viola: in *Twelfth Night*.

PAGE 262.

16. **"lusty brimmers"** . . . **Mr. Cotton**: in Lamb's essay on "New Year's Eve" he used the phrase "hearty, cheerful Mr. Cotton," and quoted a poem by him, *The New Year*, which contains the lines:

> Then let us welcome the New Guest
> With lusty brimmers of the best.

Charles Cotton (1630–1687) is known as a poet, the translator of Montaigne's *Essais*, and the continuator of Walton's *Compleat Angler*.

PAGE 263.

17. **Crœsus**: the fabulously wealthy King of Lydia in the sixth century B.C.

18. **great Jew R——**: probably Nathan Meyer Rothschild (1777–1836), the founder of the English branch of the famous banking family.

POOR RELATIONS

Note the conformity of the first two paragraphs of this essay to the pattern of the seventeenth-century "characters."

PAGE 264.

1. **Agathocles' pot**: Agathocles, who became Tyrant of Syracuse, was the son of a humble potter.

2. **a Mordecai in your gate**: Esther iii, 2.

3. **a Lazarus at your door**: Luke xvi, 20.

4. **a lion in your path**: 1 Kings xiii, 24.

5. **a frog in your chamber**: Exodus viii, 3.

6. **a fly in your ointment**: Ecclesiastes x, 1.

7. **a mote in your eye**: Matthew vii, 3.

8. **the one thing not needful**: Luke x, 42.

9. **the hail in harvest**: Proverbs xxvi, 1; the phrase there, however, is "rain in harvest."

PAGE 265.

10. **tide waiter**: customs inspector.

PAGE 266.

11. **aliquando sufflaminandus erat**: the Latin equivalent of the preceding phrase, "He may require to be repressed sometimes."

12. **Richard Amlet**: a character in the comedy *The Confederacy*, by Sir John Vanbrugh (1664–1726).

13. **Poor W——:** the F—— (Favel) of "Christ's Hospital"; see note 78 to page 220.

PAGE 267.

14. **servitor's gown:** a servitor is at Oxford a student partly supported by the college; the corresponding term at Cambridge is "sizar." It was formerly the duty of such students to wait at table.

15. **Nessian venom:** Hercules was killed by wearing a shirt that had been dipped in the poisonous blood of the centaur Nessus.

16. **Latimer . . . Hooker:** Hugh Latimer (1485–1555), Bishop of Worcester and powerful in the English Reformation, had been a sizar at Cambridge, and Richard Hooker (cir. 1553–1600), the famous theologian, a servitor at Oxford.

PAGE 268.

17. **Artist Evangelist:** St. Luke, according to tradition, was a painter as well as a physician.

18. **like Satan, "knew his mounted sign — and fled ":** see *Paradise Lost*, iv, 1013–1015.

PAGE 269.

19. **at Lincoln:** the Lambs came from Lincolnshire.

20. **young Grotiuses:** Hugo Grotius (1583–1645), the famous Dutch jurist, wrote *De Jure Belli et Pacis*.

THE SUPERANNUATED MAN

The account of himself that Lamb gives in this essay is substantially true to fact, except that he had actually been employed in the East India House instead of by a private firm. On March 29, 1825, after thirty-three years of service, he was retired on an annual pension of £441.

PAGE 271.

1. **Motto:** "Freedom has at last looked upon me": somewhat adapted from Virgil's *Eclogues* i, 28.

2. **O'Keefe:** John O'Keefe (1747–1833), a prolific writer of light stage pieces.

3. **Mincing Lane:** a London street, the center of the colonial trade.

PAGE 272.

4. **native fields of Hertfordshire:** Lamb was a Londoner born and bred, but his mother was from Hertfordshire and he had frequently visited his grandmother in that county. See "Mackery End."

5. **the wood had entered into my soul:** "The iron entered into his soul." — Psalm cv, 18 (Prayer-book version).

PAGE 273.

6. **L——** : the Lacy, as **B——** is the Boldero of " the house of Boldero, Merryweather, Bosanquet, and Lacy." Under the disguise of a private firm of merchants are represented the directors of the India House.

PAGE 274.

7. **Esto perpetua** : Be thou perpetual.

8. **Old Bastile** : the infamous state prison in Paris, stormed by the Revolutionary mob on July 14, 1789.

9. **like the man — "that's born," etc.** :

> I know no more the way to temporal rule,
> Than he that's born and has his years come to him
> In a rough desert.

The lines are from *The Mayor of Quinborough*, I, i, 102–103, a comedy by Thomas Middleton (1570–1627).

PAGE 275.

10. **passage . . . in a Tragedy by Sir Robert Howard** : from *The Vestal Virgin*, V, i. Sir Robert Howard (1626–1698) was Dryden's brother-in-law, and his collaborator in the *Indian Queen*.

PAGE 276.

11. **Ch—— . . . Do—— . . . Pl——** : Chambers, probably Dodwell (possibly Dowley), and Plumley, three of Lamb's colleagues at the India House.

12. **a Gresham or a Whittington** : Sir Thomas Gresham (d. 1579) founded the Royal Exchange. Sir Richard Whittington (d. 1423), the hero of popular tales, was thrice Lord Mayor of London.

13. **Aquinas** : St. Thomas Aquinas (d. 1274), an Italian theologian and scholastic philosopher, the first printed edition of whose works filled seventeen folio volumes.

14. **Carthusian** : the Carthusians are a very strict monastic order, whose principal monastery was until recently at Chartreux, France.

PAGE 277.

15. **Elgin marbles** : the finest existing collection of ancient Greek sculptures. They were brought by Lord Elgin from Athens to England about 1800 and placed in the British Museum.

16. **cantle** : piece, slice.

17. **Lucretian pleasure** : Lucretius (d. 55 B.C.) was a Roman philosophical poet. The reference here is to the opening lines of Book II of *De Rerum Natura* :

Suave, mari magno turbantibus æquora ventis,
E terra magnum alterius spectare laborem.

Bacon, in his essay " Of Truth," roughly translates: " It is a pleasure to stand upon the shore, and to see ships tossed upon the sea."

18. **carking**: being concerned, anxious.

PAGE 278.

19. **"As low as to the fiends "**: see *Hamlet*, II, ii, 519.

20. **Retired Leisure**: see Milton's *Il Penseroso*, 49–50.

21. **cum dignitate**: dignified — from the phrase *otium cum dignitate*, dignified leisure.

22. **Opus operatum est**: My work is finished. The phrase is probably employed here for the sake of the pun on " opera."

JAMES HENRY LEIGH HUNT

AUTUMNAL COMMENCEMENT OF FIRES

PAGE 279.

1. **"the web of our life,"** etc.: see *All's Well that Ends Well*, IV, iii, 83–84.

2. **Theocritus**: (third century B.C.), the famous Greek idyllic and pastoral poet.

3. **Petrarch**: Francesco Petrarca (1304–1374), the first great poet of the Renaissance in Italy.

4. **Ariosto**: Ludovico Ariosto (1474–1533), a great Italian poet of the Renaissance; his chief work is the *Orlando Furioso*.

5. **Montaigne**: see Introduction, pages xi–xvi.

6. **Marcus Aurelius**: Marcus Aurelius Antoninus (121–180), a celebrated Roman emperor and the author of the *Meditations of Marcus Aurelius*.

7. **Molière**: the stage name of Jean Baptiste Poquelin (1622–1673), the greatest French writer of comedies.

8. **Poussin**: Nicolas Poussin (1594–1665), a famous French landscape and historical painter.

9. **Raphael**: Raphael Sanzio (1483–1520), a great Italian painter, especially of religious subjects.

PAGE 280.

10. **great bed at Ware**: a bed about twelve feet square, in an inn at Ware in Hertfordshire; it is referred to in *Twelfth Night*, III, ii, 51.

11. **Hounslow Heath**: formerly a waste tract on the great Western Road from London, haunted by highwaymen.

12. **Archbishop of Toledo . . . Marquis Marialva:** probably the Archbishop of Granada and the Marquis de Marialva are meant; Gil Blas served both of these as secretary; see *Gil Blas*, Bk. VII, chaps. ii–xi.

PAGE 281.

13. **Duodenarian:** apparently coined by Hunt, as an epithet denoting small means, from *duo denarii*, twopence.

14. **Montaigne "of that ilk":** Montaigne, lord of the estate of Montaigne.

15. **"And let my lamp at midnight hour,"** etc.: *Il Penseroso*, 85–92.

GETTING UP ON COLD MORNINGS

PAGE 282.

1. **Giulio Cordara:** Giulio Cesare Cordara (1704–1785), an Italian poet and historiographer of the Jesuits.

PAGE 283.

2. **decumbency:** lying down, as " incumbency " is etymologically lying in ; see " incumbent," p. 284.

3. **"haled" out of their "beds,"** etc.: see *Paradise Lost*, ii, 596.

PAGE 284.

4. **the Queen of France . . . that degenerate King:** Eleanor of Aquitaine (1122?–1204), wife of Louis VII of France and later of Henry II of England. Louis VII, "The Pious" (cir. 1120–1180), had shaved his beard in obedience to an archiepiscopal edict.

5. **Emperor Julian:** Julian the Apostate, Roman emperor, 361–363.

6. **Cardinal Bembo:** Pietro Bembo (1470–1547), a celebrated Italian man of letters.

7. **Michael Angelo:** Michelagnolo Buonarroti (1475–1564), the most famous Italian artist — sculptor, painter, architect, and poet.

8. **Titian:** Tiziano Vecelli (1477?–1576), the great Venetian painter.

9. **Fletcher:** John Fletcher, Beaumont's collaborator; see note 23 to page 249.

10. **Haroun al Raschid:** Caliph of Bagdad (786–809); a great Eastern sovereign, known in the West, however, chiefly through the *Arabian Nights*.

11. **Bed-ridden Hassan:** Bedreddin Hassan, the son of Noureddin Ali, in the *Arabian Nights* tale of that name.

12. **Wortley Montague:** Edward Wortley Montagu (1713–1776), English writer and traveler, son of the more famous Lady Mary Wortley Montagu (1689–1762), the traveler, letter-writer, and poetess of " the Town."

13. **"Sweetly recommends itself,"** etc.: *Macbeth*, I, vi, 2–3.

PAGE 285.

14. **"Falsely luxurious! Will not man awake?"**: Thomson, *Summer*, 67; see note 11 to page 248.

15. **Holborn**: it is not to-day, and was not in Hunt's time, the longest street in London.

THE OLD GENTLEMAN

PAGE 286.

1. **Lady M. W. Montague**: see note 12 to page 284.

2. **Churchill**: Charles Churchill (1731-1764), writer of satirical verse.

3. **George Anne Bellamy**: (1731?-1788), an Irish-English actress, the illegitimate daughter of Lord Tyrawley.

PAGE 287.

4. **Blair's Works**: Hugh Blair (1718-1800) was a Scotch divine and man of letters whose *Sermons* were once extremely popular.

5. **Junius**: the pseudonym of the unknown author of a series of brilliant satirical *Letters* published 1769-1772.

6. **American War**: the Revolution.

7. **Lord George Gordon**: an English agitator, tried for treason in connection with the No-Popery rioting in London in 1780.

8. **Hogarth**: see note 7 to page 242.

9. **Sir Joshua**: Sir Joshua Reynolds (1723-1792), the celebrated English portrait painter, first president of the Royal Academy, and one of the founders of the Literary Club.

10. **Marquis of Granby**: an English general in the Seven Years' War.

11. **Comte de Grasse . . . Admiral Rodney**: the Comte de Grasse commanded the French fleet that coöperated with Washington in the capture of Cornwallis at Yorktown in 1781. He was defeated in the West Indies in 1782 by the English under Admiral Rodney.

12. **Dr. Johnson's criticism on Hanway**: see Boswell's *Life*, *anno* 1756 (Vol. I, pp. 313-314 in Hill's edition).

PAGE 288.

13. **Mr. Oswald . . . Mr. Lampe**: the first is probably James Oswald, an eighteenth-century musician and dancing master; the second is John Frederick Lampe (cir. 1703-1751), a German composer of songs and light operas, resident in England after about 1725.

14. **Lord North . . . Lord Rockingham**: the former was the English prime minister during the American Revolution; he was succeeded in office by Rockingham.

PAGE 289.

15. **Garrick, Woodward . . . Clive:** David Garrick (1717–1779), probably the greatest English actor-manager; Dr. Johnson said of him that "his death eclipsed the gaiety of nations." Henry Woodward (1714–1777), a noted comedian and mimic. Catherine Clive (1711–1785), an actress especially famous in light parts.

16. **Vauxhall . . . Raneiagh:** both were formerly amusement gardens on the Thames near London.

17. **Newmarket:** the site of a famous English race course where races have been run for the last three hundred years.

DEATHS OF LITTLE CHILDREN

PAGE 290.

1. **a Grecian philosopher:** Solon (cir. 638–cir. 559 B.C.), the great Athenian statesman. For the incident referred to, see chapter xvi of his *Life* by Diogenes Laertius.

PAGE 294.

2. **"of these are the kingdom of heaven":** see Matthew xix, 14.

3. **"knowledge of good and evil":** Genesis ii, 9.

SHAKING HANDS

PAGE 296.

1. **two really kind men, who evinced this soreness of hand:** the first one described is unidentified, the second was Hazlitt.

WILLIAM HAZLITT

ON READING OLD BOOKS

PAGE 297.

1. **Tales of My Landlord:** several of Scott's novels were published in series under this general title.

2. **Lady Morgan:** (1783 ?–1859) a writer of lively Irish novels.

3. **Anastasius:** an Eastern romance, on its first publication in 1819 attributed to Byron, but actually written by Thomas Hope (1770–1831).

4. **Delphine:** a novel published in 1802 by Madame de Staël, the celebrated French bluestocking and miscellaneous writer.

5. **"in their newest gloss":** *Macbeth*, I, vii, 34.

6. **black-letter:** the so-called Gothic type used in the earlier printed books; it closely resembled the type used to-day in German books.

7. **Andrew Millar:** Andrew Millar (1707–1768), Thomson's and Fielding's publisher.

8. **Thurlow's State Papers:** John Thurloe (1616–1668) was Secretary of State during the Protectorate of Cromwell. His *State Papers* were published in 1742.

9. **Sir William Temple's Essays:** Sir William Temple (1628–1699) was an English statesman and miscellaneous writer. See introduction to the present volume, p. xxii.

10. **Sir Godfrey Kneller:** Sir Godfrey Kneller (1646–1723), a portrait painter, had as patrons Charles II, James II, William III, and Queen Anne.

PAGE 298.

11. **rifaccimentos:** *rifacimento* is literally "remaking." The term is usually applied to a literary work which has been made out of another work.

PAGE 299.

12. **"for thoughts and for remembrance":** see *Hamlet*, IV, v, 175–177.

13. **Fortunatus's Wishing Cap:** Fortunatus, in the widely current popular tale, receives a magic cap, which will place him wherever he wishes to be.

14. **My father Shandy . . . Bruscambille:** see Sterne's *Tristram Shandy*, Bk. III, chap. xxxv.

15. **Peregrine Pickle:** one of the novels of Tobias Smollett (see note 14 to page 248). The "Memoirs of Lady Vane" are in chapter lxxxi.

16. **Tom Jones:** see note 12 to page 248. The Masquerade is in Bk. XIII, chap. vii; Thwackum and Square, Bk. III, chap. iii; Molly Seagrim, Bk. IV, chap. viii; Sophia and her muff, Bk. V, chap. iv; her aunt's lecture, Bk. VII, chap. iii.

17. **"the puppets dallying":** *Hamlet*, III, ii, 257.

18. **let this hump, like Christian's burthen, drop:** in *Pilgrim's Progress* Christian's burden fell off when he reached the cross.

PAGE 300.

19. **"ignorance was bliss":** Thomas Gray (1716–1771), *Ode on a Distant Prospect of Eton College*, 99–100:

> — where ignorance is bliss
> 'T is folly to be wise.

20. **raree-show:** a peep show.

21. **Ballantyne press . . . Minerva press:** the former was the Edinburgh printing house with which Scott was associated, the latter a London center for the issuance of cheap, popular fiction.

22. **the time "when I was in my father's house, and my path ran down with butter and honey"**: the source of this quotation has not been determined. It may be a confused recollection of Job xx, 17, "streams of honey and butter," with the frequently occurring Biblical phrase "my father's house."

23. **Mrs. Radcliffe's Romance of the Forest**: Mrs. Ann Radcliffe (1764–1823) was the most important of the late eighteenth- and early nineteenth-century novelists of mystery and terror. The *Romance of the Forest* was published in 1791.

24. **"sweet in the mouth"** . . . **"bitter in the belly"**: see Revelations x, 9.

25. **"gay creatures"** . . . **"of the element"** . . . **"living in the clouds"**: see Milton's *Comus*, 299–301.

PAGE 301.

26. **Tom Jones discovers Square**: *Tom Jones*, Bk. V, chap. v.

27. **Parson Adams . . . Mrs. Slip-slop**: *Joseph Andrews*, Bk. IV, chap. xiv.

28. **Major Bath, etc.**: the names are those of famous characters of fiction: Major Bath in Fielding's *Amelia*; Commodore Trunnion in Smollett's *Peregrine Pickle*; Trim and Uncle Toby in Sterne's *Tristram Shandy*; Don Quixote, Sancho, and Dapple in Cervantes' *Don Quixote*, the last name being that of Sancho's ass; Gil Blas, Dame Lorenza Sephora, Laura, and Lucretia in Le Sage's *Gil Blas de Santillane*.

29. **O Memory! etc.**: these lines have not been identified as a quotation; they are perhaps by Hazlitt himself.

30. **Chubb's Tracts**: Thomas Chubb (1679–1747) was a tallow chandler, who wrote much on the deistic controversy.

PAGE 302.

31. **"fate, free-will, etc."** . . . **"found no end"**: see *Paradise Lost*, ii, 558–561.

32. **"Would I had never seen Wittenberg, never read book"**: *Faustus* xvi, 20–21, in Bullen's edition; ll. 1376–1377 in Tucker Brooke's edition.

33. **Hartley, etc.**: David Hartley (1705–1757), David Hume (1711–1776), Bishop George Berkeley (1685–1753), John Locke (1632–1704), and Thomas Hobbes (1588–1679) were all philosophical writers. Hazlitt was at one time deeply interested in metaphysics.

34. **New Eloise**: Rousseau's sentimental romance. On this and Rousseau's other works see note 29 to page 316.

35. **I have spoken elsewhere**: in the *Round Table* essay, "On the Character of Rousseau."

36. **"scattered like stray-gifts o'er the earth"**: probably an inexact recollection of lines 27–28 in Wordsworth's *Stray Pleasures*:

> Thus pleasure is spread through the earth
> In stray gifts to be claimed by whoever shall find.

PAGE 303.

37. **Sir Fopling Flutter**: a character in Etherege's *The Man of Mode*. See also note 34 to page 318.

38. **leurre de dupe**: decoy for a simpleton; the phrase occurs in Book IV of Rousseau's *Confessions*.

39. **"a load to sink a navy"**: see *Henry VIII*, III, ii, 383.

40. **a friend, who had some lottery puffs, etc.**: Charles Lamb.

PAGE 304.

41. **Marcian Colonna is a dainty book**: *Marcian Colonna* is a verse tale by Bryan Waller Procter — "Barry Cornwall" — (1787–1874). The quotation is from a sonnet addressed to Procter by Lamb.

42. **Keats's Eve of St. Agnes**: John Keats (1795–1821). *The Eve of St. Agnes* is a richly colored verse romance. The bits Hazlitt quotes here are both from stanza 24:

> The tiger moth's deep damasked wings;

and

> A shielded scutcheon blushed with blood of queens and kings.

43. **"come like shadows — so depart"**: *Macbeth*, IV, i, 111.

44. **"Words, words, words"**: *Hamlet*, II, ii, 194.

45. **great preacher in the Caledonian Chapel**: Edward Irving (1792–1834).

46. **"as the hart that panteth," etc.**: see Psalm xlii, 1.

47. **Goethe's Sorrows of Werter and Schiller's Robbers**: the first is a sentimental novel, published 1774; the second a "Storm and Stress" play published 1781, according to Hazlitt the first play he read.

48. **"giving my stock of more," etc.**: see *As You Like It*, II, i, 48–49.

PAGE 305.

49. **Authors of the Lyrical Ballads**: in the spring of 1798 Hazlitt visited Wordsworth and Coleridge at Nether-Stowey and Alfoxden. His essay "On My First Acquaintance with Poets" presents an extremely interesting account of this visit.

50. **Valentine, Tattle . . . Miss Prue**: characters in *Love for Love*, by William Congreve (1670–1729), the wittiest and cleverest of the Restoration comic dramatists.

51. **"know my cue without a prompter"**: see *Othello*, I, ii, 83–84.

52. **Intus et in cute:** "Intimately, and under the skin"; from Persius, *Satires* III, 30.

53. **Sir Humphry Davy:** Sir Humphry Davy (1778–1829), famous chemist and man of letters.

PAGE 306.

54. **Richardson . . . Clarissa . . . Clementina . . . Pamela:** Samuel Richardson (1689–1761) was the first of the great English novelists. His novels are *Pamela* (1740–1741), *Clarissa Harlowe* (1747–1748), and *Sir Charles Grandison* (1753–1754). They are tediously elaborated, but excel in analysis of feminine emotion and of motives of conduct. Pamela and Clarissa are the heroines of the two earlier novels; Clementina is the beautiful Italian who went mad from love of the impeccable Sir Charles Grandison; Lovelace, named in the footnote, was the betrayer of Clarissa.

55. **"with every trick and line,"** etc.: see *All's Well That Ends Well*, I, i, 104–107.

56. **Mackenzie's Julia de Roubigné . . . Man of Feeling:** Henry Mackenzie (1745–1831) was an essayist and sentimental novelist. His novels are *The Man of Feeling* (1771), *The Man of the World* (1773), and *Julia de Roubigné* (1777).

57. **"that ligament, fine as it was, was never broken":** *Tristram Shandy*, Bk. VI, chap. x.

58. **Boccaccio . . . story of the Hawk:** the *Decameron*, fifth day, ninth story.

59. **Farquhar:** George Farquhar (1678–1707), a comic dramatist of the Restoration school.

PAGE 307.

60. **"at one proud swoop":** cf. "at one fell swoop" — *Macbeth*, IV, iii, 219.

61. **"with all its giddy raptures":** cf. "all its dizzy raptures" — Wordsworth, *Tintern Abbey*, 85.

62. **"embalmed with odours":** *Paradise Lost*, ii, 843.

63. **His form had not yet lost,** etc.: *Paradise Lost*, i, 591–594.

64. **"falls flat upon the grunsel edge, and shames its worshippers":** see *Paradise Lost*, i, 460–461.

65. **Junius's:** see note 5 to page 287.

PAGE 308.

66. **"he, like an eagle in a dove-cot,"** etc.: see *Coriolanus*, V, vi, 115–116.

67. **Wordsworth . . . Essay on Marriage:** no such essay by Wordsworth is known.

PAGE 309.

68. "**worthy of all acceptation**": I Timothy i, 15.

69. **Lord Clarendon's History of the Grand Rebellion**: Edward Hyde (1608–1674), first Earl of Clarendon, was an English statesman who remained loyal to the king in the Civil War, of which he afterwards wrote the history from the Royalist point of view.

70. **Froissart's Chronicles**: Jean Froissart (1337–cir. 1410) wrote an extremely picturesque *Chronique de France, d'Angleterre, d'Écosse, et d'Espagne*, which relates the events of history in western Europe from 1325 to 1400. A spirited English translation was made by Lord Berners in 1523–1525.

71. **Holinshed and Stowe**: Raphael Holinshed (d. 1580?) wrote *Chronicles of England, Scotland, and Ireland*, which furnished Shakespeare material for many plays. John Stowe (1525–1605) wrote or edited several chronicles of English history and a *Survey of London*.

72. **Fuller's Worthies**: see note 21 to page 249.

73. **Beaumont and Fletcher**: see note 23 to page 249.

74. **Thucydides**: (471?–401? B.C.), a celebrated Greek historian.

75. **Guicciardini**: Francesco Guicciardini (1483–1540) was the author of a *History of Italy* from 1494 to 1532.

76. **Don Quixote**: the great burlesque romance of chivalry, by Miguel de Cervantes Saavedra (1547–1616).

77. "**another Yarrow**": see Wordsworth's *Yarrow Unvisited*, stanza 7.

ON GOING A JOURNEY

PAGE 310.

1. **The fields his study, etc.**: from *The Farmer's Boy, Spring*, 32, by Robert Bloomfield (1766–1823).

2. **a friend in my retreat, etc.**: from *Retirement*, 741–742, by William Cowper (1731–1800).

3. **Contemplation may plume her feathers, etc.**: see Milton's *Comus*, 378–380.

4. **a Tilbury**: a light two-wheeled vehicle.

PAGE 311.

5. "**sunken wrack and sumless treasuries**": *Henry V*, I, ii, 165.

6. "**Leave, oh, leave me to my repose**": see Thomas Gray's (1716–1771) *The Descent of Odin*, 50.

7. "**very stuff o' the conscience**": *Othello*, I, ii, 2.

8. "**Out upon such half-faced fellowship**": *1 Henry IV*, I, iii, 208.

9. **Mr. Cobbett's :** William Cobbett (1762–1835), a political journalist and essayist.

10. **"Let me have a companion of my way," says Sterne, etc. :** somewhat inaccurately quoted from the eighteenth of the *Sermons of Mr. Yorick*. On Sterne see note 15 to page 248.

PAGE 313.

11. **"give it an understanding, but no tongue " :** *Hamlet*, I, ii, 250.

12. **Pindaric ode :** after the manner of Pindar (522–443 B.C.), the greatest Greek lyric poet.

13. **"He talked far above singing " :** see Beaumont and Fletcher's *Philaster*, V, v, 165–166.

14. **All-Foxden :** see note 49 to page 305.

15. **"that fine madness in them which our first poets had " :** probably an inexact recollection of lines 105–110 of Michael Drayton's (1563–1631) *To Henry Reynolds — Of Poets and Poesie*:

> Next Marlowe, bathed in the Thespian springs,
> Had in him those brave translunary things
> That the first poets had : his raptures were
> All air and fire, which made his verses clear;
> For that fine madness still he did retain
> Which rightly should possess a poet's brain.

16. **Here be woods as green, etc. :** Fletcher's *Faithful Shepherdess*, I, iii, 26 ff.

17. **Phœbe :** goddess of the moon and sister of Phœbus, god of the sun. Latmos is a mountain range in Asia Minor.

PAGE 314.

18. **"take one's ease at one's inn " :** see *1 Henry IV*, III, iii, 92–93.

19. **The cups that cheer, but not inebriate :** Cowper's *Task*, iv, 39–40.

20. **Sancho . . . once fixed upon cow-heel :** *Don Quixote*, Part II, chap. lix. Sancho Panza was the esquire and counterpart of Don Quixote.

21. **Shandean contemplation :** the adjective is formed from *Tristram Shandy*, the title of Sterne's novel, and means digressive, reflective.

22. **Procul, O procul este profani :** "Away, away, ye unhallowed" : *Æneid* VI, 258.

PAGE 315.

23. **"unhoused free condition is put into circumscription and confine " :** see *Othello*, I, ii, 26–27.

24. **"lord of one's self, uncumbered with a name " :** Dryden's *Epistle to John Driden*, 18, has " Lord of yourself, uncumbered with a wife."

25. **association of ideas :** the psychological principle according to which an idea calls related ideas into consciousness. The " proof " Hazlitt speaks of is not known.

PAGE 316.

26. **the Cartoons :** the drawings of religious subjects by the great Italian painter Raphael (1483–1520), made to be reproduced in tapestry. They are now in the South Kensington Museum, London.

27. **Paul and Virginia :** a sentimental romance by Bernardin de Saint Pierre, published 1788.

28. **Madame D'Arblay's Camilla :** Madame D'Arblay, or Frances Burney (1752–1840), an extremely popular realistic English novelist, wrote *Evelina*, *Cecilia*, and *Camilla*, of which the last was the least successful.

29. **New Eloise :** the letter referred to is number 17 of Part IV. The author, Jean Jacques Rousseau (1712–1778), was the great Swiss-French sentimentalist and social philosopher and the most powerful personal force in the revolutionary movement of the late eighteenth century. His most important works are *La Nouvelle Héloïse* (1761), *Le Contrat social* (1762), *Émile, ou de l'Éducation* (1762), and *Les Confessions* (1782–1788). *La Nouvelle Héloïse* recounts in a series of letters the love of Julie, a young woman of rank, for St. Preux, a man of low birth. Its interest lies largely in its passages of fervid passion and of landscape description. *Le Contrat social* is a political work, whose theories formed the basis of Jacobin politics in the French Revolution. Upon *Émile* see note 36 to page 224. *Les Confessions* is Rousseau's autobiography, largely concerned with sentimental affairs and remarkably frank in its presentation of them.

30. **bon bouche :** a titbit, dainty morsel.

31. **"green upland swells,"** etc. . . . **"glittered green with sunny showers " :** see Coleridge's *Ode on the Departing Year*, stanza 7.

32. **Liberty, Genius, Love, Virtue :** this passage reflects the enthusiasm kindled by Hazlitt's just-formed acquaintance with Coleridge and by his belief in the triumph of the principles of the French Revolution.

PAGE 317.

33. **The beautiful is vanished, and returns not :** Coleridge's translation of Schiller's *Wallenstein's Tod*, V, i, 68.

PAGE 318.

34. **"Beyond Hyde Park,"** etc.: from *The Man of Mode*, V, ii, a comedy by Sir George Etherege (1635?–1691).

35. **Stonehenge :** see note 9 to page 231.

PAGE 319.

36. "The mind is its own place ": *Paradise Lost*, i, 254.

37. With glistering spires and pinnacles adorn'd : *Paradise Lost*, iii, 550.

38. the Bodleian . . . Blenheim : the former is the university library at Oxford; the latter, the magnificent house of the Duke of Marlborough.

39. when I first set my foot on the laughing shores of France : in 1802, after the Peace of Amiens, Hazlitt went to Paris to study and copy the masterpieces of art collected there by Napoleon. At the time Hazlitt's enthusiasm was about evenly divided between Napoleon and painting.

PAGE 320.

40. "the vine-covered hills and gay regions of France ": from a *Song* by William Roscoe (1753–1831).

41. the Bourbons : the reigning French dynasty from 1589 to the French Revolution and from the downfall of Napoleon to 1830. The name has become synonymous for excessive political conservatism and repression.

42. " jump ": risk, take chances on; see *Macbeth*, I, vii, 4–7.

43. Dr. Johnson remarked how little foreign travel, etc. : Boswell's *Life*, *anno* 1778 (Hill's edition, Vol. III, p. 352).

44. Out of my country and myself I go : the source of this quotation — if it is a quotation and not by Hazlitt himself — has not been located.

ON THE FEELING OF IMMORTALITY IN YOUTH

PAGE 321.

1. Motto : from *Hydriotaphia, or Urn-Burial,* chap. v ; see note 34 to page 224.

2. The vast, the unbounded prospect lies before us : see Addison's *Cato*, V, i, 13.

3. " bear a charmed life ": *Macbeth*, V, viii, 12.

4. Bidding the lovely scenes at distance hail : see line 32 of the ode *The Passions*, by William Collins (1721–1759).

PAGE 322.

5. "this sensible, warm motion," etc. : *Measure for Measure*, III, i, 120–121.

6. " wine of life is drank up ": see *Macbeth*, II, iii, 100.

PAGE 323.

7. "as in a glass, darkly ": see 1 Corinthians, xiii, 12.

8. the foolish fat scullion, in Sterne : see *Tristram Shandy*, Bk. V, chap. vii.

PAGE 324.

9. "**the feast of reason and the flow of soul**": Pope's *Imitations of Horace*, Satire I, 128.

10. "**brave sublunary things**": see note 15 to page 313.

11. **Sidon ... Tyre ... Babylon ... Susa**: Sidon was earlier the richest and most powerful Phœnician city, as Tyre was later; Babylon and Susa were once capitals of great empires. All four are now mere small towns or only heaps of rubbish.

12. **The stockdove plain amid the forest deep, etc.**: slightly adapted from James Thomson's *Castle of Indolence*, i, 33–34.

PAGE 326.

13. "**the purple light of love**": Gray's *Progress of Poesy*, 41.

14. **Rubens**: Peter Paul Rubens (1577–1640), the great Flemish painter, particularly famed as a colorist.

PAGE 327.

15. "**the Raphael grace, the Guido air**": cf: "Match Raphael's grace with thy loved Guido's air," Pope's *Epistle to Mr. Jervas*, 36. Raphael Santi (1483–1520) was the great Italian painter of religious subjects in particular; Guido Reni (1575–1642) was also an Italian painter.

16. "**gain new vigour at our endless task**": see Cowper's *Charity*, 104.

17. **divinæ particula auræ**: particles of divine ether.

18. **Rembrandt**: Rembrandt Hermanzoon Van Rijn (1607–1669), the greatest of the Dutch school of painters.

PAGE 328.

19. "**beguile the slow and creeping hours of time**": see *As You Like It*, II, vii, 112.

PAGE 329.

20. **Robbers ... Don Carlos**: plays by Schiller, the first published 1781, the second 1787.

21. **From the dungeon of the tower time-rent, etc.**: from Coleridge's sonnet *To the Author of the Robbers*, 3–4.

22. "**That time is past with all its giddy raptures**": see Wordsworth's *Tintern Abbey*, 83–85.

PAGE 330.

23. "**Even from the tomb the voice of nature cries,**" etc.: Gray's *Elegy*, 91–92.

24. "**all the life of life is flown**": see Burns's *Lament for James, Earl of Glencairn*, 46.

25. **From the last dregs of life, etc.**: see Dryden's *Aurengzebe*, IV, i, 41–42.

PAGE 331.

26. **"treason domestic, foreign levy, nothing could touch us farther"** : see *Macbeth*, III, ii, 24–26.

27. **"reverbs its own hollowness"** : adapted from *Lear*, I, i, 155–156.

WILLIAM MAKEPEACE THACKERAY

The three essays in this selection originally appeared as Nos. 7, 12, and 23 of the *Roundabout Papers* in the *Cornhill Magazine*.

TUNBRIDGE TOYS

PAGE 333.

1. **hardbake** : a kind of candy.

2. **prodigal little son** : see Luke xv, 11–32.

PAGE 334.

3. **bull's-eyes** : glass marbles.

4. **form** : class.

PAGE 335.

5. **Eutropius** : (fourth century A.D.), the author of a concise history of Rome.

6. **Bartlemytide** : the time of the festival of St. Bartholomew, August 24.

PAGE 337.

7. **Mr. Sala** : George Augustus Sala (1828–1895), novelist and miscellaneous writer.

PAGE 338.

8. **Tyburn** : the site of the public gallows until its transfer to Newgate Prison in 1783.

9. **stumps** : the uprights forming the wicket in cricket.

10. **Valancour** : one of the principal characters in *The Mysteries of Udolpho*, a romance of mystery and terror, by Mrs. Ann Radcliffe (1764–1823).

11. **Manfroni** : apparently the chief figure in the tale twice named later in this essay. The editors cannot make any further identification, but the story is evidently of the same character as *The Mysteries of Udolpho*.

12. **Thaddeus of Warsaw** : the principal character in a pseudo-historical romance of the same name by Jane Porter (1776–1850).

13. **Corinthian Tom . . . Jerry Hawthorn** : characters in the once extremely popular *Life in London*, by Pierce Egan the elder (1772?–1849).

14. **a lecture on George II. in the Cornhill Magazine** : Thackeray's lectures on *The Four Georges*, first delivered in America (1855–1856), were printed in the *Cornhill* in the issues from July to October, 1860.

On Being Found Out

PAGE 341.

1. **coram populo**: in the presence of the public.

2. **cried his peccavi**: acknowledged his fault; *peccavi* is literally "I have sinned."

3. **Siste tandem, carnifex**: Cease, pray, O executioner!

PAGE 342.

4. **Jack Ketch**: a famous English executioner (d. 1686). His name was applied to the hangman in *Punch and Judy*, and then became synonymous with hangman.

5. **one of your Bluebeards**: in the famous nursery story Bluebeard gives his young wife the keys to his castle with permission to enter all the rooms but one. Her curiosity compels her to enter the forbidden room, in which she finds the bodies of six former wives, whom Bluebeard had murdered for disobeying the same prohibition.

PAGE 343.

6. **Abbé Kakatoes . . . Marquis de Croquemitaine**: apparently invented names; *kakatoes* is a French form for "cockatoo," and *croquemitaine* means "bugbear."

7. **Palsambleu**: an archaic French oath; a corruption of *par le sang Dieu*.

PAGE 344.

8. **put the cap out . . . put his head into it**: suggested by the proverb, "If the cap fits, wear it."

PAGE 345.

9. **κτῆμα ἐς ἀεί**: an immortal possession.

10. **dies iræ**: Day of Judgment, literally "day of wrath"; from the famous Latin hymn beginning:

Dies iræ, dies illa.

PAGE 346.

11. **Bardolph . . . Nym . . . Doll Tearsheet . . . Mrs. Quickly**: Bardolph is a rascally companion of Falstaff's in *Henry IV*. In *Henry V* he accompanies the king's army into France, where he is executed for stealing a pàx (or pyx) from a church (*Henry V*, III, vi, 41–51). Nym is his companion thief in *Henry V* (III, ii, 44–57). Doll Tearsheet is a woman of the town and a friend of Mrs. Quickly's in *2 Henry IV*, and Mrs. Quickly is the hostess of the Boar's Head Tavern, the meeting place of Prince Hal and Falstaff.

12. **de la société**: of the company.

De Finibus

Page 347.

1. **De Finibus:** literally, "about endings."

2. **Stella:** Esther Johnson, whom Swift is said to have secretly married in 1716. From 1710 to 1713, while Swift was in London and Stella in Ireland, he wrote her daily letters, which were later published as the *Journal to Stella*. These letters show a playful tenderness and a capacity for feeling not hinted at in Swift's other works.

3. **some commentator or other:** Thackeray himself in his lecture on Swift in the *English Humourists*.

4. **Mr. Johnson . . . touching the posts:** see Boswell's *Life, anno* 1764 (Vol. I, p. 485, note 1 in Hill's edition).

5. **Dodsley's:** a famous eighteenth-century printing house, by which many of Dr. Johnson's works were published.

6. **Green Arbour Court:** the *Cornhill* was printed in Green Arbour Court.

7. **Pendennis, Clive Newcome . . . Philip Firmin:** the principal characters in Thackeray's novels *Pendennis*, *The Newcomes*, and *The Adventures of Philip*. The final section of the last named and *De Finibus* appeared in the same number of the *Cornhill*.

8. **tamen usque recurro:** "yet I always come back"; see Horace, *Epistles* I, x, 24.

Page 348.

9. **Woolcomb . . . Twysden:** characters in *The Adventures of Philip*.

Page 349.

10. **Angels and ministers of grace:** *Hamlet*, I, iv, 39.

11. **Goethe . . . Weissenborn . . . Weimar:** Weimar, the capital of a small German principality, was for more than forty years the home of Goethe. Through the residence there of Goethe, Schiller, Herder, and Wieland, it became the center of German literature. Thackeray resided in Weimar for some time in 1831, and had three interviews with Goethe. During his stay he had lessons from Dr. Weissenborn.

Page 350.

12. **as different . . . as Lord Palmerston and Mr. Disraeli:** Lord Palmerston, for instance, was of Irish, and Disraeli (later Lord Beaconsfield), of Jewish descent; the former was prominent as a Whig, the latter as a Tory.

Page 352.

13. **once on the Mississippi:** Thackeray lectured in America in 1852-1853 and again in 1855-1856.

14. **Jacob Faithful:** a lively sea story by Frederick Marryatt (1792–1848).

15. **Vingt Ans Après:** *Twenty Years After*, a sequel to *The Three Musketeers*; both by Alexandre Dumas *père* (1802–1870). D'Artagnan, named below, is the adventurous hero of both romances.

16. **Woman in White:** a novel of thrills and mystery, by William Wilkie Collins (1824–1889).

17. **à la mode le pays de Pole:** "according to the Polish custom"; the internecine quarrels of the Poles were marked by the utmost barbarity.

18. **Doctor F—— . . . Mr. T. H——:** Doctor Firmin and Tufton Hunt were villainous characters in the *Adventures of Philip*.

PAGE 353.

19. **dilectissimi fratres:** most dearly beloved brethren.

20. **"Miserere nobis miseris peccatoribus":** "Have mercy upon us, miserable sinners!"

21. **libera me:** deliver me.

PAGE 354.

22. **peccavi:** see note 2 to page 341.

23. **perennial brass:** see Horace, *Odes* III, xxx, 1: *Exegi monumentum ære perennius* — "I have wrought myself a monument more lasting than bronze."

24. **Pythoness:** the priestess at the oracle of Apollo at Delphi; she was supposed to be inspired by the god with a spirit of divination.

PAGE 355.

25. **Mignon . . . Knight of La Mancha:** the persons named in this paragraph are all among the greatest characters of fiction. Mignon is the mysterious Italian maiden, the daughter of the old harper, in Goethe's *Wilhelm Meisters Lehrjahre*; Margaret is Gretchen, the heroine of his *Faust*; Goetz von Berlichingen is the hero of his early drama by that name, a play patterned after Shakespeare's historical plays. Dugald Dalgetty is a soldier of fortune in Scott's *Legend of Montrose*, and Ivanhoe is the hero of the novel of the same name. Uncas is the young Indian chief, the hero of Cooper's *Last of the Mohicans*, and Leatherstocking is Natty Bumpo, the backwoodsman who plays a prominent part in the series of novels of Indian and pioneer life — *The Leatherstocking Tales*. Athos, Porthos, and Aramis are Dumas's "Three Musketeers," the companions of D'Artagnan. Amelia Booth is the title character of Fielding's *Amelia*, loving and generous. Uncle Toby is the whimsical, tender-hearted uncle of Tristram in Sterne's *Tristram Shandy*. Tittlebat Titmouse is the vulgar and simple

shopman, who for a time enjoys a great estate in *Ten Thousand a Year*, by Samuel Warren (1807–1877). Crummles is an eccentric actor and the manager of a cheap theatrical company in Dickens's *Nicholas Nickleby*. Gil Blas is the title character in the famous picaresque romance by Alain René Le Sage (1668–1747); the reference is to a traveling company of comedians, with whose fortunes those of Gil Blas are for a time involved. Sir Roger de Coverley is the good-natured and somewhat eccentric old country gentleman of the *Spectator*. The Knight of La Mancha is Don Quixote, the hero of Cervantes' romance. He is crack-brained from reading romances of chivalry, while his blessed squire, Sancho Panza, is intensely material and matter-of-fact.

ROBERT LOUIS STEVENSON

WALKING TOURS

This essay was originally published in the June, 1876, number of the *Cornhill Magazine*; it was reprinted in *Virginibus Puerisque* (London, 1881).

PAGE 357.

1. **a brown john :** apparently a confusion of "brown george," a large earthenware vessel, and "demijohn," a large glass or earthenware bottle.

PAGE 358.

2. **"I cannot see the wit," says Hazlitt :** the source of this, as of the other quotations from Hazlitt later in the essay, is the paper "On Going a Journey." See pages 310–311 and 316 of the present collection.

3. **a peace that passes comprehension :** perhaps a disguised quotation of Philippians iv, 7.

4. **like Christian on a similar occasion :** after Christian had lost his burden at the cross, he "gave three leaps for joy, and went on singing" (*Pilgrim's Progress*, Part I).

PAGE 359.

5. **the merchant Abudah's chest :** an allusion to a character in *Tales of the Genii*, by the Reverend James Ridley, who was haunted in his dreams by an old hag, and was freed only after learning to "fear God and keep his commandments."

PAGE 362.

6. **"Though ye take from a covetous man all his treasure," says Milton :** in *Areopagitica*, near the middle of the work.

PAGE 363.

7. **a volume of Heine's songs :** the lyrics of Heinrich Heine (1797–1856) were among the few German works in Stevenson's reading. His fondness for Heine began apparently during his university days. See Balfour's *Life*, Vol. I, p. 117.

8. **Tristram Shandy :** Sterne's *Tristram Shandy* is so discursive as to invite browsing instead of continuous reading.

9. **joviality to the full significance of that audacious word :** joviality is derived from Jove, the chief of the gods.

10. **Burns, numbering past pleasures :** cf. " The Rigs of Barley," stanza 4 :

> I hae been blythe wi' comrades dear ;
> I hae been merry drinking ;
> I hae been joyfu' gath'rin gear ;
> I hae been happy thinking.

PAGE 364.

11. **Philistines perspiring after wealth :** a " Philistine," according to Matthew Arnold, who popularized the term in England, is one of those people "who believe most that our greatness and welfare are proved by our being very rich, and who most give their lives and thoughts to becoming rich " (*Culture and Anarchy*, chap. i).

On Falling in Love

Stevenson contributed this essay to the February, 1877, number of the *Cornhill*; it was reprinted in *Virginibus Puerisque* (1881) as the third of a series of four papers bearing the title of the volume.

PAGE 365.

1. Motto : *Midsummer Night's Dream*, III, ii, 115.

2. **cénacle :** a gathering of men of letters, artists, and the like.

PAGE 366.

3. **the Apollo Belvedere :** a famous antique statue in the Vatican, representing the god as a handsome youth.

4. **Leonardo da Vinci :** an Italian painter, architect, sculptor, and scientist of the Renaissance (1452–1519).

5. **Goethe in his youth :** perhaps Stevenson had in mind here the following sentences of Lewes's *Life of Goethe* (Bk. II, chap. v), a work to which, in his essay on " Books Which Have Influenced Me " (1887), he acknowledged a particular indebtedness : " He was now turned twenty, and a more magnificent youth never perhaps entered the Strassburg gates. Long before he was celebrated, he was likened to an Apollo : when he

entered a restaurant the people laid down their knives and forks to stare at him. . . . The features were large and liberally cut, as in the fine sweeping lines of Greek art."

PAGE 367.

6. **the difficulty Shakespeare was put into**: according to the tradition first recorded by Dennis in 1702, Queen Elizabeth was so much pleased with Falstaff in *Henry IV* that she commanded Shakespeare to write a play showing the fat knight in love; and as a result of this command Shakespeare in a fortnight wrote *The Merry Wives of Windsor*.

7. **Henry Fielding**: see note 12 to page 248.

8. **a passage or two in Rob Roy**: perhaps the following passages were in Stevenson's mind (the references are to the edition by Andrew Lang, London, 1893): Vol. I, pp. 215–216, 217–219; Vol. II, pp. 241–244.

PAGE 368.

9. **nonchaloir**: apathy, lack of strong interest or feeling.

10. **unhorsed, like St. Paul, from his infidel affectation**: see Acts ix, 1–9.

PAGE 369.

11. **Adelaide**: a lyric by Friedrich von Matthisson (1761–1831), set to music by Beethoven. Stevenson's admiration for the poem and its setting appears in a letter to Mrs. Sitwell, dated September 16, 1873 (*Letters*, Vol. I, p. 60–61).

12. **Heine's songs**: see note 7 to page 363.

13. **Mercutio**: the quick-spirited friend of Romeo.

14. **Poor Antony**: his infatuation for Cleopatra cost him his empire and his life; see *Antony and Cleopatra*.

15. **Les Misérables**: the best-known novel of Victor Hugo (1802–1885), a work greatly admired by Stevenson for its "masterly conception and . . . development," its pathos, truth, and "high eloquence." See his paper on "Victor Hugo's Romances."

16. **George Sand**: the nom de plume of Baroness Dudevant (1804–1876), one of the most eminent of nineteenth-century French novelists.

17. **George Meredith**: George Meredith (1828–1909), an English poet and realistic novelist. A number of Stevenson's letters are addressed to him, and in the essay on " Books Which Have Influenced Me " his *Egoist* stands with such works as Montaigne's *Essais*, Whitman's *Leaves of Grass*, and Hazlitt's " Spirit of Obligations " as a potent factor in the moral and intellectual development of his younger Scotch contemporary.

18. **that land of Beulah**: in the *Pilgrim's Progress* the beautiful land in which " the Shining Ones commonly walked, because it was upon the borders of Heaven."

Page 370.

19. **magnifico :** properly a Venetian nobleman or grandee.

20. **Grandisonian airs :** Sir Charles Grandison, the faultless hero of Richardson's novel of that name (see note 54 to page 306), is the quintessence of respect and chivalrous delicacy toward women.

21. **Daniel Deronda :** George Eliot's last novel (1876–1877), one of the literary events of the year in which Stevenson's essay was first published.

Page 371.

22. **the marriage of Cana :** there are three famous paintings of the marriage at Cana, two by Paolo Veronese (1528–1588) and one by Tintoretto (1518–1594).

Page 373.

23. **" The blind bow-boy " :** the phrase occurs in *Romeo and Juliet*, II, iv, 16.

The Lantern-Bearers

This essay first appeared in *Scribner's Magazine* in February, 1888. It was later reprinted in *Across the Plains, with other Memories and Essays* (1892).

Page 374.

1. **a certain easterly fisher-village :** probably North Berwick, a small village on the Firth of Forth, about twenty miles east of Edinburgh. Many of Stevenson's vacations as a boy were spent here (see Balfour's *Life*, Vol. I, pp. 36, 67), and the place served as a background for episodes in at least two of his later works of fiction — *David Balfour* (cf. especially Pt. I, chaps. xiii and xiv) and *The Pavilion on the Links*.

2. **penny pickwicks :** cheap cigars of a type well known in England in Stevenson's boyhood.

3. **cocknify :** imbue with cockney qualities, citify.

Page 375.

4. **the Bass Rock :** a rock island lying about a mile and a half off shore, a short distance east of North Berwick. In the Rebellion of 1745 it was one of the last strongholds of the Stuart cause. Cf. Stevenson's description of it in *David Balfour*, Pt. I, chap. xiv.

5. **Tantallon :** a castle (now in ruins) about three miles east of North Berwick. It formerly belonged to the earls of Douglas, one of whom (Archibald, d. cir. 1514) bore the nickname of Bell-the-Cat. There is a spirited description of Tantallon as it was in the days of this earl, in Scott's *Marmion* (Canto V, stanza xxxiii).

6. **the Law :** a steep hill at the back of North Berwick.

PAGE 376.

7. **geans**: wild cherries (Stevenson's note).

8. **Canty Bay**: about two and a half miles east of North Berwick.

PAGE 377.

9. **coil**: tumult, confusion.

10. **a tragic Maenad**: in Greek mythology the mænads, or priestesses of Bacchus, were characterized by their frenzied dancing and singing.

PAGE 379.

11. **the Old Bailey Reports**: the Old Bailey Court, in London, was, until 1905, the principal criminal court in England.

PAGE 380.

12. **"His mind to him a kingdom was"**: a modified quotation of the first line of Sir Edward Dyer's (cir. 1550–1607) "My Mind to me a Kingdom is."

13. **thimble-rigger**: an adept at thimblerig, hence a swindler.

PAGE 381.

14. **the fable of the monk**: a widespread popular story, known commonly as the story of Monk Felix. See the references given in R. Köhler, *Kleinere Schriften*, Vol. II (1900), pp. 239–240. Stevenson may have read it in the version in Longfellow's *Golden Legend* (Pt. II), though the time of the monk's absence is there given as a hundred instead of fifty years. For the material of this note the editors are indebted to Professor G. L. Hamilton.

PAGE 382.

15. **(a murrain on the word!)**: a curse on it; the expression has not been in common use since the early eighteenth century.

16. **Whitman**: for the work of this American poet Stevenson professed throughout life a warm, though not uncritical, admiration. See especially his paper on Whitman in *Familiar Studies of Men and Books*, and the essay "Books Which Have Influenced Me."

17. **a kind of Birmingham sacredness**: the meaning apparently is that Whitman gave to the term "average man" the same kind of authority that the name Birmingham confers on the manufactured goods upon which it is stamped.

18. **Harrow boys**: students at Harrow, one of the great public schools of England.

PAGE 383.

19. **Zola**: Émile Zola (1840–1902), perhaps the best-known of modern French realistic novelists. Stevenson, while recognizing his power, had

little sympathy with his artistic ideals and methods. "Diseased anyway and black-hearted and fundamentally at enmity with joy" he called him in a letter written in 1882 (*Letters*, Vol. I, p. 275).

PAGE 384.

20. **By his fireside, as impotent fancy prompts, etc.**: the editors have been unable to find the source of this quotation.

21. **a voice far beyond singing**: perhaps a reminiscence of Beaumont and Fletcher's "He talked far above singing," quoted by Hazlitt in "On Going a Journey." See page 313 of the present collection, and note.

22. **jibbing**: balking, contrary.

PAGE 385.

23. **Tolstoi's Powers of Darkness**: a drama in five acts by Count Leo Tolstoi (1828–1910), the great Russian novelist and religious writer. In the crucial situation of the play, Mikita, a peasant who has prospered by marrying the widow of his former master, murders the child of his step-daughter, Akulina, whom he has seduced, and then, overcome by remorse, confesses his crime and gives himself up to the police.

24. **when Levine labours in the field**: in Tolstoi's *Anna Karenina*, Pt. III, chaps. iv, v.

25. **when André sinks beyond emotion**: in Tolstoi's *War and Peace*, Pt. XII, chap. xvi.

26. **when Richard Feverel and Lucy Desborough meet beside the river**: in George Meredith's *The Ordeal of Richard Feverel*, chap. xv.

27. **when Antony, "not cowardly, puts off his helmet"**: in *Antony and Cleopatra*, IV, xv, 56. The quoted phrase is from Antony's dying words to Cleopatra.

28. **when Kent has infinite pity on the dying Lear**: in *King Lear*, V, iii.

29. **Dostoieffsky's Despised and Rejected**: a novel by the Russian writer Feodor Dostoieffsky (1821–1881).

30. **Itur in antiquam silvam**: "Here is the road to the virgin forest." The source of the phrase is Virgil, *Æneid* vi, 179.